NUREG-1806, Vol. 1

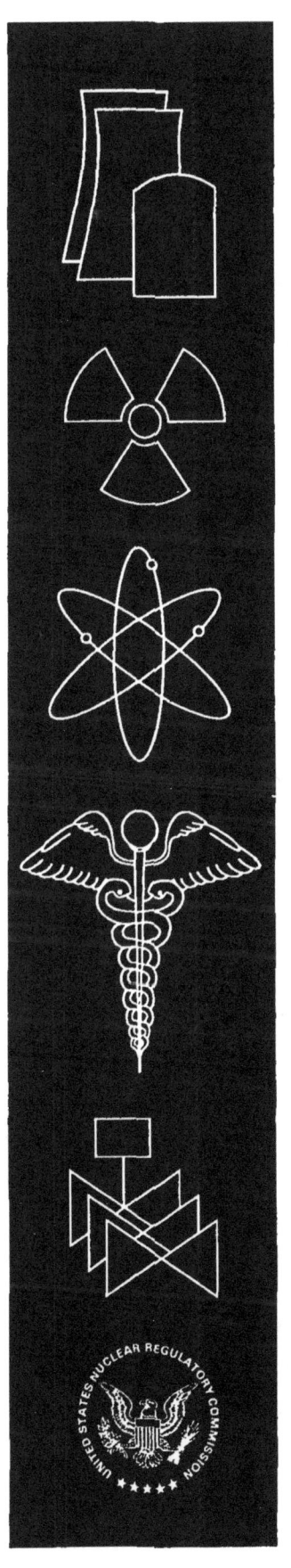

Technical Basis for Revision of the Pressurized Thermal Shock (PTS) Screening Limit in the PTS Rule (10 CFR 50.61)

I0413226

Summary Report

U.S. Nuclear Regulatory Commission
Office of Nuclear Regulatory Research
Washington, DC 20555-0001

AVAILABILITY OF REFERENCE MATERIALS
IN NRC PUBLICATIONS

NRC Reference Material

As of November 1999, you may electronically access NUREG-series publications and other NRC records at NRC's Public Electronic Reading Room at http://www.nrc.gov/reading-rm.html.
Publicly released records include, to name a few, NUREG-series publications; *Federal Register* notices; applicant, licensee, and vendor documents and correspondence; NRC correspondence and internal memoranda; bulletins and information notices; inspection and investigative reports; licensee event reports; and Commission papers and their attachments.

NRC publications in the NUREG series, NRC regulations, and *Title 10, Energy*, in the Code of *Federal Regulations* may also be purchased from one of these two sources.
1. The Superintendent of Documents
   U.S. Government Printing Office
   Mail Stop SSOP
   Washington, DC 20402–0001
   Internet: bookstore.gpo.gov
   Telephone: 202-512-1800
   Fax: 202-512-2250
2. The National Technical Information Service
   Springfield, VA 22161–0002
   www.ntis.gov
   1–800–553–6847 or, locally, 703–605–6000

A single copy of each NRC draft report for comment is available free, to the extent of supply, upon written request as follows:
Address: U.S. Nuclear Regulatory Commission
          Office of Administration
          Mail, Distribution and Messenger Team
          Washington, DC 20555-0001
E-mail: DISTRIBUTION@nrc.gov
Facsimile: 301–415–2289

Some publications in the NUREG series that are posted at NRC's Web site address http://www.nrc.gov/reading-rm/doc-collections/nuregs are updated periodically and may differ from the last printed version. Although references to material found on a Web site bear the date the material was accessed, the material available on the date cited may subsequently be removed from the site.

Non-NRC Reference Material

Documents available from public and special technical libraries include all open literature items, such as books, journal articles, and transactions, *Federal Register* notices, Federal and State legislation, and congressional reports. Such documents as theses, dissertations, foreign reports and translations, and non-NRC conference proceedings may be purchased from their sponsoring organization.

Copies of industry codes and standards used in a substantive manner in the NRC regulatory process are maintained at—
          The NRC Technical Library
          Two White Flint North
          11545 Rockville Pike
          Rockville, MD 20852–2738

These standards are available in the library for reference use by the public. Codes and standards are usually copyrighted and may be purchased from the originating organization or, if they are American National Standards, from—
          American National Standards Institute
          11 West 42nd Street
          New York, NY 10036–8002
          www.ansi.org
          212–642–4900

NUREG-1806, Vol. 1

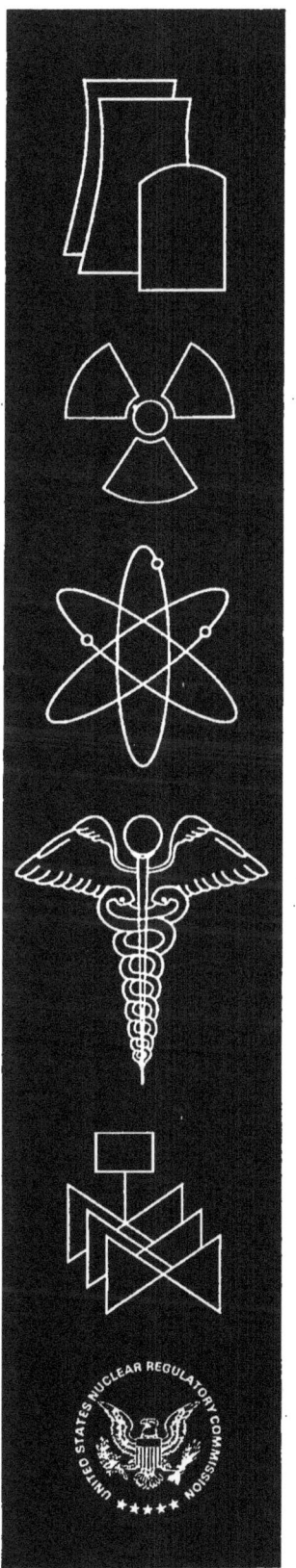

Technical Basis for Revision of the Pressurized Thermal Shock (PTS) Screening Limit in the PTS Rule (10 CFR 50.61)

Summary Report

Manuscript Completed: May 2006
Date Published: August 2007

Prepared by
M. EricksonKirk, M. Junge, W. Arcieri,
B.R. Bass, R. Beaton, D. Bessette,
T.H.J. Chang, T. Dickson, C.D. Fletcher,
A. Kolaczkowski, S. Malik, T. Mintz,
C. Pugh, F. Simonen, N. Siu,
D. Whitehead, P. Williams, R. Woods,
S. Yin

Division of Fuel, Engineering and Radiological Research
Office of Nuclear Regulatory Research
U.S. Nuclear Regulatory Commission
Washington, DC 20555-0001

Abstract

During plant operation, the walls of reactor pressure vessels (RPVs) are exposed to neutron radiation, resulting in localized embrittlement of the vessel steel and weld materials in the core area. If an embrittled RPV had a flaw of critical size and certain severe system transients were to occur, the flaw could very rapidly propagate through the vessel, resulting in a through-wall crack and challenging the integrity of the RPV. The severe transients of concern, known as pressurized thermal shock (PTS), are characterized by a rapid cooling of the internal RPV surface in combination with repressurization of the RPV. Advancements in our understanding and knowledge of materials behavior, our ability to realistically model plant systems and operational characteristics, and our ability to better evaluate PTS transients to estimate loads on vessel walls led the NRC to realize that the earlier analysis, conducted in the course of developing the PTS Rule in the 1980s, contained significant conservatisms.

This report summarizes 21 supporting documents that describe the procedures used and results obtained in the probabilistic risk assessment, thermal hydraulic, and probabilistic fracture mechanics studies conducted in support of this investigation. Recommendations on toughness-based screening criteria for PTS are provided.

Foreword

The reactor pressure vessel is exposed to neutron radiation during normal operation. Over time, the vessel steel becomes progressively more brittle in the region adjacent to the core. If a vessel had a preexisting flaw of critical size and certain severe system transients occurred, this flaw could propagate rapidly through the vessel, resulting in a through-wall crack. The severe transients of concern, known as pressurized thermal shock (PTS), are characterized by rapid cooling (i.e., thermal shock) of the internal reactor pressure vessel surface that may be combined with repressurization. The simultaneous occurrence of critical-size flaws, embrittled vessel, and a severe PTS transient is a very low probability event. The current study shows that U.S. pressurized-water reactors do not approach the levels of embrittlement to make them susceptible to PTS failure, even during extended operation well beyond the original 40-year design life.

Advancements in our understanding and knowledge of materials behavior, our ability to realistically model plant systems and operational characteristics, and our ability to better evaluate PTS transients to estimate loads on vessel walls have shown that earlier analyses, performed some 20 years ago as part of the development of the PTS rule, were overly conservative, based on the tools available at the time. Consistent with the NRC's Strategic Plan to use best-estimate analyses combined with uncertainty assessments to resolve safety-related issues, the NRC's Office of Nuclear Regulatory Research undertook a project in 1999 to develop a technical basis to support a risk-informed revision of the existing PTS Rule, set forth in Title 10, Section 50.61, of the Code of Federal Regulations (10 CFR 50.61).

Two central features of the current research approach were a focus on the use of realistic input values and models and an explicit treatment of uncertainties (using currently available uncertainty analysis tools and techniques). This approach improved significantly upon that employed in the past to establish the existing 10 CFR 50.61 embrittlement limits. The previous approach included unquantified conservatisms in many aspects of the analysis, and uncertainties were treated implicitly by incorporating them into the models.

This report summarizes a series of 21 reports that provide the technical basis that the staff will consider in a potential revision of 10 CFR 50.61; it includes a description of analysis procedures and a detailed discussion of findings. The risk from PTS was determined from the integrated results of the Fifth Version of the Reactor Excursion Leak Analysis Program (RELAP5) thermal-hydraulic analyses, fracture mechanics analyses, and probabilistic risk assessment. These calculations demonstrate that, even through the period of license extension, the likelihood of vessel failure attributable to PTS is extremely low ($\approx 10^{-8}$/year) for all domestic pressurized water reactors. Limited analyses are continuing to further evaluate this finding. Should the $\approx 10^{-8}$/year value be confirmed, this would provide a basis for significant relaxation, or perhaps elimination, of the embrittlement limit established in 10 CFR 50.61. Such changes would reduce unnecessary conservatism without affecting safety because the operating reactor fleet has little probability of exceeding the limits on the frequency of reactor vessel failure established from NRC guidelines on core damage frequency and large early release frequency through the period of license extension.

Brian W. Sheron, Director
Office of Nuclear Regulatory Research
U.S. Nuclear Regulatory Commission

Contents

Appendices

Figures

xv

Tables

Executive Summary

This report summarizes the results of a 5-year study conducted by the U.S. Nuclear Regulatory Commission (NRC), Office of Nuclear Regulatory Research (RES). The aim of this study was to develop the technical basis for revision of the Pressurized Thermal Shock (PTS) Rule, as set forth in Title 10, Section 50.61, of the *Code of Federal Regulations* (10 CFR 50.61), "Fracture Toughness Requirements for Protection Against Pressurized Thermal Shock Events," consistent with the NRC's current guidelines on risk-informed regulation. This report, together with other supporting reports documenting the study details and results, provides this basis.

This executive summary begins with a description of PTS, how it might occur, and its potential consequences for the reactor pressure vessel (RPV). This is followed by a summary of the current regulatory approach to PTS, which leads directly to a discussion of the motivations for conducting this project. Following this introductory information, we describe the approach used to conduct the study, and summarize our key findings and recommendations, which include a proposal for revision of the PTS screening limits. We then conclude the executive summary with a discussion of the potential impact of this proposal on regulations other than 10 CFR 50.61.

Description of PTS

During the operation of a nuclear power plant, the RPV walls are exposed to neutron radiation, resulting in localized embrittlement of the vessel steel and weld materials in the area of the reactor core. If an embrittled RPV had an existing flaw of critical size and certain severe system transients were to occur, the flaw could propagate very rapidly through the vessel, resulting in a through-wall crack and challenging the integrity of the RPV. The severe transients of concern, known as pressurized thermal shock (PTS), are characterized by a rapid cooling (i.e., thermal shock) of the internal RPV surface and downcomer, which may be followed by repressurization of the RPV. Thus, a PTS event poses a potentially significant challenge to the structural integrity of the RPV in a pressurized-water reactor (PWR).

A number of abnormal events and postulated accidents have the potential to thermally shock the vessel (either with or without significant internal pressure). These events include a pipe break or stuck-open valve in the primary pressure circuit, a break of the main steam line, etc. During such events, the water level in the core drops as a result of the contraction produced by rapid depressurization. In events involving a break in the primary pressure circuit, an additional drop in water level occurs as a result of leakage from the break. Automatic systems and operators must provide makeup water in the primary system to prevent overheating of the fuel in the core. However, the makeup water is much colder than that held in the primary system. As a result, the temperature drop produced by rapid depressurization coupled with the near-ambient temperature of the makeup water produces significant thermal stresses in the thick section steel wall of the RPV. For embrittled RPVs, these stresses could be sufficient to initiate a running crack, which could propagate all the way through the vessel wall. Such through-wall cracking of the RPV could precipitate core damage or, in rare cases, a large early release of radioactive material to the environment. Fortunately, the coincident occurrence of critical-size flaws, embrittled vessel steel and weld material, and a severe PTS transient is a very low-probability event. In fact, only a few currently operating PWRs are projected to closely approach the current statutory limit on the level of embrittlement during their planned operational life.

Current Regulatory Approach to PTS

As set forth in 10 CFR 50.61, the PTS Rule requires licensees to monitor the embrittlement of their RPVs using a reactor vessel material surveillance program qualified under Appendix H to 10 CFR Part 50, "Reactor Vessel Material Surveillence Program Requirements." The surveillance results are then used together with the formulae and tables in 10 CFR 50.61 to estimate the fracture toughness transition temperature (RT_{NDT}) of the steels in the vessel's beltline and how those transition temperatures increase as a result of irradiation damage throughout the operational life of the vessel. For licensing purposes, 10 CFR 50.61 provides instructions on how to use these estimates of the effect of irradiation damage to estimate the value of RT_{NDT} that will occur at end of license (EOL), a value called RT_{PTS}. 10 CFR 50.61 also provides "screening limits" (maximum values of RT_{NDT} permitted during the plant's operational life) of +270°F (132°C) for axial welds, plates, and forgings, and +300°F (149°C) for circumferential welds. These screening limits correspond to a limit of 5×10^{-6} events/year on the annual probability of developing a through-wall crack [RG 1.154]. Should RT_{PTS} exceed these screening limits, 10 CFR 50.61 requires the licensee to either take actions to keep RT_{PTS} below the screening limit (by implementing "reasonably practicable" flux reductions to reduce the embrittlement rate, or by deembrittling the vessel by annealing [RG 1.162]), or perform plant-specific analyses to demonstrate that operating the plant beyond the 10 CFR 50.61 screening limit does not pose an undue risk to the public [RG 1.154].

While no currently operating PWR has an RT_{PTS} value that exceeds the 10 CFR 50.61 screening limit before EOL, several plants are close to the limit (3 are within 2°F, while 10 are within 20°F). Those plants are likely to exceed the screening limit during the 20-year license renewal period that is currently being sought by many operators. Moreover, some plants maintain their RT_{PTS} values below the 10 CFR 50.61 screening limits by implementing flux reductions (low-leakage cores, ultra-low-leakage cores), which are fuel management strategies that can be economically deleterious in a deregulated marketplace. Thus, the 10 CFR 50.61 screening limits can restrict both the licensable and economic lifetime of PWRs.

Motivation for this Project

It is now widely recognized that the state of knowledge and data limitations in the early 1980s necessitated conservative treatment of several key parameters and models used in the probabilistic calculations that provided the technical basis for the current PTS Rule. The most prominent of these conservatisms include the following factors:

- highly simplified treatment of plant transients (very coarse grouping of many operational sequences (on the order of 10^5) into very few groups (≈ 10), necessitated by limitations in the computational resources needed to perform multiple thermal-hydraulic calculations)

- lack of any significant credit for operator action

- characterization of fracture toughness using RT_{NDT}, which has an intentional conservative bias

- use of a flaw distribution that places *all* flaws on the interior surface of the RPV, and, in general, contains larger flaws than those usually detected in service

- a modeling approach that treated the RPV as if it were made entirely from the most brittle of its constituent materials (welds, plates, or forgings)

- a modeling approach that assessed RPV embrittlement using the peak fluence over the entire interior surface of the RPV

These factors indicate the high likelihood that the current 10 CFR 50.61 PTS screening limits are unnecessarily conservative. Consequently, the NRC staff believed that reexamining the technical basis for these screening limits, based on a modern understanding of all the factors that influence PTS, would most likely provide strong justification for substantially relaxing these limits. For these reasons, RES undertook this study with the objective of developing the technical basis to support a risk-informed revision of the PTS Rule and the associated PTS screening limit.

Approach

As illustrated in the following figure, three main models (shown as solid blue squares), taken together, allow us to estimate the annual frequency of through-wall cracking in an RPV:

- probabilistic risk assessment (PRA) event sequence analysis
- thermal-hydraulic (TH) analysis
- probabilistic fracture mechanics (PFM) analysis

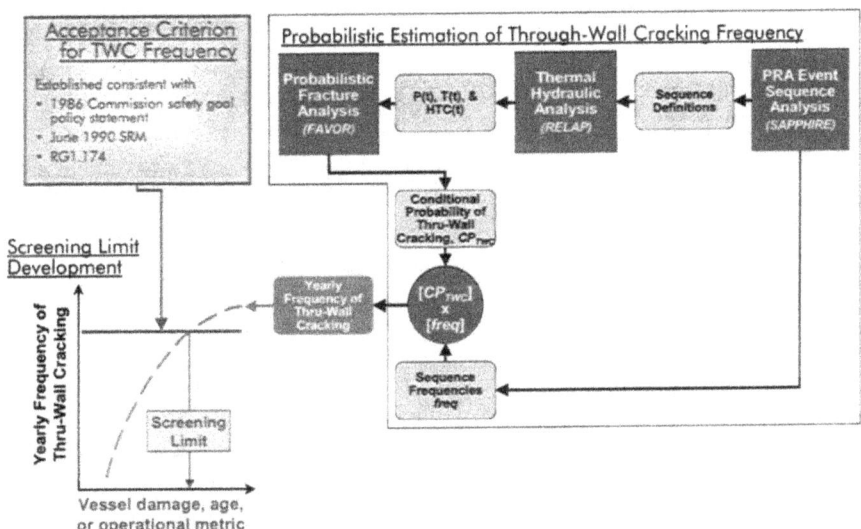

Schematic showing how a probabilistic estimate of through-wall cracking frequency (TWCF) is combined with a TWCF acceptance criterion to arrive at a proposed revision of the PTS screening limit

First, a PRA event sequence analysis is performed to define the sequences of events that are likely to cause a PTS challenge to RPV integrity, and estimate the frequency with which such sequences can be expected to occur. The event sequence definitions are then passed to a TH model that estimates the temporal variation of temperature, pressure, and heat-transfer coefficient in the RPV downcomer, which is characteristic of each sequence definition. These temperature, pressure, and heat-transfer coefficient histories are then passed to a PFM model that uses the TH output, along with other information concerning plant design and construction materials, to estimate the time-dependent "driving force to fracture" produced by a particular event sequence. The PFM model then compares this estimate of fracture driving force to the fracture toughness, or fracture resistance, of the RPV steel. This comparison allows us to estimate the probability that a crack could grow to sufficient size that it would penetrate all the way through the RPV wall if that particular sequence of events actually occured. The final step in the analysis involves a simple matrix multiplication of the probability of through-wall cracking (from the PFM analysis) with the frequency at which a particular event sequence is expected to occur (as defined by the event-tree analysis). This product establishes an estimate of the annual frequency of through-wall cracking that can be expected for a particular plant after a particular period of operation when subjected to a particular sequence of events. The annual frequency of through-wall cracking is then summed for all event sequences to estimate the total annual frequency of through-wall cracking for the vessel. Performance of such analyses for various operating lifetimes provides an estimate of how the annual frequency of through-wall cracking can be expected to vary over the lifetime of the plant.

The probabilistic calculations just described are performed to establish the technical basis for a revised PTS Rule within an integrated systems analysis framework. Our approach considers a broad range of factors that influence the likelihood of vessel failure during a PTS event, while accounting for uncertainties in these factors across a breadth of technical disciplines. Two central features of this approach are a focus on the use of realistic input values and models (wherever possible), and an *explicit* treatment of uncertainties (using currently available uncertainty analysis tools and techniques). Thus, our current approach improves upon that employed in developing SECY-82-465, which included intentional and unquantified conservatisms in many aspects of the analysis, and treated uncertainties *implicitly* by incorporating them into the models.

Key Findings

The findings from this study are divided into the following five topical areas: (1) the expected magnitude of the through-wall cracking frequency (TWCF) for currently anticipated operational lifetimes, (2) the material factors that dominate PTS risk, (3) the transient classes that dominate PTS risk, (4) the applicability of these findings (based on detailed analyses of three PWRs) to PWRs *in general*, and (5) the annual limit on TWCF established consistent with current guidelines on risk-informed regulation. In this summary, *the conclusions are presented in boldface italic*, while the supporting information is shown in regular type.

TWCF Magnitude for Currently Anticipated Operational Lifetimes

- ***The degree of PTS challenge is low for currently anticipated lifetimes and operating conditions.***

  - Even at the end of license extension (60 operational years, or 48 effective full-power years (EFPY) at an 80% capacity factor), the mean estimated TWCF does not exceed 2×10^{-8}/year for the plants analyzed. Considering that the RPVs at the Beaver Valley Power Station and Palisades Nuclear Power Plant are constructed from some of the most irradiation-sensitive materials in commercial reactor service today, these results suggest that, provided that operating practices do not change dramatically in the future, the operating reactor fleet is in little danger of exceeding either the TWCF limit of 5×10^{-6}/yr expressed by Regulatory Guide 1.154 [RG 1.154] or the value of 1×10^{-6}/yr recommended in Chapter 10 of this report — even after license extension.

Material Factors and their Contributions to PTS Risk

- ***Axial flaws, and the toughness properties that can be associated with such flaws, control nearly all of the TWCF.***

  - Axial flaws are much more likely than circumferential flaws to propagate through the RPV wall because the applied fracture driving force increases continuously with increasing crack depth for an axial flaw. Conversely, circumferentially oriented flaws experience a driving force peak mid-wall, providing a natural crack arrest mechanism. It should be noted that crack initiation from circumferentially oriented flaws is likely; it is only their through-wall propagation that is much less likely (relative to axially oriented flaws).

  - It is, therefore, the toughness properties that can be associated with axial flaws that control nearly all of the TWCF. These include the toughness properties of plates and axial welds at the flaw locations. Conversely, the toughness properties of both circumferential welds and forgings have little effect on the TWCF because these can be associated only with circumferentially oriented flaws.

Transients and their Contributions to PTS Risk

- *Transients involving primary side faults are the dominant contributors to TWCF, while transients involving secondary side faults play a much smaller role.*

  - The severity of a transient is controlled by a combination of three factors:
    - initial cooling rate, which controls the thermal stress in the RPV wall
    - minimum temperature of the transient, which controls the resistance of the vessel to fracture
    - pressure retained in the primary system, which controls the pressure stress in the RPV wall

  - The significance of a transient (i.e., how much it contributes to PTS risk) depends on these three factors and the likelihood that the transient will occur.

  - Our analysis considered transients in the following classes (as shown in the following table):
    - primary side pipe breaks
    - stuck-open valves on the primary side
    - main steam line breaks
    - stuck-open valves on the secondary side
    - feed-and-bleed
    - steam generator tube rupture
    - mixed primary and secondary initiators

Factors contributing to the severity and risk-dominance of various transient classes

Transient Class		Transient Severity			Transient Likelihood	TWCF Contribution
		Cooling Rate	Minimum Temperature	Pressure		
Primary Side Pipe Breaks	Large-Diameter	Fast	Low	Low	Low	Large
	Medium-Diameter	Moderate	Low	Low	Moderate	Large
	Small-Diameter	Slow	High	Moderate	High	~0
Stuck-Open Valves, Primary Side	Valve Recloses	Slow	Moderate	High	High	Large
	Valve Remains Open	Slow	Moderate	Low	High	~0
Main Steam Line Break		Fast	Moderate	High	High	Small
Stuck-Open Valve(s), Secondary Side		Moderate	High	High	High	~0
Feed-and- Bleed		Slow	Low	Low	Low	~0
Steam Generator Tube Rupture		Slow	High	Moderate	Low	~0
Mixed Primary & Secondary Initiators		Slow	Mixed		Very Low	~0
Color Key		Enhances TWCF Contribution	Intermediate		Diminishes TWCF Contribution	

  - The table above provides a qualitative summary our results for these transient classes in terms of both transient severity and the likelihood that the transient will occur. The color-coding of table entries indicates the contribution (or lack thereof) of these factors to the TWCF of the various classes of transients. This summary indicates that the risk-dominant transients (medium- and large-diameter primary side pipe breaks, and stuck-open primary side valves that later reclose) all have multiple factors that, in combination, result in their significant contributions to TWCF.

    - For medium- to large-diameter primary side pipe breaks, the fast to moderate cooling rates and low downcomer temperatures (generated by rapid depressurization and emergency injection of low-temperature makeup water directly to the primary) combine to produce a high-severity transient. Despite the moderate to low likelihood that these transients will occur, their severity (if they do occur) makes them significant contributors to the total TWCF.

- For stuck-open primary side valves that later reclose, the repressurization associated with valve reclosure coupled with low temperatures in the primary combine to produce a high-severity transient. This, coupled with a high likelihood of transient occurrence, makes stuck-open primary side valves that later reclose significant contributors to the total TWCF.

- The small or negligible contribution of all secondary side transients (main steam line break, stuck-open secondary valves) results directly from the lack of low temperatures in the primary system. For these transients, the minimum temperature of the primary for times of relevance is controlled by the boiling point of water in the secondary (212°F (100°C) or above). At these temperatures, the fracture toughness of the RPV steel is sufficiently high to resist vessel failure in most cases.

Applicability of These Findings to PWRs in General

- *Credits for operator action, while included in our analysis, do not influence these findings in any significant way.* Operator action credits can dramatically influence the risk-significance of *individual* transients. Therefore, appropriate credits for operator action need to be included as part of a "best estimate" analysis because there is no way to establish *a priori* if a particular transient will make a large contribution to the total risk. Nonetheless, the results of our analyses demonstrate that these operator action credits have a small *overall effect* on a plant's *total TWCF*, for reasons detailed below.

  o Medium- and Large-Diameter Primary Side Pipe Breaks: No operator actions are modeled for any break diameter because, for these events, the safety injection systems do not fully refill the upper regions of the reactor coolant system (RCS). Consequently, operators would never take action to shut off the pumps.

  o Stuck-Open Primary Side Valves that May Later Reclose: Reasonable and appropriate credit for operator actions (throttling of the high-pressure injection (HPI) system) has been included in the PRA model. However, these credits have a small influence on the estimated values of vessel failure probability attributable to transients caused by a stuck-open valve in the primary pressure circuit (SO-1 transients) because the credited operator actions only prevent repressurization when SO-1 transients initiate from Hot Zero Power (HZP) conditions and when the operators act promptly (within 1 minute) to throttle the HPI. Complete removal of operator action credits from the model only slightly increases the total risk associated with SO-1 transients.

  o Main Steam Line Breaks: For the overwhelming majority of transients caused by a main steam line break (MSLB), vessel failure is predicted to occur between 10 and 15 minutes after transient initiation because the thermal stresses associated with the rapid cooldown reach their maximum within this timeframe. Thus, all of the long-term effects (isolation of feedwater flow, timing of HPSI control) that can be influenced by operator actions have no effect on vessel failure probability because such factors influence the progression of the transient *after failure has occurred* (if it occurs at all). Only factors affecting the initial cooling rate (i.e., plant power level at time of transient initiation, break location inside or outside of containment) can influence the conditional probability of through-wall cracking (CPTWC), and operator actions do not influence such factors in any way.

- *Because the severity of the most significant transients in the dominant transient classes is controlled by factors that are common to PWRs in general, the TWCF results presented herein can be used with confidence to develop revised PTS screening criteria that apply to the entire fleet of operating PWRs.*

  o Medium- and Large-Diameter Primary Side Pipe Breaks: For these break diameters, the fluid in the primary cools faster than the wall of the RPV. In this situation, *only* the thermal conductivity of the steel and the thickness of the RPV wall control the thermal stresses and, thus, the severity of the fracture challenge. Perturbations in the fluid cooldown rate controlled by break diameter, break location, and season of the year do not play a role. Thermal conductivity is a physical property, so it is very consistent for all RPV steels, and the thicknesses of the three RPVs analyzed are typical of PWRs. Consequently, the TWCF contribution of medium- to large-diameter primary side pipe breaks is expected to be consistent from plant-to-plant and can be well represented for all PWRs by the analyses reported herein.

- o Stuck-Open Primary Side Valves that May Later Reclose: A major contributor to the risk-significance of SO-1 transients is the return to full system pressure once the valve recloses. The operating and safety relief valve pressures of all PWRs are similar. Additionally, as previously noted, operator action credits only slightly affect the total risk associated with this transient class.

- o Main Steam Line Breaks: Since MSLBs fail early (within 10–15 minutes after transient initiation), only factors affecting the initial cooling rate can have any influence on the CPTWC values. These factors, which include the plant power level at event initiation and the location of the break (inside or outside of containment), are not influenced by operator actions in any way.

- *Sensitivity studies performed on the TH and PFM models to investigate the effect of credible model variations on the predicted TWCF values revealed no effects significant enough to recommend changes to the baseline RELAP and FAVOR models, or to recommend cautions regarding the robustness of those models.*

- *An investigation of design and operational characteristics for five additional PWRs revealed no differences in sequence progression, sequence frequency, or plant thermal-hydraulic response significant enough to call into question the applicability of the TWCF results from the three detailed plant analyses to PWRs in general.*

- *An investigation of potential external initiating events (e.g., fires, earthquakes, floods) revealed that the contribution of those events to the total TWCF can be regarded as negligible.*

Annual Limit on TWCF

- *The current guidance provided by Regulatory Guide 1.174 [RG 1.174] for large early release is appropriately applied to setting an acceptable annual TWCF limit of $1x10^{-6}$ events/year.*

- o While many post-PTS accident progressions led only to core damage (which suggests a TWCF limit of $1x10^{-5}$ events/year limit in accordance with Regulatory Guide 1.174), uncertainties in the accident progression analysis led to our recommendation to adopt the more conservative limit of $1x10^{-6}$ events/year based on LERF.

Recommended Revision of the PTS Screening Limits

We recommend using different reference temperature (RT) metrics to characterize an RPV's resistance to fractures initiating from different flaws at different locations in the vessel. Specifically, we recommend a reference temperature for flaws occurring along axial weld fusion lines (RT_{AW} or RT_{AW-MAX}), another for flaws occurring in plates or in forgings (RT_{PL} or RT_{PL-MAX}), and a third for flaws occurring along circumferential weld fusion lines (RT_{CW} or RT_{CW-MAX}). In each of these reference temperature pairs, the first metric is a weighted value that accounts for the differences between plants in weld fusion line area or plate volume, while the second metric is a maximum value that can be estimated based only on the information in the NRC's Reactor Vessel Integrity Database (RVID). We also recommend using different RT values together to characterize the fracture resistance of the vessel's beltline region, in recognition of the fact that the probability of vessel fracture initiating from different flaw populations varies considerably in response to factors that are both understood and predictable. Correlations between these RT metrics and the TWCF attributable to axial weld flaws, plate flaws, and circumferential weld flaws show little plant-to-plant variability because of the general similarity of PTS challenges among plants.

RT-based screening limits were established by setting the total TWCF (i.e., that attributable to axial weld flaws and plate flaws and circumferential weld flaws) equal to the reactor vessel failure frequency acceptance criterion of 1×10^{-6} events per year. The following figures graphically represent these screening limits (for the maximum *RT* metrics), along with an assessment of all operating PWRs relative to these limits. In these figures, the region of the graphs between the red locus and the origin has TWCF values below the 1×10^{-6} acceptance criterion, so these combinations of reference temperatures would be considered acceptable and require no further analysis. By contrast, the region of the graph outside of the red locus has TWCF values above the 1×10^{-6} acceptance criterion, indicating the need for additional analysis or other measures to justify continued plant operation. Clearly, operating PWRs do not closely approach the 1×10^{-6}/year limit. At EOL, at least 70°F, and up to 290°F, (39 to 161°C) separate plate-welded PWRs from the proposed screening limit; this separation between plant-specific values and the proposed screening limit reduces by 10–20°F (5.5 to 11°C) at end of license extension (EOLE, defined as 60 operating years or 48 EFPY). Additionally, no forged plant is anywhere close to the limit of 1×10^{-6} events per year at either EOL or EOLE. This separation of operating plants from the screening limit contrasts markedly with the current situation, where the most embrittled plants are within 1°F (0.5°C) of the screening limit set forth in 10 CFR 50.61. These differences in the "proximity" of operating plants to the current (10 CFR 50.61) and proposed screening limits are illustrated by the bar graph on the next page.

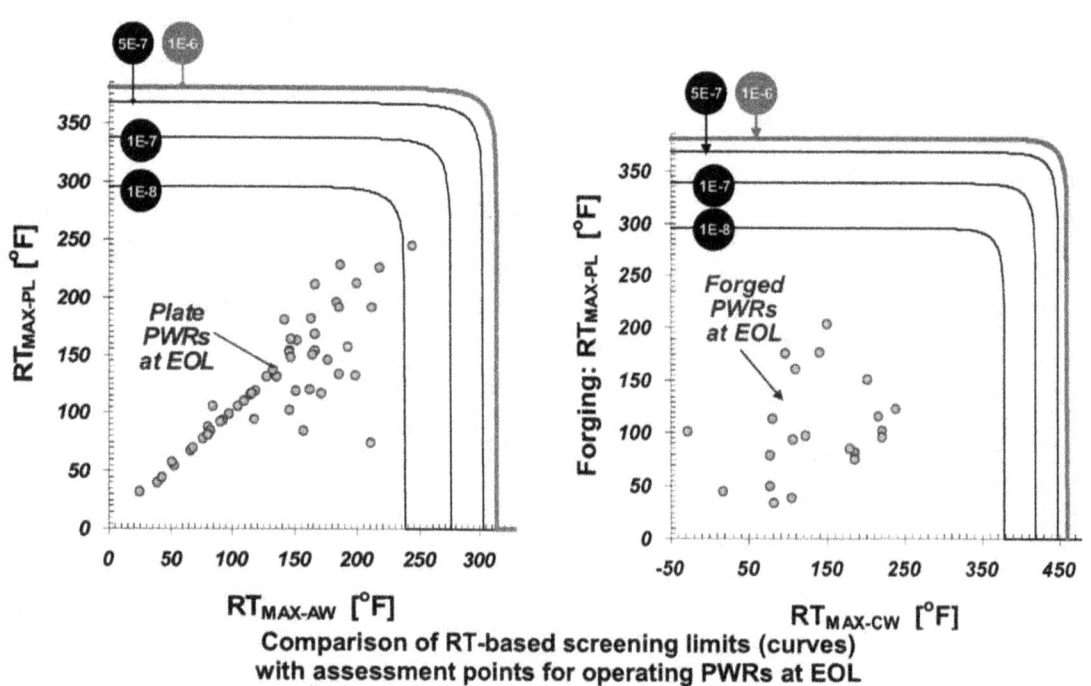

**Comparison of RT-based screening limits (curves)
with assessment points for operating PWRs at EOL
(Left: plate vessels, Right: forged vessels)**

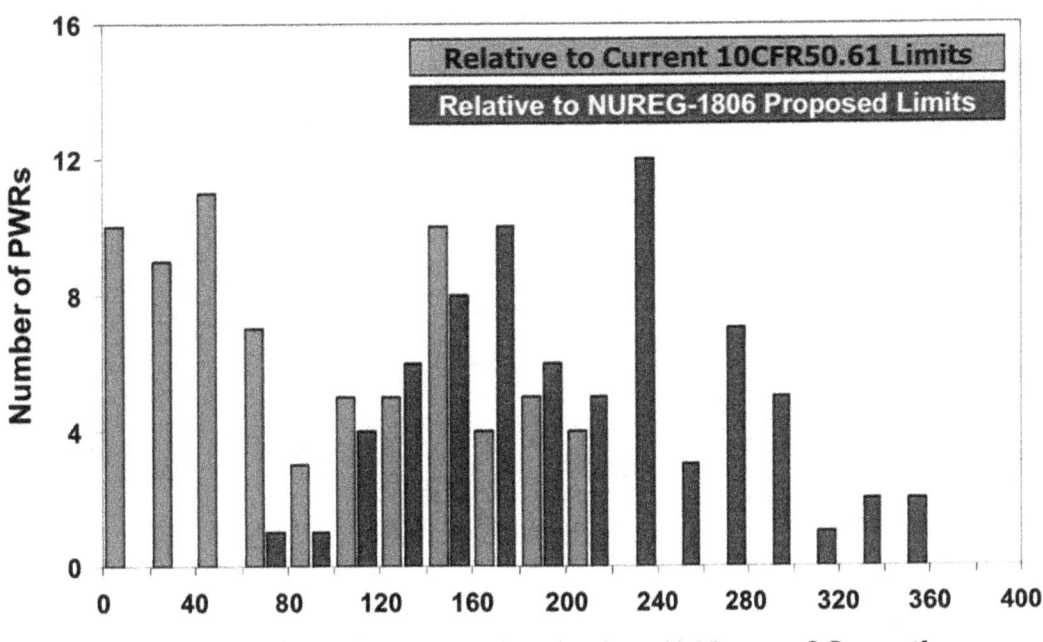

°F from PTS Screening Limit after 40 Years of Operation
Difference between the proximity of operating PWRs to the current RT_PTS screening limits and to the screening limits proposed based on the work presented in this report.

These *RT*-based screening limits (and similar limits described in the text for application to weighted *RT* values) apply to PWRs in general, subject only to the following provisos:

- When assessing a forged vessel where the forging has a very high reference temperature (RT_{PL} above 225°F (107°C)) **and** the forging is believed to be susceptible to subclad cracking, a plant-specific analysis of the TWCF produced by the subclad cracks should be performed. However, no forging is projected to reach this level of embrittlement, even at EOLE.

- When assessing an RPV having a wall thickness of 7-in. (18-cm) or less (7 vessels), the proposed *RT* limits are conservative.

- When assessing an RPV having a wall thickness of 11-in. (28-cm) or greater, the proposed *RT* limits may be nonconservative. For the three plants meeting this criterion, either the *RT* limits would need to be reduced or known conservatisms in the current analysis would have to be removed to demonstrate compliance with the TWCF limit of 1×10^{-6} event/year. However, because these three plants are Units 1, 2, and 3 of the Palo Verde Nuclear Generating Station, which have vessels with very low embrittlement projected at EOL and EOLE, there is little practical need for such plant-specific analysis.

Aside from relying on different *RT* metrics than 10 CFR 50.61, this proposed revision of the PTS screening limit differs from the current screening limit in the absence of a "margin term." Use of a margin term is appropriate to account (at least approximately) for factors that occur in application but were not considered in the analysis upon which the screening limit is based. For example, the 10 CFR 50.61 margin term accounts for uncertainty in copper, nickel, and initial RT_{NDT}. However, our model explicitly considers uncertainty in all of these variables, and represents these uncertainties as being larger (a conservative representation) than would be appropriate in any plant-specific application of the proposed screening limit. Consequently, use of the 10 CFR 50.61 margin term with the new screening limits is inappropriate. In general, the following additional reasons suggest that use of *any* margin term with the proposed screening limits is inappropriate:

(1) The *TWCF* values used to establish the screening limit represent 90th percentile values or greater.

(2) The results from our three plant-specific analyses apply to PWRs *in general*, as demonstrated in Chapters 8 and 9 of this report.

(3) Certain aspects of our modeling cannot reasonably be represented as "best estimates." On balance, there is a conservative bias to these non-best-estimate aspects of our analysis because residual conservatisms in the model far outweigh residual nonconservatisms.

Abbreviations

¼-T FLAW	Surface-breaking flaw defined by ASME Boiler and Pressure Vessel Code as having a depth equal to one-quarter of the vessel wall thickness and a length equal to six times the flaw depth
1D	One-Dimensional
ABAQUS	Commercial finite element code developed by Hibbett, Karlsson, and Sorenson in Pawtucket, Rhode Island
ACRS	Advisory Committee on Reactor Safety (NRC)
ADV	Atmospheric Dump Valve
AFW	Auxiliary Feedwater
APET	Accident Progression Event Tree
APEX	Advanced Plant Experiment
ASME	American Society of Mechanical Engineers
ASTM	American Society for Testing and Materials
ATWS	Anticipated Transient without Scram
B&W	Babcock and Wilcox
BWOG	Babcock and Wilcox Owners' Group
BCC	Body-Centered Cubic
BWR	Boiling-Water Reactor
CDF	Core Damage Frequency
CE	Combustion Engineering
CEOG	Combustion Engineering Owners' Group
CFD	Computational Fluid Dynamics
CL	Cold Leg
CFR	*Code of Federal Regulations*
CFT	Core Flood Tank
CPI	Conditional Probability of Crack Initiation
CPTWC	Conditional Probability of Through-Wall Cracking
CSAU	Code Scaling, Applicability, and Uncertainty Methodology
CSNI	Committee on the Safety of Nuclear Installations
CST	Condensate Storage Tank
CVN	Charpy V-Notch
ECC	Emergency Core Cooling
ECCS	Emergency Core Cooling System
EFPY	Effective Full-Power Years
EFW	Emergency Feedwater
EOL	End of License (40 operating years, 32 EFPY)
EOLE	End of License Extension (60 operating years, 48 EFPY)

EPRI	Electric Power Research Institute
ESFAS	Engineered Safety Features Actuation System
F&B	Feed-and-Bleed
FAVOR	Fracture Analysis of Vessels, Oak Ridge
FCI	Frequency of Crack Initiation
GMAW	Gas Metal Arc Weld
H2TS	Hierarchical, Two-Tiered Scaling
HCLPF	High Confidence of Low Probability of Failure
HEP	Human Error Probability
HFE	Human Failure Event
HPI	High-Pressure Injection
HPSI	High-Pressure Safety Injection
HRA	Human Reliability Analysis
HSSI	Heavy Section Steel Irradiation (Project)
HZP	Hot Zero Power
IAEA	International Atomic Energy Agency
ID	Inner Diameter
IPE	Individual Plant Examination
IPEEE	Individual Plant Examination of External Events
IPTS	Integrated Pressurized Thermal Shock
ISLOCA	Interfacing Systems Loss-of-Coolant Accident
ITV	Intermediate Test Vessel
IVO	Imatran Voima Oy
LAS	Low-Alloy Steel
LBLOCA	Large-Break Loss-of-Coolant Accident (pipe diameters above ~8-in. (~20-cm))
LEFM	Linear Elastic Fracture Mechanics
LER	Licensee Event Report
LERF	Large Early Release Frequency
LOCA	Loss-of-Coolant Accident
LOF	Lack of Inter-Run Fusion
LOFT	Loss-of-Fluid Test facility
LPI	Low-Pressure Injection
LPSI	Low-Pressure Safety Injection
MBLOCA	Medium-Break Loss-of-Coolant Accident (pipe diameters of ~4 to 8-in. (~10 to 20-cm))
MFIV	Main Feedwater Isolation Valve
MFW	Main Feedwater
MIST	Multi-loop Integral System Test
MRJ	Materials Reliability Project
MSIV	Main Steam Isolation Valve
MSLB	Main Steam Line Break

NDT	Nil-Ductility Temperature
NEA	Nuclear Energy Agency (OECD)
NRC	U.S. Nuclear Regulatory Commission
NRR	Office of Nuclear Reactor Regulation (NRC)
NUREG/CR	NRC Technical Report Designator (Contractor-prepared Report published by the U.S. Nuclear Regulatory Commission)
OD	Outer Diameter
OECD	Organization for Economic Cooperation and Development
ORNL	Oak Ridge National Laboratory
PFM	Probabilistic Fracture Mechanics
PIRT	Phenomena Identification and Ranking Table
PNNL	Pacific Northwest National Laboratories
PORV	Power-Operated Relief Valve
Ppb	Parts per Billion
PRA	Probabilistic Risk Assessment
PRODIGAL	Probability of Defect Initiation and Growth Analysis
PTS	Pressurized Thermal Shock
PTSE	Pressurized Thermal Shock Experiment
PVRUF	Pressure Vessel Research Users' Facility
PWR	Pressurized-Water Reactor
QHO	Quantitative Health Objective, as defined by the Commission's Safety Goal Policy Statement [NRC FR 86]
RCP	Reactor Coolant Pump
RCS	Reactor Coolant System
RELAP	Reactor Leak and Power excursion code
REMIX	a computer program used to determine the temperature of a plume in the downcomer when the flow in the loops is stagnant
RES	Office of Nuclear Regulatory Research (NRC)
RG	Regulatory Guide
RLE	Review-Level Earthquake
ROSA	Rig of Safety Assessment
RPS	Reactor Protection System
RPV	Reactor Pressure Vessel
RT	Reference Temperature
RVFF	Reactor Vessel Failure Frequency
RVID	Reactor Vessel Integrity Database
RWST	Refueling Water Storage Tank
SAPHIRE	Systems Analysis Programs for Hands-on Integrated Reliability Evaluations
SAW	Submerged Arc Weld
SBLOCA	Small-Break Loss-of-Coolant Accident (pipe diameters below ~4-in. (~10-cm))
SCC	Stress Corrosion Cracking
SECY	Secretary of the (U.S. Nuclear Regulatory) Commission

SEMISCALE	a 1:1705 scaled experimental facility that simulates the primary system of a 4-loop PWR plant
SG	Steam Generator
SGTR	Steam Generator Tube Rupture
SIAS	Safety Injection Actuation Signal
SIT	Safety Injection Tank
SMAW	Submerged Metal Arc Weld
SO-1	Stuck-open valve in the primary pressure circuit
SO-2	Stuck-open valve in the secondary pressure circuit
SQA	Software Quality Assurance
SRM	Staff Requirements Memorandum
SRV	Safety/Relief Valve
SSC	System, Structure, or Component
SSE	Safe-Shutdown Earthquake
SSRV	Secondary System Relief Valve
TBV	Turbine Bypass Valve
TH	Thermal-Hydraulics
TMI	Three Mile Island
TSE	Thermal Shock Experiment
TWCF	Through-Wall Cracking Frequency
UMD	University of Maryland
UPTF	Upper Plenum Test Facility
USE	Charpy V-Notch Upper-Shelf Energy
V&V	Verification and Validation
VCIF	Vessel Crack Initiation Frequency
(W)	Westinghouse
WOG	Westinghouse Owners' Group
WPS	Warm Pre-Stress

Nomenclature

Symbols Used in Thermal-Hydraulics

α	thermal diffusivity, m^2/s
β	bulk coefficient of expansion, $1/C$
μ	viscosity, $kg/m\text{-}s$
ν	kinematic viscosity, m^2/s
ρ	density, kg/m^3
σ	stress, kg/s^2
τ	characteristic time
C_p	heat capacity, $m^2/s^2\text{-}C$
g	gravitational acceleration, m/s^2
Gr	Grashof Number
h	convective heat transfer coefficient, $W/m^2\text{-}C$
D	diameter, m
J	joules, $kg\text{-}m^2/s^2$
k	conductivity, $W/m\text{-}C$
l	length, m
Nu	Nusselt Number
Pr	Prandtl Number
P	pressure, $kg/m\text{-}s^2$
q	heat flux, W/m^2
Re	Reynolds Number
Ri	Richardson Number
s	seconds
t	thickness, m
t	time, s
u	velocity, m/s
T	temperature, C
W	watts, $kg\text{-}m^2/s^3$

Symbols Used in Fracture Mechanics

$2a$	Flaw depth measured through the vessel wall thickness
$2c$	Flaw length measured parallel to the axial or circumferential direction of the vessel
Cu	Copper content, weight%
J_{Ic}	A fracture toughness measure defined by ASTM E1820, which quantifies the resistance of metals to crack initiation by the initiation, growth, and coalescence of microvoids
$J\text{-}R$	A fracture toughness measure defined by ASTM E1820, which quantifies the resistance of metals to ductile tearing
K_{Jc}	A fracture toughness measure defined by ASTM E1921, which quantifies the resistance of metals to crack initiation by cleavage mechanisms
K_{Ia}	A fracture toughness measure defined by ASTM E1221, which quantifies the ability of metals to arrest (stop) a running cleavage crack
K_{Ic}	A fracture toughness measure defined by ASTM E399, which quantifies the resistance of metals to crack initiation under plane strain conditions
$K_{Ic(min)}$	The minimum K_{Ic} fracture toughness possible at a particular temperature
$K_{APPLIED}$	Linear elastic crack driving force
$\mathcal{L}$	For a buried defect, distance from the wetted clad surface on the vessel ID to the inner crack tip
l	The length of the fusion line of an axial weld
Ni	Nickel content, weight%
P	Phosphorus content, weight%
RT_{AW}	A fracture toughness reference temperature, which characterizes the RPV's resistance to fractures initiating from flaws found along the axial weld fusion lines. It corresponds to the maximum RT_{NDT} of the plates/welds that lie to either side of the weld fusion lines, and is weighted to account for differences in weld fusion line length (and, therefore, number of simulated flaws) between vessel courses.
RT_{PL}	A fracture toughness reference temperature, which characterizes the RPV's resistance to fractures initiating from flaws found in plates that are not associated with welds. It corresponds to the maximum RT_{NDT} occurring anywhere in the plate.
RT_{CW}	A fracture toughness reference temperature, which characterizes the RPV's resistance to fractures initiating from flaws found along the circumferential weld fusion lines. It corresponds to the maximum RT_{NDT} of the plates/welds that lie to either side of the weld fusion lines.
RT_{NDT}	Transition fracture toughness reference temperature defined by ASME NB-2331
$RT_{NDT(u)}$	Unirradiated value of RT_{NDT}
RT_{PTS}	RT_{NDT} projected end of license to account for the effects of irradiation (defined in 10 CFR 50.61)
t_{WALL}	Vessel wall thickness
t_{CLAD}	Stainless steel cladding thickness

T_{30}	The temperature at which the mean CVN energy is 30 ft-lbs (41J)
$T_{35/50}$	Charpy V-notch energy transition temperature defined as the temperature at which the CVN energy is at least 50 ft-lbs (68J) and the lateral expansion of the specimen is at least 0.035-in. (0.89-mm) [See the definition on page 2-7]
T_{NDT}	Nil-ductility temperature defined by ASTM E-208
ΔT_{30}	The shift in the CVN 30 ft-lb (41J) transition temperature produced by radiation damage
σ_{flow}	Flow strength, average of tensile yield and tensile ultimate strength
ϕt	Fluence

Glossary

Terms Used in Probabilistic Risk Assessment

Abnormal operating procedure	A procedure (i.e., list of actions) used to address unique or special plant circumstances identified while using emergency operating procedures (EOPs). These abnormal operating procedures are usually called by EOPs, but may be indicated directly by some plant conditions.
.Accident progression event tree	The event tree used to model the part of the accident sequence that follows the onset of core damage, including containment response to severe accident conditions, equipment availability, and operator performance.
Binning	The process of taking a large number of sequences and combining then into a smaller number of groups, that are expected to have similar characteristics (e.g., TH conditions), to allow effective utilization of limited resources.
Core damage	Uncovery and heatup of the reactor core to the point at which prolonged oxidation and severe fuel damage is anticipated and involving enough of the core to cause a significant release.
Dominant scenario	An accident sequence (scenario) that is usually represented by the top 10 or 20 events or groups of events modeled in a PRA, which accounts for a large fraction of the specified end state.
Emergency operating procedure	The primary procedure (i.e., list of actions) used to respond to a plant disturbance resulting from an initiating event.
Event tree	A logic diagram that begins with an initiating event or condition and progresses through a series of branches that represent expected system or operator performance that either succeeds or fails and arrives at either a successful or failed end state.
Fault tree	A deductive logic diagram that depicts how a particular undesired event can occur as a logical combination of other undesired events.
Large Early Release	The rapid, unmitigated release of airborne fission products from the containment to the environment occurring before the effective implementation of offsite emergency response and protective actions, such that there is a potential for early health effects.
Latin Hypercube sampling	A stratified sampling technique, in which the random variable distributions are divided into equal probability intervals, and probabilities are then randomly selected from within each interval.
Mitigating equipment	Systems or components, used to respond to an initiating event, of which successful operation prevents the occurrence of an undesired event or state.
Pre-initiator human failure event	Human failure events that represent the impact of human errors committed during actions performed prior to the initiation of an accident (e.g., during maintenance or the use of calibration procedures).
Post-initiator human failure event	Human failure events that represent the impact of human errors committed during actions performed in response to an accident initiator.

Prompt fatality	A fatality that results from substantial radiation exposures incurred during short time periods (usually within weeks, though up to 1 year for pulmonary effects).
PTS bin	A group of sequences that are expected to have similar TH characteristics and are represented by one unique set of TH characteristics during a FAVOR calculation.
Risk-informed	An approach to analyzing and evaluating activities, which bases decisions on the results of traditional engineering evaluations, supported by insights derived from the use of PRA methods.
Scenario	See Sequence.
Screening	The process of eliminating items from further consideration based on their negligible contribution to the probability of an undesired end state or its consequences.
Sequence	A representation in terms of an initiating event followed by a sequence of failures or successes of events (i.e., system, function, or operator performance) that can lead to undesired consequences, with a specified end state (e.g., potential for PTS).

Terms Used in Thermal-Hydraulics

Blowdown	Rapid depressurization of a system in response to a break.
Break flow	Flow of water (liquid and vapor) out a pipe break or a valve.
Break energy	Energy content of the fluid flow out a break.
Bottom-up	To break up a complex system into its subsystems, and then break up each subsystem into its components, examine individual local phenomena and processes that most affect each component, and build up the total complex system from these individual pieces (like manufacturing a car).
Coast down	Time required for a pump to stop rotating once power is shut off due to inertia.
Decay heat	Heat generated from radioactive decay of fission products.
Enthalpy	Sum of internal energy and volume multiplied by pressure.
Flash	Change of phase from saturated liquid to vapor resulting from decrease in pressure.
Flow quality	Mass fraction of flow stream that is steam. Higher quality flow would have a high mass fraction of steam.
Forced flow	Flow driven by a pump.
Inventory	Mass of water.
Loop flow	Mass flow rate of coolant in a circuit.
Makeup water	Water reservoir available for inventory control.
Natural circulation	Flow driven by buoyancy (gravity).
Pressure drop	Change in pressure due to conversion of mechanical energy to internal energy.
Protection system	Electrical controls to actuate engineering safety features.
Quality	Mass fraction of steam in a two-phase steam-water mixture.

Saturation temperature	A temperature corresponding to phase change from liquid to vapor.
Sensible heat	The product of specific heat and temperature change of subcooled liquid.
Subcooled	A system is *subcooled* if it exists entirely in a liquid state. The *degree of subcooling* is the number of degrees that the temperature of the system would have to be raised to cause boiling.
Throttled	Operation of a control valve to regulate flow.
Top-down	To characterize a complex system by establishing the governing behavior, or phenomenon, that is most important, and then proceed from that starting point to successive lower levels, by identifying the processes that have the greatest influence on the top-level phenomenon.
Trip	A "trip" occurs when a breaker opens in response to its trip mechanism (an arm that holds the breaker closed moves to allow the breaker to open). When a reactor trips, all of the breakers that provide power to the rod control system open, causing the rods to be inserted in the core and stopping the nuclear reaction. When a pump trips, the breaker opens, thereby disconnecting power and causing the pump to stop.
Water solid	A situation in which there is no steam in the system (i.e., it is all liquid). A "water solid" system is *subcooled*.

Terms Used in Fracture Mechanics

Brittle	Fracture occurring without noticeable macroscopic plastic deformation (stretching) of the material.
Cleavage fracture	Microscopically, cleavage is a fracture mode that occurs preferentially along certain atomic planes through the grains of the material. Cleavage can only occur in ferritic steels (i.e., steels having a body-centered cubic lattice structure). Macroscopically, cleavage fracture is often called "brittle" fracture because little noticeable plastic deformation (stretching) of the material occurs. (Note, however, that plastic flow at the micro-scale is a necessary precursor to cleavage.) Macroscopically, cleavage fracture is also characterized as being a sudden event, with cracks of very large dimensions developing over durations measured in fractional seconds. A useful, although inexact, analogue for cleavage fracture in common experience is the breaking of glass.
Ductile fracture	Microscopically, ductile fracture occurs through the initiation, growth, and eventual coalescence of micro-voids in the material into a macroscopic crack. These micro-voids tend to initiate at local heterogeneities in the material (e.g., inclusions, carbides, clusters of dislocations). Macroscopically, ductile fracture is associated with considerable plastic deformation (stretching) of the material. Relative to cleavage fracture, ductile fracture occurs very slowly, with crack growth rates measured in seconds rather than in micro-seconds (for cleavage).
Fracture toughness	A general term referring to a material's resistance to fracture. The term may be modified to refer to fractures by different mechanisms: Arrest fracture toughness measures a material's ability to stop a running cleavage crack. Cleavage fracture toughness measures a material's ability to resist crack initiation in cleavage. Ductile fracture toughness measures a material's ability to resist crack initiation attributable to ductile mechanisms on the upper shelf.

Lower shelf	At low temperatures, the toughness behavior of steels occurs by transgranular cleavage and is said to be on the lower shelf. On the lower shelf, a fracture is unstable, and is often referred to as a "brittle" fracture.
Reference temperature	A characteristic temperature used to locate the transition curve of a ferritic steel on the temperature axis.
Transition (or transition curve)	Between lower shelf and upper shelf temperatures, the fracture behavior of a ferritic material is said to be in "transition." At low temperatures in transition, fracture occurs by cleavage. As temperature increases through the transition regime, fracture occurs by ductile crack initiation and growth, a process which is terminated by cleavage. At still higher temperatures, cleavage cannot occur, and upper shelf conditions exist.
Upper shelf	At high temperatures, the toughness behavior of steels occurs by ductile mechanisms (micro-void initiation, growth, and coalescence) and is said to be on the upper shelf. On the upper shelf, afracture is stable and dissipates considerable amounts of energy.

Terms Used in Uncertainty Analysis

Aleatory	Aleatory uncertainties arise as a result of the randomness inherent in a physical or human process. Consequently, aleatory uncertainties are fundamentally irreducible. If the uncertainty in a variable is characterized as being aleatory, the entire distribution of the variable is carried through each simulation run.
Epistemic	Epistemic uncertainties are caused by limitations in our current state of knowledge (or understanding) of a given process. Epistemic uncertainties can, in principle, be reduced by an increased state of knowledge. If the uncertainty in a variable is characterized as being epistemic in a probabilistic simulation, individual values of the variable are randomly selected from a distribution and propagated through the calculation. This procedure models the understanding that the "correct" value of the variable is knowable, at least in principal. Thus, for epistemic uncertainties, individual simulation runs are deterministic, while the totality of all simulation runs captures the uncertainty characteristic of the epistemic variable.

1 Motivation for and Objective of this Study

1.1 Description of Pressurized Thermal Shock

During the operation of a nuclear power plant, the walls of the reactor pressure vessel (RPV) are exposed to neutron radiation, resulting in localized embrittlement of the vessel steel and weld materials in the area of the reactor core. If an embrittled RPV had an existing flaw of critical size and certain severe system transients were to occur, the flaw could very rapidly propagate through the vessel, resulting in a through-wall crack and challenging the integrity of the RPV. The severe transients of concern, known as pressurized thermal shock (PTS), are characterized by a rapid cooling (i.e., thermal shock) of the internal RPV surface and downcomer, which may be followed by repressurization of the RPV. Thus, a PTS event poses a potentially significant challenge to the structural integrity of the RPV in a pressurized-water reactor (PWR).

A number of abnormal events and postulated accidents have the potential to thermally shock the vessel (either with or without significant internal pressure). These events include a pipe break or stuck-open valve in the primary pressure circuit, or a break of the main steam line, among others. During such events, the water level in the core drops as a result of the contraction produced by rapid depressurization. In events involving a break in the primary pressure circuit, an additional drop in water level occurs as a result of leakage from the break. Automatic systems and operators must provide makeup water in the primary system to prevent overheating of the fuel in the core. However, the makeup water is much colder than that held in the primary system. As a result, the temperature drop produced by rapid depressurization coupled with the near-ambient temperature of the makeup water produces significant thermal stresses in the thick section steel wall of the RPV. For embrittled RPVs, these stresses could be sufficient to initiate a running crack, which could propagate all the way through the vessel wall. Such through-wall cracking of the RPV could precipitate core damage or, in rare cases, a large early release of radioactive material to the environment. Fortunately, the coincident occurrence of critical-size flaws, embrittled vessel steel and weld material, and a severe PTS transient is a very low-probability event.

1.2 PTS Limits on the Licensable Life of a Commercial Pressurized Water Reactor

In the early 1980s, attention was focused on the possibility that PTS events could challenge the integrity of the RPV wall for two reasons:

- Operational experience suggested that overcooling events, while not common, did in fact occur.

- The results of in-reactor materials surveillance programs suggested that the steels used in RPV construction were prone to loss-of-toughness over time as a result of neutron irradiation-induced embrittlement.

This possibility of accident loading combined with degraded material conditions motivated investigations aimed at assessing the risk of vessel failure posed by PTS for the purpose of establishing the operational limits needed to ensure that the likelihood of RPV failures caused by PTS transients is kept sufficiently low. These efforts led to the publication of a Commission paper [SECY-82-465], which provided the technical basis for subsequent development of what has come to be known as the "PTS Rule," as set forth in Title 10, Section 50.61, of the *Code of Federal Regulations* (10 CFR 50.61), "Fracture Toughness

Requirements for Protection Against Pressurized Thermal Shock Events" [10 CFR 50.61].

Currently, 10 CFR 50.61 requires licensees to monitor the embrittlement of their RPVs using a reactor vessel material surveillance program qualified under Appendix H to 10 CFR Part 50, "Domestic Licensing of Production and Utilization Facilities." The surveillance results are used together with the formulae and tables in 10 CFR 50.61 to estimate the fracture toughness transition temperature (RT_{NDT}[†]) of the steels in the vessel's beltline and how those transition temperatures increase as a result of irradiation damage throughout the operational life of the vessel. For licensing purposes, 10 CFR 50.61 provides instructions on how to use these estimates of the effect of irradiation damage to estimate the value of RT_{NDT} that will occur at end of license (EOL), a value called RT_{PTS}. 10 CFR 50.61 also provides "screening limits" (maximum values of RT_{NDT} permitted during the plant's operational life) of +270°F (132°C) for axial welds, plates, and forgings, and +300°F (149°C) for circumferential welds. These screening limits correspond to a limit of 5×10^{-6} events/year on the annual probability of developing a through-wall crack [RG 1.154]. Should RT_{PTS} exceed these screening limits, 10 CFR 50.61 requires that the licensee to either take actions to keep RT_{PTS} below the screening limit (by implementing "reasonably practicable" flux reductions to reduce the embrittlement rate, or by deembrittling the vessel by annealing [RG 1.162]), or perform plant-specific analyses to demonstrate that operating the plant beyond the 10 CFR 50.61 screening limit does not pose an undue risk to the public [RG 1.154]. While no currently operating PWR has an RT_{PTS} value that exceeds the 10 CFR 50.61 screening limit before EOL, several plants are close to the limit

(3 are within 2°F while 10 are within 20°F, see Figure 1.1). Those plants that are close to are likely to exceed the screening limit during the 20-year license renewal period that is currently being sought by many operators. Moreover, some plants maintain their RT_{PTS} values below the 10 CFR 50.61 screening limits by implementing flux reductions (low-leakage cores, ultra-low-leakage cores), which are fuel management strategies that can be economically deleterious in a deregulated marketplace. Thus, the 10 CFR 50.61 screening limits can restrict the licensable and the economic lifetime of PWRs. As detailed in the next section, there is considerable reason to believe that these restrictions are not necessary to ensure public safety and, in fact, place unnecessary burden on licensees.

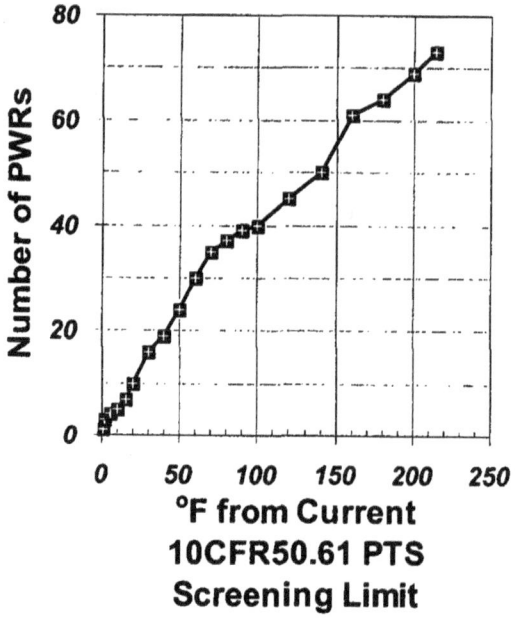

Figure 1.1. Proximity of currently operating PWRs to the 10 CFR 50.61 screening limit for PTS

[†] The RT_{NDT} index temperature was intended to correlate with the fracture toughness transition temperature of the material. Fracture toughness, and how it is reduced by neutron irradiation embrittlement, are key parameters controlling the RPV's resistance to any loading challenge. For a more detailed description of RT_{NDT} (in specific) and fracture toughness (in general), see [**EricksonKirk PFM**].

1.3 Technical Factors Suggesting Conservatism of the Current PTS Rule

It is now widely recognized that state of knowledge and data limitations in the early 1980s necessitated conservative treatment of several key parameters and models used in the probabilistic calculations that provided the technical basis [SECY-82-465] of the current PTS Rule [10 CFR 50.61]. The most prominent of these conservatisms include the following factors:

- highly simplified treatment of plant transients (very coarse grouping of many operational sequences (on the order of 10^5) into very few groups ($\approx$10), necessitated by limitations in the computational resources needed to perform multiple thermal-hydraulic calculations)

- lack of any significant credit for operator action

- characterization of fracture toughness using RT_{NDT}, which has an intentional conservative bias [ASME NB2331]

- use of a flaw distribution that places *all* flaws on the interior surface of the RPV, and, in general, contains larger flaws than those usually detected in service

- a modeling approach that treated the RPV as if it were made entirely from the most brittle of its constituent materials (welds, plates, or forgings)

- a modeling approach that assessed RPV embrittlement using the peak fluence over the entire interior surface of the RPV

These factors indicate the high likelihood that the current 10 CFR 50.61 PTS screening limits are unnecessarily conservative. Consequently, the staff of the U.S. Nuclear Regulatory Commission (NRC) believed that reexamining the technical basis for these screening limits, based on a modern understanding of all the factors that influence PTS, would most likely provide strong justification for substantially relaxing these limits.

1.4 Statement of Objective

For the reasons stated in Section 1.3, the NRC's Office of Nuclear Regulatory Research (RES) undertook this study with the objective of developing the technical basis to support a risk-informed revision of the PTS Rule and the associated PTS screening limit, and thereby providing the basis for potential rulemaking.

1.5 Guide to this Report

As discussed in Chapter 4, this report summarizes a much larger documentary package, and updates a previous report [*Kirk 12-02*]. We begin in Chapter 2 by describing PTS, its potential precursors, and the historical occurrence of PTS in reactor operations. We also summarize the key findings on which the current rule is based, and we detail the provisions of the current rule. Chapter 3 describes this study in detail and discusses its guiding principles, our investigative approach, and our fundamental assumptions. Additionally, we detail the many organizations and individuals that have contributed to this project. Chapter 4 provides a "map" to the documents from which this summary report was drawn and describes the information available in each of those detailed reports. In Chapters 5, 6, and 7, we synopsize the key features of our probabilistic risk assessment (PRA) and human reliability analysis (HRA), our thermal-hydraulic (TH) analysis, and our probabilistic fracture mechanics (PFM) analysis, respectively. Chapters 6 and 7 also address experimental validation of our TH and PFM methodologies. Chapter 8 presents the results of our baseline plant-specific analysis of three PWRs, while Chapter 9 examines the general applicability of these results to the larger population of all commercial PWRs. In Chapter 10, we develop a limit on the risk posed by PTS that is consistent with current regulatory guidance. Chapter 11 combines the information from Chapters 8 through 10 to develop a proposed revision to the 10 CFR 50.61 screening limit. Finally, Chapter 12 summarizes our findings and discusses some considerations for rulemaking.

2 Pressurized Thermal Shock Background

In this chapter, we provide background information on PTS. We begin with a general description of the progression of a PTS event, including its precursors and their effect on both the primary pressure circuit and the RPV itself (Section 2.1). We then discuss the historical incidence of PTS (Section 2.2). Finally, we summarize the findings of SECY-82-465, which provide the technical basis for the current PTS Rule (Section 2.3), and we review the rule's provisions (Section 2.4).

2.1 General Description of the Progression of a PTS Event

In the following sections, we describe the event sequence that can give rise to a PTS event (Section 2.1.1), the effect of those events on both the primary and secondary pressure circuits (Section 2.1.2), and the challenge that these transients can pose to the structural integrity of the RPV (Section 2.1.3).

2.1.1 Precursors

Normally, the RPV is very hot because of the high temperature of the water it contains (600°F 315°C)). Several types of malfunctions or accidents can cause the vessel to suddenly fill with cool water or cause the reactor coolant water temperature to decrease rapidly. Such rapid cooling causes the vessel to experience thermal shock. If the RPV is then subjected to high pressure, the phenomenon is referred to as PTS.

Most significant PTS scenarios fall into one of the following two categories:
- breaks in the primary side of the reactor coolant system (RCS) (see Sections 2.1.2.1 and 2.1.2.2)
- breaks in the secondary system (see Section 2.1.2.3).

Here, we use the term "break" to refer to pipe breaks (e.g., hot leg break, cold leg break, main steam line break, steam generator tube rupture), as well as stuck-open valves. Initially, a stuck-open valve transient behaves much like a transient initiated by a pipe break. However, later in stuck-open valve transients the valve can unstick (and, therefore, reclose), so repressurization is possible. Our analysis considers potential failures of the following valves:
- Primary Side/RCS: Power-operated relief valves (PORVs) and safety relief valves (SRVs)
- Secondary Side: Main steam isolation valves (MSIVs), steam generator atmospheric dump valves (ADVs), main steam safety valves (MSSVs), and so on.

Figure 2.1 illustrates the arrangement of the major components of both the primary and secondary systems in a PWR.

2.1.2 Thermal-Hydraulic Response of the Vessel

2.1.2.1 Pipe Breaks in the Primary System

When a break occurs in the primary system, mass is lost from the RCS. The level of water in the pressurizer (PZR) decreases, thereby causing a decrease in RCS pressure. If the RCS pressure or PZR level decreases too far, the reactor protection system (RPS) will generate a reactor trip signal, which in turn will insert the control rods and stop the fission process. Additionally, the engineered safety features actuation system (ESFAS) will generate a safety injection actuation signal (SIAS). The SIAS will start the high-pressure injection (HPI) and low-pressure injection (LPI) pumps, which will start the supply of emergency core cooling (ECC) water to the RCS, as pressure allows.

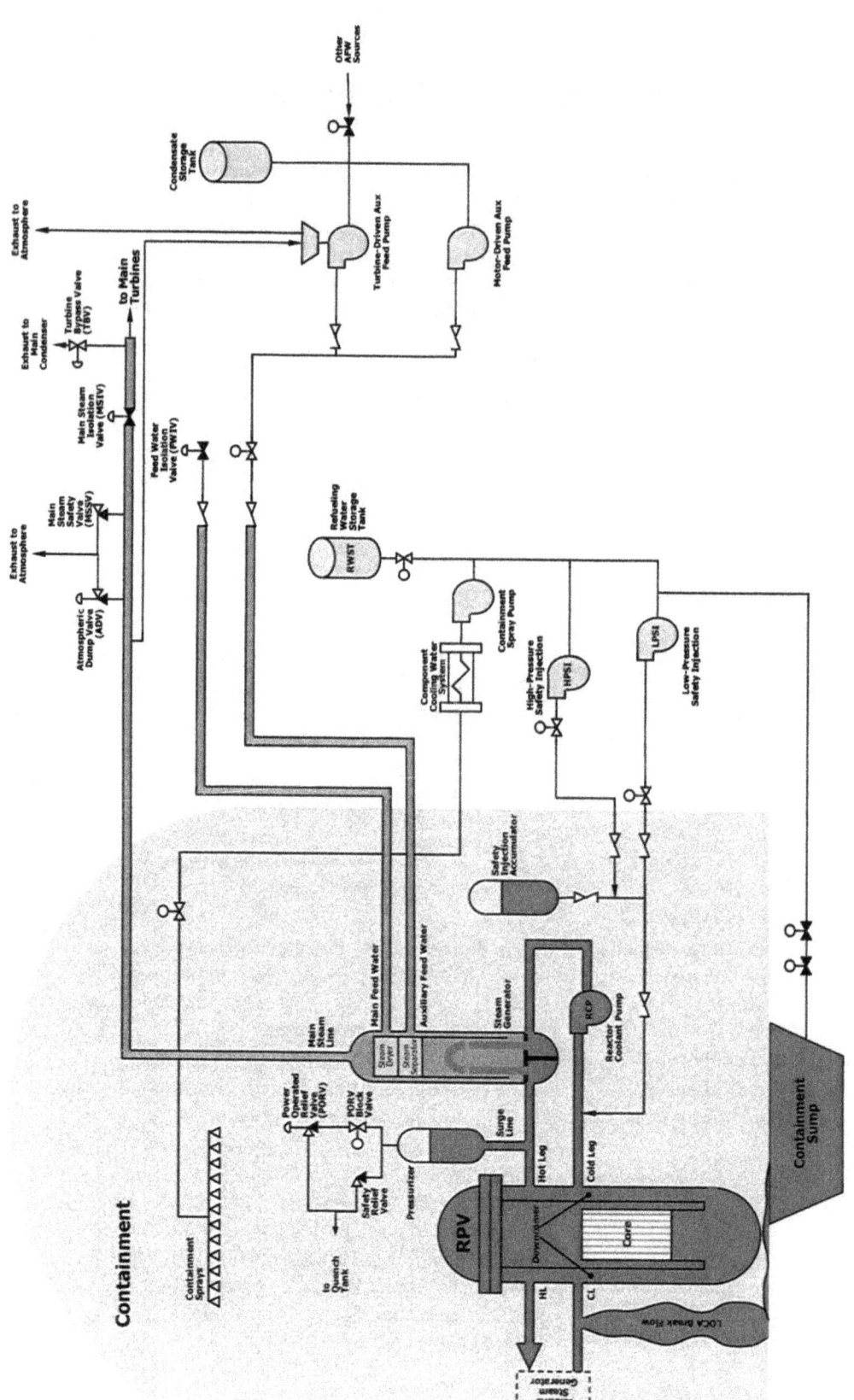

Figure 2.1. Schematic illustration of the main components of the primary (red) and secondary (blue) systems in a pressurized-water reactor

2-2

Further progress of the transient depends upon the ability of HPI to make up for the mass lost through the break.

For very small breaks (less than ~1.4-in. (3.5-cm) in diameter), HPI is sufficient to make up the lost mass and, thereby, maintain RCS mass and pressure control. For larger breaks, HPI is insufficient to replace the lost mass, so PZR level and RCS pressure continue to fall. As the pressure continues to fall, the safety injection tanks (SITs) discharge and, eventually, the LPI begins injecting colder water into the RCS. The ECC injection rates are substantially greater for large breaks (compared to small breaks), and result in much greater cooldown of the primary system and subsequently the RPV wall.

The controlling feature of such loss-of-coolant accidents (LOCAs) is the size of the break. The larger the break, the faster the transient proceeds, and the more severe the cooldown. Larger breaks cause a greater pressure decrease, which results in larger ECC flows. This causes the downcomer temperature to drop rapidly. The rate of temperature decrease (which is controlled by the break size) and the minimum temperature achieved (which is controlled by the temperature of the ECC water and whether ECC water is recirculated from the sump) are the dominant TH factors that influence the severity of the transient. Since RCS pressure is low, it not a significant factor.

2.1.2.2 Stuck-Open Primary Safety Relief Valves

During stuck-open valve transients, a primary SRV is assumed to stick open as a result of mechanical binding or other possible causes. This binding of the valve may release later in the transient, resulting in valve reclosure. Phenomenologically, stuck-open valve scenarios are similar to small hot leg break LOCAs, until the valve recloses. The "break" areas of stuck-open valve scenarios are typically in the small-break LOCA range of ≈1.5 to 2+-in. (≈3.8 to 5+-cm).

Following valve reclosure, HPI will gradually fill the RCS. As the RCS fills, the primary system pressure will increase above the saturation pressure of the coolant, thereby reestablishing subcooling in the loops. When operating procedures allow, the HPI can be controlled to avoid overfilling the RCS. If, however, the operator fails to attend to HPI control in a timely manner, the RCS can continue to fill until the primary system is water solid, meaning there is no longer any steam in the system. Since water is nearly incompressible, the RCS pressure rises very rapidly, and the pressure created by HPI will reopen the SRVs. RCS pressure will then remain at the SRV setpoint of 17.25 MPa (2500 psi) for as long as the HPI remains on.

The controlling features of stuck-open valve scenarios are the length of time the valve is open, and the repressurization associated with the primary system becoming water solid. The longer the SRV stays open, the cooler the downcomer temperature becomes. Timely operator control of HPI is an important factor influencing transient severity because it determines the maximum pressure achieved in the primary system. Thus, for these scenarios, both downcomer temperature and RCS pressure are important.

2.1.2.3 Breaks in the Secondary System

Secondary side breaks can include both actual breaks of the steam line and the sticking-open of one or more of the numerous control and safety valves in the steam system. A stuck-open valve is, therefore, also referred to as a "break," consistent with the terminology adopted to describe stuck-open valves in the primary system Break sizes can range from a single valve sticking open to a complete main steam line break (MSLB). Similar to LOCAs, *time* and *break size* are directly related. The larger the break, the faster the transient proceeds, and the more severe the cooldown.

Following break initiation, the response of engineered safety features systems may result in safety injection actuation, actuation of main feedwater isolation valves (MFIVs) and/or MSIVs, as well as automatic control of auxiliary feedwater (i.e., through isolation of a turbine-driven pump). If the break is downstream of the MSIVs, the steam line break will be terminated when the MSIV shuts. For larger MSLBs, MSIV closure is automatic and occurs rapidly after break initiation. For smaller steam line breaks, however, the operators will isolate the affected steam generator by securing flow to the generator and manually isolating the MSIVs. Therefore, downstream breaks are not PTS-significant. However, the main steam SRVs and ADVs are upstream of the MSIVs and, consequently, are not affected by an MSIV closure. For breaks occurring upstream of the MSIVs, steam will continue to blowdown until the affected steam generator is completely depressurized.

Steam generator depressurization causes cooling of the primary system. As steam continues leaking out of the break, the secondary side pressure continues to decrease, and the water in the generator remains saturated. Consequently, as the secondary side pressure decreases, the secondary side temperature also decreases. The primary side and secondary side remain "thermally coupled" during secondary side break scenarios, meaning that the primary system temperature will track the temperature of the affected steam generator. This primary system cooling increases the density of the primary water, so the volume of the water in the RCS shrinks. For sufficiently large secondary breaks, the shrinkage may be sufficient to actuate the emergency core cooling system (ECCS), causing direct injection of water at a temperature between that of external storage tanks ($\approx$40°F (4.4°C)) and that of water recirculated from the sump (~120°F (49°C)). The flow of this colder water increases the cooling rate of the primary, thereby increasing transient severity. However, HPI does not reduce the minimum temperature of the primary below the boiling point of water in the secondary because the large heat transfer area in the affected steam generator (which is now at saturated conditions) is more than sufficient to bring the HPI water temperature up to the boiling point in the secondary system.

If the break is outside of containment, the lowest temperature expected would be 212°F (100°C) (saturation for atmospheric pressure); however, the final temperature could be higher (~250°F

(120°C)) if the break is in containment. In this case, the minimum temperature of the primary system depends on the final containment pressure following blowdown of the steam generator.

The controlling features of steam line break scenarios are the size of the break, control of feedwater to the broken steam generator, proper steaming of the unaffected generator, and control of HPI if HPI is actuated. Large steam line breaks resemble large LOCAs in terms of the rate of downcomer cooling. The differences between large steam line breaks and primary system pipe breaks (LOCAs) are as follows:

- The downcomer does not get as cold during secondary side breaks. Temperatures typically range from 212°F to 250°F (100°C to 121°C) for secondary side breaks, depending on whether the break is outside or inside of containment and, if inside, what the containment pressure is. By contrast, temperatures for primary system pipe breaks (LOCAs) can be as low as $\approx$40°F (4.4°C) for LOCAs because the minimum temperature is controlled by the boiling point of water, rather than ambient outside temperatures.

- Natural circulation flow rates (characteristic of large steam line breaks) are higher than loop stagnation flow rates (characteristic of large LOCAs). This higher flow ensures thorough mixing in the downcomer of the reactor coolant and ECCS flow (provided that coolant flow is initiated). The need to consider thermal plumes or streaming effects can thus be eliminated *a priori* for breaks in the secondary system.

2.1.3 Response of the Vessel to PTS Loading

As detailed in Section 2.1.2, all PTS precursors cause rapid cooling of the primary system. Depending on the transient, this cooling may or may not be accompanied by significant pressure. Both of these factors (rapid cooling and pressure) produce stresses in the vessel wall. The thermal stresses are (approximately) equal both along the axis of the vessel and around its circumference because of its cylindrical geometry. At the beginning of the cooldown, the thermal stresses are tensile on the inner diameter (ID) of the vessel, and are equilibrated by compressive stresses on its outer diameter (OD). As the transient continues, these thermal stresses reduce to zero to the extent that isothermal conditions are achieved in the vessel wall. The pressure stresses are twice as large in the circumferential direction as they are in the axial direction (again as a direct consequence of the cylindrical vessel geometry). Also, pressure stresses are constant through the thickness of the RPV wall.

The degree to which these stresses challenge the integrity of the vessel is controlled by a number of factors, the most important of which are as follows:

- the existence of a crack in the RPV, as well as its location, orientation, and size

- the material's resistance to cracking at the location of the flaw, which is measured by its "fracture toughness." Fracture toughness depends on a number of other factors (each defined at the flaw location), the most important of which are as follows:
  o temperature
  o irradiation damage (fluence)
  o chemical composition
  o fracture toughness before irradiation

Qualitatively, when high stresses occur in the presence of a large crack at a low temperature, and when the material at the location of the crack has low fracture toughness, initiation of the crack becomes more likely. The likelihood that this initiated crack will propagate all the way through the vessel wall (thereby producing a breach in the primary system and leading to a condition we have defined as "failure") again depends on the interplay between the applied stresses (and how they vary through the wall) with the material's ability to stop a running crack (known as "arrest fracture toughness"). The factors that influence fracture toughness (listed above) also influence arrest fracture toughness. While arrest is by no means certain, it is true that as the crack propagates into the vessel wall, arrest becomes progressively more

likely for transients where the stresses are primarily thermal. For these "mostly thermal" transients (medium- and large-diameter primary side pipe breaks, for example) arrest becomes more likely as the crack progresses into the vessel wall because temperature tends to increase while irradiation damage tends to decrease. (Both of these changes increase arrest fracture toughness.) Conversely, the progression of a crack initiated by a transient that produces both thermal and pressure stresses is fundamentally different. In this situation, the stresses remain higher through the wall because of the contribution of the pressure stress. Additionally, the fracture driving force tends to increase as the crack travels through the wall, as a result of the effect of primary system pressure on the crack faces. For these reasons, in transients that produce both thermal and pressure stresses, almost all cracks that initiate also propagate all the way through the vessel wall.

2.2   Historical Incidence of PTS

In the technical basis document written to support the current PTS Rule [SECY-82-465], the staff summarized the operational events that had, to that date, presented PTS challenges to operating plants. These events are depicted in Figure 2.2, which illustrates the three key operational parameters influencing event severity. Specifically, those parameters are the final RCS temperature, severity of the thermal shock (dT/dt) caused by the event, and existence (or lack thereof) of high pressure. A more recent search of licensee event reports (LERs) submitted between 1980 and 2000 reveals the occurrence of 128 "potentially PTS-significant" events. Approximately half of those LERs report the minimum temperature reached by the RCS, and the data suggest that the most recent transients are nearly all benign, with all but one having minimum RCS temperatures above 500°F (260°C). Thus, while overcooling events have occurred, they have only rarely been severe enough to challenge the structural integrity of the RPV.

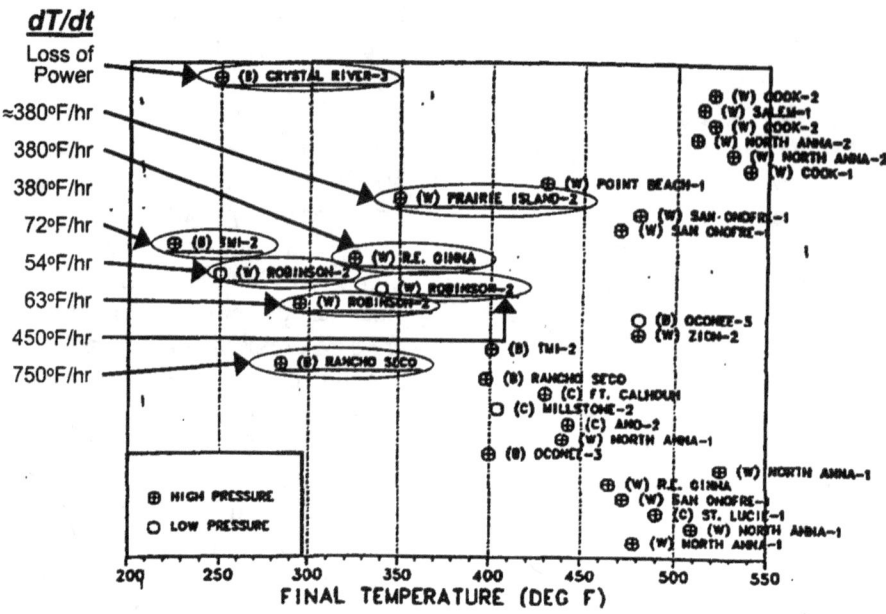

Figure 2.2. Figure 2.13 from SECY-82-465, depicting the final temperatures for 32 PTS precursor events experienced in commercial reactor service prior to 1982 (Cooling rates associated with the most significant transients have been superimposed on this graph.)

2.3 Summary of SECY-82-465 Findings

In the early 1980s, the nuclear industry and the NRC staff performed a number of investigations to assess the risk of vessel failure posed by PTS, and to establish the operational limits needed to ensure that the likelihood of RPV failures caused by PTS transients is maintained at an acceptably low level. These efforts led to the publication of a Commission paper [SECY-82-465] that provided the technical basis for subsequent development of what has come to be known as the "PTS Rule" [10 CFR 50.61]. The Commission paper included a number of probabilistic calculations performed to assess the influence of both contributory and mitigating factors (e.g., plant design, operator actions, operator training, material toughness, flaw population, and so on) on the outcome (vessel failure or non-failure) of a PTS event. The results of these calculations were used to develop a relationship between the probability of a through-wall crack developing in the RPV and the RT_{NDT} index temperature of the RPV. Regulatory Guide 1.154 [RG 1.154] later used this relationship, together with the judgment that

an annual through-wall cracking frequency of 5×10^{-6} is acceptable, to establish "screening limits," or maximum values of RT_{NDT} permitted during the operating life of the plant. Specifically, the established limits were +270°F (132°C) for axial welds, plates, and forgings, and +300°F (149°C) for circumferential welds [10 CFR 50.61].

In the mid-1980s, the NRC conducted a number of follow-on studies concerning the risk associated with PTS events [ORNL 85a, 85b, 86]. These studies, featuring plant-specific analyses of H.B. Robinson Steam Electric Plant, Calvert Cliffs Nuclear Power Plant, and Oconee Nuclear Station, demonstrated that plants embrittled to the PTS screening limit of +270°F (132°C) had an annual probability of developing a through-wall crack below 5×10^{-6} events/reactor year. These plant-specific analyses demonstrate the conservatism of the generic analyses reported in SECY-82-465, which served as the basis for the provisions of 10 CFR 50.61.

2.4 Current Provisions of 10 CFR 50.61

As previously stated, 10 CFR 50.61 establishes "screening limits" (or maximum values of RT_{NDT} permitted during the operating life of the plant) of +270°F (132°C) for axial welds, plates, and forgings, and +300°F (149°C) for circumferential welds. Here, we discuss in greater detail the provisions of 10 CFR 50.61, as follows:

- Section 2.4.1: why an index-temperature approach is adopted to characterize transition fracture toughness in ferritic steels

- Section 2.4.2: the approach used to characterize irradiation effects on the index temperature

- Section 2.4.3: the specific provisions of 10 CFR 50.61

- Section 2.4.4: an evaluation of currently operating PWRs, relative to the PTS screening limits In 10 CFR 50.61

2.4.1 Index Temperature Approach to Characterize Transition Fracture Toughness in Ferritic Steels

"Fracture toughness" is a measure of a material's ability to deform without breaking in the presence of preexisting cracks. Physical evidence and numerous experimental observations demonstrate that the temperature dependence of the cleavage initiation fracture toughness of ferritic steels (K_{Ic} or K_{Jc}) does not depend on composition, heat treatment, material forming techniques (weld, plate, or forging), or irradiation conditions [Kirk 01a]. These factors influence only the position of the toughness transition curve on the temperature axis. This has led to widespread use of transition temperature approaches to characterize the cleavage fracture toughness of ferritic materials [WRC 175, Wallin 93a]. Such approaches employ empirical and/or physical evidence to establish the temperature dependence of fracture toughness that is common to all ferritic steels. Figure 2.3 shows the data used to establish the ASME K_{Ic} curve, one of the earliest transition temperature characterizations

developed specifically using nuclear grade ferritic steels and weldments [WRC 175]. The formula for the curve in Figure 2.3 is as follows:

Eq. 2-1 $K_{Ic} = 33.2 + 2.806 \cdot \exp[0.02 \cdot (T - RT_{NDT} + 100)]$

where

RT_{NDT} is defined in accordance with ASME NB2331, as follows: $RT_{NDT} = MAX\{T_{NDT}, T_{35/50} - 60\}$.

T_{NDT} is the nil-ductility temperature (NDT) determined by testing specimens in accordance with ASTM E208.

$T_{35/50}$ is the transition temperature at which Charpy-V notch (CVN) specimens tested in accordance with ASTM E23 exhibit lateral expansion of at least 0.035-in. (0.89-mm) and absorbed energy of at least 50 ft-lbs (68J).

In Eq. 2-1, RT_{NDT} serves as an "index temperature" (i.e., a single value that characterizes the combined effects of alloying heat treatment, irradiation, etc. on fracture toughness)[‡]. Combining an index temperature with the (independently established) temperature dependence of fracture toughness (Eq. 2-1) defines the variation of toughness with temperature throughout the transition regime. The ease with which an index temperature can be experimentally established (relative to the much greater testing burden necessary to establish the complete toughness transition curve) makes transition temperature approaches attractive in applications where extensive material characterization is either economically infeasible or, for practical reasons, impossible.

[‡] While RT_{NDT} is an index temperature that has customarily been used along with a fracture toughness transition curve (i.e., the ASME K_{Ic} curve), RT_{NDT} is **not** a *fracture toughness* index temperature. As specified by ASME NB-2331 (and as represented in Eq. 2-1), RT_{NDT} is defined based on non-fracture toughness tests that can, at best, be correlated with fracture toughness. [*EricksonKirk PFM*] provides a more detailed description of RT_{NDT}.

The monitoring of neutron irradiation embrittlement falls into both categories because of the expense associated with the testing of irradiated materials and the limited volumes of material that can be irradiated as part of a surveillance program.

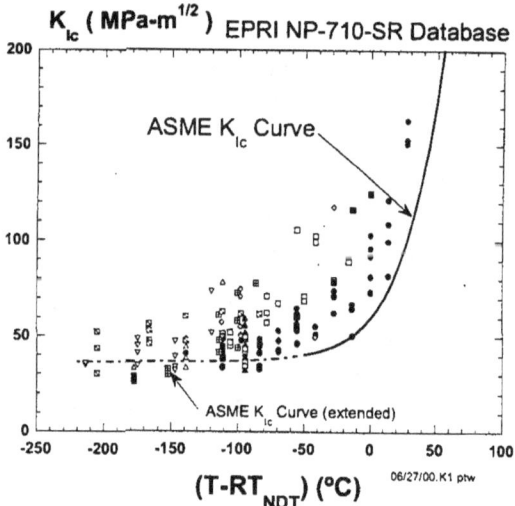

Figure 2.3. The empirical data used to establish the ASME K_{Ic} curve

2.4.2 Irradiation Effects on Index Temperature

As part of their required reactor vessel material surveillance programs qualified under Appendix H to 10 CFR Part 50, licensees attach surveillance capsules to the inner diameter and/or internal structures of the RPV. These capsules, which contain Charpy V-notch (CVN) specimens [ASTM E23], are removed over the lifetime of the RPV [ASTM E185], and the CVN specimens are tested to establish the index temperature T_{30} (the temperature at which the energy consumed in fracturing the CVN specimen is 30 ft-lbs). The difference between T_{30} after some amount of irradiation and T_{30} before irradiation begins is called ΔT_{30}, a metric which has long been used to assess the degree of irradiation damage imparted to the steel. (ΔT_{30} is closely related to the irradiation-induced shift in fracture toughness transition temperature. See [Kirk 01b] and [*EricksonKirk-PFM*].) These ΔT_{30} values from RPV surveillance programs provide the empirical basis to establish embrittlement trend curves that correlate the effect of irradiation exposure and chemical composition on ΔT_{30}. 10 CFR 50.61 adopts the following embrittlement trend curve [Randall 87]:

Eq. 2-2 $\qquad \Delta T_{30} = (CF) f^{(0.28-0.1\log f)}$

where

CF is a "chemistry factor" that characterizes the irradiation sensitivity of the steel. CF depends on copper content, nickel content, and product form. 10 CFR 50.61 includes tables of CF values.

f is the fast neutron fluence in neutrons per cm^2 (E>1Mev) divided by 10^{19}. For the purposes of 10 CFR 50.61, f is defined as the peak fluence at the clad-to-base metal interface at EOL.

2.4.3 Provisions of the Current Rule

10 CFR 50.61 uses the RT_{NDT} index temperature and the ΔT_{30} index temperature shift to estimate the effect of irradiation on RT_{NDT}, as follows:

Eq. 2-3 $\qquad RT_{NDT(f)} = RT_{NDT(u)} + \Re \cdot \Delta T_{30} + M$

where

$RT_{NDT(f)}$ is the estimated RT_{NDT} of the vessel material after irradiation to the fluence f. Toughness is determined from $RT_{NDT(f)}$ through its use as an index temperature for the ASME K_{Ic} and K_{IR} curves.

$RT_{NDT(u)}$ is the unirradiated RT_{NDT}. It can be determined based on either ASME NB2331 or other alternative techniques [NRC MEMO 82, NRC MTEB 5.2].

$\Re$ is 1 if ΔT_{30} is calculated from chemistry and fluence using Eq. 2-2. If ΔT_{30} is evaluated based on surveillance CVN data, $\Re$ is the ratio of the CF value estimated from the chemistry of the surveillance capsule to the CF value estimated from the heat average chemistry.

ΔT_{30} is defined by Eq. 2-2.

M   is defined by **Eq. 2-4**.

Eq. 2-4 $M = 2\sqrt{\sigma_I^2 + \sigma_\Delta^2}$

where

σ_I is the standard deviation in the value of $RT_{NDT(u)}$.

σ_Δ is the standard deviation in the value of ΔT_{30}.

According to 10 CFR 50.61, a nuclear power plant licensee is required to estimate $RT_{NDT(f)}$ at EOL using **Eq. 2-2** for all materials in the vessel beltline. The highest of these values, defined as RT_{PTS}, is compared to the 10 CFR 50.61 PTS screening limit of +300°F (149°C) for circumferential welds and +270°F (132°C) for all other materials. If RT_{PTS} exceeds the screening limit, the licensee is required to either (1) implement flux reduction techniques to keep RT_{PTS} below the screening limit, (2) anneal the vessel according to Regulatory Guide 1.162 [RG 1.162], or (3) submit a safety analysis to the NRC demonstrating that the plant is safe to operate beyond the screening limit.

2.4.4 Evaluation of Operating Plants Relative to the Current PTS Screening Limits

Figure 1.1 compares RT_{NDT} values for all currently operating PWRs evaluated at the end of their originally licensed life (40 years) using Eq. 2-3 with the current 10 CFR 50.61 PTS screening limits. A number of points should be noted:

- No plants currently exceed the screening limit. However, since the operators of the Yankee Rowe Nuclear Power Plant failed to persuade the staff to permit operation in excess of the screening limit using the probabilistic procedures outlined in Regulatory Guide 1.154 [RG 1.154], all plants that have predicted that they would exceed the screening limit before EOL have elected to remain in statutory compliance by (1) implementing flux reduction, (2) pursuing new technological approaches coupled with exemption requests, or (3) using a combination of the two approaches.

- Currently, 10 plants project an RT_{NDT} at EOL ($\equiv RT_{PTS}$) within 20°F of the screening limit.

- While the most embrittled region in one-third of the operating PWRs is the circumferential weld, less than half of those plants (11 of 23) have their operation limited by the circumferential weld because of the higher PTS screening limit currently used to assess these plants (+300°F (149°C) *vs.* the +270°F (132°C) value used for axial welds, plates, and forgings).

3 PTS Reevaluation Project

This chapter describes the PTS Reevaluation Project, which the NRC's Office of Nuclear Regulatory Research (RES) initiated in 1999. The chapter is structured as follows:

- Model Structure: Section 3.1 provides an overview of the model used to evaluate the technical basis for a revised PTS screening limit.

- Uncertainty Treatment: Since the objective of this study is to develop the technical basis for a risk-informed revision of 10 CFR 50.61, a systematic treatment of uncertainties is a central feature of this project. Section 3.2 describes our framework for uncertainty treatment and propagation and provides an overview of how uncertainties were addressed in the PRA, TH, and PFM.

- Assumptions: Section 3.3 summarizes the fundamental assumptions made in developing our model.

- Contributors: Section 3.4 describes the organizations and individuals that have made key contributions over the course of this project.

- Peer Review: Given the complex interdisciplinary nature of this project, and at the request of the NRC's Advisory Committee on Reactor Safeguards (ACRS), the staff convened a panel of external experts to review the study's methodologies, findings, and recommendations. Section 3.5 describes the conduct of this review group and the staff's approach to addressing their comments.

3.1 Model Used to Evaluate a Revised PTS Screening Limit

3.1.1 Restrictions on the Model

The desired outcome of this study is to establish the technical basis for a new PTS screening limit. To enable all commercial PWR licensees to assess the state of their RPVs relative to such a new criterion without the need to make new material property measurements, the fracture toughness properties of the RPV steels need to be estimated using only information that is currently available (i.e., RT_{NDT} values, upper-shelf energy values, and chemical composition of beltline materials). All of this information is summarized in the NRC's Reactor Vessel Integrity Database [RVID2].

3.1.2 Overall Structure of the Model

Our overall model involves three major components, which are illustrated (along with their interactions) in Figure 3-1:

Component 1. *Probabilistic Evaluation of Through-Wall Cracking Frequency*: Estimate frequency of through-wall cracking as a result of a PTS event given the operating, design, and material conditions in a particular plant.

Component 2. *Acceptance Criterion for Through-Wall Cracking Frequency*: Establish a value of reactor vessel failure frequency (RVFF) consistent with current guidance on risk-informed decision-making.

Component 3. *Screening Limit Development*: Compare the results of the two preceding steps to determine if some simple, materials-based PTS screening limit can be established. Conceptually, plants falling below the screening limit would be deemed adequately resistant to a PTS challenge and would not require further analysis. Conversely, more detailed, plant-specific analysis would be needed to assess the safety of plant operation beyond the screening limit.

Each of these components is described in the following subsections.

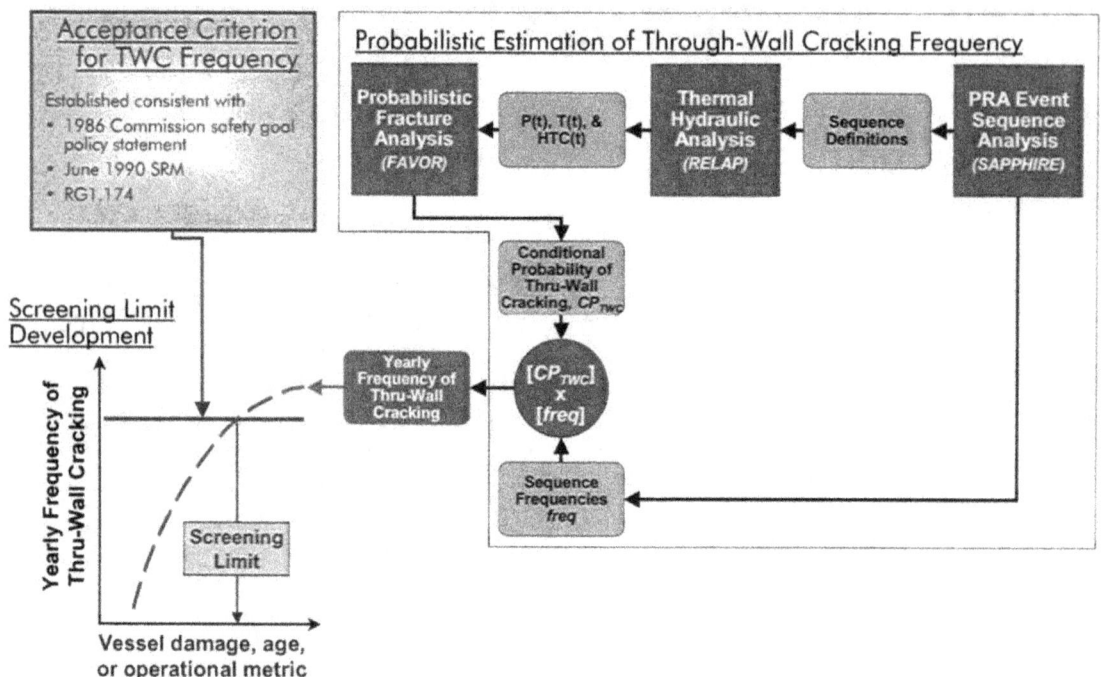

Figure 3-1. High-level schematic showing how a probabilistic estimate of through-wall cracking frequency (TWCF) is combined with a TWCF acceptance criterion to arrive at a proposed revision of the PTS screening limit.

3.1.2.1 Component 1: Probabilistic Estimation of Through-Wall Cracking Frequency

As illustrated in Figure 3-1, three main models (shown as solid blue squares), taken together, allow us to estimate the annual frequency of through-wall cracking in an RPV:

- PRA event sequence analysis
- TH analysis
- PFM analysis

In the following subsections, we first describe these three models and their sequential execution to give the reader an appreciation of their interrelationships and interfaces (Section 3.1.2.1.1). Secondly, we describe the iterative process we undertook, which involved repeated execution of all three models in sequence, to arrive at final models for each plant (Section 3.1.2.1.2). We then discuss the three

specific plants we analyzed in detail (Section 3.1.2.1.3). Finally, we conclude with a discussion of the steps taken to ensure that our conclusions based on these three analyses apply to domestic PWRs *in general* (Section 3.1.2.1.4).

3.1.2.1.1 Sequential Description of How PRA, TH, and PFM Models are Used To Estimate TWCF

First, a PRA event sequence analysis is performed to define the sequences of events that are likely to cause a PTS challenge to RPV integrity, and estimate the frequency with which such sequences can be expected to occur. The event sequence definitions are then passed to a TH model, which estimates the temporal variation of temperature, pressure, and heat-transfer coefficient in the RPV downcomer characteristic of each sequence definition. These temperature, pressure, and heat transfer coefficient histories are then passed to a PFM model that uses the TH output, along with other information concerning plant design and construction materials, to estimate the time-dependent "driving force to fracture" produced by a particular event sequence. The PFM model then compares this estimate of fracture driving force to the fracture toughness, or fracture resistance, of the RPV steel. This comparison allows us to estimate the probability that a crack would be created and would penetrate all the way through the RPV wall if that particular sequence of events actually occurred. The final step in the analysis involves a simple matrix multiplication of the probability of through-wall cracking (from the PFM analysis) with the frequency at which a particular event sequence is expected to occur (as defined by the event-tree analysis). This product establishes an estimate of the annual frequency of through-wall cracking that can be expected for a particular plant after a particular period of operation when subjected to a particular sequence of events. The annual frequency of through-wall cracking is then summed for all event sequences to estimate the total annual frequency of through-wall cracking for the vessel. Performance of such analyses for various operating lifetimes provides an estimate of how the annual through-wall cracking frequency can be expected to vary over the lifetime of the plant.

3.1.2.1.2 Iterative Process Used To Establish Plant-Specific Models

The set of transients used to represent a particular plant are identified using a PRA event-tree approach, in which many thousands of different overcooling sequences are "binned" together into groups of transients believed to produce similar thermal-hydraulic outcomes. Judgments regarding which transients to put into which bin were guided by such characteristics as similarity of break size, operator action, etc., and resulted in "bins" such as medium-break primary system LOCAs, MSLBs, etc. From each of the tens or hundreds of individual event sequences in each bin, a single sequence was then selected and programmed into the Reactor Leak

and Power (RELAP) TH excursion code to define the variation of pressure, temperature, and heat transfer coefficient *vs.* time. These TH transient definitions were then passed to the Fracture Analysis of Vessels, Oak Ridge (FAVOR) PFM code, which estimated the conditional probability of through-wall cracking (CPTWC) for each transient. When multiplied by the bin frequency estimates from the PRA, these CPTWCs become TWCF values, which (when rank-ordered) estimate the degree to which each bin contributes to the total TWCF of the vessel. At this stage, many bins were found to contribute very little or nothing at all to the total TWCF, and so received little further scrutiny. However, some bins invariably dominated the TWCF estimate. These bins were further subdivided by partitioning the bin frequency, and selecting a TH transient to represent each part of the original bin. This refined model was then reanalyzed using FAVOR, and the bins that provide significant contributions to TWCF are again examined. This process of bin partitioning, and selection of a TH transient to represent each newly partitioned bin, continued until the total estimated TWCF for the plant no longer changes significantly.

3.1.2.1.3 Plant-Specific Analyses Performed

In this study, we performed detailed calculations for three operating PWRs (Oconee 1, Beaver Valley 1, and Palisades), as shown in Figure 3-2. Together, these three plants sample a wide range of design and construction methods, and they contain some of the most embrittled RPVs in the operating fleet.

3.1.2.1.4 Generalization to All Domestic PWRs

Since the objective of this study is to develop the technical basis for revision of the 10 CFR 50.61 PTS screening limit that applies *in general* to all PWRs, we must understand the extent to which the three plant-specific analyses adequately address (in either a representative or a bounding sense) the range of conditions experienced by domestic PWRs *in general*.

- High embrittlement plant
- Westinghouse design

- High embrittlement plant
- Combustion Engineering design

- Plant used in 1980s PTS study
- Babcox & Wilcox design

Figure 3-2. The three plants analyzed in detail in the PTS reevaluation effort.

To achieve this goal, we have took the following measures:

- We performed sensitivity studies on both the TH and PFM models to address the effect of credible changes to the models and/or their input parameters. The results of these studies provide insights regarding the robustness of our conclusions (based on three plants), when applied to the PWR population in general.

- We examined plant design and operational characteristics of five additional plants. In so doing, our aim was to determine whether the design and operational features identified as being important in our three plant-specific analyses vary significantly enough in the population of PWRs to question the generality of our results.

- In our three plant-specific analyses, we assumed that the only possible origins of PTS events are caused by events *internal* to the plant. However, the PRA categorized *external* events (such as fires, floods, and earthquakes), which can also be PTS precursors. We, therefore, examined the potential for external initiating events to create significant additional risk relative to the internal initiating events we already modeled in detail.

3.1.2.2   Component 2: Acceptance Criterion for Through-Wall Cracking Frequency

Since the issuance of SECY-82-465 and the original PTS Rule, the NRC has established a considerable amount of guidance on the use of risk metrics and risk information in regulation [e.g., NRC FR 86, and RG 1.174]. To ensure consistency with this guidance, the PTS Reevaluation Project staff identified and assessed options for a risk-informed criterion for RVFF (which Regulatory Guide 1.154 currently specifies in terms of TWCF).

As described in a May 2002 status report on risk metrics and criteria for PTS [SECY-02-0092], the options developed involved both qualitative concerns (the definition of RPV failure) and quantitative concerns (a numerical criterion for the reactor vessel failure frequency). These options reflected uncertainties in the margin between PTS-induced RPV failure, core damage, and large early release. The options also incorporated input received from the ACRS [NRC LTR 02], regarding concerns related to the potential for large-scale oxidation of reactor fuel in an air environment.

Our assessment of the options involved identifying technical issues unique to PTS accident scenario development, developing an accident progression event tree to structure consideration of the issues, performing a scoping study of containment performance during PTS accidents, and reviewing the options in light of this information. The scoping study involved collecting and evaluating available information, performing a few limited-scope thermal-hydraulic and structural calculations, and conducting a semi-quantitative analysis of the likelihood of various accident progression scenarios.

3.1.2.3   Component 3: Screening Limit Development

As illustrated schematically in the lower left corner of Figure 3-1, a screening limit for PTS can be established based on a simple comparison of *TWCF* estimates as a function of an appropriate measure of RPV embrittlement with the *TWCF* acceptance criterion (see Chapter 10). Beyond the work to establish both the *TWCF vs.* embrittlement curve and the limit value for *TWCF*, it is also necessary to establish a suitable vessel damage metric that, ideally, allows different conditions in different materials at different plants to be normalized. From a practical standpoint, "suitable" implies that the metric needs to be based on readily available information regarding plant operation and materials.

3.2   Uncertainty Treatment

At the outset of this project (1999), a staff member reviewed the NRC's existing approach for PRA modeling, focusing on how uncertainties should be treated, how they were propagated through the PRA, TH, and PFM models, and how that approach compared with the NRC's guidelines on work supporting risk-informed regulation [*Siu 99*]. This review established the general framework for model development and uncertainty treatment adopted in this study. In the following two sections, we first review this recommended framework (Section 3.2.1), and then discuss its actual implementation (Section 3.2.2). Section 3.2.2 provides an overview of the uncertainty treatment implemented in the PRA, TH, and PFM analyses and discusses how uncertainties are "passed" between these three main technical modules. Details of these implementations appear elsewhere in this report (Sections 5.2.6–5.2.7, 6.8.2, and 7.4, respectively) and in other documents [*Whitehead-PRA, Chang*, and *EricksonKirk-PFM*, respectively].

3.2.1   Recommended Framework

In this study, we performed probabilistic calculations to establish the technical basis for a revised PTS Rule within an integrated systems analysis framework [Woods 01]. Our approach considers a broad range of factors that influence the likelihood of vessel failure during a PTS event, while accounting for uncertainties in these factors across a breadth of technical disciplines [*Siu 99*]. Two central features of this approach are a focus on the use of realistic input values and models (wherever possible), and *explicit* treatment of uncertainties (using currently available uncertainty analysis tools and techniques). Thus, our current approach improves upon that employed in developing SECY-82-465, in which many aspects of the analysis included intentional and unquantified conservatisms, and uncertainties were treated *implicitly* by incorporating them into the models (RT_{NDT}, for example).

Our probabilistic models distinguish between aleatory and epistemic uncertainties. Aleatory uncertainties arise as a result of the randomness inherent in a physical or human process, whereas epistemic uncertainties are caused by limitations in our current state of knowledge (or understanding) of a given process. A practical way to distinguish between aleatory and epistemic uncertainties is that the latter can, in principle, be reduced by an increased state of knowledge. Conversely, because aleatory uncertainties arise as a result of randomness at a level below which a particular process is modeled, they are fundamentally irreducible. The distinction between aleatory and epistemic uncertainties is an important part of PTS analysis because different mathematical and/or modeling procedures are used to represent these different types of uncertainty.

3.2.2 Implementation

In this section, we describe our implementation of the uncertainty framework synopsized in Section 3.2.1, focusing specifically on the following aspects:

- How the framework was implemented in of the PRA, TH, and PFM analyses. Consistent with the framework, we systematically identify uncertainties and characterize their nature (as aleatory or epistemic). These uncertainties are then either quantified or addressed as part of the overall structure of the mathematical model.

- How uncertainties are "propagated" through the major components of the computational model used to estimate the TWCF illustrated in the upper right corner of Figure 3-1. This includes propagating uncertainties from PRA to TH, PRA to PFM, and TH to PFM.

- How the uncertainties considered in all three models (i.e., PRA, TH, and PFM) become manifest in the uncertainties in the estimated value of TWCF.

The first two points are described in Sections 3.2.2.1 through 3.2.2.3, for PRA, TH, and PFM, respectively. The final point is addressed in Section 3.2.2.4. Finally, Section 3.2.2.5 addresses the uncertainties associated with the potential "incompleteness" of our mathematical model relative to the physical reality we are trying to represent.

3.2.2.1 PRA

As illustrated in Figure 3-1, the PRA analysis has two major outputs:

- Bin Definition: the representation (or model) of the total PTS challenge using a finite number of event "bins," each of which represents an assortment of TH scenarios (that are believed to be similar)

- Bin Frequency: an estimate (central tendency and distribution) of the frequency with which the events represented by each bin are expected to occur

Each of these outputs has an associated uncertainty, as described in the following sections.

3.2.2.1.1 Bin Definition

Each bin represents an assortment of TH scenarios (i.e., PTS sequences) for the following reasons:

- Like most PRAs, ours includes the usual idealization that both equipment failures and operator actions are binary (i.e., a valve either sticks open or it does not, an operator either acts or fails to act)[§]. Clearly, reality is continuous; valves may stick open by various amounts and operators may act, but after some delay. This idealization leads to the situation where our mathematical representation (a single bin) represents a spectrum of potential outcomes, with each outcome having a distinct TH characteristic.

- Another common PRA feature that we adopt is to group "similar" transients together in a single bin. For example, all primary system pipe breaks having a break diameter of 8-in. (20-cm) and above are placed in a single bin called "large-break LOCAs." This approach is motivated by previous experience indicating that transients grouped in this manner have "similar" severity. Nonetheless, such "similarity" is an approximation. To continue with the large-break LOCA example, hot leg and cold leg breaks have different severities for the same break diameter, break diameter changes above 8-in. (20-cm) cause slightly different severities, and so on. All of these unmodeled effects occur for well-recognized physical reasons. Again, this idealization leads to the situation where our model (a single bin) represents a spectrum of potential outcomes, with each outcome having a distinct TH characteristic.

---

§   As detailed in Section 5.2.6.1, this statement is not always true. When judged to be important, certain equipment failures and operator actions were further subdivided (e.g., 30% stuck-open valves, operator actions at 1 vs. 10 minutes, etc.). Nonetheless, the PRA model is still a discrete representation of a continuum, and each PRA bin still represents a spectrum of TH responses.

Thus, the structure of the PRA representation of the PTS challenge contains within it an uncertainty that is random and (hence) aleatory, having to do with all the ways that a PTS challenge could occur (i.e., PTS sequences). Discretizing the continuum of potential PTS sequences (which number in the tens or hundreds of thousands) into a tractable number of bins for detailed analysis (~hundreds) means that each bin contains many sequences, each of which can (in principle) produce a different TH response and, thereby, a different effect on the vessel.

As is often the case in PRA, only a portion of the entire aleatory uncertainty significantly affects the overall results of the analysis. The important part of the aleatory uncertainty is determined by the way the PRA model was developed and how the bins were defined. As described in Section 3.1.2.1.2, an initial PRA model is developed and individual TH sequences are selected to represent each bin. These TH definitions are then passed to the FAVOR PFM code, which estimates the CPTWC for each transient. When multiplied by the frequency estimates for each bin, these CPTWC values become TWCF values, which (when rank-ordered) estimate the degree to which each bin contributes to the total TWCF of the vessel. At this stage, many bins are found to contribute very little or nothing at all to the total TWCF. However, some bins invariably dominate the TWCF estimate. These bins are then further subdivided by partitioning the frequency of the bin, and selecting a TH transient to represent each part of the original bin. This refined model is then reanalyzed using FAVOR, and the bins that provide significant contributions to TWCF are again examined. This process of bin partitioning, and selection of a TH transient to represent each newly partitioned bin, continues until the total estimated TWCF for the plant no longer changes significantly. At this point, that portion of all possible PTS sequences (and, hence, the aleatory uncertainty) that significantly affects the overall results is determined and remains in the final model as representing the aleatory uncertainty associated with how a PTS challenge might occur.

3.2.2.1.2   Bin Frequency

For each bin, there is uncertainty regarding the true frequency of occurrence. The uncertainty in the frequency with which the events represented by each bin occurs depends upon the following three factors, each of which is also uncertain:

- uncertainty in the initiating event and its associated frequency

- uncertainty in the series of equipment successes and/or failures that may follow the initiating event, and the uncertainty in their associated probabilities

- uncertainty in the operator actions that may or may not be taken following the initiating event, and the uncertainty in their associated probabilities

Thus, the frequency of occurrence of each bin is a function of the frequencies and probabilities of these factors. (The bin frequency is estimated from the individual frequencies and probabilities using Latin Hypercube sampling techniques to develop the bin frequency histogram that is provided as input to the FAVOR post-processor (FAVPOST).) Each of these factors has an associated epistemic uncertainty, which is described by a distribution. These uncertainties are epistemic in nature because our belief as to the estimates of these frequencies and probabilities is influenced by our limited state of knowledge about these rare events; and better knowledge would clearly lead to reduced uncertainty.

3.2.2.2   TH

The approach used to address uncertainty in the TH analysis principally utilized sensitivity studies to quantify the effects of phenomenological and boundary condition uncertainties/variations on the severity of a TH sequence. The results of these studies were used in two ways:

(1) They were combined with probability estimates of the sensitivity parameters being evaluated to adjust the bin frequencies from the PRA analysis.

(2) They were used to justify further subdivision of the PRA bins. (See the discussion in Section 3.2.2.1.1.)

In this way, the TH uncertainty analysis accounts for certain parameters that can affect the thermal-hydraulic response of the plant, which were not explicitly considered in the PRA analysis (e.g., season of the year). Because the uncertainty analysis also produced insights regarding the effects of various system parameters and TH models on event severity, it also helped to identify the transient used to represent each PRA bin to the PFM analysis.

This method of accounting for TH uncertainty does not quantify the uncertainties associated with each TH sequence. Rather, it characterizes the uncertainties associated with each PRA bin. This is appropriate because, as illustrated in Figure 3.3, each TH sequence that is passed to the PFM analysis represents a much larger number of TH sequences that, together, constitute a PRA "bin." Provided the combined effects of the TH parameter and modeling uncertainties on the severity of this one representative sequence is small relative to both

- the uncertainty in the frequency of occurrence of all of sequences in the bin, and

- the variability in severity between the different sequences in the bin

then, the uncertainty associated with TH parameter and modeling uncertainties of the representative sequence can be considered negligible. The appropriateness of not accounting for these uncertainties because they are negligibly small is ensured by the iterative process used to define the PRA bins.

As described in Section 3.2.2.1.1, PRA bins that contribute significantly to the estimated TWCF were continually partitioned (including appropriate partitioning of the bin frequencies and selection of new TH sequences to represent each partitioned bin) until the total estimated TWCF for the plant did not change significantly with continued partitioning. Thus, any errors caused by not explicitly accounting for the TH parameter and modeling uncertainties associated with the TH sequence used to represent each PRA bin are not expected to influence the outcome of the analysis (i.e., the estimated values of TWCF).

3.2.2.3   PFM

Development of the PFM model featured a comprehensive review of all model components (both sub-models and parameters) with the aim of identifying, classifying, and quantifying the uncertainties in each [*EricksonKirk-PFM*]. In the great majority of cases, the best-estimate models (and associated uncertainties) were quantified, and these were propagated through the calculation. In some cases, inadequate empirical and/or physical evidence existed to support creation of a best-estimate with uncertainties. In these cases, conservative models and parameters were adopted [*EricksonKirk-SS*]). The judgment to include these conservatisms as part of the overall model is itself a treatment of uncertainty, not through quantification, but rather by influencing the structure of the overall PFM model.

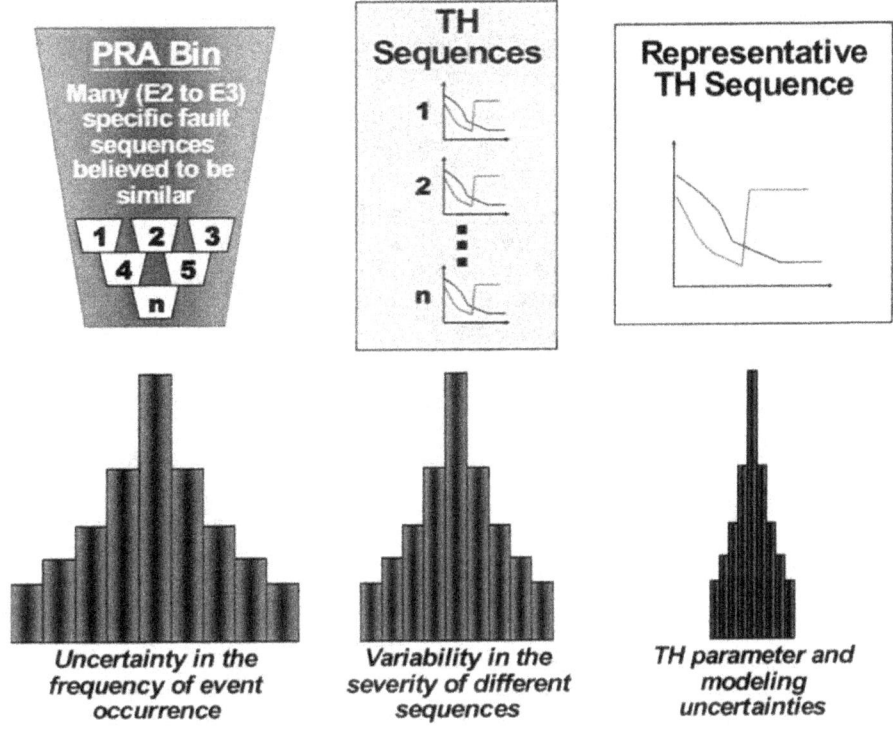

Figure 3.3. Characterization of TH uncertainties

The great majority of the parameters in the PFM model (e.g., RT_{NDT}, Cu, Ni, fluence, flaw parameters) were determined to have epistemic uncertainties. Statistical distributions were developed to characterize these uncertainties from representative data. In some cases, physical models guided these characterizations.

Conversely, the various fracture toughness parameters in the PFM model were all determined to have aleatory (irreducible) uncertainties. These alleatory uncertainties are a direct and natural consequence of the heterogeneity of the material at the same size scale as the crack-tip deformation fields. They also arise because the interaction of two factors (material resistance *vs.* applied loading) produces the measured parameter called fracture toughness (again, see [*EricksonKirk-PFM*] for full details).

The output of the PFM model is distributions quantifying the CPTWC for each transient analyzed. (This value is termed "conditional" because occurrence of the transient is assumed in the PFM calculation.) These distributions account for the uncertainties in the various toughness parameters, non-toughness parameters, and sub-models that together make up the PFM model.

3.2.2.4 What the Uncertainties in TWCF Represent

Sections 3.2.2.1, 3.2.2.2, and 3.2.2.3 described the uncertainties in the PRA, TH, and PFM models, respectively. Table 3.1 summarizes that discussion, and indicates that in each of these three areas, the important uncertainties have been either "accounted for" (in that they influenced the structure of the computational model) or "numerically quantified" (as part of the model). Thus, a description of what the uncertainties in the reported values of TWCF represent requires more than a strictly numerical answer. As described in a NUREG-series report on the theory and implementation of the FAVOR code [*Williams*], FAVPOST estimates the numerical value of TWCF by performing a matrix multiplication of the distribution of the frequency of each bin defined in the PRA analysis with the distribution of CPTWC estimated by the PFM analysis. However, these uncertainties and their quantifiable distributions arise as a direct consequence of the particular model we have used to calculate them and, as indicated in Table 3.1, the structure of the model itself accounts for a number of uncertainties that have not been numerically quantified. Thus, the uncertainties in our reported TWCF values represent all of the uncertainties discussed in this section and in the detailed companion reports [*Whitehead-PRA*, *Chang*, and *EricksonKirk-PFM*].

Table 3.1. Summary of uncertainty treatment in the three major technical areas

Technical Area	Uncertainty Type	Uncertainties that were accounted for in the structure of the model	Uncertainties that were numerically quantified
PRA	Aleatory	Discretization of all of the ways a PTS challenge could occur into a finite number of "bins"	---
	Epistemic	---	Bin frequency
TH	Aleatory	Boundary condition uncertainties	The effects of certain boundary condition uncertainties are reflected in the frequencies assigned to certain PRA bins.
	Epistemic	Model uncertainties	---
PFM	Aleatory	---	Uncertainties in fracture toughness values (e.g., K_{Ic}, K_{Ia}, J_{Ic})
	Epistemic	Adoption of conservative models (e.g., RT_{NDT}, flaw distribution, fluence attenuation)	Uncertainties in non-toughness values (e.g., Cu, Ni)

3.2.2.5 Incompleteness Uncertainty

As with any attempt to represent a complex physical system using a mathematical model, the question of "incompleteness uncertainty" arises. That is, "What has been left out of the model and, as a result, how confident should a decision-maker be in using the results of the analysis?". It is fundamentally impossible to quantitatively address uncertainties arising from unknown factors. However, our process for model building, verification and validation (V&V) of our computational models, conservatisms known to remain in the models, the various reviews to which our work has been subjected, and the potential implementation of our results in future rules all provide qualitative assurance that any incompleteness in the model should have a negligible effects on the results. We discuss each of these factors below:

- Process for Model Building: The PRA, TH, and PFM models were developed and continually improved throughout this study. Licensees from the three study plants provided input and review of both the PRA and TH models. The commercial nuclear power industry, working under the auspices of the Electric Power Research Institute (EPRI) Materials Reliability Project, was involved in reviewing all three models from the inception of the study. Additionally, subject-matter experts from the industry played a key role in both developing and reviewing the PFM model. To address uncertainties in a manner consistent with the framework proposed by Siu and synopsized in Section 3.2.1, various new models of both flaws and fracture toughness behavior were created for the PFM model. These new models have been presented for review and comment in various public and international venues, and have been published in both peer-reviewed journals and conference proceedings [Kirk 01a, Kirk 02a, Natishan 01, EricksonKirk 04].

- Computational V&V: Calculations made in PRA, TH, and PFM are performed using computer codes referred to as SAPHIRE, RELAP, and FAVOR, respectively. SAPHIRE and RELAP are commercially available programs and have been subjected to extensive review and V&V. The FAVOR PFM code was developed by RES for the express purpose of performing probabilistic simulations of PTS. Accordingly, we have performed and reported V&V of FAVOR according to the software quality assurance (SQA) guidance in NUREG/BR-0167 [*Malik*].

- Known Conservatisms: While we devoted considerable effort throughout this study to perform "best estimate" analyses, it is nonetheless true that a number of conservatisms remain. Primary among these is the decision to treat through-wall cracking of the RPV as *equivalent to* occurrence of a large early release of radioactivity to the atmosphere. Chapter 10 discusses the reason for, and conservatism implicit in, this assumption. Furthermore, throughout the development of all the PRA, TH, and PFM models, there has been a tendency to address uncertainties by adopting conservative models or input values when the weight of physical and empirical evidence was inadequate to construct a "best-estimate" model. These types of conservatisms are discussed throughout Chapters 5–7 and in the supporting detailed reports [*Whitehead-PRA, Bessette, EricksonKirk-PFM*], and are summarized in Section 11.4.4.

- Reviews: As described under *Process for Model Building* above, our models were subjected to both internal and external review during their development. Additionally, we solicited and received reviews of the entire project from three sources. In December 2002, we published an interim report summarizing the results of computations performed up to that time [*Kirk 12-02*]. This report was reviewed by both the commercial nuclear power industry and staff from the NRC's Office of Nuclear Reactor Regulation (NRR), with both groups providing written comments [NEI Comments, NRR Comments]. These reviews indicated the need for numerous minor revisions, remodeling of some Oconee transients, and (most significantly) a fundamental restructuring and expansion of the documentation to improve both clarity and completeness. Addressing these comments resulted in this document (and the supporting documents, see Section 4.1),

which have been subjected to review by an international group of experts. The comments provided by this panel (see Section 3.5 and Appendix B) have, again, resulted in improvements in both our documentation and our mathematical models. It is important to recognize that the combined effect of all of these changes (i.e., changes made in response to NEI, NRR, and external review panel comments) to the TWCF results [*Kirk 12-02*] has been to reduce the total TWCF by, on average, approximately one-third. Thus, while the comments received from the review panels have improved both the clarity of our documentation and the overall completeness and correctness of our models, the changes have not substantially altered either the overall structure of the models or the TWCF results that could be used to establish a new numerical value for the PTS screening criterion.

- Potential Implementation: Should NRR elect to use the information presented in this and supporting documents as the basis for rulemaking to revise the requirements of 10 CFR 50.61, it must be remembered that it is only a *screening limit* that is being revised. Exceeding a screening limit does not suggest that failure is imminent (or even likely). It merely signals the need for the licensee to take additional actions (either analytical or mitigative) to assure NRR that plant operation beyond the screening limit does not unduly increase the risk to the public. Additionally, the current structure of 10 CFR 50.61 requires that these actions be taken three years before the limits are actually exceeded. It also requires continued surveillance (according to the requirements of Appendix H to 10 CFR Part 50) to ensure the continued validity of assumptions made during development of the screening limit regarding irradiation embrittlement mechanisms. Maintenance of this rule structure mitigates the practical impact on the overall public risk posed by PTS, as a result of any incompleteness uncertainties associated with the recommended numerical value of the screening limit.

3.3 Fundamental Assumptions and Idealizations

Any mathematical model of a physical system inherently involves some level of assumption and/or idealization to make estimates of the parameters of interest tractable within the practical constraints associated with the particular problem of interest. As discussed in greater detail in Chapters 5, 6, and 7, the PRA, TH, and PFM models each involve a large number of sub-models and, thus, a large number of possible assumptions and/or idealizations. Assumptions and idealizations that occur within each of the PRA, TH, and PFM sub-models are, therefore, addressed in Chapters 5, 6, and 7, respectively, or within their supporting reports. In the following subsections, we discuss the fundamental assumptions and idealizations that pertain to the PRA, TH, and PFM sub-models *as a whole*.

3.3.1 Probabilistic Risk Assessment

As with any PRA or HRA, the analysis team found it necessary to make assumptions in this study. In addition to the typical assumptions made as part of a PRA (e.g., actual plant system configuration is represented by the as-built as-operated documented information), the analysis team made various additional assumptions during the detailed PTS analyses. These assumptions are grouped into seven categories, as follows:

1. Project execution

    a. Lessons learned from the Oconee analysis and preliminary PFM calculations for Beaver Valley and Palisades were used to simplify the model construction for Beaver Valley and Palisades.

2. Possible PTS Initiating Events

    a. Scenarios initiated by an anticipated transient without scram (ATWS) were screened from the PTS analyses for two reasons. First, ATWS events generally begin with severe undercooling (i.e., there is too much power for the heat removal capability) and likely involve other failures to achieve an overcooling situation. Second, with typical ATWS frequency estimates in the range of 10^{-5}/yr to 10^{-6}/yr combined with the need for other failures to occur to *possibly* cause a continuing and serious overcooling situation, ATWS-initiated sequences should not be significant contributors to PTS risk when compared to other modeled scenarios with initiator frequencies commonly in the range of 1/yr to 10^{-3}/yr.

    b. Interfacing systems loss-of-coolant accidents (ISLOCAs) could involve overcooling from the start of the event. However, significant ISLOCAs often fail, or are assumed to fail, mitigating equipment in PRAs, which ultimately causes an undercooling event, rather than an overcooling event; thus, ISLOCAs were not analyzed. Also, similar to ATWS, frequency estimates for ISLOCAs of sufficient size to cause a sever cooldown are in the range of 10^{-5}/yr to 10^{-6}/yr. Therefore, ISLOCAs should not be significant contributors to PTS risk when compared to other modeled scenarios with initiator frequencies commonly in the range of 1/yr to 10^{-3}/yr.

    c. It was asssumed that the frequency of inadvertent reactor/turbine trips under hot zero power (HZP) conditions is 20% of that occuring under full power conditions. The basis of this 20% factor is as follows:

        i. The plant operates at HZP approximately 2% of the time.

        ii. Except for inadvertent reactor/turbine trips attributable to transient conditions that arise while purposely changing feedwater and steam conditions along with changing power and other parameters in the plant, a review of transients occurring while at HZP provided no evidence that initiators are significantly more prone to occur at HZP than at full power. While no statistical treatment of this observation was attempted, engineering judgment was used to suggest that reactor/turbine trips seem more likely under HZP than under full power conditions because operators are often adjusting feedwater and steam conditions during HZP, factors that increase the likleyhood of tripping the plant. On this baisis, a factor of 10 increase in the likelihood of trips under HZP (vs. full power condtions) was assumed.

   iii.   2% x 10 = 20%

3. Scenario development

   a. Medium- and large-break LOCAs were modeled as leading directly to a significant thermal transient for the reactor vessel without the need to consider the response of mitigating systems.

   b. The status of pressurizer PORVs and SRVs (i.e., whether they were open or closed) was assumed to be unimportant in the development of small LOCA scenarios. The basis for this assumption was that the pressure drop resulting from the LOCA initiating event should preclude the demand to open a primary side PORV or SRV.

   c. The PTS models excluded certain systems, structures, and components (SSCs) (e.g., pressurizer sprays and heaters) because they typically were found to have little impact on PTS risk.

   d. The functions of some SSCs were simply assumed for certain scenarios (e.g., accumulators were assumed to inject their inventory if conditions in the primary were such that injection should occur—failure of accumulator check valves was not modeled).

   e. The analysts recognized the importance of *when* an operator action occurred or

when a piece of equipment changed state to the degree of overcooling experienced during a PTS scenario. To account for this, the scenarios incorporated a ***limited*** set of important operator actions (e.g., operator fails to throttle high-pressure injection) and equipment state changes (e.g., stuck-open pressurizer SRV recloses).

4. Systems analysis

   a. The impact of heating and ventilation failures on equipment performance can be ignored because of the relatively slow effects on PTS-relevant equipment (e.g., failure of a pump as a result of room cooling failure typically takes a few hours by which time the PTS event is most likely over).

5. Data

   a. Engineering judgment was used to estimate the failure probabilities for some SSCs. The numerical values provided by these judgments were typically conservative (i.e., the values were chosen such that potential PTS scenarios would not be inadvertently eliminated).

6. Human reliability analysis

   a. Pre-initiator human failure events (HFEs) were not explicitly modeled in the Oconee and Beaver Valley PTS PRAs. Such human events were assumed to be included in the industry-wide data that was used to model system unavailabilities. For the Palisades analysis, pre-initiator HFEs were left "as-is" (i.e., the existing pre-initiator HFEs in the Palisades PRA model used in the PTS analysis were not modified).

   b. The time at which operators perform an action is taken to be either the earliest the action can be performed or the latest the action can be performed, whichever exacerbates PTS conditions (e.g., if the action involves the operator successfully throttling a pump by 20 minutes, then the action would be modeled as occurring at 20 minutes).

   c. Given the uncertainty associated with the various plant conditions that could exist during hot shutdown, some human error probabilities (HEPs) were assumed to be greater than their corresponding full-power HEPs.

7. PTS bin development

   a. The assignment of the large number of potential PTS scenarios (tens of thousands) to a more limited number of PTS TH bins (tens to over one hundred) involved the analysts' judgments as to how various combinations of equipment and operator successes affected the TH response of the plant when compared to a limited set of initial TH calculations. If the analysts judged that a scenario's response would be similar to an existing TH calculation, the scenario was "binned" into the existing calculation's bin. If the analysts judged that a scenario's response could be sufficiently different from the existing calculations, a new TH calculation was requested, thereby creating a new bin.

   b. Typically, the analysts estimated the impact of the various equipment and operator combinations on two parameters (i.e., minimum downcomer temperature and primary pressure).

   c. Minimum downcomer temperature was the most important parameter that the analysts used to decide whether an existing TH bin could represent a scenario, or whether a new TH bin should be created.

   d. If the analysts determined that a PTS scenario could "fit" into more than one TH bin having similar characteristics (i.e., minimum downcomer temperatures approximately the same), they assigned the scenario to the bin believed to be more conservative (i.e., the scenario was assigned to the bin with the highest primary pressure).

3.3.2 Thermal-Hydraulics

The appropriateness of the RELAP TH analysis to assess PTS rests on the validity of the following fundamental assumptions:

• We assume that the TH methodology implemented in RELAP is appropriate to assess the conditions in the downcomer during a PTS event. RELAP estimates fluid temperatures and wall-to-fluid heat transfer coefficients that represent well-mixed conditions in the downcomer at the core elevation. This approach assumes that jets, thermal plumes, and thermal streaming are not significant factors for PTS-type loadings.

• We assume that it is appropriate to use the variation of pressure, temperature, and heat transfer coefficient with time characteristic of a *single* TH transient to represent an entire PRA bin (which may contain many tens or hundreds of transients).

In the following subsections, we discuss the appropriateness of each of these assumptions.

3.3.2.1 Appropriateness of the RELAP TH Model, in General

At the most basic level, a TH analysis requires calculation of conservation of mass and energy, from which pressure and temperature follow from the equation of state. From this information, the analysis then estimates the distribution of energy within the RCS. Within the downcomer, the interface between the thermal-hydraulic and fracture mechanics calculations is the heat flux between the downcomer fluid and the vessel wall. Heat flux quantifies the RCS energy distribution, which depends on both the temperature and heat transfer characteristics of the downcomer region. In this study, we used RELAP5/MOD3.2.2γ to estimate the heat flux and pressure boundary conditions. RELAP5 is a best-estimate systems code that models heat transfer and hydrodynamic processes without any intentional conservative or nonconservative modeling features. The code has been extensively documented [RELAP 01]. Our specific validation of RELAP5 addressed its ability to accurately estimate pressure, downcomer fluid temperature, and wall-to-fluid heat transfer coefficients for PTS loading conditions [*Fletcher*]. In these validation studies, which are summarized in Section 6.2, we compared RELAP5/MOD3.2.2γ predictions of pressure and temperature to measurements made in the most ideally scaled integral systems test facilities. These comparisons demonstrate that RELAP5/MOD3.2.2γ predictions of pressure and temperature appropriately characterize PTS loading events.

3.3.2.2 Appropriateness of the TH Model

RELAP5 calculates fluid temperatures and wall-to-fluid heat transfer coefficients that are characteristic of a well-mixed downcomer (at the core elevation). Dickson evaluated the suitability of this assumption using a predecessor of FAVOR [Dickson 87]. In that study, the base-case calculation represented a hot leg break with a diameter of 2-in. (5-cm) and a "nominal" plume strength of 140°F (60°C). (Plume strength equals the temperature difference between the colder water below the cold legs and the balance of the downcomer.) It should be noted that this "nominal" plume strength greatly exceeds any plumes that have been measured, as detailed in the following paragraph, and this "nominal" plume had no discernable effect of (relative to no plume at all) on the probability of through-wall cracking estimated by FAVOR. Furthermore, a doubling of the nominal plume strength produces only a 30% increase in the estimated probability of through-wall cracking. This study provided an indication that the well-mixed downcomer assumptions made by both RELAP and FAVOR are appropriate.

More recently, we have performed additional work to establish the adequacy of the assumption of a one-dimensional (1D) temperature boundary condition, as follows:

- A new integral experimental program was conducted at the APEX-CE test facility at Oregon State University to study cold leg and downcomer mixing [*Reyes-APEX*].

- We reviewed existing experimental databases, including integral system tests in the Loss-of-Fluid Test (LOFT) facility and the Rig of Safety Assessment (ROSA), as well as full-scale tests in the Upper Plenum Test Facility (UPTF), and reduced-scale mixing tests at Creare, Purdue University, and Imatron Voimy Oy (Finland).

- We performed mixing calculations using the REMIX code and computational fluid dynamics (CFD) codes.

In thermal-hydraulic evaluations of PTS [*Bessette*], we compare these experimental data and RELAP5/MOD3.2.2γ predictions of pressure and temperature to establish the adequacy of the uniform temperature approximation. As seen consistently in the experimental data, the downcomer is well-mixed. In integral system test data, the temperature variations seen in the in the axial or azimuthal directions is on the order of 9°F (5°C). Large temperature gradients (i.e., on the order of 180°F, or 100°C) are often seen in the cold leg following loop flow stagnation. However, temperature gradients in the cold leg do not translate to corresponding temperature variations in the downcomer because of the large eddy mixing occurring in the downcomer.

In summary, the maximum plume measured in any integral test facility representation of a PTS transient is on the order of 9°F (5°C). Probabilistic fracture mechanics calculations show that much larger plumes (strengths of ≈ 216°F, or 120°C) are needed to have even small effects on the estimated probability of through-wall cracking [*Bessette*, Section 5.5]. For these reasons, the modeling approaches of both the RELAP and FAVOR codes with regard to temperature uniformity throughout the downcomer are viewed as both appropriate and non-biasing for this application.

3.3.2.3 Appropriateness of a Using a Single TH Transient To Represent an Entire PRA Bin

In Section 3.1.2.1.2, we described the iterative process used to establish the single TH transient that represents an entire PRA bin (which may contain many tens or hundreds of transients). This process includes continual partitioning of the PRA bins that contribute significantly to the estimated TWCF until the total estimated TWCF for the plant does not change significantly with continued partitioning. Given that process, the appropriateness of using a single TH transient to represent an entire bin (which may contain tens or hundreds of sequences that can produce, in principal, a like number of different TH responses) is not justified based on the exact agreement of the representative TH transient to all of the other transients in the bin (which is not, and cannot, be guaranteed). Rather, the appropriateness is justified by the procedure detailed in Section 3.1.2.1.2, which ensures that further subdivision of the bins would not result in significant changes to the TWCF (the desired output of the analysis).

3.3.3 Probabilistic Fracture Mechanics

The appropriateness of the FAVOR PFM analysis to assess PTS rests on the validity of the following four fundamental assumptions:

- We assume (in general) that linear elastic fracture mechanics (*LEFM*) is an appropriate methodology to use in assessing the structural integrity of RPVs subjected to PTS loadings, and (in particular) that FAVOR predictions of the fracture response of RPVs in response to PTS loading are accurate.

- We assume that the effect of crack growth by subcritical mechanisms (i.e., environmentally assisted cracking and/or fatigue) is negligible and, consequently, the flaw population of interest is that associated with initial vessel fabrication.

- We assume that the fracture toughness of the stainless steel cladding is adequately high, and remains so even after irradiation, so there is no possibility of cladding failure

as a result of the loading imposed by PTS transients.

- We assume that stresses are sufficiently low at locations in the vessel wall between $3/8 \cdot t_{wall}$ from the vessel ID and the OD, so the probability of failure associated with postulated defects in this region does not have to be calculated because it is zero.

- We assume that if a particular transient does not achieve a temperature in the downcomer below 400°F (204°C), it does not contribute to the vessel failure probability.

In the following subsections, we discuss the appropriateness of each of these assumptions.

3.3.3.1 Use of Linear Elastic Fracture Mechanics

One fundamental assumption in constructing our PFM model is that a linear elastic stress analysis of the vessel, and consequent fracture integrity assessment using the techniques of linear elastic fracture mechanics (*LEFM*), are accurate. Evidence supporting the appropriateness of this assumption is available in the following areas:

(1) In Section 7.10, we summarize the results of studies aimed at experimentally validating the appropriateness of *LEFM* techniques when applied to assessing the integrity of RPVs under thermal shock and PTS experiments. The results of three experimental series performed on scaled pressure vessels at ORNL in the 1970s and 1980s demonstrate the accuracy of *LEFM* techniques in these applications.

(2) One fundamental requirement for LEFM validity is that the dimensions of the plastic zone at the tip of a loaded crack must be very small compared with the dimensions of the crack being assessed and the structure in which the crack resides [Rolfe]. Under these conditions, the error introduced by plastic flow (which is not accounted for within LEFM theories) is acceptably small. To assess plastic zone sizes characteristic of the PTS problem, we had the FAVOR probabilistic fracture mechanics code report

all of the applied driving force to fracture ($K_{applied}$) values from an analysis of Beaver Valley Unit 1 at 60 EFPY, which contribute to the *TWCF*, (i.e., those that have a conditional probability of crack initiation greater than 0). The top graph in Figure 3-4 shows these $K_{applied}$ values overlaid on the K_{Ic} transition curve, while the bottom graph shows these same values expressed in the form of a cumulative distribution function. The lower graph indicates that 90% of the $K_{applied}$ values that contribute to the *TWCF* estimate lie between 20 and 35 ksi√in (22 – 38.5 MPa√m). Using these stress intensity factor values together with Irwin's equation for the plastic zone size under plane strain conditions [Rolfe] indicates that the plastic zone radii characteristic of PTS loading range from ~0.03 to ~0.13-in. (~0.76 to ~3.30-mm) depending upon the value of $K_{applied}$ (here taken to range from 20 to 35 ksi√in, or 22 – 38.5 MPa√m), and the value of the yield strengths (here taken to be 70 ksi (on average) for unirradiated materials and 90 ksi (on average) for irradiated materials (483 and 621, respectively). These values of plastic zone radii are small compared with the thickness of a PWR reactor vessel, indicating the appropriateness of LEFM techniques. Moreover, it can be noted that as the vessel ages, irradiation damage causes the yield strength to increase. Thus, as vessels approach EOL and extended EOL conditions, LEFM techniques become, if anything, more appropriate.

3.3.3.2 Assumption of No Subcritical Crack Growth

3.3.3.2.1 Due to Environmental Effects on the Low-Alloy Pressure Vessel Steel

Stress corrosion cracking (SCC) requires the presence of three factors: an aggressive environment, a susceptible material, and a significant tensile stress. If these three factors exist and SCC can occur, growth of intrinsic surface flaws in a material is possible. Since an accurate PTS calculation for the low-alloy steel

(LAS) pressure vessel should address realistic flaw sizes, the potential for crack growth in the reactor vessel LAS as a result of SCC needs to be analyzed, in principle. However, for the reasons detailed in the following paragraphs, SCC for LAS in PWR environments is highly unlikely and, therefore, is appropriately assumed not to occur for the purposes of the FAVOR calculations reported herein.

The first line of defense against SCC of LAS is the cladding that covers much of the LAS surface area of the reactor vessel and main coolant lines. This prevents the environment from contacting the LAS and, therefore, obviates any possibility of SCC of the pressure boundary.

Additionally, several test programs have been conducted over the past three decades, all of which show that SCC in LAS cannot occur in normal PWR or boiling-water reactor (BWR) operating environments. SCC of LAS in the reactor coolant environment is controlled by the electrochemical potential (often called the free corrosion potential). The main variable that controls the LAS electrochemical potential is the oxygen concentration in the coolant. During normal operation of a PWR, the oxygen concentration is below 5ppb. The electrochemical potential of LAS in this environment cannot reach the value necessary to cause SCC [IAEA 90, Hurst 85, Rippstein 89, Congleton 85]. During refueling conditions, the oxygen concentration in the reactor coolant does increase. However, the temperature during an outage is low, rendering SCC kinetically unfavorable. During refueling outage conditions with higher oxygen concentrations but lower temperatures, the electrochemical potential of the LAS would still not reach the values necessary for SCC to occur [Congleton 85].

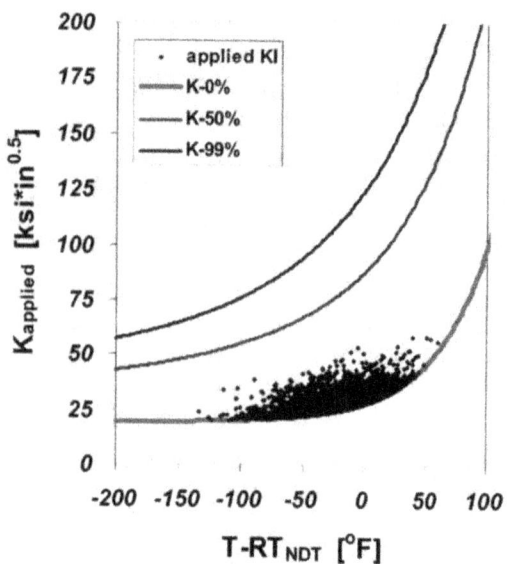

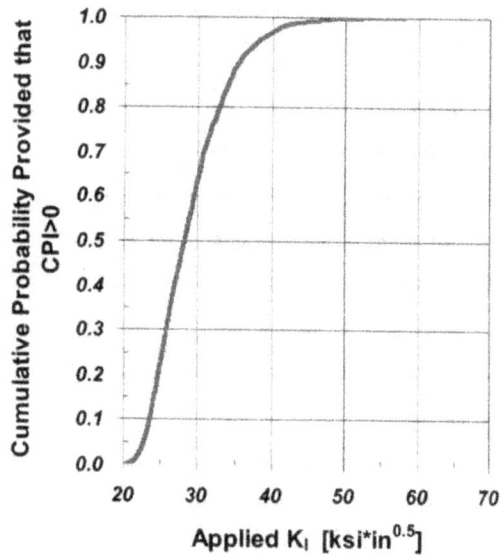

Figure 3-4. Illustration of the magnitude of $K_{applied}$ values that contribute to TWCF because they have a conditional probability of crack initiation > 0. The top graph shows all $K_{applied}$ values with $CPI > 0$ overlaid on the K_{Ic} transition curve from an analysis of Beaver Valley Unit 1 at 60 EFPY. The bottom graph shows these same results expressed in the form of a cumulative distribution function.

3.3.3.2.2 Due to Environmental Effects on the Austenitic Stainless Steel Cladding

As stated in Section 3.3.3.2.1, one assurance of the negligible effects of environmentally assisted crack growth on the low-alloy pressure vessel steel is the integrity of the austenitic stainless steel cladding that provides a corrosion-resistant barrier between the LAS and the primary system water. Under conditions of normal operation, the chemistry of the water in the primary pressure circuit is controlled with the express purpose of ensuring that SCC of the stainless steel cladding cannot occur. Even under chemical upset conditions (during which control of water chemistry is temporarily lost), the rate of crack growth in the cladding is exceedingly small. For example, Ruther et al. reported an upper bound crack growth rate of $\approx 10^{-5}$ mm/s ($\approx 4 \times 10^{-7}$ in/s) in poor-quality water (i.e., high oxygen) environments [Ruther 84]. The amount of crack extension that could occur during a chemical upset is therefore quite limited, and certainly not sufficient to compromise the integrity of the clad layer.

3.3.3.2.3 Due to Fatigue

Fatigue is a mechanism that initiates and propagates flaws under the influence of fluctuating or cyclic applied stress and can be separated into two broad stages: fatigue damage accumulation (potentially leading to crack initiation), and fatigue crack growth.

Fatigue is influenced by variables that include mean stress, stress range, environmental conditions, surface roughness, and temperature. Thermal fatigue can also occur as thermal stresses develop when a material is heated or cooled. Generally, fatigue failures occur at stresses having a maximum value less than the yield strength of the material. The process of fatigue damage accumulation, crack initiation, and crack growth closely relates to the phenomenon of slip attributable to static shear stress. Following a period of fatigue damage accumulation, crack initiation will occur by the progressive development and linking of intrusions along slip bands or grain boundaries. Growth of these initiated cracks includes fracture deformation sequences, plastic blunting followed by resharpening of the crack tip, and alternate slip processes.

The PWR vessel is specifically designed so that all of its components satisfy the fatigue design requirements in Section III of the Boiler and Pressure Vessel Code promulgated by the American Society of Mechanical Engineers (ASME), or equivalent. Several studies have shown that the 60-year anticipated fatigue "usage" of the vessel beltline region attributable to normal plant operations, including plant heatup/cooldown, design-basis transients, etc. is low, so fatigue-initiated cracks will not occur. Similarly, fatigue loading of the vessel is considered insufficient to result in propagation of any existing fabrication defects [EPRI 94, Kasza 96, Khaleel 00].

3.3.3.3 Assumption that the Stainless Steel Cladding will not Fail as a Result of the Loads Applied by PTS

Stainless steel, even in the clad form, typically exhibits initiation fracture resistance (J_{Ic} and $J\text{-}R$) values that far exceed those of the ferritic steels from which the RPV wall is made (see [Bass 04] for cladding data, compared to [EricksonKirk 04] for ferritic steel data). This is especially true for the levels of embrittlement at which vessel failure becomes a (small) probability because, at the fluences characteristic of the vessel ID location, the fracture toughness of ferritic steels can be considerably degraded by neutron damage, while the fracture toughness of austenitic stainless steels are essentially unaffected by these same levels of irradiation damage [Chopra 06]. This high toughness of the stainless steel cladding coupled with the small characteristic size of defects found in the cladding [**Simonen**] justifies the assumption that the stainless steel cladding will not fail as a result of the loads applied by PTS.

3.3.3.4 Non-Contribution of Flaws Deep in the Vessel Wall to Vessel Failure Probability

In FAVOR, flaws simulated to exist further than $\frac{3}{8} \cdot t_{wall}$ from the inner diameter surface are eliminated, *a priori*, from further analysis. This screening criterion is justified based on deterministic fracture mechanics analyses, which demonstrate that for the embrittlement and loading conditions characteristic of PTS, such flaws have zero probability of crack initiation. As illustrated in Figure 3.5, in practice, crack initiation almost always occurs from flaws that having their inner crack tip located within $0.125 \cdot t_{wall}$ of the inner diameter, further substantiating the appropriateness of eliminating cracks deeper than $\frac{3}{8} \cdot t_{wall}$ from further analysis.

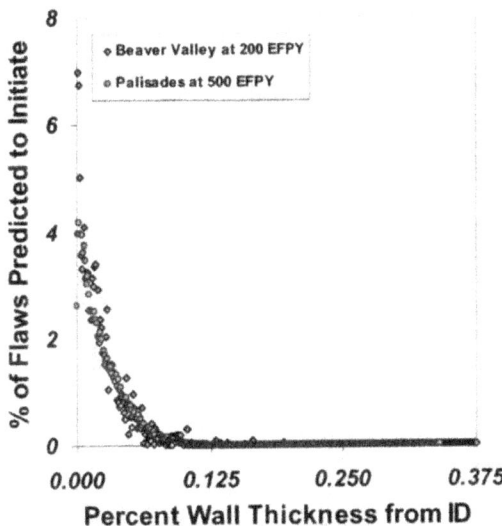

Figure 3.5. Distribution of crack initiating depths generated by FAVOR Version 03.1

3.3.3.5 Non-Contribution of Certain Transients to Vessel Failure Probability

When running a plant-specific analysis using FAVOR, we only calculated the CPTWC for TH transients that reach a minimum temperature at or below 400°F (204°C). This *a priori* elimination of transients is justified based on experience and deterministic calculations, both of which demonstrate that such transients lack adequate severity to have non-zero values of CPTWC, even for very large flaws and very large degrees of embrittlement. Additionally, the results of our plant-specific analyses (reported in Chapter 8) show that a minimum transient temperature of 352°F (178°C) must be reached before CPTWC will rise above zero, validating that our elimination of transients with minimum temperatures above 400°F (204°C) does not influence our results in any way.

3.4   Participating Organizations

This study could not have succeeded without the cooperation of a large number of individuals both within and outside the NRC. From its inception, the commercial nuclear power industry, working under the auspices of EPRI, has been a key participant in this project. Table 3.2 summarizes the key organizations and individuals, and their contributions to this study.

3.5   External Review Panel

In response to a letter [Bonaca 03] from the Chairman of the ACRS, the NRC's Executive Director for Operations (EDO) [Travers 03] identified a need to conduct formal peer review of the technical basis developed for potential revision of the screening criteria in the PTS Rule (10 CFR 50.61). In response to the EDO's direction, RES solicited a panel of experts to perform an independent review of this report, and all supporting documentation that comprises the basis for our recommended revisions to the PTS Rule. Two peer reviewers were selected from each of the three key technical areas (PRA, TH, and PFM). Each peer reviewer was asked to provide his or her individual comments on the entire PTS technical basis without developing a consensus on a unified set of comments, to satisfy the requirement that this peer review panel must not constitute a Federal advisory committee. The following individuals served on the peer review panel.

- **Dr. Ivan Catton:** Professor at the University of California, Los Angeles. Prof. Catton is an internationally recognized expert

in thermal-hydraulics, and has served as a member of the NRC's ACRS.

- **Dr. David Johnson:** Vice President of ABS Consulting Inc., Irvine, California. Dr. Johnson is an internationally recognized expert in PRA. He is involved in major risk studies and in using those studies to support decision-making.

- **Dr. Thomas E. Murley:** The chair of this peer review panel, Dr. Murley is a former Director of the NRR. Dr. Murley played a key role in regulating the operation of nuclear power plants for many years in comprehensive, high-level, broad-scope management of programs on water-cooled nuclear reactor power plants' safety and risk assessments.

- **Dr. Upendra Rohatgi:** A researcher at the U.S. Department of Energy's Brookhaven National Laboratory, Upton, NY. Dr. Rohatgi has been extensively involved in the development of thermal-hydraulic computer codes for nuclear power plant applications. In the mid-1980s, he reviewed the thermal-hydraulic analyses performed for two of the plants analyzed in developing the current PTS Rule.

- **Mr. Helmut Schulz:** Head of the Department of Structural Integrity of Components at Gesellschaft fuer Anlagen-und Reaktorsicherheit (GRS), Cologne, Germany. As a senior manager, Mr. Schulz has been involved in directing the development of PFM methodologies and managing various international cooperative research projects concerning fracture mechanics under the auspices of the Committee on the Safety of Nuclear Installations (CSNI) and the Nuclear Energy Agency (NEA) of the Organization for Economic Cooperation and Development (OECD) in Europe.

- **Dr. Eric vanWalle:** Head of the Reactor Materials Research Department, Belgian Nuclear Research Center (SCK-CEN), Mol, Belgium. Dr. vanWalle is extensively involved in irradiation embrittlement characterization of RPV materials, and various International Atomic Energy Agency (IAEA) and OECD/NEA cooperative research projects in fracture mechanics related to ensuring the structural integrity of nuclear power plants.

Appendix B provides more details of the peer review, including both the reviewers' comments regarding our technical basis and recommendations, and the staff's responses to those comments.

Table 3.2. Participating organizations

	Sponsor/Organization	Individuals	Responsibilities
NRC	RES/DET/MEB	Mark EricksonKirk, Shah Malik, Tanny Santos, Debbie Jackson, Todd Mintz	Project management, materials, fracture mechanics
	RES/DRAA/PRAB	Roy Woods, Nathan Siu, Lance Kim, Mike Junge	PRA, human reliability analysis, event sequence analysis, risk goal
	RES/DSARE/SMSAB	Dave Bessette	Thermal-hydraulics analysis
	Oak Ridge National Laboratory	Terry Dickson, Richard Bass, Paul Williams	PFM Code FAVOR
	Pacific Northwest National Laboratory	Fred Simonen, Steve Doctor, George Schuster	Flaw distribution
	Brookhaven National Laboratory	John Carew	Fluence
	Sandia National Laboratories	Donnie Whitehead, John Forester, Vincent Dandini	PRA, human reliability analysis, event sequence analysis, external events analysis, generalization task
	SAIC	Alan Kolaczkowski, Susan Cooper, Dana Kelly	PRA, human reliability analysis, event sequence analysis, external events analysis, generalization task
	University of Maryland	Mohammad Modarres, Ali Mosleh, Fei Li, James Chang	Uncertainty analysis of PFM and TH
	The Wreathwood Group	John Wreathall	Human reliability analysis
	Buttonwood Consulting	Dennis Bley	Human reliability analysis
	INEEL	William Galyean	PRA, event sequence analysis
	ISL	Bill Arcieri, Robert Beaton, Don Fletcher	Thermal-hydraulic calculations using RELAP

Sponsor/Organization		Individuals	Responsibilities
EPRI	EPRI	Stan Rosinski	Program Management
	EPRI Materials Reliability Program (MRP) RPV Integrity Issue Task Group	Robert O. Hardies	ITG Chairman – Constellation Nuclear
	Westinghouse Electric Company	Ted Meyer, Bruce Bishop, Randy Lott, Steve Byrne, Robert Lutz, Barry Sloan, Eric Frantz	PRA, risk goal, PFM Code FAVOR, Fracture mechanics, materials, uncertainty analysis of PFM and TH
	Framatome ANP	Ken Yoon	Materials, fracture mechanics
	Sartrex Corporation	Ron Gamble	PRA, risk goal, PFM Code FAVOR
	Phoenix Engineering Associates	Marjorie EricksonKirk	Uncertainty analysis of PFM, fracture mechanics
	Constellation Nuclear – Calvert Cliffs	Robert O. Hardies	Plant-specific PTS
	First Energy – Beaver Valley	Dennis Weakland	Plant-specific PTS
	Duke Energy – Oconee	Jeff Gilreath, Steve Nadar	Plant-specific PTS
	Nuclear Management Company – Palisades	John Kneeland, Brian Brogan, Christer Dahlgren, Gary Pratt	Plant-specific PTS
	Applied Reliability Engineering	Dave Blanchard	Palisades PRA

4 Structure of this Report, and Changes Relative to Previous Reports

4.1 Report Structure

This report summarizes information found in a collection of other documents. As illustrated in Figure 4-1, various reports that concern either procedures or calculated results are available in each of three main technical areas (PRA, TH, and PFM). In this report, we do not attempt to provide a comprehensive summary of all aspects of the PFM, TH, and PRA procedures or results. Rather, in Chapters 5, 6, and 7, we focus on the key features of the PRA, TH, and PFM models, respectively, placing particular emphasis on changes between these models and those that were used to establish the technical basis for the current PTS Rule [10 CFR 50.61]. Chapter 8 goes on to detail the results of our "baseline" probabilistic calculations for Oconee Unit 1, Beaver Valley Unit 1, and Palisades. Chapter 9 summarizes various studies we have performed that collectively demonstrate the applicability of the results in Chapter 8 to PWRs in general, rather than just to the specific conditions analyzed herein. In Chapter 10, we discuss considerations associated with selecting an acceptable annual limit on TWCF, while in Chapter 11, we compare this limit to the results from Chapter 8 to establish a revision to the RT_{PTS} screening criteria currently expressed in 10 CFR 50.61.

4.2 Changes Relative to Previous Studies

To assist readers familiar with the details of calculations that form the basis for the current PTS rule [SECY-82-465] or the calculations previously reported from this effort [*Kirk 12-02*], we provide a guide to where our methodology and results differ from the previous studies, and provide pointers to locations in this and other documents where those changes are discussed in greater detail

4.2.1 Studies Providing the Technical Basis of the Current PTS Rule

As detailed in Section 3.2, one fundamental difference between our approach and that of SECY-82-465 is that here we consider all of the known factors that influence the likelihood of vessel failure during a PTS event, while accounting for uncertainties in these factors in a consistent manner across a breadth of technical disciplines (see [*Siu 99*] for details). Two central features of this approach are a focus on the use of realistic input values and models (wherever possible), and *explicit* treatment of uncertainties (using currently available uncertainty analysis tools and techniques). Thus, our current approach improves upon that employed in developing SECY-82-465, in which many aspects of the analysis included intentional and unquantified conservatisms, and uncertainties were treated *implicitly* by incorporating them into the models.

In addition to this overall change in modeling approach, the following specific changes were made in the three main technical areas:

Modifications to PRA

Table 5.1 (in Section 5.2.2) summarizes the differences between the current PRA and that used to support the current PTS Rule. These differences fall into the following three major categories:

(1) greater refinement and detail in the current PRA

(2) more realistic treatment of operator actions in the current PRA

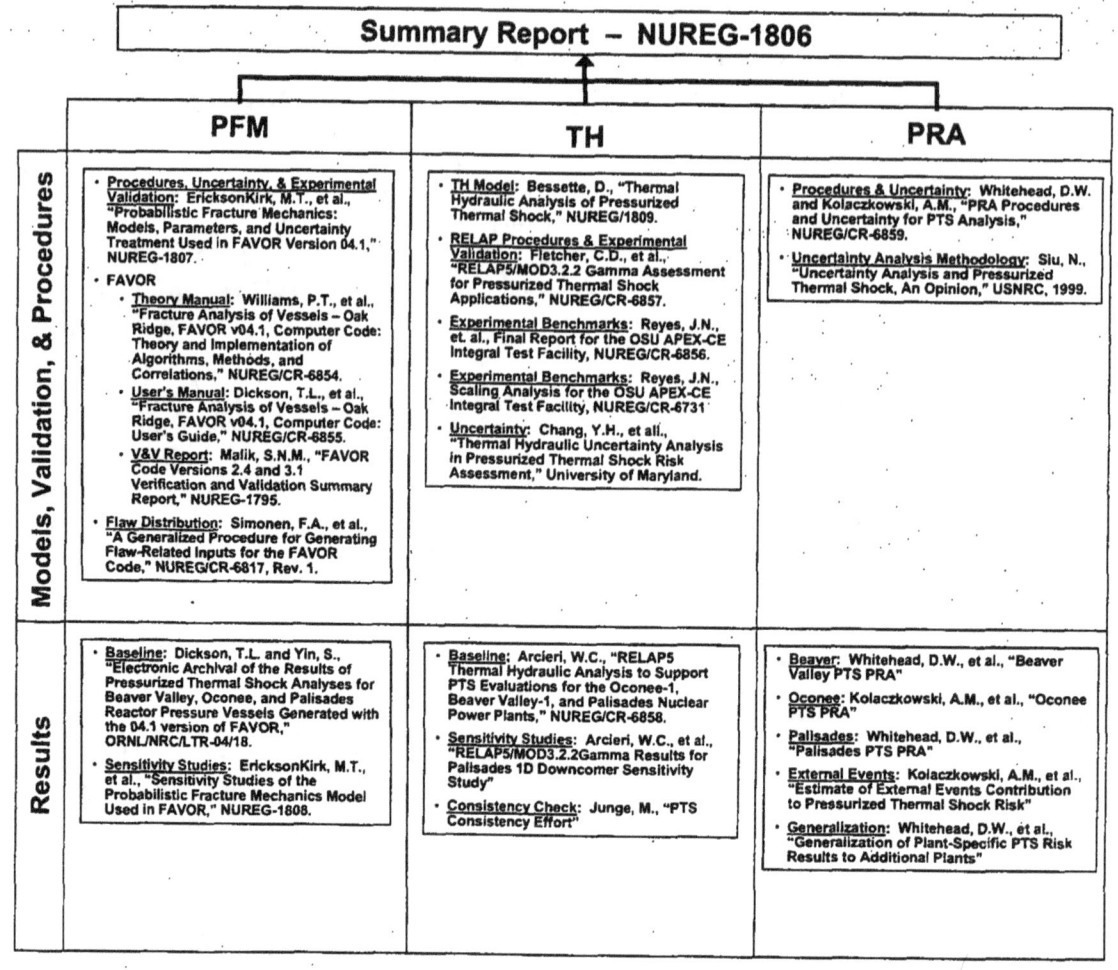

Figure 4-1. Structure of documentation summarized by this report. When these reports are cited in the text, the citation appears in *italicized boldface* to distinguish them from literature citations.

(3) Use of the latest available data on initiating event frequencies and equipment failure probabilities in the current PRA

As noted in the table, since these improvements were made with the intent of increasing both the accuracy and comprehensiveness of the PRA representation of the plants, they neither systematically increase nor reduce the estimated risk from PTS.

Modifications to TH

The first PTS study was performed during the early 1980s. In that study, TH calculations were performed for Oconee Unit 1 with RELAP5/MOD1.5 (circa 1982) and for H.B. Robinson Unit 2 with RELAP5/MOD1.6 (circa 1984). The results of those calculations were documented in [ORNL 86, ORNL 85b].

By contrast, the TH calculations performed in the current study employed RELAP5/MOD3.2.2Gamma, which was released in 1999 [RELAP 99]. The changes in the RELAP5 code in the intervening 20 years have been extensive [RELAP 99:

- RELAP5/MOD3.2.2Gamma uses a revised treatment of non-equilibrium modeling, including wall heat transfer models and coupling of the wall heat transfer and vapor generation models.

- Interphase friction models were revised, and now incorporate a new interphase drag model for the vertical bubbly and slug flow regimes.

- A general cross-flow modeling capability was installed, allowing cross-flow connections between most types of components and among the cell faces on those components.

Other changes were implemented as a result of the code assessments related to the RELAP5 analysis for the AP600 advanced passive reactor:

- The Henry-Fauske critical flow model was added to provide a standard-reference critical flow model upon which code calculations are based.

- Changes were made in code numerics to greatly reduce recirculating flows within model regions nodalized with a multidimensional approach.

- A mechanistic interphase heat transfer model was implemented to include the effects of noncondensible gases. This change greatly improved the simulation of condensation, preventing erratic behavior and code execution failures. This change is particularly important for situations where the plant accumulators empty and nitrogen is discharged into the reactor coolant system (a situation that typically led to code execution failure at the time of the first PTS study).

In the current study, no major changes were made from the RELAP5 plant input modeling approach used in the first PTS study [ORNL 86, ORNL 85a]. With only a few exceptions, the plant input models use the same nodalization schemes as before. Those nodalization schemes reflect plant modeling recommendations and guidance for the general modeling of plant transients, which evolved over years of RELAP4 and RELAP5 experimental assessments and plant applications preceding the first PTS study.

However, the current study used capabilities in RELAP5/MOD3.2.2Gamma, including renodalization of the reactor vessel downcomer (using the general cross-flow modeling capability), conversion of the vessel/hot and cold leg connections and the hot leg-to-pressurizer surge line connection to the cross-flow format, and addition of junction hydraulic diameter input data as required by the conversion of the code to junction-based interphase drag. [**Bessette, Fletcher** document how these RELAP5/MOD3.2.2Gamma capabilities influence the models used in the current study.]

Current computer calculation speeds and data storage capabilities exceed greatly those used during the first PTS study, allowing the number of transients that can be reasonably evaluated directly using RELAP5 to be expanded by more than an order of magnitude. In the first PTS study, budget and schedule considerations limited the number of transients evaluated per plant to about 10 to 15. By contrast, the current study used more than 500 RELAP5 transient calculations to characterize the risk of vessel failure.

Enormous advances in analysis tools (automated processes and plotting and data extraction routines) have also occurred. These tools lead to more comprehensive analyses, better communication and sharing of data, and more effective reporting of results.

Modifications to PFM

(1) A significant conservative bias in the unirradiated toughness index temperature (RT_{NDT}) model was removed. (See item 3 in Section 7.7.2.2 of this report and Section 3.2.2.3.1 of [**EricksonKirk-PFM**].)

(2) The spatial variation in fluence was recognized. (See item 1 in Section 7.7.2.2 of this report and Section 3.2.3.1 of [**EricksonKirk-PFM**].)

(3) Most flaws are now embedded, rather than on the surface, and are also smaller than before. (See Section 7.5 of this report and [**Simonen**].)

(4) Material region-dependent embrittlement properties were used. (See item 1 in Section 7.7.2.2 and Table 8.2 of this report.)

(5) Non-conservatisms in the crack arrest model were removed. (See item 2 in Section 7.8.2 of this report, Section 4.1 of [*EricksonKirk-PFM*], and [Kirk 02a].)

(6) Non-conservatisms in the embrittlement model were removed. (See Section 3.2.3 of [*EricksonKirk-PFM*]).

(7) The possibility of fracture on the upper shelf has been accounted for. (See item 1 in Section 7.8.2 of this report, Section 4.2 of [*EricksonKirk-PFM*], and [EricksonKirk 04].)

(8) The effect of warm pre-stress (WPS) has been accounted for. (See Section 7.7.1.1 of this report, Appendix B to [*EricksonKirk-PFM*])

(9) Uncertainties on chemical composition and $RT_{NDT(u)}$, which bound all known individual materials, have been included. (See Appendix D to [*EricksonKirk-PFM*].)

4.2.2 December 2002 Draft Report

In December 2002, we issued a draft report that detailed the results of plant-specific analyses performed on Oconee Unit 1, Beaver Valley Unit 1, and Palisades [*Kirk 12-02*]. Since that report was issued, we have made the following significant changes to our model:

Modifications to PRA

No significant changes were made to the PRA/HRA models since [*Kirk 12-02*].

Modifications to TH

The RELAP5 Oconee model was revised to incorporate comments received from Duke Power [*Arcieri-Base*]. In addition, momentum flux modeling in the downcomer was changed to avoid the erroneous prediction of recirculating flows in the downcomer that, for a small number of cases, were unphysically high. When erroneous predictions of recirculating flows occurred, the high liquid velocity resulted in correspondingly high calculations of the heat

transfer coefficient. The entire set of Oconee cases was rerun.

Modifications to PFM

We revised the FAVOR PFM code. The information presented in [*Kirk 12-02*] was generated with FAVOR Version 02.4, whereas the information presented herein was generated with FAVOR Version 04.1. We made the following significant changes to FAVOR between these versions:

(1) As part of our V&V effort, we identified a bug in how FAVOR associated material properties with cracks that lie on the fusion line of welds. This bug was most significant when the toughness properties of the plates adjacent to the weld are lower and, thus, control the fracture response, as is the case with Beaver Valley Unit 1. Details of this bug fix can be found [*Malik*].

(2) FAVOR now considers the possibility of failure occurring by ductile tearing on the upper shelf. Section 7.8 of this report describes the upper-shelf model we used and our rationale for its introduction, while Section 4.2 of [*EricksonKirk-PFM*] and [*Williams*] provide full details of the FAVOR Version 04.1 upper-shelf model.

(3) FAVOR now models the effects of crack face pressure loading, as described in [*Williams*].

(4) FAVOR now accounts for the temperature dependence of thermal-elastic material properties, as described in [*Williams*].

5 Probabilistic Risk Assessment and Human Reliability Analysis

5.1 Introduction

This section describes the analysis activities associated with performing the PRA and HRA portions of the PTS reanalysis project.
As depicted in Figure 5.1, the PTS reanalysis project was a closely integrated effort among three primary technical disciplines:

(1) PRA (including HRA),
(2) TH modeling, and
(3) PFM.

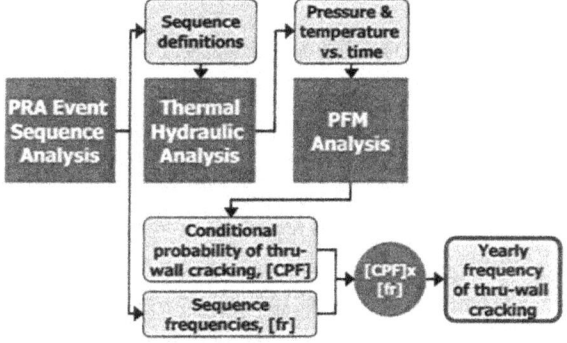

Figure 5.1. Integrated technical analyses comprising the PTS reanalysis project

As such, while this section focuses on the PRA and HRA (hereafter referred to as PRA unless specifically dealing with HRA) aspects of the reanalysis, important interfaces with the other technical disciplines are noted and cannot be completely separated from what was done in the PRA portion of the PTS reanalysis project.

A key final product of this reanalysis project is the estimation of TWCFs associated with severe overcooling scenarios. The PRA portion of the reanalysis project had three primary purposes:

(1) Define the overcooling scenarios (sequences) with the potential for being PTS challenges.

(2) Direct the TH analysis as to the specific sequences to be modeled to obtain plant TH response information to be forwarded to the PFM analysts.

(3) Estimate the frequencies, including uncertainties, for those overcooling sequences that are potentially important to the PTS results and provide that information to the PFM analysts.

In fulfilling the above purposes, the PRA analysts followed an iterative process.
The iterations were the result of (1) additional information becoming available from the other disciplines as the analyses evolved, and (2) feedback from the licensees participating in the three plant analyses (Oconee Unit 1, Beaver Valley Unit 1, and Palisades Unit 1).

For each purpose listed above, a specific product was produced. The first product, definition of the overcooling sequences, is in the form of event trees constructed by the PRA analysts for each of the three plant PTS analyses. Event tree construction is a well-known and well-established PRA modeling tool that has been used in identifying and analyzing core damage scenarios, such as in the Individual Plant Examination (IPE) program. In this case, the same tool was used to identify and model overcooling sequences, rather than core damage sequences that could occur as a result of undercooling events. The sequences depicted by the PTS event trees represent those combinations of initiating events that disrupt normal plant operation (e.g., turbine trip), and subsequent plant equipment and operator responses that are included in each plant model to represent overcooling sequences with the potential to be a PTS challenge.

The second product, direction by the PRA analysts to the TH analysts as to specific sequences to be modeled in their phase of the overall PTS analyses, was provided in the form of written and oral communications among the analysts. Each TH-modeled sequence was assigned a "case" number for identification purposes. For a given plant analysis, each TH "case" is a scenario that broadly represents many possible sequences on the event trees for that plant whose characteristics are similar enough that the sequences can be collectively represented by a single TH sequence (case). The TH analysts modeled each case to derive the time histories for reactor coolant pressure, reactor vessel downcomer temperature, vessel wall heat transfer characteristics, and other parameters important to defining the plant TH response during each case. This response information was subsequently provided to the PFM analysts to determine the vessel wall response (i.e., crack initiation and propagation) for the TH conditions. The modeling of multiple event tree sequences by a smaller number of "case" sequences involved a manual *binning* process that is summarized later in more detail.

The third product, sequence frequencies including uncertainties, was provided to the PFM analysts by the PRA analysts for those overcooling "case" bins that are potentially important to the PTS results. This information was provided in the form of electronic files containing a "case" bin identifier and statistical frequency information associated with that bin. These bin frequencies correspond to the "case" sequences modeled by the TH analysts and represent the combined frequencies of all event tree sequences combined into each bin. The PFM analysts then used the statistical frequency information, along with the TH information representing each bin, to estimate the TWCFs.

5.2 Methodology

A multi-step approach was followed to produce the PRA products for the PTS reanalysis project. Figure 5.2 depicts the steps followed to define the sequences of events that may lead to PTS (for input to the TH model), as well as the frequencies with which these sequences are expected to occur (for combination with the PFM results to estimate the annual frequency of through-wall cracking). Although the approach is illustrated in a serial fashion, its implementation involved multiple iterative passes through the various steps as the analyses and mathematical representations of each plant evolved. The following sections describe seven steps that together comprise the PRA analysis:

Step 1: Collect information (Section 5.2.1)

Step 2: Identify the scope and features of the PRA model (Section 5.2.2)

Step 3: Construct the PRA models (Section 5.2.3)

Step 4: Quantify and bin the PRA modeled sequences (Section 5.2.4)

Step 5: Revise PRA models and quantification (Section 5.2.5)

Step 6: Perform uncertainty analysis (Section 5.2.6)

Step 7: Incorporate uncertainty and finalize results (Section 5.2.7)

The reader should recognize that the PRA models described in this section consider *only* events internal to the operating plant (stuck-open valves, pipe breaks, etc.) as possible PTS precursors. A scoping study aimed at assessing the frequency and consequences of external initiating events (e.g., fires, floods, etc.) is detailed in a separate document [*Kolaczkowski-Ext*] and summarized in Section 9.4 of this report.

5.2.1 Step 1: Collect Information

During the initial phase of the PTS project, significant resources were expended to collect information regarding PTS in general and each plant in particular. General information-gathering activities included reviewing the basis for the current PTS Rule [10 CFR 50.61], and searching LERs for the years 1980–2000 to gain an understanding of the frequency and severity of real overcooling events [INEEL 00a]. Plant-specific information sources included the PRA analyses performed during the 1980s in support of the Integrated Pressurized Thermal Shock (IPTS) studies and the current PTS Rule [ORNL 85a, 85b, 86], as well as plant-specific design and operational information. Familiarity with all of this information provided the bases upon which the PRA analysis of each plant was conducted.

5.2.1.1 Generic Information

5.2.1.1.1 LER Review

The LER review identified a total of 128 events, demonstrating that overcooling events, or at least their precursors, do occur from time to time. These events are dominated by failure to properly control or throttle secondary side feed, a precursor that leads to relatively minor overcooling. Still, a few events have been associated with actual or potential loss of portions of secondary pressure control. These events predominantly involve equipment failures in the main feedwater, feed and steam control, and main steam systems. The results of the LER review also demonstrate that both active and passive (i.e., latent) human errors play a role, as many of the equipment failures were caused by improper maintenance or testing. Additionally, equipment in non-normal configurations can be an aggravating factor because contributing equipment faults have occurred that operators must identify, and for which they must compensate, to prevent overcooling.

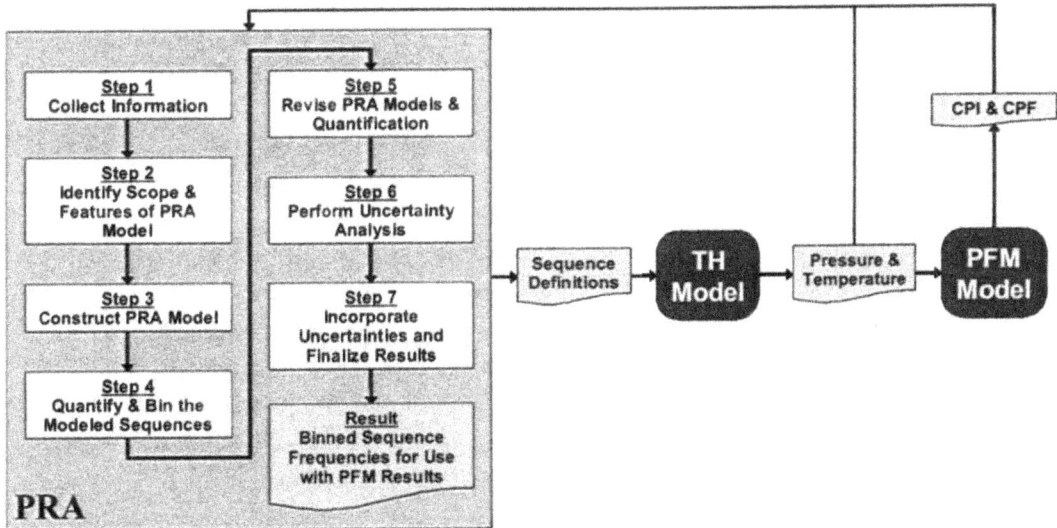

Figure 5.2. Diagrammatic representation of the PRA approach

5.2.1.1.2 Initiator Frequency and Probability Data

Initiator frequency and failure probability data are needed for initiating events, systems, and components as input to the PRA model. Since the goal of the PTS reevaluation project was to provide a PTS risk perspective for the operating fleet of PWRs, it was deemed appropriate to apply industry-wide PWR data for initiator frequencies and equipment failure probabilities in the plant-specific analyses. Hence, while the PRA model structure and the operational considerations it represented were based on plant-specific information, initiator frequencies and equipment failure probability data were generally based on industry-wide data.

Generic PWR data were obtained from two main sources. The first source, NUREG/CR-5750 [Poloski 99], summarizes industry-wide initiator experience for the years 1987–1995, along with failure probabilities for selected components. This information was updated twice. The first update was performed in an unpublished (at the time) addendum to NUREG/CR-5750 [Poloski 99], which extended the experience base through 1998. The second update dealt with loss-of-coolant initiators and was based on input intended to account for time-dependent material aging mechanisms that were not included in the experiential data [Tregoning 05]** The second source, NUREG/CR-5500 [Poloski 98], summarizes industry-wide experience for selected systems.

5.2.1.2 Specific Information

5.2.1.2.1 Previous PTS-PRA Analyses

Review of the PRA analyses performed in support of the IPTS studies and the current PTS Rule was another important input to the analyses.

** Generic initiator frequency and system failure probability information (as described in Section 5.2.1.1.2) was used for Oconee 1 and Beaver Valley 1, whereas the plant-specific PRA conducted by Consumers' Energy personnel (for Palisades) incorporated plant-specific information.

Of particular relevance were NUREG/CR-3770 [ORNL 86] and WCAP-15156 [Westinghouse 99] (a more recent 1999 study) since these are past analyses of two of the plants covered in this work, Oconee 1 and Beaver Valley 1, respectively. Information in NUREG/CR-4183 [ORNL 85b] concerning H.B. Robinson, and NUREG/CR-4022 [ORNL 85a] concerning Calvert Cliffs, was also considered since these documents provided additional perspectives and analytical considerations useful to this work.

5.2.1.2.2 Plant-Specific Information

At the outset of each plant-specific analysis, information was requested from the licensees pertaining to plant design, procedures, training, and other aspects of plant operation relevant to building a PRA model for analyzing PTS. Information provided in response to these requests was supplemented by information gained during plant visits and ongoing interactions (oral, written, and email exchanges) with each licensee as the analyses evolved. In total, plant-specific information was derived from the following sources:

- summaries of any recent past actual overcooling events
- current PRA model and write-ups
- final safety analysis report sections
- piping and instrument diagrams and electrical drawings
- emergency and abnormal operating procedures
- miscellaneous system design-basis information and related material
- PTS-relevant training material
- operational aspects associated with hot-shutdown conditions
- observed multiple simulator exercises at each plant involving overcooling events that were setup and run as part of a collaborative effort between each licensee and the NRC contractor PRA analysts
- periodic interactions with the licensees regarding modeling details as each analysis evolved

- feedback from each licensee as interim results from the analyses became available

5.2.2 Step 2: Identify the Scope and Features of the PRA Model

The format, structure, and details considered in the current analyses draw considerably from the earlier PRA analyses of PTS. Aside from recognition of the results and the reasons for the results from these past analyses, limitations and conservatism associated with the past studies were identified and, to the greatest possible extent, alleviated. Other improvements were adopted with the intent of increasing both the accuracy and comprehensiveness of the PRA representations of the plants. Table 5.1 summarizes the differences between the current PRA and that used to support the current PTS Rule. These differences fall into the following three major categories:

(1) greater refinement and detail in the current PRA

(2) more realistic treatment of operator actions in the current PRA

(3) use of the latest available data on initiating event frequencies and equipment failure probabilities in the current PRA

As noted in the table, since these improvements were made with the intent of increasing both the accuracy and comprehensiveness of the PRA representations of the plants, they neither systematically increase nor reduce the estimated risk from PTS.

In addition to identifying the areas for improvement of the PRA models that are addressed in Table 5.1, review of past PRA analyses of PTS provided information in four other areas:

(1) identifying the types of sequences that needed to be included in the PRA

(2) identifying what types of initiating events should be included

(3) identifying what functions and equipment status needed to be included

(4) identifying what human actions needed to be considered

The following four subsections describe the general features of the PRA models in each area. These features were established by a team approach involving analysts skilled in both system/sequence considerations and HRA considerations. Thus, the process for building PRA models involved integrated consideration of both system/sequence and human reliability factors.

5.2.2.1 Types of Sequences

The following list details the types of sequences included in the PRA models:

- overcooling scenarios
  - at full/nominal-power operation
  - under hot-shutdown conditions
- loss of RCS pressure scenarios
- virtually sustained RCS pressure scenarios (i.e., scenarios where RCS pressure initially decreases, necessitating start of HPI to restore pressure)
- late repressurization scenarios
- scenarios that provide immediate overcooling, as well as those that begin as loss-of-cooling scenarios (i.e., undercooling) and subsequently become overcooling scenarios

Two types of scenarios commonly modeled in PRAs are not included in the current PTS analyses (as previously discussed in Section 3.3.1):

(1) ATWS scenarios

(2) ISLOCA scenarios

Sequences resulting from such scenarios were not included, based on the following considerations. First, ATWS events generally initially begin as a severe undercooling event (i.e., there is too much power for the heat removal capability) and likely involve other failures to achieve an overcooling situation. While ISLOCAs, like the LOCAs modeled in the PTS study, could involve overcooling from the start of the event, significant ISLOCAs are often assumed to fail mitigating equipment in PRAs, which ultimately causes an undercooling event and core damage. Second, with typical ATWS and sizeable (not just small leaks), ISLOCA frequency estimates in the range of 10^{-5}/yr to 10^{-6}/yr (or even lower) and with the need

**Table 5.1. Comparison of PRA analyses used in this study
with the PRA analyses that supported 10 CFR 50.61**

	Difference Between Current PRA Analyses and the PRA Analyses that Supported 10 CFR 50.61		Effect on Calculated Risk	Comments
1	Refinement of Detail Considered by the Analysis	Slight expansion of the types of sequences and initiators considered	Increase	
2		Slight expansion of support systems both as initiators and as dependencies affecting equipment response	Increase	
3		Less gross binning of TH sequences because there are more "cases" into which to bin individual TH runs	Reduce	Current work features 50–100 cases per plant whereas previous studies only considered about a dozen cases (e.g., small steamline breaks and the opening of 1–2 secondary valves were previously binned with a large guillotine steamline break, thereby treating the cooling effects of the smaller scenarios much too conservatively).
4		External initiating events considered as potential PTS precursors	Increase	See Section 9.4.
5	Treatment of Operator Actions	Credit for operator actions is based on detailed consideration of numerous contextual factors associated with the modeled sequences, on multiple simulator observations at each plant, on the latest procedures and relevant training, and on numerous discussions with operating and training staffs. Detrimental acts of commission are also considered based on these same inputs, including procedural steps that call for operator actions that can exacerbate overcooling in certain situations.	Both Increase and Reduce	
6		A greater number of discrete operator action times are considered.	Reduce	Previous studies considered success or failure of operator action generally at 1 or 2 times after the start of the event. Currently, we consider up to 3 discrete times for some operator action.
7	Use of New Data	Includes the latest industry-wide (and some plant-specific) data for initiating event frequencies, equipment failure probabilities, and common-cause considerations.	Reduce	Largest factor is the significant drop in the initiator frequencies as a result of the decrease in scram rates resulting from institutional programs executed in the 1980s and 1990s.

for other failures to occur to possibly cause a continuing and serious overcooling situation, sequences involving ATWS or ISLOCAs should not be significant contributors to PTS risk. This is because other modeled scenarios that are likely to be significant contributors to PTS risk commonly have initiator frequencies in the range of 1/yr to 10^{-3}/yr, including other LOCAs that are already modeled in the PTS study.

5.2.2.2   Initiating Events

The following internal initiating events were included in the PRA models:

- small-, medium-, and large-break LOCAs
- transients commonly modeled in PRA analyses, including:
  o reactor-turbine trip
  o loss of main feedwater
  o loss of main condenser
  o loss of offsite power (including station blackout)
  o loss of support systems, such as AC or DC buses
  o loss of instrument air
  o loss of various cooling water systems
- steam generator tube rupture (SGTR)
- small and large steam line breaks with and without subsequent isolation

5.2.2.3   Functional/Equipment Considerations

The event trees in the PRA models that depict potential overcooling sequences are based on the status and interactions of four plant functions and associated plant equipment. Figure 5.3 presents a function-level event tree depicting the four functions and resultant general types of sequences treated in the PRA models. Each plant analysis features much more detailed event trees constructed at the initiator and equipment response level that incorporate the plant-specific design and operational features. These four functions (i.e., primary integrity, secondary pressure, secondary feed, and primary flow/pressure) are important to treat in the PTS analyses for the following reasons:

- Primary integrity: The status of this function influences the potential RCS pressure, which in turn influences the rate of cooldown (in some situations), the injection source capability, and the incoming and outgoing flow rates. All of these factors influence the vessel downcomer temperature.

- Secondary pressure: The status of this function influences the pressure and temperature in the RCS, since the RCS and the secondary side of the plant are thermal-hydraulically coupled in most scenarios. For example, a rapid drop in secondary pressure can cause rapid cooling of the RCS, affecting both the downcomer temperature and, potentially, the RCS pressure (depending on subsequent RCS injection flow and heat removal).

- Secondary feed: The status of this function influences the pressure and temperature in the RCS, since the RCS and the secondary side of the plant are thermal-hydraulically coupled in most scenarios. For example, overfeed can contribute to enhanced cooling of the RCS, affecting both the downcomer temperature and, potentially, the RCS pressure (depending on subsequent RCS injection flow and heat removal).

- Primary pressure/flow: The status of this combination of conditions influences the RCS pressure and flow conditions (forced flow or natural circulation) during the overcooling event as well as the nature of the injection that can add cooling to the vessel wall. The flow characteristics either exacerbate or mitigate flow stagnation, which can also affect the downcomer temperature.

In the plant event trees, the status of equipment relevant to each function is modeled in each PRA. This means that for each plant, the status of equipment relevant to each function is identified and included in the sequence modeling. For illustrative purposes, the following list summarizes the equipment associated with each function in the PRA models:

- Primary integrity: Status of pipe breaks, PORVs and associated block valves, pressurizer SRVs, and pressurizer heaters and spray considerations where appropriate.

- Secondary pressure: Status of steam line breaks, MSIVs and associated non-return valves, as well as related bypass and drain valve considerations where appropriate, turbine throttle and governor valves, steam dump/turbine bypass valves and associated isolation valves (if any), ADVs and associated isolation valves, and secondary steam relief valves (SSRVs).

- Secondary feed: Status of main feedwater (MFW), condensate, and auxiliary/emergency feedwater (AFW/EFW) systems.

- Primary pressure/flow: Status of high head safety injection, charging pumps and letdown considerations, accumulators/safety injection tanks, low head safety injection, and reactor coolant pumps (RCPs).

The status of other equipment that is relevant because of interactions with the equipment in this list is also modeled as appropriate. Such equipment includes the actuation and protection/isolation circuitry associated with the equipment in the preceding list, and support systems including cooling water, instrument air, and electric power and instrumentation. Heating and ventilation equipment was not considered in the analyses because of the slow effects of such a loss, and since the loss can often be easily identified and recovered.

5.2.2.4   Human Action Considerations

Plant records of overcooling events that have actually occurred demonstrate that operator actions and inactions can significantly influence the degree of overcooling and the RCS pressure for many types of overcooling events. Consequently, operator action directly influences, in both beneficial and detrimental ways, the potential for many types of event sequences to become serious PTS challenges. For example, early operator action to isolate the feed to a faulted (depressurizing or already depressurized) steam generator directly affects the amount of overcooling that occurs and/or how long such cooling is sustained.

Consequently, any "realistic" PTS analysis needs to consider operator actions and inactions that influence overcooling sequences. Therefore, consistent with the guiding principles of this project to adopt best-estimate models and treat uncertainties explicitly whenever practicable, a rigorous treatment of human actions is included in the PRA models. The process to identify, model, and probabilistically quantify human factors derives largely from NUREG-1624, Revision 1 [NRC 00], which uses an expert elicitation approach. In this study, the experts included both NRC contractors and licensees. These individuals considered both errors of omission and acts of commission. This process identified several general classes of human failures (see Table 5.2), which have been incorporated into the PRA models. Table 5.2 also details which of the four primary functions (identified in Section 5.2.2.3) these failures most affect.

5.2.3   Step 3: Construct the PTS-PRA Models

The well-known and well-established event tree-fault tree PRA methodology was adopted as the basis for all plant-specific analyses. However, the modeling approach varied somewhat from plant-to-plant because of the order in which the plants were analyzed (lessons learned in the Oconee analysis impacted the Beaver Valley and Palisades modeling approach, for example). Additionally, the availability of information from TH and PFM at the time PRA modeling began influenced how the PRA model evolved. A summary is provided below of the modeling approaches for Oconee, Beaver Valley, and Palisades.

Table 5.2 General classes of human failures considered in the PTS analyses

Primary Integrity Control	Secondary Pressure Control	Secondary Feed Control	Primary Pressure/ Flow Control
I. Operator fails to isolate an isolable LOCA in a timely manner (e.g. close a block valve to a stuck-open PORV) II. Operator induces a LOCA (e.g., opens a PORV) that induces/enhances a cooldown	I. Operator fails to isolate a depressurization condition in a timely manner II. Operator isolates when not needed (may create a new depressurization challenge, lose heat sink...) III. Operator isolates wrong path/SG (depressurization continues) IV. Operator creates an excess steam demand such as opening turbine bypass/atmospheric dump valves	I. Operator fails to stop/throttle or properly align feed in a timely manner (overcooling enhanced or continues) II. Operator feeds wrong (affected) SG (overcooling continues) III. Operator stops/throttles feed when inappropriate (causes underfeed, may have to go to feed and bleed possibly causing overcooling)	I. Operator does not properly control cooling and throttle/terminate injection to control RCS pressure II. Operator trips RCPs when not appropriate and/or fails to restore them when desirable III. Operator does not provide sufficient injection or fails to trip RCPs appropriately (failure to provide sufficient injection is modeled as leading to core damage; thus, such sequences are not PTS-relevant)

5.2.3.1 PRA Modeling Differences Attributable to the Organization Constructing the Model

Both the Oconee and Beaver Valley PTS analyses use the same large event tree-small fault tree modeling format adopted by the PRAs that formed the technical basis for the current PTS Rule. This approach makes best use of the earlier work in constructing updated PRA models. Since the desired outputs do not require the explicit component faults for some systems included in the model, very simple system fault trees were used with corresponding system-level failure data to represent the failure or unavailability of these systems.

In contrast, a plant-specific PRA model developed by the licensee was used to provide the starting point for the PRA model of the Palisades plant used in this project. The licensee's PRA includes more detailed component-level fault trees for all the systems included in the PTS-PRA model. However, in all three analyses, the level of resolution in the results is sufficient for the purposes of assessing the PTS risk.

5.2.3.2 PRA Modeling Differences Attributable to the Order of Plant Analysis

The PRA model of Oconee was constructed first (at a time when feedback information from the TH analysis and from the PFM analysis was not yet available). Consequently, it was not possible to screen out of the model overcooling sequences having a benign TH response or very low estimated conditional probabilities of through-wall cracking (from the PFM analysis). Hence, the Oconee PRA model contains virtually all the possible overcooling sequences with virtually no *a priori* screening out of "low significance" sequences. Subsequent feedback from both TH and PFM verified that many of the sequences included in the Oconee model could justifiably been omitted from the PRA model.

Work on the Beaver Valley PRA model was initiated after the Oconee model had been constructed, at a time when the Oconee analysis results, while still evolving, were generally well-understood. Also, as the Beaver Valley PRA model was being constructed, some advanced TH and PFM results were already available for Beaver Valley sequences (identified from "lessons learned" from the Oconee analysis). Consideration of this TH/PFM information on Beaver Valley permitted *a priori* screening of the following general categories of sequences from the Beaver Valley PRA model:

- Sequences involving certain combinations of stuck-open pressurizer PORVs or SRVs were not modeled.

- Sequences involving certain combinations of secondary valve and simultaneous pressurizer PORV/SRV stuck-open events were not modeled.

- Sequences involving only secondary valve (single or multiple) stuck-open events were not modeled.

- Sequences involving overfeed of various steam generator (SG) combinations were not modeled.

- Sources of secondary depressurization downstream of the MSIVs were not explicitly modeled.

- SGTR sequences (including those involving lack of proper feed control and even with RCPs shutdown, possibly inducing RCS loop stagnation) were not modeled.

- Other sequences were screened from modeling on a case-by-case basis if the sequence frequency could be conservatively estimated as less than $\sim 10^{-8}$/yr. This screening limit was used because, when coupled with the maximum CPTWC (i.e., failure) calculated for any type of sequence (in the 10^{-3} range) a TWCF of $<10^{-11}$/yr would be generated. Such frequencies would clearly not be important to the overall PTS results, since some other sequences were known to involve TWCFs in the 10^{-8}/yr range.

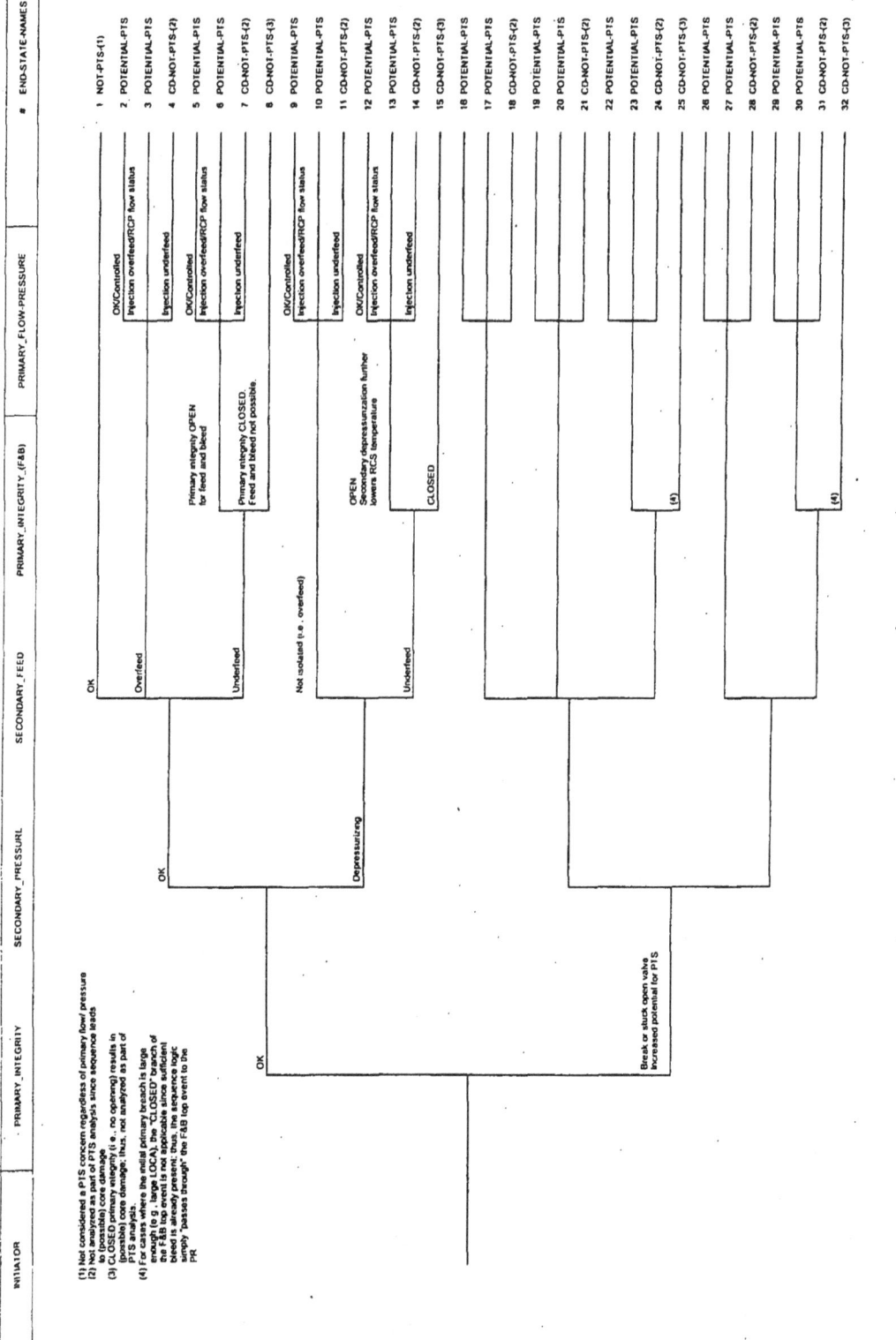

Figure 5.3. Functional event tree as the basis for PTS PRA analysis

Because the Palisades model was built starting with an already established licensee component-level PRA model with overcooling sequences, it is the most detailed model of the three. This preexisting Palisades model was augmented by the licensee, on the basis of NRC contractor review and input, to include possible scenarios and other factors not already in the preexisting model. Consequently, the "lessons learned" from the Oconee PRA also influenced the Palisades PRA model. In general, the Palisades PRA model addresses the same types of initiators and sequences, as do the Oconee and Beaver Valley models. However, the initiating event frequencies, equipment failure probability data, and human failure estimates are specific to Palisades.

5.2.4 Step 4: Quantify and Bin the PTS-PRA Modeled Sequences

For each plant, two conditions were modeled: full operating power and hot zero power (HZP). As identified in Section 5.2.3.2, little information was available to screen out potential PTS sequences for Oconee. Thus, because of a SAPHIRE code [SAPHIRE] limitation (i.e., the inability to store more than 100,000 sequences in a database); it became necessary to produce separate SAPHIRE models for full-power and HZP. Once the models (i.e., the event trees and fault trees) were constructed, the SAPHIRE code was used to generate the sequence logic for each event tree, and to solve the resulting sequences (90,629 sequences for each model) with no truncation attributable to frequency.

Given the number of potential PTS sequences for Oconee (181,258), it was necessary to group (i.e., bin) sequences with like characteristics into representative TH cases that could be analyzed with the RELAP TH code [RELAP].

Initial bins were constructed by developing event tree partitioning rules in SAPHIRE, and then applying those rules to produce the TH bins. Development of the partitioning rules required the analysts to examine the TH information available from preliminary analyses

to identify the characteristics that would be important to the binning process.

Using this information, the analysts then made judgments as to whether existing TH characteristics could be used to represent new groups of sequences. If the analysts judged that existing characteristics were appropriate, either because they matched the examined sequences exactly or because the TH conditions from the new sequences were expected to be similar to, but not be worse than, the conditions from the existing analysis, the uniquely defining characteristics associated with the existing TH analyses were written in rule form for application in SAPHIRE. For those cases where the analysts were sufficiently unsure as to the appropriateness of using existing characteristics, new TH characteristics were identified. These new sets of characteristics were discussed with the TH analysts. If those discussions led to the conclusion that the expected TH conditions could be sufficiently different from prior TH analyses and the frequency of occurrence of the conditions was such that they could not be "added" to some existing TH bin without being unnecessarily conservative, a new TH calculation (and hence, TH "case") was identified. The TH characteristics associated with this new calculation were then written in rule form for subsequent application in SAPHIRE.

This iterative process continued until all accident sequence cut sets were associated with a specific TH bin. Thus, the final application of the developed rules involved the examination of each sequence cut set to determine which rule the cut set met, the subsequent "tagging" of the cut set, and the gathering of like-tagged cut sets into initial TH bins. Once all cut sets were gathered into the initial TH bins, the bins were re-quantified using a truncation limit of 10^{-10}/yr.

For Beaver Valley, essentially the same process was followed. The major difference between the Oconee and Beaver Valley analyses was in the number of sequences developed and solved (a total of 8,298 sequences for Beaver Valley for power and HZP). As discussed in the previous subsection, knowledge about what was and was not important in the Oconee analysis was used with preliminary sequence frequency estimates and CPTWC results from early Beaver Valley TH and PFM calculations to minimize the number of sequences actually modeled in the corresponding SAPHIRE databases. Given the significantly lower number of sequences, no truncation was performed on the initial TH bins.

For Palisades, the process was somewhat different, in that the SAPHIRE model included both power and HZP sequences in the same database (only 3,425 sequences total) and the sequences were solved using truncation value of a 10^{-9}/yr. Another difference between the Palisades and Oconee or Beaver Valley analyses was how the TH bins were created. In the Palisades analysis, each sequence end state was defined to a specific TH bin and all resulting cut sets were placed in the defined bin. (Note: use of this binning process rather than the one used in the Oconee or Beaver Valley analyses did not have any significant impact on the results, which are similar across the three plant analyses. It is simply that the binning process was somewhat less refined for bins that, based on experience with Oconee and Beaver Valley, were not expected to significantly influence the estimated TWCF values.)

5.2.5 Step 5: Revise PTS-PRA Models and Quantification

With preliminary results available, reviews were conducted by both licensee and internal project staff. This allowed for formal feedback from the licensee with regard to the PTS-PRA models, inputs, assumptions, and results, and gave the analysts an opportunity for self-review of the PRA performed to date. The purposes of the reviews were to determine the following:

- whether inaccuracies existed in the models, and whether additional potential PTS sequences needed to be modeled

- whether additional TH bins should be created to reduce unnecessary conservatism based on new or updated information obtained from preliminary CPTWC calculations or needs identified by the uncertainty analysis

- which human actions were associated with the important TH bins

- which of those human actions should be reexamined to produce even more realistic (i.e., less conservative) HEPs

- what combination of the above could be accomplished within the constraints of the project

For Oconee, the reviews identified the following needs:

- to add one more type of potential PTS sequence

- to add more TH bins to address uncertainty issues and reduce conservatism (note that conservatism is reduced by not having too many sequences represented by a bin that is described by plant conditions that are too conservative for the actual conditions of the sequences)

- to reexamine some human actions to produce updated HEPs to account for more specific conditions

The Beaver Valley reviews identified the following needs:

- to add more TH bins to address uncertainty issues and reduce conservatism

- to reexamine some human actions to produce updated HEPs to account for more specific conditions

Because the Palisades analysis was performed by the utility, the results of the review described here dealt only with issues identified by the NRC review of the licensees' PTS model. The review identified the following needs:

- to add more break sizes to the LOCA class of initiating events

- to modify probabilities for a few selected basic events

- to add more TH bins to address uncertainty issues

It should be mentioned that while formal reviews were performed, such as during the second plant visits at both Oconee and Beaver Valley, informal periodic reviews were conducted through frequent written and oral communications among the licensees and project staff. Appropriately, the models were revised and requantification was performed on the basis of these licensee inputs and as a result of self-evaluations by the project staff.

5.2.6 Step 6: Perform Uncertainty Analyses

The primary objective of the PRA portion of the PTS analyses was to produce frequencies of the set of representative plant responses to plant upsets (i.e., scenarios). These scenarios involve mitigating equipment successes and failures, as well as operator actions that result in various degrees of overcooling of the internal reactor vessel downcomer wall. The major areas of uncertainty associated with the PRA can be grouped into two broad categories:

- modeling of the representative plant scenarios

- estimation of the frequency of each modeled scenario

These areas of uncertainty and the techniques used to deal with the uncertainties are discussed in the following two subsections.

5.2.6.1 Modeling of Representative Scenarios to Characterize Aleatory Uncertainty

Each scenario in the PRA is represented by a collection of events described by the logic of the event tree and relevant fault trees for each initiating event identified in the analysis. The model initially assumed binary logic (e.g., the valve either fully recloses or sticks wide open with no intermediate states) for the events. The only explicit modeling of event timing involved the timing of operator actions (i.e., failure to take an action is modeled as failure to take that action in multiple discrete times — for example, by 10 minutes, by 20 minutes — each with a probability). Most uncertainties with regard to model structure (e.g., completeness, intermediate states) were

not quantified. However, where deemed potentially important, a few aleatory uncertainties were addressed by purposely changing the model and assigning a probability to the applicability of the model change. Each of these changes became a different scenario (TH bin) with an associated frequency (e.g., area associated with a stuck-open SRV reduced 30%, timing of enclosure of a stuck-open SRV (3,000 s vs. 6,000 s), actual break size of small and medium LOCAs). Since it is unknown which scenario will occur following an initiating event, the complete set of scenarios, as represented by the event trees, characterize a large part of the aleatory uncertainty associated with the occurrence of a PTS challenge. The most important of these uncertainties that were explicitly handled in the analyses are addressed further in the next step, Step 7.

In addition, there is the overall uncertainty regarding the completeness of the PRA model(i.e., have all scenarios that potentially lead to PTS conditions been identified and modeled). This uncertainty issue was addressed non-quantitatively through both internal (i.e., NRC and its contractors) and external (i.e., licensee) reviews of the PRA model. As a result of this peer review process, the models are expected to produce a sufficiently complete set of potential PTS sequences and thus, any incompleteness in the models is expected to have a negligable effect on the results.

5.2.6.2 Quantification of Scenario Frequencies to Characterize Epistemic Uncertainty

Each scenario from the set of modeled scenarios is the interaction of what are treated as random events:

- initiating event (plant upset)

- series of mitigating equipment successes/failures (e.g., MFW trips, AFW starts, ADV challenges when one sticks open)

- operator actions (e.g., fails to close the ADV isolation valve by 20 minutes after the ADV sticks open)

Thus, the occurrence of each scenario is random, and the frequency of each scenario is obtained using the following equation:

Eq. 5-1

$$f_{scenario} = f_{initiating-event} \cdot Py_{equipment-response} \cdot Py_{Operator-Actions(s)}$$

where f denotes a frequency and Py denotes a probability.

Each of the variables used to obtain the scenario frequency has an epistemic uncertainty described by a distribution. The source of this information came primarily from the input data used in the analysis (i.e., the addendum to NUREG/CR-5750 [Poloski 99] for Oconee and Beaver Valley, and the plant-specific data used in the Palisades analysis). For a few specific model inputs, other data sources were also used to derive these uncertainty estimates. For the HEPs, both best-estimate values and uncertainty ranges and distributions were derived through the expert elicitation processes carried out in the human reliability analyses. Latin Hypercube sampling techniques were used to propagate these epistemic uncertainties to generate a probability distribution for each scenario frequency. Thus, the frequencies provided by the PRA analysts to the PFM analysts were described by histograms representing the resulting frequency distributions. In this way, these PRA uncertainty distributions were propagated through and combined with the PFM uncertainties to ultimately derive uncertainty distributions in the estimated TWCFs.

5.2.7 Step 7: Incorporate Uncertainty and Finalize Results

This section discusses important uncertainties (largely aleatory in nature) specifically addressed in the PRA and describes how each was handled. As described in the previous subsection, epistemic uncertainty in the frequency for each of the final TH bins was estimated using Latin Hypercube sampling techniques and is not described in this subsection.

The uncertainties discussed below were dealt with quantitatively; however, the degree of resolution

associated with each specific uncertainty was limited. These uncertainties include:

- size of the LOCA within a LOCA category plus other factors (e.g., initial injection water temperature)

- size of the opening associated with single or multiple stuck-open SRV(s)

- time at which a stuck-open SRV recloses

- time at which operators take or fail to take action

These uncertainties were highlighted for specific treatment in the analysis based on (1) the scenarios found to be most important to the PTS results, and (2) a series of uncertainty analyses performed by the University of Maryland (UMD) project team members on many of the inputs and parameters potentially affecting the PTS results to see which uncertainties would most affect those results. The specific UMD analyses are discussed in [*Chang*]. The results of that work concluded that the above uncertainties are sufficiently important that they needed to be treated explicitly in the PRA model. These uncertainties and how they were addressed are discussed in the following paragraphs.

The actual break size of a LOCA for a specific LOCA class (i.e., small, medium, or large) can be any point on the spectrum of sizes defined by the two end points for that class. In addition, other factors (e.g., initial injection water temperature, break location, and injection flow rate) can contribute to the overall PTS model uncertainty, since these factors along with the specific break size affect the rate of cooling and subsequent plant response. Numerical probability results from the UMD uncertainty analysis were used to model and estimate the importance of the various modeling uncertainties examined in the UMD analysis, including different break sizes within a given class (which were assumed to be uniformly distributed). These numerical analyses provided a spectrum of different plant TH responses arising from uncertainties in these key parameters including break size. This spectrum of results was then represented by a number of discrete cases to cover the total spectrum of results (typically, five cases for small LOCAs, three for medium

LOCAs, and one for large LOCAs). Each case was assigned a probability by the UMD analysts based on how much of the total spectrum the discrete case represented. Each discrete case was assigned a new TH case number with corresponding TH curves, and the frequency of each new case was adjusted using the UMD assigned probability for that case. This was accomplished through the following steps:

- gather all cut sets from all sequences generated for a specific LOCA class into one bin

- reproduce the gathered cut sets a specified number of times corresponding to the number of discrete cases defined to represent the spectrum of results

- modify each set of reproduced cut sets to include the probability assigned to that discrete case

Thus, the new modified cut sets account for the uncertainty associated with various parameters examined in the UMD analysis, including possible variation of break sizes within a given LOCA class.

Just as with the LOCAs, the size of the opening associated with a stuck-open SRV can vary from sizes that are not PTS-significant to the valve fully stuck open. To deal with this and other relevant issues examined in the UMD analysis, the cut sets (and their associated frequencies) from stuck-open SRV sequences were modified to include a fraction that represented the uncertainty from the UMD work. In this case, it was assumed that the SRV opening size is uniformly distributed (any specific opening is equally likely) and the resulting fraction was included in the sequence frequency estimates to account for that fraction of possible SRV size openings that would be sufficient, from a cooling perspective, to be potentially important.

The time at which a stuck-open SRV recloses is unknown and can occur at any point after the valve sticks open. To approximate this, the frequencies associated with stuck-open SRV sequences with subsequent closure of the SRV were divided equally between two specific SRV reclosure times (i.e., 3,000 s and 6,000 s). These

two time points were chosen after reviewing stuck-open SRV TH conditions. The 6,000 s point was chosen to coincide with the time when the change in downcomer wall temperature had "flattened out." The 3,000 s point was chosen to coincide with the time when sufficient cooling had occurred to the downcomer wall such that PTS could become an issue. Use of these two times provides a mechanism for determining some measure of the uncertainty associated with reclosure of stuck-open SRVs. Each case was assigned a 50% chance of occurring[††].

Just as the time at which a stuck-open SRV recloses is unknown, so too are the times at which operators perform actions. To address this issue, the times at which selected operator actions (i.e., those believed to be relatively important to PTS) were performed was varied. Typically, two or three different times were chosen to represent the uncertainty in when the action would be performed. Once the times were defined, typically (1) as early as could be expected, (2) as late as possible that would still affect the outcome, and (3) for some actions, some intermediate time, the probability of failing to perform the action by the specified time was developed. Use of these operator action times provides a means of estimating the uncertainty associated with when the operators actually perform their actions.

For the Oconee analysis, all issues identified above were incorporated into the analysis. For the Beaver Valley and Palisades analyses, results from the UMD analysis indicated that little uncertainty came from the sequences involving stuck-open SRVs that remained stuck open; thus, no modifications were made to those types of sequences in the Beaver Valley and Palisades analyses. However, all other

---

[††] Subsequent sensitivity analyses demonstrated that the 6,000 s time is nearly the worst time from a PTS challenge point of view. The worst conditional probabilities of vessel failure typically occur if the SRV is assumed to close at 7,000 s or a little beyond, but the vessel failure probabilities are within a factor of ~2 of those calculated for 6,000 s. See also the discussion in Section 8.5.3.3.2 and Comment #76 in Appendix B.

modifications were made for the analyses of Beaver Valley and Palisades.

6 Thermal-Hydraulic Analysis

6.1 Introduction and Chapter Structure

This section describes the thermal-hydraulic analysis performed on the Oconee-1, Beaver Valley-1, and Palisades nuclear power plants:

- The Oconee-1 coolant system is a lowered-loop, Babcock & Wilcox design with two steam generators, two hot legs, and four cold legs.

- The Beaver Valley-1 coolant system is a Westinghouse design with three steam generators, three hot legs, and three cold legs.

- The Palisades coolant system is a Combustion Engineering design with two steam generators, two hot legs, and four cold legs.

The discussion in this section begins in Section 6.2 with a general discussion of thermal-hydraulic issues for transients that contribute to the risk of vessel failure attributable to reactor coolant system overcooling. This section is followed by a description of the RELAP5 code and its implementation in the TH analysis in Section 6.3. The general structure of the RELAP5 code and an overview of the physical models contained in RELAP5 are included in this section.

The modeling of the plant primary and secondary systems including model initialization is discussed in Section 6.4. Section 6.5 presents an overview of the types of transients simulated, while Section 6.6 presents an overview of the results.

A summary discussion of the experimental validation of RELAP5 is presented in Section 6.7. Section 6.8 presents a discussion of sensitivity analysis and the analysis of uncertainty.

6.2 Thermal-Hydraulic Analysis of PTS Transients

The PTS analysis combines the thermal-hydraulic response of the reactor coolant system with the thermal response of the reactor vessel. These parameters, when combined with the PFM analysis, are used to estimate the probability of unstable crack propagation leading to possible vessel failure. The principal purpose of the TH analysis is to generate the time histories for key parameters for use in the FAVOR fracture mechanics analysis code, for various plant transients. The parameter responses passed to the FAVOR code are the reactor vessel downcomer fluid temperature, primary system pressure, and heat transfer coefficient on the inside of the vessel wall.

A wide variety of transients that could contribute to the risk of vessel failure were analyzed. These transients include reactor system overcooling attributable to a LOCA or a stuck-open primary side relief valve, a component failure that results in an uncontrolled release of steam from the secondary side (e.g., MSLB or stuck-open secondary side relief valve), or a control system failure that results in overfilling the steam generators. Combinations of failures are also of concern and were analyzed. The transients analyzed were defined from an event and fault tree analysis to determine possible transients (or accident sequences) and their frequencies of occurrence (see Chapter 5). Each transient and its associated frequency of occurrence are factored into the PFM analysis to estimate the risk of vessel failure.

As part of the analysis, key parameters and processes that affect the reactor vessel downcomer fluid temperature, primary system pressure and heat transfer coefficient on the inside of the vessel wall were defined. The Phenomena Identification and Ranking Table (PIRT) methodology was used to identify the most important processes that impact reactor system thermal-hydraulic response to a transient [Shaw 88, Zuber 89].

The PIRT methodology considered number of phenomenological processes and reactor system and plant boundary condition parameters. Examples of phenomenological processes include wall-to-fluid heat transfer in the downcomer, natural circulation flow, and steam generator heat transfer. Boundary condition examples include ECCS water injection temperature, break location (in the case of a LOCA), and timing of valve reclosure (for transients involving a stuck-open relief valve).

The PIRT methodology has been applied to the Yankee Rowe and H.B. Robinson plants for PTS events. In the case of Yankee-Rowe, the PIRT is based on a 1.3-in. [3.3-cm] cold leg break. This break is approximately equivalent to a 2.8-in. [7.1-cm] break when scaled up to the larger diameter of the three current plants. The H.B. Robinson PIRT was based on a 2-in. [5.08-cm] hot leg break. A PIRT was also performed as part of the assessment of RELAP5/MOD3.2.2Gamma against data from tests performed at experimental facilities that considered the wide variation in thermal-hydraulic conditions that can occur in PTS transients. This assessment is discussed in the RELAP5 PTS Assessment Report [*Fletcher*]. Table 6.1, excerpted from that report, provides a list of the parameters and processes considered and their ranking. This list considers a broader view of the types of transients that were analyzed, rather than focusing on a single transient.

The PIRT table presented in Table 6.1 was used to focus the RELAP5/MOD3.2.2Gamma assessment on the following parameters that can be observed in the experiments:

- break flow
- primary system pressurization
- natural circulation/flow stagnation
- boiler-condensation mode and reflux condensation
- mixing in the downcomer
- condensation, mixing, and stratification in the cold leg

- integral system response

These parameters were selected because of their primary or secondary importance on downcomer conditions. The following three phenomena were deemed to be most important to downcomer conditions during PTS events:

- natural circulation/flow stagnation
- integral system response
- primary system pressurization

Natural circulation/flow stagnation is important because if loop flow continues (or restarts during a transient), warm water at the average coolant system temperature will be flushed through the reactor vessel downcomer, increasing the downcomer fluid temperature. In contrast, if the loop flow is stagnant, the cold ECCS water will not be mixed with water from other parts of the reactor system and the downcomer temperature will be colder relative to the natural circulation case. Integral system response is important because the ECCS injection behavior (flow rates, timing, and to some extent temperatures) are functions of the overall system behavior. System pressurization is itself a primary figure of merit in the PTS analysis. The other phenomena listed above were considered because of their effect on these main phenomena or because they potentially impact downcomer conditions. Fluid mixing in the downcomer is among these phenomena. These phenomena as well as the overall RELAP5/MOD3.2.2Gamma assessment are further discussed in Section 6.7.

6.3 RELAP5 Code Description

6.3.1 RELAP5 Analysis Process

The RELAP5/MOD3.2.2Gamma computer code released in June 1999 was used for transient analysis to determine downcomer fluid conditions. The RELAP5 code was developed for best-estimate transient simulation of light-water reactor coolant systems during postulated accidents and transients. The code models the coupled behavior of the reactor coolant system, core, and secondary side system for loss-of-coolant accidents and operational transients such as anticipated transients without scram, loss of offsite power, loss of feedwater, and loss of flow. With RELAP5, a generic modeling approach is used that permits simulating a variety of thermal-hydraulic systems. Control system and secondary system components are included to permit modeling of plant controls, turbines, condensers, and secondary feedwater and steam systems.

Figure 6.1 and Figure 6.2 present top-level schematics of the RELAP5 modeling process and code structure.

The RELAP5 model input development process is portrayed on the left side of Figure 6.1. When modeling fluid systems with RELAP5, the physical systems are subdivided into networks of fluid cells that are interconnected by junctions. The RELAP5 model represents the fluid volumes, flow areas, path lengths and other characteristics of the physical system using a nodalization scheme of the fluid cells and junctions.

A RELAP5 input model is developed by assembling data that describes the thermal-hydraulic parameters of the physical system, such as pipe lengths, flow areas, volumes, and coefficients that simulate the pressure losses for flow through irregular geometry. The input model also requires the user to select various modeling options appropriate for the specific application, such as the critical flow model to be used and the locations in the model where it is to be activated.

The user must specify the initial conditions (pressures, temperatures, flow rates, etc.) for every model feature. In practice, RELAP5 plant transient event simulations begin from conditions that represent steady-state conditions. The initial condition input specifications cannot be made to an acceptable degree of accuracy using a manual approach. Instead, the user typically enters initial conditions that only approximate the desired ones and executes the plant model with RELAP5 in a steady-state mode until a smooth solution is attained with initial conditions that acceptably represent steady-state conditions. RELAP5 transient event simulations are then begun, starting from

the accurate set of RELAP5-calculated steady-state initial conditions.

The user must specify the thermo-physical properties (such as thermal conductivity and heat capacity) for the materials of the model features that represent structures.

The user also defines the timing information for the calculation. This includes the problem start time, problem end time, a range of time step size and the interval between data points for the calculation printed and plotted output.

The RELAP5 code is executed using the input model described above and the code execution process is summarized in Figure 6.2. RELAP5 simultaneously solves the equations for the conservation of mass, momentum and energy for the fluid conditions and flows among the cells and junctions in the nodalization grid.

The code employs a set of steam tables to represent the steam, water and noncondensible gas physical properties (pressure, temperature, void fraction, quality, density, internal energy, etc.) in each cell as the transient calculation proceeds.

The transient calculation is advanced in time using discrete time steps, the selection of which is made to assure a stable solution. The code automatically makes this selection of time step size within the minimum and maximum time step range that is defined by the user via the input.

Table 6.1   Phenomena Identification and Ranking Table for Pressurized Thermal Shock in PWRs

Rank	Description	Comments
1	Break flow/diameter (or valve capacity)	Importance of LBLOCA has increased, pressure is less important
2	ECCS flow rate (Accumulator, HPI, LPI)	State on/off, shutdown head of pumps, accumulator initial pressure
3	Operator actions	Includes operating procedures, RCP trip, HPI throttling, feedwater isolation, etc.
4	Time of stuck valve reclosure	Pressurizer safety relief valves which reclose after sticking open
5	Plant initial state	Hot full power vs. hot zero power operation
6	Break location	Primary LOCA (hot leg, cold leg), MSLB (inside/outside containment, upstream/downstream MSIVs), SGTR
7	Unique plant features/design	Difference in steam generator design, number of loops, vent valves, etc.
8	Vessel to downcomer fluid heat transfer	Affects the rate at which heat is transferred from the vessel wall to the downcomer fluid. Affects risk of vessel failure in non-conduction limited situations.
9	ECCS injection temperatures	Seasonal/operational variations
10	Sump recirculation	ECCS temperature/flow changes after RWST drained
11	Feedwater control (or failure)	Post trip main feedwater behavior, steam generator overfeed events
12	Feedwater temperature	Oconee (using AFW instead of MFW during transient).
13	Reactor vessel wall heat conduction	In conjunction with vessel to downcomer fluid heat transfer, affects the rate at which heat is transferred from the vessel wall to the downcomer fluid. Important particularly on those situations where heat transfer from the wall is conduction limited.
14	Loop flow upstream of HPI	Scenario dependent, not as important for LBLOCAs
15	ECCS – RCS mixing in cold legs	Affects potential for formation of cold plumes in the downcomer
16	Flow distribution in downcomer	Affects mixing and potential for formation of cold plumes in the downcomer
17	Jet behavior, cold leg pipe to downcomer	
18	Loop injection upstream of safety injection	Scenario dependent, important for MSLB, not for LBLOCA
19	Steam generator energy exchange	
20	Timing of manual RCP trips	Risk of vessel failure lower if pumps remain on. Operator assumed to trip RCPs in accordance with plant procedures.
21	Interphase condensation and non-condensibles	RELAP5 overprediction of condensation
22	DC to core inlet bypass	Less important for LBLOCAs
23	Downcomer to upper plenum bypass	Less important for LBLOCAs
24	Upper head heat transfer coefficient under voided conditions	Less important for LBLOCAs

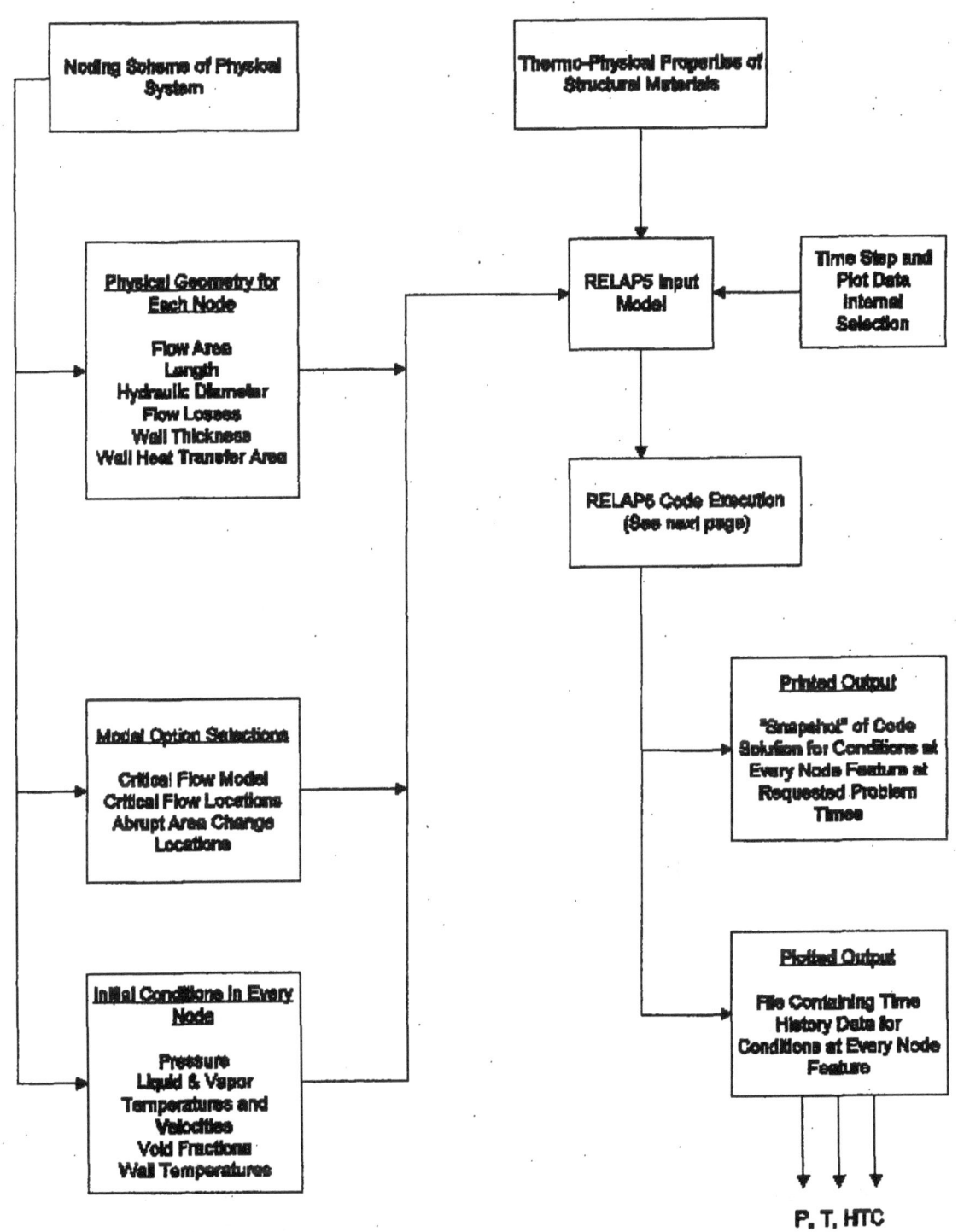

Figure 6.1.   Schematic of RELAP5 Input and Output Processing

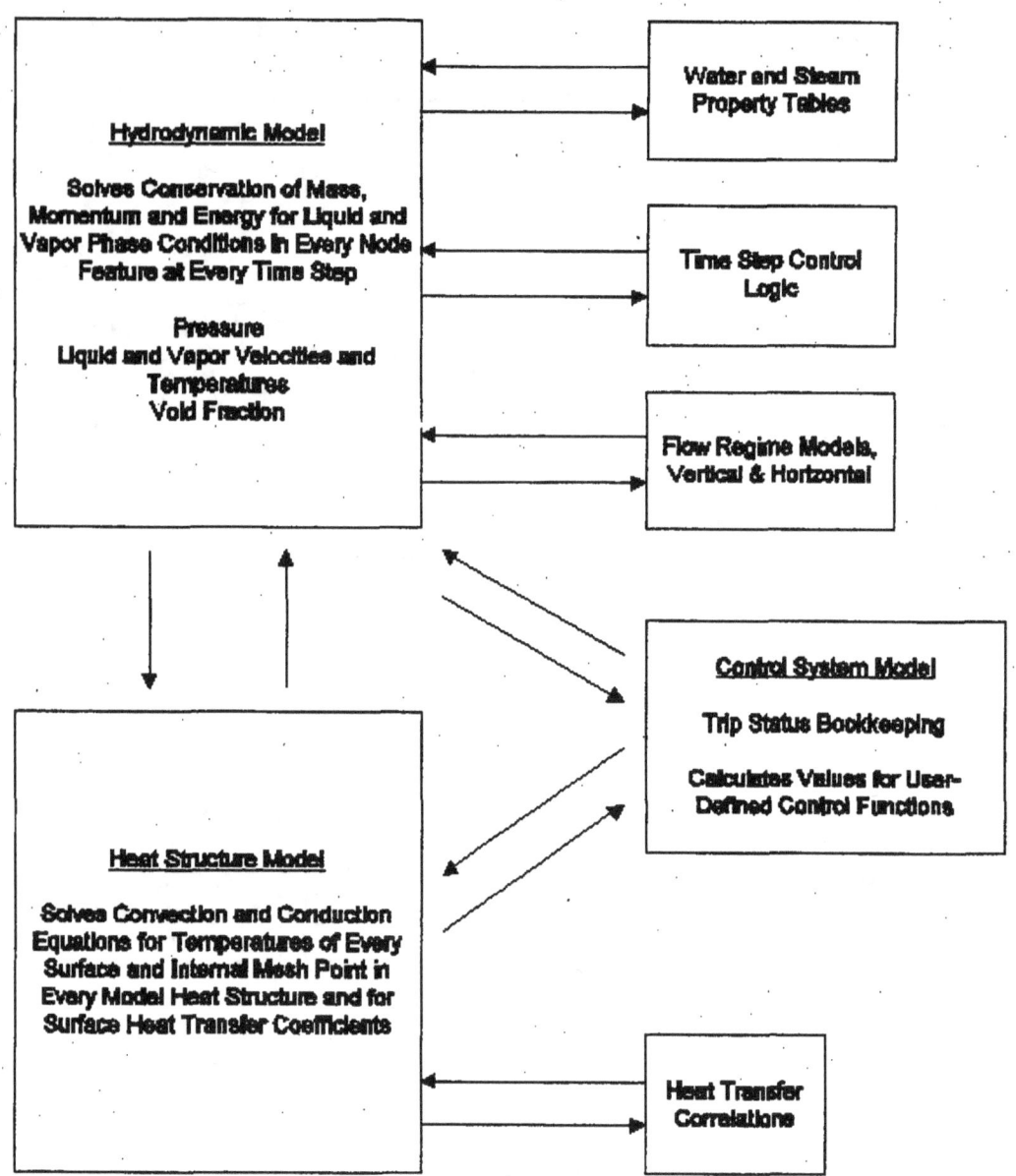

Figure 6.2.   Schematic of RELAP5 Execution Processing

RELAP5 is based on a hydrodynamic model for single-phase and two-phase systems involving steam-water-noncondensible fluid mixtures in enclosed regions. The model is non-homogeneous (that is, the liquid and vapor phases at the same location may flow at different velocities) and non-equilibrium (that is, the liquid and vapor phases within the same region may exist at different temperatures).

The RELAP5 solution is based on a staggered-mesh arrangement in which the conditions representing the fluid state (pressures, temperatures, void fractions, etc.) are calculated at the center of each cell and the fluid flow behavior (liquid and vapor velocities and mass flow rates) is calculated at the junctions between the cells. The RELAP5-calculated behavior, therefore, represents flow of liquid and vapor from the center of one cell, through one-half of the length of that cell to the interconnecting junction, and through one-half of the length of the adjacent cell to the center of the adjacent cell.

The flow through the cell regions of the flow path is subjected to the influence of losses attributable to wall friction, and the flow through the junctions may be subjected to the influence of losses attributable to the presence of irregular configurations, such as pipe bends, valves, and orifices. In addition, the model considers the effects of friction between the liquid and vapor phases.

Flow regime maps that provide characteristics for fluid behavior in vertical and horizontal cell orientations are used to determine the distribution of steam and liquid within each cell. This distribution is considered consistently throughout the RELAP5 model (for example, influencing interphase friction, liquid and steam velocities, condensation, and vaporization and fluid-to-wall heat transfer).

The RELAP5 heat structure model is used to represent the structures of the physical system, such as fuel rods, steam generator tubes, and piping walls. Heat structures may include the effects of internal heating, such as with fuel rods or electrically powered pressurizer heaters. Heat structures are connected to the fluid cells and may be "single-sided" (connecting to a fluid cell on only one side, for example when modeling a cold leg piping wall) or "two-sided" (connecting to fluid on both sides, for example, when modeling the passage of heat from the primary to secondary coolant system through the steam generator tubes).

RELAP5 calculates wall-to-fluid heat transfer on a consistent basis, with the heat transfer based on the wall surface temperature and the fluid conditions (pressure, temperatures, velocities) in the fluid cell connected to the wall. The flow of heat within the heat structure is based on the wall surface temperature and a solution of the one-dimensional conduction heat transfer equation. A wall heat transfer mode map (analogous to the flow regime map described above) is used to determine the fluid-to-wall

heat transfer process based on the wall temperature and fluid conditions (pressure, steam and liquid temperatures, void fraction, steam and liquid velocities).

RELAP5 capabilities include trip and control functions that allow the system model to represent the functions of automatic and operator actions in a plant. Examples of these actions include reactor trips, feedwater termination, relief valve operation, reactor coolant pump trips, and initiation of emergency core coolant flows. The RELAP5 trip and control features are also particularly important because they provide great flexibility for linking the hydrodynamic and heat structure models together and using them for simulating transient events that realistically represent the expected behavior the prototype plant systems.

RELAP5 output, as portrayed on the right side of Figure 6.1, includes both printed and plotted output. The printed output consists of a snapshot of the RELAP5 solution for the conditions of every model feature at user-selected times during the transient calculation. The plotted output consists of a file containing the time histories of the calculated solutions for every condition in every model feature. The user specifies the data interval of the plotted output. For the PTS application, it is the RELAP5-calculated time histories for reactor vessel downcomer fluid temperature, pressure, and wall heat transfer coefficient that are passed to the fracture mechanics analysts for use as boundary conditions in their analyses.

The RELAP5 plant and code assessment calculations for the PTS project were performed consistently using the same version of the code, which is RELAP5/MOD3.2.2Gamma. Complete documentation regarding the RELAP5 code and its application is found the RELAP5 Code Manuals [RELAP, various citations].

6.3.2 RELAP5 Numerics Issues

Two potential RELAP5 problems related to unphysical flow circulations exist that are significant for PTS analysis. These problems are discussed as follows.

The first potential problem relates to circulations for plants with two cold legs per coolant loop during event sequences that result in complete stagnation of the coolant loops (LOCAs with break diameters larger than 2 inches). Potential flow networks exist for these plants, consisting of the two common cold legs and the steam generator outlet plenum on each coolant loop and the reactor vessel downcomer. Circulating flows within these networks have been observed in RELAP5 calculations during periods when cold ECC injection water is injected into the cold legs. The calculated solution initially becomes unstable, resulting in the onset of a continuous flow through the network (with forward flow through one of the cold legs and reverse flow through the other cold leg).

Recirculating cold leg flows are believed to be numerically initiated as a result of round-off error, although once initiated, physically based buoyancy forces are created that could sustain such flows. The data from certain MIST and APEX tests used in the RELAP5 assessments (discussed later) provide potential, but inconclusive, evidence of circulating flows in cold leg networks in the test facilities. If present, cold leg network flow increases the downcomer fluid temperature as a result of mixing of the ECC injection water before it enters the downcomer. Because cold leg network flow is nonconservative for PTS, and because it is not clear whether such flows are physical, large artificial reverse flow loss coefficients were added in the cold legs near the reactor coolant pumps in the Oconee and Palisades models used for the LOCA cases. These artificial flow loss coefficients prevent negative flow in either of the two cold legs, thereby preventing circulating flows within the cold network and ensuring a solution for PTS that is conservative in this respect.

The second potential problem relates to large circulating flows calculated by RELAP5 to exist within the reactor vessel downcomer region that are not physically realistic. As with cold leg network circulation (described above), downcomer circulations were noted for LOCA sequences with break diameters greater than 2-in. (5-cm). The source of the circulation was

traced to the application of the RELAP5 momentum flux model within downcomer regions that are represented using two-dimensional nodalization schemes (in the axial and azimuthal directions). The root cause of this problem in the RELAP5 code has not yet been determined; however, it was found that deactivating momentum flux for the junctions within the downcomer region prevented these physically unrealistic circulating flows. As a result, momentum flux was deactivated in the downcomer regions of the plant models used for the LOCA cases.

6.4 Plant Model Development

For all three plants examined, the thermal-hydraulic analysis methodology is similar. For each plant, the best available RELAP5 input model was used as the starting point. For Oconee, the base model was that used in the code scaling, applicability, and uncertainty [CSAU] study. For Beaver Valley, the base model was the H.B. Robinson-2 model used in the original PTS study in the mid-1980s. This model was reviewed by Westinghouse and revised and updated based on the review comments to reflect the Beaver Valley plant configuration. For Palisades, the base model was obtained from CMS Energy Corporation, the operators of the Palisades plant. This model was originally developed and documented by Siemens Power Corporation to support analysis of the loss of electrical load event for Palisades. The RELAP5 models are detailed representations of the power plants and include all major components for both the primary and secondary plant systems. RELAP5 heat structures are used throughout the models to represent structures such as the fuel, vessel wall, vessel internals, and steam generator tubes. The reactor vessel nodalization includes the downcomer, lower plenum, core inlet, core, core bypass, upper plenum and upper head regions. Plant-specific design features, such as the Oconee reactor vessel vent valves, are included. To illustrate the model features and level of detail, a nodeing diagram for the Palisades plant is included in Figure 6.3, Figure 6.4, and Figure 6.5. The modeling approaches used for Oconee and Beaver Valley are similar.

The downcomer model used in each plant was revised to use a two-dimensional nodalization. This approach was used to capture the possible temperature variation in the downcomer resulting from the injection of cold ECCS water into each cold leg. Capturing this temperature variation in the downcomer is not possible with a one-dimensional downcomer nodalization. In the revised models, the downcomer is divided into six azimuthal regions for each plant. The reason for choosing six azimuthal regions is to match the geometry of the hot and cold legs around the circumference of the reactor vessel and so that water from each of the cold legs would flow into a separate downcomer node.

The safety injection systems modeled for the Oconee, Palisades, and Beaver Valley plants include high-pressure injection (HPI), low-pressure injection (LPI), other ECCS components (e.g., accumulators, core flood tanks (CFTs), and/or safety injection tanks (SITs), depending on the plant designation), and makeup/letdown as appropriate. The secondary coolant system models include steam generators, main and auxiliary/emergency feedwater, steam lines, safety valves, main steam isolation valves (as appropriate) and turbine bypass and stop valves. Each of the models was updated to reflect the current plant configuration, including updating system setpoints (to best estimate values) and modifying control logic to reflect current operating procedures. Other model changes include adding control blocks to calculate parameters for convenience or information only (e.g., items such as minimum downcomer temperature).

Detailed information regarding the specific individual RELAP5 input models for the Oconee, Beaver Valley and Palisades plants can be found in [*Arcieri-Base*].

The RELAP5 model does not include an explicit containment model. A volume held at constant atmospheric pressure is used to represent the containment. This approach was used for the simulation of adverse containment conditions during a main steam line break in the containment. In this situation, the reactor coolant pumps are tripped because of high containment pressure.

The RELAP5 analysis considers the increase in injection water temperature resulting from switchover of the ECCS suction from the refueling water storage tank (RWST) to the containment sump. This switchover occurs when the water inventory in the RWST is depleted as a result of the combined pumping of the ECCS and containment spray pumps. After switchover, the ECCS and containment sprays operate in a recirculation mode, taking suction from the containment sump. At the point of suction switchover, ECCS injection water temperature will increase from a typical range of 283 to 305 K (50 to 90°F) to 325 to 335 K (120 to 140°F) or higher. Increase in ECCS injection temperature resulting from switchover to the containment sump is modeled to reflect the change in ECCS injection temperatures.

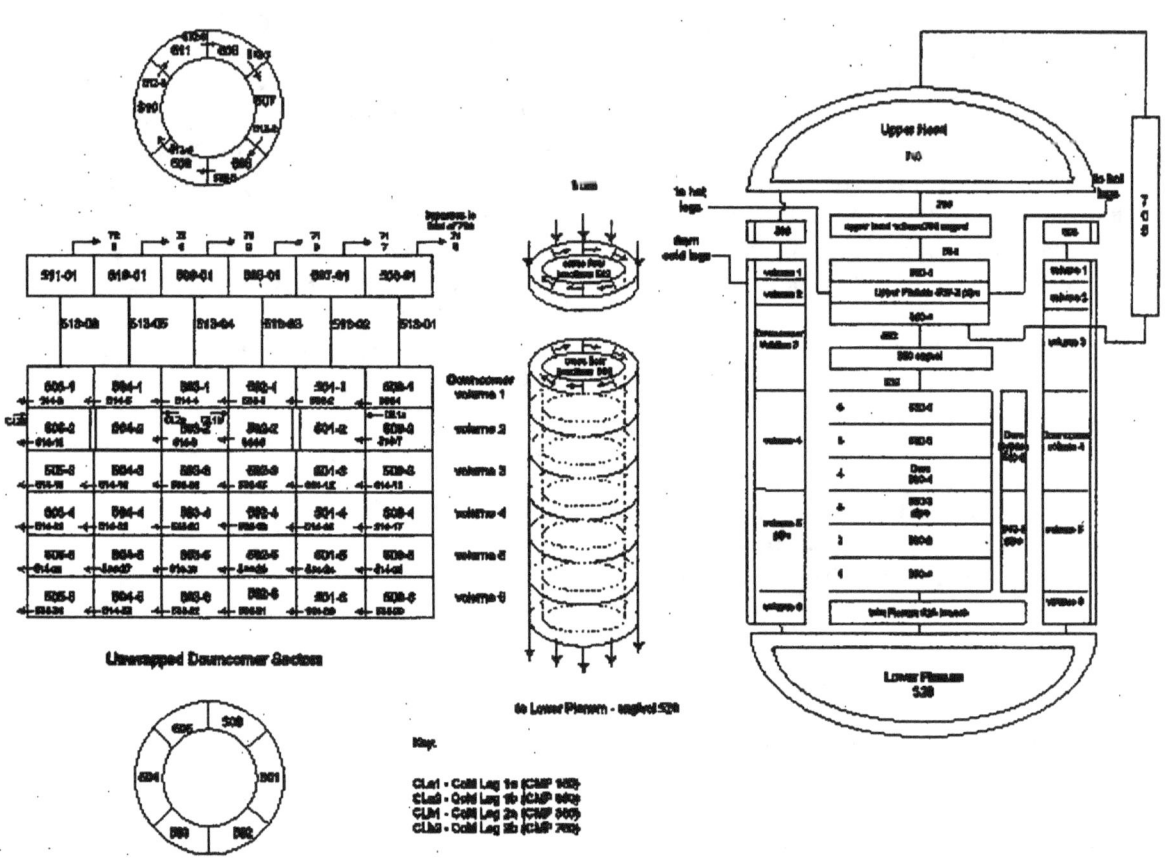

Figure 6.3.   Palisades Reactor Vessel Nodalization

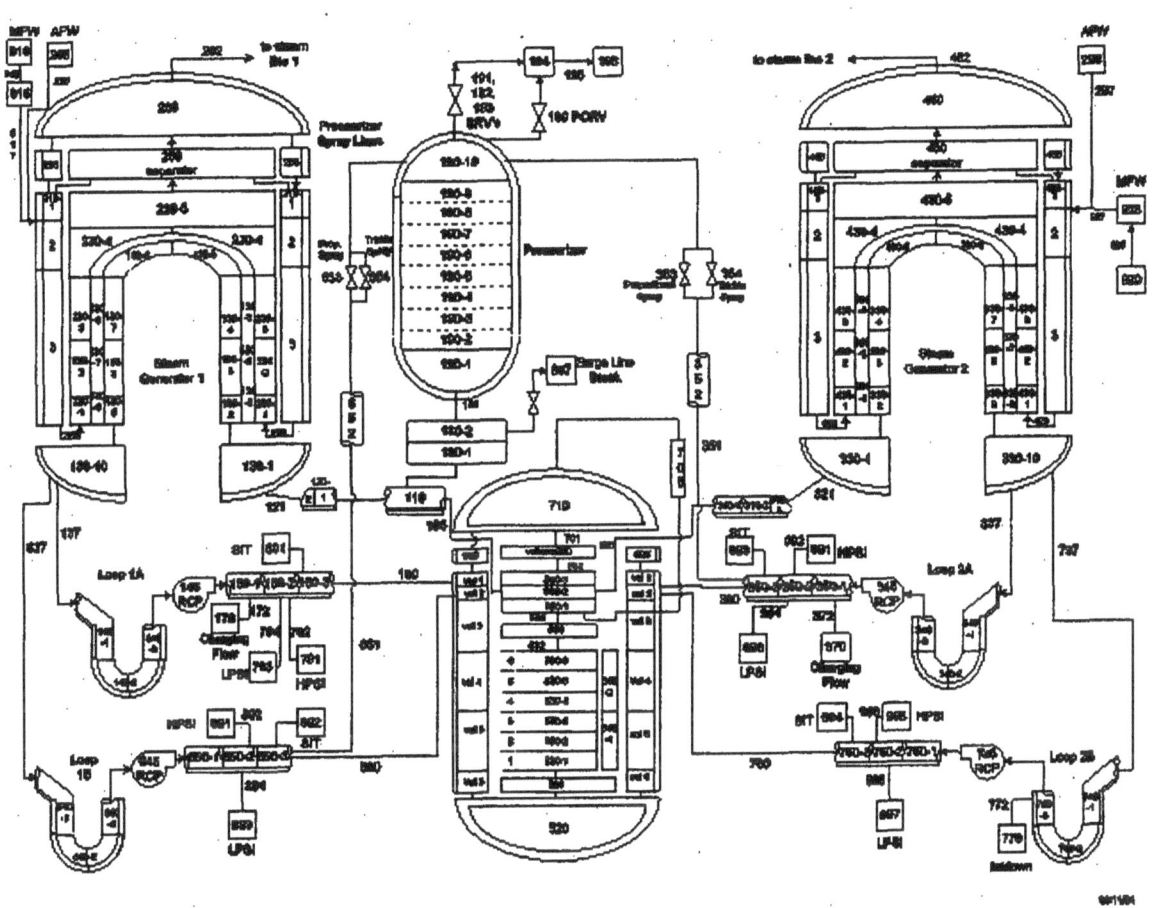

Figure 6.4. Palisades Coolant Loop Nodalization

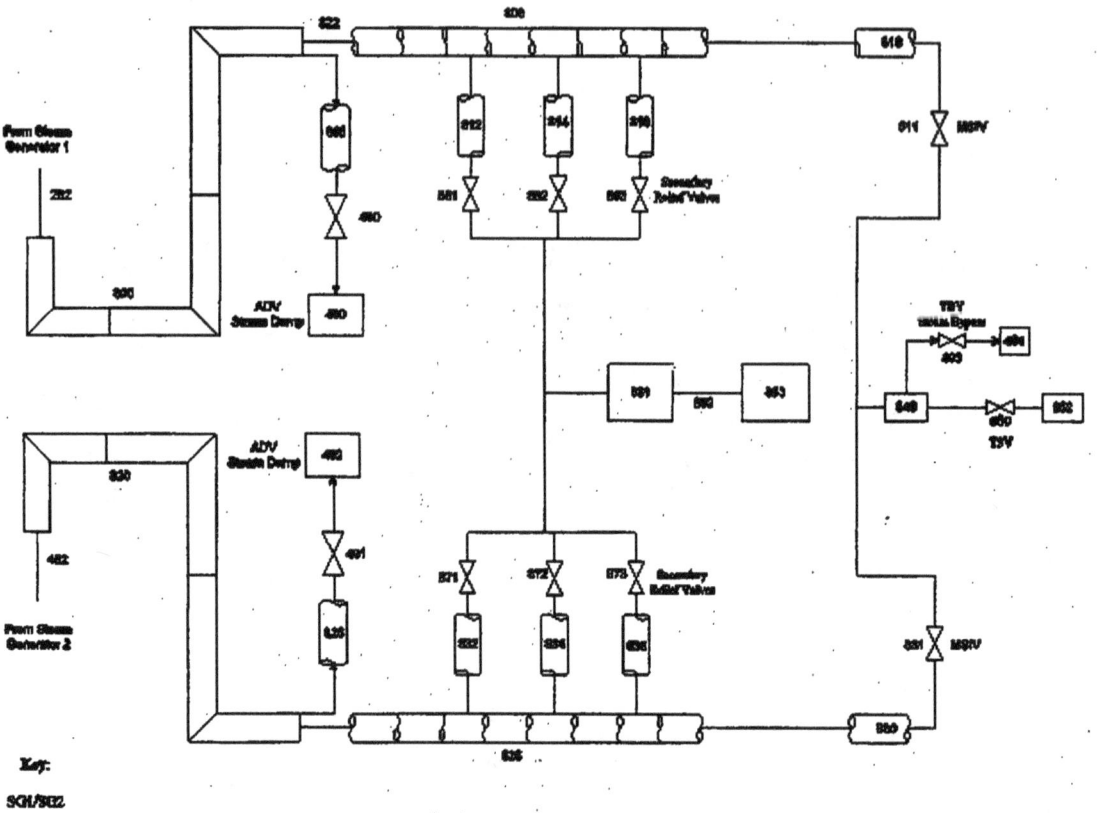

Figure 6.5. Palisades Main Steam System Nodalization

6.5 Transient Event Simulations

Transient events were selected for evaluation based on probabilistic risk assessment (PRA) analysis. Since each plant possesses unique thermal-hydraulic, hardware failure, and operational characteristics, there necessarily was variation in the transients events analyzed for the three plants. Examples of plant-to-plant differences important for PTS that affect transient selection include variations in shutoff heads for HPI pumps; initial pressure and temperature conditions in the accumulator (safety injection tank, core flood tanks); initial ECCS fluid temperature and allowed range; initial steam generator (SG) water masses; sizes and configurations of various valves and automatic controllers; and plant-specific operating procedures.

The development of the transient case list for each plant was an evolutionary process defined by the transient or sequence definition analysis. Generally, transients were selected based on the rate of primary system cooldown after transient initiation. Most transient event cases simulated generally fell into the categories of LOCAs and reactor/turbine trips with various complicating hardware and operator failures. Scenarios that consider stuck-open relief valves that either remain open or subsequently reclose later in the transient, system failures that cause steam generator overfeed, main steam line breaks, and others were analyzed. Evaluations were also performed for other types of events, such as steam generator tube rupture, recovery from a loss-of-all-feedwater event, and feed-and-bleed recovery from a LOCA with HPI failure.

The transient event simulations were run as RELAP5 restart calculations beginning from steady plant operating conditions. Total simulation time is 15,000 seconds for Palisades and Beaver Valley. For Oconee, the total simulation time is 10,000 seconds.

6.5.1 Loss of Coolant Accidents

The smallest LOCA break size evaluated was 1.0-in. (2.54-cm) in diameter. Larger break diameters were also evaluated where the break flow area was progressively doubled, up to 22.63-in. (57.47-cm) in diameter. Break diameters considered in the analysis, therefore, range over the full break spectrum. The breaks for most LOCA cases are assumed to be on the hot side of the reactor coolant system (in the pressurizer surge line for smaller breaks and in the hot leg for larger breaks). The hot leg break location was selected for most evaluations because it results in the greatest reactor coolant system cooldown rate, an intentionally conservative treatment. The ECCS injection rates are also maximized in this situation. Evaluation of cold leg break LOCAs was also performed.

For all LOCA cases, the discharge and flow loss coefficients used for break junctions are assumed to be equivalent to those used in AP600 work. While these coefficients may not be appropriate for a specific break, the wide spectrum of break diameters accounts for any uncertainties in loss coefficients.

6.5.2 Reactor/Turbine Trips

The majority of cases analyzed are initiated by a reactor/turbine trip followed by various primary or secondary side failures. These failures include relief valve failures, steam generator level control failures, and others. In the RELAP5 model for all cases, a reactor trip is considered the same as a turbine trip. In reality, if a reactor trip signal is generated, there is a small delay before a turbine trip is generated. Since the long-term downcomer temperature and pressure are of interest, this delay is considered negligible. There are numerous cases where stuck-open valves (pressurizer or steam generator PORVs, safety relief valves, etc.) are modeled as failures following a reactor/turbine trip. In these cases, the valve is assumed to spuriously open at transient initiation. Primary side stuck valves (pressurizer SRVs or PORVs) are similar to LOCAs where the "break" is located at the top of the pressurizer, rather than in the surge line, hot leg, or cold leg. In most cases, the RELAP5 models use a single valve component to model several valves in parallel. For example, in Beaver Valley, three pressurizer PORVs are modeled with a single RELAP5 valve component. In order to have a single PORV fail by sticking open, the RELAP5 valve component is opened to one-third of the full flow area.

In a number of cases, the valve that stuck open was assumed to reclose at some later time. The time of reclosure was defined as either 3,000 seconds or 6,000 seconds depending on the transient definition from the PRA analysis. (Occasionally, a different time was chosen.) Various times were chosen since it would not be known when the valve would reclose (if it were to reclose). The 6,000-second reclosure time was selected as a point far enough out in time where the primary pressure and temperature reached a minimum.

Another set of failures is overfeeding of the steam generators. As with other cases, the initiating event is the reactor/turbine trip. These cases will result in an overcooling event. The failure could be anything from equipment/component failure to control failure or operator error. Cases have been run where a single steam generator is filled to the top, and the water level is maintained at that level. There are cases where multiple steam generators are filled to the top. Cases were run where the steam generator was filled to the top, then feedwater was stopped and the steam generator was allowed to boil dry.

6.5.3   Main Steam Line Break

Main steam line break cases were selected because they cause rapid depressurization of the steam generator. This rapid depressurization is one of the most limiting overcooling transients from a single failure on the secondary side. Large breaks considered were modeled as double-ended guillotine breaks. These breaks were assumed to occur at the connection of the steam line to the steam generator (upstream of the main steam isolation valves). Smaller steam line breaks were simulated with stuck secondary

side valves (SRVs, ADVs, etc.) Turbine bypass valves were also assumed to stick open. In plants with main steam isolation valves, some of these stuck valves (breaks) were isolated by the MSIVs.

6.5.4   Operator Actions

Various operator actions are considered in the RELAP5 analyses based on the transient definition from the PRA analysis. For cases involving a primary system LOCA, the operator is assumed to take no action since automatic systems are presumed to operate and provide the core and primary system cooling. In these situations, the primary operator function is to monitor system conditions. For various transients involving reactor/turbine trips combined with component failures that lead to primary system overcooling, operator actions are a major factor and were modeled. Generally, the two categories of operator actions considered are (1) the operator correctly diagnoses the plant situation and performs the correct actions based on the emergency operating procedures, and (2) the operator fails to correctly diagnose the situation or takes an incorrect action.

A significant operator action for the plants analyzed is HPI control/throttling. Depending on the transient scenario, continued HPI injection can cause the system to refill and repressurize to the HPI pump shutoff pressure and/or the pressurizer PORV opening setpoint pressure. A good example of a transient where system repressurization can occur is a stuck-open primary safety valve that recloses after the system has depressurized. Continued HPI will cause the primary system to repressurize in this case unless the operator recognizes that the faulted valve has reclosed and takes action to control HPI injection.

Different plants have different HPI control methods. In Oconee, the operator can throttle HPI flow to obtain a desired flow rate and maintain a certain pressurizer water level. In Beaver Valley, however, the operator can either have a pump running or not. There is no "throttling"; rather, pumps are turned off if conditions are met. In Palisades, the operator can throttle HPI if auxiliary feedwater is operating with the steam generator wide-range level greater than -84% and the reactor coolant system subcooling greater than 13.9 K (25°F). In this case, HPI is throttled to maintain pressurizer level between 40 and 60%. HPI control is a crucial component in the overall PTS risk. An event where there is no HPI control can produce a much greater challenge to vessel integrity because of primary system repressurization than would the same event with HPI control because system repressurization does not occur. One significant variable in the HPI control is operator timing. Since the time that the operator will take control of the HPI is variable depending on the transient situation, several times are analyzed based on PRA input to determine the variation in overall system (downcomer) conditions. As an example, for Beaver Valley, cases were run where the operator does not control HPI, controls HPI 1 minute after the criteria for control are met, and controls HPI 10 minutes after the criteria are met.

Another example of an operator action is control of the reactor coolant pumps. The different plants use different criteria for tripping the RCP. At Oconee, the operator is assumed to trip the RCPs on low subcooling. At Beaver Valley, the RCP trip criterion is based on the difference between steam generator and pressurizer pressures. At Palisades, RCP trip criteria are based on primary system pressure and subcooling margin. In some events, the RCPs were not predicted to trip; however, various operating procedures could have caused the operators to trip the pumps. Therefore, in some cases, the RCPs were set to trip as an operator action. An additional note about RCPs is that they will be tripped if there are adverse containment conditions (i.e., main steam line break). Since the RELAP5 models used do not include the containment, the pumps were tripped manually if it was deemed necessary.

Failure of the operator to correctly diagnose the situation and take the correct action was also considered in the transient analysis. Failure to isolate the auxiliary/emergency feedwater to a faulted steam generator during a steam line

break is an example of an operator failure considered in this analysis. This failure will result in an overcooling event where the faulted generator continues to remove heat, thus lowering the primary temperature. Timing of operator action was also analyzed. As an example, analyses were performed assuming that the operator stops AFW/EFW to the faulted generator (at 30 minutes for Beaver Valley). Time of operator action was determined by PRA analysis.

6.6 RELAP5 Analysis Results

The parameters that are used in the probabilistic fracture mechanics analysis are the reactor vessel downcomer fluid temperature, primary system pressure and reactor vessel wall heat transfer coefficient as a function of transient time. Post-processing of the RELAP5 results is performed to generate files that are transmitted to ORNL for analysis. Averaged values for the downcomer fluid temperature, system pressure, and downcomer fluid to vessel wall heat transfer coefficient were provided.

A large number of cases were analyzed for the Oconee, Beaver Valley, and Palisades plants to meet the requirements of the PRA analysis. A total of 177 cases were run for Oconee, 67 cases for Palisades, and 130 cases for Beaver Valley. These cases were needed to support the PRA model, particularly to support the development of transient bins needed to categorize the large number of transients that must be considered in developing a nuclear plant risk model. Because of the large number of cases, the results that are used in the probabilistic fracture mechanics analysis are separately presented in [*Arcieri-Base*].

6.7 RELAP5 Assessment Against Experimental Data

Assessments are performed to establish the suitability of the RELAP5/Mod 3.2.2Gamma code for analyzing plant transients that are significant risk contributors for PTS. The RELAP5 code version used for the assessment calculations is the same that is used for the PTS plant calculations. Assessment principally consists of performing an analysis for a particular experimental facility for a specific transient test. The results from a RELAP5 simulation of the test are compared against measurements from the experiment and conclusions are drawn regarding the code capabilities for predicting the physical behavior of the test.

Prior assessments of RELAP5 have been performed for a wide variety of transients over the 20-year development history of the code. Many of those assessments focused on tests representing LOCAs, for which the key system response is the integrity of the reactor core. It is noted that LOCAs as an event category are also an important vessel failure risk contributor for PTS, and so the extensive LOCA experimental database remains relevant and very useful for PTS applications. However, in contrast to the focus on core behavior during LOCAs, the focus for PTS-related transients is on the temperature and pressure conditions in the reactor vessel downcomer. Hence, the assessments discussed here focus on comparing RELAP5 results to experimental data for conditions in the downcomer.

The assessment of RELAP5/MOD3.2Gamma for representing PTS behavior, performed in the context of the PIRT discussion presented in Section 6.2, are summarized in the following sections. The assessments are documented in detail in the RELAP5 PTS Assessment Report [*Fletcher*].

6.7.1 Separate Effects Tests

RELAP5 was assessed against separate-effects experiments to evaluate RELAP5 capabilities for predicting specific localized behavior that is relevant for PTS. These separate-effects experiments included Marviken tests for assessing critical flow models, MIT pressurizer facility tests for assessing steam condensation and RCS pressurization behavior, UPTF full-scale tests for assessing condensation and steam-water flow phenomena and semiscale tests for assessing coolant loop natural circulation flow behavior. These assessments are discussed in this section.

6.7.1.1 Marviken Tests

Critical flow assessments were performed using data obtained from two experiments conducted at the Marviken facility. Marviken is a full-scale test facility fabricated from the 14,830-ft^3 (420-m^3) pressure vessel that was part of the Marviken nuclear power plant. RELAP5 is assessed against Marviken Tests 22 and 24.

During the experiments, the vessel is pressurized, the desired temperatures and liquid levels are established, and the break is opened, allowing a blowdown of the vessel to occur through a discharge pipe. The two tests differ mainly in the length of the discharge pipe that is employed.

The RELAP5 code utilizes the Henry-Fauske critical flow model to determine the break flow rate during periods when critical flow occurs.

A comparison of the measured and RELAP5-calculated vessel discharge flow rates for Marviken Test 22 is presented in Figure 6.6. The RELAP5 prediction of mass flow rate is in excellent agreement with the test data. The comparison of results for Test 24 is similar.

The Marviken assessments indicate that RELAP5 is capable of predicting critical break flow in an experimental system of the prototype scale. However, issues related to the exact configuration of breaks in PWR piping result in an additional general break flow prediction uncertainty. In order to account for this general uncertainty, the PTS plant calculations were performed using a spectrum of break diameters and locations. Break diameters from 1-in. (2.54-cm) to 22.63-in. (57.5-cm) in equal flow area increments were analyzed in the PTS plant evaluations.

6.7.1.2 MIT Pressurizer Test ST4

The MIT test facility is a small-scale, low-pressure representation of a PWR pressurizer. The insulated test vessel is 3.74-ft (1.14-m) tall with an inner diameter of 0.667-ft (0.203-m). Test ST4 was initialized with 1.41-ft (0.432-m) of saturated water in the bottom of the vessel at a pressure of 0.493 MPa [71.5 psia]. During the test, subcooled water is injected into the bottom of the vessel, increasing both the water level and pressure.

The capabilities of RELAP5 for simulating the steam condensation and the interfacial heat transfer between the stratified liquid and the vapor above the liquid were tested using comparisons to the measured data from this test. The mixing of the cold incoming water with hot water initially in the tank affects the prediction of the pressure increase, which for PTS is an important phenomenon. The simulation of this test is included in the set of standard problems that is executed routinely for RELAP5 developmental assessment.

A comparison of the measured and RELAP5-calculated pressure behavior is shown in Figure 6.7. The pressure increases as a result of the compression of the steam volume above the water surface. As the pressure increases, so too does the saturation temperature, leading to condensation of steam on the tank walls and liquid interface. RELAP5 predicted the trend of the pressure increase well, but somewhat

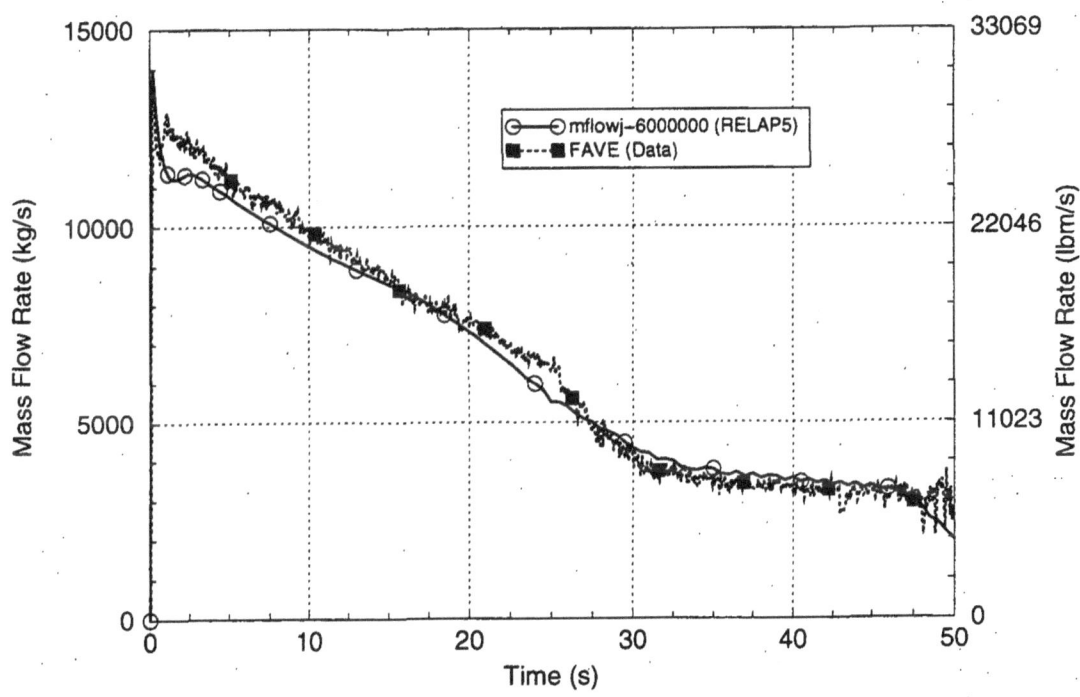

Figure 6.6.   Mass Flow Rate at Nozzle Outlet (Marviken Test 22)

overpredicted the pressure. The pressure overprediction is attributed to an underprediction of the environmental heat losses with the model. Heat losses in a small facility like the MIT test facility can have a significant impact on system parameters such as pressure. Overall, the assessment indicates that RELAP5 is capable of well-predicting the pressure increases experienced when steam regions within the RCS of a PWR are compressed.

6.7.1.3   Upper Plenum Test Facility

The Upper Plenum Test Facility (UPTF) is a full-scale model of a four-loop 1,300 MWe PWR. Components included in this facility are the reactor vessel, downcomer, lower plenum, core simulator, upper plenum, and four coolant loops, each with reactor coolant pump and steam generator simulators. The test vessel, core barrel, and internals are a full-size representation of a PWR reactor vessel.

RELAP5 assessment was performed for Run 131 of UPTF Test 6. This test represents the interaction of steam and water in the reactor vessel downcomer and lower plenum regions of a PWR during the end-of-blowdown and refill portions of a large cold-leg break LOCA. The test investigates the behavior as the ECC water injected into the cold legs penetrates downward into the reactor vessel downcomer.

The test is run by injecting steam at a constant rate through the core and steam generator simulators at pressure and temperature conditions of 0.258 MPa [37.4 psia] and 458 K (364°F). The steam flows in the reverse direction, upward through the reactor vessel downcomer, toward the broken cold leg. When the steam flow behavior becomes steady, slightly subcooled emergency core cooling water at 392 K [246°F] is injected into the cold legs of the three intact loops.

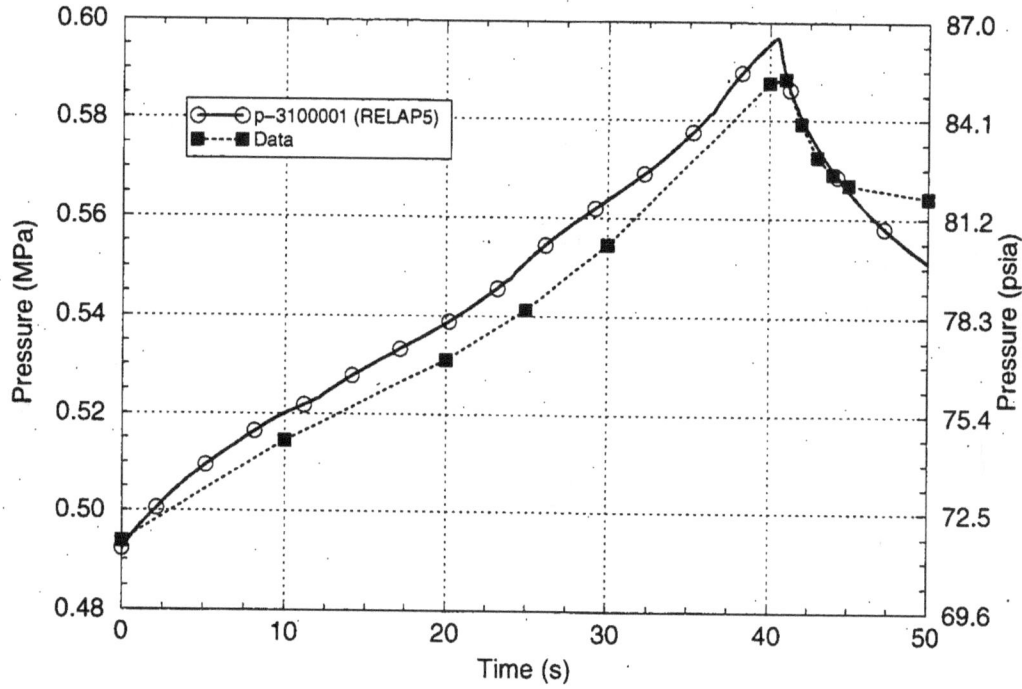

Figure 6.7. Pressure Rise (MIT Pressurizer Test ST4)

The RELAP5 simulation for UPTF Test 6, Run 131 indicates that the code well-predicts the measured downcomer pressure, lower plenum liquid level, and downcomer fluid temperature responses during the test. RELAP5 under predicted the downcomer fluid temperature by an average of 8 K (15°F) over the test period.

6.7.1.4   Semiscale Tests

Experiments were performed in the Semiscale Mod-2A test facility to evaluate single-phase, two-phase, and reflux steady-state coolant loop natural circulation behavior. This facility is a small-scale model of the primary coolant system of a four-loop PWR. The scaling factor between the test facility and full-scale plant is 1:1705. Two Semiscale Mod-2A tests, S-NC-2 and S-NC-3, are used for RELAP5 assessment.

The test facility represents the major components of a PWR, including, steam generators, reactor vessel, downcomer, reactor coolant pumps, pressurizer, and loop piping. The natural circulation experiments conducted at the facility utilized a single-loop configuration where the intact loop pump was replaced with a spool piece containing an orifice that simulated the hydraulic resistance of a locked pump rotor. The reactor vessel was also modified for these experiments to ensure a uniform heatup of the entire system and to avoid condensation in the vessel upper head region.

In Test S-NC-2, the steady-state loop natural circulation flow rate is measured as a function of the primary-side mass inventory. Single-phase, two-phase, and reflux steady-state modes were examined by varying the primary-side system mass while holding the SG secondary side conditions constant. During the test, a total of 17 separate steady-state conditions with different primary-side inventories ranging from 100 % to 61.2% of the full or maximum inventory were evaluated.

The RELAP5-calculated loop flow rates for Test S-NC-2 compare well with the test data for primary system inventories above 97% (single-phase liquid circulation and low-void two-phase circulation) and below 70% (reflux cooling circulation). For two-phase loop circulation, RELAP5 tended to overpredict the measured circulation rate for inventories between 70% and 90% and to underpredict it for inventories between 90% and 97%. The disagreement between the calculated and measured flow rates. for inventories between 70% and 97% is attributed to overprediction of interphase drag by RELAP5.

In Test S-NC-3, the SG secondary side inventory is varied and the primary-side natural circulation flow rate is measured as a function of the reduced effective SG heat transfer area. As the SG inventory declines, the SG heat removal capability and the driving potential for primary-side loop circulation (the density difference between the core and the SG) is diminished, causing the primary flow rate to decline.

RELAP5 well-predicted the measured primary-side flow at effective SG heat transfer areas above 55% but overpredicted the primary-side flow at lower inventories.

In summary, RELAP5 well-predicted the two semiscale natural circulation tests for the

conditions associated with high primary- and secondary-side coolant system inventories. The code also well-predicted the transitions to lower primary-side flow rates resulting from reduced primary- and secondary-side inventories. However, at reduced primary- and secondary-side inventories, the code generally tended to overpredict the primary-side flow rate and these overpredictions are believed to result from an overprediction of interphase drag.

Overpredicting the primary-side flow rate generally is nonconservative from the viewpoint of PTS analysis. Since the temperature of the coolant loop flow typically is much higher than the ECCS injection temperature, faster loop flows result in warmer temperatures for coolant entering the reactor vessel. The assessments indicate that under degraded inventory conditions, the primary-side flow rate may be overpredicted by a factor of about two. The maximum downcomer fluid temperature uncertainty that results from overpredicting the loop flow is estimated to be 19 K (34°F). However, it is noted that this uncertainty applies only during simulation of event sequences involving natural circulation, and then only during specific time periods within them when the primary or secondary system inventories are degraded. This uncertainty is evaluated as part of the integral system assessments that follow.

6.7.2 Integral System Response

RELAP5 was assessed against integral-effects experiments to evaluate code capabilities for predicting the system response in facilities scaled to pressurized water reactors. The assessments focus on the code capabilities for predicting the behavior of the reactor vessel downcomer conditions, which are of greatest significance for PTS analysis. The integral-effects experiments address phenomena in coolant system configurations specifically representing the geometries of Westinghouse, Combustion Engineering, and Babcock & Wilcox PWR plant designs. The integral-effects tests simulated PWR behavior under conditions expected during small, medium, and large break LOCAs; stuck-open pressurizer SRV events; and feed-and-bleed cooling operation scenarios.

These sequence categories make up the majority of the risk-dominant sequences in the PTS evaluation study for the Oconee-1, Beaver Valley-1 and Palisades PWRs.

The integral tests used in the assessments were performed in the ROSA-IV, ROSA/AP600, OSU-APEX, LOFT, and MIST experimental facilities. Comparisons of pressures and temperatures measured in these experiments to those predicted by RELAP are made in Sections 6.7.2.1 through 6.7.2.5. Section 6.7.2.6 makes comparisons between heat transfer coefficient estimates from these and other experimental data and those predicted by RELAP.

6.7.2.1 ROSA-IV Experiments

The ROSA-IV facility is a 1/48 volume-scaled, full-pressure representation of a Westinghouse 3,423 MWt four-loop PWR. The facility utilizes a full-height electrically heated core. The four PWR coolant loops are represented with two equal-volume loops. Components included in the loops are the hot leg, steam generator, reactor coolant pump, cold leg, pressurizer (on the intact loop) and ECCS systems (HPI, LPI, and accumulators).

RELAP5 was assessed against two ROSA IV experiments, SB-CL-18 and SB-HL-06.

ROSA-IV Test SB-CL-18 represents a 5% 6-in. (15.24-cm) equivalent diameter scaled break on the side of a cold leg with the reactor in full-power operation. The HPI and AFW systems are assumed to fail and a LOOP is assumed to occur at the time of the reactor trip.

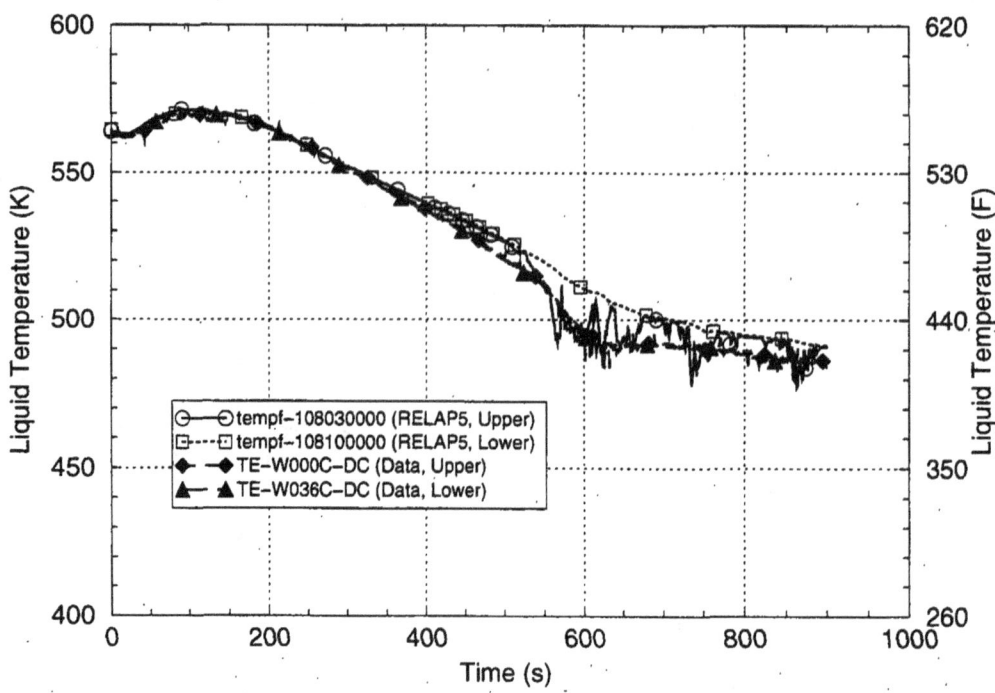

Figure 6.8. Reactor Vessel Downcomer Fluid Temperatures (ROSA-IV Test SB-CL-18)

The assessment of RELAP5 against the test data from ROSA-IV Test SB-CL-18 indicates that the code is capable of acceptably simulating the experiment behavior including the parameters of key importance for PTS (RCS pressure, coolant loop flow, and reactor vessel downcomer

temperatures). Figure 6.8 compares the measured and RELAP5-calculated reactor vessel downcomer fluid temperatures. The data shown are for elevations within the downcomer corresponding to the top and bottom of the reactor core. RELAP5 overpredicted the downcomer fluid temperature by a maximum of 13 K (23°F) and underpredicted it by a maximum of 23 K (41°F). Over the test period, RELAP5 overpredicted the downcomer fluid temperature by an average of 0.16 K (0.29°F).

ROSA-IV Test SB-HL-06 represents a 0.5% 2-in. (5.08-cm) equivalent diameter scaled break on the top of the hot leg with the reactor in full-power operation. The HPI and AFW systems are assumed to fail and a LOOP is assumed to occur at the time of the reactor trip. When the core uncovered and the heatup began, the pressurizer PORV was opened to depressurize the primary system and initiate accumulator injection.

The assessment of RELAP5 against the test data from ROSA-IV Test SB-HL-06 indicates that the code is capable of acceptably simulating the experimental behavior including the parameters of key importance for PTS (RCS pressure, coolant loop flow, and reactor vessel downcomer temperatures). Figure 6.9 compares the measured and RELAP5-calculated reactor vessel downcomer fluid temperatures. The data shown are for elevations within the downcomer corresponding to the top and bottom of the reactor core. The large drop in the measured downcomer temperature at about 8,000 s resulted from a condensation-driven rapid movement of water into the pressurizer; this water movement was not seen in the RELAP5 calculation. Condensation is an expected uncertainty in code calculations and the current state of the art in thermal-hydraulic modeling does not allow accurate predictions of extreme transient condensation events. RELAP5 underpredicted the downcomer fluid temperature by a maximum of 70 K (126°F) and by an average of 10 K (18°F) over the test period.

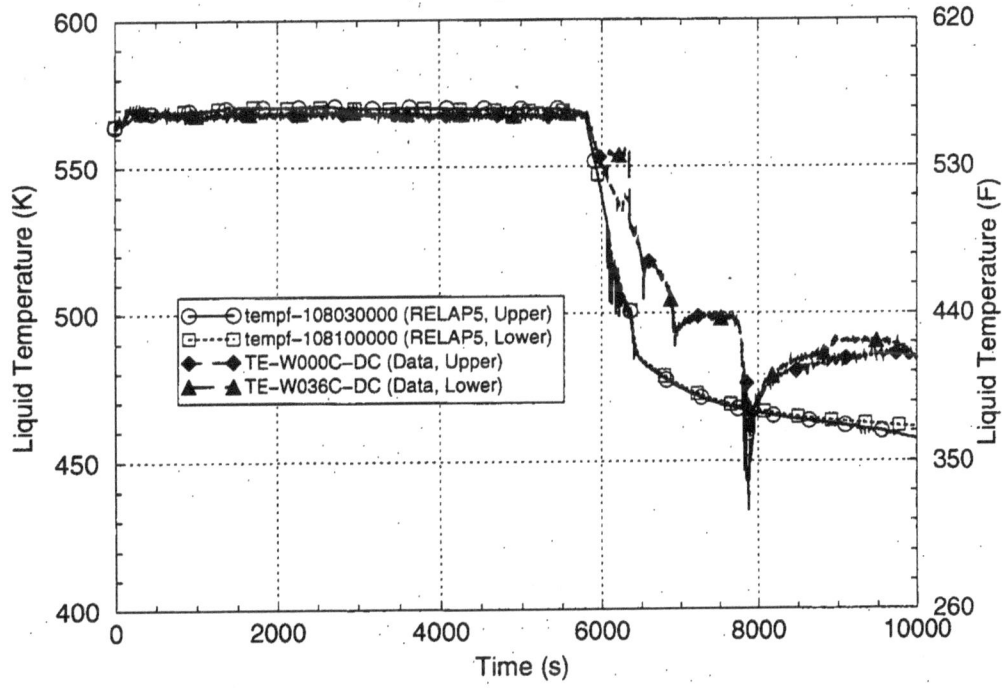

Figure 6.9.   Reactor Vessel Downcomer Temperatures (ROSA-IV Test SB-HL-06)

6.7.2.2   ROSA AP-600 Experiments

The ROSA-AP600 facility is a 1/30 volume-scaled, full-pressure representation of a Westinghouse AP600 PWR. The facility utilizes a full-height electrically heated core. The two AP600 coolant loops are represented with two equal-volume loops in the test facility. Components represented in the loops are the hot leg, steam generator, one reactor coolant pump (compared with two pumps in the plant design),

6-21

one cold leg (compared with two in the plant design), pressurizer (on one loop), and core makeup tanks (CMTs) on the other loop. The passive residual heat removal (PRHR) system, ADS, and IRWST are also represented in the test facility.

While there are configuration differences between the designs of AP600 and currently operating PWRs, assessments against ROSA/AP600 data are useful for PTS because the cold leg and reactor vessel downcomer regions of the facility are particularly well-instrumented and activation of the ADS effectively causes a transition from a small-break LOCA event sequence to a large-break LOCA event sequence, both of which are of

interest for the PTS application. RELAP5 was assessed against two ROSA-AP600 experiments, AP-CL-03 and AP-CL-09.

Test AP-CL-03 represents a 0.1% 1-in. (2.54-cm) diameter scaled break on the bottom of a cold leg in the CMT loop. The reactor is operating at full power when the break opens. An additional failure, where one of the two ADS-4 valves on the CMT loop fails to open, is also assumed.

The comparisons of RELAP5-calculated and measured data for this experiment show that the complex system behavior and timing of the test are well-predicted with RELAP5. The RELAP5 prediction of coolant loop flow stagnation and draining are in good agreement with the test data.

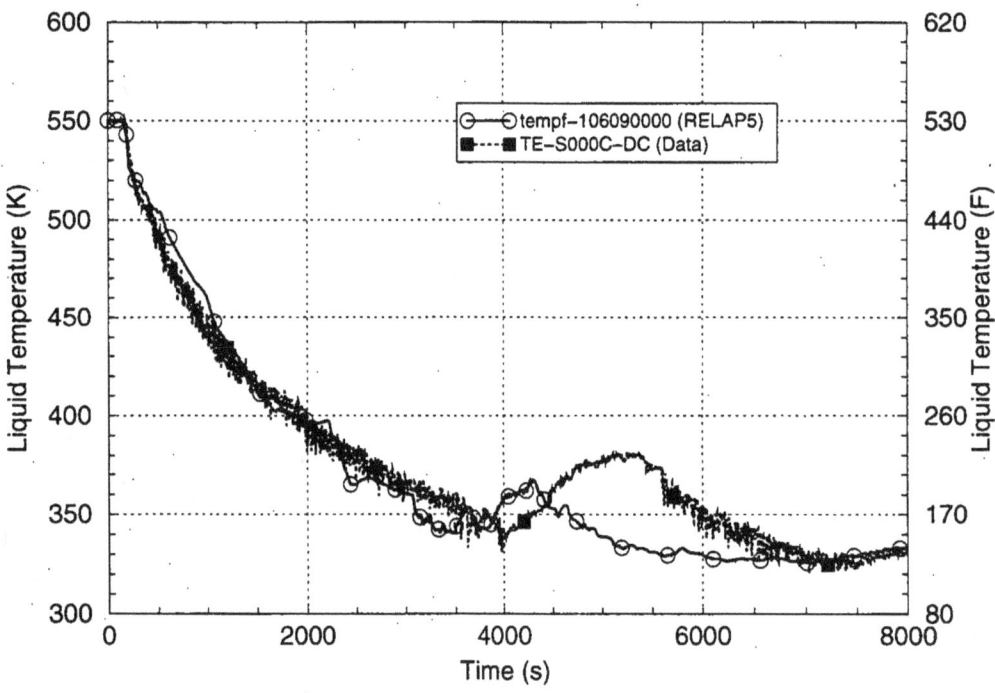

Figure 6.10. Reactor Vessel Downcomer Fluid Temperatures (ROSA/AP600 Test AP-CL-03)

The test exhibits thermal stratification within the cold legs; a layer of cold ECCS water resides under a layer of warmer water within the horizontal cold leg pipes. This thermal-stratification behavior cannot be represented with a one-dimensional computer code such as RELAP5. However, the assessment indicates only minimal effects of this code limitation on the calculated reactor vessel downcomer prediction. Figure 6.10 compares the RELAP5-

calculated and measured reactor vessel downcomer fluid temperatures on the pressurizer-loop side of the downcomer at an elevation corresponding to the bottom of the reactor core. The fluid temperature code-data comparisons at other locations in the downcomer are similar. RELAP5 overpredicted the downcomer fluid temperature by a maximum of 59 K (106°F) and underpredicted it by a maximum of 72 K (130°F). RELAP5 underpredicted the downcomer fluid temperature by an average of 4 K (7°F) over the test period.

Test AP-CL-09 also represents a 0.1% 1-in. (2.54-cm) diameter scaled break on the bottom of a cold leg in the CMT loop. The reactor is operating at full power when the break opens. Although similar to Test AP-CL-03, Test AP-CL-09 represents additional passive safety system failures:

- Both CMT discharge valves fail closed.

- Half of the valves in each ADS stage fail closed.

- ADS (normally activated by low CMT level) activated 30 minutes after a low-low pressurizer pressure signal is generated.

- Check valve in accumulator discharge line on the CMT loop fails closed.

- Check valve in the IRWST discharge line on the CMT loop fails closed.

- Only one-half of the PRHR heat exchanger capability is available.

The comparisons of RELAP5-calculated and measured data for this experiment show that the complex system behavior and timing of the test are well-predicted with RELAP5.

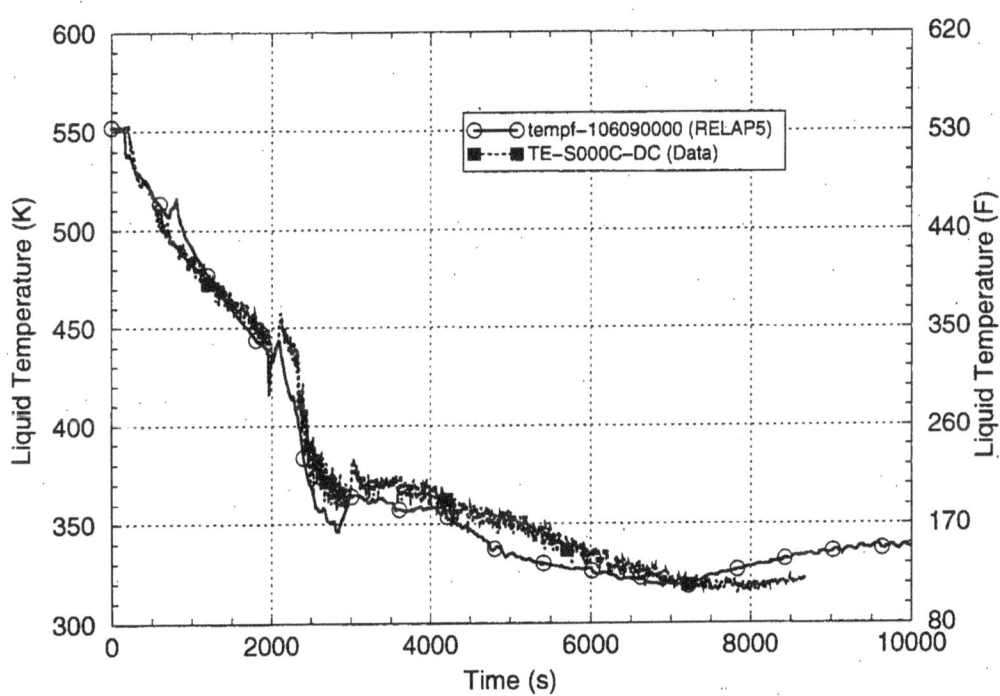

Figure 6.11. Reactor Vessel Downcomer Fluid Temperatures (ROSA/AP600 Test AP-CL-09)

As in Test AP-CL-03, thermal stratification behavior within the horizontal cold legs (which cannot be represented with RELAP5) is observed in Test AP-CL-09. Because of cold leg thermal stratification effects, the sequence order in which two loops stagnated in the RELAP5 calculation was the reverse of that seen in the test. However, good agreement is seen between the calculated and measured first-loop and second-loop stagnation times. The

assessment indicates only minimal effects of this code limitation on the prediction of vessel downcomer fluid temperatures. Figure 6.11 compares the RELAP5-calculated and measured reactor vessel downcomer fluid temperatures on the pressurizer-loop side of the downcomer at an elevation corresponding to the bottom of the reactor core. The fluid temperature code-data comparisons at other locations in the downcomer are similar. RELAP5 overpredicted the downcomer fluid temperature by a maximum of 39 K (71°F) and underpredicted it by a maximum of 49 K (88°F). RELAP5 overpredicted the downcomer fluid temperature by an average of 1 K (2°F) over the test period.

6.7.2.3   APEX Tests

A series of tests specific for plants of Combustion Engineering (CE) design was conducted at the APEX facility operated by Oregon State University. The APEX facility is a ¼-height scale low-pressure integral systems facility that has been configured to model the thermal-hydraulic phenomena of CE plants. The purpose of these tests was to investigate mixing of high-pressure injection fluid in the cold leg and the downcomer and to evaluate the onset of coolant loop flow stagnation, which can lead to low temperatures in the reactor vessel downcomer. Two APEX tests were used for RELAP5 assessment, APEX-CE-13 and APEX-CE-05.

Test APEX-CE-13 represents a stuck-open pressurizer safety relief valve event with the reactor operating at full power. The stuck-open valve is subsequently assumed to reclose. This type of transient event is a significant contributor to PTS risk event because the RCS is first significantly cooled and then repressurized after the relief valve closes. To start the test, the ADS-2 valve atop the pressurizer was opened to simulate a stuck-open pressurizer safety relief valve. Simultaneously, two reactor coolant pumps were tripped, the HPI system was actuated and reactor core power was tripped. The ADS-2 valve was closed at 1 hour into the test and the test was terminated about 20 minutes later after the RCS had refilled.

The comparisons of RELAP5-calculated and measured data from Test APEX-CE-13 indicate that the code is capable of acceptably simulating the behavior of the key PTS parameters for this test. RELAP5 overpredicted the RCS cooldown rate during the period when the relief valve is open as shown in Figure 6.12. RELAP5 predicted a delayed onset of the repressurization and underpredicted the pressurization rate after

the relief valve closed as seen in Figure 6.13. These differences between the calculated and measured responses are considered to be moderate and to result from difficulties in adequately modeling the system heat losses of small-scale facilities such as APEX. RELAP5 underpredicted the downcomer fluid temperature by an average of 2 K (4°F) over the test period.

Test APEX-CE-05 was performed to provide baseline mixing data for the injection of cold ECC water into the cold legs of the RCS. During the test, RCS temperatures and pressures consistent with full-power plant operation are first established and then the steam generators, RCPs and reactor core heaters are secured to create stagnant conditions in the RCS. High-pressure injection is initiated into the four cold legs and a pressurizer drain valve is opened to accommodate the injected fluid and control the pressurizer level and RCS pressure. For this test, the behavior of interest is the manner in which the cold water entering the vessel through the cold legs spreads downward and around the reactor vessel downcomer annulus. The thermocouple instrumentation of the facility was upgraded in order to observe this behavior.

The test data exhibit only very small variations in the downcomer temperatures around the periphery of the downcomer. The maximum azimuthal downcomer temperature variations are 9 K (16°F) at the elevation corresponding to the top of the core and are 5 K (9°F) at the elevation corresponding to the bottom of the core. No significant plumes were observed in the downcomer based on the temperature results of this test. Larger variations are seen in the axial direction in the downcomer, but these variations, which are related to the time required for fluid to transit though the downcomer, are short-lived. The downcomer temperature variations observed in the RELAP5 simulation of the test similarly are small.

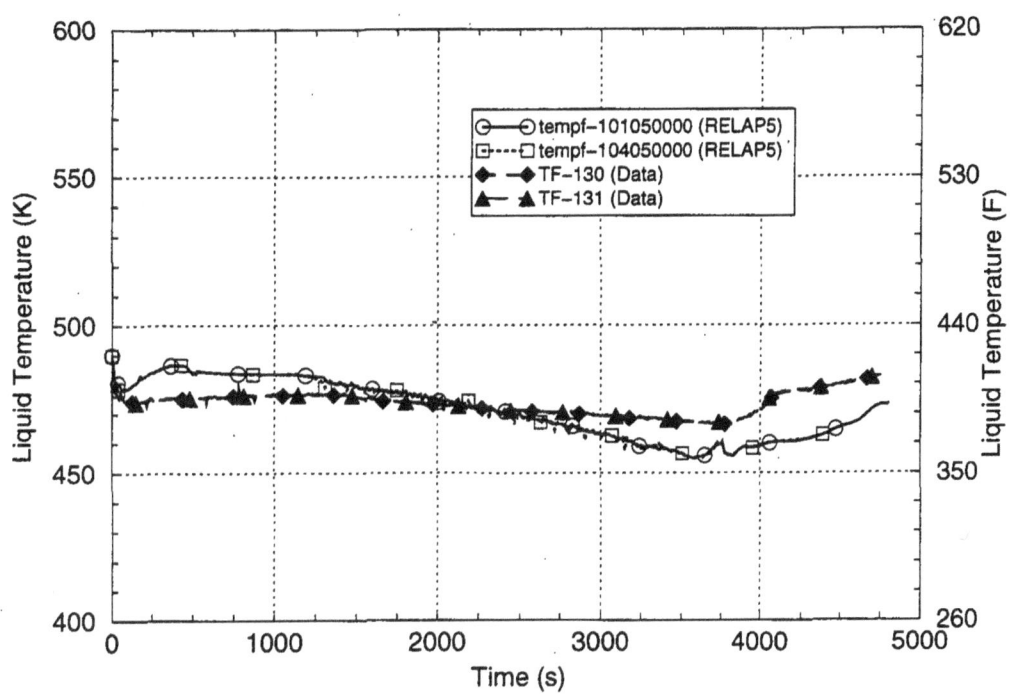

Figure 6.12. Reactor Vessel Downcomer Fluid Temperatures (Test APEX-CE-13)

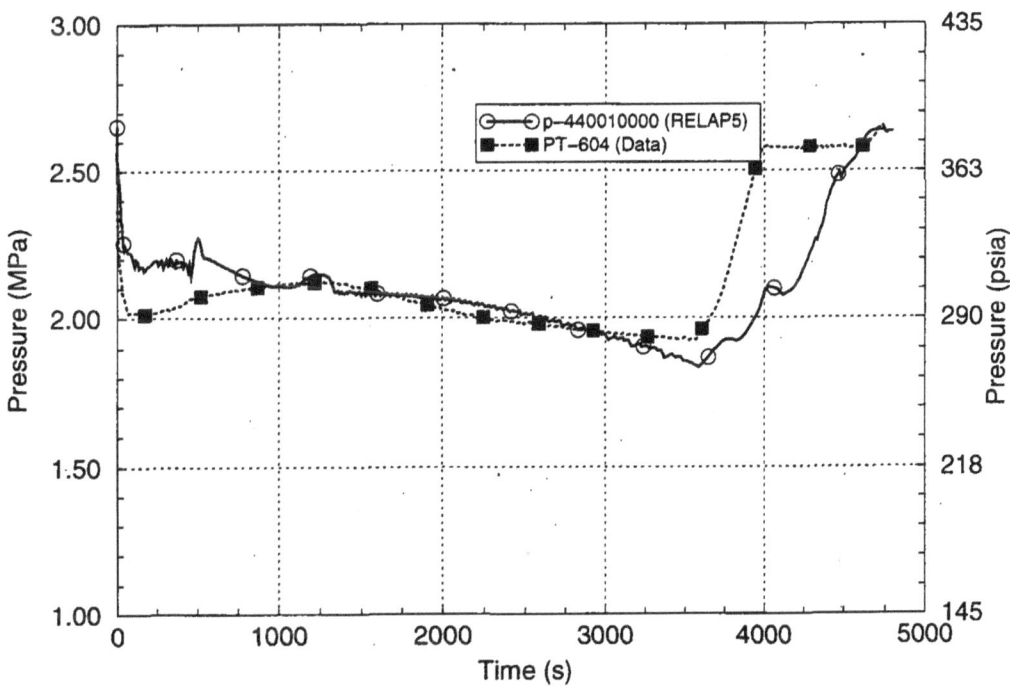

Figure 6.13. Pressurizer Pressure (Test APEX-CE-13)

Figure 6.14 compares the RELAP5-calculated and measured reactor vessel downcomer fluid temperature responses for Test APEX-CE-05 at a representative location (directly under one of the cold legs at an elevation corresponding to the top of the core). The figures show that RELAP5 predicts the downcomer fluid temperature excellently up to about 2,000 s, but then underpredicts it afterward. Over the test period, RELAP5 underpredicted the downcomer fluid temperature by an average of 5 K (9°F). The underprediction is attributed to more involvement of warm fluid residing within the cold legs in the mixing process in the experiment than in the calculation.

A second sensitivity RELAP5 calculation for Test APEX-CE-05 was performed in which large artificial flow loss coefficients for reverse flow were added in the reactor coolant pump suction regions of each cold leg. This modeling approach is used in PTS plant calculations to suppress circulations through the cold legs on the same coolant loop (in the forward direction through one cold leg and in the reverse direction in the other) for certain types of PTS events. This model change resulted in RELAP5-calculated reactor vessel downcomer fluid temperatures that were additionally lower (compared with the above calculation) by an average of 8 K (14°F) over the test period. This difference represents the expected downcomer temperature conservatism resulting from using the high artificial reverse flow loss coefficient modeling approach.

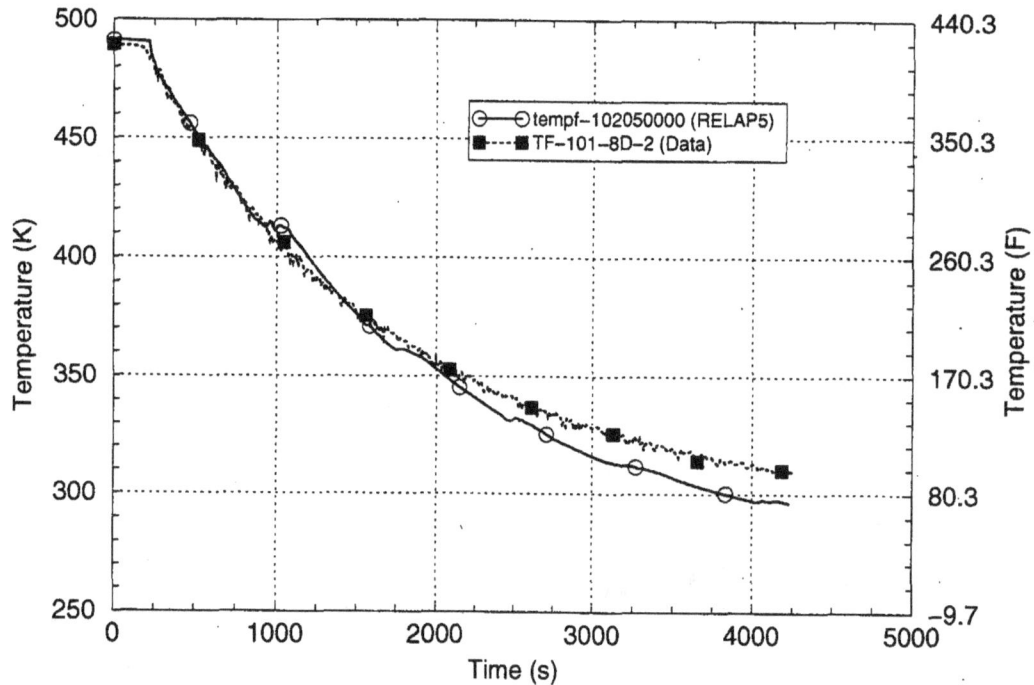

Figure 6.14. Reactor Vessel Downcomer Fluid Temperatures (Test APEX-CE-05)

6.7.2.4 LOFT Tests

The Loss-of-Fluid Test Facility (LOFT) is a 50-MWt volumetrically scaled PWR system. The LOFT facility was designed to obtain data on the performance of the engineered safety features of a commercial PWR system for postulated accidents, including LOCAs.

The LOFT nuclear core is approximately 5.51-ft (1.68-m) tall and 2-ft (0.61-m) in diameter, and is composed of nine fuel assemblies containing 1,300 nuclear fuel rods of representative PWR design. Three intact loops are simulated using a volume/power ratio scaling by the single circulating (intact) loop in the LOFT primary system. The broken loop is simulated by the scaled LOFT blowdown loop.

An ECCS is provided to simulate the engineered safety features in PWRs. An HPI system centrifugal pump and a nitrogen-pressurized accumulator supply emergency core cooling. The LPI system and accumulator discharge lines are orificed as required to simulate the delivery characteristics of various PWR emergency core cooling systems.

RELAP5 assessment was performed using three LOFT experiments, Test L3-7, Test L2-5 and Test L3-1.

Loft Test L3-7 represents plant recovery actions following a 1-in. (2.54-cm) equivalent diameter break in the cold leg of a PWR operating at full power. The primary purpose of this test is to establish a break flow approximately equal to the HPI flow at an RCS pressure of approximately 6.9 MPa [1,000 psia], to isolate the break and to demonstrate the stabilization of the plant at cold shutdown conditions.

During Test L3-7, the break was opened, the reactor and reactor coolant pumps were tripped, leading to coolant loop natural circulation flow. At 1,800 s, the AFW and HPI flows were terminated to hasten the loss of RCS fluid inventory and to establish the conditions leading into the system recovery to cold shutdown conditions. At 3,603 s, the AFW flow was reinstated and a SG steam bleed operation begun to effect a controlled depressurization of the

intact loop SG secondary system. The HPI flow was reinstated at 5,974 s, and the test was terminated at 7,302 seconds.

The assessment indicates that RELAP5 is capable of acceptably simulating the behavior of the key PTS parameters for LOFT Test L3-7. The RELAP5 prediction of the RCS pressure is in good-to-excellent agreement with the measured data. The RELAP5 prediction of the reactor vessel downcomer fluid temperature is in good agreement with the measured data. Figure 6.15 shows a comparison of the measured and calculated reactor vessel downcomer fluid temperatures for this test at representative locations in the downcomer (on the broken loop and intact loop sides of the downcomer and at elevations in the downcomer corresponding to the elevations of the top and middle of the core). Over the test period, RELAP5 underpredicted the downcomer fluid temperature by an average of 8 K (14°F).

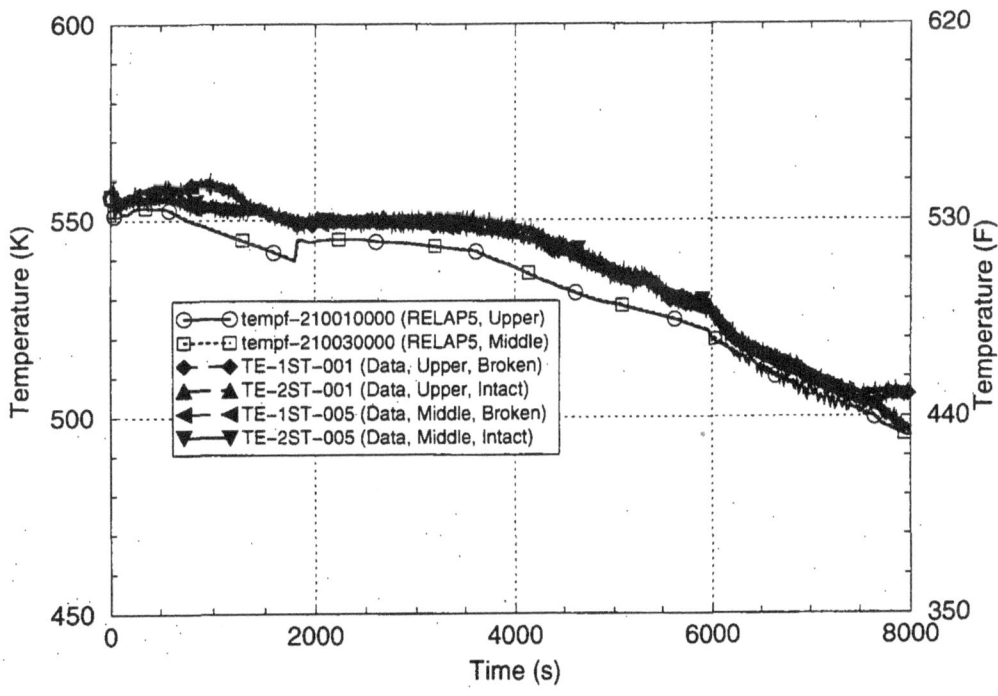

Figure 6.15. Reactor Vessel Downcomer Fluid Temperatures (LOFT Test L3-7)

Test LOFT L2-5 represents a double-ended offset guillotine break LOCA in the cold leg of a PWR operating at full power. The primary

purpose of this test was to evaluate the performance of the ECCS for cooling the core. For the purposes of the PTS assessment, this test provides data for the very rapid blowdown and refilling of the RCS with cold ECCS which accompanies a very large break in the RCS. During the test, the break was opened and the reactor and reactor coolant pumps were tripped. Accumulator injection began when the RCS pressure had declined below the initial accumulator pressure and delayed injection of HPI and LPI ECC coolant began at 24 s and 37 s, respectively after the break opened.

The assessment indicated no major differences between the RELAP5-calculated and measured responses for LOFT Test L2-5. The RELAP5 predictions of the reactor vessel downcomer fluid temperature and RCS pressure are in good agreement with the measured data. Figure 6.16 shows a comparison of the measured and calculated reactor vessel downcomer fluid temperatures for this test at representative locations in the downcomer (on the broken loop side of the downcomer at elevations in the downcomer corresponding to the elevations of the top, middle and bottom of the core). Over the test period, RELAP5 underpredicted the downcomer fluid temperature by an average of 4 K (7°F).

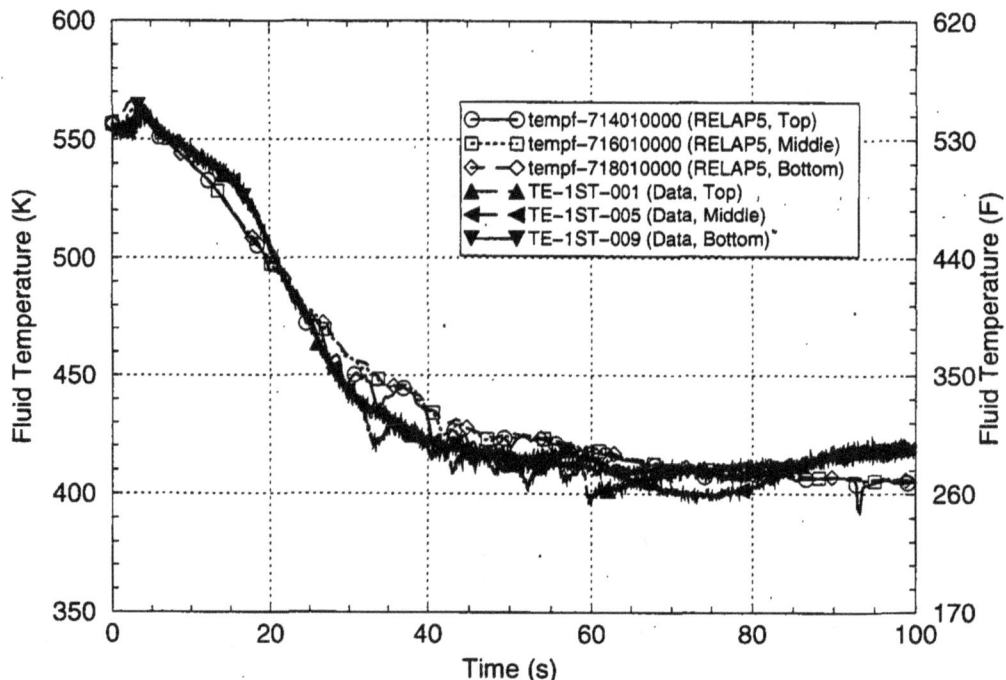

Figure 6.16. Reactor Vessel Downcomer Fluid Temperatures (LOFT Test L2-5)

LOFT Test L3-1 represents an equivalent 4-in. (10.16-cm) diameter break LOCA in the cold leg of a PWR operating at full power. The primary purpose of this experiment was to evaluate the performance of the ECCS for cooling the core.

During the experiment, the reactor and the reactor coolant pumps were tripped and ECC flows from the HPI and accumulator systems were initiated as the RCS pressure declined. The accumulator water inventory was fully discharged and the experiment was continued until 3,623 s using the HPI ECC flow alone.

At that time a feed-and-bleed SG cooling process was implemented; the experiment was concluded at 4,368 s.

For the purposes of the PTS assessment, this test provides data for the rapid blowdown and stabilization of the RCS with ECCS injection for a break diameter that is toward the larger end of the small-break LOCA spectrum.

Test L3-1 also provides data useful for comparing RELAP5 simulation capabilities when using one-dimensional and two-dimensional reactor vessel downcomer modeling approaches. RELAP5 PTS plant simulations have shown considerable variation in calculated downcomer temperatures for cold leg LOCAs with break diameters near 4-in. (10.2-cm), depending upon whether the 1-dimensional or 2-dimensional RELAP5 downcomer modeling approach is used. RELAP5 calculations for LOFT Test L3-1 are performed using both downcomer modeling approaches in order to judge which approach is better for simulating cold leg breaks of this approximate size.

The assessment indicated that the behavior in the reactor vessel downcomer region is particularly difficult to predict for a break of this size and location. Accumulator injection has a potential for directly influencing the downcomer temperature, but mixing within the cold leg and upper downcomer regions significantly affects that influence. The prediction of mixing within the thermally stratified cold leg regions is beyond the capability of RELAP5. The break is large enough that the RCS depressurizes sufficiently to result in accumulator injection, but not so large as to allow for an accumulator discharge that is insensitive to the RCS pressure. Finally, the break location in the cold leg adds to the prediction difficulty because the most direct path for steam to reach the break is upward through the downcomer, against the downward flow of cold accumulator water. Therefore, interphase condensation modeling, known to be a weakness of RELAP5, appears to be particularly important for predicting the behavior for this particular break size and location

The assessment indicates that RELAP5 is capable of acceptably predicting the reactor coolant system parameters for this test. The downcomer fluid temperatures in the test were underpredicted using both the 1- and 2-dimensional downcomer modeling approaches. Over the test period, the underprediction is by an average of 7 K (13°F) when using the one-dimensional downcomer modeling scheme and by an average of 13 K

(23°F) when using the 2-dimensional downcomer modeling scheme. Figure 6.17 compares the measured and calculated fluid temperatures for Test LOFT L3-1 at a representative location in the reactor vessel downcomer. The data shown are for a location on the broken loop side of the downcomer at an elevation corresponding to the middle of the reactor core. The code-data comparisons at other locations in the downcomer are similar.

The 2-dimensional reactor vessel downcomer modeling approach is judged to be the more appropriate approach for RELAP5 PTS applications because of (1) the better accumulator injection behavior it produced, (2) the ability it provides for predicting different fluid behavior in the intact and broken-loop sides of the reactor vessel downcomer, which has the potential to affect break flow and downcomer mixing, and (3) the more conservative downcomer fluid temperature predictions it produced.

More detailed information regarding the assessment of RELAP5 for LOFT Test L3-1 is found in Section 3.9 of [*Fletcher*].

6.7.2.5   MIST Tests

The Multi-loop Integral System Test (MIST) facility is a scaled full-pressure experimental facility that represents the B&W lowered-loop plant design with two hot legs and four cold legs. The plant-to-facility power scaling factor is 817, and the plant-to-facility volume scaling factor is 620 for the total primary system volume, excluding the core flood tanks. Major components include two once-through steam generators with full length tubes, two hot leg pipe segments, four cold leg pipe segments, four coolant pumps, a reactor vessel with an external downcomer, a pressurizer with spray and PORV connections, and one core flood tank. Boundary systems provide simulation of the HPI, auxiliary feedwater, and various types of failures such as steam generator tube ruptures and LOCAs.

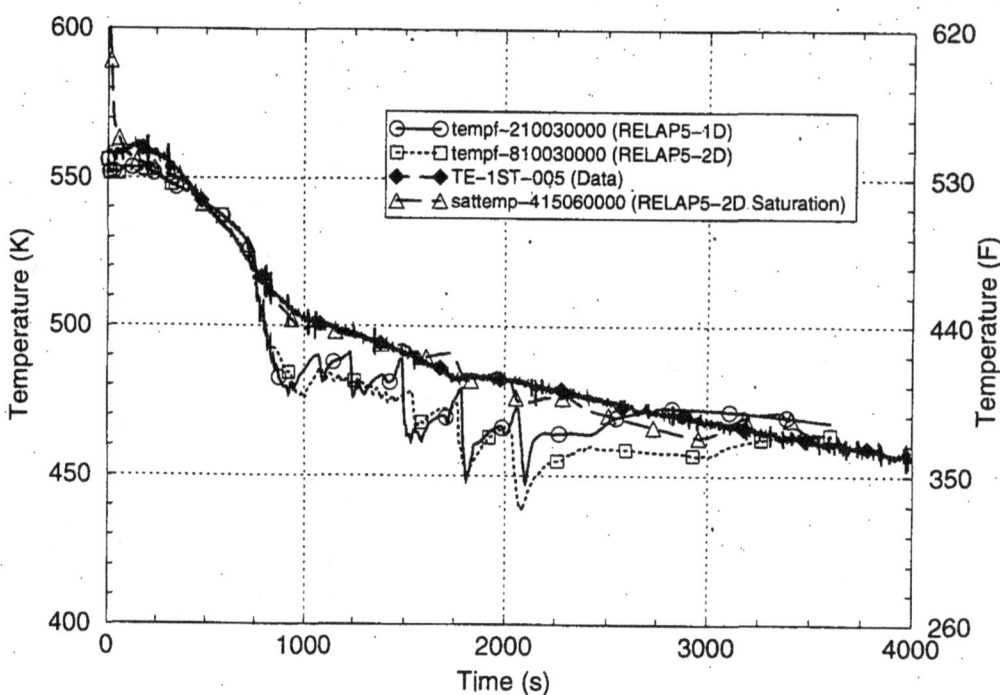

Figure 6.17. Reactor Vessel Downcomer Fluid Temperatures (LOFT Test L3-1)

RELAP5 assessment was performed for three MIST experiments, Test 360499, Test 3109AA, and Test 4100B2.

MIST Test 360499 is a HPI-power operated relief valve (HPI-PORV) feed-and-bleed simulation, starting from 110% flow, 10% scaled-power conditions. The system behavior for this test resembles a stuck-open pressurizer PORV event sequence with continued HPI injection and operator throttling based upon the RCS subcooling margin. Events such as this are significant contributors to the risk of PTS vessel failure.

The assessment for this test indicated that the RELAP5 prediction of the RCS pressure was excellent. However, the assessment indicated major differences between the calculated and measured responses within the cold legs on the two coolant loops. RELAP5 overpredicted the cold leg temperature in Loop A, and did not predict the coolant loop flow stagnation seen in the test. RELAP5 underpredicted the cold leg temperature in Loop B and did predict the coolant loop flow stagnation seen in the test.

Despite these difficulties, the RELAP5 prediction of the reactor vessel downcomer fluid temperature, which represents a mixture of the cold leg temperatures, was judged to be good. Figure 6.18 compares the calculated and measured reactor vessel downcomer fluid temperatures for MIST Test 360499 at a representative location in the downcomer (at an elevation corresponding to the bottom of the core). The code-data comparisons at other downcomer locations are similar. Over the test period, RELAP5 overpredicted the downcomer fluid temperature by an average of 3 K (5°F).

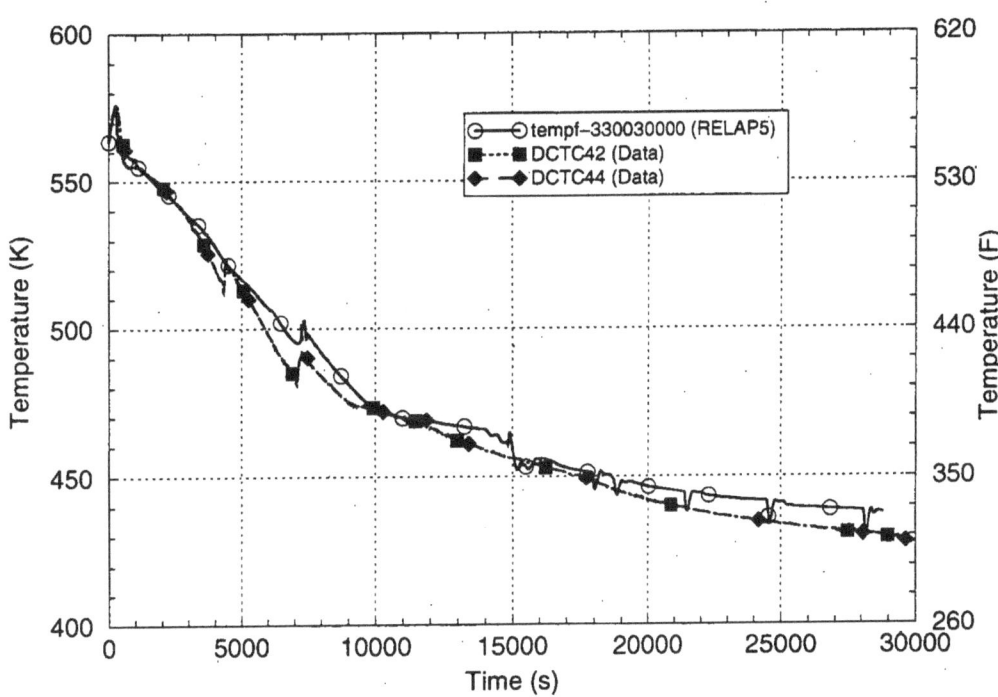

Figure 6.18. Reactor Vessel Downcomer Fluid Temperatures (MIST Test 360499)

MIST Test 3109AA represents a 1.6-in.[2] (10-cm[2]) break in the RCP discharge section of a PWR cold leg. This break size corresponds to a 1.4-in. (3.59-cm) diameter break in the PWR and is sufficiently small that HPI flow can compensate for break flow. At the start of the test, the facility is operating under natural-circulation loop flow conditions, with the RCP rotors locked.

The assessment indicated no major differences between the calculated and measured data for MIST Test 3109AA. The RELAP5 prediction of the RCS pressure is in good agreement with the measured data. The code well-predicted the interruption of loop natural circulation flow in both of the coolant loops. RELAP5 overpredicted the reactor vessel downcomer fluid temperature after about 1,000 s. Figure 6.19 compares the calculated and measured reactor vessel downcomer fluid temperatures for MIST Test 3109AA at a representative location in the downcomer (at an elevation corresponding to the top of the core). The code-data comparisons at other downcomer locations are similar. Over the test period, RELAP5

overpredicted the downcomer fluid temperature by an average of 10 K (18°F).
MIST Test 4100B2 represents a 15.5-in.[2] (100-cm[2]) [4.4-in. (11.2-cm) diameter] equivalent break in the RCP discharge section of a PWR cold leg. The break size is sufficiently large that HPI cannot compensate for the break flow. The test is initiated at conditions representing 3.5% scaled power and coolant loop natural circulation conditions with the RCPs tripped and their rotors locked. During the test, the core power is tripped and HPI and EFW flows are initiated.

The assessment for MIST Test 4100B2 shows moderate differences between the calculated and measured data for the most important parameters for PTS (RCS pressure and downcomer fluid temperature). Following the RCS blowdown, basic limitations of RELAP5 resulted in an underprediction of the stable RCS pressure by about 0.68 MPa [98 psi]. RELAP5 slightly underpredicted the downcomer fluid temperatures during the blowdown period, up to about 2,100 s. However, during the refill period RELAP5 overpredicted the reactor vessel

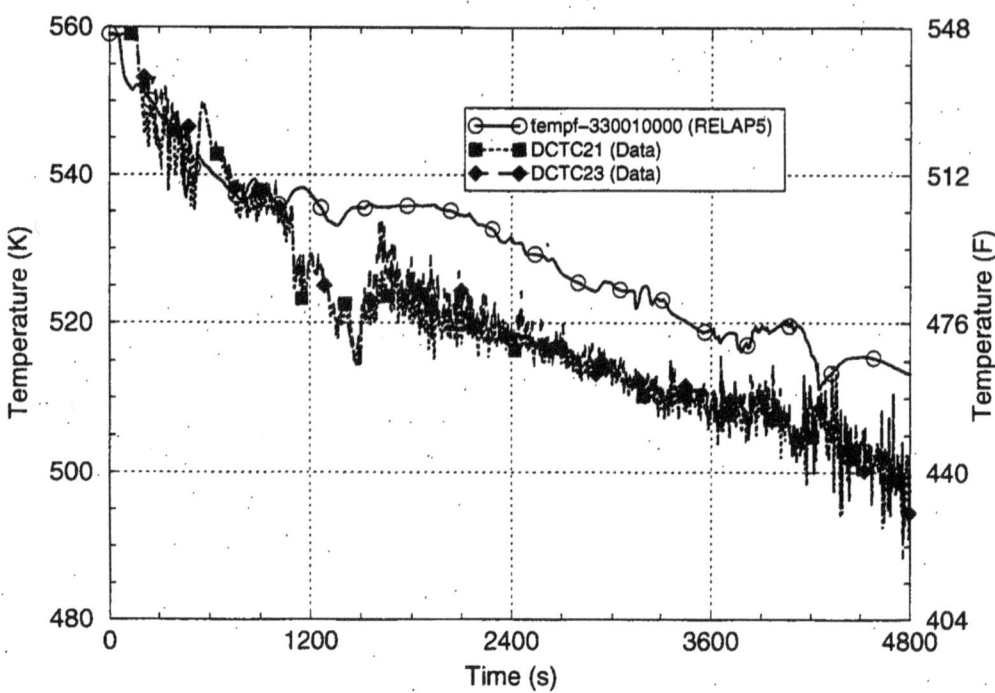

Figure 6.19. Reactor Vessel Downcomer Fluid Temperatures (MIST Test 3109AA)

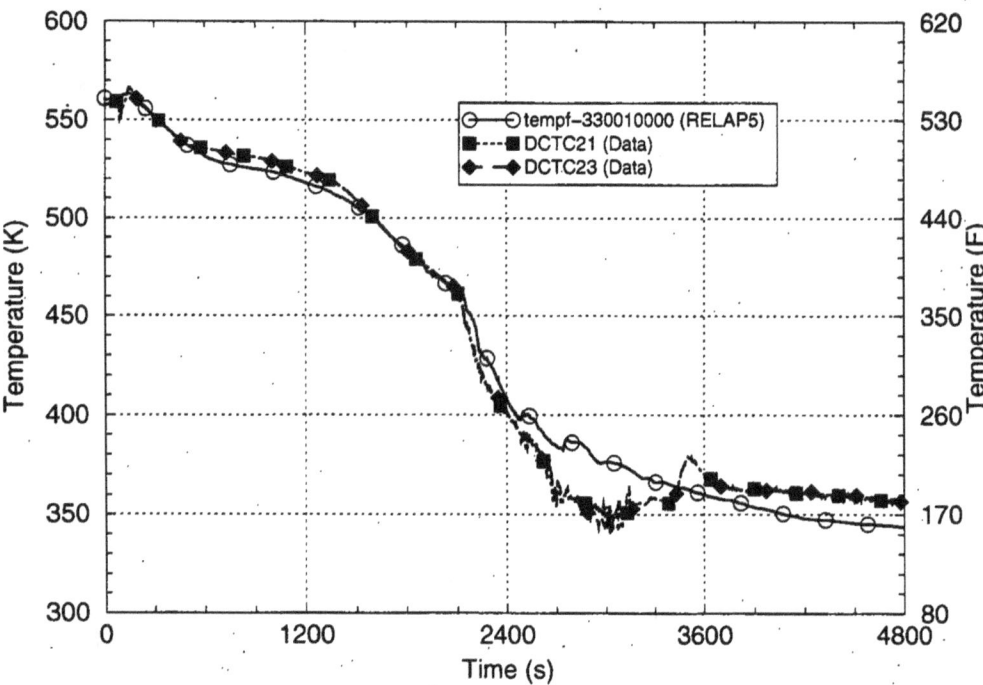

Figure 6.20. Reactor Vessel Downcomer Fluid Temperatures (MIST Test 4100B2)

downcomer fluid temperature by up to 32 K (58 °F). Figure 6.20 compares the calculated and measured reactor vessel downcomer fluid temperatures for MIST Test 4100B2 at a representative location in the downcomer (at an elevation corresponding to the top of the core). The code-data comparisons at other downcomer locations are similar. Over the test period,

RELAP5 overpredicted the downcomer fluid temperature by an average of 0.37 K (0.67°F).

6.7.2.6   Reactor Vessel Wall Inside-Surface Heat Transfer Coefficient

For the reactor vessel wall heat transfer coefficient, quantitative assessment comparisons are more difficult than for RCS pressures and downcomer fluid temperatures because heat transfer coefficients are not directly measured in the experiments. Further, since most of the test facilities were designed to study core-coolability safety issues and not vessel downcomer overcooling issues, experimental instrumentation related to downcomer wall heat transfer (wall and fluid thermocouples, wall heat fluxes and downcomer fluid velocities) is generally limited. Quantitative assessments of RELAP5 capabilities for predicting the vessel wall heat transfer coefficient and other heat transfer-related parameters are provided in this section to the extent feasible considering the limited available data. Other investigations into reactor vessel wall heat transfer in general and RELAP5 capabilities in particular are also presented here to support the assessment conclusions regarding the wall heat transfer coefficient. The information in this section summarizes that presented in greater detail elsewhere [*Bessette*].

As described below, for the PTS application, the wall heat transfer regime of greatest interest is for wall-to-fluid convection for Reynolds numbers toward the low end of the turbulent range. This regime corresponds to the reactor vessel downcomer situation during periods with low coolant-loop natural circulation flow or periods after the coolant-loop flows have stagnated as a result of voiding in the upper regions of the RCS (as is caused by draining during LOCA events). Other heat transfer regimes are also experienced during portions of the PTS transient accident scenarios. Highly turbulent forced convection is experienced when reactor coolant pumps are operating or when there is robust coolant-loop natural circulation flow. Saturated and subcooled nucleate boiling

are generally experienced for events where the RCS rapidly depressurized, the fluid saturation temperature quickly drops and the hot vessel wall passes heat to a flashing and boiling fluid. The attention is given here to the regime for convection because it (1) is frequently encountered in the PTS scenarios, and (2) results in a relatively low heat transfer coefficient. The other regimes (highly turbulent convection and boiling) result in large heat transfer coefficients. A detailed assessment of the accuracy of RELAP's heat transfer models is not warranted in these other regimes because the process of wall-to-fluid heat transfer is dominated by the surface boiling transport mechanism and not by the convective movement of fluid. Therefore, the heat transfer is less influenced by details of bulk fluid motion

6.7.2.6.1   Effect of Heat Transfer Coefficient on Wall Heat Flux

During normal steady plant operation, the reactor vessel wall temperature is the same as the downcomer fluid temperature (which is core inlet temperature). During PTS scenarios, the fluid temperature falls. The wall-to-fluid heat transfer processes from the hotter vessel wall to the colder fluid in the downcomer are of significance. The RCS cooldowns experienced in the PTS accident scenarios generally fall into three categories of (1) secondary-side events, such as main steam line breaks, (2) small primary-side LOCAs, such as hot or cold leg breaks or stuck-open pressurizer relief valve events, and (3) large primary-side LOCAs, such as double-ended hot or cold leg breaks. Each of these event categories is separately discussed in the following subsections.

6.7.2.6.1.1   Secondary Side Events

For secondary-side events, the RCS is rapidly cooled by overcooling to the steam generators but the RCS remains at high pressure and, often, forced flow of coolant through the RCS loops continues. The RCS fluid cools, but the extent of the cooldown is limited because the ultimate heat sink temperature is the saturation temperature at atmospheric pressure, which represents the final state in the secondary coolant system. The reactor vessel wall heat transfer coefficient remains high as a result of pump-forced flow or a robust coolant-loop natural circulation flow for cases where the reactor coolant pumps are tripped. As a result, the wall-to-fluid heat transfer process is controlled by heat conduction through the reactor vessel wall.

6.7.2.6.1.2   Small Primary Side LOCAs

For small primary-side LOCA events, the RCS depressurizes at a rate that is proportional to the break size. Fluid flashing caused by the RCS depressurization cools the RCS fluid as the saturation temperature falls. The ECC systems add cold water to the RCS at rates that increase with decreasing RCS pressure. This pressure dependency results because the ECC systems are made up of (1) tanks (accumulators, core flood tanks, and safety injection tanks) with cold water inventory stored at intermediate pressures, and (2) centrifugal pump systems (HPI, LPI, etc.) for which no flow is delivered above the pump shutoff heads and for which lower RCS pressures lead to greater cold water injection flow rates.

For the small LOCAs, the system pressure is defined by the RCS mass and energy balances associated with core heat addition, cold water injection, steam generator heat removal, and break flow. There is much interdependence among the PTS parameters of interest (pressure, fluid temperature, and heat transfer coefficient).

Larger break sizes lead to lower pressures (which tend to mitigate the PTS risk) while at the same time leading to higher ECC injection rates and lower fluid temperatures (which tend to increase the PTS risk). Further, the variations in the injection flow rate can directly affect the break flow (which, in turn, affects RCS pressure) and the RCS inventory, which affects tripping of reactor coolant pumps, coolant loop natural circulation and stagnation, vessel downcomer velocities and wall heat transfer coefficients. For small primary-side LOCA events, the potential for vessel failure as a

consequence of PTS arises as a result of incomplete RCS depressurization and RCS draining, which causes the stagnation of the coolant-loop natural circulation flows and leads to pooling of cold water in the cold leg and downcomer regions.

Because for small breaks, the injection of cold ECC water is at a low rate, the RCS cooldown experienced for this category of LOCA events is relatively slow and there is a feedback between the heat transfer from the wall to the fluid and the fluid temperature itself. For this category of events, the downcomer wall heat transfer regimes generally fall into the range of turbulent forced convection from wall to subcooled liquid (even following coolant loop flow stagnation, the downcomer flow rates remain sufficiently high to resemble forced convection).

6.7.2.6.1.3   Large Primary Side LOCAs

For large primary-side LOCA events, the RCS completely depressurizes and the injections of cold ECC water from the HPI, LPI, and accumulator systems are at very high rates. The rapid decline in the fluid saturation temperature leads to limited periods of fluid flashing and boiling on the hot vessel wall. Heat transfer coefficients are very high for conditions of nucleate boiling. As a result of the large break size, the RCS cannot repressurize from the ECC injection. The high injection rate floods the cold legs and vessel downcomer regions with cold water and this quickly terminates the boiling process.

6.7.2.6.2   Comparison of Measured and RELAP5-Calculated Reactor Vessel Wall Heat Transfer Data

Only limited pertinent data are available from integral system tests for assessing RELAP5 reactor vessel wall-to-fluid heat transfer for geometries consistent with the plants and the conditions present in the PTS accident scenarios. Instruments are often not available for directly measuring heat transfer coefficient or heat flux. However, downcomer fluid and vessel wall thermocouple data along with fluid velocity data are occasionally available that permit a quantified comparison between the measured and RELAP5-calculated wall heat transfer process. This section summarizes vessel wall-to-fluid heat transfer comparisons pertinent for the PTS for tests performed in the UPTF, APEX-CE, and Creare test facilities.

6.7.2.6.2.1   UPTF Test 1 Run 21

The UPTF featured a full-scale representation of the reactor vessel, downcomer, and cold legs of a PWR. Test 1 Run 21 consisted of injecting cold HPI water into one of the four cold legs (Cold Leg 2) into a system that was initially filled with hot pressurized water. The experimental conditions are comparable to those experienced in a PWR following stagnation of the coolant loop natural circulation flow. This experimental facility and test were modeled with RELAP5 and the calculated results were compared with the measured test data. The RELAP5 model included a 2-dimensional nodalization scheme, comparable to those employed in the PTS plant analyses.

The measured velocity data at the core-bottom elevation in the downcomer exhibited a downward flow below Cold Leg 2 and upward flows through other azimuthal sectors of the downcomer as shown in Figure 6.21. (The direction of positive velocity is downward.) The RELAP5 simulation also showed a downward water flow below Cold Leg 2 (Figure 6.22), but with the cold water spreading into sectors adjacent to Cold Leg 2 by the time the flow reached the core bottom elevation. As a result, the RELAP5-calculated velocities are seen in these figures to be lower than the measured velocities. The fluid velocities in the downcomer (in both the test and calculation) were much greater than the superficial fluid velocity based on only the HPI flow in the downcomer. The test data indicated that the downcomer velocity is ~16 times the downcomer HPI superficial velocity.

An assessment of the RELAP5-calculated vessel wall heat transfer coefficient was made using fluid and wall thermocouple data. In

downcomer regions away from Cold Leg 2, RELAP5 was found to underpredict the rates of decline in both the fluid and vessel wall temperatures by a similar extent and therefore to predict the heat transfer coefficient well (within ~15%). Below Cold Leg 2, RELAP5 was found to underpredict the wall-to-fluid differential temperature of the test as shown in Figure 6.23 and to also underpredict the wall-to-fluid heat flux (as indicated by the slower cooldown rate at the location of a thermocouple embedded 1-in. (25-mm) into the vessel wall at the core top elevation; see Figure 6.24). Since the RELAP5 underprediction of the differential temperature was much greater than the RELAP5 underprediction of the heat flux, RELAP5 was found to overpredict the wall-to-fluid heat transfer coefficient under Cold Leg 2 for UPTF Test 1-21 by a factor of ~2.

6.7.2.6.2.2   APEX-CE Test 5

The Advanced Plant Experiment facility (APEX-CE) is a reduced-height, pressure, and temperature facility scaled to Palisades, a CE-designed plant. The test consisted of injecting cold HPI water into all four cold legs of a system that was initially filled with hot pressurized water. The experimental conditions are comparable to those experienced in a pressurized water reactor following stagnation of the coolant loop natural circulation flow. This experimental facility and test were modeled with RELAP5 and the calculated results were compared with the measured test data. The RELAP5 model included a two-dimensional nodalization scheme, comparable to those employed in the PTS plant analyses.

The RELAP5 assessment concentrated on the first 1,700 s of the test period. There was excellent agreement between measured and calculated fluid and wall temperatures as shown in Figure 6.25 and Figure 6.26. The excellent match between the measured and calculated wall temperatures indicated that RELAP5 also predicts the wall heat flux well. However, a comparison between the measured and calculated wall-to-fluid differential temperatures indicated that RELAP5 underpredicted the test differential temperature by a factor of ~2 and, therefore, overpredicted the wall-to-fluid heat transfer coefficient for APEX-CE-5 by the same factor.

There are no direct measurements for downcomer flow velocity in the APEX-CE facility, but flow velocity indications were derived from thermocouple data. The calculations indicated that the RELAP5 and measured flow velocities are in good agreement and that (after scaling up for a full-height downcomer) the data indicate that the downcomer circulating flow velocity is a factor of ~20 greater than the superficial velocity of the HPI flowing alone in the downcomer region.

6.7.2.6.2.3   Creare Fluid Mixing Tests

Creare performed experiments in a one-half linear scale facility to investigate fluid mixing in a downcomer region for a stagnant coolant-loop situation. The facility represents the region of a single cold leg and one-fourth of the reactor vessel downcomer. The downcomer configuration included a thermal shield installed in the center of the downcomer span. Two NRC tests, MAY105 and MAY106 were performed to simulate cold water injection into an initially hot downcomer (RELAP5 simulations for these tests were not performed). Velocity measurements for two tests indicated velocity ratios (downcomer velocity to superficial downcomer velocity based on HPI flow) of 21 and 26. The downcomer flow was found to contain regions of up-flow and down-flow, with the down-flow velocities greater than the up-flow velocities. The downcomer flow pattern was found to be buoyancy induced.

Figure 6.27 shows that the heat transfer data for the Creare tests are proportional to the Dittus-Boelter correlation. An enhancement of the heat transfer by a factor of ~1.55 above the Dittus-Boelter correlation is seen in the figure for down flow regions but not elsewhere. The enhancement is attributed to entrance effects to which the thermal shield configuration may contribute. In modeling convective heat transfer, RELAP5 applies the maximum of Churchill-Chu for free convection and Dittus-Boelter for forced convection. At low flow

velocities (e.g., < ~1 m/s), Churchill-Chu provides higher heat transfer coefficients than Dittus-Boelter.

6.7.2.6.2.4   Summary and Discussion

Three sets of experiments related to injection of cold water into stagnant initially hot water in the reactor vessel downcomer region of a pressurized water reactor have been described in this section. The situation represented by these tests is consistent with that following coolant-loop stagnation in many of the PTS accident scenario categories. The experiments all indicate that the buoyancy effects of cold water entering the downcomer through the cold legs set up a circulation within the downcomer region. The downcomer circulation velocities are seen to be larger than the superficial velocity (that which would result in the downcomer from the ECC injection flow alone) by factors of ~16 to 26.

In the UPTF and APEX-CE assessments, RELAP5 with a two-dimensional downcomer nodalization is seen to be able to capture on a first-order basis the flow pattern and velocities in the downcomer region. Based on comparison between measured and RELAP5-calculated wall and fluid temperature data, RELAP5 is seen to provide reasonable representations of the vessel wall inside surface heat transfer coefficient. For the UPTF test, RELAP5 is seen to provide a good representation (within ~15%) of the heat transfer coefficient for downcomer regions away from Cold Leg 2 (the only cold leg through which the cold water enters the vessel) and to overpredict the heat transfer coefficient by a factor of ~2 for the region under Cold Leg 2. For the APEX-CE test (for which cold water enters the vessel through all cold legs), RELAP5 is seen to overpredict the heat transfer coefficient for all downcomer regions, again by a factor of ~2. Creare data corroborate UPTF and APEX-CE data in showing enhanced large eddy circulating flows in the downcomer. The relatively high velocities result in good heat transfer as seen in the data and predicted by RELAP5. The integrated assessment of RELAP5 for downcomer heat transfer shows the predictions of the RELAP code to be either realistic or conservative.

6.7.2.6.3 Comparison of RELAP5-Calculated and CFD-Calculated Downcomer Flows

A comparison was made between RELAP5 and COMMIX CFD code solutions for the flow patterns experienced in the reactor vessel downcomer. The comparison was made during the coolant-loop flow stagnation period following a 2-inch (5.1-cm) hot-side break accident scenario in a three-loop Westinghouse plant.

The comparison indicated that RELAP5 adequately captured the overall flow patterns but not finer-scale eddy-flow behavior seen in the COMMIX run. The flow velocities from the COMMIX and RELAP5 calculations were similar and on the order of 19.7 to 39.4 in/s (0.5 to 1.0 m/s).

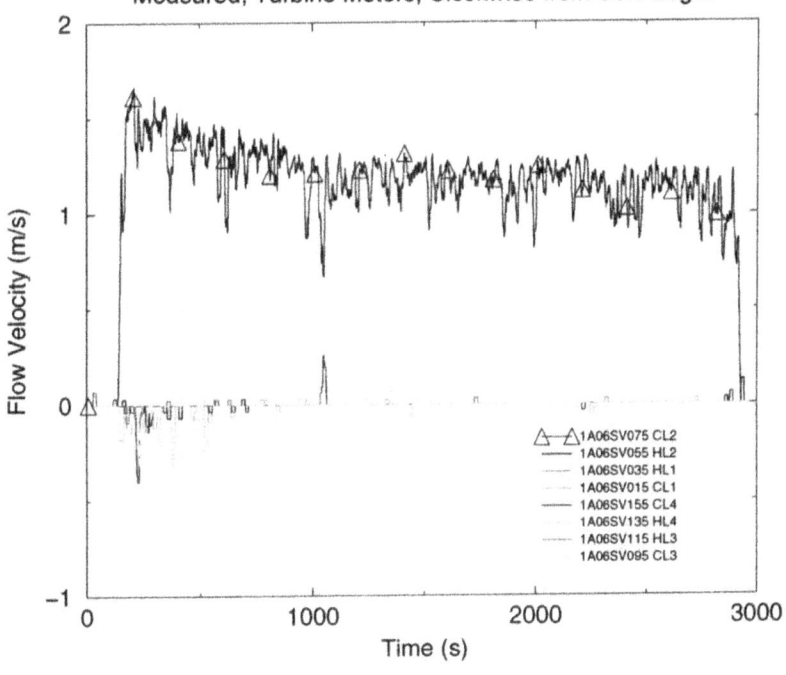

Figure 6.21. UPTF 1-21 DC Velocities at Bottom-Core Elevation Measured, Turbine Meters, Clockwise from Cold Leg 2, Filtered

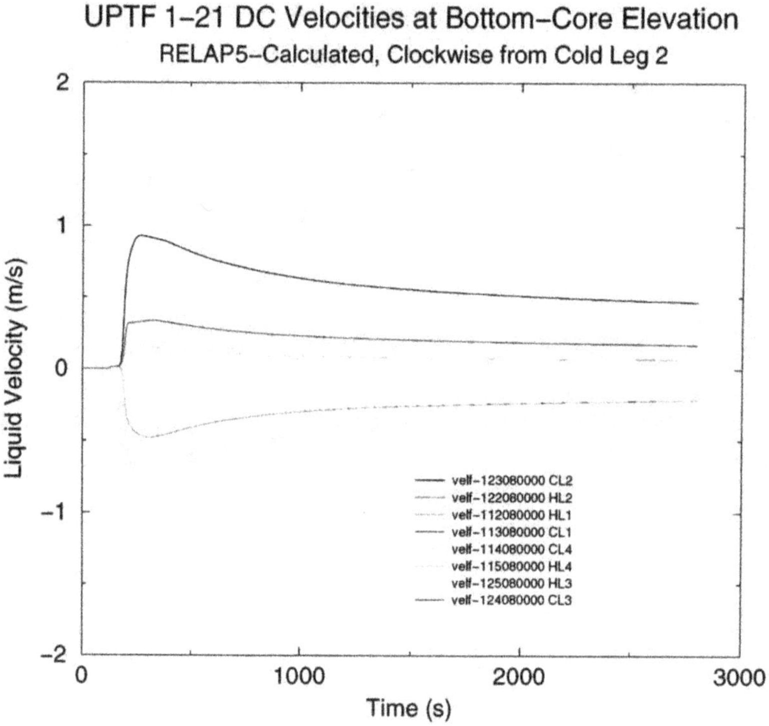

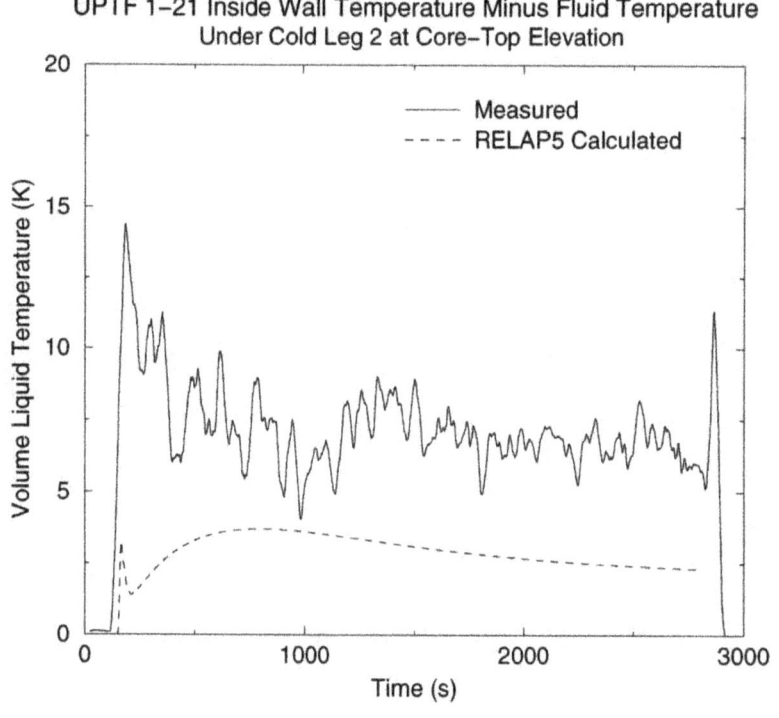

Figure 6.22. UPTF 1-21 DC Velocities at Bottom-Core Elevation RELAP5 (Calculated, Clockwise from Cold Leg 2)

UPTF 1-21 Inside Wall Temperature Minus Fluid Temperature
Under Cold Leg 2 at Core-Top Elevation

Figure 6.23. UPTF 1-21 Wall Temperature Minus Fluid Temperature Under Cold Leg 2 at Core-Top Elevation

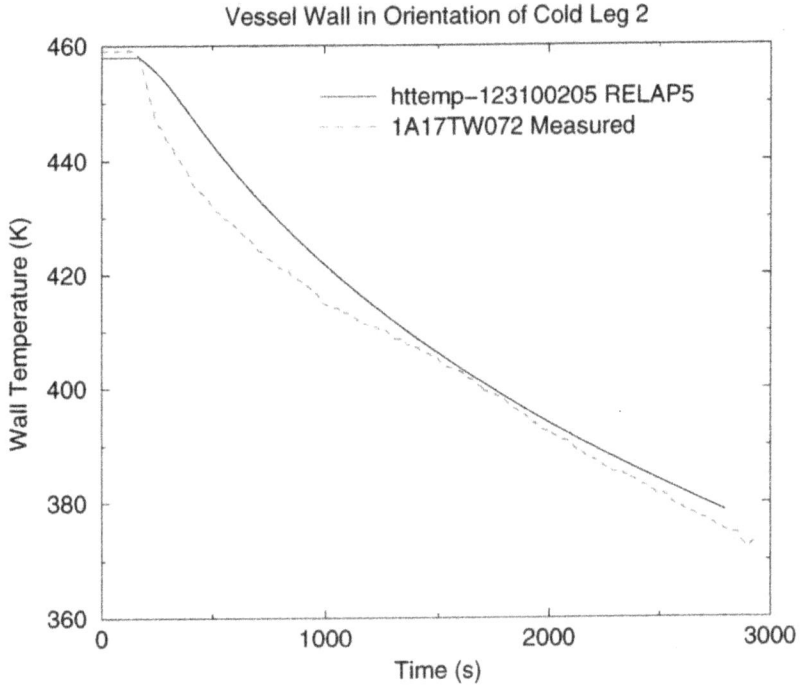

Figure 6.24. UPTF Test 1-21 Wall Temperatures at 25 mm Depth Vessel Wall in Orientation of Cold Leg 2

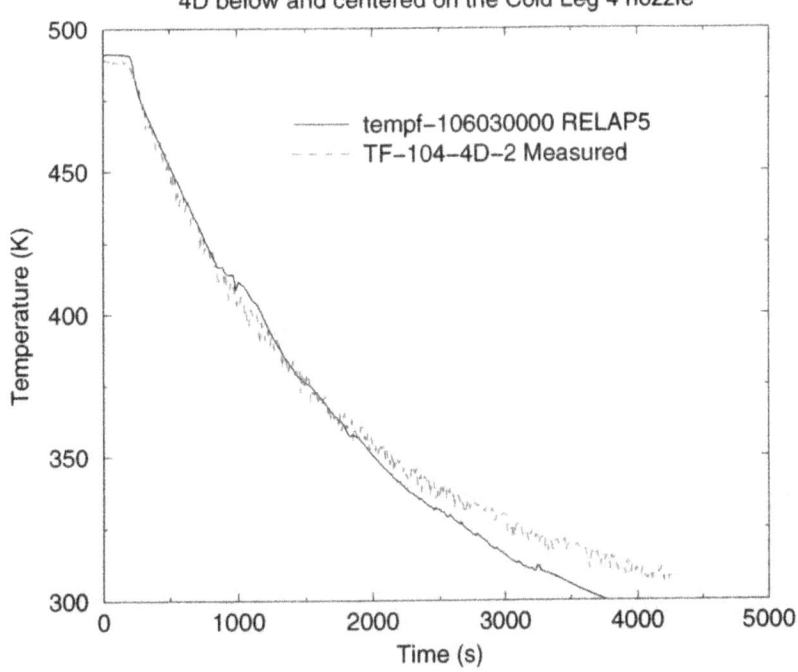

Figure 6.25. APEX–CE–05 Measured and RELAP5 Fluid Temperatures 4D below and centered on the Cold Leg 4 nozzle

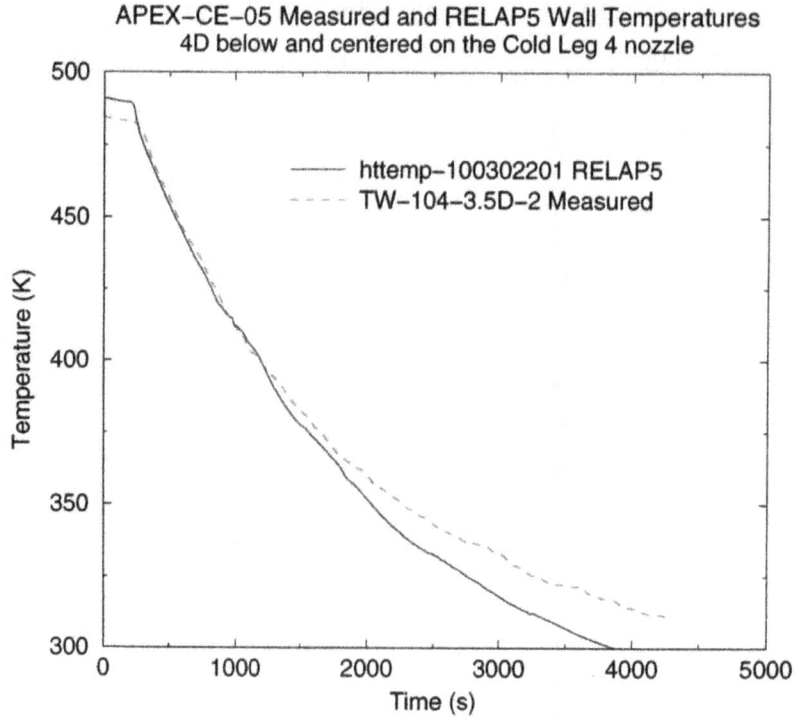

Figure 6.26. APEX–CE–05 Measured and RELAP5 Wall Temperatures
4D below and centered on the Cold Leg 4 nozzle

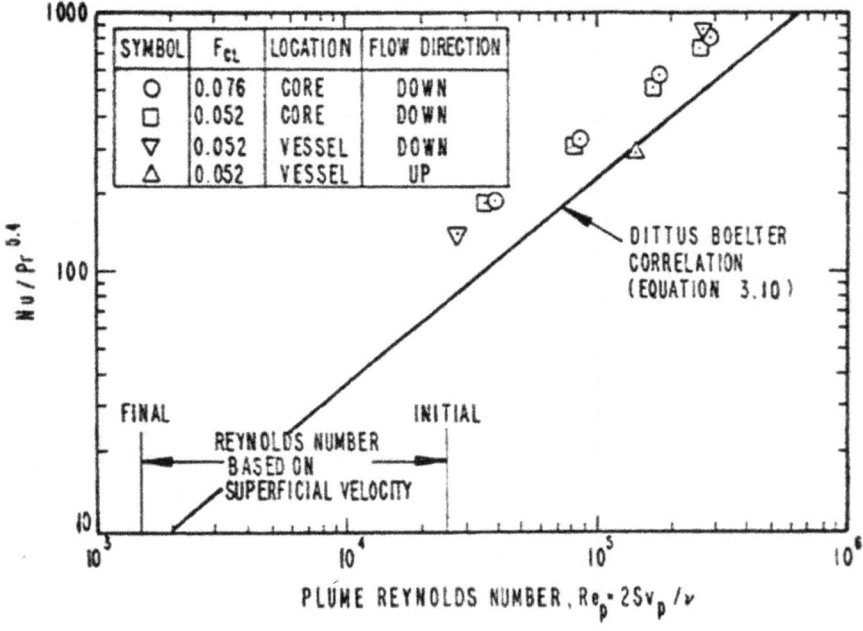

Figure 6.27. Creare Data Compared to Dittus-Boelter

6.7.3 RELAP5 Assessment Conclusions

An assessment has been performed of the RELAP5/MOD3.2.2Gamma computer code capabilities for predicting the parameters of importance for evaluating PTS risk during PWR plant accident scenarios, focusing on the RCS pressure and the temperature of the fluid in the reactor vessel downcomer region. The assessment is performed by comparing the results from RELAP5 simulations of pertinent separate-effects and integral-effects tests with measured test data for experiments in facilities scaled to PWRs. Qualitative judgments are made regarding the overall fidelity of the RELAP5 test predictions. Quantitative estimates also are made of the average uncertainties in the RELAP5 predictions for the important PTS parameters.

The RELAP5 PTS assessment uses data from six experiments in four different separate-effects experimental facilities and from eleven experiments in five different integral-effects experimental facilities.

The separate-effects experiments specifically address (1) pressurizer draining and filling; (2) critical break flow; (3) steam and water behavior in the reactor vessel lower plenum and downcomer regions during the end-of-blowdown and refill periods of LBLOCAs; and (4) single-phase, two-phase, and reflux cooling mode loop natural circulation phenomena under primary-side and secondary-side degraded inventory conditions. These represent phenomena that are significant for the prediction of the important PTS parameters.

The results of the 18 assessment cases generally indicated good and excellent agreement between the RELAP5 calculations and the measured test data. The conclusion from the RELAP5/MOD3.2.2Gamma PTS assessment is that the code is capable of well-predicting the phenomena of importance for evaluating PTS risk in PWRs. The average uncertainty in the RCS pressure prediction is characterized as ±0.2 MPa (±29 psi). The average uncertainty in the reactor vessel downcomer fluid temperature prediction is characterized as ±10 K (±18°F).

6.8 Sensitivity and Uncertainty Analysis

Sensitivity studies were performed to evaluate the effect of key parameters on the RELAP5 prediction of downcomer conditions. These sensitivity studies formed the basis for the assessment of uncertainty in the thermal-hydraulic analysis. The purpose of the uncertainty analysis was to provide adjustments to PRA bin probabilities based on key thermal-hydraulic parameters that significantly affect downcomer conditions, principally temperature.

6.8.1 Sensitivity Analysis

Table 6.2 presents a summary of the results of the sensitivity studies performed as part of the thermal-hydraulic analysis. Many of these sensitivity studies were used to guide the definition of the transients analyzed in this study and to guide the uncertainty assessment discussed later in this section. In addition to the sensitivity studies listed in Table 6.2, evaluations were performed on convective heat transfer from the reactor vessel to the downcomer fluid and on the effect of the in-vessel circulation flows on downcomer conditions.

The heat transfer coefficient model for mixed convection used in RELAP5/MOD3.2.2Gamma is computed as the maximum of the forced convection, laminar convection, and natural convection values. The correlations used are by Dittus-Boelter, Kays, and Churchill-Chu. However, the flow and heat transfer in the downcomer during flow stagnation conditions are more accurately described as buoyancy opposed mixed convection. In this situation, heat transfer is from the hot walls to subcooled fluid flowing downward under low flow conditions. Under these conditions, heat transfer may be enhanced compared to free convection as modeled in RELAP5, which would promote more rapid cooling of the vessel walls.

Sensitivity studies utilizing the Petukhov correlation for parallel plates (known as the ORNL ANS Interphase Model in

RELAP5/MOD3.2.2Gamma) in lieu of the Dittus-Boelter correlation were performed. Additionally, RELAP5/MOD3.2.2Gamma was modified to apply a multiplier to compensate for buoyancy effects in forced turbulent convection published by Swanson and Catton [Swanson 87]. This model was later refined to utilize the Petukhov-Gnielinski heat transfer correlation along with the multiplier proposed by Swanson and Catton.

Other studies were performed where the heat transfer coefficient calculated by RELAP5 was varied by ±30%. The results of these RELAP5 calculations were analyzed using FAVOR to determine the direct impact of heat transfer uncertainty on vessel failure probability. The results of the heat transfer coefficient sensitivity studies are discussed in Chapter 9.

In-vessel circulation flows that deliver water from the upper plenum region to the upper downcomer can occur during a transient (particularly a LOCA). Such flows would tend to warm the water in the upper downcomer and the cold legs. Experiments and CFD studies have shown that there can be significant counter-flow of warm water from the upper downcomer, and energy exchange in the cold leg between the warm stream and the cold ECC injection. These in-vessel flows tend to increase the downcomer temperature.

The B&W vent valve design allows for significant in-vessel circulation once the reactor coolant pumps are tripped. While the pumps are on, the vent valves are held shut by differential pressure. After the pumps are tripped, flow stagnation conditions can occur, and the resulting pressure difference between the upper plenum and the downcomer will cause the vent valves to open, resulting in significant flow of warm water from the upper plenum to the downcomer. The impact of vent valve function on the downcomer fluid temperature is transient-dependent, but can be on the order of 50 K (90°F) based on a 2.83-in. (7.18-cm) surge line break, as seen in the next section.

While Westinghouse and CE plants do not have vent valves, they do have a bypass flow path

between the upper downcomer and the upper plenum. The area of this path is generally not precisely characterized in power plants, but amounts to approximately 3% of the total core flow during normal plant operation. Assuming typical values of entrance and exit loss coefficients, the approximate flow area becomes 0.580-ft^2 (0.054-m^2) (10-in. [25.4-cm] diameter equivalent). This value is about 7% of the flow area of the Oconee vent valves, which is 8.45-ft^2 (0.785-m^2). The RELAP5 results were reviewed to evaluate bypass flows, for a large number of Palisades and Beaver Valley transients. The calculations indicate that the flow through the bypass region is small compared to the B&W vent valve flow, implying that the effect of bypass flow on downcomer temperature is small for Westinghouse and CE plants.

6.8.2 Treatment of Uncertainties

6.8.2.1 Overview

The approach used to address uncertainty in the thermal-hydraulic analysis principally utilized sensitivity studies to quantify the effect of phenomenological and boundary condition uncertainties/variations on the severity of a TH sequence. The results of these studies were used in either of the following two ways:

(1) They were combined with probability estimates on the sensitivity parameters being evaluated to adjust the bin probabilities from the PRA analysis.

(2) They were used to justify further subdivision of the PRA bins.

In this way, the TH uncertainty analysis accounted for certain parameters that can affect the thermal-hydraulic response of the plant that were not explicitly considered in the PRA analysis (e.g., season of the year). Because the uncertainty analysis also produced insights regarding the effects of various system parameters and TH models on event severity, it also helped to identify the transient used to represent each PRA bin to the PFM analysis.

Table 6.2   Summary of PTS Sensitivity Studies

Parameter	Significance	Sensitivity Evaluation	Results
Break flow (or valve capacity)	Most important factor in determining the RCS cooldown and depressurization rate. Directly impacts ECCS injection flow.	Break spectrum analysis performed for the three plants analyzed. Range of break diameters considered is 1-in. (2.54-cm) to 22-in. (56-cm), sequentially increasing the flow area by a factor of 2. Analyses where the flow area was varied by ±30% were also performed.	Significant effect on downcomer conditions. Can be significant contributor to vessel failure risk. Uncertainty in break flow for a given break area is small, given the range of break areas evaluated.
Break location	Downcomer temperature generally warmer for cold leg breaks vs. hot leg breaks. Hot leg breaks generally result in lower downcomer temperatures because the break flow enthalpy is higher for a hot leg break than for the same size cold leg break. In addition, for cold leg breaks, the ECC flow into the broken cold leg tends to flow out the break. Therefore, less cold ECC water is delivered to the downcomer.	Effect of break location evaluated by analyzing both cold leg and hot leg breaks.	Significant effect on downcomer conditions. Either hot leg or cold leg breaks can be significant contributors to vessel failure risk.
HPI Flow (BC)	ECCS flow rates are specified from pump flow curves which are pressure dependent.	HPI flow rate varied by ±10%. Evaluations also done considering HPI pump failure.	Effect of flow rate sensitivity found to have an insignificant impact on downcomer conditions and is not a significant contributor to vessel failure risk. Transients involving pump failure resulted in warmer downcomer temperatures, but are generally small contributors to vessel failure risk.

Parameter	Significance	Sensitivity Evaluation	Results
Accumulator Injection Temperature	Injection of large volume of cold water as the system pressure reaches the injection pressure of the accumulators. Injection temperature is dependent upon the season (winter or summer) assumed.	Temperature varied from 294 K (70°F) to 314 K (105°F) depending on the plant analyzed and season assumed.	Significant effect on downcomer conditions, principally temperature in conjunction with HPI and LPI injection temperature sensitivity evaluation. Can be significant contributor to vessel failure risk.
Accumulator Injection Rate	Injection of large volume of cold water as the system pressure reaches the injection pressure of the accumulators.	The effect of pressure on flow was examined by varying the initial pressure from 3.8 MPa [550 psi], 4.1 MPa [600 psi] (nominal) and 4.5 MPa [650 psi].	Insignificant effect on downcomer conditions.
HPI and LPI Injection Temperature	Seasonal effect on the injection water temperature, which affects the downcomer water temperature. Done in conjunction with the accumulator injection temperature sensitivity.	Oconee – Temperature range considered is 278 K (40°F) to 303 K (85°F). Palisades – Temperature range considered is 278 K (40°F) to 311 K (90°F). Beaver Valley – summer temperature of 286 K (55°F) considered. Note that Beaver Valley maintains ECC water temperature at a constant 300 K (50°F) in accordance with Technical Specifications.	Significant effect on downcomer conditions. Affected transients can be significant contributors to vessel failure risk.
Decay Heat Load	Decay heat load directly affects downcomer conditions.	Hot full power conditions and hot zero power conditions considered. Hot zero power defined as 0.2% of full core power (~5.2 MWth).	Uncertainties in decay heat load small compared to the range of conditions considered.
HPI Flow Control	Direct impact of HPI flow rate on downcomer conditions. HPI throttling generally reduces downcomer temperature and system pressure.	For transients involving either closure of a stuck-open pressurizer SRV or main steam line break, the RCS may reach conditions for which operating procedures require HPI throttling or termination. For these transients, the scenarios analyzed varied the timing and conditions under which the operator controlled HPI flow.	Significant effect on downcomer conditions, principally temperature. Affected transients can be significant contributors to vessel failure risk.

Parameter	Significance	Sensitivity Evaluation	Results
Feedwater Control	Direct impact on downcomer conditions particularly if the steam generator is overfilled.	Various feedwater control scenarios ranging from normal control of steam generator level to failure of level control or operator error, resulting in filling of the steam generators until water entered the steam lines.	Range of sequences analyzed covers uncertainty in feedwater control. Generally, effects are insignificant unless combined with a valve failure or MSLB.
Secondary Pressure Control	Direct impact on downcomer conditions for MSLB or stuck-open secondary relief valve sequences.	A spectrum of PRA sequences were analyzed for failures of secondary side valves, including steam dump, steam generator safety/relief, and atmospheric release valves. The failures were combined in some instances with failure of feedwater control such that the faulted steam generator continued to be fed with auxiliary feedwater.	Significant effect on downcomer conditions. Affected transients can be significant contributors to vessel failure risk.

This method of accounting for TH uncertainty does not quantify the uncertainties associated with each TH sequence; rather, it characterizes the uncertainties associated with each PRA bin. This is appropriate because, as illustrated in Figure 3.3, each TH sequence that is passed on to the PFM analysis represents a much larger number of TH sequences that, together, constitute a PRA "bin." Provided the combined effects of the TH parameter and modeling uncertainties on the severity of this one representative sequence is small relative to both

- the uncertainty in the frequency of occurrence of all of the sequences in the bin, and

- the variability in severity between the different sequences in the bin, then

the uncertainty associated with TH parameter and modeling uncertainties of the representative sequence can be considered negligible. The appropriateness of not accounting for these uncertainties because they are negligibly small is ensured by the iterative process used to define the PRA bins. PRA bins that contribute significantly to the estimated TWCF were continually partitioned (including appropriate partitioning of their frequencies and selection of new TH sequences to represent each partitioned bin) until the total estimated TWCF for the plant did not change significantly with continued partitioning. Thus, any errors caused by not explicitly accounting for the TH parameter and modeling uncertainties associated with the TH sequence used to represent each PRA bin are not expected to influence the outcome of the analysis (i.e., the estimated values of TWCF).

The following section summarizes the TH uncertainty analysis. Full details can be found in a companion report [*Chang*].

6.8.2.2 Approach

The TH uncertainty characterization begins with identification of the event categories (e.g., LOCAs) that are expected to significantly challenge vessel integrity. If necessary, each of these event categories was then subdivided. For example, the LOCA event category called was subdivided as follows:

- Small LOCA: between 1.5-in. (3.8-cm) and approximately 4-in. (10-cm)

- Medium LOCA: approximately 4-in. (10-cm) and approximately 8-in. (20-cm)

- Large LOCA: greater than approximately 8-in. (20-cm)

- Stuck-open pressurizer safety relief valves
  - Without subsequent reclosure
  - With subsequent reclosure, resulting in system repressurization

The aim of event category subdivision was to better bound the uncertainty by not having one category attempt to represent too broad a range of thermal-hydraulic conditions. However, even within these subdivided event categories the response of the plant can vary due to sequence to sequence differences within each subdivision. To quantify this, the following uncertainties were identified:

- Aleatory Uncertainties
  (1) Break diameter (1- to 22-in. (2.5- to 56-cm)): variation of ±30% considered.
  (2) Break location (surge line or hot leg, cold leg)
  (3) Decay heat level (full power, low (hot zero) power)
  (4) Reactor coolant pump status (tripped vs. operating)
  (5) Heat structure sensible heat (variation of ±30% considered)
  (6) HPI state (normal operation, failed)
  (7) HPI flow rate (±10%)
  (8) Accumulator pressure ± 345 kPa (±50 psi), accumulator temperature: 21°C, 43°C (70°F, 110°F)
  (9) Effect of seasonal variation on downcomer temperature (summer, winter)

- Epistemic Uncertainties
  (1) In-vessel circulation attributable to vent valve function in Oconee (cases where valves failed were considered)
  (2) Vessel wall-to-downcomer fluid heat transfer
  (3) Flow resistance (loop flow)
  (4) Break flow

6.8.2.2.1 Break Diameter and Location (Aleatory 1 and 2)

Downcomer conditions are strongly influenced by the break diameter (break flow) and break location. Various diameters (1.5-in. (3.8-cm) to 22-in. (56-cm)) and break locations (surge line, hot leg, and cold leg) are considered.

The thermal-hydraulic response of the reactor system is considerably different as the break diameter increases from 2-in. (5.08-cm) to 16-in. (40.64-cm). For the larger break cases of 8-in. (20.32-cm) or more, maximum ECCS delivery will occur (the HPI and LPI systems will be operating at pump runout conditions), resulting in the maximum rate of reactor coolant system (downcomer) cooldown and depressurization.

For smaller breaks in the range of 5.6-in (14.37-cm) or less, ECCS delivery flow will be limited by the break flow so that the rate at which reactor coolant system cooldown and depressurization will occur is more strongly tied to break diameter and location. In this range, the rate of reactor system cooldown and depressurization decreases with break diameter. Transients involving stuck-open primary side safety valves fall into this category.

ECCS performance is also affected by the break location. For hot leg or surge line breaks, the ECCS will flow from the cold legs through the downcomer to the break. For cold leg breaks, some of the ECCS flow will be discharged through the break.

Inherently, the rate of reactor system cooldown and depressurization is more uncertain in this range relative to break diameters greater than 8-in. (20.32-cm). Hence, the uncertainty analysis focused on break diameters less than 5.6-in (14.37-cm). A ±30% variation on break area to account for break flow uncertainty was considered for LOCA and stuck-open primary safety valve transients.

6.8.2.2.2 Heat Sources (Aleatory 3, 4, and 5)

Heat sources affecting downcomer conditions include the decay heat load, reactor coolant pump status, and the sensible heat in the reactor plant heat structures.

In the case of decay heat load, three sets of decay heat data corresponding to full-power operation, 0.7% of full-power operation, and 0.2% of full-power operation were analyzed. Later in the analysis, the low-power operations were combined into the hot zero power initiating state. Probabilities assigned to these states are 0.98 for hot full-power conditions and 0.02 for hot zero power conditions. Uncertainties in heat load due to RCP operation were considered by evaluating transients where the pumps are tripped vs. when they remain operating.

The principal effect of sensible heat in the heat structures is the rate at which heat is transferred from the system structure to the system fluid. A range of ±30% is considered in the uncertainty analysis.

6.8.2.2.3 High-Pressure Injection (Aleatory 6 through 9)

ECCS performance considered four factors, including (1) failure on demand, (2) injection flow rate, (3) injection temperature, and (4) injection timing. System failures include a partial or full system failure, where the injection flow at the required rate is not delivered. Failures of this type result in warmer downcomer temperatures. Transients involving HPI failure have been considered in the uncertainty analysis. Flow rate uncertainty was assessed using a ±10% variation in HPI flow. Flow rate uncertainties in the LPI or accumulators (or core flood tank) were also considered.

Uncertainty in injection temperature considers the effect of seasonal variations on the injection water source, which is the refueling water storage tank located outdoors. Table 6.2 lists the values used. Probabilities assigned to the seasonal variation are 0.25 for summer and winter and 0.50 for fall/spring. Uncertainty in injection timing of the accumulators was considered by varying the injection pressure over a range of ±50 psi. The pressures at which high- and low-pressure injection is initiated are judged to have a small uncertainty. Uncertainty in the RCS coolant loop total flow resistance focuses on the loop flow resistance. A 100% increase in flow resistance was considered.

6.8.2.2.4   Vent Valves (Epistemic 1)

Uncertainty in the in-vessel circulation, which affects the energy distribution in the reactor coolant system, focuses principally on Oconee because of the presence of the vent valves. For the uncertainty evaluation, failure of the valves to open was considered.

6.8.2.3   Definition of Sensitivity Indicator

Sensitivity analyses were performed with RELAP5 for each of the parameters discussed in Section 6.8.2.2. Downcomer temperature is the most important of the three thermal-hydraulic boundary conditions in the fracture analysis and therefore is the focus of the sensitivity analysis. The sensitivity indicator is the effect on the average downcomer temperature due to the change in a single sensitivity parameter over the transient time of interest, which is 10,000 seconds for this analysis. Each sensitivity indicator has an associated probability of occurrence determined from the parameter being varied. The following equation is used to compute the sensitivity indicator:

$$\Delta T = \overline{T}_{sen} - \overline{T}_{nom}$$

where $\overline{T}_{sen}$ is the sensitivity case downcomer temperature averaged over the 10,000 seconds interval and $\overline{T}_{nom}$ is the base case downcomer temperature averaged over the 10,000 second interval. To compute the sensitivity indicator, each sensitivity parameter is varied (one at a time) to an upper and lower

bound and the average temperature difference is determined. This approach is called the nominal range sensitivity analysis and is described in more detail in [*Chang*].

The impact on the sensitivity indicator of a given sensitivity parameter depends strongly on the transient and therefore a large number of transients that include the types of transients considered in the PTS analysis (LOCAs, stuck-open primary safety valves, MSLBs, etc.) need to be considered.

6.8.2.4   Example of Results for a Surge Line Break

The case of a 2.83-in. (7.18-cm) surge line break LOCA for Oconee is used to illustrate the development of the sensitivity indicator. Figure 6.28 presents the sensitivity parameter ranking for the 2.83-in. (7.18-cm) surge line break LOCA for Oconee. For this case, the sensitivity indicator ranges from an increase of 100K (180°F) when HPI is assumed to fail to a decrease of 35 K (63°F) for hot zero power initialization. The sensitivity indicator depends on the transient being considered and sensitivity indicators were developed for the range of transients considered in the PTS analysis.

The uncertainty evaluation requires consideration of the effect of multiple parameters on the downcomer conditions. As an example, a transient may be initiated from hot zero power during the summertime. The sensitivity studies only evaluated the effect of increasing or decreasing a single parameter. To combine the effect of multiple parameters on the downcomer fluid temperature, the sensitivity indicators are added together. This approach is based on the assumption that the effect of any sensitivity parameter is independent of the effect of any other parameter so that the sensitivity indicators become linearly additive. Application of the linearly additive assumption avoids performing RELAP5 sensitivity studies on the large number of sensitivity parameter combinations. The linear additive assumption was applied to the various types of transients considered in the uncertainty analysis.

Validation of the linear additive assumption (LAA) was done by varying multiple sensitivity parameters in a single RELAP5 run based on a 2.83-in. (7.18-cm) surge line break LOCA model for Oconee. Five different combinations of sensitivity parameters were selected to cover a downcomer temperature range of 111 K (200°F).

Table 6.3 lists the five combinations of sensitivity parameters considered and the results of T_{sens} computed applying the linear additive assumption compared to direct computation using RELAP5. A plot of the results is shown in Figure 6.29. The 45-degree line in Figure 6.29 represents the perfect scenarios in which the expected values are same as the RELAP5 calculated values. The solid dots represent the realities. The difference between the solid dots and the squares on the 45-degree line is the deviation of the LAA from the RELAP5 results. Figure 6.29 shows that downcomer temperature computed using the linear additive assumption is in good agreement with the RELAP5 calculated results.

Given the important sensitivity indicators and associated probabilities, a statistical analysis is carried out to finalize selection of representative transients for each bin and to refine the frequencies for the bins defined during the front-end risk modeling. This statistical analysis is performed in two parts. First, the downcomer temperature is determined by adjusting the nominal downcomer temperature for each subcategory identified in Step 5 by the sensitivity indicator (downcomer temperature adjustment) for all combinations of sensitivity parameters being considered for that subcategory using the linear additive approach. Then, the probability of occurrence for each combination of sensitivity parameters is determined. Note that thousands of temperature points are generated for all of the combinations of sensitivity parameters considered.

Table 6.3   List of Combined Sensitivity Indicators Varied for LAA Verification

No.	Sensitivity Parameters Varied	T_{sens} (°K) using LAA	T_{sens} (°K) using RELAP5	$T_{sens,\,RELAP5}$ − $T_{sens,\,LAA}$ (°K)
1	Winter conditions; p(CFT) +50 psi; 70% A_{brk}; RVVVs Close; 70% HTC	331.7	345.3	13.6
2	Summer; vent valves failed closed; 200% loop flow resistance	360.0	362.3	2.7
3	p(CFT) +50 psi; 110% nominal HPI mass flow; 70% nominal break area; 130% nominal heat transfer coefficient	387.6	391.4	3.8
4	Summer conditions; p(CFT) +50 psi ; 90% nominal HPI mass flow; 130% nominal break area; normal vent valve function; 200% loop flow resistance	415.5	406.9	-8.6
5	Summer conditions; 90% nominal HPI mass flow; 70% nominal break area; normal vent valve function; 130% nominal heat transfer coefficient.	438.2	448.8	10.7

Given the downcomer temperature and corresponding probability, a probability density function is constructed. The development of this function is illustrated in Figure 6.30 for Oconee for LOCAs between 1.5-in. (3.81-cm) and 4-in. (10.16-cm) in diameter. This figure shows the resulting cumulative distribution function found from integrating the probability density function that is used to obtain the probabilities used to adjust the bin frequencies.

The representative scenarios are determined from the probability density function by subdividing the probability into five bands between the 0.05 and 0.95 probability levels and determining the temperature at the median point in each band. The probabilities in the two regions near the tails are increased by 0.05. This adjustment is made because of potentially large errors in the sensitivity indicator in the tails of the probability density function (below 0.05 and above 0.95 probability level). In Figure 6.30, there are five bands shown on the cumulative density function plots along with the median values identified and the downcomer temperature corresponding to each median.

Selection of the representative scenario corresponding to the median temperature in each probability band in the cumulative density distribution plot is done by picking the sensitivity indicator result that corresponds to the median temperature and using the

corresponding set of RELAP5 results for probabilistic fracture mechanics analysis. An example of the selection of representative scenarios along with the corresponding probabilities is presented in Table 6.4.

The uncertainty analysis was performed for the transients considered for the Oconee, Beaver Valley, and Palisades plants. There were some variations in the thermal-hydraulic categories considered, the sensitivity indicators evaluated and in the set of representative transients selected. These variations are attributable to differences principally in plant design and plant operating conditions. Otherwise, the approach used is the same for the three plants. Adjustments were made to the bin probabilities and representative sequences were selected based on the uncertainty analysis conducted for the three plants. Details can be found in [*Chang*].

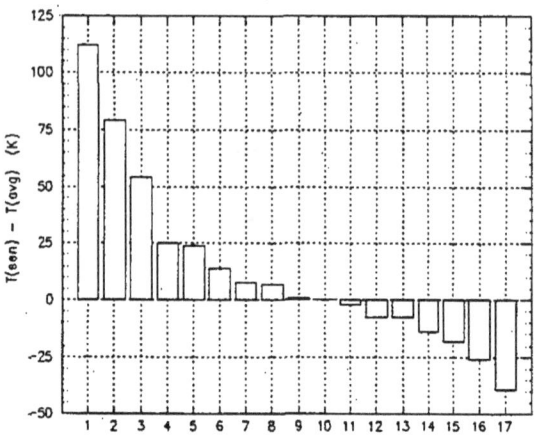

1	100% HPI fail
2	50% HPI fail
2	50% HPI fail
3	25% HPI fail
4	RVVVs Open
5	CL LOCA
6	90% m(HPI)
7	130% CHTC
8	Summer
9	P(CFT) -= 50 psi
10	Nominal
11	P(CFT) += 50 psi
12	110% m(HPI)
13	70% CHTC
14	Winter
15	High CL rev. K
16	RVVV Close
17	HZP

Figure 6.28.   Sensitivity parameter ranking of a 2.8-in. (7.18-cm) surge line break LOCA

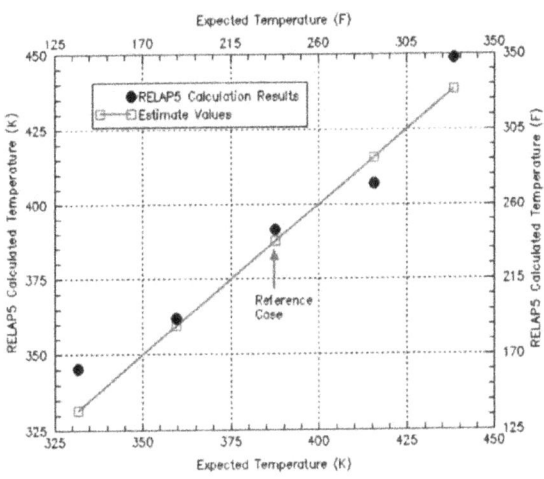

Figure 6.29. Confirmation of the Linearly Additive Assumption for a 2.8-in. (7.18-cm) surge line break LOCA

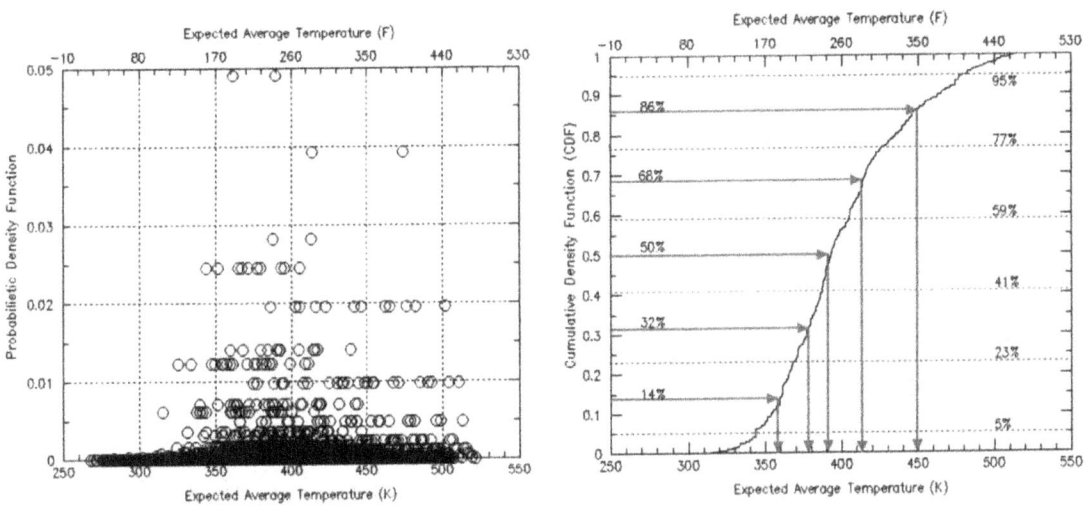

Figure 6.30.   Illustration of the Statistical Results for Downcomer Temperature Distribution

Table 6.4   Example of Representative Scenario Selection

#	TH Bin #	Probability	Scenario Specification Descriptions
1	145	0.23	1E-3 m² cold leg LOCA with increased 30% break area (Winter)*
2	142	0.18	4E-3m² surge line with 30% reduced break area
3	141	0.18	4E-3m² surge line with 30% increased break area
4	172	0.18	8E-3m² cold leg LOCA
5	154	0.23	8E-3m² surge line LOCA with 30% reduced break area RPV vent valves closed

7 Probabilistic Fracture Mechanics Analysis

7.1 Interaction of PFM Model with PRA and TH models

Figure 7.1 illustrates how the PFM model connects to both the PRA and TH models discussed in Chapters 5 and 6, respectively. Specifically, the PFM model takes as input from TH the pressure, temperature, and heat transfer coefficient time histories that have been defined by TH for the sequences defined by PRA. The PFM model uses this TH information along with other information concerning plant design and materials of construction to estimate the time-dependent driving force to fracture produced by a particular event sequence. The PFM model compares this estimate of fracture driving force to the fracture toughness, or fracture resistance, of the RPV steel. This comparison allows us to estimate the probability that a particular sequence of events will produce a crack all the way through the RPV wall were that sequence of events actually to occur. The final step in the analysis involves a matrix multiplication of these through-wall cracking frequency estimates with the frequency at which a particular event sequence is expected to occur (as defined by PRA). This product establishes an estimate of the annual frequency of through-wall cracking that can be expected for a particular plant after a particular period of operation when subjected to a particular sequence of events. The annual frequency of through-wall cracking is then summed for all event sequences specified by PRA to estimate the total annual frequency of through-wall cracking for the vessel. Performance of such analyses for various operating lifetimes provides an estimate of how the annual through-wall cracking frequency can be expected to vary over the lifetime of the plant.

7.2 Components of the PFM Model

Figure 7.1 also shows that the PFM model is itself composed of four major sub-models (which themselves are composed of yet more sub-models and parameter inputs). The four major sub-models that make up the PFM model are as follows:

- A flaw distribution model: see Section 7.5 for an overview and [*Simonen*] for details.

- A neutronics model: see Section 7.6 for an overview and [*EricksonKirk-PFM*] for details.

- A crack initiation model: see Section 7.7 for an overview and [*EricksonKirk-PFM*] for details.

- A through-wall cracking model: see Section 7.8 for an overview and [*EricksonKirk-PFM*] for details.

Together, these four sub-models provide the information necessary to estimate both the fracture driving force ($K_{applied}$) generated by the PTS loading and the resistance of the material to fracture ($K_{Resistance}$). $K_{applied}$ depends upon the thermal-hydraulic inputs of pressure, temperature, and heat transfer coefficient (all *vs.* time), on the vessel dimensions, and on the location and size of the flaws that are quantified by the flaw distribution model. $K_{Resistance}$, more commonly called "fracture toughness," depends upon the chemical composition of the steel, the downcomer temperature from the thermal-hydraulics calculations combined with the heat conduction properties of the steel, and on the degree of neutron irradiation exposure experienced by the steel. Our calculations consider the potential for cracks to initiate in either a brittle manner by cleavage or in a ductile manner by microvoid initiation and coalescence. (The type of crack initiation that occurs depends upon the temperature.) We also consider the potential for cleavage cracks to stop, which is a phenomenon referred to as "crack arrest." These different failure modes all have different characteristics fracture toughness ($R_{esistance}$) values, as follows:

- K_{lc} quantifies the resistance of the material to crack initiation in cleavage.

- J_{lc} and J-R quantifies the resistance of the material to crack initiation by micro-void coalescence. Furthermore, the J-R curve describes the resistance of the material to further ductile crack growth.

- K_{la} quantifies the ability of the material to stop (arrest) a running cleavage crack.

These various values of $K_{Resistance}$ (K_{lc}, J_{lc}, J-R, and K_{la}) and their dependencies on chemical composition, temperature, and neutron irradiation exposure are estimated by a combination of the neutronics model, the crack initiation model, and the through-wall cracking model. Also, the crack initiation model and the through-wall cracking models estimate, respectively, the probability of crack initiation and the probability of through-wall cracking by comparing the value of $K_{applied}$ to the appropriate value of $K_{Resistance}$.

7.3   Objectives of this Chapter

The objectives of this chapter are as follows:

(1) Section 7.4: Describes our approach to model development and uncertainty characterization.

(2) Sections 7.5 through 7.8: Provide a summary discussion of the four major sub-models that make up the PFM model.

(3) Section 7.9: Provides a summary discussion of how all of these sub-models are implemented in the FAVOR probabilistic fracture mechanics code. (See [*Dickson-UG*] and [*Williams*] for details.)

(4) Section 7.10: Provides a summary discussion of an experimental validation of the linear elastic fracture mechanics (LEFM) techniques that underlie our approach.

(See Appendix A of [*EricksonKirk-PFM*] for details.)

7.4   Approach to Model Development and Uncertainty Characterization

As discussed in Section 3.2, our approach to developing a risk-informed revision of 10 CFR 50.61 requires explicit identification of the type of uncertainty (aleatory or epistemic) to enable the development of an appropriate mathematical model. To do so, it is first necessary to establish independent, physically motivated, models that account for the effects of irradiation damage and temperature. We achieved this goal by the following three-step process:

(1) Uncertainty Identification: We began by constructing a graphical description of the current toughness model. This description, called a "root cause diagram," is illustrated schematically in Figure 7.2. Diagrams of this type show *all* of the parameters (shaded boxes) and *all* of the relationships (nodes) used to estimate the fracture toughness for a particular set of conditions. Decomposing the toughness / embrittlement model in this way permitted identification of individual sources of uncertainty, both in the parameters and in the relationships assumed between the parameters.

(2) Uncertainty Classification: Uncertainties were classified through an understanding of the basic physical mechanisms responsible for crack initiation, for crack arrest, and for irradiation damage. Without this physical understanding, it was impossible to distinguish the irreducible (i.e., aleatory) uncertainties associated with variability of the material from reducible (i.e., epistemic) uncertainties caused by limited data, imperfect models, and so on.

(3) Uncertainty Quantification: The physical understanding developed to classify uncertainty types also played a pivotal role in uncertainty quantification because a model of fracture toughness that can be regarded as representing the true behavior

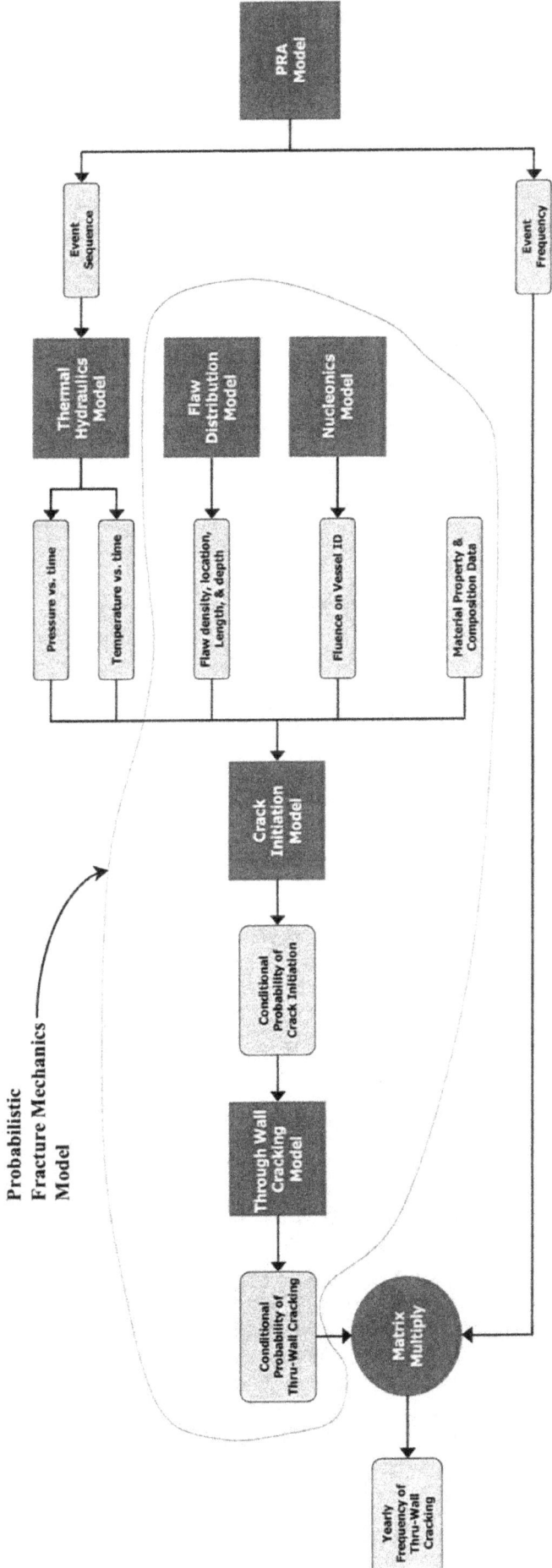

Figure 7.1. Illustration of the interrelationships between PFM model and the TH and PRA models, and the four principal sub-models that comprise the PFM model

of the material is needed to quantify the uncertainties present in any other model. Therefore, uncertainty quantification was achieved by comparing the RT_{NDT}-based toughness model developed for use in the PTS reevaluation project to this best-estimate model.

To be consistent with LEFM principles, LEFM-valid K_{Ic} and K_{Ia} values were used to calibrate the parameters of this best estimate model. However, the best-estimate model cannot be constructed as a purely empirical fit to these K_{Ic} and K_{Ia} values. Without the insights available from a physically based understanding it was impossible to discern if the trends demonstrated by the laboratory data can be expected to apply to the material and loading conditions of interest in commercial PWRs. Consequently, the "best estimate models" each had a form motivated by the physical processes responsible for the underlying phenomena.

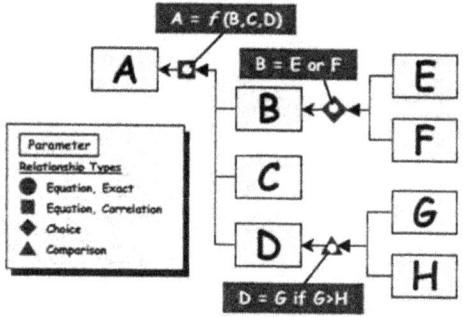

Figure 7.2. **Illustration of a root cause diagram showing how uncertainties in input variables (E, F, G, and H) propagate through models (nodes), themselves potentially having uncertainty, to produce uncertainty in a resultant value (A)**

7.5   Flaw Model

The flaw model provides estimates of the density (flaws per unit area or volume), size, and location in the vessel wall of initial fabrication defects[‡‡]. This flaw distribution, reported in

---

[‡‡] Growth of initial fabrication defects attributable to sub-critical cracking mechanisms does not need to be considered; see Section 3.3.3.2.

detail by [*Simonen*], represents a major improvement in realism relative to that adopted in previous studies of PTS risk. Indeed, one of the major unknowns/uncertainties identified in the last comprehensive evaluation of PTS [SECY-82-465] was the distribution of flaws assumed to exist in the RPV wall. SECY-82-465 used flaw models based on the Marshall study, which included data from a limited population of nuclear vessels and from many non-nuclear vessels [Marshall 82]. These flaw measurements were part of routine pre-service NDE examinations performed 25 or more years ago at vessel fabrication shops. Given the limitations of the NDE technology available at the time, the Marshall flaw distribution provides a reasonable representation only for flaws having depth dimensions larger than ≈1-in. (2.54-cm). The Marshall distribution was nonetheless applied in SECY-82-465 and in the IPTS studies [ORNL 85a, 85b, 86] by extrapolating fits to the data to the much smaller flaws of concern in PTS calculations (less than ≈0.25-in. (0.64-cm)). Additionally, all flaws in the Marshall distribution were assumed to break the inner-diameter surface of the RPV despite the fact that the observations rarely, if ever, revealed surface breaking flaws in nuclear grade construction.

Table 7.1 summarizes the various sources of experimental data used by Simonen et al. to develop the flaw distributions used in FAVOR. While the volume of material represented in Table 7.1 improve greatly on the Marshall flaw distributions [Marshall 82], an inescapable conclusion is also that the quantity of available data is also quite small compared with the volume of RPV material in service. Consequently, it is not possible to ensure on an empirical basis alone that the flaw distributions developed based on these data apply to all PWRs in general. However, the flaw distributions proposed in [*Simonen*] rely on the experimental evidence gained from inspections of the materials summarized in Table 7.1 do not rest solely on this empirical evidence. Along with these data Simonen et al. used both physical models and expert opinions when developing their recommended flaw distributions. Additionally, where detailed information was lacking Simonen et al. made conservative judgments (for example, all NDE indications were modeled as cracks and, therefore, potentially deleterious to RPV integrity). This combined use of empirical evidence, physical models, expert opinions, and conservative judgments allowed Simonen et al. to propose flaw distributions for use in FAVOR that are believed to be appropriate/conservative representations of the flaw population existing in PWRs in general. (See Appendix C and [*Simonen*] for details.)

Table 7.1. **Summary of sources of experimental data sources for the flaw distribution**

Vessel	Weld	Plate	Clad
PVRUF	9150	855	1650
Shoreham	10375	975	--
Hope Creek	245	550	--
River Bend	2440	1465	--
Table entries represent volume of material examined in in³.			

In the following sections, we summarize the findings of this study for buried flaws in welds (Section 7.5.1), buried flaws in plates (Section 7.5.2), and surface flaws in both plates and welds (Section 7.5.3). Section 7.5.4 contrasts our flaw distribution the results with the Marshall distribution used in SECY-82-465.

7.5.1 Buried Flaws in Welds

The Simonen study made the following observations regarding flaws that form as part of the axial or circumferential weld fabrication process:

(1) Flaws in welds are distributed uniformly through the thickness of the RPV weld. There is no tendency for a greater density of flaws to occur either near the root or cap passes.

(2) No surface breaking flaws were identified in all of the weld material examined, nor was a credible physical mechanism for surface flaw generation identified. Consequently, the flaw distributions used herein contain *only* buried flaws. This is a significant change from the Marshall flaw distribution, which contained *only* surface breaking flaws.

(3) Virtually all non-volumetric flaws found in welds were lack of side-wall fusion defects that exist on the fusion line between the deposited weld metal and the plate or forging being joined. Consequently, the number of flaws in a particular weld scales in proportion to the fusion line area. Additionally, this observation implies that axial welds contain *only* axially oriented flaws whereas circumferential welds contain *only* circumferentially oriented flaws.

(4) Data on flaw density exhibited statistically significant differences depending upon the welding process used (SAW, SMAW, GMAW, or repair weld). However, it is difficult in practice to ascertain from records precisely where different weld processes were used, or where repair welds were made. For this reason, we decided that the flaw distributions used in this study would represent blended combinations of the SAW, SMAW, and REPAIR flaw distributions. Percentages of SAW and SMAW were established on a vessel specific basis. The percentage of repair weld was assumed to be 2% for all vessels analyzed. A repair weld volume of 2% exceeds slightly the repair percentage of 1.5% that was observed by PNNL for both the Shoreham and PVRUF vessels.

(5) Flaw densities exhibited statistically significant differences depending upon the vessel examined (PVRUF or Shoreham). Since Simonen did not establish a model capable of explaining why the density and size of flaws can be expected to vary from vessel to vessel, it was decided to adopt for FAVOR calculations flaw densities based only on observations of the Shoreham vessel because the Shoreham welds had a higher flaw density than the PVRUF welds.

(6) Flaw depth dimensions did not exhibit statistically significant differences for the different welding process and vessels examined, so in this case the data from the different processes and vessels were pooled.

There was, however, clear differences in the distributions of flaws length depending on the welding processes and vessels examined, so the flaw length distributions were established on a case-by-case basis.

It should also be noted that the empirical data used as the primary evidence to establish the distribution of embedded weld flaws do not, and cannot, provide any information about the maximum size a flaw can be. For this reason, it was decided to truncate the non-repair flaw distribution at 1-in. (2.54-cm) and the repair flaw distribution at 2-in. (5.08-cm). In both cases, the selected truncation limit exceeds the maximum observed flaw size by a factor of 2. We performed a sensitivity study with FAVOR and ascertained that, within reasonable bounds on truncation limit dimension, the estimated through-wall cracking frequency is not influenced in any significant way by the truncation limit [Dickson 03].

7.5.2   Buried Flaws in Plates

As reflected by the information in Table 7.1, the empirical evidence available to support a plate flaw distribution is much more limited than the available information for welds. Data on flaw rates and sizes from these sources agree well with two flaw distributions for plates derived by applying flaw density adjustment factors to weld flaw distributions. These adjustment factors, which were proposed by a group of experts [*Simonen*], are as follows:

- The density of plate flaws of depth less than 0.24-in. (6-mm) is 10% of that for weld flaws.

- The density of plate flaws of depth above 0.24-in. (6-mm) is 2.5% of that for weld flaws.

Since reasonable agreement exists between the limited experimental data on plate flaws and the adjusted weld distributions it was decided to use the adjusted weld distributions as input to FAVOR. A truncation limit of 0.43-in. (1.09-cm) was selected because it exceeds the largest observed plate flaw by a factor of 2. Again, a FAVOR sensitivity study demonstrates that this truncation limit does not influence significantly the estimated TWCF [Dickson 03].

Finally, the data reported by [*Simonen*] failed to reveal any preferred orientation for plate flaws. To model this finding in the most accurate way possible without performing mixed-mode fracture calculations, half of the simulated plate flaws are orientated axially, while the remaining half are oriented circumferentially in the vessel.

7.5.3   Surface Flaws in Welds and Plates

The entire inner-diameter of a nuclear RPV is clad with a thin layer of stainless steel to prevent corrosion of the underlying ferritic steel. Lack of inter-run fusion (LOF) can occur between adjacent weld beads, resulting in circumferentially oriented cracks. (All cladding in RPVs was deposited circumferentially.) While the data in [*Simonen*] shows a high probability (1 to 10 flaws per meter of deposited cladding weld bead) of obtaining very shallow LOF defects (1% of the clad layer thickness), only two deep LOF defects, having depths of ~50% and ~63% of the clad layer thickness, were found in all of the cladding inspected. Simonen found no evidence of LOF defects that completely compromised the clad layer.

The only flaws we expect to challenge the integrity of the RPV during PTS loading are those that completely penetrate the clad layer because it is only in this situation that the crack has its tip residing in the ferritic RPV steel, which is subject to neutron irradiation embrittlement. Despite the lack of empirical evidence for such deep flaws, it was not believed appropriate to completely exclude such flaws from the flaw model used in our PFM analysis owing to the limited amount of clad material examined. For this reason, we developed a distribution for small *buried* cladding flaws based on a combination of the data available, expert judgment, and the predictions of the PRODIGAL weld flaw simulation code [PRODIGAL]. This distribution was adjusted as follows to estimate the number of the clad flaws that fully penetrate the cladding thickness:

- We estimated that only 1/1000th of the observed density of *buried* cladding flaws would fully penetrate the cladding thickness.

- We assumed that these surface breaking defects exist only in single layer cladding. Multi-layer cladding was assumed to have no surface breaking flaws because the likelihood of two LOF defects aligning in two different weld layers is quite remote.

- Based on the physical mechanism of their formation, all LOF defects are aligned with the clad welding direction (circumferential).

In FAVOR, these surface-breaking circumferential flaws in the cladding can be simulated to occur anywhere in the vessel (i.e., in any weld, plate, and forging).

7.5.4 Comparison of the Current Flaw Distribution with that Proposed by the Marshall Committee

Figure 7.3 compares of the Marshall flaw distribution with the three components of the flaw distribution developed by Simonen. The following observations can be made:

- In general, the individual contributions to the new flaw distribution contain more flaws than the Marshall distribution, but the flaws in the new distribution are considerably smaller.

- While all of the flaws in the Marshall distribution are surface-breaking, only flaws associated with the cladding are surface-breaking in our new distribution, and these comprise only a small percentage of the total. Also, these cladding flaws are all circumferentially oriented because they follow the direction of weld deposition.

- The Marshall distribution focused on flaws in welds and did not distinguish between flaws in different product forms. The new distribution does, and it demonstrates that flaws in base metal are considerably smaller and occur less frequently than flaws in welds.

As illustrated in Figure 7.4, Dickson and Simonen report that the estimated TWCF drops by a factor of between 20 and 70 when the new flaw distribution is adopted instead of the Marshall distribution [Dickson 03].

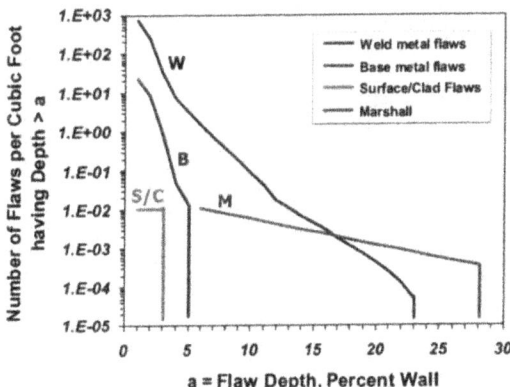

Figure 7.3. Comparison of the new flaw distribution to the Marshall flaw distribution

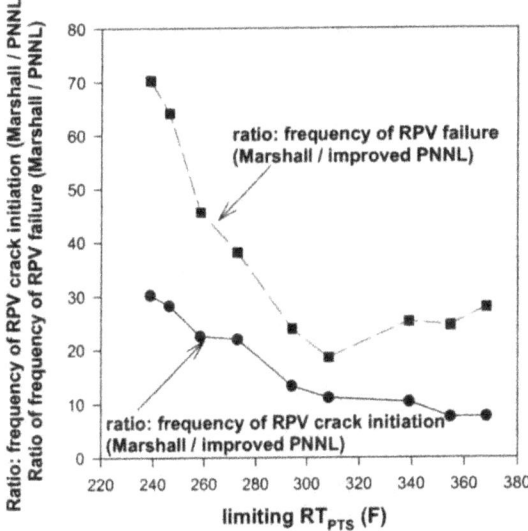

Figure 7.4. Illustration of the impact of the flaw distribution adopted in this study (improved PNNL) with that used in previous PTS calculations (Marshall flaw characterization) [Dickson 02] (analysis performed on Oconee at 60 EFPY)

7.6 Neutronics Model

The neutronics model is itself composed of two major components:

- a calculation of the fluence on the ID of the vessel performed according to NRC Regulatory Guide 1.190 [RG 1.190]

- attenuation of this fluence through the wall of the vessel to the location of the crack of interest using the attenuation formula in Regulatory Guide 1.99 [RG 1.99].

7.6.1 ID Fluence

The variation of fluence over the inner diameter of the vessel is estimated using modeling procedures based on the guidance provided in the NRC Regulatory Guide 1.190 [RG 1.190], "Calculational and Dosimetry Methods for Determining Pressure Vessel Neutron Fluence." Fluences so calculated are considered best estimates because they are based on the most up-to-date calculational procedures.

While procedures used to calculate fluence have been updated from those that provided the basis of the current PTS Rule, the more significant change in our fluence treatment has been the refinement of our discretization of the circumferential and azimuthal variation of fluence. In previous studies, each major region in the beltline of the vessel (i.e., each weld, plate, or forging) was assigned a value of fluence equal to the peak value estimated to occur anywhere in the region. In contrast, our models capture the detailed azimuthal and axial variation of fluence, resulting in a much more realistic model of the fluence variation in the beltline region.

7.6.2 Through-Wall Fluence Attenuation

Similar to previous PTS calculations [SECY-82-465, ORNL 85a, ORNL 85b, ORNL 86] FAVOR adopts the Regulatory Guide 1.99, Revision 2, model of fluence attenuation through the thickness of the vessel [RG 1.99]. This model assumes that the fluence (and thus the damage caused by irradiation) drops exponentially as the through-wall distance from the inner radius of the RPV increases. The exponential coefficient adopted (-0.24) assumes that fluence attenuates at the same rate as displacements per atom (DPA) (a conservative assumption). A recent review of attenuation models [English 02] concluded that while the RG1.99R2 attenuation model is widely regarded

as conservative, no better alternative model exists at the current time.

7.7 Crack Initiation Model

The crack initiation model is itself composed of the following major components:

- Fracture driving force model
  - LEFM driving force
  - Warm pre-stress
- Crack initiation resistance model
  - Unirradiated cleavage crack initiation toughness index temperature
  - Irradiation-induced shift in the cleavage crack initiation toughness index temperature
  - Cleavage crack initiation fracture toughness transition behavior

The probability of a crack initiating is determined by comparing the fracture driving force ($K_{applied}$) and the crack initiation resistance (K_{Ic}). If $K_{applied}$ for a given set of conditions (i.e., a particular TH transient and a particular flaw) exceeds the minimum value of the K_{Ic} distribution, the conditional probability of crack initiation (*CPI*) takes on a value greater than zero, which is calculated by FAVOR. Conversely, if $K_{applied}$ for a given set of conditions falls below the minimum value of the K_{Ic} distribution then *CPI*=0 (exactly zero, not a very small number).

In the following two subsections, we discuss the key features of the crack initiation model (Section 7.7.1) and the major differences between the current crack initiation model and that used in previous investigations of PTS risk (Section 7.7.2) [SECY-82-465, ORNL 85a, ORNL 85b, ORNL 86]. [*EricksonKirk-PFM*] provides a detailed discussion of the crack initiation model.

7.7.1 Key Features

7.7.1.1 Fracture Driving Force Model

Warm pre-stress (WPS) effects were first noted in the literature in 1963 [Brothers 63]. These investigators reported (as have many since them) that the apparent fracture toughness of a ferritic steel can be elevated in the fracture mode transition regime if the specimen is first "pre-stressed" at an elevated temperature. Once a specimen is subjected to a certain $K_{applied}$ and has not failed, the temperature can be reduced and the specimen will remain intact despite the fact that the process of reducing the temperature has also reduced the initiation fracture toughness (K_{Ic} or K_{Jc}) to values smaller than $K_{applied}$. In the past four decades, the physical mechanisms responsible for the WPS effect have been identified, studied extensively, and validated.

The types of loading that produce PTS challenges are characterized (generally) by a rapid cooldown on the inside the RPV. This type of loading produces values of $K_{applied}$ that initially increase, but later decrease as the transient progresses. Thus, depending upon the specifics of the transient (temperature gradients, flaw location, and so on) WPS may be effective, thereby preventing initiation of a cleavage crack even though $K_{applied}$ exceeds K_{Ic}. Nonetheless, to date, investigations of PTS have not included WPS as part of the PFM model [SECY-82-465, ORNL 85a, ORNL 85b, ORNL 86] for the following two reasons:

(1) TH transients were previously represented as smooth variations of both pressure and temperature with time. However, data taken from operating nuclear plants demonstrate that actual TH transients are not always so well behaved. This created the possibility that the short duration fluctuations of pressure and/or temperature with time characteristic of real transients might nullify the beneficial effect of WPS while the companion idealized transient might show WPS to be effective.

(2) In the past, the probabilistic risk assessment (PRA) models of human reliability (HR) were not sufficiently sophisticated to capture the potential for plant operators to repressurize the primary system as part of their response to an overcooling event. Since such a repressurization would usually nullify the benefit of WPS, it was viewed as nonconservative to account for the benefit produced by WPS within a model that may

also ignore the potentially deleterious effects of operator actions.

This reevaluation of the PTS Rule features both more realistic representations of the TH transients and a much more sophisticated PRA/HR models that consider explicitly both acts of omission and commission on the part of plant operators. Consequently, we have incorporated WPS effects into the PFM model. Thus, in this model the following two requirements must **both** be met for a crack to initiate:

Eq. 7-1 $K_{applied} \geq K_{Ic(min)}$

            $dK_{applied}/dt > 0$

7.7.1.2   Crack Initiation Resistance Model

Our model of the resistance of ferritic steels to cleavage crack initiation includes the following characteristics:

- a temperature dependency of fracture toughness that is universal to all ferritic steels and is uninfluenced by irradiation

- a scatter in fracture toughness that is universal to all ferritic steels and is not influenced by irradiation

- a finite lower bound to the distribution of (scatter in) crack initiation toughness values (i.e., a value of fracture driving force below which cleavage fracture *cannot* occur)

- an irradiation damage model that recognizes that the effects of irradiation are purely athermal (i.e., affecting *only* the position of the fracture toughness transition curve on the temperature axis)

These characteristics are all motivated by an understanding of the physical processes responsible for cleavage fracture. While the numerical coefficients of our model are obtained empirically (i.e., obtained by fitting toughness data) the functional forms of the fits are physically motivated. This physical basis provides an additional benefit in that it helps provide assurance that the models apply to all conditions of interest (i.e., to a variety of RPV steels and welds subject to range of irradiation conditions.

Our physical understanding of cleavage fracture also provides important guidance regarding how the uncertainty in fracture toughness should be modeled. Specifically, it is recognized that the distribution of non-coherent particles throughout the BCC iron lattice establishes the scatter in K_{Ic} and K_{Jc} data [Natishan 01, EricksonKirk 04]. It is possible, at least in principle, to know if a non-coherent particle exists at a particular point in the matrix, or not. This might suggest an epistemic nature to K_{Ic} and K_{Jc} scatter, were it not for the fact that K_{Ic} and K_{Jc} do not exist as point properties. K_{Ic} and K_{Jc} values always have an associated size scale, that being the plastically deformed volume. Upon loading, the presence of the crack elevates the stress state along the entire length of the crack front to the point that dislocations begin to move in the surrounding volume of material, which contains a distribution of dislocation barriers (e.g., non-coherent particles, grain boundaries, twin boundaries, etc.). Sufficient accumulation of dislocations at a barrier can elevate the local stress-state sufficiently to initiate a crack in the barrier, and, if the criteria for fracture are satisfied, propagate the crack through the entire surrounding test specimen or structure. Thus, the existence of a particular dislocation barrier at a particular location does not control K_{Ic} and K_{Jc}. Rather K_{Ic} and K_{Jc} are controlled by the *distribution* of these barriers throughout the lattice, and how this *distribution* interacts with the elevated stresses along the crack front. Since the distribution of these barriers throughout the lattice is random and occurs at a size-scale below that considered by the crack initiation toughness model, the uncertainty in K_{Ic} and K_{Jc} is irreducible. For this reason, the uncertainty in K_{Ic} is modeled as aleatory in FAVOR [*Williams*].

Beyond the aleatory uncertainty in K_{Ic}, our model of crack initiation toughness accounts for uncertainties in both the model and in the input parameters that are epistemic in nature. The major epistemic model uncertainty is the RT_{NDT} bias correction, which is discussed in the next section, because this represents a major change in the crack initiation model relative to that adopted in previous investigations of PTS. Epistemic uncertainties in input data (i.e., Cu, Ni, and P content, initial RT_{NDT}, and un-irradiated CVN upper-shelf energy) are accounted for and propagated through the FAVOR calculation. While the mean values of these distributions are the values the licensees have docketed [RVID2], the statistical distributions assumed to exist around these mean values were derived from *all data available* for the entire population of RPV-grade ferritic steels and their weldments. Consequently, these distributions overestimate (sometimes significantly so) the degree of uncertainty in these input variables relative to that which would characterize a *particular* weld, plate, or forging that would exist in the beltline of a *particular* PWR. While plant-specific studies might appropriately adopt less-scattered distributions, we have used generic distributions of the input variables to support our goal of developing a revision to 10 CFR 50.61 that applies to all PWRs.

7.7.2 Major Changes

In this section, we summarize the major changes between the calculational models adopted here and those used to support the current version of 10 CFR 50.61.

7.7.2.1 Fracture Driving Force Model

As discussed in Section 7.7.1.1, our models incorporate the effects of WPS, whereas previous studies of PTS have not. Adopting a WPS model can reduce the TWCF estimated for certain classes of transients. For example, the TWCF estimated for a primary side pipe break will be significantly smaller when the effects of WPS are considered, while the TWCF estimated for a stuck-open valve that recloses later during the transient (thereby repressurizing the primary system) may not be affected by WPS at all. In plant analyses of Oconee Unit 1 based on a complete set of transients (i.e., considering the potential for vessel failure from all potential PTS precursors), inclusion of WPS in the model reduces the estimated TWCF by between a factor of 2½ and 3 [Dickson 03]. Dickson's results show that while the degree of "benefit" associated with adopting a WPS model depends on the transients considered to produce PTS risk it is reasonably insensitive to the degree of embrittlement.

7.7.2.2   Crack Initiation Resistance Model

Relative to the models used in the studies that established the technical basis to the current PTS Rule [SECY-82-465, ORNL 85a, ORNL 85b, ORNL 86], our model has the following *major* differences (see [*EricksonKirk-PFM*] for a comprehensive discussion of *all* differences):

(1) Consideration of Systematic Material Property and Fluence Variations throughout the Beltline Region: In previous studies, the known systematic variations of material properties and fluence throughout the beltline region were treated in a highly simplified fashion. Specifically, the effect of radiation damage on each major region (i.e., each plate, weld, or forging) of the vessel was assessed assuming that the entire region was subjected to the maximum fluence occurring anywhere in the region. This approach led to significant overpredictions of the embrittlement of the vessel, and consequent overestimates of the PTS risk. These conservatisms are absent from our model.

(2) Treatment of Fracture Toughness Scatter as Aleatory: The aleatory model of fracture toughness uncertainty described in Section 7.7.1.2 differs from the epistemic treatment of toughness uncertainty adopted in all pervious probabilistic studies of PTS. In these studies the result of a particular trial in the calculation was the prediction that the vessel *had* or *had not* failed. While this epistemic treatment is inconsistent with our current understanding of the physics of cleavage fracture, the difference in the mean TWCF estimates produced by these two different approaches is small (all other factors being held constant).

(3) RT_{NDT} Bias Correction: While the restrictions on model development detailed in Section 3.1.1 require that the basis of our model be non-toughness metrics (i.e., RT_{NDT}) our model recognizes that RT_{NDT} is not a direct measure of the fracture toughness transition temperature. Indeed RT_{NDT} is by intention a conservative approximation to the true fracture toughness transition temperature, overestimating this value (an implicit conservatism) by 65°F (18°C) on average, and up to 200°F (93°C) in some cases. Our model removes this conservative bias (on average), but in the process, introduces a non-physical model uncertainty. This model uncertainty, which cannot be removed as long as we rely on RT_{NDT}-based metrics, should be regarded as an implicit conservatism in our results. This bias correction significantly reduces the estimated annual through-wall cracking frequency.

7.7.2.3   Method for Estimating Vessel Crack Initiation Probability from the Probability of Initiation of Individual Cracks in the Vessel

Our treatment of the uncertainty in crack initiation fracture toughness (K_{Ic}) as aleatory necessitates use of a different methodology for estimating the probability of crack initiation in the vessel from the probabilities of initiation of the many individual cracks throughout the vessel from that adopted in the calculations used in [SECY-82-465][§§]. In previous probabilistic studies of PTS, the uncertainty in K_{Ic} was modeled as being epistemic, meaning that for any individual simulation, there existed a single value of K_{Ic}. Consequently, if the probabilistic computer code simulated that the applied fracture driving force ($K_{applied}$) resulting from a PTS transient ever exceeded K_{Ic} for any of the

---

[§§]   The discussion in this section also applies to the mathematical combination the probability of individual cracks propagating through-wall to estimate the probability of the vessel developing a through-wall crack.

flaws in the vessel, the vessel failure probability was set to 1 (a certainty) and further calculations for that vessel were not performed because a vessel cannot fail twice. When K_{Ic} uncertainty is correctly modeled as being aleatory (as it is in our model), a different approach is needed because the result of each simulation run is not vessel non-failure (probability 0) or vessel failure (probability 1), but rather vessel non-failure (probability 0) or vessel failure *probability* ($0 <$ probability ≤ 1; in practical terms vessel failure probability is usually a very small number that is *not* close to 1). In this situation, the appropriate representation of the vessel failure probability is the complement (meaning the difference from 1) of the joint (meaning combined) probability of non-failure of all of the flaws in the vessel [Fang 03], which can be expressed mathematically as follows:

$$\text{Eq. 7-2} \quad P_{FAIL(VESSEL)} = 1 - \prod_{j=1}^{n}\left(1 - P_{FAIL(j)}\right)$$

where n is the total number of flaws simulated to exist in the pressure vessel. This equation can be stated in words as follows: *the probability that the vessel will fail is 1 minus the probability that all of the cracks in the vessel do not fail*, or, even more simply: *in order for the vessel to not fail all of the cracks in it must not fail*.

During the many public meetings that have been held during the course of the PTS reevaluation project, concerns have been expressed that this methodology for estimating the vessel failure probability is both inappropriate and overly conservative. The following alternative probability formula has been proposed:

$$\text{Eq. 7-3} \quad P_{FAIL(VESSEL)} = \underset{j=1}{\overset{n}{MAX}}\left(P_{FAIL(j)}\right)$$

This equation states that the failure probability of the vessel is the maximum of the individual failure probabilities associated with the many individual cracks in the vessel. The appropriateness of Eq. 7-2 rather than Eq. 7-3 when estimating the total probability associated with system failures (vessels) that might result from many individual causes (cracks) can be

easily understood by way of analogy. Consider the "system" to be an individual human life and consider the "failure" to be death. Below, we provide two examples to illustrate the differences between Eq. 7-2 and Eq. 7-3, and the appropriateness of Eq. 7-2:

Example 1: Hypothetical individual #1 leads a very controlled life and (so) is subject to only one cause of death (cancer). The individual's annual risk of dying of cancer is 2%. In this situation, this individual's total annual risk of death is estimated to be 2% by either Eq. 7-2 or by Eq. 7-3.

Example 2: Hypothetical individual #2 is less careful than hypothetical individual #1 and (so) is at risk from more than one cause of death. The individual's annual risk of dying from any one of four causes is as follows: cancer=2%, AIDS=1%, skydiving=½%, gunshot=¼%. Clearly individual #2 has a greater annual death risk than individual #1, yet Eq. 7-3 estimates their annual death risks to be identical: MAX(2%, 1%, ½%, ¼%), or 2%. Conversely, Eq. 7-2 estimates individual #2's annual death risk to be {1-(1-0.02)*(1-0.01)*(1-0.005)*(1-0.0025)}, or 3.7%.

It can also be noted that for the particular situation of interest here (PTS-induced failures of nuclear RPVs containing cracks), the numerical differences between the failure probabilities estimated by Eq. 7-2 and Eq. 7-3 is actually very small because, as illustrated in Figure 7.5, for the great majority of the time, only one crack in a vessel has a probability of through-wall cracking that exceeds zero. It was for this reason, that Meyer assessed the differences between Eq. 7-2 and Eq. 7-3 to be practically insignificant [Meyer 03].

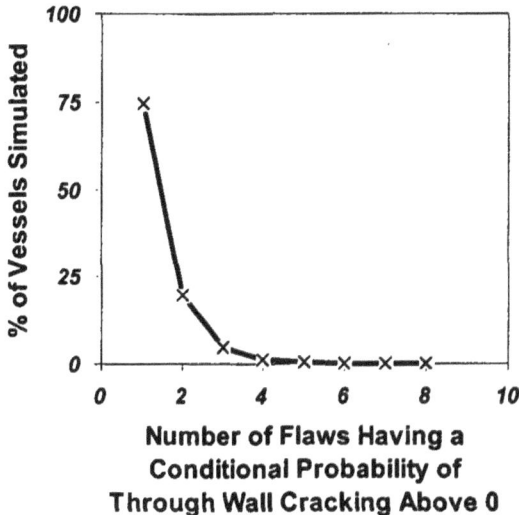

Figure 7.5. Number of flaws simulated that have a conditional probability of through-wall cracking that exceeds zero (Oconee at 60 EFPY).

7.8 Through-Wall Cracking Model

Provided that the results of a particular trial for a particular simulated flaw result in an estimation of *CPI* > 0, FAVOR will check to see how far the simulated crack will propagate into the vessel wall before it arrests permanently (if it arrests at all). The through-wall cracking model is itself composed of the following component models:

- Fracture driving force
  - LEFM driving force
- Crack growth resistance
  - cleavage crack arrest
  - upper shelf ductile tearing model
  - property gradient model

The probability of through-wall cracking is determined by comparing the fracture driving force ($K_{applied}$) to the resistance to further crack growth, which is expressed as a value of cleavage crack arrest toughness (K_{Ia}). Additionally, once a propagating crack has arrested the potential for re-initiation at some later time in the transient is assessed relative to the material's resistance to crack initiation in either cleavage (K_{Ic}) or by ductile tearing ($K\{J_{Ic}\}$, and the associated *J-R* curve). For each

simulation where FAVOR calculates a value of *CPI* > 0, it then conducts 100 deterministic through-wall cracking analyses. The outcome of each of these deterministic simulations is either that the crack propagates all the way through the thickness of the vessel[***], or that the crack arrests before it reaches the outer diameter. The percentage of the trials that result in through-wall cracking is then multiplied by the *CPI* value to estimate the *CPTWC*.

In the following two subsections, we discuss the key features of the through-wall cracking model (Section 7.8.1) and the major differences between our model and that used in previous investigations of PTS risk (Section 7.8.2) [SECY-82-465, ORNL 85a, ORNL 85b, ORNL 86]. These sections address only the crack growth resistance models because the fracture driving force models are the same as used for crack initiation. [*EricksonKirk-PFM*] provides a detailed discussion of the through-wall cracking model.

7.8.1 Key Features

Our model of the resistance of ferritic steels to through-wall cracking includes both a cleavage crack arrest model and a model for re-initiation of a crack by ductile tearing on the upper shelf[†††]. These models include the following characteristics:

- Crack arrest toughness model
  - a temperature dependency of crack arrest toughness that is universal to all ferritic steels and is not influenced by irradiation
  - a scatter in crack arrest toughness that is universal to all ferritic steels and is not influenced by irradiation

---

[***] In practice, when the crack extends 90% of the way through the wall thickness the vessel is considered to have failed.

[†††] The through-wall cracking model also accounts for the possibility of re-initiation in cleavage, but for these purposes the crack initiation model described previously in Section 7.7 is used.

- a finite lower bound to the distribution of (scatter in) crack arrest toughness values (i.e., a value of fracture driving force below which cleavage fracture *cannot* occur)

- a model that positions the crack arrest transition temperature depending on the crack initiation transition temperature, and recognizes that the temperature differential between the crack initiation and crack arrest transition temperatures depends on the amount of prior hardening (i.e., irradiation damage) experienced by the material

- Upper shelf ductile initiation and tearing model

  - a temperature dependency of upper-shelf toughness that is universal to all ferritic steels and is not influenced by irradiation

  - a scatter in upper-shelf toughness that is universal to all ferritic steels and is not influenced by irradiation

  - a linkage between the magnitude of the fracture toughness on the upper shelf and the fracture toughness transition temperature

These characteristics are all motivated by an understanding of the physical processes responsible for both cleavage crack arrest and for ductile crack initiation on the upper shelf. While the numerical coefficients of our models are obtained empirically (i.e., obtained by fitting toughness data), the functional forms of the fits are physically motivated. This physical basis provides an additional benefit in that it helps provide assurance that the models apply to all conditions of interest (i.e., to a variety of RPV steels and welds subject to range of irradiation conditions).

Our physical understanding of both cleavage crack arrest and of ductile crack initiation also provides important guidance regarding how the uncertainty in fracture toughness should be modeled. As was the case for cleavage crack initiation toughness, it is recognized that the

physical processes responsible for both cleavage crack arrest and for ductile crack initiation make the uncertainty in these toughness values aleatory in nature [*EricksonKirk-PFM*], and it is so modeled in FAVOR [*Williams*].

7.8.2 Major Changes

Relative to the models used in the studies that established the technical basis to the current PTS Rule [SECY-82-465, ORNL 85a, ORNL 85b, ORNL 86], our model has the following *major* differences (see [*EricksonKirk-PFM*] for a comprehensive discussion of *all* differences):

(1) Allowance of Ductile Tearing and Inclusion of Crack Arrest Resistance at $K_{applied}$ Values Above 200 ksi√in (220 MPa√m): In all former studies of PTS (including our own study reported in [*Kirk 12-02*]) the resistance to crack arrest was truncated at 200 ksi√in (220 MPa√m) because this is the highest value allowed by the ASME code K_{Ia} curve. However, ample evidence from large-scale experiments exists demonstrating that crack arrest above 200 ksi√in (220 MPa√m) does occur, indicating the inappropriateness and over-conservatism of the 200 ksi√in (220 MPa√m) limit. Moreover, no allowance was ever made in former studies of the possibility for an arrested crack to re-initiate by ductile tearing on the upper shelf despite the fact that the resistance to crack initiation on the upper shelf ranges between 100 and 200 ksi√in (110-220 MPa√m) for ferritic RPV steels both before and after irradiation. We have eliminated this apparent oversight in our through-wall cracking model. As shown in Figure 7.6, the combined effect of these two changes is a reduction in the TWCF by a factor of 4–5 (at lower levels of embrittlement) down to a reduction factor of ~1.5 as embrittlement increases. Allowing cracks to arrest at $K_{applied}$ values above 200 ksi√in has resulted in cracks being arrested at shallower depths, which in turn makes re-initiation by either cleavage or ductile fracture more difficult. Thus, removing the conservatism of the 200 ksi√in (220 MPa√m) limit on K_{Ia} more than

compensated for the non-conservatism associated with assuming that re-initiation in a ductile mode cannot occur.

(2) A Separation between the K_{Ic} and K_{Ia} Curves that Depends on the Degree of Irradiation Embrittlement: In all studies of PTS risk predating this reevaluation, the temperature separation between the K_{Ic} and K_{Ia} transition curves was held fixed irrespective of the material condition, as has always been the practice for the ASME K_{Ic} and K_{Ia} curves. However, because ferritic steels harden to an absolute limit [Wagenhofer 01], the separation between the two curves depends upon the degree to which the material is hardened, with more hardened (more irradiated) materials having smaller separations [Kirk 02a]. This is also supported by ample empirical evidence [Wallin 98b]. We have not performed a sensitivity study to assess the effect of this model change. However, comparison of the temperature differential between the K_{Ic} and K_{Ia} curves adopted by our current model (see curve of Figure 7.7) with the constant temperature differential of ~30°C (~86°F) previously assumed (i.e., the temperature separation between the ASME K_{Ic} and K_{Ia} curves) demonstrates our new model reduces the crack arrest capacity of higher toughness materials (i.e., materials having a T_o value of ~60°C (~140°F) or less) because the greater K_{Ic} to K_{Ia} curve separation adopted by our model reduces the of value of K_{Ia} at a fixed K_{Ic}. Conversely, the crack arrest capacity of more embrittled materials (i.e., materials having a T_o value of ~60°C (~140°F) or more) is greater in our model than it is in the ASME model.

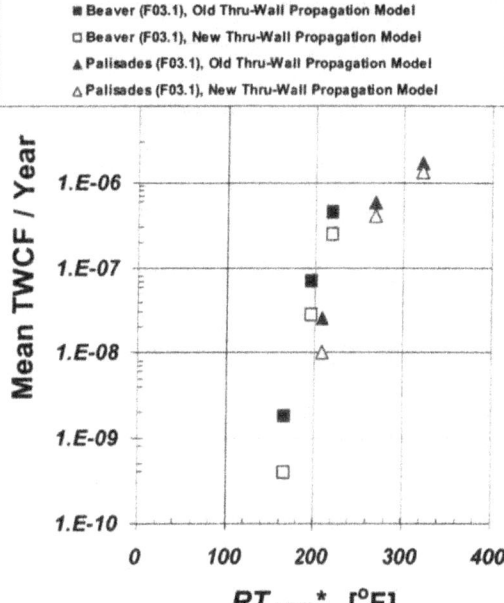

Figure 7.6. Combined effects of allowing K_{Ia} to exceed 200 ksi√in and allowing for ductile crack re-initiation on the upper shelf. Open points show TWCF results when K_{Ia} is allowed to exceed 200 ksi√in and ductile crack re-initiation is permitted. $RT_{NDT}*$ is defined in [Kirk 12-02].

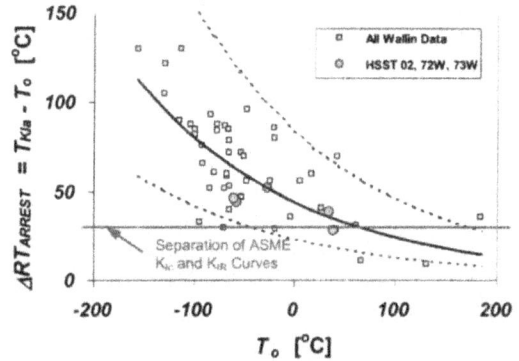

Figure 7.7. Comparison of temperature separation between crack initiation and crack arrest toughness transition curves assumed in our current calculations (blue curve) with the constant separation of ~30°C (~86°F) assumed by previous calculations

7.9 Probabilistic Fracture Mechanics Code FAVOR

7.9.1 Implementation of PFM Model

As shown in Figure 7.8, FAVOR is composed of three computational modules: (1) a deterministic load generator (**FAVLoad**), (2) a Monte Carlo PFM module (**FAVPFM**), and (3) a post-processor (**FAVPost**). Figure 7.8 also indicates the nature of the data streams that flow through these modules.

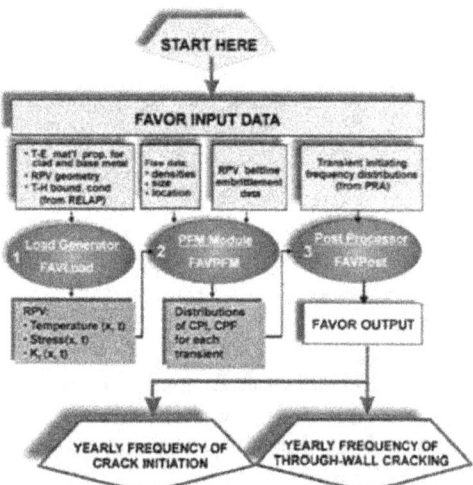

Figure 7.8. FAVOR data streams flow through three modules: (1) FAVLoad, (2) FAVPFM, and (3) FAVPost

FAVLoad takes as input the time histories of pressure, temperature, and heat transfer coefficient defined by the RELAP TH analysis. These inputs are used along with a 1D transient heat conduction equation to estimate the time-dependent variation of temperature through the vessel wall. These time-dependent temperature profiles are used, along with the RELAP pressure history, in a linear elastic stress analysis to estimate the time history of applied-K_I, which is passed to FAVPFM for further analysis.

The FAVPFM module implements the logical specification of the PFM model within a series of nested loops illustrated in Figure 7.9. These loops step through the TH time history and implement the Monte-Carlo trials necessary to estimate the conditional probabilities of crack initiation and of though wall cracking. The probabilities estimated by FAVOR (complete with uncertainties) are *conditional* in the sense that, within the FAVPFM module, the TH transients are assumed to occur.

The FAVPFM module provides the capability to model the variation of radiation damage in the *beltline region* of an RPV with as much detail as the analyst considers necessary. Only that portion of the beltline that is proximate to the active core need be modeled because the fast-neutron flux, and thus the radiation damage, drops to nearly zero within a foot beyond the fuel region. Within this region (active core ±1-ft. (0.3-m), the vessel is represented as a combination of "major regions," with each major region representing a different plate, weld, or forging each having (potentially) a unique combination of mean copper content, mean nickel content, mean phosphorus content, and unirradiated RT_{NDT}. Each major region may be divided into as many "sub-regions" as the analyst feels are necessary to represent accurately both the axial and azimuthal variation of fluence. Sufficient discretization is adopted so that each sub-region is effectively subjected to the same fluence throughout. In this way, the complex variation of embrittlement throughout the vessel wall that is caused by variations in both material and radiological conditions is represented to the model. It should be noted that this material/radiological model is a considerably more accurate representation of reality than the models adopted in the calculations performed to support SECY-82-465 and the IPTS studies. In these earlier calculations, the entire vessel was presumed to be made out of the most irradiation-sensitive material, and all of this material was assumed to be subjected to the peak fluence that occurred anywhere in the vessel.

The last FAVOR module, FAVPost, combines the conditional initiation and through-wall cracking probabilities and combines these, through a matrix multiplication, with the frequency histograms for each TH sequence provided by the PRA analyses. In this way, the complete distribution of TWCF (per operating year) is estimated.

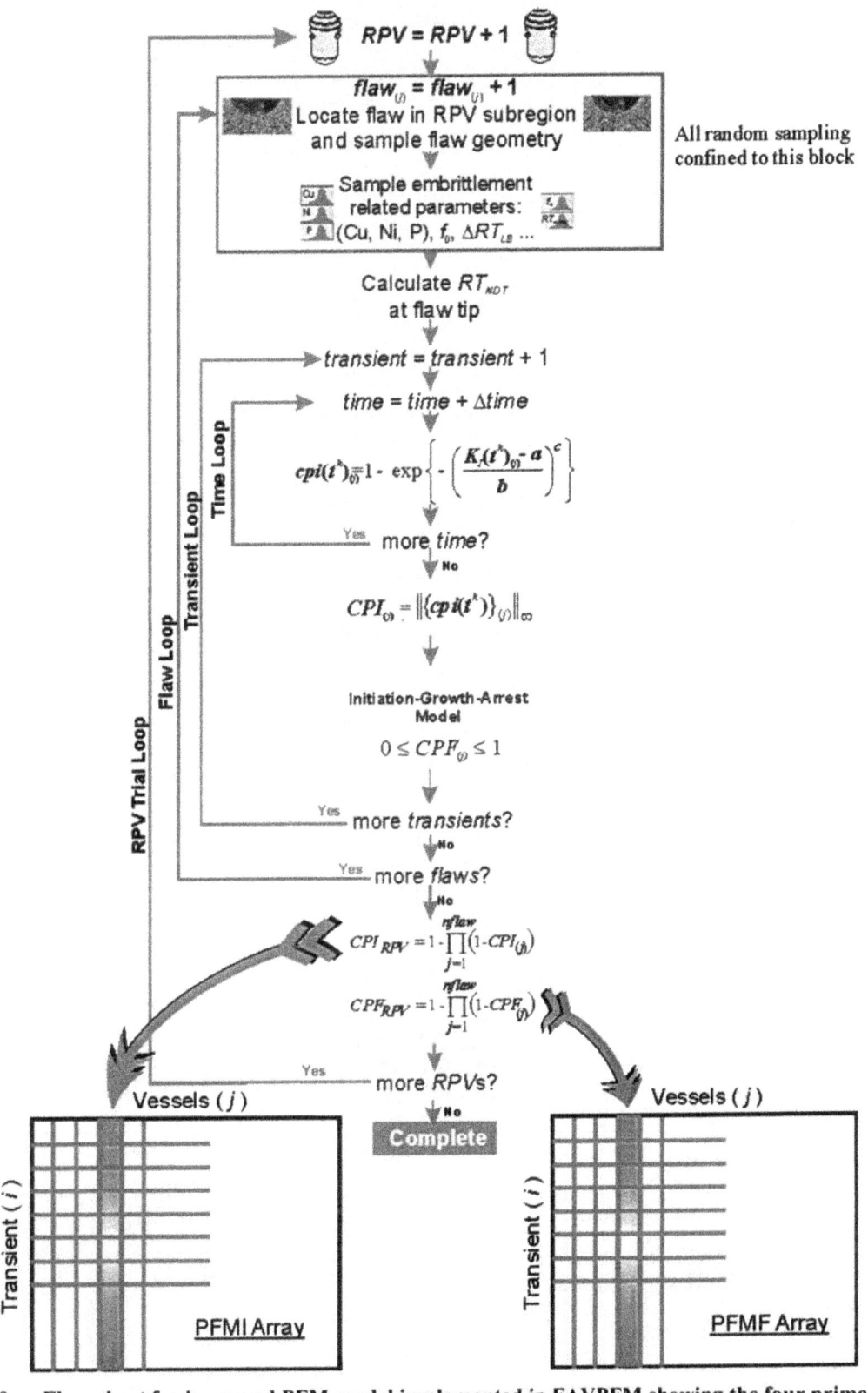

Figure 7.9. Flow chart for improved PFM model implemented in FAVPFM showing the four primary nested loops – (1) *RPV Trial Loop*, (2) *Flaw Loop*, (3) *Transient Loop*, and (4) *Time Loop*

7.9.2 Discretization of the Reactor Pressure Vessel

FAVOR utilizes discretizes the RPV beltline into one "major regions" for each axial weld, circumferential weld, plate, and forging. The major regions are further subdivided into iso-fluence "subregions." To model accurately the complex variation of fluence with azimuth and axial location (see Figure 7.10) a large number of sub-regions was necessary (15280, 19651, and 67076 subregions for Beaver Valley, Oconee, and Palisades, respectively). The neutron fluence maps were provided for 32 and 40 EFPY were used, and were linearly extrapolated to estimate fluence for longer operational durations.

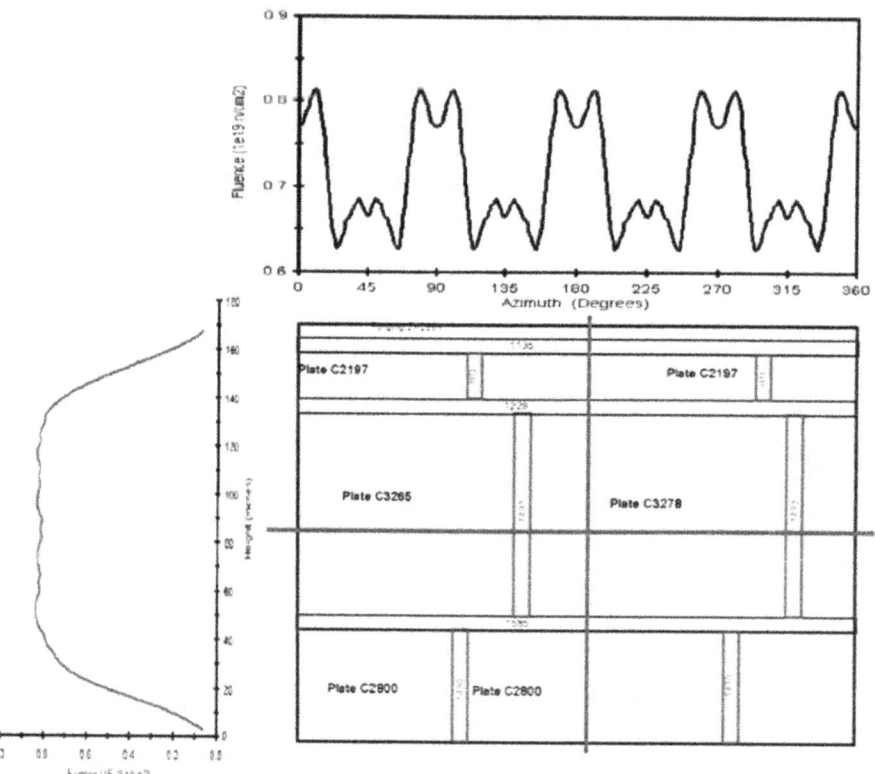

Figure 7.10. Rollout diagram of beltline materials and representative fluence maps for Oconee Unit 1

7.10 Experimental Validation of Linear Elastic Fracture Mechanics

Extensive experimental/analytical investigations performed at ORNL during the 1970s and 1980s examined the accuracy with which LEFM models could be expected to predict the failure of nuclear RPVs subjected to both simple loadings (pressure only) and to much more complex loadings (PTS conditions) [Cheverton 85a, Cheverton 85b]. These investigations all featured tests on thick-section pressure vessels (see Figure 7-11), and aimed to reproduce, as closely as practical in a laboratory setting, the conditions that characterize thermal shock of a nuclear RPV. These conditions include the following:

- fracture initiation from small flaws

- severe thermal, stress, and material toughness gradients

- biaxial loading

- effects of cladding (including residual stresses)

- conditions under which warm pre-stress may be active

- combined stress and toughness gradient conditions that can promote crack initiation, arrest, re-initiation, and re-arrest all during the same transient

- due to these various gradients, the possibility of conversion of fracture mode from cleavage to ductile and back again all during the same TH transient

The three test series were as follows:

- The first series of tests employed ten intermediate test vessels (ITVs), three with cracks located at a cylindrical nozzle and seven with cracks located remote from any geometric discontinuities. These tests were aimed at investigating the ability of LEFM to predict the fracture response of thick section vessels containing relatively deep flaws (20 to 83% of the 6-in. (152.4 mm) vessel wall) at test temperatures ranging from lower shelf to upper shelf. A variety of nuclear grade RPV plates, forgings, and weldments were tested.

- The second series of tests comprised eight thermal-shock experiments (TSEs). The purpose of these experiments was to investigate the behavior of surface cracks under thermal-shock conditions similar to those that would be encountered during a large-break loss of coolant accident (LBLOCA) (i.e., a rapid cooldown in the absence of internal pressure).

- The third series of tests included two experiments that subjected ITV specimens to concurrent pressure and thermal transients. These "pressurized thermal shock experiments," or PTSEs, sought to simulate the effects of a rapid cooldown transient combined with significant internal pressure. Thus, these experiments simulated TH conditions characteristic of smaller break LOCAs.

These investigations support the following conclusions:

- ITV Experiments:
  - LEFM analyses very closely predicted actual fracture pressures for thick-wall pressure vessels.
  - Methods for calculating fracture toughness from small specimens were successfully used in applications of fracture analysis of thick flawed vessels.

- Thermal Shock Experiments (TSEs):
  - Multiple initiation-arrest events with deep penetration into the vessel wall were predicted and observed.
  - Surface flaws that were initially short and shallow were predicted and observed to grow considerably in length before increasing significantly in depth.
  - Warm pre-stress was observed to limit crack extension through the wall under LOCA conditions.
  - Small-specimen fracture mechanics data successfully predicted the fracture behavior of thick pressure vessels.
  - Crack arrest occurred in a rising stress field.

- Pressurized Thermal Shock Experiments (PTSEs):
  - Warm pre-stress is effective at inhibiting crack initiation for conditions under which crack initiation would otherwise be expected (i.e., $K_{applied} > K_{Ic}$).
  - Crack arrest toughness values (K_{Ia}) inferred from conditions prototypic of PTS loading agree well with other experimental measurements, suggesting the transferability of laboratory toughness data to structural loading conditions.

o   LEFM predictions of crack initiation, growth, and arrest behavior successfully captured the response of the vessel to the transient; however some details were not exactly predicted (two initiation-run-arrest events were predicted whereas one was observed).

With regard to this final bullet item, it should be noted that exact agreement between deterministic predictions and individual experiments cannot be expected when the physical processes that underlie those experiments produce large aleatory uncertainties (as is the case with K_{Ic} and K_{Ia} data; see Sections 7.7.1.2 and 7.8.1, respectively). Such disagreement does not in itself condemn the methodology, but rather reveals that the precision of any single prediction is limited by the precision in our knowledge of the controlling material properties.

Figure 7-11. Test vessels used in the ITV and PTSE test series (top) and in the TSE test series (bottom)

8 Vessel Failure Frequencies Estimated for Oconee Unit 1, Beaver Valley Unit 1, and Palisades

8.1 Chapter Structure

In this chapter, we describe the results of our probabilistic calculations for Oconee Unit 1, Beaver Valley Unit 1, and Palisades. Section 8.2 details the plant-specific features of each analysis, including both methodology and input variables. In Section 8.3, we present the values of frequency of crack initiation (FCI) and through-wall cracking frequency (TWCF) that we have estimated for these three plants, and we discuss the characteristics of the distributions from which these values are derived.

In Section 8.4, we examine the material features that contribute most significantly, and those that do not contribute at all, to the magnitude of the FCI and TWCF values. A key output of this section is a methodology to express the embrittlement level of different plants on an equivalent basis. In Section 8.5, we both identify the classes of transients (e.g., LOCAs, MSLBs, and so on) that contribute most significantly, and those that do not contribute at all, to the level of PTS challenge at a particular plant. Using this information along with methodology developed in Section 8.4 allows us to determine if plant-specific factors need to be considered when assessing the level of challenge posed to plants by different transient classes. The chapter concludes with Section 8.6, which summarizes our findings and indicates factors that need to be considered if these findings are to be considered generally applicable to all PWRs. Issues of general applicability are examined in more detail in Chapter 9.

8.2 Plant-Specific Features of Analysis

8.2.1 PRA

8.2.1.1 Analysis Methodology

In the case of both the Oconee and Beaver Valley PRA analyses, NRC contractors were responsible for both constructing the PRA models and binning the overcooling sequences into "case" sequences. The PRA models were constructed from scratch, largely based on information learned from the 1980s PTS work, but with numerous improvements. The HRA portion of the PRA was also initially performed by the NRC contractors. The corresponding licensees provided information about each plant and answered both written and verbal questions as the PRA model and the PRA/HRA evolved. In each case, two plant visits took place: one early in the process to gather plant information, and a second when interim results were available to allow licensee review and input.

In contrast, the PRA/HRA analysis for Palisades derived mostly from an existing licensee PRA model that already included overcooling sequences. NRC contractors provided comments on the existing PRA model, a model that was subsequently modified by the licensee in response to these comments. Once the revised PRA model was satisfactory to both the licensee and NRC contractors, the HRA portion of the analysis was conducted as a collaborative effort. This HRA information was included in the Palisades PRA model, and sequence binning and frequency estimates were subsequently performed primarily by the licensee with NRC contractor review, input, and slight modification. Two plant visits were also conducted for the Palisades analysis: the first for initial project and plant familiarization, and the second for conducting the collaborative HRA. As for the other two plant analyses, numerous discussions were held between the Palisades staff and NRC Contractors as the PRA model and PRA/HRA evolved. Hence, while the same overall approach was followed to construct all three PRA/HRA models, the origin of these models and the key personnel responsible for constructing them varied from plant-to-plant

8.2.1.2   Inputs

The plant-specific PRAs described in Section 8.2.1.1 led to the definition of a master list of thermal-hydraulic transients. A sub-set of these transients from this list was defined as the "base case" for each plant, which represents our best mathematical description of the conditions at the plant that could produce a PTS challenge to vessel integrity. TH cases from the master list were eliminated from the base case for a number of reasons, including the following:

- Certain transients were binned together, making some TH runs redundant, or

- Sensitivity studies revealed that certain TH cases did not need to be passed on, or

- The minimum temperature remained above 400°F (204°C) within the first ≈170 minutes. Experience gained from previous analysis of PTS has repeatedly demonstrated that transients need to be at least this severe to make any contribution at all to the calculated through-wall cracking frequency. Later examination of TWCF estimates for all base case transients revealed that many transients having lower minimum temperatures still made no contribution to TWCF, thus demonstrating the appropriateness of this screening limit.

The details of each plant-specific PRA are summarized in other reports [*Kolaczkowski-Oco, Whitehead-BV, Whitehead-Pal*]. Appendix A provides the master list of transients for all three plants, and also lists the frequency values for the base-case transients.

8.2.2   TH

This section describes the RELAP5 models developed for the Oconee-1, Beaver Valley Unit 1, and Palisades plants. The TH analysis methodology is similar for the three plants. In each case, the best available RELAP5 input model was used as the starting point to expedite the model development process. For Oconee, the base model was that used in the code scaling, applicability and uncertainty (CSAU) study. For Beaver Valley, the base model was the H.B. Robinson-2 model used in the original PTS study in the mid 1980s. This model was revised by Westinghouse to reflect the Beaver Valley plant configuration. For Palisades, the base model was obtained from Nuclear Management Corporation, the operators of the Palisades plant. This model was originally developed and documented by Siemens Power Corporation to support analysis of the loss of electrical load event for Palisades.

The RELAP5 models for the Oconee, Beaver Valley, and Palisades plants are detailed representations of the power plants and include all major components for both the primary and secondary plant systems. RELAP5 heat structures are used throughout the models to represent structures such as the fuel, vessel wall, vessel internals, and steam generator tubes. The reactor vessel nodalization includes the downcomer, lower plenum, core inlet, core, core bypass, upper plenum and upper head regions. Plant-specific features, such as the reactor vessel vent valves, are included as appropriate.

The downcomer model used in each plant utilizes a two-dimensional nodalization. This approach was used to capture the possible temperature variation in the downcomer due to the injection of cold ECCS water into each of the cold legs. Capturing this temperature variation in the downcomer is not possible with the original one-dimensional downcomer. In the revised models, the downcomer is divided into six azimuthal regions for each plant.

The safety injection systems modeled for the Oconee, Palisades, and Beaver Valley plants include high-pressure injection (HPI), low-pressure injection (LPI), other ECCS components (e.g., accumulators, core flood tanks (CFTs), safety injection tanks (SITs) depending on the plant designation), and makeup/letdown, as appropriate.

The secondary coolant system models include steam generators, main and auxiliary/emergency feedwater, steam lines, safety valves, main steam isolation valves (as appropriate), and turbine bypass and stop valves.

Each of the models was updated to reflect the current plant configuration including updating system setpoints (to best estimate values) and modifying control logic to reflect current operating procedures. Other changes to the models include the addition of control blocks to calculate parameters for convenience or information only (e.g., items such as minimum downcomer temperature). The Oconee, Beaver Valley, and Palisades models were then initialized to simulate hot full power and hot zero power plant operation for the purpose of establishing satisfactory steady-state conditions from which the PTS transient event sequence calculations are started.

In RELAP5 simulations of LOCA event sequences for the Oconee and Palisades plants during which all of the reactor coolant pumps are tripped and the loss of primary coolant system inventory is sufficient to interrupt coolant loop natural circulation flow, a circulating flow was observed between the two cold legs on the same coolant loop. The circulations mix coolant in the reactor vessel downcomer, cold leg and SG outlet plenum regions. These RELAP5 cold-leg circulations were originally reported during the first PTS evaluation study [Fletcher 84, Spiggs 85] and are significant for the PTS application. When the circulation is present the calculated reactor vessel downcomer fluid temperature benefits from the warming effects created by mixing the cold HPI fluid with the warm steam generator outlet plenum fluid. When the circulation is not present the calculated reactor vessel downcomer fluid temperature more directly feels the influence of the cold HPI fluid. Note that both the Oconee and Palisades plants have a "2x4"

configuration with two cold legs and one hot leg in each coolant loop. In contrast, the Beaver Valley plant has a single hot and cold leg per coolant loop and this type of circulating flow is not seen. (See Section 6.3.2 for a further discussion of this issue.)

Certain experiments used in the assessment exhibited apparent indications of cold leg circulations very similar to those simulated with RELAP5. However, the experimental evidence was not judged to be conclusive and concerns (related to circulation initiation and the scalability of the behavior from the sub-scale experiment to full-scale plant configurations) remain regarding the veracity of these circulations. Because of these concerns and because the effect of including cold leg circulations in the RELAP5 simulations is nonconservative for PTS (i.e., it results in warmer reactor vessel downcomer temperatures), same-loop cold leg circulations were prevented in the RELAP5 PTS plant simulations for LOCA events. The cold leg circulations were prevented by implementing large reverse flow loss coefficients (1.0E5, based on the cold leg pipe flow area) in the reactor coolant pump regions of the RELAP5 model. The model change is implemented at the time during the event sequence when the reactor coolant pump coast-down is complete.

A tabulation of the key parameters for the three study plants relevant to PTS is presented in Table 8.1, while [*Arcieri-Base*] explains the TH models in detail.

8.2.3 PFM

A separate report [*Dickson-Base*] provides full details of the plant-specific input values for each of the three plants. These inputs include the following:

- Composition and Mechanical Property Data: As detailed in Section 7.7.1.2 of this report and in Appendix D of [*EricksonKirk-PFM*] FAVOR models the uncertainty in the input variables of Cu, Ni, P, unirradiated RT_{NDT}, and unirradiated Charpy upper shelf energy. The data on which the distributions that

FAVOR samples are based are drawn from *all data available* for the entire population of RPV-grade ferritic steels and their weldments. Consequently, these distributions overestimate (sometimes significantly so) the degree of uncertainty in these input variables relative to that characteristic of a *particular* weld, plate, or forging in a *particular* PWR. The mean values of Cu, Ni, P, unirradiated RT_{NDT}, and unirradiated Charpy upper shelf energy about which these distributions are located are modeled as being specific to the particular welds, plates, and forgings in the particular plants. These input values, which are summarized in Table 8.2 are drawn from the NRC's Reactor Vessel Integrity Database [RVID2]. RVID2 was developed based on information obtained from licensee responses to NRC Generic Letter 92-01, Revision 1 and its 1995 supplement [GL9201R1, Strosnider 94, GL9201R1S1]. GL-92-01 was issued to resolve questions arising out of the staff's review of the Yankee Rowe PWR in the early 1990s. In reviewing the licensee's submittal, the staff noted that chemical composition and reference temperature information was not available for the specific materials from which Yankee was constructed. To prevent occurrence of this problem at other plants GL-92-01 required licensees to provide to the NRC all of their vessel-specific composition and mechanical property data. The 1995 supplement to GL-92-01 [GL9201R1S1] continued and broadened this data collection effort when the staff noted that licensees were not always able to consider all pertinent data in their submittals because of both proprietary issues associated with some data sets and because no single source of all the material property data needed to support reactor vessel integrity evaluations existed. As the consolidation of all the data obtained in response to GL-92-01 Rev. 1 (and its 1995 supplement) the information in RVID2 (and, consequently, in Table 8.2) provides a sound basis for the compositional and mechanical property models adopted in FAVOR.

- Flaw Data: As described in Section 7.5 and detailed by [*Simonen*], flaw distributions have been derived that apply to domestic PWRs in general. Nonetheless, these distributions have certain plant-specific aspects. Table 8.3 summarizes the variables that quantify the plant-specific features of the flaw distribution, and the basis for these variables.

- Locations of Welds, Plates, and Forgings within the Vessel Beltline, and Fluence: Plant-specific information is needed regarding the spatial arrangement of the different welds, plates, and forgings and on the variation of fluence throughout the beltline region of the vessels. Figure 8.1 provides an example of such information for Oconee Unit 1; see [*Dickson-Base*] for full details. Information regarding the spatial arrangement of the different welds, plates, and forgings is taken from construction drawings while fluence estimates are based on RG1.190 procedures. (See Section 7.6 of this report and [*EricksonKirk-PFM*] for details.)

Only those factors discussed above are defined on a plant-specific basis in this analysis. All other features not mentioned are justified as generic and treated as such. Details on models and variables treated generically can be found in Chapter 7, as well as in [*EricksonKirk-PFM, EricksonKirk-SS*].

8.3   Estimated Values of FCI and TWCF

This section begins with a presentation of our estimates of the annual frequencies of crack initiation (FCI) and through-wall cracking (TWCF) resulting from PTS for our three study plants for a range of embrittlement conditions (Section 8.3.1). We then examine the characteristics of the distributions that underlie these FCI and TWCF values (Section 8.3.2).

8.3.1 Overall Results

Table 8.4 presents FAVOR Version 04.1 estimates of the mean annual *FCI* and mean annual *TWCF* for Oconee Unit 1, Beaver Valley Unit 1, and Palisades at 32 and 60 EFPY[‡‡‡]. To estimate values of these metrics close to the *TWCF* limit of 1×10^{-6} events/year proposed in Chapter 10, it was necessary to increase the amount of irradiation damage beyond that likely during operational lifetimes currently considered possible. To do so, we performed analyses for some very long operating lifetimes (designated as Ext-A and Ext-B in the table), thereby increasing the fluence and, consequently, the irradiation damage. The range of irradiation exposures examined includes conditions both below and above the current 10 CFR 50.61 RT_{PTS} screening limits.

The results in Table 8.4 demonstrate that even at the end of license extension (60 operational years, or 48 EFPY at an 80% capacity factor) the mean estimated through-wall cracking frequency (*TWCF*) does not exceed 2×10^{-8}/year. Considering that the Beaver Valley and Palisades RPVs are constructed from some of the most irradiation-sensitive materials in commercial reactor service today, these results suggest that, provided operating practices do not change dramatically in the future, the operating reactor fleet is in little danger of exceeding the *TWCF* acceptance criterion of 5×10^{-6}/yr expressed by Regulatory Guide 1.154 [RG 1.154][§§§], even after license extension.

8.3.2 Distribution Characteristics

To present our analysis results for all three plants in as compact a format as possible, we report only mean values of FCI and TWCF in Table 8.4. Nonetheless, since a systematic treatment of uncertainties is key to our objective of developing a risk-informed revision to 10 CFR 50.61, it is important to examine the characteristics of the distributions that underlie these mean values. As illustrated in Figure 8.2 using Beaver Valley as a characteristic example, the TWCF distributions are both very broad and highly skewed toward zero. As described in the following sections, both the skewness and the spread in these results are expected because both of these characteristics result directly from the physical features of cleavage fracture.

8.3.2.1 Skewness in the TWCF Distribution

The skewness in the TWCF distributions illustrated in Figure 8.2 results directly from the physical nature of cleavage crack initiation and arrest. The crack initiation (K_{Ic}) and crack arrest (K_{Ia}) toughness distributions both have finite lower bound values that are physically justified [*EricksonKirk-PFM*]. The following three mathematical conditions all lead to a likelihood of through-wall cracking that is zero *by definition* (not just a very small number):

- If the applied-K_I value for a particular FAVOR simulation run (i.e., a particular crack in a particular location subjected to a particular TH transient) never exceeds the 0th percentile K_{Ic} value, then the crack has zero probability of crack initiation and (consequently) zero probability of through-wall cracking.

- If the applied-K_I value for a particular simulation run exceeds the 0th percentile K_{Ic} value, but exceeds it at a time when the applied-K_I value is dropping with time (i.e., $dK_I/dt \leq 0$), then warm pre-stress has occurred and the crack has zero probability of crack initiation and (consequently) zero probability of through-wall cracking.

[‡‡‡] The table also includes a number of different reference temperature metrics, the significance of which is discussed in Section 8.4.

[§§§] Specifically, Section 9 of Regulatory Guide 1.154 makes the following statement: *"This Regulatory Guide outlines the analyses that should be performed in support of any request to operate at RT_{PTS} values in excess of 270°F ... and states that the staff's primary acceptance criterion will be licensee demonstration that through-wall cracking frequency will be below 5×10^{-6} per reactor year for such operation."*

- If the applied-K_I value for a particular simulation run exceeds the minimum K_{Ic} at a time when the applied-K_I value is increasing with time (i.e., $dK_I/dt > 0$), then the crack has a non-zero probability of crack initiation. However, if while the crack is propagating through the RPV wall, the applied-K_I value falls below the minimum K_{Ia} value then the crack arrest must occur. Such a crack would provide no contribution to the through-wall cracking frequency.

Table 8.1.   Summary of Plant Parameters Relevant to the PTS Evaluation

Description	Oconee	Beaver Valley	Palisades
Reactor thermal power	2568 MWt	2660 MWt	2530 MWt
Primary code safety valve opening pressure	17.34 MPa (2515 psia)	17.27 MPa (2505 psia)	Three valves with staggered opening setpoints of 17.24, 17.51 and 17.79 MPa (2500, 2540 and 2580 psia).
Primary code safety valve capacity	Two valves each with a capacity of 43.47 kg/s (345,000 lbm/hr) at 16.89 MPa (2450 psia).	Three valves each with a capacity of 62.77 kg/s (498,206 lbm/hr) at 17.24 MPa (2500 psia).	Three valves each with a capacity of 28.98 kg/s (230,000 lbm/hr) at 17.75 MPa (2575 psia).
Pressurizer PORV opening pressure	17.0 MPa (2465 psia)	The first PORV is controlled by a compensated error signal. The error [pressurizer pressure − 15.51 MPa (2250 psia) is processed with a proportional plus integral controller. This PORV begins to open when the compensated error is ≥ 0.69 MPa (100 psi) and closes when the compensated pressure error < 0.62 MPa (90 psi). The second and third PORVs open when the pressurizer pressure is ≥ 16.2 MPa (2350 psia) and close when pressure < 16.1 MPa (2340 psia).	Two valves, both with an opening setpoint pressure of 16.55 MPa (2400 psia). Note that closed block valves prevent the function of pressure relief through these valves during normal plant operation.
PORV capacity	Estimated flow rate is 16.03 kg/s (127,000 lbm/hr) at 16.9 MPa (2450 psia).	Three valves each with a capacity of 26.46 kg/s (210,000 lbm/hr) at 16.2 MPa (2350 psia)	Two valves each with a capacity of 61.46 kg/s (487,800 lbm/hr) at 16.55 MPa (2400 psia).

Description	Oconee	Beaver Valley	Palisades
LPI injection actuation setpoint	3.89 MPa (550 psig).	SIAS signal: pressurizer pressure ≤ 12.72 MPa (1845 psia), high steamline DP (steamline pressure < header pressure by 0.69 MPa (100 psi) or more), or steamline pressure ≤ 3.47 MPa (503 psia).	Pressurizer pressure less than 10.98 MPa (1593 psia) with a 27-second time delay.
LPI pump shutoff head	1.48 MPa (214 psia)	1.48 MPa (214.7 psia)	1.501 MPa (217.7 psia).
LPI pump runout flow	504.5 kg/s (1110 lbm/s) total for two pumps.	313.4 kg/s (690.84 lbm/s) total for the three loops.	433.5 kg/s (955.7 lbm/s) total for the four loops.
HPI injection actuation setpoint	11.07 MPa (1605 psia)	SIAS signal: pressurizer pressure ≤12.72 MPa (1845 psia), high steamline DP (steamline pressure < header pressure by 0.69 MPa (100 psi) or more), or steamline pressure ≤3.47 MPa (503 psia).	Pressurizer pressure less than 10.98 MPa (1593 psia) with a 27-second time delay.
HPI pump shutoff head	> 18.61 MPa (2700 psia)	>17.93 MPa (2600 psia)	8.906 MPa (1291.7 psia).
HPI pump runout flow	80.9 kg/s (178.2 lbm/s) total for the four loops.	61.12 kg/s (134.7 lbm/s) total for the three loops.	86.49 kg/s (190.7 lbm/s) total for the four loops.
Reactor coolant pump trip setpoint	No automatic trips on the reactor coolant pump. Operator is assumed to trip RCPs at 0.28 K (0.5°F) subcooling.	No automatic trips on the reactor coolant pumps. Operator is assumed to trip RCPs when the differential pressure between the RCS and the highest SG pressure was less than 2.59 MPa (375 psig).	No automatic pump trips. Procedures instruct the operators to trip two RCPs (one in each loop) if pressurizer pressure falls below 8.96 MPa (1300 psia) and to trip all pumps if RCS subcooling falls below 13.9 K (25°F) or if containment pressure exceeds 0.127 MPa (18.4 psia).
SG safety valve bank opening pressure	The lowest relief valve setpoint is 6.76 MPa (980 psia).	The lowest relief valve setpoint is 7.51 MPa (1090 psig).	The lowest MSSV opening setpoint pressure is 7.097 MPa (1029.3 psia).
SG atmospheric steam dumps opening criteria	Not included in the RELAP5 model.	Opening pressure of 7.24 MPa (1050 psia).	Open to control the RCS average temperature to 551 K (532°F)

Description	Oconee	Beaver Valley	Palisades
Number of main steam isolation valves	None.	One per steam line.	One per steam line.
Location of steamline flow restrictors	None.	Located in SG outlet nozzles.	Located in SG outlet nozzles.
Isolation of turbine-driven EFW/AFW pump during MSLB	Isolated during MSLB by isolation circuitry	Requires manual operator action and would be done if needed to maintain SG level	Requires manual operator action and would be done if needed to maintain SG level.
Analyzed range of SI water temperature	Base case model assumptions for HPI and LPI nominal feed temperature is 294.3 K (70°F). CFT temperature is 299.8 K (80°F). Sensitivity cases for ECCS temperature due to seasonal variation: Summer Conditions HPI, LPI - 302.6 K (85°F) CFT - 310.9 K (100°F) Winter Conditions HPI, LPI - 277.6 K (40°F) CFT - 294.3 K (70°F)	Base case model assumptions for HPI and LPI nominal feed temperature is 283.1 K (50°F). CFT temperature is 305.4 K (90°F). Sensitivity cases for ECCS temperature due to seasonal variation: Summer Conditions HPI, LPI – 285.9 K (55°F) CFT – 313.7 K (105°F)	Base case model assumptions for HPI and LPI nominal feed temperature is 304.2 K (87.9°F). SIT temperature is 310.9 K (100°F). Sensitivity cases for ECCS temperature due to seasonal variation: Summer Conditions HPI, LPI - 310.9 K (100°F) SIT - 305.4 K (90°F) Winter Conditions HPI, LPI - 277.6 K (40°F) SIT - 288.7 K (60°F)
Refueling water storage tank water volume	Borated water storage tank water volume is 327,000 gallons (1,237,695 l)	Tank's useable volume is between 1627.7 and 1669.4 m³ (430,000 and 441,000 gallons).	889.5 m³ (235,000 gallons)
Containment spray actuation setpoint and flow rate	Total containment spray flow rate is 3,000 gpm (11355 lpm (1500 gpm/pump, 5678 lpm/pump)	Total containment spray flow is 334.4 liter/s (5300 gpm)	Containment spray is activated on high containment pressure at 0.127 MPa (18.4 psia). Total containment spray rate is 229.8 liters/s (3643 gpm).
CFT/accumulator water volume	2 tanks each with a water volume of 28,579 liters (7550 gallons)	3 accumulators each with a liquid volume of 29,299 liters (7740 gallons)	4 SITs each with a water volume of 29450 liters (7780 gallons).
CFT/SIT/ accumulator discharge pressure	4.07 MPa (590 psia)	4.47 MPa (648 psia)	1.48 MPa (214.7 psia)

Table 8.2. Plant specific material values drawn from the RVID2 database [RVID2]

Product Form	Heat	Beltline	$\sigma_{flow(u)}$ [ksi]	$RT_{NDT(u)}$ [°F] Method	$RT_{NDT(u)}$ Value	$\sigma_{(u)}$ Value	Cu	Ni	P	$USE_{(u)}$ [ft-lb]
Beaver Valley 1, (Designer: Westinghouse, Manufacturer: CE) Coolant Temperature = 547°F, Vessel Thickness = 7-7/8-in.										
PLATE	C4381-1	INTERMEDIATE SHELL B6607-1	83.8	MTEB 5-2	43	0	0.14	0.62	0.015	90
	C4381-2	INTERMEDIATE SHELL B6607-2	84.3	MTEB 5-2	73	0	0.14	0.62	0.015	84
	C6292-2	LOWER SHELL B7203-2	78.8	MTEB 5-2	20	0	0.14	0.57	0.015	84
	C6317-1	LOWER SHELL B6903-1	72.7	MTEB 5-2	27	0	0.2	0.54	0.01	80
LINDE 1092 WELD	305414	LOWER SHELL AXIAL WELD 20-714	75.3	Generic	-56	17	0.337	0.609	0.012	98
	305424	INTER. SHELL AXIAL WELD 19-714	79.9	Generic	-56	17	0.273	0.629	0.013	112
LINDE 0091 WELD	90136	CIRC WELD 11-714	76.1	Generic	-56	17	0.269	0.07	0.013	144
Oconee 1, (Designer and Manufacturer: B&W) Coolant Temperature = 556°F, Vessel Thickness = 8.44-in.										
FORGING	AHR54 (ZV2861)	LOWER NOZZLE BELT	(4)	B&W Generic	3	31	0.16	0.65	0.006	109
PLATE	C2197-2	INTERMEDIATE SHELL	(4)	B&W Generic	1	26.9	0.15	0.5	0.008	81
	C2800-1	LOWER SHELL	(4)	B&W Generic	1	26.9	0.11	0.63	0.012	81
	C2800-2	LOWER SHELL	69.9	B&W Generic	1	26.9	0.11	0.63	0.012	119
	C3265-1	UPPER SHELL	75.8	B&W Generic	1	26.9	0.1	0.5	0.015	108
	C3278-1	UPPER SHELL	(4)	B&W Generic	1	26.9	0.12	0.6	0.01	81
LINDE 80 WELD	1P0962	INTERMEDIATE SHELL AXIAL WELDS SA-1073	79.4	B&W Generic	-5	19.7	0.21	0.64	0.025	70
	299L44	INT./UPPER SHL CIRC WELD (OUTSIDE 39%) WF-25	(4)	B&W Generic	-7	20.6	0.34	0.68	(3)	81
	61782	NOZZLE BELT/INT. SHELL CIRC WELD SA-1135	(4)	B&W Generic	-5	19.7	0.23	0.52	0.011	80
	71249	INT./UPPER SHL CIRC WELD (INSIDE 61%) SA-1229	76.4	ASME NB-2331	10	0	0.23	0.59	0.021	67
	72445	UPPER/LOWER SHELL CIRC WELD SA-1585	(4)	B&W Generic	-5	19.7	0.22	0.54	0.016	65
	8T1762	LOWER SHELL AXIAL WELDS SA-1430	75.5	B&W Generic	-5	19.7	0.19	0.57	0.017	70
	8T1762	UPPER SHELL AXIAL WELDS SA-1493	(4)	B&W Generic	-5	19.7	0.19	0.57	0.017	70
	8T1762	LOWER SHELL AXIAL WELDS SA-1426	75.5	B&W Generic	-5	19.7	0.19	0.57	0.017	70
Palisades, (Designer and Manufacturer: CE) Coolant Temperature = 532°F, Vessel Thickness = 8½-in.										
PLATE	A-0313	D-3803-2	(4)	MTEB 5-2	-30	0	0.24	0.52	0.01	87
	B-5294	D-3804-3	(4)	MTEB 5-2	-25	0	0.12	0.55	0.01	73
	C-1279	D-3803-3	(4)	ASME NB-2331	-5	0	0.24	0.5	0.011	102
	C-1279	D-3803-1	74.7	ASME NB-2331	-5	0	0.24	0.51	0.009	102
	C-1308A	D-3804-1	(4)	ASME NB-2331	0	0	0.19	0.48	0.016	72
	C-1308B	D-3804-2	(4)	MTEB 5-2	-30	0	0.19	0.5	0.015	76

Product Form	Heat	Beltline	$\sigma_{flow(u)}$ [ksi]	RT$_{NDT(u)}$ [°F]			Composition[2]			USE$_{(u)}$ [ft-lb]
				RT$_{NDT(u)}$ Method	RT$_{NDT(u)}$ Value	$\sigma_{(u)}$ Value	Cu	Ni	P	
LINDE 0124 WELD	27204	CIRC. WELD 9-112	76.9	Generic	-56	17	0.203	1.018	0.013	98
LINDE 1092 WELD	34B009	LOWER SHELL AXIAL WELD 3-112A/C	76.1	Generic	-56	17	0.192	0.98	(3)	111
	W5214	LOWER SHELL AXIAL WELDS 3-112A/C	72.9	Generic	-56	17	0.213	1.01	0.019	118
	W5214	INTERMEDIATE SHELL AXIAL WELDS 2-112 A/C	72.9	Generic	-56	17	0.213	1.01	0.019	118

Notes:

(1) Information taken directly from the July 2000 release of the NRC's Reactor Vessel Integrity (RVID2) database.

(2) These composition values are as reported in RVID2. In FAVOR calculations these values should be treated as the central tendency of the Cu, Ni, and P distributions detailed in [*EricksonKirk-PFM*].

(3) No values of phosphorus are recorded in RVID2 for these heats. A generic value of 0.012 should be used, which is the mean of 826 phosphorus values taken from the surveillance database used by Eason et al. to calibrate the embrittlement trend curve.

(4) No values strength measurements are available in PREP4 for these heats [PREP]. A value of 77 ksi should be used, which is the mean of other flow strength values reported in this Table.

Table 8.3.   Summary of vessel specific inputs for the flaw distribution

Variable		Oconee	Beaver Valley	Palisades	Calvert Cliffs	Notes
Inner Radius (to cladding)	[in]	85.5	78.5	86	86	Vessel specific info
Base Metal Thickness	[in]	8.438	7.875	8.5	8.675	Vessel specific info
Total Wall Thickness	[in]	8.626	8.031	8.75	8.988	Vessel specific info

	Variable		Oconee	Beaver Valley	Palisades	Calvert Cliffs	Notes
SAW Weld	Volume fraction	[%]	97%				100% - SMAW% - REPAIR%
	Thru-Wall Bead Thickness	[in]	0.1875	0.1875	0.1875	0.1875	All plants report plant-specific dimensions of 3/16-in.
	Truncation Limit	[in]	1				Judgment. Approx. 2X the size of the largest non-repair flaw observed in PVRUF & Shoreham.
	Buried or Surface	--	All flaws are buried				Observation
	Orientation	--	Circ flaws in circ welds, axial flaws in axial welds.				Observation: Virtually all of the weld flaws in PVRUF & Shoreham were aligned with the welding direction because they were lack of sidewall fusion defects.
	Density basis	--	Shoreham density				Highest of observations
	Aspect ratio basis	--	Shoreham & PVRUF observations				Statistically similar distributions from Shoreham and PVRUF were combined to provide more robust estimates, when based on judgment the amount data were limited and/or insufficient to identify different trends for aspect ratios for flaws in the two vessels.
	Depth basis	--	Shoreham & PVRUF observations				Statistically similar distributions combined to provide more robust estimates

	Variable		Oconee	Beaver Valley	Palisades	Calvert Cliffs	Notes
SMAW Weld	Volume fraction	[%]	1%				Upper bound to all plant-specific info provided by Steve Byrne (Westinghouse – Windsor).
	Thru-Wall Bead Thickness	[in]	0.21	0.20	0.22	0.25	Oconee is generic value based on average of all plants specific values (including Shoreham & PVRUF data). Other values are plant-specific as reported by Steve Byrne.
	Truncation Limit	[in]	1				Judgment. Approx. 2X the size of the largest non-repair flaw observed in PVRUF & Shoreham.

	Variable						Notes
	Buried or Surface	--	All flaws are buried				Observation
	Orientation	--	Circ flaws in circ welds, axial flaws in axial welds.				Observation: Virtually all of the weld flaws in PVRUF & Shoreham were aligned with the welding direction because they were lack of sidewall fusion defects.
	Density basis	--	Shoreham density				Highest of observations
	Aspect ratio basis	--	Shoreham & PVRUF observations				Statistically similar distributions from Shoreham and PVRUF were combined to provide more robust estimates, when based on judgment the amount data were limited and/or insufficient to identify different trends for aspect ratios for flaws in the two vessels.
	Depth basis	--	Shoreham & PVRUF observations				Statistically similar distributions combined to provide more robust estimates

	Variable		Oconee	Beaver Valley	Palisades	Calvert Cliffs	Notes
Repair	Volume fraction	[%]	2%				Judgment. A rounded integral percentage that exceeds the repaired volume observed for Shoreham and for PVRUF, which was 1.5%.
	Thru-Wall Bead Thickness	[in]	0.14				Generic value: As observed in PVRUF and Shoreham by PNNL.
	Truncation Limit	[in]	2				Judgment. Approx. 2X the largest repair flaw found in PVRUF & Shoreham. Also based on maximum expected width of repair cavity.
	Buried or Surface	--	All flaws are buried				Observation
	Orientation	--	Circ flaws in circ welds, axial flaws in axial welds.				The repair flaws had complex shapes and orientations that were not aligned with either the axial or circumferential welds; for consistency with the available treatments of flaws by the FAVOR code, a common treatment of orientations was adopted for flaws in SAW/SMAW and repair welds.
	Density basis	--	Shoreham density				Highest of observations

Aspect ratio basis	--	Shoreham & PVRUF observations				Statistically similar distributions from Shoreham and PVRUF were combined to provide more robust estimates, when based on judgment the amount data were limited and/or insufficient to identify different trends for aspect ratios for flaws in the two vessels.
Depth basis	--	Shoreham & PVRUF observations				Statistically similar distributions combined to provide more robust estimates

	Variable		Oconee	Beaver Valley	Palisades	Calvert Cliffs	Notes
Cladding	Actual Thickness	[in]	0.188	0.156	0.25	0.313	Vessel specific info
	# of Layers	[#]	1	2	2	2	Vessel specific info
	Bead Width	[in]	1				Bead widths of 1 to 5-in. characteristic of machine deposited cladding. Bead widths down to ½-in. can occur over welds. Nominal dimension of 1-in. selected for all analyses because this parameter is not expected to influence significantly the predicted vessel failure probabilities. May need to refine this estimate later, particularly for Oconee who reported a 5-in bead width.
	Truncation Limit	[in]	Actual clad thickness rounded to the nearest 1/100th of the total vessel wall thickness				Judgment & computational convenience
	Surface flaw depth in FAVOR	[in]	0.259	0.161	0.263	0.360	
	Buried or Surface	--	All flaws are surface breaking				Judgment. Only flaws in cladding that would influence brittle fracture of the vessel are brittle. Material properties assigned to clad flaws are that of the underlying material, be it base or weld.
	Orientation	--	All circumferential.				Observation: All flaws observed in PVRUF & Shoreham were lack of inter-run fusion defects, and cladding is always deposited circumferentially
	Density basis	--	No surface flaws observed. Density is 1/1000th that of the observed buried flaws in cladding of vessels examined by PNNL. If there is more than one clad layer then there are no clad flaws.				Judgment
	Aspect ratio basis	--	Observations on buried flaws				Judgment
	Depth basis	--	Depth of all surface flaws is the actual clad thickness rounded up to the nearest 1/100th of the total vessel wall thickness.				Judgment.

	Variable		Oconee	Beaver Valley	Palisades	Calvert Cliffs	Notes
Plate	Truncation Limit	[in]	0.433				Judgment. Twice the depth of the largest flaw observed in all PNNL plate inspections.
	Buried or Surface	--	All flaws are buried				Observation
	Orientation	--	Half of the simulated flaws are circumferential, half are axial.				Observation & Physics: No observed orientation preference, and no reason to suspect one (other than laminations which are benign.
	Density basis	--	1/10 of small weld flaw density, 1/40 of large weld flaw density of the PVRUF data				Judgment. Supported by limited data.
	Aspect ratio basis	--	Same as for PVRUF welds				Judgment
	Depth basis	--	Same as for PVRUF welds				Judgment. Supported by limited data.

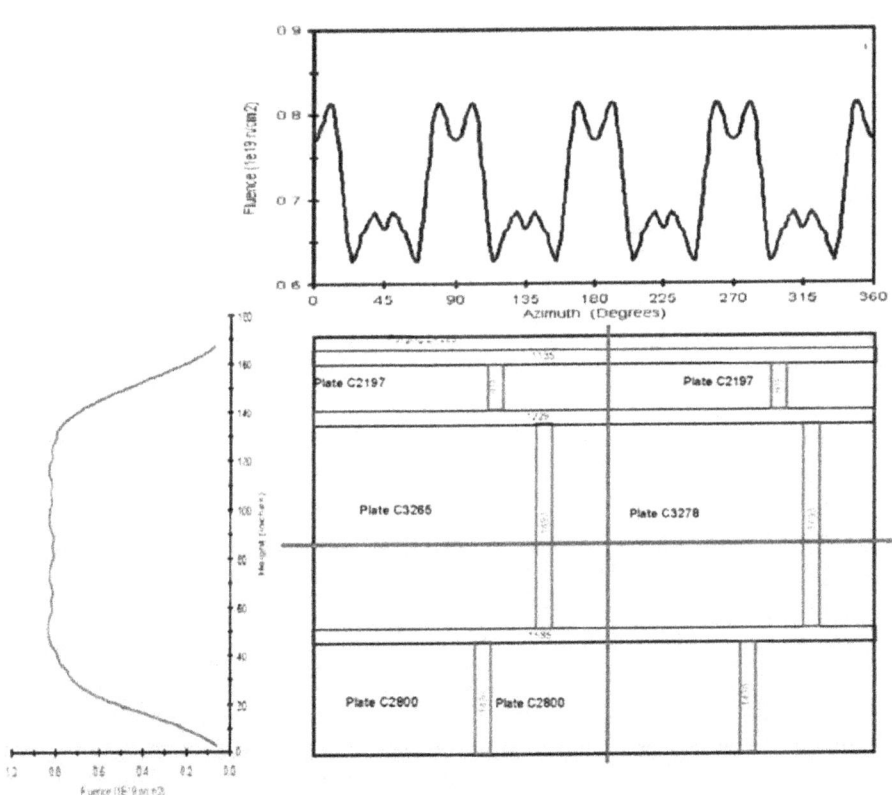

Figure 8.1.   Rollout diagram of beltline materials and representative fluence maps for Oconee

Table 8.4. Mean crack initiation and through-wall cracking frequencies estimated for Oconee Unit 1, Beaver Valley Unit 1, using FAVOR Version 04.1

Plant	EFPY[1]	RT_{PTS} [°F][2]	Axial Weld Fusion Line Reference Temperatures [°F]			Reference Temperatures Evaluated at Max Fluence on Vessel ID [°F]		Mean FCI [events/ year]	Mean TWCF [events/ year]
			Max RT_{NDT} in an Axial Weld	Max RT_{NDT} in a Plate	Weld Length Weighted Max RT_{NDT}	Plate	Circ Weld		
Oconee	32	221	152	76	134	79	175	1.29E-10	2.30E-11
	60	250	171	86	149	89	193	1.02E-09	6.47E-11
	Ext-Oa	323	232	131	200	136	251	1.01E-07	1.30E-09
	Ext-Ob	329	263	161	227	170	281	5.24E-07	1.16E-08
Beaver Valley	32	280	155	192	171	243	83	1.32E-07	8.89E-10
	60	299	175	210	188	272	102	5.19E-07	4.84E-09
	Ext-Ba	308	188	225	203	301	121	1.71E-06	2.02E-08
	Ext-Bb	312	207	250	226	354	155	8.87E-06	3.00E-07
Palisades	32	283	212	180	210	189	201	5.22E-08	4.90E-09
	60	311	230	196	227	205	215	1.23E-07	1.55E-08
	Ext-Pa	358	277	246	271	259	254	7.46E-07	1.88E-07
	Ext-Pb	372	333	316	324	335	301	4.47E-06	1.26E-06

1. All plants were analyzed for operational durations of 32 and 60 EFPY (or 40 and 75 operational years, respectively, at an 80% capacity factor. Each plant was also analyzed at two extended embrittlement levels (Ext-Oa and Ext-Ob for Oconee, for example) with the aim of obtaining mean through-wall cracking frequency values closer to the 1×10^{-6} limit proposed in Chapter 10.
2. RT_{PTS} is defined as per the equations and procedures of 10 CFR 50.61. Limiting materials in Oconee, Beaver Valley, and in Palisades are circumferential weld SA-1229, plate 6317-1, and axial weld 2-112 A/C, respectively.

In practice, these mathematical conditions are satisfied most of the time in the Monte Carlo simulations conducted using FAVOR (78% of the time in Beaver Valley at 32 EFPY, for example) because the simulated crack is small, the simulated toughness is high, and the simulated TH transient does not produce a very severe stress state in the RPV wall. However, on rare occasions, a larger crack will be simulated in a lower toughness material and subjected to a more severe transient. In these situations, the likelihood of developing a through-wall crack is higher. However, this combined sampling of the upper tails of many distributions happens only rarely.

8.3.2.2 Large Spread in the TWCF Distribution

The TWCF distributions illustrated in Figure 8.2 are very broad, spanning three or mode orders of magnitude from minimum to maximum. This characteristic again relates to the physics of cleavage fracture. As discussed in Section 8.3.2.1, the absolute lower bounds associated with both the K_{Ic} and K_{Ia} distributions leads to a large number of the Monte Carlo simulations producing a through-wall cracking probability that is, *by definition*, zero. However, on rare occasions, the tails of many distributions are sampled in the same simulation run, resulting in a larger crack being simulated to occur in a lower toughness material. This combined possibility of both zero and higher probabilities of TWCF leads to TWCF distributions that are naturally broad. As illustrated in Figure 8.2, the TWCF distributions tend to compress as the plants age because the more embrittled materials in these plants are less likely to produce through-wall cracking frequencies that are either very low, or zero.

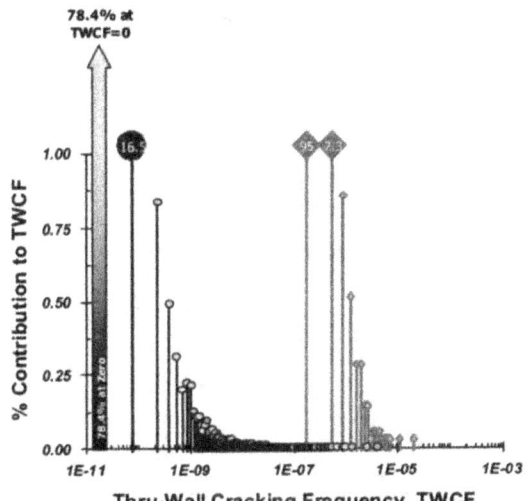

Figure 8.2. **Typical distribution of through-wall cracking frequency (as calculated for Beaver Valley at 32 EFPY (blue circles) and for extended embrittlement conditions (red diamonds)**

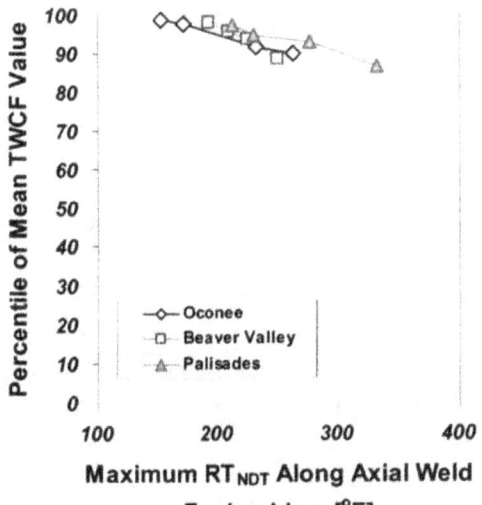

Figure 8-3. **TWCF distribution percentile corresponding to the mean value**

Because of the skewness characteristic of the TWCF distributions, the mean values reported in Table 8.4 do not lie close to the median value of the underlying distributions. In fact, as illustrated in Figure 8-3, mean TWCF values generally correspond to the ~90th percentile (and usually higher) over the range of embrittlement studied. Thus, the mean TWCF values are appropriately used to establish a revised PTS screening limit suitable for regulatory use.

8.4 Material Factors Contributing to FCI and TWCF

This section begins (in Section 8.4.1) with a discussion of the flaws simulated by FAVOR to exist in the RPV and the toughness properties that control the behavior of those flaws (i.e., if the flaw initiates, if the flaw propagates through the RPV wall). These considerations lead to several proposed "reference temperature metrics" that are can be used to correlate and/or predict the likelihood of fracture occurring in the various regions (axial weld, circumferential weld, plate) of the RPV beltline. We then discuss (in Section 8.4.2) the contribution of the various RPV beltline regions to the estimated FCI and TWCF values. In Section 8.4.3, we propose a procedure that accounts, at least approximately, for the different embrittlement levels in the three study plants to enable the comparison of similar transients at different plants presented in Section 8.5. We conclude in Section 8.4.4 with a discussion of how these results differ from those reported in December 2002 [*Kirk 12-02*].

8.4.1 Flaws Simulated by FAVOR, and Reference Temperature Metrics

When performing a structural flaw assessment, the location of the flaw or flaws being assessed needs to be known (along with many other factors) so that the resistance to fracture of the material at the flaw location can be either measured or estimated. The situation in this study differs somewhat from a routine flaw assessment because the flaws are simulated, and because hundreds upon thousands of flaws are being assessed. Nonetheless, the objective here is to correlate and/or predict the metrics that quantify the vessel's resistance to fracture:

CPI Conditional Probability of Crack Initiation. This is the probability that a crack will grow from its original size, conditioned on the assumed occurrence of a particular transient.

CPTWC Conditional Probability of Through-Wall Cracking. This is the probability that a crack will grow from its original size to the point that it propagates completely through the vessel wall, conditioned on the assumed occurrence of a particular transient.

FCI Frequency of Crack Initiation. This is the matrix product of the CPI value for each transient (including its uncertainty distribution) with the estimated frequency of that transient occurring (including its uncertainty distribution). FCI values are expressed per year.

TWCF Through-Wall Cracking Frequency. This is the matrix product of the CPTWC value for each transient (including its uncertainty distribution) with the estimated frequency of that transient occurring (including its uncertainty distribution). TWCF values are expressed per year.

In order to correlate and/or predict these metrics to quantify the vessel's resistance to fracture, some measure of the resistance of the materials in the vessel to fracture at the location of these many flaws is needed. A reference temperature (RT) establishes the resistance of a material to fracture, the variability in this resistance, and how this resistance varies with temperature. As described in [**EricksonKirk-PFM**] and as illustrated schematically in Figure 8-4, a reference temperature is commonly thought of as positioning the cleavage fracture toughness transition curve on the temperature axis. However, because relationships exist that establish the position of the arrest transition curve and of the upper shelf curve with respect to the cleavage reference temperature (see [**EricksonKirk-PFM**] for a full discussion), the toughness of ferritic steels can be fully descried by this single reference temperature. Since RT values can be estimated from information on vessel materials available in the RVID database [RVID2] and from information available from surveillance programs implemented under Appendix H to 10 CFR Part 50, they provide a way to estimate the resistance of vessel materials to fracture and how this resistance diminishes with increased neutron irradiation.

Figure 8-5 illustrates the location and orientation of the flaws that are simulated to exist in the RPV and the relationship between these flaw locations and the azimuthal and axial variations of fluence. (See [**EricksonKirk-PFM**] and [**Simonen**] for a more detailed explanation of the technical bases for these flaw locations and orientations.) The information in Figure 8-5 is summarized as follows for each of the simulated flaw populations:

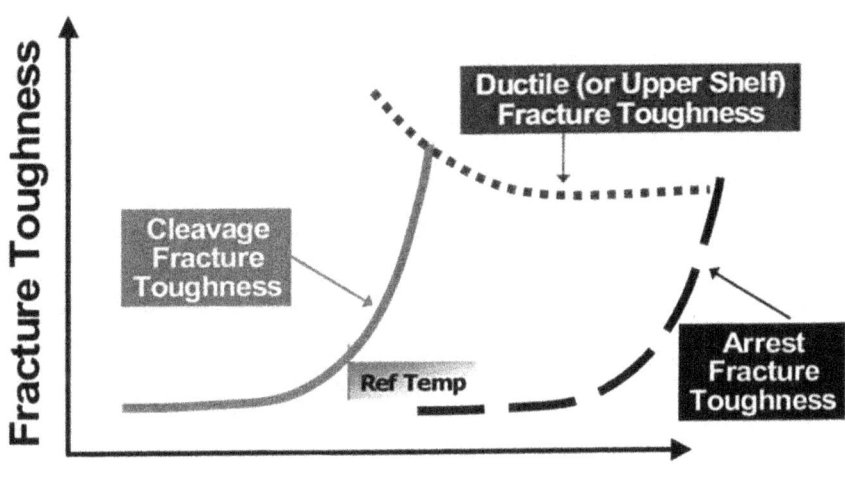

Figure 8-4. Relationship between a reference temperature (RT) and various measure of resistance to fracture (fracture toughness). This is a schematic illustration of temperature dependence only; scatter in fracture toughness is not shown.

- Embedded Axial Weld Flaws: The overwhelming majority of flaws in axial welds are lack of fusion defects, which occur on the weld fusion lines. Consequently, all of these flaws are oriented axially. The behavior of these flaws (i.e., if the flaw initiates, if the flaw propagates through the RPV wall) is controlled by the less tough of the plate or weld that lie on either side of the flaws. As illustrated in Figure 8-5, the axial fluence variation is relatively minor along most of the axial weld fusion line length. However, the large azimuthal fluence variation can expose each axial weld fusion line to have different fluences. The likelihood of vessel fracture from axial weld flaws depends upon (1) the total number of axial weld flaws (which scales with fusion line area), and (2) the fluence to which these flaws are subjected. Consequently, an appropriate metric to correlate/predict the likelihood of fracture from axial weld flaws would be weighted to account for variations in axial weld length and fluence level. Mathematically, the reference temperature metric for axial welds (RT_{AW}) is defined as follows:

$$\text{Eq. 8-1} \quad RT_{AW} = \frac{\sum_{i=1}^{nafl} RT_{MAX-AW}^{i} \cdot \ell_{FL}^{i}}{\sum_{i=1}^{nfl} \ell_{FL}^{i}}$$

where

$nafl$ is the number of axial weld fusion lines in the vessel beltline region,

ℓ_{FL} is the length of a particular fusion line in the vessel beltline region, and

RT_{MAX-AW} is evaluated for each of the axial weld fusion lines using the following formula. In the formula the symbol ϕt_{FL} refers to the maximum fluence occurring along a particular axial weld fusion line, and ΔT_{30} is the shift in the Charpy V-Notch 30-ft-lb energy produced by irradiation at ϕt_{FL}.

$$RT_{MAX-AW} \equiv MAX\left\{\left(RT_{NDT(u)}^{plate} + \Delta T_{30}^{plate}\left(\phi t_{FL}\right)\right), \left(RT_{NDT(u)}^{axialweld} + \Delta T_{30}^{axialweld}\left(\phi t_{FL}\right)\right)\right\}$$

- Embedded Circumferential Weld Flaws: The overwhelming majority of flaws in circumferential welds are lack of fusion defects, which occur on the weld fusion lines. Consequently, all of these flaws are oriented circumferentially. The behavior of these flaws (i.e., if the flaw initiates, if the flaw propagates through the RPV wall) is controlled by the less tough of the plate or weld that lie on either side of the flaws. As illustrated in Figure 8-5, the azimuthal fluence variation ensures that these circumferential weld cracks will somewhere be subjected to the maximum fluence that occurs anywhere on the vessel ID.

Flaws are equally likely to occur at any position around the circumference of the RPV, and the initiation / propagation of fracture from such flaws is more likely at higher fluences. Consequently, an appropriate metric to correlate/predict the likelihood of fracture from circumferential weld flaws would be a weighted average of the largest RT_{NDT} value associated with each circumferential weld fusion line when irradiated to the maximum ID fluence. Mathematically, the reference temperature metric for circumferential welds (RT_{CW}) is defined as follows:

$$\text{Eq. 8-2} \quad RT_{CW} = \frac{\sum_{i=1}^{ncfl} RT_{MAX-CW}^{i}}{ncfl}$$

where

$ncfl$ is the number of circumferential weld fusion lines in the vessel beltline region,

RT_{MAX-CW} is evaluated for each of the circumferential weld fusion lines using the following formula. In the formula the symbol ϕt_{MAX} refers to the maximum fluence occurring over the ID in the vessel beltline region, and ΔT_{30} is the shift in the Charpy V-Notch 30 ft-lb energy produced by irradiation at ϕt_{MAX}.

$$RT_{MAX-CW} \equiv MAX\left\{\left(RT_{NDT(u)}^{plate} + \Delta T_{30}^{plate}(\phi t_{MAX})\right), \left(RT_{NDT(u)}^{circweld} + \Delta T_{30}^{circweld}(\phi t_{MAX})\right)\right\}$$

It should be noted that at an equivalent embrittlement level, the likelihood of a circumferential weld flaw leading to through-wall cracking of the vessel is much lower than for an axial weld flaw. Even though circumferential and axial weld flaws are the same size because they are drawn from the same distribution, the variation of crack driving force through the wall of a cylindrical RPV differs considerably for circumferential and for axial flaws. Cheverton et al. describe how the application of a cold thermal shock to the inner diameter of a cylinder containing a flaw produces bending of the cylinder wall [Cheverton 85a]. This bending, originating from the contraction of the cold metal at and near the ID and the resistance to this contraction provided by the hotter metal deeper into the thickness of the cylinder, tends to be much larger for infinite length axial flaws than for infinite length circumferential flaws. A cylindrical geometry with an infinite axial flaw is asymmetric while a cylindrical geometry with an infinite circumferential flaw is symmetric. The asymmetry associated with the axial flaw degrades the cylinder's resistance to bending much more than the symmetric circumferential flaw (see Figure 8-6). It is for this reason that the applied-K_I of an axially oriented flaw continues to increase for cracks extending much deeper into the vessel wall than does the applied-K_I for a circumferentially oriented flaw (see Figure 8.7). The driving force peak that occurs for circumferential cracks provides a natural crack arrest mechanism that occurs in all RPVs because of their cylindrical geometry. Conversely, the applied driving force for axial flaws continues to increase as their depth increases, which leads directly to the ability of axial flaws to propagate all the way through the RPV wall.

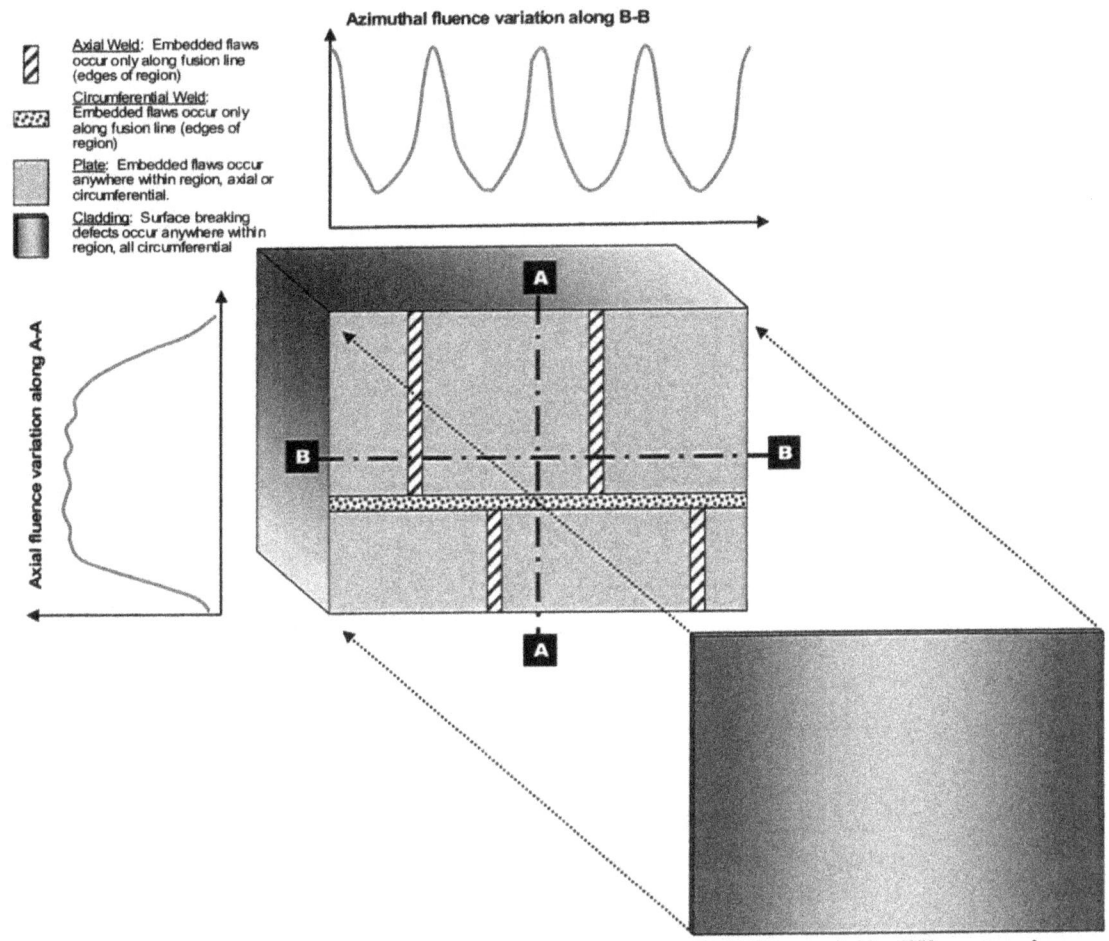

Figure 8-5. Location and orientation of flaws simulated by FAVOR to exist in different regions of the RPV beltline

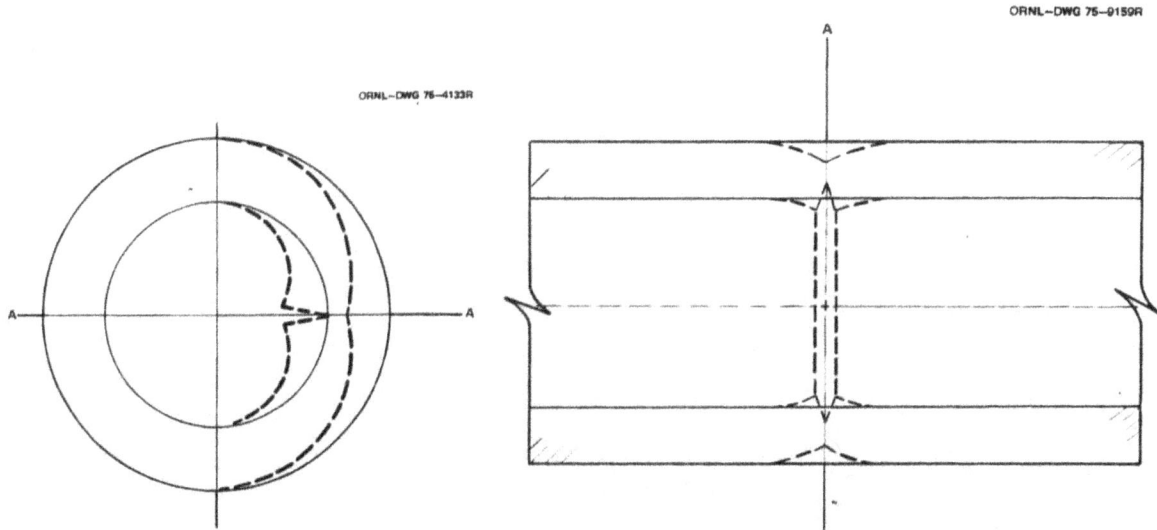

Figure 8-6. Effect of flaw orientation on the bending experienced by a cylinder subjected to a cold thermal shock on the inner diameter.

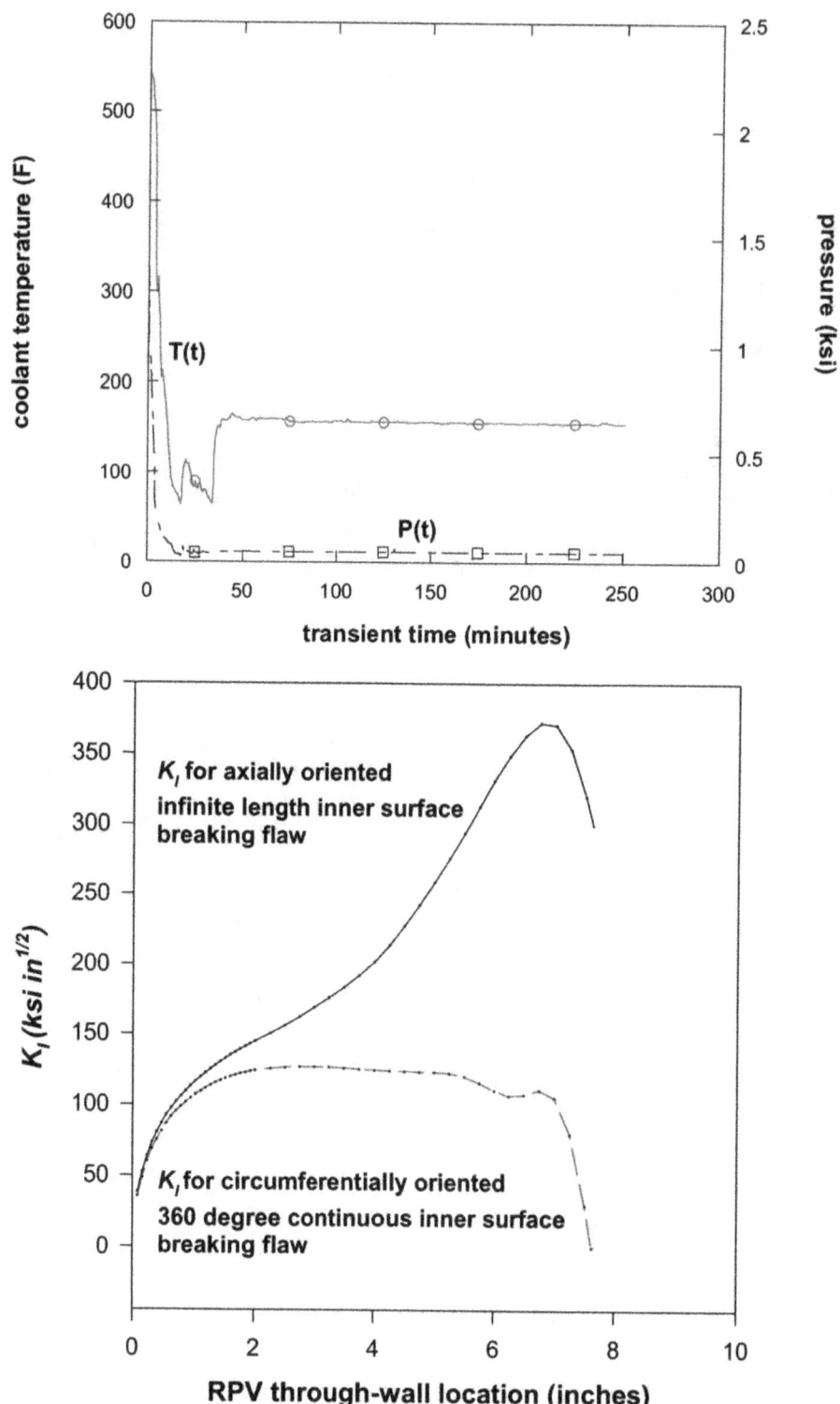

Figure 8.7. Through-wall variation of crack driving force (K_I): axially oriented flaws compared to circumferentially oriented flaws
(Comparison is shown for an 8-inch diameter surge line break in Beaver Valley (Transient #7 – see top plot) at a time 11 minutes after the start of the transient (see bottom plot).)

- Embedded Plate Flaws: Flaws in plates occur predominantly due to no-metallic inclusions. These can occur anywhere within the plate; they have no preferred orientation (i.e., they are equally likely to be axial or circumferential). As illustrated in Figure 8-5, the azimuthal fluence variation makes it certain that every plate will somewhere be subjected to the maximum fluence occurring on the vessel ID. Plate flaws are equally likely to occur at any position in the plate, so initiation / propagation of fracture from such flaws is more likely at higher fluences. Consequently, an appropriate metric to correlate / predict the likelihood of fracture from plate flaws would be a weighted average of the largest RT_{NDT} value associated with each plate when irradiated to the maximum ID fluence. Mathematically, the reference temperature metric for plates (RT_{PL}) is defined as follows:

$$\text{Eq. 8-3} \quad RT_{PL} = \frac{\sum_{i=1}^{npl} RT_{MAX-PL}^{i} \cdot V_{PL}^{i}}{\sum_{i=1}^{npl} V_{PL}^{i}}$$

where

npl	is the number of plates in the vessel beltline region,
V_{PL}	is the volume of each of these plates,
RT_{MAX-PW}	is evaluated for each plate using the following formula. In the formula the symbol ϕt_{MAX} refers to the maximum fluence occurring over the ID in the vessel beltline region, and ΔT_{30} is the shift in the Charpy V-Notch 30 ft-lb energy produced by irradiation at ϕt_{MAX}.

$$RT_{MAX-PL} \equiv RT_{NDT(u)}^{plate} + \Delta T_{30}^{plate}\left(\phi t_{MAX}\right)$$

It should be noted that at an equivalent embrittlement level, the likelihood of a plate flaw leading to through-wall cracking of the vessel is much lower than for an axial weld flaw for two reasons. First, half of all simulated plate flaws are oriented circumferentially, which reduces their driving force relative to axial flaws (see Figure 8.7). Additionally, plate flaws are generally much smaller than weld flaws. However, the azimuthal variation of fluence makes it virtually certain that some region of the plates will be subjected to a higher fluence (often a much higher fluence) than will the axial weld fusion lines. At some point, this added embrittlement to which the plate flaws are subjected will overcome the smaller plate flaw driving force caused by their smaller size (vs. axial weld flaws), causing the fracture of plate flaws to become more likely than the fracture of axial weld flaws.

- Surface-Breaking Flaws in the Stainless Steel Cladding: The only flaws simulated to break the inner diameter surface of the RPV occur because of lack of inner-run fusion between adjacent beads of weld-deposited stainless steel cladding. Since this cladding is always deposited circumferentially, these flaws are always oriented circumferentially, and they can occur anywhere over the entire ID surface of the vessel. All of the simulated flaws have a crack depth equal to the thickness of the cladding layer, so the toughness properties that control the behavior of these flaws (i.e., if the flaw initiates, if the flaw propagates through the RPV wall) are those of the axial weld, circumferential weld, or plate region that lie under the simulated location of the surface flaw. As discussed later in this section, FAVOR reports the contribution of these flaws to FCI and TWCF along with the contribution of the underlying axial weld, circumferential weld, or plate region. Thus, the contribution of these flaws to FCI and TWCF is addressed by the combination of RT_{AW}, RT_{CW}, and RT_{PL} making an independent reference temperature metric for flaws in cladding unnecessary. Furthermore, the circumferential orientation of these flaws makes their contribution to FCI and TWCF very small[****].

8.4.2 Effect of RPV Beltline Region on FCI and TWCF Values

As illustrated in Figure 8-5, the beltline region of a nuclear RPV is fabricated from different material product forms. All three vessels analyzed here are plate vessels and, therefore, are fabricated from heavy section ferritic steel plates roll formed to produce 120° or 180° degree segments. These segments are joined by axial welds to form a shell course, and then different shell courses are joined by circumferential welds to make the vessel. Two to three shell courses generally make up the beltline region of the vessel. An alternative fabrication practice, which avoids the need for axial welds, is to join ring-forged cylinders with circumferential welds. In Section 9.2, we address application of the results presented in this chapter (for plate vessels) to forged vessels.

In this report, we use the term "regions" to refer to the different product forms (i.e., plates, axial welds, circumferential welds, and forgings) that make up each RPV. As detailed in Table 8.2, each region has unique properties of chemical composition (which controls susceptibility to irradiation embrittlement), strength, and toughness. These properties also vary within the each region, see [*EricksonKirk-PFM*] and [*Williams*], respectively, for a description of our bases for characterizing this variation and of the statistical

models we have adopted in FAVOR for this purpose. Table 8.5 details the relative contributions these different regions make to the FCI and TWCF values reported in Table 8.4, demonstrating that these different regions (and their associated flaw populations) make widely varied contributions to the FCI and TWCF values, as follows:

- Circumferential Flaws: Circumferential flaws are responsible for a large portion of the FCI because the maximum ID fluence always interacts with a potential location of a circumferential flaw, but almost never with the potential location of an axial flaw. The consequential higher embrittlement frequently associated with circumferential flaws ($RT_{CW} > RT_{AW}$) leads directly to their role as dominant initiators[††††]. However, as illustrated in Figure 8.7, differences in how the driving force to fracture varies through-wall in a cylindrical vessel causes most of these initiated circumferential cracks to arrest before they propagate completely through the vessel wall and contribute to the TWCF. For this reason, circumferential cracks do not contribute to TWCF except in a very minor way at very high RT_{CW} values.

- Axial Flaws: Axial flaws are responsible for nearly all of the TWCF. In both Oconee and in Palisades, the toughness associated with the axial weld flaws is less than the toughness associated with the plate flaws ($RT_{AW} > RT_{PL}$) so the axial weld flaws control nearly all of the TWCF. In Beaver Valley, the toughness associated with the plate flaws is less than the toughness associated with the axial weld flaws

---

[****] At the extremely high embrittlement level simulated by the Ext-Ob analysis of Oconee Unit 1, cladding flaws contributed only 2.5% and 0.01% to the total FCI and TWCF (respectively). At the more realistic embrittlement levels represented by the 32 and 60 EFPY analyses, these flaws made no contribution to either FCI or TWCF.

[††††] This observation regarding the general dominance of circumferential flaws in controlling FCI does not apply to Palisades. In Palisades, the toughness along the axial weld fusion line is less than the toughness along the circumferential weld fusion line (i.e., $RT_{AW} > RT_{CW}$). This occurs because the chemistry of the axial welds in Palisades is more irradiation-sensitive than that of the circumferential welds, increasing their embrittlement despite the lower fluence along the axial weld fusion lines.

$(RT_{PL} > RT_{AW})$. Thus, in Beaver Valley, the plate flaws are responsible for some portion of the TWCF. However, they do not completely control the TWCF because weld flaws are much larger than plate flaws. Nonetheless, it is *always* the toughness properties that can be associated with axial flaws (i.e., the toughness properties of either the plate or of the axial weld: RT_{AW} and/or RT_{PL}) that control the TWCF. The toughness properties of the circumferential weld (RT_{CW}) play only a minor role and this only for highly embrittled materials (high RT_{CW}).

Table 8.5. Relative contributions of various flaw populations to the FCI and TWCF values estimated by FAVOR Version 04.1

EFPY	Reference Temperatures [°F]			Mean FCI	Mean TWCF	Apportionment by Originating Flaw Population					
						FCI[1]			TWCF[1]		
	RT_{AW}	RT_{CW}	RT_{PL}			Axial Welds	Circ Welds	Plates	Axial Welds	Circ Welds	Plates
Oconee Unit 1											
32	134	136	72	1.29E-10	2.30E-11	33.83%	66.16%	0.00%	100.00%	0.00%	0.00%
60	149	156	83	1.02E-09	6.47E-11	18.64%	81.35%	0.01%	99.90%	0.10%	0.00%
Ext-Oa	200	207	134	1.01E-07	1.30E-09	8.82%	90.82%	0.35%	99.83%	0.16%	0.00%
Ext-Ob	227	229	164	5.24E-07	1.16E-08	8.52%	90.78%	0.71%	99.81%	0.11%	0.08%
Beaver Valley Unit 1											
32	171	243	217	1.32E-07	8.89E-10	2.37%	96.01%	1.61%	68.44%	0.33%	31.23%
60	188	272	244	5.19E-07	4.84E-09	3.01%	94.26%	2.73%	39.19%	0.72%	60.09%
Ext-Ba	203	301	273	1.71E-06	2.02E-08	2.64%	93.04%	4.33%	15.69%	1.74%	82.55%
Ext-Bb	226	354	324	8.87E-06	3.00E-07	2.23%	91.02%	6.75%	9.21%	6.18%	84.62%
Palisades											
32	210	201	165	5.22E-08	4.90E-09	93.79%	6.22%	0.00%	99.95%	0.05%	0.00%
60	227	215	181	1.23E-07	1.55E-08	92.56%	7.44%	0.00%	99.97%	0.04%	0.00%
Ext-Pa	271	259	231	7.46E-07	1.88E-07	84.45%	15.41%	0.15%	99.91%	0.02%	0.08%
Ext-Pb	324	335	293	4.47E-06	1.26E-06	60.24%	38.58%	1.18%	98.62%	0.01%	1.37%

Note: (1) FCI and TWCF percentages may not add to 100% due to rounding.

8.4.3 Embrittlement Normalization between Different Plants

Section 8.5 examines the classes of transients that have the greatest contribution to FCI and TWCF. Part of this discussion focuses on the similarity/difference of the severity associated with the same type of transient at different plants (e.g., does a 4-in. hot leg break have a similar severity at the different analyzed plants, or must plant-specific factors be considered to accurately predict the severity of the transient?). These discussions form the beginning of our assessment of the general applicability of our results to all PWRs — a topic that Chapter 9 addresses in more detail. To perform these plant-to-plant comparisons of transient severity on an equivalent basis, it is important to be able to account for the differences in embrittlement level between the different analyses we performed. We use the reference temperature metrics RT_{AW}, RT_{CW}, and RT_{PL} introduced in Section 8.4.2 for this purpose.

As discussed in Section 8.4.2, the development of a single reference temperature to serve as an embrittlement metric for all plants is complicated by the following two factors:

- The fracture toughness varies widely throughout the pressure vessel (because of the combined influences of different chemistries in different regions and the fluence variation over the vessel ID).

- The distribution of flaws throughout the vessel; their size, location, and orientation; is non-homogeneous (for physically understood reasons).

Nonetheless, the toughness properties associated with axial cracks control the likelihood of developing a through-wall crack. In Oconee and in Palisades, these properties are described completely by RT_{AW} because ~100% of the TWCF is associated with the axial weld flaw population in these plants, irrespective of embrittlement level.

The situation in Beaver Valley is more complex because the high fluence levels remote from the axial weld fusion lines and the high irradiation susceptibility of the Beaver Valley materials create a situation where plate flaws and (at very high levels of embrittlement) circumferential weld flaws contribute to the TWCF. To reflect this, the reference temperature for Beaver Valley should lie between RT_{AW} and RT_{PL}. These considerations are reflected in the final column of

Table 8.6, which provides the reference temperature values used in Section 8.5. *It should be noted this approach to obtaining a single reference temperature is developed here **only** to support the transient comparisons performed in Section 8.5. Embrittlement metrics useful for estimating the level of PTS risk in PWRs **in general** are discussed and developed in Chapter 11.*

8.4.4 Changes in these Results Relative to those Reported in December 2002

While the specific numerical results reported herein differ from those in our interim report [*Kirk 12-02*], the general trends discussed in this section have not changed substantively from those reported earlier.

8.5 Contributions of Different Transients to the Through-Wall Cracking Frequency

8.5.1 Overview

As a first step toward assessing the transients that contribute most prominently to the overall TWCF, we divided the transients analyzed for each plant (see Appendix A for a complete list) into the following transient classes:

Table 8.6. Reference temperature metric used in Section 8.5.

Plant	EFPY	Reference Temperatures [°F]			TWCF Apportioned by Originating Flaw Population			Reference Temperature for Section 8.5 Comparisons [°F]
		RT_{AW}	RT_{CW}	RT_{PL}	Axial Welds	Circ Welds	Plates	
Oconee	32	134	136	72	100.00%	0.00%	0.00%	134 (=RT_{AW})
	60	149	156	83	99.90%	0.10%	0.00%	149 (=RT_{AW})
	Ext-Oa	200	207	134	99.83%	0.16%	0.00%	200 (=RT_{AW})
	Ext-Ob	227	229	164	99.81%	0.11%	0.08%	227 (=RT_{AW})
Beaver Valley	32	171	243	217	68.44%	0.33%	31.23%	185 (=RT_{AW} + 0.31·{RT_{PL}-RT_{AW}})
	60	188	272	244	39.19%	0.72%	60.09%	222 (=RT_{AW} + 0.61·{RT_{PL}-RT_{AW}})
	Ext-Ba	203	301	273	15.69%	1.74%	82.55%	262 (=RT_{AW} + 0.85·{RT_{PL}-RT_{AW}})
	Ext-Bb	226	354	324	9.21%	6.18%	84.62%	315 (=RT_{AW} + 0.91·{RT_{PL}-RT_{AW}})
Palisades	32	210	201	165	99.95%	0.05%	0.00%	210 (=RT_{AW})
	60	227	215	181	99.97%	0.04%	0.00%	227 (=RT_{AW})
	Ext-Pa	271	259	231	99.91%	0.02%	0.08%	271 (=RT_{AW})
	Ext-Pb	324	335	293	98.62%	0.01%	1.37%	324 (=RT_{AW})

Note: In Section 8.5, when the TWCFs of different plants are compared at "roughly equivalent" embrittlement levels, the results associated with the shaded rows are used.

LOCA Pipe breaks of any diameter on the primary side (see Tables A.1 and A.2)

SO-1 Stuck-open valves (that may later reclose) on the primary side (see Tables A.3 and A.4)

F&B Feed & bleed "LOCA" (see Table A.8)

MSLB Large diameter (or "main") steam line break (see Table A.5)

SO-2 Smaller diameter secondary side breaks, including stuck-open valves (see Table A.7)

SGTR Steam generator tube rupture (see Table A.8)

OVR Overfeed (see Table A.8)

MIX Mixed primary and secondary initiators (see Table A.9)

Figure 8-8, Figure 8-9, and Figure 8-10 illustrate the contribution to the total TWCF of each transient analyzed for Oconee. Beaver Valley, and Palisades, respectively. (Descriptions of the

transients that contribute more than 1% to the total TWCF are provided in Table 8.7, Table 8.8, and Table 8.9 for each plant.) These graphical depictions demonstrate that many of the transients analyzed contribute little or nothing to the TWCF while a limited number of transients dominate TWCF. In general, the contributions of primary side pipe breaks (LOCAs) and stuck-open valves on the primary side that may later reclose (SO-1) are the most important, collectively accounting for 70% or more of the total risk (see Figure 8-11). Stuck-open valves on the secondary side (SO-2) and breaks in the main steam line (MSLB) also contribute to TWCF, but to a more limited extent. Feed-and-bleed LOCAs (F&B) and steam generator tube ruptures (SGTR) do not contribute to TWCF in any significant way.

Figure 8-12 illustrates the annual frequencies of occurrence of the most risk-significant classes of events, where risk-significance is based on the information in Figure 8-8 through Figure 8-10. In Figure 8-12 the division between small and medium and medium and large break LOCAs occurs at approximately 4 and 8-inches (10.16 and 20.32-cm), respectively. Based on this information, the following observations can be made:

- Plant Effects on Frequency: The frequencies associated with Oconee and Beaver Valley are identical because these frequencies were established by the NRC's PRA contractors based on industry-wide data [INEEL99, INEEL00b] and based on limited plant-specific data. It was the view of these analysts that there were not enough differences between these plants and/or plant-specific data to support adoption of plant-specific frequencies. The Palisades frequencies differ slightly from those adopted for the other two plants for several reasons. Different analysts performed the Palisades PRA, so some differences are attributable to different interpretations of available data. Secondly, the Palisades PRA analysts adopted slightly different models to represent PTS risk than were used for the other two plants. Finally, the Palisades PRA analysis made use of some Palisades-specific information. Taken together, the small plant-to-plant frequency differences shown in Figure 8-12 arise, in part, because of both real differences between the plants and differences in modeling or judgment.

- Event Effects on Frequency: SO-2 events occur with the greatest frequency; approximately 0.02/yr. MSLB and SO-1 events are the next most frequent, but are approximately 10 times less likely than SO-2 events. All LOCA events are less likely still, as illustrated in Figure 8-12. The least likely event class is large-break LOCAs, which are approximately 3,000 times less likely than SO-2 events.

In the following subsections, we examine in further detail the four classes of transients that collectively account for virtually all of the TWCF: LOCA, SO-1, MSLB, and SO-2.

Sections 8.5.2 through 8.5.5 are structured as follows:

Step 1. Each section begins with a general description of transients in the class, how the transient progresses, what actions the operators take, and so on.

Step 2. We then review of all of the transients in the class that were modeled in each of the three study plants with the aim of describing how each transient class has been modeled. Additionally, this discussion points out plant-specific similarities/differences in our treatment of the transient class as regards the specific transients selected to represent the class as a whole.

Step 3. We then examine relationships between the systems-based characteristics of the transients in the class (e.g., break size, break location, HPI throttling at 1 vs. 10 minutes, etc.) and their thermal-hydraulic signature (i.e., their temporal variation of pressure, temperature, and heat transfer coefficient in the downcomer).

Step 4. The probabilistic fracture mechanics results are then discussed within the context of the thermal-hydraulic understanding developed in Step #2. Specifically we overlay on the TH transients the predicted times at which the vessel fails. This focuses attention on the part of the transient where differences in the TH signature can influence whether the vessel is predicted to fail or not. Particular attention is paid to determining the importance of operator actions in controlling the transient severity, and identifying if the results from these three study plant can be considered to apply to all PWRs in general.

Step 5. The discussion of each transient class concludes with a comparison of our current findings to those reported previously [Kirk 12-02] and those that established the basis for the current provisions of 10 CFR 50.61 [SECY-82-465].

Finally, in Section 8.5.6, we discuss classes of transients that do not contribute in any significant way to the total TWCF. These include SGTR, feed-and-bleed LOCAs, and transients that include a combination of failures in both the primary and secondary pressure circuits.

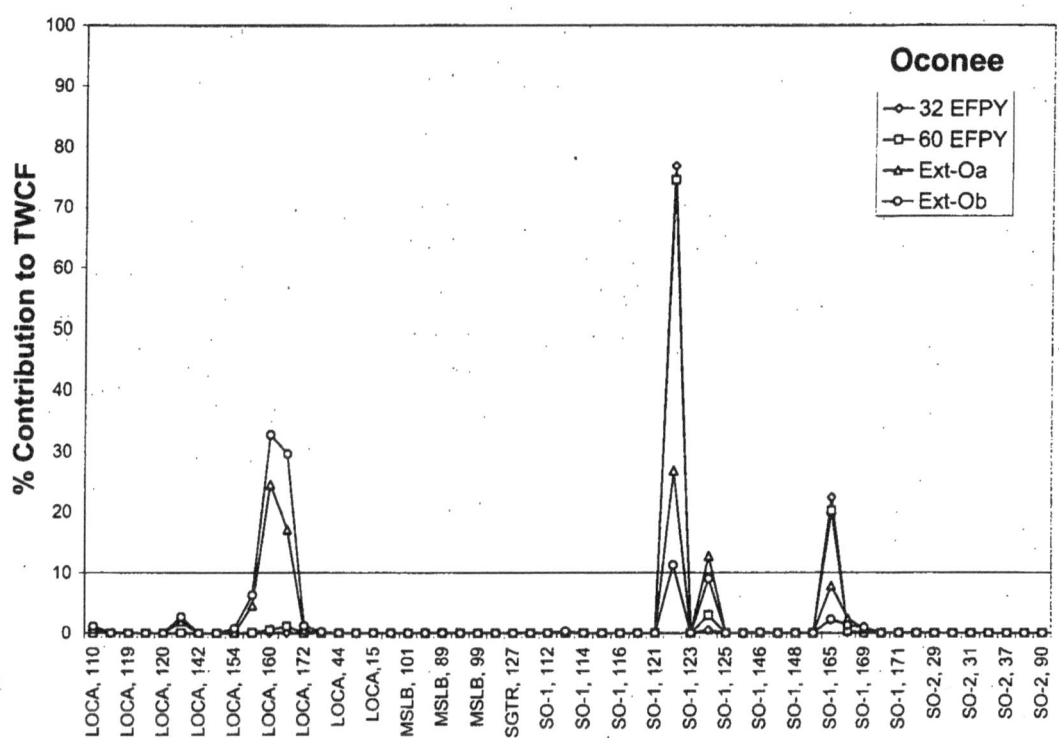

Figure 8-8. Contributions of the different transients to the TWCF in Oconee Unit 1 (Numbers on the abscissa are the TH case numbers, see Appendix A)

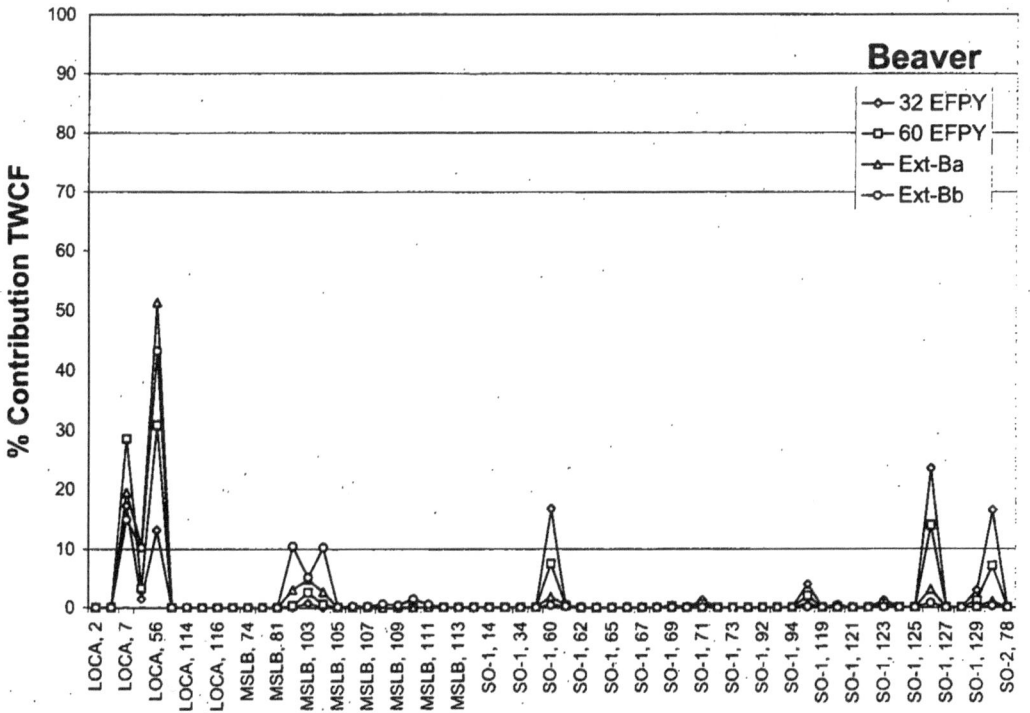

Figure 8-9. Contributions of the different transients to the TWCF in Beaver Valley Unit 1
(Numbers on the abscissa are the TH case numbers, see Appendix A)

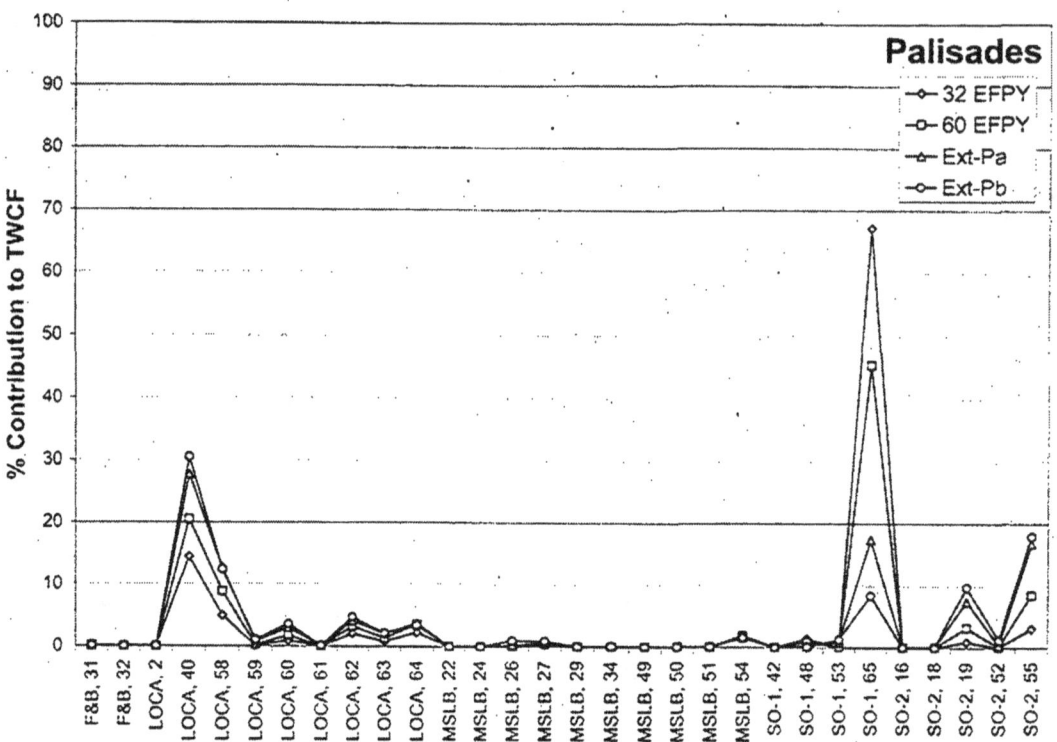

Figure 8-10. Contributions of the different transients to the TWCF in Palisades
(Numbers on the abscissa are the TH case numbers, see Appendix A)

Table 8.7. Transients that contribute most significantly to the estimated TWCF of Oconee Unit 1

Class	TH#	System Failure	Operator Action	HZP?	%
SO-1	122	Stuck-open pressurizer safety valve. Valve recloses at 6,000 secs.	Operator throttles HPI at 10 minutes after 2.7 K [5°F] subcooling and 100-in. (254-cm) pressurizer level is reached. (Throttling criteria is 27.8 K [50°F] subcooling.)	Yes	47%
SO-1	165	Stuck-open pressurizer safety valve. Valve recloses at 6,000 secs [RCS low-pressure point].	None	Yes	13%
SO-1	124	Stuck-open pressurizer safety valve. Valve recloses at 3,000 secs.	Operator throttles HPI at 10 minutes after 2.7 K [5°F] subcooling and 100-in. (254-cm) pressurizer level is reached. (Throttling criteria is 27.8 K [50°F] subcooling.)	Yes	6%
SO-1	168	TT/RT with stuck-open pzr SRV. SRV assumed to reclose at 3,000 secs. Operator does not throttle HPI.	None	Yes	1%
LOCA	160	5.66-in. (14.37-cm) surge line break. ECC suction switch to the containment sump included in the analysis.	None	No	15%
LOCA	164	8-in. (20.32-cm) surge line break. ECC suction switch to the containment sump included in the	None	No	12%

Class	TH#	System Failure	Operator Action	HZP?	%[1]
		analysis.			
LOCA	156	16-in. (40.64-cm) hot leg break. ECC suction switch to the containment sump included in the analysis.	None	No	3%
LOCA	141	3.22-in. (8.19-cm) surge line break [Break flow area increased by 30% from 2.83-in. (7.18-cm) break].	None	No	1%

Note: 1. The column headed "%" indicates the contribution of this transient to the TWCF averaged across all four embrittlement levels analyzed.

Table 8.8. Transients that contribute most significantly to the estimated TWCF of Beaver Valley Unit 1

Class	TH#	System Failure	Operator Action	HZP?	%[1]
SO-1	126	Reactor/turbine trip w/one stuck-open pressurizer SRV which recloses at 6,000 s and operator controls HHSI 10 minutes after allowed.	None	No	10%
SO-1	60	Reactor/turbine trip w/one stuck-open pressurizer SRV which recloses at 6,000 s.	None.	No	7%
SO-1	130	Reactor/turbine trip w/one stuck-open pressurizer SRV which recloses at 3,000 s at HZP and operator controls HHSI 10 minutes after allowed.	None	Yes	6%
SO-1	97	Reactor/turbine trip w/one stuck-open pressurizer SRV which recloses at 3,000 s.	None.	Yes	2%
SO-1	129	Reactor/turbine trip w/one stuck-open pressurizer SRV which recloses at 6,000 s at HZP and operator controls HHSI 10 minutes after allowed.	None	Yes	1%
SO-1	123	Reactor/turbine trip w/two stuck-open pressurizer SRVs which reclose at 3,000 s at HZP and operator controls HHSI 10 minutes after allowed.	None	Yes	1%
LOCA	56	4-in. (10.16-cm) surge line break	None	No	35%
LOCA	7	8-in. (20.32-cm) surge line break	None.	No	20%
LOCA	9	16-in. (40.64-cm) hot leg break	None.	No	6%
MSLB	102	Main steam line break with AFW continuing to feed affected generator for 30 minutes.	Operator controls HHSI 30 minutes after allowed. Break is assumed to occur inside containment so that the operator trips the RCPs as a result of adverse containment conditions.	No	4%
MSLB	104	Main steam line break with AFW continuing to feed affected generator for 30 minutes.	Operator controls HHSI 60 minutes after allowed. Break is assumed to occur inside containment so that the operator trips the RCPs as a result of adverse containment conditions.	No	3%
MSLB	103	Main steam line break with AFW continuing to feed affected generator for 30 minutes.	Operator controls HHSI 30 minutes after allowed. Break is assumed to occur inside containment so that the operator trips the RCPs as a result of adverse containment conditions.	Yes	3%

Class	TH#	System Failure	Operator Action	HZP?	%[1]

Note: 1. The column headed "%" indicates the contribution of this transient to the TWCF averaged across all four embrittlement levels analyzed.

Table 8.9. Transients that contribute most significantly to the estimated TWCF of Palisades

Class	TH#	System Failure	Operator Action	HZP?	%
SO-1	65	One stuck-open pressurizer SRV that recloses at 6,000 sec after initiation. Containment spray is assumed not to actuate.	None. Operator does not throttle HPI.	Yes	35%
SO-1	48	Two stuck-open pressurizer SRVs that reclose at 6,000 sec after initiation. Containment spray is assumed not to actuate.	None. Operator does not throttle HPI.	Yes	1%
SO-1	53	Turbine/reactor trip with two stuck-open pressurizer SRVs that reclose at 6,000 sec after initiation. Containment spray is assumed not to actuate.	None. Operator does not throttle HPI.	No	1%
LOCA	40	16-in. (40.64-cm) hot leg break. Containment sump recirculation included in the analysis.	None. Operator does not throttle HPI.	No	23%
LOCA	58	4-in. (10.16-cm) cold leg break. Winter conditions assumed (HPI and LPI injection temp = 40°F (4.44°C), Accumulator temp = 60°F (15.56°C))	None. Operator does not throttle HPI.	No	10%
LOCA	62	8-in. (20.32-cm) cold leg break. Winter conditions assumed (HPI and LPI injection temp = 40°F (4.44°C). Accumulator temp = 60°F (15.56°C))	None. Operator does not throttle HPI.	No	4%
LOCA	64	4-in. (10.16-cm) surge line break. Summer conditions assumed (HPI and LPI injection temp = 100°F (37.78°C), Accumulator temp = 90°F (32.22°C))	None. Operator does not throttle HPI.	No	3%
LOCA	60	2-in. (5.08-cm) surge line break. Winter conditions assumed (HPI and LPI injection temp = 40°F (4.44°C), Accumulator temp = 60°F (15.56°C))	None. Operator does not throttle HPI.	No	2%
LOCA	63	5.66-in. (14.37-cm) cold leg break. Winter conditions assumed (HPI and LPI injection temp = 40°F (4.44°C). Accumulator temp = 60°F (15.56°C))	None. Operator does not throttle HPI.	No	2%
LOCA	59	4-in. (10.16-cm) cold leg break. Summer conditions assumed (HPI and LPI injection temp = 100°F (37.78°C). Accumulator temp = 90°F (32.22°C))	None. Operator does not throttle HPI.	No	1%

Class	TH#	System Failure	Operator Action	HZP?	%
MSLB	54	Main steam line break with failure of both MSIVs to close. Break assumed to be inside containment causing containment spray actuation.	Operator does not isolate AFW on affected SG. Operator does not throttle HPI.	No	2%
MSLB	27	Main steam line break with controller failure resulting in the flow from two AFW pumps into affected steam generator. Break assumed to be inside containment causing containment spray actuation.	Operator starts second AFW pump.	No	1%
SO-2	55	Turbine/reactor trip with 2 stuck-open ADVs on SG-A combined with controller failure resulting in the flow from two AFW pumps into affected steam generator.	Operator starts second AFW pump.	No	12%
SO-2	19	Reactor trip with 1 stuck-open ADV on SG-A.	None. Operator does not throttle HPI.	Yes	5%
Note: 1. The column headed "%" indicates the contribution of this transient to the TWCF averaged across all four embrittlement levels analyzed.					

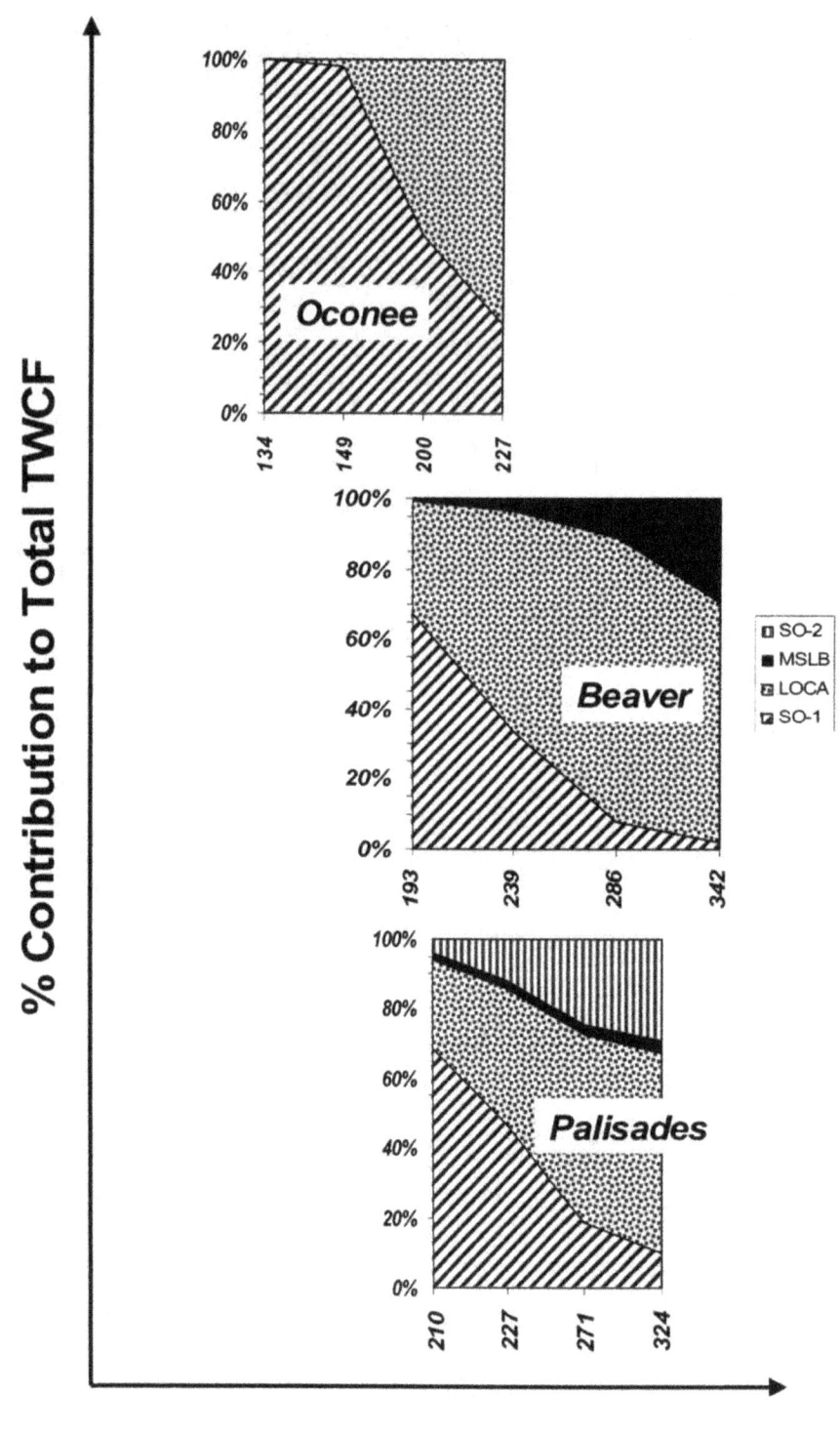

Figure 8-11. Variation in percent contribution to the total TWCF of different transient classes with reference temperature (RT) as defined in

Table 8.6. The contributions of feed-and-bleed LOCAs and steam generator tube ruptures were also assessed. These transient classes made no contribution to TWCF, with the exception that feed-and-bleed LOCAs contributed < 0.1% to the TWCF of the Palisades RPV.

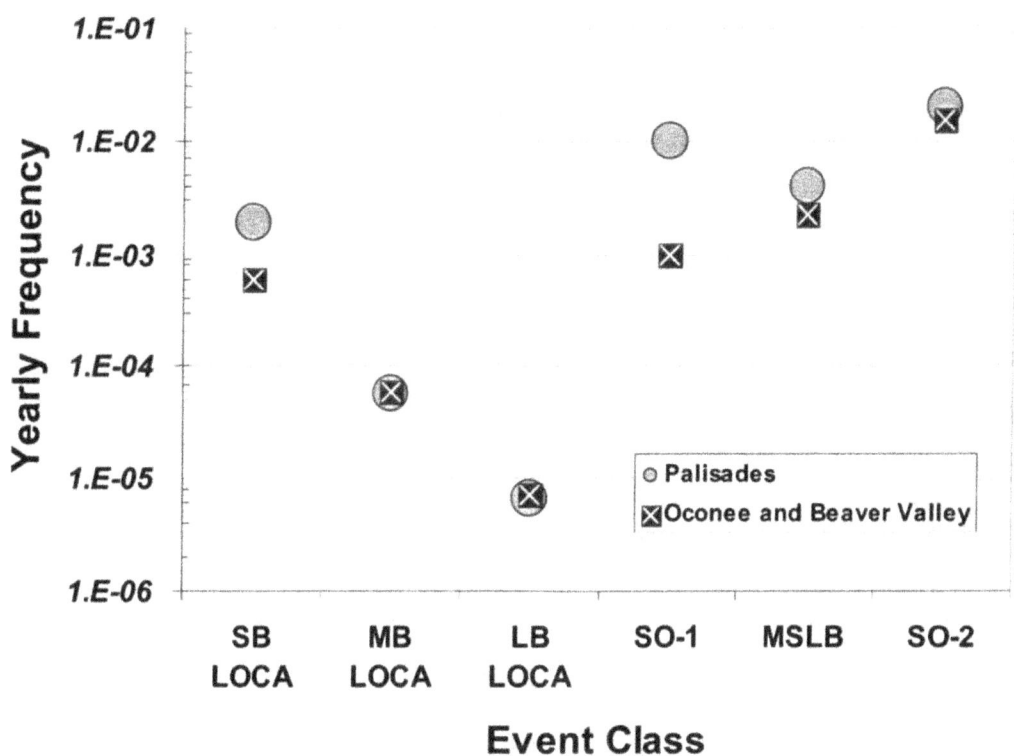

Figure 8-12. Comparison of the annual frequencies of various broad classes of events for full-power conditions

8.5.2 Primary Side Pipe Breaks

8.5.2.1 General Description of a Pipe Break Transient

Following a pipe break, the primary system cools by two mechanisms. The rapid depressurization caused by the break produces a rapid drop in system temperature because, under the saturated conditions that exist once a break occurs, pressure is linked to temperature via the ideal gas law. For large-diameter breaks, this pressure-induced temperature decrease dominates the primary system cooldown. As break size decreases, another cooling mechanism (the temperature and volume of the ECC injection water) becomes important. As indicated in Figure 2.1, ECCS pumps (e.g., HPSI, LPSI, etc.) all inject into the cold leg. Consequently, for cold leg breaks, some of the injection water is lost out of the break, never reaching (or cooling) the downcomer. In this situation, the volume of the cooling water lost is approximately proportional to the number of

cold legs. (For example, in a 3-loop plant, if one cold leg breaks, the injection flow reaching the downcomer is diminished by one-third.) Conversely, no cooling water is lost if the break occurs in either the hot leg or in the surge line. For this reason, cold leg breaks tend to be somewhat less severe (at an equivalent diameter) than hot leg or surge line breaks.

The minimum temperature to which the injection water cools the primary can depend on the ambient temperature outside the plant because both the HPSI and LPSI pumps draw from the RWST. In plants where the RWST is outside and uninsulated, the temperature of the cooling water is subject to seasonal temperature variations, which directly impact the portion of the downcomer cooling controlled by safety injection. The effect of seasonal temperature variations on cooling water temperature is a more important factor for smaller diameter breaks.

Additionally, factors such as the total volume of the inventory in the RWST and the pressures at which the safety injection pumps start can differ from plant-to-plant. These features influence the cooldown characteristics of pipe break transients for the following reasons:

- The total volume of the inventory in the RWST controls the time interval over which the ECCS can draw water from this source. If the transient continues after this time, the ECCS has to switch over to recirculation from the containment sump. Since the water in the sump has flowed out of the break, it is generally warmer (~120°F (48.9°C)) than water drawn from the RWST (as low as ~ 40°F (4.4°C) during the winter).

- For breaks of medium to small diameter (approximately 4-in. (10.16-cm) and below) the cooldown rate is sufficiently gradual that it can be influenced by the pressure at which the safety injection pumps start. Plant-specific differences can, therefore, influence the cooldown rate. Differences of this type occurred among the three study plants. Both Oconee and Beaver Valley have high-head HPSI that injects water immediately upon receiving a safety injection actuation signal (at ~ 1,700 psi). In contrast, Palisades has low-head HPSI pumps that inject water when the pressure falls below 1,300 psi.

8.5.2.2   Model of this Transient Class

As detailed in Appendix A, Tables A.1 (break diameters above 3.5-in. (8.9-cm)) and A.2 (break diameters below 3.5-in. (8.9-cm)) our modeling of primary side pipe breaks includes a spectrum of break diameters ranging from 1.4- to 16-in. (3.6- to 40.6-cm) because break size is the single most important factor that controls the rate of system depressurization and (thereby) the severity of the transient. No operator actions are modeled for any break diameter exceeding ≈3-in. (≈7.6-cm) because for these events, the safety injection systems do not fully refill the upper regions of the RCS. Consequently, operators would never take action to shut off the pumps. Other factors modeled include the following:

- break location (for smaller diameter breaks)

- season of the year (for smaller diameter breaks)

- total volume of the RWST inventory (controls the time at which cooling water begins to draw from the sump, which is warmer than the water stored in the RWST)

- pump start setpoints

8.5.2.3   Relationships between System Characteristics and Thermal-Hydraulic Response

8.5.2.3.1   Dominant vs. Secondary Factors

Primary side pipe breaks characteristically cause both a rapid cooldown and a rapid depressurization of the primary system. At long times, the temperature of the primary approaches the temperature of the injection water, which can be as low as 35°F (1°C) because it is stored in external tanks. As described in the previous section, the break area (i.e., $\pi \cdot (D_{BREAK}/2)^2$) is the main factor controlling the initial cooldown rate because break area controls the depressurization rate and the two are linked through the ideal gas law. Figure 8.13 illustrates this point for a spectrum of hot leg/surge line breaks in both Beaver Valley and Oconee.

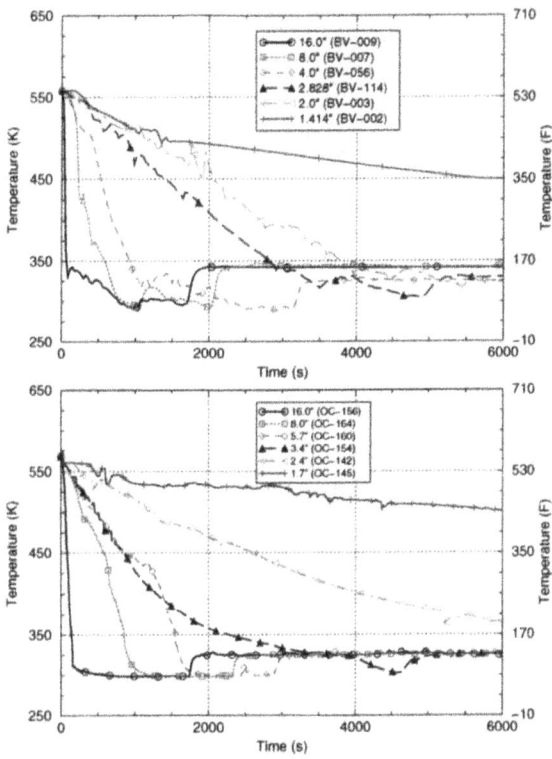

Figure 8.13. Effect of surge line and hot-leg break diameter on the cooldown characteristics of Beaver Valley (top) and Oconee (bottom)

Factors other than break size can alter the cooldown signature somewhat, but are generally less important than the dominating influence of break area. For example:

- Break Location: As described in the previous section, cold leg breaks are expected to be less severe than hot leg breaks at equivalent break diameter due to loss of injection water out of the break. However, as illustrated in Figure 8.14 the effect of break location is not so great as to take a break out of severity order as indicated by break size.

- Injection Water Temperature: Variations in injection water temperature occur both at the time in the transient when the volume of the RWST is exhausted and the HPSI/LPSI pumps start drawing off the sump and as a consequence of seasonal variations. The sudden increase in downcomer temperature evident at approximately 2000 sec. on the 8- and 16-in. diameter break curves in the top graph in Figure 8.13 indicates the time at

which the switchover to sump occurs. Figure 8.15 illustrates the effect of seasonal variations on cold leg breaks in Palisades. Again, break diameter is seen to be the dominant factor controlling the initial cooldown rate with seasonal factors playing a less important role.

Relative to differences in cooldown rate between different break sizes, differences in primary system pressure are more modest because safety injection flow cannot fully compensate for the loss of inventory out of these breaks. Figure 8.16 illustrates this point for a range of break sizes in both Oconee and Beaver Valley. Similarly, the effect of break size on differences in the heat transfer coefficient between different breaks is more modest, see Figure 8.17.

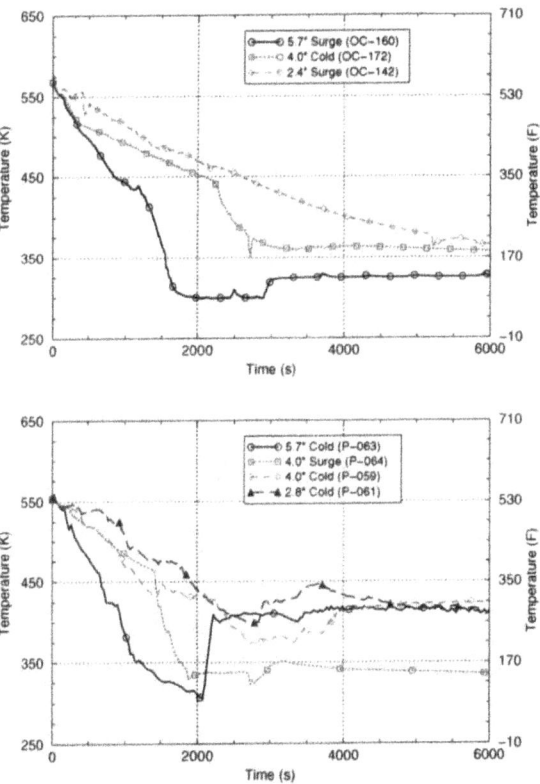

Figure 8.14. Effect of break location on the cooldown characteristics in Oconee (top) and Palisades (bottom)

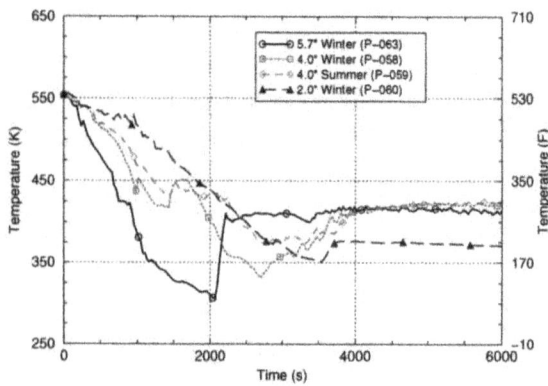

Figure 8.15. Effect of season on the cooldown characteristics of cold leg breaks in Palisades

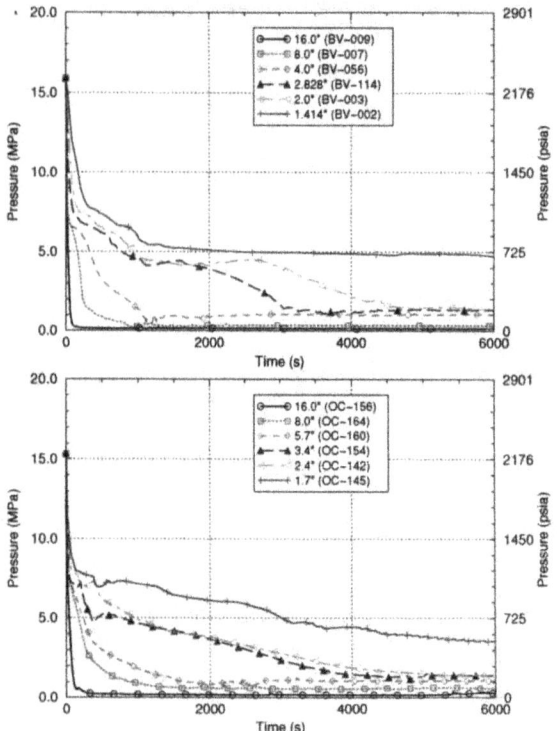

Figure 8.16. Effect of surge line and hot-leg break diameter on the depressurization characteristics of Beaver Valley (top) and Oconee (bottom)

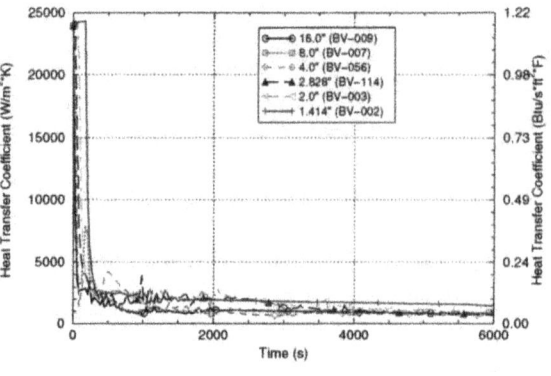

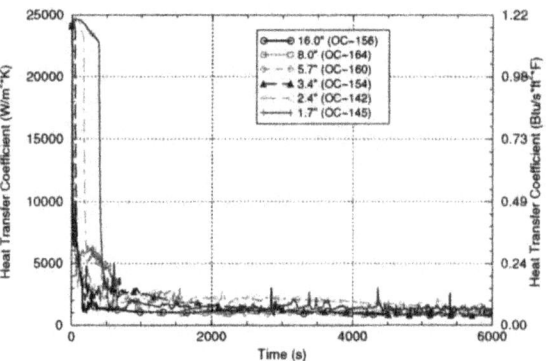

Figure 8.17. Effect of surge line and hot-leg break diameter on the heat transfer coefficient in Beaver Valley (top) and Oconee (bottom)

8.5.2.3.2   Plant-Specific Effects

Figure 8.18 compares the cooldown characteristics of different break sizes across the three plants modeled. For nominally identical conditions between plants (i.e., break size, break location, power level at transient initiation), the response of the three study plants is similar across the entire break size spectrum. This is because the cooldown rate is controlled (mostly) by the size of the break and the overall size, temperature, and pressure of the RPV in which the break occurs. In Figure 8.18, these factors are consistent plant-to-plant.

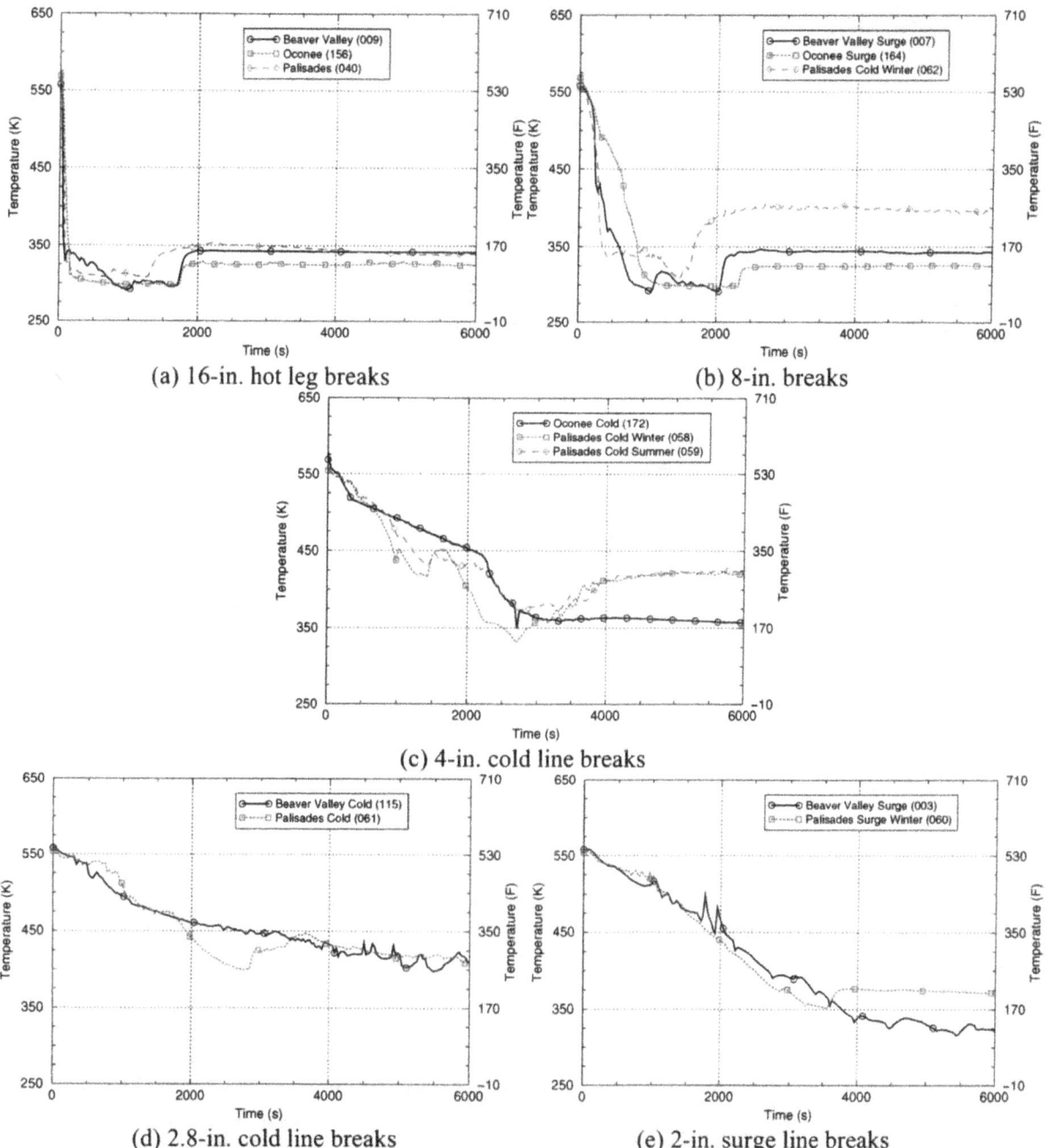

Figure 8.18. Comparison of the cooldown characteristics of the three plants modeled for a spectrum of break diameters

8.5.2.4 Estimates of Vessel Failure Probability

In Section 8.5.2.3, we identified break size as the factor that most significantly influenced the cooldown rate that results from a pipe break, with break location and season of the year playing more limited roles. We examine these

factors in the following subsections. Additionally, we discuss differences between the number of cracks initiated by pipe break transients *vs.* those that propagate through the wall, and information concerning the time differential between transient initiation (i.e., pipe break) and vessel failure. The section concludes with an assessment of the applicability of these findings to assessing the probability of vessel failure due to pipe breaks in general.

In the following subsections, we compare values of CPTWC for different transients taken from Tables A.1 and A.2. To obtain an approximately equivalent level of embrittlement across all plants these comparisons use results for Beaver Valley and for Palisades at 60 EFPY, while Oconee results are taken at the Ext-Ob embrittlement level (see Table 8.6).

8.5.2.4.1   Break Size Effects

Figure 8.19 shows the effect of break size on the CPTWC results for all three plants. Up to a break diameter of ~4- to 5-in. (~10.16- to 12.7-cm), CPTWC depends strongly on break diameter. By comparison, for larger break diameters, the CPTWC is essentially independent of further increases in break diameter. For these larger diameter breaks, the RCS fluid cools faster than the wall of the RPV. In this situation, *only* the thermal conductivity of the steel and the thickness of the RPV wall control the thermal stresses and, thus, the severity of the fracture challenge, perturbations to the fluid cooldown rate controlled by the break diameter, break location, and season of the year do not play a role. Thermal conductivity is a physical property, so it is very consistent for all RPV steels. Consequently, the single factor controlling the severity of the fracture challenge for large diameter pipe breaks is the thickness of the RPV wall because higher thermal stresses can develop in thicker walls. This effect of wall thickness is seen in Figure 8.19, where the CPTWC for the thinner vessel (Beaver Valley: 7.875-in (20-cm) thick) is consistently below that of the thicker vessels (Palisades and Oconee both have wall thicknesses of 8½-in) for break sizes above 4- to 5-in. (~10.16- to 12.7-cm). In Section 9.2, we discuss the effects of thickness on vessel failure probability in greater detail.

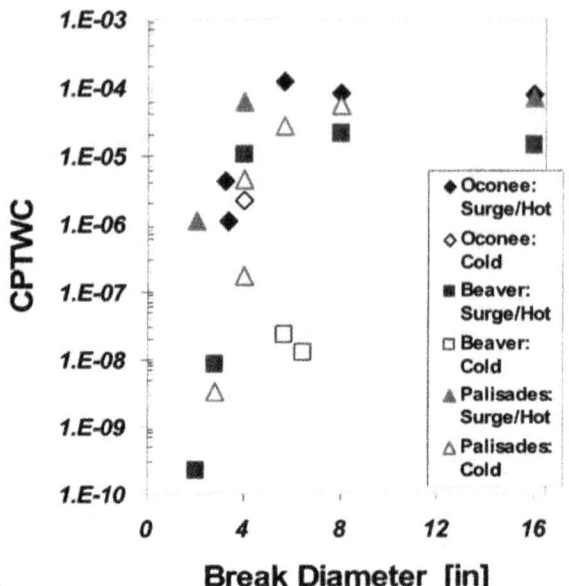

Figure 8.19. Effect of pipe break diameter and break location on the conditional probability of through-wall cracking. (CPTWC taken at approximately equivalent embrittlement levels between plants (Beaver Valley and Palisades at 60 EFPY, Oconee at Ext-Ob))

8.5.2.4.2   Break Location and Seasonal Effects

Figure 8.19 also illustrated the effect of break location. As discussed in Section 8.5.2.2 and illustrated in Figure 8.14, cold leg breaks are less severe than hot leg breaks across the entire break size spectrum because some portion of the ECC flow is lost out of a cold leg break. The magnitude of the influence of break location on CPTWC is negligible for conduction limited conditions (i.e., for large breaks) and increases with decreasing break size because it is for smaller breaks that differences in injection flow can have a significant effect on the fluid cooling rate. In the Palisades analysis the combined effects of break size and of seasonal variations were modeled in more detail than in the other two plants: Figure 8.20 shows these results. Focusing on the 4-in. (10.16-cm) diameter breaks, we see that the surge line break (summer conditions) has a CPTWC approximately 300 times greater than that of a 4-in. (10.16-cm) diameter cold leg break. The effects of seasonal variations are less important: at the 4-in. (10.16-cm) break size, a cold line break in winter has a CPTWC approximately 20 times greater than a cold line break in summer. It should be noted that seasonal variations are not important at all plants. Some plants have insulated RWSTs which mitigate the effect of outside temperature on the temperature of the ECC injection water.

breaks that contribute most significantly to the through-wall cracking frequency are ~1% for Oconee and Beaver Valley, and ~4% for Palisades. The lower ratios for Oconee and Beaver Valley are caused by the greater dominance of circumferential cracks as initiators in these plants (see Table 8.5).

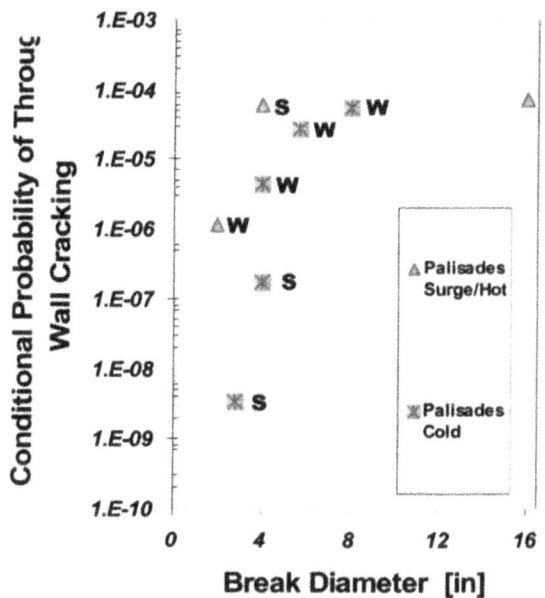

Figure 8.20. Effect of pipe break diameter, break location, and season (S=Summer, W=Winter) on the conditional probability of through-wall cracking for Palisades

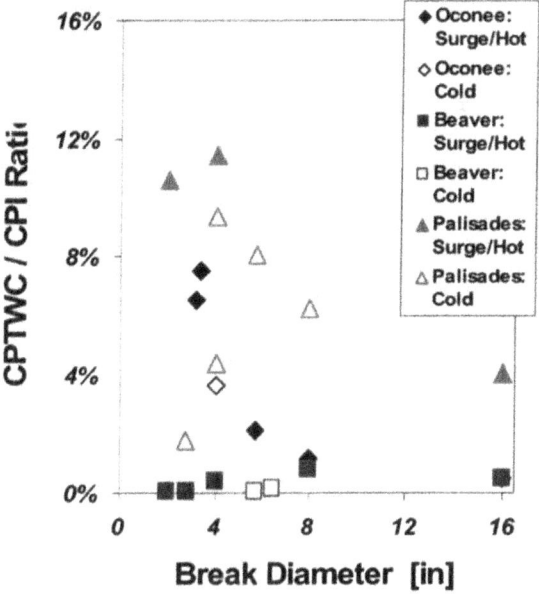

Figure 8.21. Effect of pipe break diameter and break location on the conditional proportion of initiated flaws that propagate through the wall. (CPTWC/CPI ratios taken at approximately equivalent embrittlement levels between plants (Beaver Valley and Palisades at 60 EFPY, Oconee at Ext-Ob).)

8.5.2.4.3 Differences Between Crack Initiation and Vessel Failure for Pipe Break Transients

Because of the lack of a significant pressure component during a pipe break (see Figure 8.16), these transients cause many more crack initiations than they do complete failure of the vessel wall. This is quantified in Figure 8.21 by the ratio of the conditional probability of through-wall cracking to the conditional probability of crack initiation. A ratio of 100% would indicate that all initiated cracks also propagated through the vessel wall. The maximum ratio for any pipe break analyzed is 12%. while the ratios for the large diameter

8.5.2.4.4 Time Between Pipe Break and Vessel Failure

As illustrated Figure 8.22, there is very little time (particularly for large breaks) between the initiating event (i.e., the pipe breaking) and vessel failure. If failure is going to occur as a consequence of a pipe break, it will happen within ~30 min. (1800 sec.) for 4-in. (10.16-cm) breaks. Vessel failures resulting from larger breaks occur even faster: if an 8-in. (20.32-cm) break fails the vessel, it does so within ~15 min. (900 sec.). These short failure times limit the influence of thermal-hydraulic variations that occur at much longer times (see the plots in Section 8.5.2.3); they also limit the time in which operator action can occur. Additionally, it should be noted that operator actions are not a factor for pipe break transients because for breaks of diameter ~2-in. (5.08-cm) and greater, there is no action that the operator can take: ECCS flow must continue to keep the core covered.

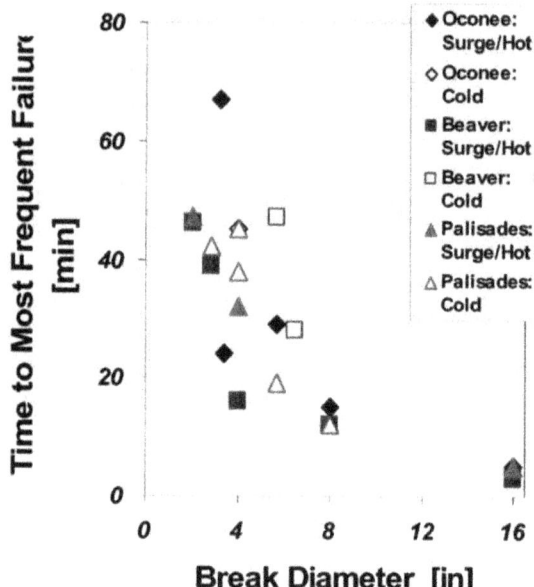

Figure 8.22. Effect of LOCA break diameter and break location on the time at which through-wall cracking occurs (Break times taken at approximately equivalent embrittlement levels between plants (Beaver Valley and Palisades at 60 EFPY, Oconee at Ext-Ob).)

8.5.2.4.5 Applicability of Findings to PWRs in General

While the information presented in this section pertains specifically to the three plants analyzed, the following three factors suggest that these results can be used with confidence to assess the risk of vessel failure arising from pipe break transients for PWRs *in general*:

(1) <u>Larger break sizes control the contribution of pipe breaks to the total estimated TWCF</u>. In the three plants studied break diameters above 5-in. (12.7-cm) account for more than 50% of the TWCF attributable to pipe breaks, with break diameters of 3.5- to 5-in. (8.9- to 12.7-cm) accounting for nearly all of the remainder. As discussed in this section, the severity of larger breaks is more

consistent from plant-to-plant than for smaller break diameters.

(2) <u>Operator actions do not play a major role in pipe break transients</u>. Consequently, the transferability of these results to other plants cannot be questioned on the basis of differences in operator training, experience, and so on.

(3) <u>At an equivalent embrittlement level, the TWCF is fairly consistent among the three plants modeled</u>. As a direct consequence of factors 1 and 2, the TWCF attributable only to primary side pipe breaks is reasonably consistent from plant-to-plant (see Figure 8.23).

In Section 9.3, we discuss the applicability of these results to PWRs *in general* in greater detail.

8.5.2.5 Comparison with Previous Studies

8.5.2.5.1 As Reported by [Kirk 12-02]

While the specific numerical results reported herein differ from those in our interim report [*Kirk 12-02*] the general trends discussed in this section have not changed substantively from those reported earlier.

8.5.2.5.2 Studies Providing the Technical Basis of the Current PTS Rule

Our results demonstrating that pipe breaks, particularly large diameter pipe breaks, are dominant contributors to PTS risk represent a substantial change relative to earlier PTS studies [SECY-82-465, ORNL 85a, 86b, 86]. It should, however, be noted that in these earlier studies, large diameter pipe breaks could not contribute to the through-wall cracking frequency because they were excluded *a priori* from the analysis. This exclusion resulted from erroneous assumptions made about the need for significant pressure to drive through-wall cracking, and erroneous interpretation of large-scale tests [Cheverton 85a, Cheverton 85b] as 1:1 surrogates for full-scale PWRs.

(See Appendix A to [*EricksonKirk-PFM*].)
Specifically, a series of thermal shock
experiments (TSEs) performed at Oak Ridge
National Laboratory in the late 1970s and early
1980s demonstrated that thermal shock alone
(no pressure was or could be applied to these
open-ended cylinders) could drive a cleavage
crack almost entirely through the wall of a
scaled RPV. (Figure 8-24 shows a post-test
photograph of the crack in TSE #6, wherein the
crack arrested after propagating 95% of the way
through the cylinder wall.) While 95% through-
wall cracking is not vessel failure, we do not feel
that this evidence adequately justifies the
previous judgment that thermal shock alone
cannot fail a pressure vessel for the following
reasons:

(1) The cylinders tested by ORNL were much
    thicker (in comparison to their diameter)
    than commercial PWRs. This increased
    stiffness makes crack arrest more likely in
    the experiment than in the actual structure.

(2) The cylinders tested in the ORNL TSEs
    were fabricated from forgings that tended to
    have material on the outer diameter that was
    tougher (lower fracture toughness transition
    temperature) than on the inner diameter.
    This toughness gradient, which resulted
    from the processes used to fabricate the
    forgings, is not typical of the axial welds
    that contribute the most to PTS failure
    frequencies. Again, qualitatively, crack arrest
    in the TSEs is more likely than in the actual
    structure.

(3) Because the ORNL TSEs used open-ended
    cylinders, the pressure component of the
    loading was zero, *by definition*. However,
    the results of our PFM calculations
    (see Figure 8-25) demonstrate that,
    while low, some pressure is retained within
    the primary system, even for large diameter
    breaks.

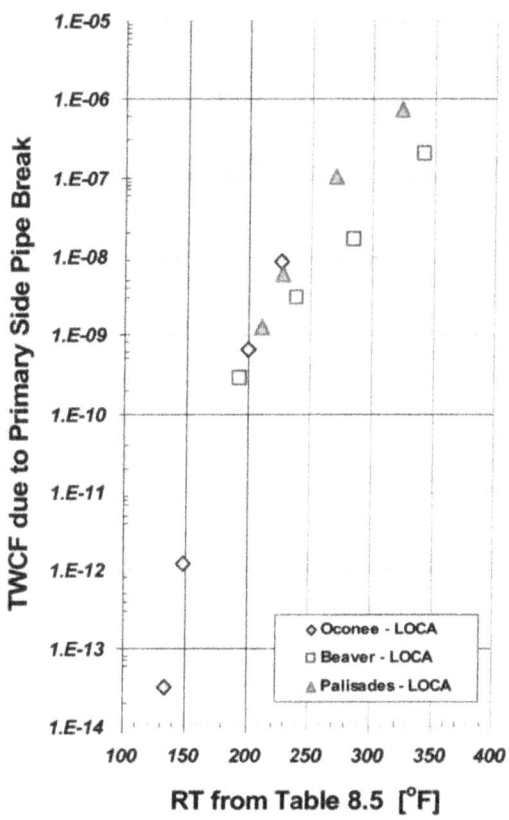

Figure 8.23. The TWCF attributable only to
primary side pipe breaks in the three study plants

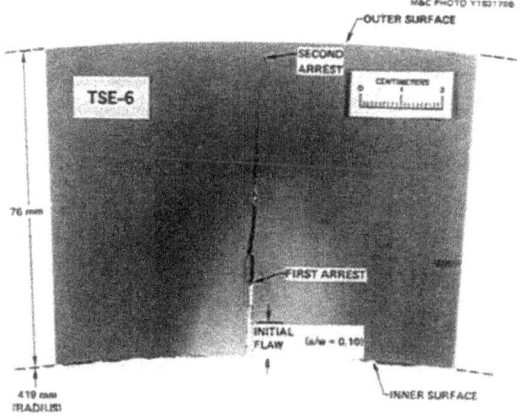

Figure 8-24. Radial profile of arrested crack
in TSE 6 [Cheverton 85a]
(The crack in this experiment arrested
after propagating 95% of the way through
the cylinder wall.)

8-43

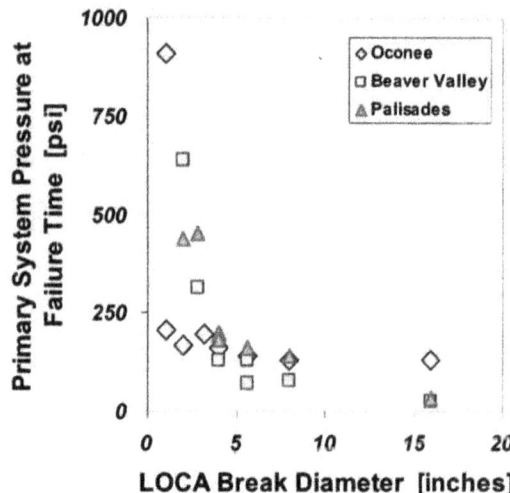

Figure 8-25. Effect of pipe break diameter on the pressure in the primary system at the most likely time of failure

8.5.3 Stuck-Open Valves on the Primary Side (SO-1)

8.5.3.1 General Description of an SO-1 Transient

An SO-1 transient begins with a demand of one or more pressurizer SRVs. In some cases, the SRV opens in response to a real demand, but more often, SRVs open because of a false demand (for example, setpoint drift). Opening of an SRV causes depressurization and consequent rapid cooldown of the RCS. At this stage, other plant equipment actuates and the operators respond in accordance with operating procedures, injecting makeup water to address the loss of primary system coolant caused by the open SRV. Since the makeup water is stored in external tanks at ambient temperature, emergency injection further cools the downcomer wall. At some (random) later time, the stuck-open SRV recloses. When the valve recloses the continued charging and high-pressure injection causes the RCS to begin to refill. For the first ~15 minutes following valve reclosure, both RCS pressure and temperature are stable or increase slightly. During this time, it is unlikely that the primary injection throttling criteria will be met because the primary system is still saturated (i.e., there is no subcooling)

and the level in the pressurizer is inadequate to satisfy the throttling criteria. After ~15 minutes, the RCS pressure will rise very quickly (over just a few minutes) as the pressurizer fills as a result of the combined effects of continued primary injection and system heatup. During this rapid repressurization, the primary system throttling criteria will be met, thereby *allowing* the operators to act to control the repressurization rate. The *ability* of operators to throttle injection once they are *allowed* to depends upon how quickly they are able to recognize and react to rapid changes in plant conditions, from a saturated system before bubble collapse to a nearly solid system as and after the bubble collapses. The rapidity of operator response once the throttling criteria are met controls whether, and for how long, the RCS becomes fully repressurized.

8.5.3.2 Model of this Transient Class

Transients modeled in this class (see Table A.3 in Appendix A) include one or more stuck-open pressurizer SRVs or PORVs that may reclose (unstick) later in the transient. The initial cooling rate in these transients is similar to that of a small (~2-in. (5.08-cm) diameter) pipe break, so it is not so rapid as to generate a considerable challenge to the RPV (see Figure 8.19). However, the potential for valve reclosure at some point in the transient leads to the possibility of system repressurization, and this coupled with the thermal stresses from the cooldown and the lowered fracture toughness of the vessel (because of the reduced temperature in the primary system) dramatically increases the severity of this transient class over that associated with small diameter pipe breaks.

Our modeling of this transient class includes the following factors:

- plant power level at transient initiation (full-power *vs.* hot zero power)

- the random time at which valve reclosure is assumed to occur (the possibility of reclosure after both 3,000 and 6,000 seconds was modeled)

- the timing of operator action (i.e., pump throttling) after valve reclosure (modeling considered action taken 1 minute, 10 minutes, and never after the throttling criteria were met)[‡‡‡‡]

- seasonal variations

- more than one valve sticking open

- less than the total number of stuck-open valves subsequently reclosing, or valves only partially sticking open

Scoping analyses revealed the first three of these factors to be of primary importance in establishing the severity of the loading challenge, while the last three factors played very minor roles. Attention, therefore, focused on a more detailed analysis of the first three factors, the effects of which are described in the following section.

8.5.3.3 Relationships between System Characteristics and Thermal-Hydraulic Response

The following three sections (8.5.3.3.1 through 8.5.3.3.3) examine the effects of the following factors, based on the results of a systematic study of these variables performed for Oconee (see Figure 8-26 and Figure 8-27):

- valve reclosure time
- plant power level at transient initiation
- timeliness of operator action once the throttling criteria are met

The results of a somewhat more limited study performed for the Beaver Valley plant can be found in Figure 8-28 through Figure 8-30. Finally, we discuss how well these trends can be expected to apply to other PWRs

---

[‡‡‡‡] This statement applies only to the models of Beaver Valley and Oconee. Because of hardware differences Palisades was modeled differently (see Section 8.5.3.4.2).

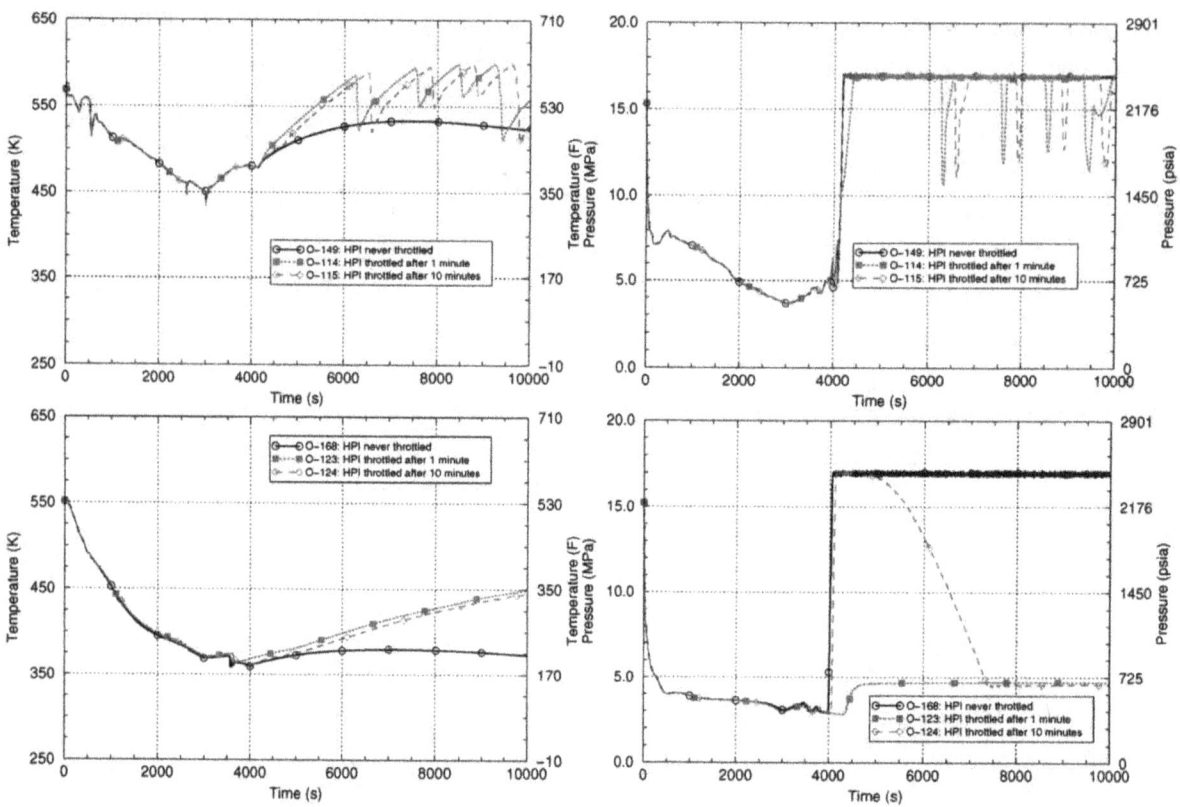

Figure 8-26. Oconee SO-1 transients where the stuck-open SRVs reclose after 3,000 seconds. (Transients in the upper graphs initiate from full power, while transients in the lower graphs initiate from hot zero power.)

8.5.3.3.1 Effect of Valve Reclosure Time on SO-1 Response

Valve reclosure is a random event that can occur at any time after the transient begins. In our model, we have discretized this continuum into the two possibilities of reclosure at 3,000 and 6,000 seconds. These possibilities were selected based on the recognition that the severity of the transient varies with valve reclosure time. Up to some time, transient severity increases with increasing time before reclosure because the temperature of the primary system is dropping (which reduces the fracture toughness) while the thermal stresses are still climbing (because the cooldown is continuing). However, once the RCS has reached its minimum temperature (established by the temperature of the HPI water), the severity of the event begins to reduce because the thermal stresses begin to decline.

The 6,000-second reclosure time was selected to coincide (approximately) with the time of maximum transient severity because it is (approximately) at this time that the RCS temperature reaches its minimum value. The 3,000-second reclosure time was selected because it is not reasonable to assume that all valve reclosures will occur at the worst possible time. The potential for valve reclosure after very long times (in excess of 7,200 seconds, or 2 hours) were not considered because by that time, operators would have initiated new procedures. Since the operators' objective is to stop the transient (i.e., stop dumping irradiated primary system water into containment), they would likely depressurize the steam generators by opening the steam dump valves to cool the secondary side, and they would start low-pressure injection and cool down the RCS to saturation conditions. These actions change the nature of the transient, making it more benign.

Also, they change the probability of operator error. Additional information on valve reclosure times can be found in response to Peer Reviewer Comment #76 in Appendix B to this report.

Figure 8-26 through Figure 8-30 illustrate the effect of valve reclosure at 3,000 vs. 6,000 seconds in both Oconee (Figure 8-26 and Figure 8-27) and Beaver Valley (Figure 8-28 through Figure 8-30). The primary difference between these two reclosure times is that the system temperature at the time of repressurization is lower for the 6,000-second case. Because the valve has been open for a longer time, HPI of cold water has continued for a longer time, leading to the colder temperatures in the downcomer. The temperature at the time of repressurization is ≈ 50–75°F (27.7 – 41.7 °C)colder when reclosure occurs after 6,000 sec. vs. when reclosure occurs after only 3,000 sec. in Oconee (compare Figure 8-26 to Figure 8-27). In Beaver Valley, the effect of a longer time before reclosure on the temperature at repressurization is more modest (≈25°F or 13.9°C) compare Figure 8-30 to Figure 8-28 and Figure 8-29). Additionally, comparing similar conditions between plants (Figure 8-27 for Oconee vs. Figure 8-28 for Beaver Valley) reveals that Beaver Valley cools faster and reaches lower temperatures than Oconee. The origins of these differences between plants are threefold:

- The presence of vent valves at Oconee allows recirculation of water in the downcomer area, leading to higher temperatures in B&W plants.

- The mass flow rate of the PORV in Beaver Valley is 65% greater than that at Oconee (see Table 8.1). Thus, more cooling water is injected into the Beaver Valley RPV in a fixed amount of time, leading to more rapid cooling of the primary system.

- The temperature of the injection water is warmer at Oconee (70°F (21°C)) than it is at Beaver Valley (50°F (10°C)), which leads directly to lower minimum temperatures at Beaver Valley.

Other features of the transient that contribute significantly to its severity (e.g., repressurization or not) are not influenced by valve reclosure time. Whether a plant repressurizes following valve reclosure depends on the plant power level at event initiation, as well as the timeliness of operator action, as discussed in the following two sections.

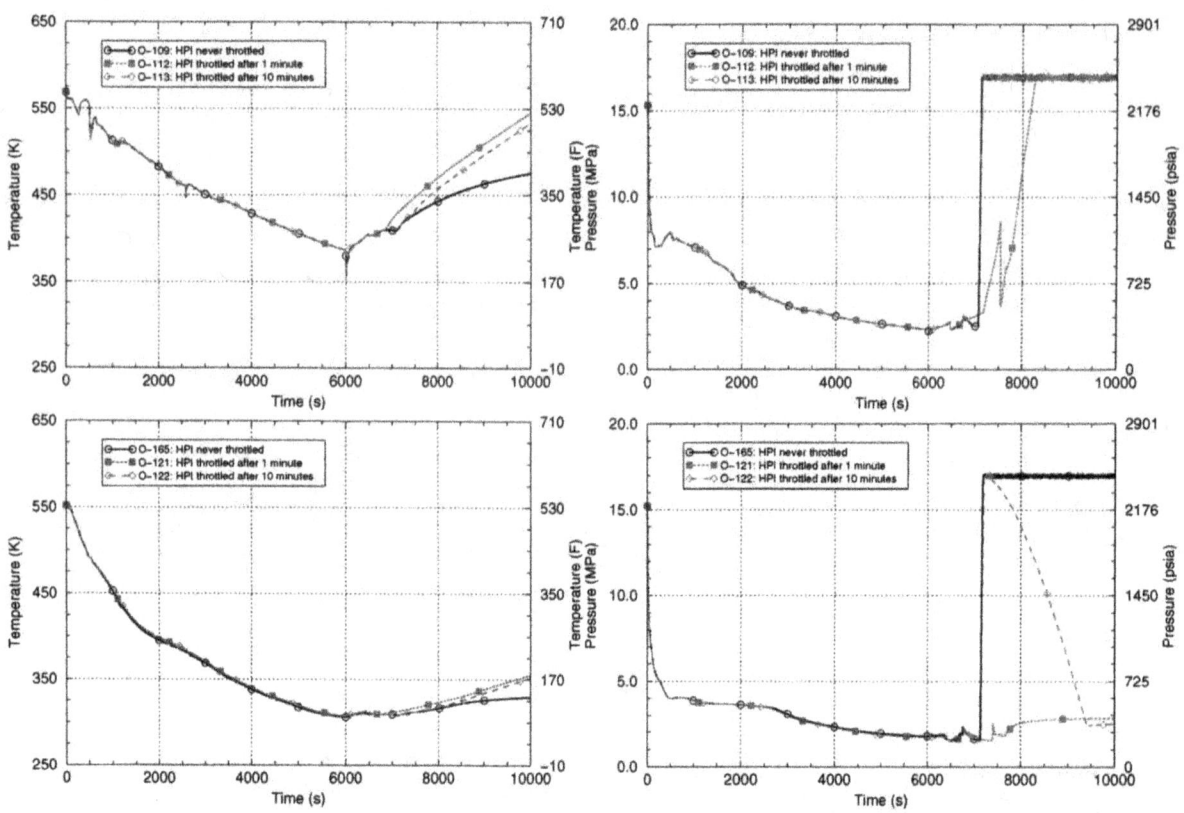

Figure 8-27. Oconee SO-1 transients where the stuck-open SRVs reclose after 6,000 seconds (Transients in the upper graphs initiate from full power, while transients in the lower graphs initiate from hot zero power.)

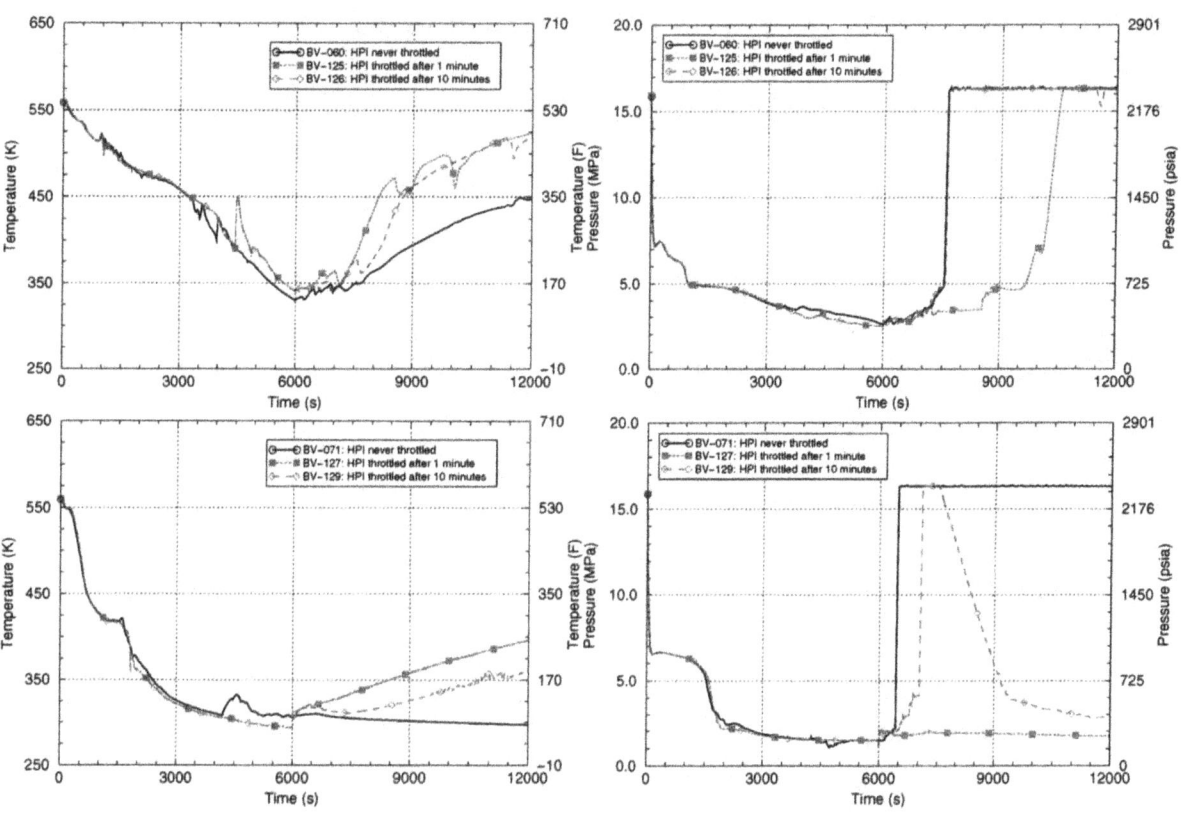

Figure 8-28. Beaver Valley SO-1 transients where a single stuck-open SRV recloses after 6,000 seconds (Transients in the upper graphs initiate from full power, while transients in the lower graphs initiate from hot zero power.)

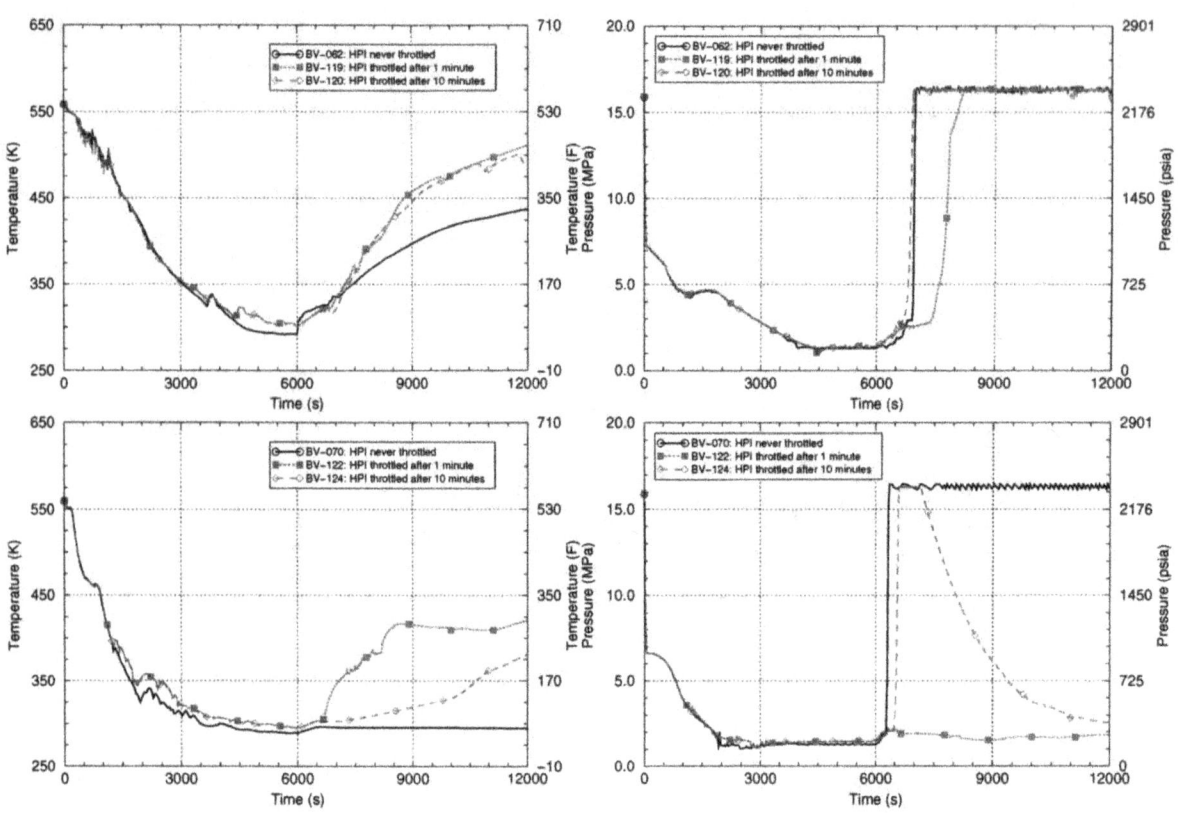

Figure 8-29. Beaver Valley SO-1 transients where a two stuck-open SRVs reclose after 6,000 seconds. (Transients in the upper graphs initiate from full power, while transients in the lower graphs initiate from hot zero power.)

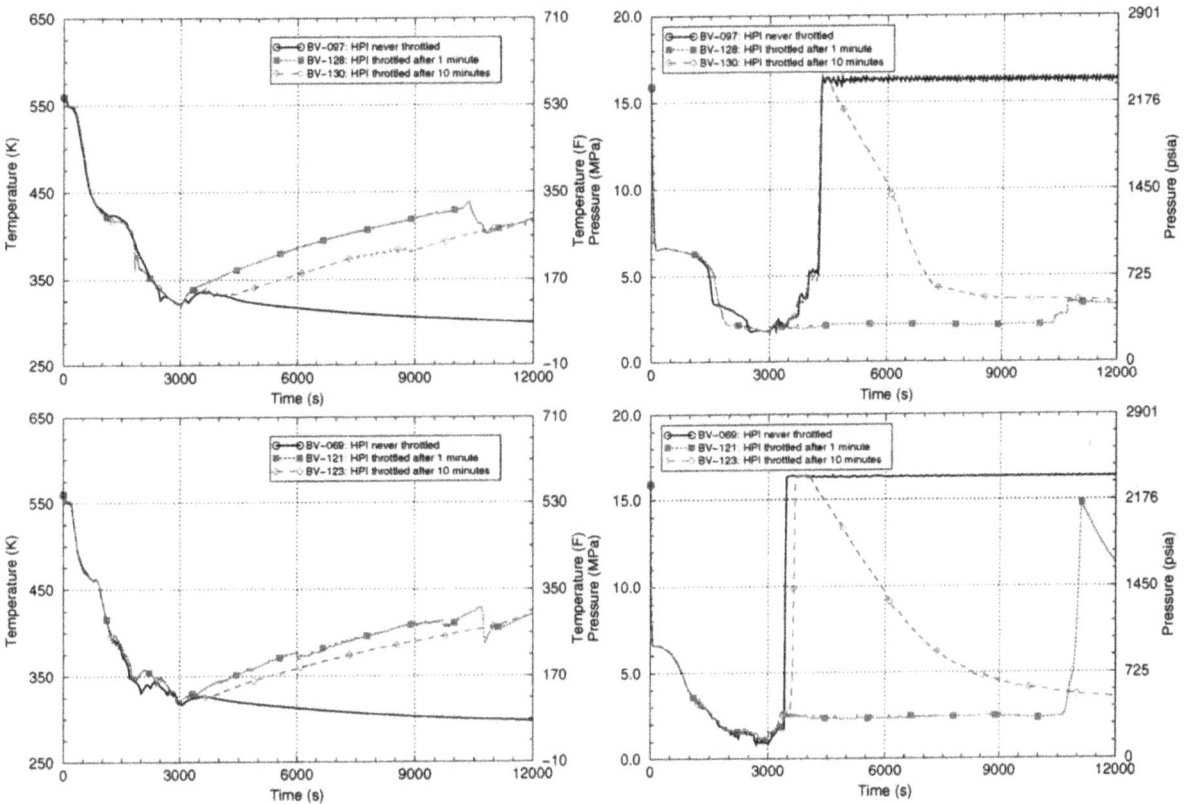

Figure 8-30. Beaver Valley SO-1 transients where stuck-open SRVs recloses after 3,000 seconds (All transients initiate from hot zero power conditions. Transients in the upper graphs have one stuck-open valve, whereas transients in the lower graphs have two stuck-open valves.)

8.5.3.3.2 Effect of Plant Power Level on SO-1 Response

If a plant experiences an SO-1 transient at HZP rather than at full-power conditions, the rate of system cooldown will be more rapid because there is less heat in the system initially. This can be seen in Figure 8-26 and Figure 8-27 by comparing the top graphs (which are initiated from full-power conditions) *vs.* the bottom graphs (which are initiated from HZP conditions). The cooling rate for the HZP transients is considerably more rapid than for the full-power transients. This more rapid cooling rate for HZP transients coupled with the fact that HZP transients begin at lower temperatures than full-power transients makes the temperature at the time or repressurization much lower for HZP transients than it is for full-power transients. These observations are true regardless of the plant considered, and can be expected to hold for all PWRs because of differences in system heat

characteristic of HZP *vs.* full-power conditions. For these reasons, SO-1 transients are always more severe when initiated under HZP conditions.

8.5.3.3.3 Effect of Timing of Operator Action on SO-1 Response

Operators are allowed to limit the injection of water to the primary system once certain "throttling criteria" are met. The specific throttling criteria vary from plant-to-plant and from manufacturer to manufacturer, but generally include the following items:

- The subcooling margin must be above some specified minimum to prevent boiling in the primary.

- The level of inventory in the pressurizer must be maintained at or above a certain elevation to keep the pressurizer heaters submerged.

- There may be requirements that the pressure not be falling, to ensure that the operators have regained pressure control of the system (and so can safely begin to reduce injection flow).

These conditions generally cannot be met in an SO-1 transient until the stuck-open valve recloses. As previously noted, how quickly the operator responds after the throttling criteria are satisfied has a significant effect on whether the system repressurizes. Our model considers three possibilities for operator action: 1 minute after the throttling criteria are met, 10 minutes after the throttling criteria are met, and never (no throttling).

The information in Figure 8-26 through Figure 8-30 demonstrates that operator action must be very rapid to prevent the primary from returning to full system pressure for at least some period of time. In all of our analyses, throttling 10 minutes after the throttling criteria were met was too late to prevent rapid repressurization shortly after valve reclosure. When operators throttled 1 minute after the throttling criteria were met and the transient was initiated from full power, the rate of repressurization was sometimes reduced or the time of repressurization delayed, but full system pressure was ultimately regained. It was only in cases where operators throttled within 1 minute *and* the transient initiated from HZP that the operator action prevented system repressurization[§§§§]. This effect of power level on the repressurization response occurs because for HZP there is less heat in the system initially, and because the system is colder at the time of valve reclosure. Pressure and temperature are linked, so the need to heat up the colder water

and having less heat to do so inhibits the sudden repressurization.

Certain plant-specific features also influence the effectiveness of operator action. Comparing the results for Oconee (Figure 8-26 and Figure 8-27) and with those for Beaver Valley (Figure 8-28 through Figure 8-30) reveals that, for a fixed throttling time, repressurization is delayed somewhat longer at Beaver Valley than at Oconee. This is a direct consequence of the differences in PORV mass flow rate (65% greater at Beaver Valley) and differences in the injection water temperature (20°F (11°C) colder because of the reduced thermal energy in the RCS (of Beaver Valley relative to Oconee) at the time of value reclosure. Consequently, a given throttling action will be more effective in preventing repressurization at Beaver Valley because throttling limits the reintroduction of thermal energy to the primary, thereby delaying the time at which water solid conditions, and therefore repressurization, occur. It should, however, be noted that these plant-specific differences do not alter significantly the risk-significance of the transient because their most important feature is the return to full system pressure (or not), not small (5–10 minute) variations in when return to full system pressure occurs. Section 8.5.3.4 discusses the risk-significance of SO-1 transients in greater detail.

8.5.3.3.4 Other Factors

In principle, factors other than the time of valve reclosure, the power level at transient initiation, and the timeliness of operator throttling of HPI can affect the TH response of the plant to an SO-1 transient. These factors can include, for example, seasonal variations, more than one valve sticking open, less than the total number of valves that stuck-open reclosing, valves that only partially stick open, and so on. We considered a number of these factors (see Table A.3 of Appendix A), but found their combined likelihood and consequence to be very small relative to the three factors discussed here in detail.

[§§§§] Figure 8-30 (bottom graphs, transient 121) illustrates one case for Beaver Valley at variance with this trend. In this case, rapid operator action has significantly delayed repressurization, but has not stopped it. However, this long delay before repressurization occurs permits considerable warming of the water in the primary system, which reduces significantly the probability of vessel failure. Thus, significant delay of repressurization is nearly as effective as preventing repressurization entirely.

8.5.3.3.5 Plant-Specific Effects on SO-1 Transients

In Sections 8.5.3.3.1 through 8.5.3.3.3, attention focused on transients in Oconee and in Beaver Valley because these plants modeled first and, consequently, the most detailed parametric study was performed on these plant. The plant-specific effects of vent valves, PORV mass flow rate, and injection water temperature have already been discussed. Certain combinations of events were eliminated from the later analyses of Palisades because the insights gained from earlier analysis suggested that the eliminated transients contributed very little or nothing at all to the overall PTS risk. Nonetheless, it is important to assess the degree to which the

observations made in Sections 8.5.3.3.1 through 8.5.3.3.3 based on Oconee and Beaver Valley apply to Palisades. Figure 8-31 shows that the cooling rate in the Palisades transient initiated from HZP is less than that at either Oconee or Beaver Valley because the low-heat HPSI pumps at Palisades don't inject as much water as the high-head HPSI pumps at Beaver Valley and Oconee. Nonetheless, this plant-to-plant difference does not alter the trends noted in Sections 8.5.3.3.1 through 8.5.3.3.3 based on Oconee and Beaver Valley results (e.g., HZP transients cool more rapidly than full-power transients, only rapid operator actions taken for transients initiated under HZP conditions can prevent (or significantly delay) repressurization, etc.).

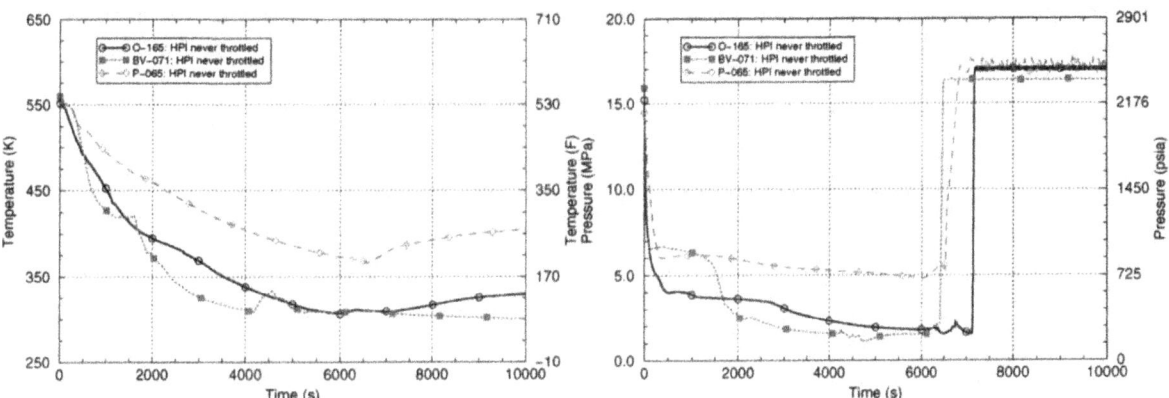

Figure 8-31. Comparison of SO-1 transients between different plants for transients initiated from HZP conditions, valve reclosure after 6,000 sec., and no HPI throttling

8.5.3.4   Estimates of Vessel Failure Probability

8.5.3.4.1   General Observations

In this section, we examine the effect that the time of valve reclosure, the power level at transient initiation, and the timeliness of operator throttling of HPI have on estimated values of CPTWC and on the predicted time of vessel failure during the transient. In Table 8.10, we examine the Oconee transients illustrated in Figure 8-26 and in Figure 8-27 focusing on various indicators of transient severity (i.e., cooling rate, if repressurization occurs or not, and the temperature at the time of repressurization), as well as the CPI, CPTWC, and time of failure values estimated by FAVOR. The following observations follow from the information in the table (these observations also apply to SO-1 transients at other plants):

Table 8.10. Transient severity indicators and estimated values of CPTWC for Oconee at Ext-Ob embrittlement conditions

HPI Throttling	Item	Transient Initiated from Full Power		Transient Initiated from HZP	
		Valve Recloses after 3,000 sec	Valve Recloses after 6,000 sec	Valve Recloses after 3,000 sec	Valve Recloses after 6,000 sec
Never	Transient #	149	109	168	165
	Average cooling rate over first 2,000 seconds (°F/hr)	308	308	486	486
	Time of repressurization (seconds)	4200	7100	4000	7100
	Temperature at repressurization (°F)	390	270	180	90
	Conditional probability of crack initiation (CPI)	0	1.83E-07	1.10E-04	1.24E-04
	Conditional probability of through-wall cracking (CPTWC)	0	1.83E-07	1.09E-04	1.24E-04
	Time of most failures (seconds)	#N/A	7140	4080	7200
10 minutes after throttling criteria satisfied	Transient #	115	113	124	122
	Average cooling rate over first 2,000 seconds (°F/hr)	308	308	486	486
	Time of repressurization (seconds)	4200	7100	4050	7100
	Temperature at repressurization (°F)	390	270	190	90
	Conditional probability of crack initiation (CPI)	0	1.42E-07	9.38E-05	1.44E-04
	Conditional probability of through-wall cracking	0	1.31E-07	9.37E-05	1.44E-04
	Time of most failures (seconds)	#N/A	7140	4140	7260
1 minute after throttling criteria satisfied	Transient #	114	112	123	121
	Average cooling rate over first 2000 seconds (°F/hr)	308	308	486	486
	Time of repressurization (seconds)	4000 – 4400	7100 - 7800	None	None
	Temperature at repressurization (°F)	400 – 440	300 - 405	#N/A	#N/A
	Conditional probability of crack initiation (CPI)	0	0	2.06E-07	2.06E-07
	Conditional probability of through-wall cracking	0	0	1.28E-08	1.28E-08
	Time of most failures (seconds)	#N/A	#N/A	1620	1620

- The occurrence of repressurization does not lead to a non-zero probability of vessel failure unless the temperature of the vessel at the time of repressurization is low enough. The information in Table 8.10 substantiates the general observation that the vessel temperature must be below 400°F (204°C) to produce a non-zero value of CPTWC.

- If a failure occurs, it most often happens between 5 and 20 minutes after the time of valve reclosure, closely following the time of repressurization.

- If repressurization occurs and a crack initiates, the initiated crack fails the vessel almost every time (i.e., the CPTWC is equal to or only slightly less than the CPI). This crack initiation/through-wall crack propagation behavior contrasts sharply with that associated with primary side pipe breaks (see Figure 8.21) where only 5–10% of initiated cracks propagated through-wall. The combination of thermal stresses and pressure in SO-1 transients makes cracks, once initiated, much more likely to propagate all the way through the RPV wall.

- SO-1 transients initiated from HZP conditions have CPTWC values that are ~1000 times higher than the same transient initiated from full-power conditions, this occurring as a consequence of the faster cooling rates and lower temperatures achieved during transients initiated from HZP.

- Valve reclosures after 6,000 seconds exhibit slightly higher CPTWC values than valve reclosures at 3,000 seconds. The effect of higher thermal stresses (for 3,000-second valve reclosures) seems to approximately offset the effect of lower toughness (for 6,000-second valve reclosures).

- For transients initiated from HZP, operator action within 1 minute of reaching the throttling criteria prevents a return to full system pressure, thereby reducing the CPTWC by a factor of ~10,000 relative to the CPTWC generated by repressurization.

8.5.3.4.2 Influence of Operator Actions

The final observation made in the preceding section indicates the potentially significant influence of operator action on the risk-significance of the transient. Consequently, in this section we review the basis for the probabilities assigned to represent the likelihood of operator action in response to this type of transient.

The probabilities assigned to reflect the likelihood of operator action (throttling HPI in this case) after certain times were established based on the expert views of three PRA analysts, with the individual analyst's judgments averaged to provide the consensus view used in our models [*Kolaczkowski-Oco, Whitehead-BV, Whitehead-Pal*]. Table 8.11 summarizes the factors that both favor and impede successful throttling considered by these analysts in formulating their opinions. Table 8.11 also provides the mean probabilities for operator action taken from the consensus distribution. These numbers reflect the analysts' view that throttling within 1 minute of meeting the throttling criteria is somewhat more likely in Oconee than in Beaver Valley, a difference motivated mostly by differences in the simulator observations and procedures followed at the different plants. The numerical throttling probabilities for Palisades are somewhat different from those of Oconee and Beaver Valley because of differences in hardware. At Palisades, HPSI can only charge to approximately 1,250 psi while pressurization between 1,250 psi and full system pressure is achieved via charging pumps. The analysts' took the view that successful throttling of HPSI was very unlikely, whereas successful throttling of charging pumps was very likely.

The plots of pressure *vs.* time (see for example Figure 8-26 and Figure 8-27) indicate that HPI must be throttled within 1 minute of meeting the throttling criteria to prevent repressurization to full system pressure for a HZP transient. Thus, in our model, operators have a 68% chance of preventing repressurization in Oconee, and a 40% chance in Beaver Valley (see Table 8.11).

Our model for Palisades deviates from that suggested by the PRA information in Table 8.11. While the PRA information suggests that repressurization to 1,250 psi is certain and further repressurization is unlikely (happening only 1 time out of 100, on average), the TH sequences selected to represent stuck-open valve transients for Palisades credit *no* operator actions[*****] and, so, all have repressurization to full system pressure. Thus, the TH sequences run and passed to PFM for analysis reflect the following operator action credits for successful throttling of HPI:

- **Oconee** operators successfully throttle HPI and, thereby, prevent return to full system pressure (on average) 68% of the time, provided that the transient initiates from HZP. Since approximately 20% of SO-1 transients occur under HZP conditions, this means that at Oconee operators prevent return to full system pressure for approximately 14% of SO-1 transients.

- **Beaver Valley** operators successfully throttle HPI and, thereby, prevent return to full system pressure (on average) 40% of the time, provided that the transient initiates from HZP. Since approximately 20% of SO-1 transients occur under HZP conditions, this means that at Beaver Valley operators prevent return to full system pressure for approximately 8% of SO-1 transients.

- **Palisades** operators never successfully throttle HPI; therefore, all stuck-open valve transients return to full system pressure once the valve recloses.

These observations indicate that while reasonable and appropriate credit for operator actions has been included in the PRA model, the actual influence of these credits on the estimated values of vessel failure probability attributable to SO-1 transients is small because the operator actions credited only prevent repressurization

when SO-1 transients initiate from HZP conditions. Complete removal of operator action credits from the model changes the total risk associated with SO-1 transients only slightly.

8.5.3.4.3   Applicability of these Findings to PWRs in General

While the information presented in this section pertains specifically to the three plants analyzed, the following factors suggest that these results can be used with confidence to assess the risk of vessel failure arising from pipe break transients for PWRs *in general*.

(1) A major contributor to the risk-significance of SO-1 transients is the return to full system pressure once the valve recloses. The operating and SRV pressures of all PWRs are similar.

(2) While our model includes reasonable and appropriate PRA credits for operator action to throttle HPI, these credits have only a small effect on the estimated probability of vessel failure because the operator actions credited only prevent repressurization when SO-1 transients initiate from HZP conditions. Complete removal of operator action credits from the model changes the total risk associated with SO-1 transients only slightly.

At an equivalent embrittlement level, the TWCF is fairly consistent between the three plants modeled. As a direct consequence of these factors, the TWCF attributable solely to stuck-open primary side valves that later reclose is reasonably consistent from plant-to-plant (see Figure 8.32). In Chapter 9, we discuss the applicability of these results to PWRs *in general* in greater detail.

[*****] The Palisades model does not subdivide the PRA bins to account for "credit" vs. "no credit" because of our understanding (at the time the model was built) that the estimated TWCF values would be sufficiently low even with this implicit conservatism.

Table 8.11. Mean operator action probabilities in our modeling of SO-1 transients

Plant	Factors that favor successful throttling	Factors against successful throttling	Mean Probability of successful throttling within x minutes after throttling criteria is satisfied		
			x = 1 minute	x = 10 minutes	x = never (no throttling)
Oconee	Crew is in loss of subcooling procedure (EP-501). Procedure contains many cautions on PTS.	Crew might have adopted a LOCA mindset and, therefore, not be attentive to the possibility of rapid repressurization.	68%	27%	5%
	Simulator observations confirm that crews are sensitized to PTS, and that they carefully monitor PTS parameters.	Emergency safeguards logic must be reset before HPI can be throttled, so throttling might be delayed while logic is being reset.			
	High pressure alarms would indicated the need to throttle HPI	Crew might not immediately throttle if they perform additional investigation to confirm that the event they are responding to is a stuck-open valve (for which throttling is appropriate) vs. a pipe break (for which throttling is not appropriate.			
	Crew would be alerted to changing plant conditions by the slow pressure rise that follows valve reclosure and precedes the rapid pressure increase.				
Beaver Valley	Before valve reclosure the crew has successfully stabilized a SLOCA, and they remain in a SLOCA condition until the valve recloses. SLOCA procedures make it reasonable to expect that the crew is thinking about PTS and is carefully monitoring plant parameters.	Simulator observations suggest that the crews do not have a sense of urgency associated with throttling/terminating HHSI. Rather, they trust that their procedures will tell them to throttle in time.	40%	56%	4%
	Simulator observations confirm that procedures are attended to and the crew carefully monitors critical parameters.	Crew might have adopted a LOCA mindset and therefore not be attentive to the possibility of rapid repressurization.			
		Emergency safeguards logic must be reset before HPI can be throttled, so throttling might be delayed while logic is being reset.			
		Crew might not immediately throttle if they perform additional investigation to confirm that the event they are responding to is a stuck-open valve (for which throttling is appropriate) vs. a pipe break (for which throttling is not appropriate.			
Palisades	Throttling of the charging system (pressurizes from 1,250 psi to full system pressure) is very likely because it is a simple action that is linked procedurally to securing HPSI.	Throttling of HPSI (pressurizes to 1,250 psi) is unlikely because the time available in which to throttle is very short.	0% for throttling HPSI within 5 minutes 99% for throttling charging system within 5 minutes		100% for never throttling HPSI 1% for never throttling charging system

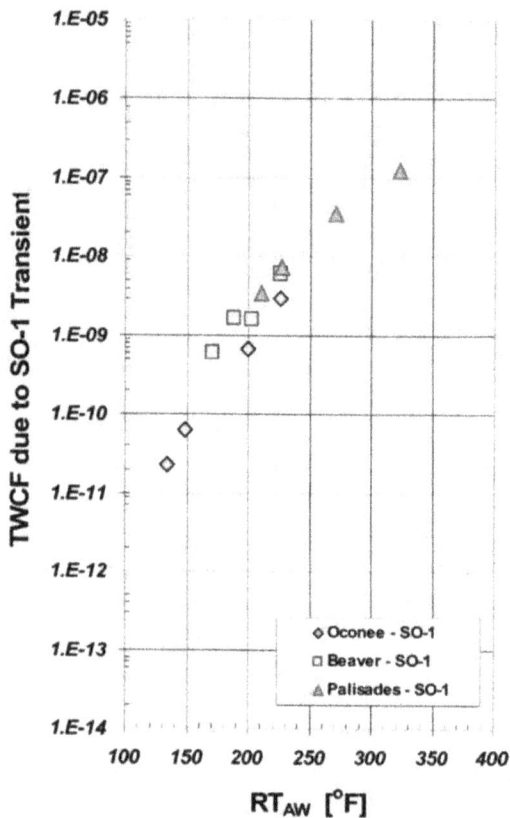

Figure 8.32. The TWCF attributable solely to stuck-open valves on the primary side that later reclose

8.5.3.5 Comparison with Previous Studies

8.5.3.5.1 As Reported by [Kirk 12-02]

Previously, we reported that stuck-open valves on the primary side were dominant contributors to TWCF only in Oconee; in both Beaver Valley and Palisades, the contribution of such transients was 20% or less [*Kirk 12-02*]. Figure 8-11 and Figure 8.32 demonstrate that stuck-open valves on the primary side now contribute significantly to the TWCF of all three plants. This change results from an inadequacy in our previous approach to determining the group of transients we use in FAVOR to represent the behavior of the plant. Previously, we performed our first FAVOR calculation for each plant for a highly embrittled condition, determined which transients contributed ~1% or more to the TWCF, and conducted analyses at lower

embrittlement levels using only this limited set of transients. As shown in Figure 8-11, our previous filtering strategy eliminated transients that provide significant contributions to PTS risk at lower embrittlement levels. Therefore, in this study, FAVOR analyses were performed on all transients at all embrittlement levels.

8.5.3.5.2 Studies Providing the Technical Basis of the Current PTS Rule

In analyses performed to establish the technical basis for the current PTS Rule, the three plants analyzed were Oconee, H.B. Robinson, and Calvert Cliffs. Analyses of Oconee and H.B. Robinson (which were performed first) did not consider the class of scenarios referred to herein as SO-1 [ORNL 85b, ORNL 86]. The Calvert Cliffs analysis, which was the last analysis performed, considered the possibility of both PORV and SRV reclosures, although not to the level of detail achieved in the current study [ORNL 85a]. Furthermore, all valve reclosure cases were binned together in the Calvert Cliffs study, which made it impossible to characterize the effects of power level, valve reclosure time, and operator action as we have in this study. Putting everything into one bin usually produces a conservative characterization; however, not investigating or understanding how various factors influence transient severity can lead to nonconservatisms when significant effects are not recognized and, therefore, not modeled.

In the 1986 analysis of Calvert Cliffs, SO-1 transients were among the two most important PTS scenarios (the other being small LOCAs) for the Calvert Cliffs analysis. This is in contrast to the 1985–1986 findings for Oconee and H.B. Robinson, which found secondary failures (either MSLBs or secondary valve openings) to be most important.

With regard to frequency estimates for SO-1 transients, our estimates rely on data that are representative of current operating practice. These estimates are lower than those used in the 1980s.

8.5.4   Large Diameter Secondary Side or Main Steam Line Breaks

8.5.4.1   General Description of MSLB Transients

MSLB transients all begin with a break in one of the main steam lines. As main steam lines are large pipes with diameters of multiple feet, the steam generator rapidly blows down (loses steam through the break). Because of the break, the affected steam generator can no longer maintain pressure above that existing at the break location. The depressurization of the generator from its 860 psi (5.92 MPa) operating pressure to the pressure at the break location causes a temperature drop in the primary from 550°F (288°C) to the saturation temperature at the pressure that exists at the break location (212°F (100°C) if the break is outside of containment, ~250°F (~121°C) if the break is inside of containment because containment is pressurized to ~50psi (345 kPa) by the steam escaping from the break). The temperature inside the still sealed primary system tracks that of the broken steam generator because of the very large heat transfer area provided by the steam generator tubes. (That is, the primary and secondary systems are coupled, so the temperature in the primary rapidly approaches that of the largest heat sink, which in this case, is the broken steam generator.) Thus, the inventory in the primary circuit cools rapidly to the temperature of the water boiling in the broken steam generator (as previously mentioned, 212°F (100°C) if the break is outside of containment, ~250°F (~121°C) if the break is inside of containment) for all durations of interest *from a PTS perspective*[ttttt].
As explained below, this is true despite the fact that both the makeup water to the primary and the feedwater to the faulted generator are

supplied at temperatures far below the boiling point of water:

- The rapid cooling of the primary in response to the MSLB shrinks the primary system inventory, causing a pressure drop. To compensate for the pressure drop, the ESFAS (an automatic function) initiates safety injection, causing the HPI pumps to supply makeup water to the primary system. HPI flow then refills and repressurizes the primary system. Even though the makeup water is drawn from external tanks and, so, is injected at a temperature far below the range of 212°F (100°C) to ~250°F (~121°C), the temperature of the primary remains at or above that of the broken steam generator because the heat transfer area provided by the steam generator tubes is so large that it overwhelms the lower temperature of the makeup water. At a later time, operators may be allowed to throttle HPI injection.

- At very long times after the beginning of an MSLB transient, the temperature in the primary system approaches that of the feed water to the faulted steam generator, or about 100°F (38°), because the reactor is no longer generating enough heat to boil the water in the faulted generator. This drop to temperatures below 212°F (100°C) does not occur until several hours or more have passed, long after isothermal conditions have been achieved in the RPV.

The primary aim of operators responding to an MSLB is to isolate the break (that is, to stop the feed to the faulted generator and/or to stop the flow out of the break). The steps the operators take to achieve this goal depends on the location of the break relative to both the main steam isolation valve and the containment structure (see Figure 2.1 for the arrangement of major plant components and a definition of the terms used in the following description):

- <u>Break downstream of the MSIV</u>: In this case, the operators' response is simply to isolate the affected generator by closing both the FWIV and MSIV. This reseals the secondary system and ends the transient. At this point, the temperature of the steam

---

[ttttt]   When the primary remains at approximately isothermal conditions for a long period of time, the temperatures of the ID and the OD of the RPV become approximately equal. Under these conditions, there is no thermal stress and, consequently, no risk of vessel failure attributable to PTS.

generator is controlled by the temperature of the primary.

- Break upstream of the MSIV outside of containment: In this case, the break flow cannot be stopped by shutting the MSIV, so the operators close both the FWIV and MSIV to isolate the affected generator. Without feedwater, the generator eventually boils dry, and the unaffected generator becomes the primary heat sink, thereby ending the transient.

- Break upstream of the MSIV inside of containment: The operators' response to this event is the same as when the break is upstream of the MSIV and outside of containment: the FWIVs are closed, stopping feed to the faulted generator. However, the venting of steam from the break inside the containment structure increases pressure inside of containment, causing an "adverse containment" condition. As a result of the increase in pressure inside of containment, the ESFAS generates a containment isolation signal. This signal automatically isolates all containment penetrations that could (potentially) lead to a radioactive release; however, the source of cooling water to the RCPs is one of these penetrations. Without cooling water, the RCPs would seize, so operators must secure (stop) the RCPs. Without RCPs to circulate water in the cold leg, the mixing of cooler and hotter water in the downcomer reduces significantly, resulting in lower downcomer temperatures.

Given the relative length of pipe runs, the ruggedness of the piping, and the pipe support system, MSLBs are most likely to occur downstream of the MSIVs. Also, as was the case with stuck-open valve transients (see Section 8.5.3), MSLBs can occur from either full power or HZP conditions.

8.5.4.2 Model of this Transient Class

As detailed in Table A.4 of Appendix A, our modeling of MSLB transients includes delayed operator actions, such as the following examples:

- allowing feed to continue to the faulted steam generator for 30 minutes or indefinitely

- throttling HPI to the primary, but only 30–60 minutes after the throttling criteria have been met

The model also includes exacerbating equipment failures, such as the following:

- failure of MSIVs to close

Additionally, the model adopts physically unrealistic temperatures, such as:

- Most MSLBs in Beaver Valley and Oconee are assumed to occur inside containment (worst case). When a main steam line breaks inside of containment, the containment building is pressurized to ~50psi (345 kPa), which elevates the boiling point of water to ~260°F (127°C). However, our model does not account for pressurization of containment by the break flow, so the boiling point of the secondary (and, consequently, the minimum temperature in the primary) is 212°F (100°C). This lower temperature increases the severity of the thermal shock to which the RPV wall is subjected and reduces the RPV's resistance against this thermal shock.

This conservative modeling approach was taken because PFM calculations performed early in the project indicated that even with these conservative assumptions, the contribution of MSLB transients to the total vessel risk was very small relative to the contribution of primary side pipe breaks and stuck-open primary side valves. Further refinement of the MSLB model to achieve increased realism would only reduce the risk-significance of the transients, and this refinement was not viewed as being necessary. Consequently, when considering the results presented in the following sections, the reader is reminded to view them as representing an upper bound to the vessel integrity challenge actually posed by MSLB transients.

8.5.4.3 Relationships between System Characteristics and Thermal-Hydraulic Response

In this section, we examine the effects of a variety of factors on the pressure and temperature transients associated with MSLBs:

- **Effect of plant power level at event initiation**: Figure 8.33 and Figure 8.34 show the effect of an MSLB initiating from full power vs. HZP conditions. The initial cooldown rate associated with the HZP transients is more rapid than for the full-power transients expected as a result of a lack of heat in the system, but only slightly so. The rapidity of the cooldown caused by the large break area of the main steam line mitigates the potential cooling rate boost associated with transient initiation from HZP.

- **Effect of break location**: Figure 8.35 shows that MSLBs occurring inside containment experience considerably faster cooldown rates than when the break is outside of containment. As previously discussed, the break of a main steam line inside containment is expected to produce more rapid cooling of the downcomer because the RCPs will be shut down, resulting in less mixing of the hot and cold water in the downcomer.

- **Isolation of feedwater flow**: Figure 8.36 shows that failure to isolate feedwater flow allows temperatures in the primary to continue to drop because feedwater flowing to the affected generator is still steaming and, therefore, still cooling the primary.

- **Timing of HHSI control**: Safety injection flow initiates automatically following an MSLB to repressurize the primary. Figure 8.37 shows that when the operators throttle HHSI effects directly how long high pressures are maintained.

In terms of plant-specific effects on MSLB transients, B&W plants (Oconee) differ from other plants because of the much smaller steam generator volume in the B&W design than in Combustion Engineering or Westinghouse designs. Consequently, the blowdown from an MSLB at Oconee concludes almost instantaneously, whereas the blowdown in Beaver Valley and Palisades takes approximately 250 seconds. The rapid blowdown in Oconee produces a much more rapid cooling rate than in the other two plants, but the minimum temperature associated with this rapid cooling is so high (far above 400°F (204°C)) that the risk of vessel failure is very very low. Thus, the vessel failure probability estimates discussed in the following section arise almost exclusively from the non-B&W plants.

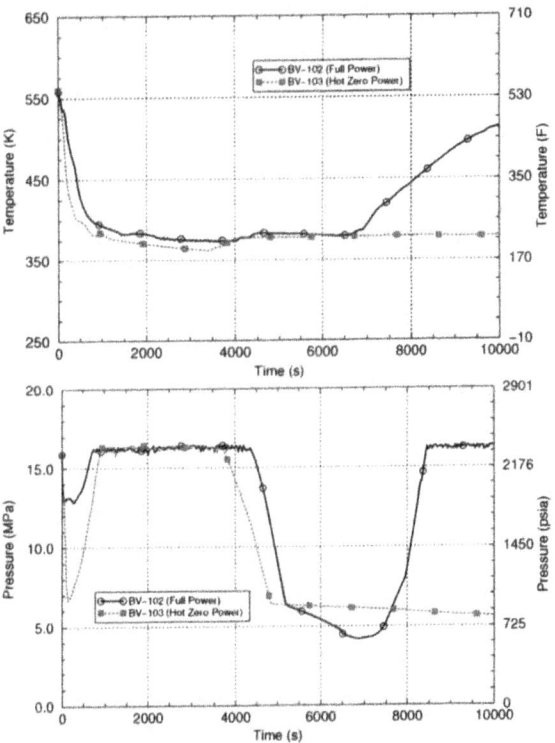

Figure 8.33. Power level effects on MSLB transients at Beaver Valley. Both breaks are in containment and have AUX feed continuing to the faulted generator for 30 minutes. The operator throttles HPSI 30 minutes after allowed.

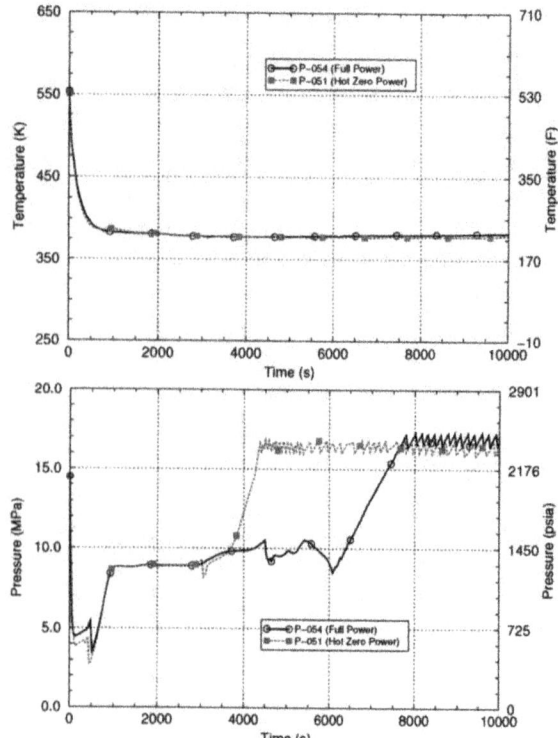

Figure 8.34. Power level effects on MSLB transients at Palisades. Both breaks are in containment and include failures of both MSIVs to close. The operator takes no actions to either isolate AUX feed or to throttle HPI.

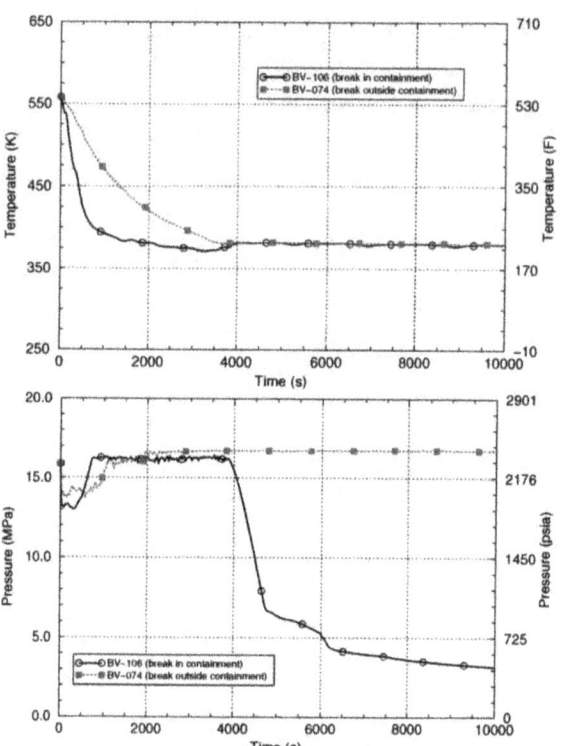

Figure 8.35. Break location effects on MSLB transients at Beaver Valley. Both breaks include continuous AUX feed and are initiated from full-power conditions. In transient 106, the operator controls HPSI 30 minutes after allowed.

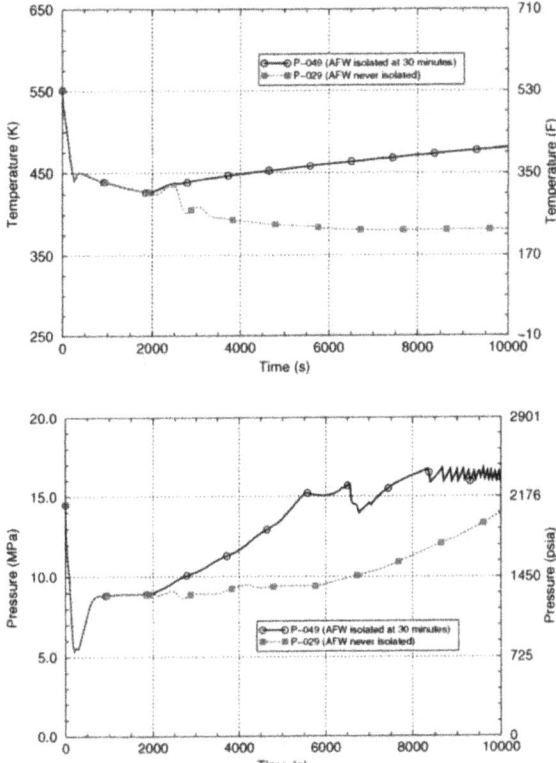

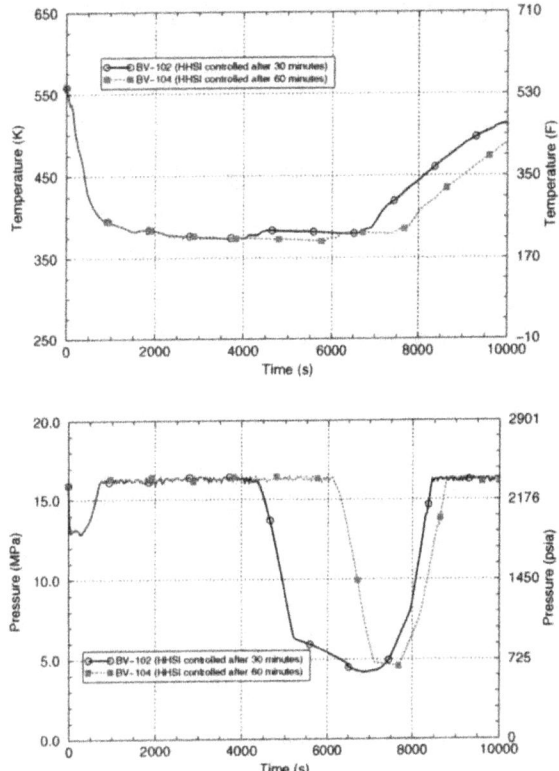

Figure 8.36. Break isolation effects on MSLB transients at Palisades. Both breaks occur inside containment and are initiated from HZP conditions.

Figure 8.37. Effect of HHSI control on MSLB transients at Beaver Valley. In both breaks, AUX feed is isolated 30 minutes after the break occurs. Both breaks are initiated from full-power conditions.

8.5.4.4 Estimates of Vessel Failure Probability

8.5.4.4.1 General Observations

In the preceding section the effect of the following factors on the pressure and temperature transients associated with main steam line breaks was examined:

- effect of plant power level at event initiation
- effect of break location
- isolation of feedwater flow
- timing of HHSI control

All of the long-time effects (isolation of feedwater flow, timing of HSSI control) have no effect on the vessel failure probability because these factors influence the progression of the thermal-hydraulic transient after failure has occurred (*if* it occurs). In almost all of the transients discussed in the previous section, vessel failure is predicted to occur between 10 and 15 minutes after transient initiation (rare cases have failures as late as 30 minutes after initiation). Thus, operator actions (as modeled) cannot affect vessel failure probability. Only factors affecting the initial cooling rate can have any influence on CPTWC values. These factors include the plant power level at event initiation and the location of the break (inside or outside of containment). As shown in Figure 8.33 and Figure 8.34, the plant power level has only a slight influence on the initial cooling rate, and (so) only a slight influence on the CPTWC (less than a factor of 2 increase). The location of the break (inside or outside of containment, see Figure 8.35) has a somewhat larger effect. For this comparison, the break inside containment has a CPTWC ~3 times higher than the break outside of containment.

Figure 8.38 presents a distribution describing the percentage of cracks initiated by MSLB transients that subsequently propagate through-wall. The large thermal component to the loading at the time of failure (10–15 minutes into the transient) allows a large percentage of the initiated cracks to experience a stable arrest. However, because there is a pressure component

to MSLB transients (the relative proportion of pressure loading to thermal loading depends on the time of failure experienced by a particular simulation), in some situations, once the cracks initiate they almost always propagate entirely through the vessel wall.

8.5.4.4.2 Applicability of these Findings to PWRs in General

These results can be applied with confidence to PWRs in general for the following reasons:

- Even though our model of MSLBs is intentionally conservative, the estimated conditional failure probabilities are low (10^{-9} to 10^{-5}); realistic estimates can be expected to be lower (perhaps considerably so) because of the physically unrealistic aspects of our modeling (e.g., we have not modeled the pressure buildup inside of containment attributable to the MSLB, which would raise the minimum temperature of the primary system, thereby reducing the severity of the transient).

- Operator actions (as modeled) have no influence whatsoever on the estimated failure probabilities reported here.

- The part of the MSLB transient responsible for the reported failure probabilities is the rapid initial cooldown caused by depressurization of the secondary through the break. Since main steam lines are so large, the rapidity of this cooldown should not vary much from plant-to-plant, nor should it be influenced by other factors (plant power level at event initiation, operator actions, etc.)

Figure 8.39 compares the portion of the TWCF attributable to MSLBs at the three study plants. Based on the factors discussed above, the plant-to-plant consistency in the level MSLBs challenge is expected.

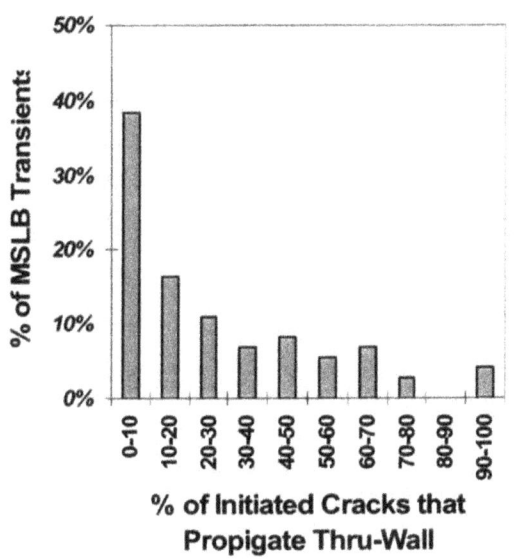

Figure 8.38. Percentage of initiated cracks that propagate through-wall for MSLB transients

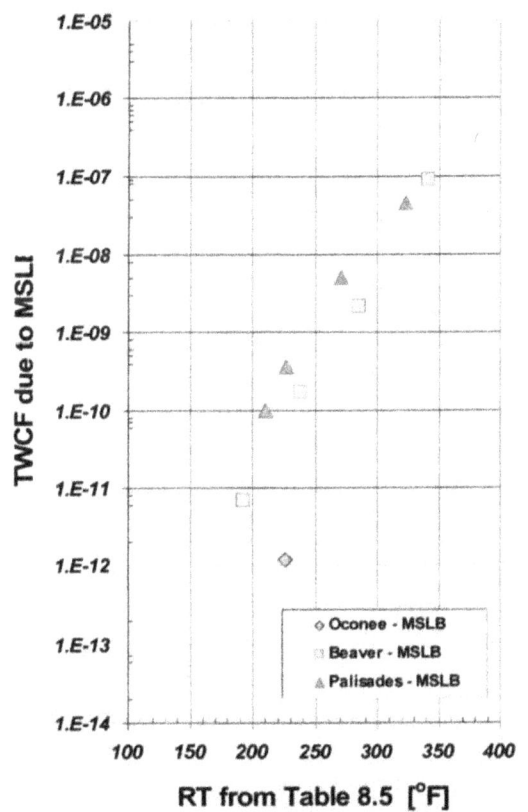

Figure 8.39. TWCF attributable to MSLB transients

8.5.4.5 Comparison with Previous Studies

8.5.4.5.1 As Reported by [Kirk 12-02]

While the specific numerical results reported herein differ from those in our interim report [*Kirk 12-02*], the general trends discussed in this section have not changed substantively from those reported earlier.

8.5.4.5.2 Studies Providing the Technical Basis of the Current PTS Rule

In analyses performed to establish the technical basis for the current PTS Rule three plants were analyzed: Oconee, H.B. Robinson, and Calvert Cliffs [ORNL-86, ORNL-85b, ORNL-85a, respectively]. Analyses of Oconee and H.B. Robinson revealed secondary failures (either MSLBs or secondary valve openings) to be the most dominant class of transient (following the "residual" categorization in Oconee), in contrast to the information reported here, which shows the contribution of MSLBs to be much less than that associated with either primary side pipe breaks or with stuck-open primary side relief valves that reclose after a significant cooling period. (See Figure 8.40 for a summary of current TWCF predictions divided by transient class.)

In the previous analyses of Oconee and H.B. Robinson, MSLBs *had to be* more risk-significant than either (1) medium–large diameter pipe breaks or (2) stuck-open relief valves on the primary side that reclose after a significant cooling period simply because these classes of transients were not modeled in the earlier studies. At the time of these previous analyses, the prevalent technical belief regarding vessel failure was that *"rapid depressurization will severely limit the potential for a vessel failure"* [ORNL-85b]. Consequently, no breaks larger than 2.5-in. (6.4-cm) in diameter were considered in these analyses. Further, while stuck-open primary side valve scenarios were analyzed, and *early* isolation of stuck-open pressurizer pilot-operated relief valve scenarios were also examined, late reclosures of primary side valves after significant cooling has occurred were not analyzed in the Oconee and H.B. Robinson analyses.

In the Calvert Cliffs analysis [ORNL-85a], the LOCAs considered included pipe diameters only up to 3-in. (7.6-cm). However, for Calvert Cliffs, "late" reclosures of stuck-open pressurizer relief valves (i.e., reclosures occurring 1½ hours into the transient) were analyzed. In the 1985 ORNL analysis of Calvert Cliffs, such a reclosure event (similar to those we analyzed in this updated study), especially at HZP, was found to be the highest or among the top three highest "dominant risk sequences" depending on the EFPY of the vessel (including being more important than steam line breaks, as we have found in this updated study). Hence, the early Calvert Cliffs analysis [ORNL-85a] shows trends similar to those reported herein.

Additionally, even though our treatment of MSLBs has been conservative, it is still more refined than in previous studies largely because of the evolution of computer capabilities and the ability to analyze many more scenarios more completely today than was available more than 20 years ago. For example, the secondary side break models adopted in the previous analyses often represented a full spectrum of secondary side breaks from small breaks and valve opening scenarios through a break of the main steam line using the bounding pressure/temperature *vs.* time transient characteristic of an MSLB. This approach overestimated both the severity of many secondary side events and the frequency of their occurrence. Furthermore, many of the

TH profiles (e.g., for downcomer temperature vs. time) were based, in part, on extrapolations of the early timing profile trends and other hand calculations that tended to conservatively predict the degree of cooling in the downcomer region.

Based on the above along with advances in our technical understanding and modeling of cooling scenarios, the associated thermal-hydraulics, and vessel fracture mechanics, it is understandable that the early belief that secondary failures dominate PTS risk has changed to that provided in this study.

8.5.5 Stuck-Open Valves on the Secondary Side (SO-2)

8.5.5.1 General Description of SO-2 Transients

The steam supply system contains several valves to control pressure. All of these valves have opening areas much smaller than the main steam line, so opening any one (or even several) of them does not produce nearly as rapid a depressurization rate (and consequently cooling rate) as that associated with MSLB transients (see Section 8.5.4). The general progress of a transient associated with one (or many) secondary side valves sticking open is, therefore, similar to that described for MSLBs (see Section 8.5.4.1), with the exception that all of these valves are outside of containment, so the considerations associated with a break in containment discussed in Section 8.5.4.1 do not apply to stuck-open secondary side valves.

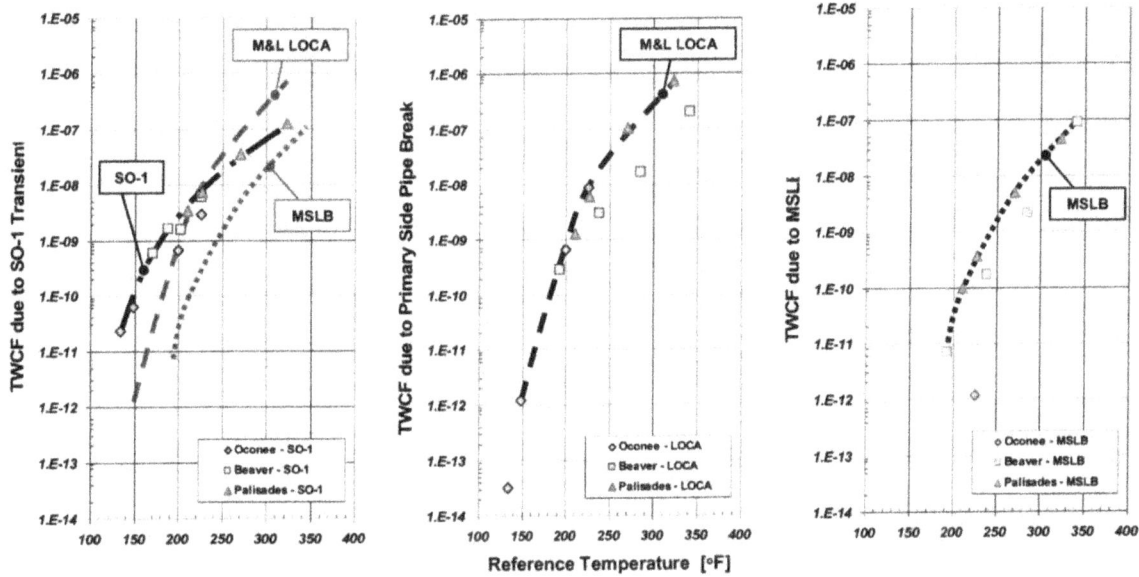

Figure 8.40. Comparison of TWCF attributable to primary side stuck-open valves, primary side pipe breaks, and MSLBs. Note that the contribution of MSLBs here overrepresents their actual contributions to TWCF because of conservatisms in their modeling. On each graph, an upper-bound curve is hand drawn to the data originally presented in Figure 8.23, Figure 8.32, and Figure 8.39. On the left hand graph, all three upper-bound curves are placed together for easy comparison.

8.5.5.2 Model of this Transient Class

Tables A.5 and A.6 in Appendix A detail the transients analyzed as SO-2s. The transients in Table A.5 include the sticking open of *all* main steam safety valves (MSSVs) or turbine bypass valves (TBVs). The opening of all TBVs is an action taken to depressurize the secondary in response to complete loss of both main and emergency feedwater to a single steam generator. Different scenarios are selected to assess the effect of smaller breaks of the steam line than those discussed in Section 8.5.4, including all MSSVs sticking open, one MSSV sticking open, or an ADV sticking open. The transients in Table A.6 begin with the trip of the reactor/turbine. This is followed by one or two of the TBVs or ADVs being opened to purge energy from the system. If these valves stick open, an overcooling transient begins. In both sets of transients (Table A.5 and A.6), the effects of operator actions and plant power level at event initiation are modeled.

Our modeling of this class of transients is not "best estimate." Rather, we have tended to examine bounding cases. This approach was motivated by the knowledge that MSLB transients (which are more severe than SO-2 transients because of the larger break area) contribute very little to the overall TWCF. (See Figure 8.41 for a comparison of cooldown rates of all transient classes.) Consequently, detailed analysis of SO-2 transients was not viewed as being warranted. When considering the results presented for SO-2 transients, the reader is reminded (1) to view them as representing an upper bound to the vessel integrity challenge actually posed by SO-2 transients, and (2) to *expect* a greater apparent risk-significance of SO-2 transients in Palisades than in the other two plants as a result of the lack of refinement in the Palisades model of this transient class.

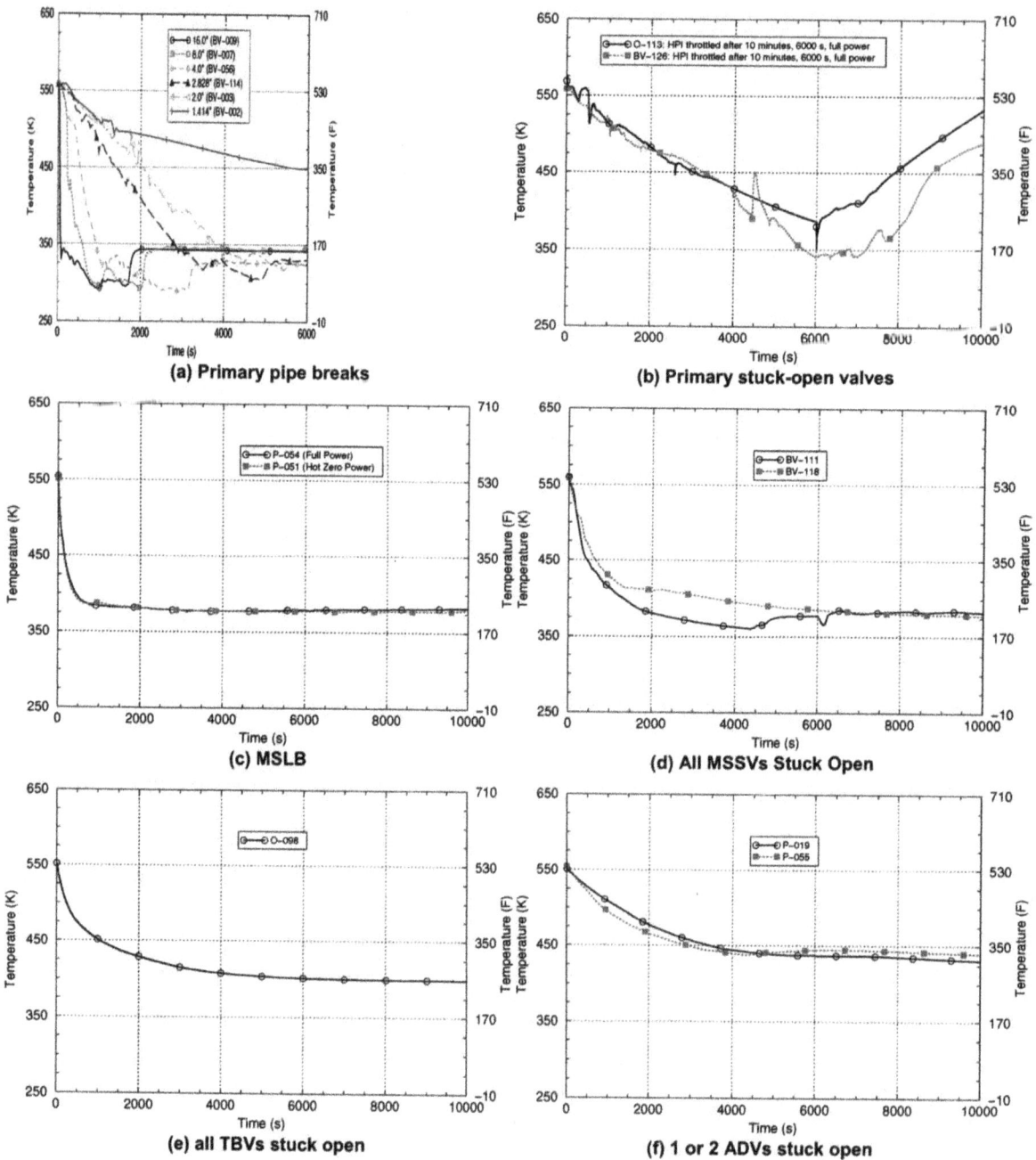

Figure 8.41. The cooldown rate of various SO-2 transients, graphs (d) through (f), compared to MSLBs, graph (c), and primary side transients, graphs (a) and (b).

8.5.5.3 Relationships between System Characteristics and Thermal-Hydraulic Response

As illustrated in Figure 8.41, the cooling rate associated with SO-2 transients is slower than for MSLBs and, in general, decreases with decreasing valve opening area. Additionally, while the minimum temperature experienced when MSSVs are open is the same as during an MSLB, the minimum temperature produced by opening TBVs or ADVs is higher (nearly 100°F (55.5°C) higher), further redacting the severity of these transients relative to MSLBs. Figure

8.42 through Figure 8.45 show both the temperature and pressure characteristics of a variety of different transients in the SO-2 category. These graphs show that for a number of different reasons (HHSI into the primary and failure to throttle same, AUX feed, etc.) SO-2 transients generally experience some (or even full) system pressure in the primary.

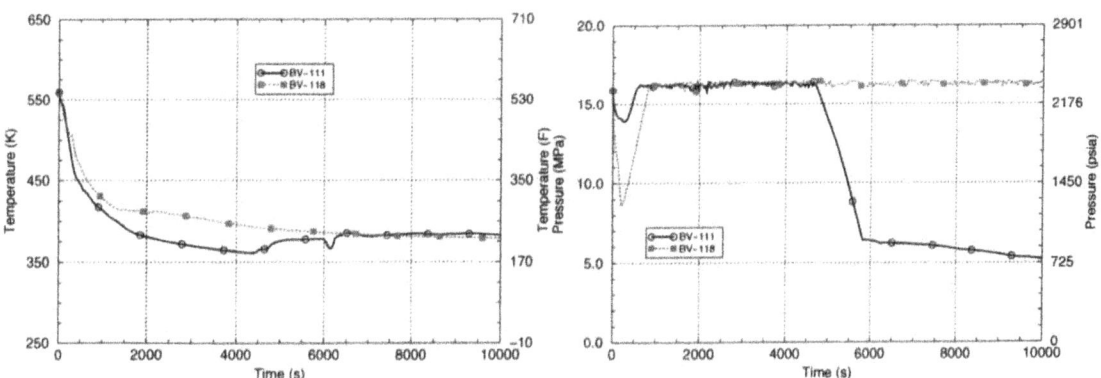

Figure 8.42. Small steam line break simulated by sticking open all MSSVs in steam generator A with AFW continuing to feed affected generator for 30 minutes. Beaver Valley transient 111 occurs at HZP, while Beaver Valley transient 118 occurs at full power.

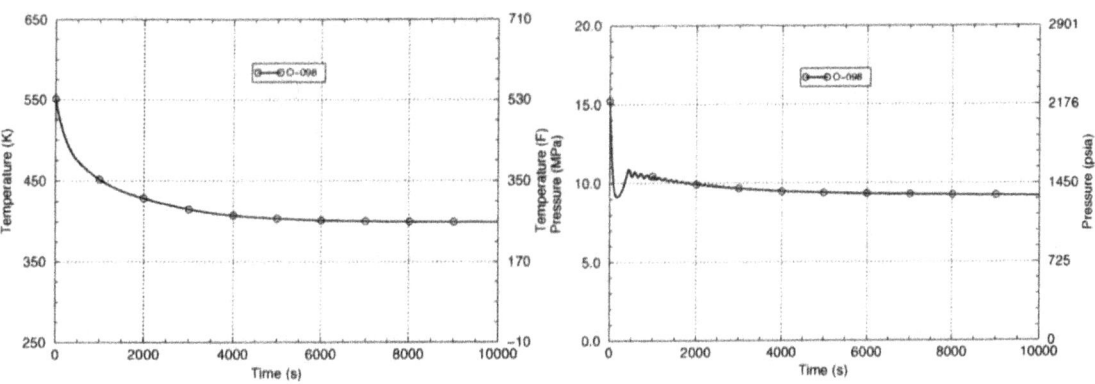

Figure 8.43. Reactor/turbine trip with loss of MFW and EFW in Oconee. Operator opens all TBVs to depressurize the secondary side.

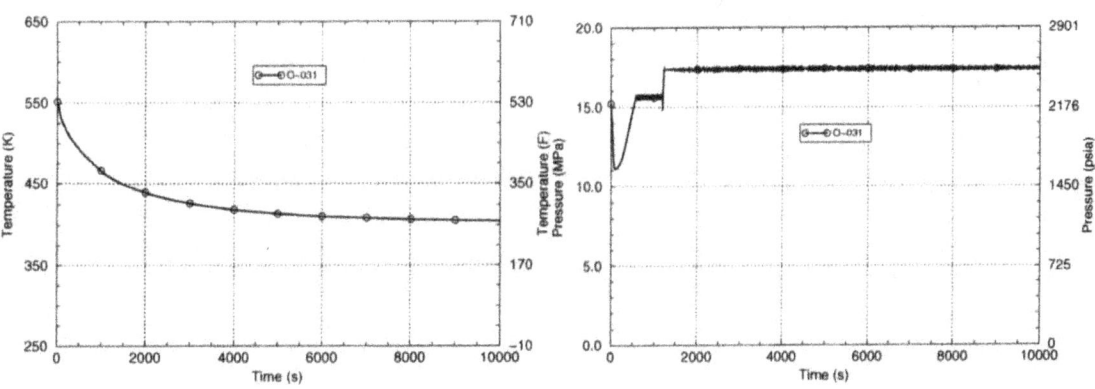

Figure 8.44. Reactor/turbine trip with two stuck-open safety valves in Oconee.

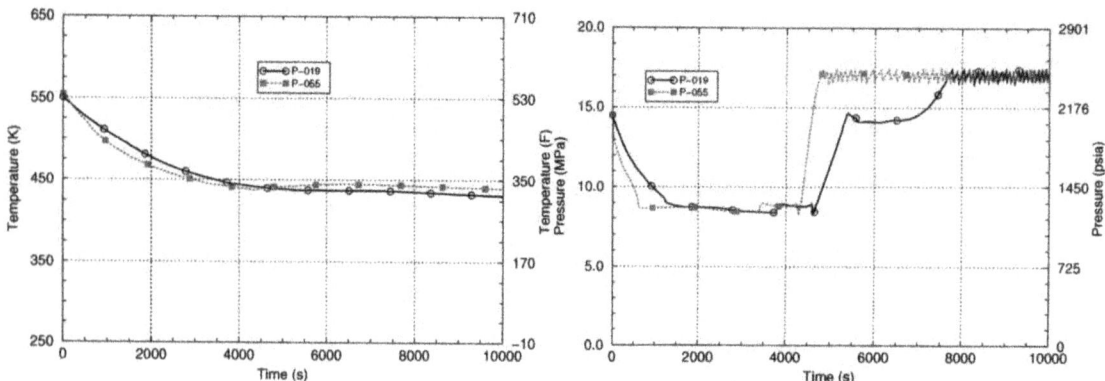

Figure 8.45. Reactor/turbine trip with one or two stuck-open ADVs (P-019 and P-055, respectively) in Palisades.

8.5.5.4 Estimates of Vessel Failure Probability

The CPTWC of SO-2 transients tends to be very low, consistent with the more gradual cooling rates caused by these transients relative to other transient classes (see Figure 8.41). Ranges of SO-2 CPTWC values for different transients are as follows (different plants are compared at roughly equivalent levels of embrittlement, see Table 8.6):

- Many stuck-open valves: CPTWC ranges from E-13 to E-10.

- One or two stuck-open valves: CPTWC ranges from E-13 to E-7.

Comparing these values with the E-5 to E-4 CPTWC values associated with the significant transients in the dominant classes (primary side pipe breaks and stuck-open valves on the primary side) provides a perspective on the limited influence of SO-2 transients to the total TWCF estimated for a vessel. As stated earlier, it is only the conservative binning of Palisades transients, this leading to high estimates of bin frequencies (see section 8.5.5.2), that has led SO-2 transients to contribute non-negligibly to the percentage total TWCF in Palisades (see Figure 8-11). More refined analysis of SO-2 transients for Palisades would reduce their influence to the point of being immeasurable, as was the case for Beaver Valley and Oconee.

Two factors in our analysis suggest that these findings can be applied to PWRs in general:

- the conservative modeling of SO-2 frequencies in Palisades

- the fact that the CPTWC values that result from *all* secondary side valves sticking open produces values that are negligible (E-13 to E-10) relative to significant transients in the dominant classes (E-5 to E-4).

Section 9.3 provides further discussion of the similarities and differences between the SO-2 modeling employed here and the general conditions in the operating fleet.

8.5.5.5 Comparison with Previous Studies

8.5.5.5.1 As Reported by [Kirk 12-02]

While the specific numerical results reported herein differ from those in our interim report [*Kirk 12-02*], the general trends discussed in this section have not changed substantively from those previously reported.

8.5.5.5.2 Studies Providing the Technical Basis of the Current PTS Rule

In the preceding analysis of the Oconee plant [ORNL 86], relevant operator action HEPs were applied to a wide spectrum of scenarios (i.e., not so scenario-specific). This analysis used generic probabilities for a limited number of operator events and did not consider all of the various times that we investigated. Thus, the preceding analysis of the Oconee plant for SO-2 transients should be viewed as being conservative relative to that reported herein. In the preceding analyses of Robinson and Calvert Cliffs [ORNL 85b, ORNL 85a], the HRA became more sophisticated, in that the HEPs were assigned on a more scenario-specific basis than for Oconee. However, these analyses still did not model different action times, as was done in our analysis. For these reasons, the preceding analysis of both Oconee and or H.B. Robinson for SO-2 transients should be viewed as being conservative relative to that reported herein.

Other generic factors contribute to the conservatism of the preceding analyses:

- Today, we have more industry experience, providing a larger data basis upon which to establish initiating event frequency estimates. The number of initiating events per year has declined since the earlier analyses were performed.

- Procedures and training have improved considerably.

- Modern PRA and HRA techniques have allowed us to do more refined analyses and model industry improvements.

- Increased computational ability has enabled finer subdivision of the challenges to the plant (more bins). This has considerably reduced the conservatism inherent to the binning process.

8.5.6 Other Transient Classes

Tables A.7 and A.8 in Appendix A summarize the transients analyzed in the following classes:

- feed-and-bleed
- steam generator tube rupture
- overfeeds
- mixed primary and secondary side failures

In all cases, the combination of the low probability of these events occurring with the low consequence of the event produces transients that are not risk-significant.

8.6   Summary

This chapter provides the results of plant-specific analyses of Oconee Unit 1, Beaver Valley Unit 1, and Palisades. In the following list, which summarizes the information presented in this chapter, the *conclusions* are shown in ***bold italics*** while supporting information is shown in regular type:

- ***The degree of PTS challenge for currently anticipated lifetimes and operating conditions is low.***

  o   Even at the end of license extension (60 operational years, or 48 EFPY at an 80% capacity factor), the mean estimated through-wall cracking frequency (*TWCF*) does not exceed 2×10^{-8}/year for the plants analyzed. Considering that the Beaver Valley and Palisades RPVs are constructed from some of the most irradiation-sensitive materials in commercial reactor service today, these results suggest that, provided that operating practices do not change dramatically in the future, the operating reactor fleet is in little danger of exceeding either the limit on *TWCF* of 5×10^{-6}/yr expressed by Regulatory Guide 1.154 [RG 1.154] or the 1×10^{-6}/yr value recommended in Chapter 10, even after license extension.

- ***Mean TWCF values are in fact upper bounds.***

  o   Because of the skewness characteristic of the *TWCF* distributions that arise as a result of the physical processes responsible for steel fracture, mean *TWCF* values correspond to the 90th percentile (or higher) of the *TWCF* distribution. Thus, the mean *TWCF* values we report in this chapter are appropriately regarded as upper bounds to the uncertainty distribution on TWCF.

- *Axial flaws, and the toughness properties that can be associated with such flaws, control nearly all of the TWCF.*

  o Axial flaws are much more likely to propagate through-wall than circumferential flaws because the applied driving force to fracture increases continuously with increasing crack depth for an axial flaw. Conversely, circumferentially oriented flaws experience a driving force peak mid-wall, providing a natural crack arrest mechanism. It should be noted that crack initiation from circumferentially oriented flaws is likely; it is only their through-wall propagation that is much less likely (relative to axially oriented flaws).

  o It is, therefore, the toughness properties that can be associated with axial flaws that control nearly all of the TWCF. These include the toughness properties of plates and axial welds at the flaw locations. Conversely, the toughness properties of both circumferential welds and forgings have little effect on TWCF because these can be associated only with circumferentially oriented flaws.

- *Transients involving primary side faults are the dominant contributors to TWCF. Transients involving secondary side faults play a much smaller role.*

  o The severity of a transient is controlled by a combination of three factors:

    - the initial cooling rate, which controls the thermal stress in the RPV wall

    - the minimum temperature of the transient, which controls the resistance of the vessel to fracture

    - the pressure retained in the primary system, which controls the pressure stress in the RPV wall

  o The significance of a transient (i.e., how much it contributes to PTS risk) depends on these three factors and on the likelihood of the transient occurring.

o Our analysis considered transients in the following classes:

  - primary side pipe breaks
  - stuck-open valves on the primary side
  - main steam line breaks
  - stuck-open valves on the secondary side
  - feed-and-bleed
  - steam generator tube rupture
  - mixed primary and secondary initiators

o Table 8.12 summarizes our results for these transient classes in terms of both transient severity indicators and the likelihood of the transient occurring. The color-coding of table entries indicates the contribution (or not) of these factors to the TWCF of the different classes of transients. This summary indicates that the risk-dominant transients (medium- and large-diameter primary side pipe breaks, and stuck-open primary side valves that later reclose) all have multiple factors that, in combination, result in their significant contribution to TWCF.

  - For medium- to large-diameter primary side pipe breaks, the fast to moderate cooling rates and the low downcomer temperatures (generated by the rapid depressurization and emergency injection of low-temperature makeup water directly to the primary) combine to produce a high-severity transient. Despite the moderate to low likelihood of transient occurrence, the severity of these transients (if they occur) makes them significant contributors to the total TWCF.

  - For stuck-open primary side valves that later reclose, the repressurization associated with valve reclosure coupled with low temperatures in the primary combine to produce a high-severity transient. This coupled with a high likelihood of transient occurrence makes stuck-open primary side valves that later reclose significant contributors to the total TWCF.

Table 8.12. Factors contributing to the severity and risk-dominance of various transient classes

Transient Class		Transient Severity			Transient Likelihood	TWCF Contribution
		Cooling Rate	Minimum Temperature	Pressure		
Primary Side Pipe Breaks	Large-Diameter	Fast	Low	Low	Low	Large
	Medium-Diameter	Moderate	Low	Low	Moderate	Large
	Small-Diameter	Slow	High	Moderate	High	~0
Primary Stuck-Open Valves	Valve Recloses	Slow	Moderate	High	High	Large
	Valve Remains Open	Slow	Moderate	Low	High	~0
Main Steam Line Break		Fast	Moderate	High	High	Small
Stuck-Open Valve(s), Secondary Side		Moderate	High	High	High	~0
Feed-and-Bleed		Slow	Low	Low	Low	~0
Steam Generator Tube Rupture		Slow	High	Moderate	Low	~0
Mixed Primary & Secondary Initiators		Slow	Mixed		Very Low	~0
Color Key	Enhances TWCF Contribution		Intermediate		Diminishes TWCF Contribution	

8-73

- The small or negligible contribution of all secondary side transients (MSLBs, stuck-open secondary valves) results directly from the lack of low temperatures in the primary system. For these transients, the minimum temperature of the primary for times of relevance is controlled by the boiling point of water in the secondary (212°F (100°C) or above). At these temperatures, the fracture toughness of the RPV steel is sufficiently high to resist vessel failure in most cases.

- *Credits for operator action, while included in our analysis, do not influence these findings in any significant way.* Operator action credits can dramatically influence the risk-significance of *individual* transients. Appropriate credits for operator action, therefore, need to be included as part of a "best estimate" analysis because there is no way to establish *a priori* if a particular transient will make a large contribution to the total risk. Nonetheless, the results of our analyses demonstrate that the *overall effect* of these operator action credits on the *total TWCF* for a plant is small, for the following reasons:

  o Medium- and Large-Diameter Primary Side Pipe Breaks: No operator actions are modeled for any break diameter because, for these events, the safety injection systems do not fully refill the upper regions of the RCS. Consequently, operators would never take action to shut off the pumps.

  o Stuck-Open Primary Side Valves that May Later Reclose: Reasonable and appropriate credit for operator actions (throttling of HPI) has been included in the PRA model. However, the influence of these credits on the estimated values of vessel failure probability attributable to SO-1 transients is small because the operator actions credited only prevent repressurization when SO-1 transients initiate from HZP conditions and when

the operators act promptly (within 1 minute) to throttle HPI. Complete removal of operator action credits from the model increases the total risk associated with SO-1 transients only slightly.

  o Main Steam Line Breaks: For the overwhelming majority of MSLB transients, vessel failure is predicted to occur between 10 and 15 minutes after transient initiation because it is within this timeframe that the thermal stresses associated with the rapid cooldown reach their maximum. Thus, all of the long-time effects (isolation of feedwater flow, timing of HSSI control) that can be influenced by operator actions have no effect on vessel failure probability because these factors influence the progression of the transient after failure has occurred (if it occurs). Only factors affecting the initial cooling rate (i.e., plant power level at transient initiation, break location inside or outside of containment) can influence the CPTWC values. These factors are not influenced in any way by operator actions.

- *Because the severity of the most significant transients in the dominant transient classes are controlled by factors that are common to PWRs in general, the TWCF results presented in this chapter can be used with confidence to develop revised PTS screening criteria that apply to the entire fleet of operating PWRs.*

  o Medium- and Large-Diameter Primary Side Pipe Breaks: For these break diameters, the fluid in the primary cools faster than can the wall of the RPV. In this situation, *only* the thermal conductivity of the steel and the thickness of the RPV wall control the thermal stresses and, thus, the severity of the fracture challenge. Perturbations to the fluid cooldown rate controlled by break diameter, break location, and season of the year do not play a role. Thermal conductivity is a physical property, so it is very consistent for all

RPV steels, and the thicknesses of the three RPVs analyzed are typical of PWRs. Consequently, the TWCF contribution of medium- to large-diameter primary side pipe breaks is expected to be consistent from plant-to-plant and can be well-represented for all PWRs by the analyses reported herein.

o Stuck-Open Primary Side Valves that May Later Reclose: A major contributor to the risk-significance of SO-1 transients is the return to full system pressure once the valve recloses. The operating and safety relief valve pressures of all PWRs are similar. Additionally, as previously noted, operator action credits affect the total

risk associated with this transient class only slightly.

o Main Steam Line Breaks: Since MSLBs fail early (within 10–15 minutes after transient initiation), only factors affecting the initial cooling rate can have any influence on CPTWC values. These factors include the plant power level at event initiation and the location of the break (inside or outside of containment). These factors are not influenced in any way by operator actions.

9 Generalization of the Baseline Results to All Pressurized-Water Reactors

In Chapter 8, we presented the results of three plant-specific analyses of Oconee Unit 1, Beaver Valley Unit 1, and Palisades. These analyses quantified the variation with material embrittlement level of the annual risk of developing a through-wall crack in an RPV. Since the objective of this project is to develop a revision to the PTS screening limit expressed in 10 CFR 50.61 that applies *in general* to all PWRs, it is critical that we understand the extent to whixh our analyses adequately address the range of conditions experienced by domestic PWRs. In this chapter, we therefore examine the generality of our results, focusing on four topics that address this goal:

- Sections 9.1 and 9.2 describe sensitivity studies performed on the TH and PFM models, respectively. These studies address the effect of credible changes to the model and/or its input parameters on the output of the model. Such results are needed to engender confidence in both the robustness of the results presented in Chapter 8 and their applicability to PWRs *in general*.

- Section 9.3 describes an effort in which we examine the plant design and operational characteristics of five additional plants. Our aim is to determine whether the design and operational features that are the key contributors to PTS risk (see Section 8.6) vary significantly enough in the general plant population to question the generality of our results.

- Throughout our analysis, we have assumed that the only possible causes of PTS events have origins that are *internal* to the plant. However, *external* events such as fires, floods, earthquakes, and so on, can also be PTS precursors. Therefore, in Section 9.4, we examine the potential for external initiating events to create significant

additional risk relative to the internal initiating events we have already modeled in detail.

9.1 Thermal-Hydraulic Sensitivity Studies

9.1.1 Introduction

This section addresses the results and observations of the thermal-hydraulic analyses and sensitivity studies performed to support the PTS analysis. The sensitivity studies were performed to evaluate the effects of variations in parameters that can affect the downcomer conditions used as boundary conditions to the probabilistic fracture mechanics analysis. These conditions are the average downcomer fluid temperature, the system pressure and the average downcomer fluid to wall heat transfer coefficient. The sensitivity studies were performed to achieve the following purposes:

(1) Determine the effect on average downcomer fluid temperature range attributable to variation of system parameters such as break size, break location, season, and others.

(2) Evaluate the impact of downcomer heat transfer coefficient on the downcomer conditions and, ultimately, on conditional probability of through-wall cracking (CPTWC).

The thermal-hydraulic analysis was performed using RELAP5/MOD3.2.2Gamma. Chapter 6 presents a discussion of RELAP5 as used in this analysis, along with a comparison of RELAP predictions of pressure, temperature, and heat transfer coefficient to the results of both separate effects and integral systems and tests (see Section 6.7). A discussion of how uncertainty was factored into the analysis is also presented in Chapter 6 (see Section 6.8.2).

9.1.2 Sensitivity Studies Performed for Uncertainty Analysis

Selection of sensitivity studies that were performed is based largely on previous experience with the types of transients being analyzed combined with variations in plant operating states that can affect the downcomer conditions. Sensitivity studies were performed for the Oconee, Beaver Valley, and Palisades plants to support the thermal-hydraulic uncertainty analyses. As previously noted, the uncertainty analysis approach is discussed in Chapter 6. This section focuses on the results of the sensitivity studies conducted to support the uncertainty analysis. [*Chang*] discusses the sensitivity and uncertainty analyses in detail.

9.1.2.1 LOCAs

Sensitivity analyses were performed on LOCAs ranging from 1.4-in. (3.59-cm) to 8-in. (20.32-cm) for the Oconee, Beaver Valley, and Palisades plants. Various sensitivity parameters were defined and a RELAP5 run was made for a selected parameter, changing only that parameter. The average downcomer fluid temperature over a 10,000-second period was then computed. The downcomer temperature difference between the nominal case (no parameters varied) and the cases where a parameter is varied is used in the uncertainty analysis.

Table 9.1, Table 9.2, and Table 9.3 present a summary of the key sensitivity parameters and the effects on downcomer temperature for the Oconee, Beaver Valley, and Palisades plants, respectively. The nominal temperatures are based on RELAP5 runs with no change in sensitivity parameters, while the other temperatures listed are the differences between the temperature results for the changed sensitivity parameter and the nominal temperature results. Several parameters were considered in the sensitivity analysis, including

season of the year, decay heat load, heat transfer coefficient, break area, and break location. Season of the year considered the impact of winter and summer on the ECCS injection water temperature. Typically, the RWST (or equivalent), which is the source of HPI and LPI injection water, is located outdoors. The temperature range analyzed is listed below:

- Oconee: The HPI and LPI injection temperature used is 303 K [85°F], and the core flood tank temperature is 311 K [100°F] during the summer. During the winter, the HPI and LPI injection temperature used is 278 K [40°F], and the core flood tank temperature is 294 K [70°F]. For the nominal case, the HPI and LPI injection temperature used is 294 K [70°F], and the core flood tank temperature is 300 K [80°F].

- Beaver Valley: HPI and LPI injection temperature used is 286 K [55°F], and core flood tank temperature is 314 K [105°F] during the summer. During the winter, the HPI and LPI injection temperature used is 281 K [45°F], and the core flood tank temperature is 297 K [75°F]. For the nominal case, the HPI and LPI injection temperature used is 283 K [50°F], and core flood tank temperature is 305 K [90°F]. Note that Beaver Valley currently cools the RWST to meet LOCA safety limits.

- Palisades: The HPI and LPI injection temperature used is 311 K [100°F], and the safety injection tank temperature is 305 K [90°F] during the summer. During the winter, the HPI and LPI injection temperature used is 278 K [40°F], and the safety injection tank temperature is 289 K [60°F]. For the nominal case, the HPI and LPI injection temperature used is 304 K [87.9°F], and the safety injection tank temperature is 300 K [80°F].

Table 9.1. Summary of Oconee Downcomer Fluid Temperature Sensitivity Results for LOCA

Parameter	Break Diameter					
	3.6-cm [1.4 in]	5.1-cm [2 in]	7.2-cm [2.8 in]	10.2-cm [4 in]	14.4-cm [5.7 in]	20.3-cm [8 in]
Nominal	*414 K [285°F]*	*394 K [250°F]*	*388 K [239°F]*	*363 K [194°F]*	*329 K [133°F]*	*317 K [111°F]*
Winter	-12 K [-22°F]	-	-14 K [-25°F]	-	-15 K [-27°F]	-3 K [-5°F]
Summer	-	-	7 K [13°F]	-	7 K [13°F]	0 K [0°F]
0.7% Decay Heat Load	-16 K [-29°F]	-	-39 K [-70°F]	-	-8 K [-14°F]	-5 K [-9°F]
130% Heat Transfer Coeff	-	6 K [11°F]	8 K [14°F]	-	2 K [4°F]	-
70% Heat Transfer Coeff	-	-7 K [-13°F]	-8 K [-14°F]	-	-5 K [-9°F]	-
Cold Leg Break		61 K [110°F]	24 K [43°F]	13 K [23°F]	16 K [29°F]	0 K [0°F]

Note: The *nominal* temperatures listed above are based on RELAP5 runs with no change in sensitivity parameters. Other temperatures listed are the difference between the temperature results for the changed sensitivity parameter and the nominal temperature results.

Table 9.2. Summary of Beaver Valley Downcomer Fluid Temperature Sensitivity Results for LOCA

Parameter	Break Diameter					
	3.6-cm [1.4 in]	5.1-cm [2 in]	7.2-cm [2.8 in]	10.2-cm [4 in]	14.4-cm [5.7 in]	20.3-cm [8 in]
Nominal	*459 K [367°F]*	*377 K [219°F]*	*336 K [145°F]*	*319 K [115°F]*	*313 K [104°F]*	*300 K [80°F]*
Winter	-2 K [-4°F]	-11 K [-20°F]	-3 K [-5°F]	-1 K [-2°F]	3 K [5°F]	-3 K [-5°F]
Summer	1 K [2°F]	-7 K [-13°F]	8 K [14°F]	12 K [22°F]	5 K [9°F]	3 K [5°F]
0.7% Decay Heat Load	-99 K [-178°F]	-29 K [-52°F]	-11 K [-20°F]	-7 K [-13°F]	-9 K [-16°F]	-1 K [-2°F]
0.2% Decay Heat Load	-106 K [-191°F]	-40 K [-72°F]	-16 K [-29°F]	-10 K [-18°F]	-11 K [-20°F]	-2 K [-4°F]
130% Heat Transfer Coeff	3 K [5°F]	-3 K [-5°F]	6 K [11°F]	5 K [9°F]		0 K [0°F]
70% Heat Transfer Coeff	-4 K [-7°F]	-15 K [-27°F]	-5 K [-9°F]	2 K [4°F]		
130% Break Area		-48 K [-86°F]	-11 K [-20°F]	-12 K [-22°F]	-13 K [-23°F]	1 K [2°F]
70% Break Area		-18 K [-32°F]	23 K [41°F]	4 K [7°F]	-7 K [-13°F]	6 K [11°F]
Cold Leg Break	-4 K [-7°F]	76 K [137°F]	79 K [142°F]	50 K [90°F]	34 K [61°F]	40 K [72°F]

Note: The *nominal* temperatures listed above are based on RELAP5 runs with no change in sensitivity parameters. Other temperatures listed are the difference between the temperature results for the changed sensitivity parameter and the nominal temperature results.

Table 9.3. Summary of Palisades Downcomer Fluid Temperature Sensitivity Results for LOCA

Parameter	Break Diameter					
	3.6-cm [1.4 in]	5.1-cm [2 in]	7.2-cm [2.8 in]	10.2-cm [4 in]	14.4-cm [5.7 in]	20.3-cm [8 in]
Nominal	*482 K [408°F]*	*427 K [309°F]*	*391 K [244°F]*	*350 K [170°F]*	*320 K [116°F]*	*310 K [98°F]*
Winter	-6 K [-11°F]	-8 K [-14°F]	-17 K [-31°F]	-16 K [-29°F]	-16 K [-29°F]	-16 K [-29°F]
Summer	8 K [14°F]	10 K [18°F]	13 K [23°F]	14 K [25°F]	13 K [23°F]	15 K [27°F]
0.7% Decay Heat Load	-32 K [-58°F]	-21 K [-38°F]	-27 K [-49°F]	-17 K [-31°F]	-1 K [-2°F]	0 K [0°F]
0.2% Decay Heat Load	-66 K [-119°F]	-47 K [-85°F]	-40 K [-72°F]	-20 K [-36°F]	-2 K [-4°F]	-1 K [-2°F]
130% Heat Transfer Coeff	4 K [7°F]	6 K [11°F]	11 K [20°F]	5 K [9°F]		
70% Heat Transfer Coeff	-3 K [-5°F]	-2 K [-4°F]	-2 K [-4°F]	-4 K [-8°F]		
130% Break Area		13 K [23°F]	24 K [43°F]	20 K [36°F]	14 K [25°F]	3 K [5°F]
70% Break Area		-9 K [-16°F]	-18 K [-32°F]	-12 K [-22°F]	-6 K [-11°F]	-1 K [-2°F]
Cold Leg Break	9 K [16°F]	38 K [68°F]	39 K [70°F]	23 K [41°F]	32 K [58°F]	22 K [40°F]

Note: The *nominal* temperatures listed above are based on RELAP5 runs with no change in sensitivity parameters. Other temperatures listed are the difference between the temperature results for the changed sensitivity parameter and the nominal temperature results.

As listed in Table 9.1 through Table 9.3, the two levels of decay heat considered were 0.7% and 0.2% of full power. The heat transfer coefficient was varied by 70% and 130% of the RELAP5 computed value in the primary system except for the core and the steam generator tubes. The nominal break area was varied by a factor of 0.7 and 1.3 to evaluate possible uncertainty in the break flow. Finally, breaks of various sizes in the cold leg as well as the hot leg are considered.

Some overall trends in the results are seen from the results in Table 9.1, through Table 9.3. First, the magnitude of the variation from nominal generally decreases with increasing break size for all three plants regardless of the parameter being evaluated, because of the combined effects of increased break and ECCS flow that occurs as the break size increases. For break diameters of 4-in. (10.2-cm) or more, ECCS flow is at a maximum since the HPI and LPI pumps are generally operating at pump runout conditions. For breaks diameters less than 2.8-in. (7.2-cm), the pump flow begins to become limited by the break flow, with decreasing pump flow as the break diameter is decreased. In this range of break diameters, the downcomer fluid temperature is more sensitive to changes in break diameter.

Cold leg breaks generally show the greatest increase in downcomer fluid temperature for the three plants, principally because of partial ECCS bypass through the break.

The assumed decay heat load between hot full power and hot zero power cases shows the greatest decrease in downcomer fluid temperature. These sensitivity parameters are part of the definition of the boundary conditions that typically are provided as part of the transient definition.

Parameters that involve model sensitivity such as change in break area, change in heat transfer coefficient (system-wide) also significantly affect the downcomer fluid temperature. Of the two parameters, downcomer fluid temperature is more sensitive to changes in break flow. As a result, a number of transients with adjustments in break area were included in the baseline models discussed in Chapter 8.

9.1.2.2 Stuck-Open Pressurizer SRVs That Reclose

Sensitivity cases for stuck-open primary side SRVs considered the following parameters:

- Number of valves stuck open (i.e., one or two valves)

- Timing of valve reclosure (Reclosure times of 3,000 s, 6,000 s, and no reclosure were analyzed. Additional sensitivity studies were conducted for longer reclosure times; see response to Peer Review Comment #76 in Appendix B.)

- Time for operator to start HPI throttling (i.e., 1 minute, 10 minutes, and not throttled)

- Decay heat (i.e., full-power and HZP)

The number of stuck-open valves analyzed for the three plants depended on the plant characteristics. For Oconee, analysis was performed for one stuck-open SRV, since the probability of two stuck-open valves was screened out on the basis of low probability. For Palisades, sensitivity analysis was not performed on the stuck-open valve scenarios.

For Beaver Valley, sensitivity studies were performed for one and two stuck-open valves considering various parameters, similar to the approach used for LOCA transients. The range used for each parameter is the same as used for the LOCA. The sensitivity of downcomer fluid temperature to each parameter is listed in Table 9.4. As in the LOCA case, the nominal temperatures are based on RELAP5 runs with no change in sensitivity parameters while the other temperatures listed are the difference between the changed and the nominal sensitivity parameter.

Table 9.4. Summary of Downcomer Fluid Temperature Sensitivity Results for Stuck-Open Primary Side Valves

| | Number of Stuck-Open SRVs | |
	1 valve	2 valves
Nominal	393 K [248°F]	349 K [169°F]
Winter	-5 K [-9°F]	-3 K [-5°F]
Summer	0 K [0°F]	6 K [11°F]
0.7% Decay Heat Load	-42 K [-76°F]	-15 K [-27°F]
0.2% Decay Heat Load	-52 K [-93°F]	-27 K [-49°F]
130% Heat Transfer Coeff	3 K [-5°F]	6 K [-11°F]
70% Heat Transfer Coeff	-8 K [-14°F]	-4 K [-7°F]
130% Valve Flow Area		-22 K [-40°F]
70% Valve Flow Area		10 K [18°F]

Some overall trends in the results are seen in Table 9.4. The largest change in temperature is from the variation in decay heat, a finding consistent with the observations made in Section 8.5.3.3.2 concerning the differences between HZP and full-power transients. This sensitivity parameter is part of the definition of the transient boundary conditions that are part of the definition of the transient being analyzed. Changes in valve flow area also significantly affect the downcomer fluid temperature. Parameters that involve model sensitivity such as change in break area, change in heat transfer coefficient (system-wide) also significantly affect the downcomer fluid temperature. Of the two parameters, downcomer fluid temperature is more sensitive to changes in break flow. Changes in these parameters are considered in defining the transients used in the risk assessment.

9.1.2.3 CPTWC Sensitivity During LOCA Transients

One of the trends identified in the sensitivity and uncertainty analysis performed in [*Chang*] is the relationship between the conditional probability of vessel failure (CPF) and the LOCA break diameter; see the related discussion in Sections 8.5.2.4.1 and 8.5.2.4.2. Figure 9.1 presents the Oconee, Beaver Valley, and Palisades CPTWC results at an approximately equivalent embrittlement level. The CPTWC data presented in Figure 9.1 for Oconee and Beaver Valley are for surge line or hot leg breaks with the indicated diameter. The transients were initiated from hot full-power conditions. The data presented for Palisades are for cold leg breaks, with the exception of the 16-in. (40.6-cm) results which represent a hot leg break. All of the Palisades cases are initiated from full-power conditions.

The results in Figure 9.1 show that CPTWC is relatively insensitive to thermal-hydraulic conditions in the primary system during LOCAs with a break diameter greater than 5.656-in. (14.4-cm). For these break diameters, the primary system cooldown rate is governed by the high rate of break and ECCS injection flow, which is a maximum at this break size range. The safety injection tanks discharge within a few minutes of accident initiation. Additionally, the high pressure and low-pressure injection systems will be at or near pump runout conditions. The combined flow of the injection systems and safety injection tank discharge will fill the downcomer with subcooled water after the initial blowdown for the duration of the transient. In this range of break sizes, the blowdown flow of the break is much greater than the ECCS flow delivery rate. The downcomer fluid temperature will be determined principally by the flow from the high and low-pressure injection systems, the safety injection tank discharge, and the initial temperature of the water used in the injection systems. In this range of break sizes, CPTWC reaches a maximum.

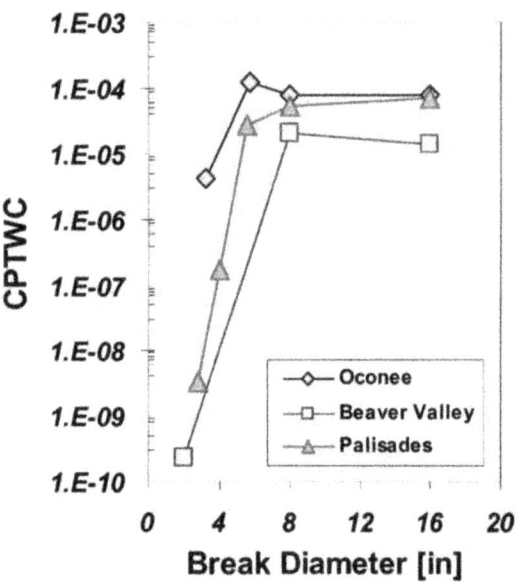

Figure 9.1. CPTWC Behavior for LOCAs of Various Break Diameters

The sensitivity of CPTWC to break size increases for break sizes below 5.656-in. (14.4-cm). This trend is seen for all of the results presented in Figure 9.1. For these smaller break diameters, the balance between break flow and the ECCS injection flow governs the primary system cooldown and depressurization rates. System depressurization is slower relative to the larger breaks (greater than 5.656-in. (14.4-cm)). As a result, safety injection tank discharge and initiation of low-pressure system injection begins later in the transient, and the injection rate is lower. At the lower end of this break diameter range (i.e., ≈2.5-in. or ≈5-cm), low-pressure system injection flow may not even be initiated, and the safety injection tanks may not totally discharge. In this range of break sizes, the depressurization limits the rate of high- and low-pressure injection system injection to the reactor system. The downcomer fluid temperature is principally determined by the break diameter (break flow), the flow from the high- and low-pressure injection systems, the safety injection tank discharge, and the initial temperature of the water used in these systems as in the larger breaks. However, water is injected at a slower rate, resulting in a slower cooldown and relative to the larger breaks.

One significant aspect of the results shown in Figure 9.1 is that there is a limit to the CPTWC value for each plant and, hence, to the risk of vessel failure produced by a primary side pipe break. Additionally, this limiting CPTWC behavior would be similar for any plant because the designs of the different vendors all have similar ratios of initial energy to RCS volume and core power to RCS volume.

The observations on CPTWC behavior suggest that the same CPTWC trend will occur for any plant with a shift in the break diameter at which the CPTWC curve bends over and reaches a maximum. This behavior is expected to occur regardless of plant power level given that the ECCS system for any plant is designed to cool the core under a wide variety of LOCA conditions. This observation is relevant to the applicability of these results to PWRs *in general*.

9.2 Fracture mechanics sensitivity studies

We have performed sensitivity studies on our PFM model (and on PFM-related variables) with two aims in mind:

- To provide confidence in the **_robustness_** of our PFM model, we assessed the effect of credible model and input perturbations on TWCF estimates.

- To provide confidence that the results of our calculations for three specific plants can be **_generalized_** to apply to all PWRs, we performed sensitivity studies to assess the influence of factors not fully considered in our baseline TWCF estimates (see Chapter 8).

Full details of sensitivity studies of our PFM model are available in a companion report [**_EricksonKirk-SS_**]. This section provides a brief summary of that information.

9.2.1 Sensitivity Studies Performed To Assess the Robustness of the PFM Model

9.2.1.1 Approach

The model used to generate TWCF estimates is a complex assemblage of many sub-models and parameter inputs. These combine to produce intermediate calculated results that, upon passing through yet more sub-models, eventually become an estimated distribution of TWCF. The existence of each sub-model and parameter input in the PFM model, and their arrangement with respect to one another, represents a decision to structure the overall model in a particular way. Changing any one of these decisions can, in principal, change the estimated output of the model (i.e., the distribution of TWCF values). Therefore, we investigated the degree to which the selection of *credible* alternative sub-models may influence the TWCF estimates. Additionally, many of the inputs parameters to the PFM cannot be known precisely. Therefore, we also investigated the degree to which *credible* variations in the input parameters change the TWCF estimates. This approach of basing sensitivity studies on *credible* alternative sub-models and/or on *credible* variations of the input parameters follows directly from two principles of our overall approach to model building (see Section 3.2):

- the use of realistic input values and sub-models

- an *explicit* treatment of uncertainties

These principles permitted calculation of TWCF estimates that are systematically biased neither high nor low (i.e., values that represent a *"best estimate"*) to the greatest extent practicable. By basing sensitivity studies on *credible* alternative sub-models and *credible* variations of the input parameters, we maintain these principals and, thereby, allow our TWCF estimates to maintain their "best estimate" label.

This approach to performing sensitivity studies deviates from that taken previously [SECY-82-465], wherein sensitivity studies either focused on "important" parameters and sub-models (i.e., those to which the TWCF was believed to be sensitive), or were performed seemingly without consideration of either the technical justification for the baseline sub-model or the credibility of the alternative sub-model used to motivate the sensitivity study. We feel it is, in most cases, important to avoid such *ad hoc* justifications for performing sensitivity studies. Low sensitivity of the output TWCF to a change in a sub-model or input having an inadequate technical justification does not provide a rational basis for accepting that sub-model or input as part of the overall model. Similarly, high sensitivity of the output to a well justified sub-model or input does not provide a basis for either condemning that sub-model/input or adopting arbitrary margins in an effort to compensate for the high sensitivity.

9.2.1.2 Sensitivity Studies Performed

As detailed in [*EricksonKirk-SS*], the following sensitivity studies were performed to provide confidence in the robustness of the PFM model:

- flaw distribution (size and density of simulated flaws)

- residual stresses assumed to exist in the RPV wall

- embrittlement shift model used and treatment of uncertainties

- re-sampling of chemical composition variables at the ¼T, ½T, and ¾T locations for welds

- crack face pressure

- upper shelf toughness model

The results of these sensitivities are summarized in the following sections.

9.2.1.2.1 Flaw Distribution

As detailed in Appendix C, the distributions of flaws that FAVOR simulates provide a conservative representation of both the sizes and densities of crack-like defects that exist in the general population of PWRs. Additionally, these flaw distributions were based on what is generally regarded as among the most comprehensive studies of flaws in RPV fabrication that is currently available [*Simonen*]. Consequently, it is difficult to find a *credible* alternative flaw model on which to motivate a sensitivity study. Nonetheless, it is informative to understand the characteristics of the flaws drawn from these distributions that contribute most significantly to the estimated values of FCI and TWCF. For example, the information presented in Figure 8.7 indicated that only axial flaws can contribute significantly to the TWCF atributable to differences in the through-wall variation of crack driving force between axial and circumferentially oriented flaws. Two other general statements can be made regarding the flaws that contribute most significantly to the estimated TWCF values:

(1) They are located close to the inner diameter surface of the vessel. The tensile thermal stresses produced by rapid cooling along the vessel ID do not penetrate far into the wall thickness of the RPV. A natural consequence of this, which is illustrated in Figure 9.3, is that the great majority of the cracks that are predicted to initiate and subsequently propagate through the vessel wall lie very close to the inner diameter surface. The information in Figure 9.3 indicates that almost all flaws that initiate lie less than 1/8-T from the vessel ID. Since they are driven by the thermal stresses characteristic of cooldown transients, these observations hold true independent of embrittlement level.

(2) They have a small through-wall dimension. This again occurs as a direct consequence of the fact that cooldown transients produce thermal stresses that (together with the pressure stresses) are only high enough to initiate cracks at locations close to the inner diameter of the vessel. Consequently, larger

flaws (which would generally be considered more deleterious in a fracture evaluation than would small flaws) tend to not initiate very frequently because their crack tips lie too far away from the inner diameter surface and, so, are subjected to low tensile loads, or even to compressive loads. In Figure 9.4 and Figure 9.5, we examine the effect of duration of irradiation exposure, flaw location (in plate or weld), and transient type on the flaw sizes that initiate fracture in our analyses. This information demonstrates that the combined effects of the duration of irradiation exposure and flaw location are small, and are entirely as expected for they correlate well with relative embrittlement levels. Transient type plays a minor role, with predominantly thermal transients such as large pipe breaks generally initiating fracture from smaller flaws while transients that involve a significant pressure component (such as stuck-open valves that may later reclose) tend to initiate fracture from larger flaws. Nonetheless, the flaws that contribute to the estimated through-wall cracking frequency are small, having median depths ranging from 0.1 to 0.3-in. (2.54 to 7.62-mm).

In combination, these observations help to allay concerns that the flaw distributions sampled in FAVOR do not simulate enough flaws of large dimensions, or that the postulated future discovery of a large (previously undetected) flaw in service could invalidate the results of this study. Neither of these concerns is valid because, given the dominant effects of thermal stresses in controlling crack driving force, large flaws do not play a role in establishing the risk of RPV failure attributable to PTS.

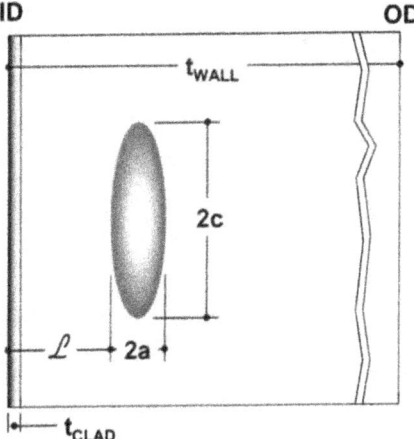

Figure 9.2. Flaw dimension and position descriptors adopted in FAVOR

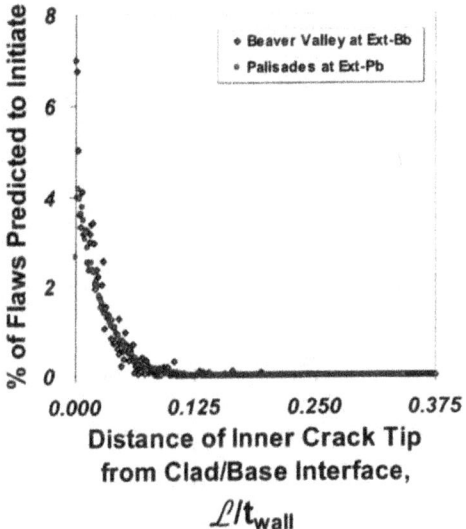

Figure 9.3. Distribution of through-wall position of cracks that initiate

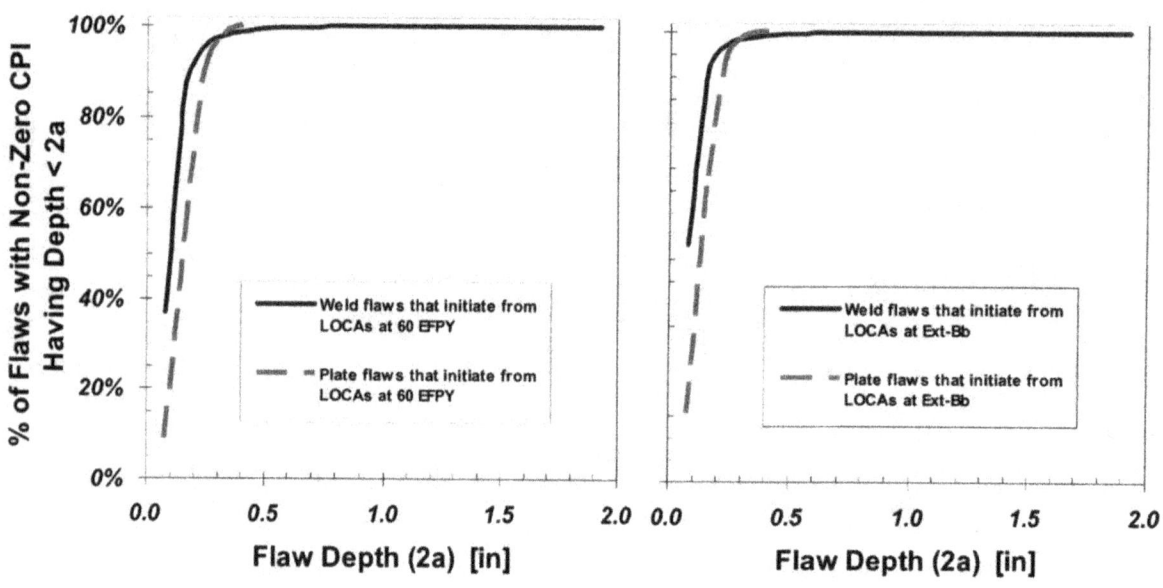

Figure 9.4. Flaw depths that contribute to crack initiation probability in Beaver Valley Unit 1 when subjected to medium- and large-diameter pipe break transients at two different embrittlement levels

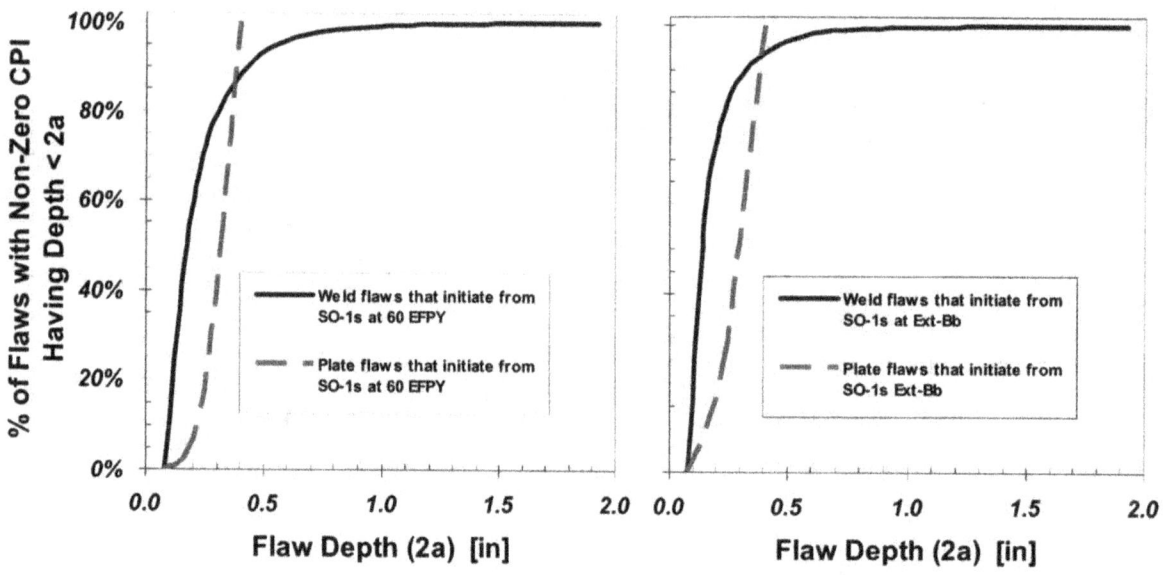

Figure 9.5. Flaw depths that contribute to crack initiation probability in Beaver Valley Unit 1 when subjected to stuck-open valve transients at two different embrittlement levels

9.2.1.2.2   Residual Stresses

FAVOR assumes that a single distribution quantifies the residual stresses produced by welding in both axial and circumferential welds [*Williams*]. These residual stresses were estimated from measurements made of how the width of a radial slot cut in the longitudinal weld in a shell segment from an RPV change with cut depth. These measurements were processed through a finite element analysis to determine the residual stress profile used by FAVOR [Dickson 99]. FAVOR also assumes that this residual stress distribution is not relieved by cracking of the vessel, (i.e., the residual stresses in the figure to the right are applied equally irrespective of a/t). Since residual stresses would have to be relieved were a crack to develop through the weld in an RPV, the effect of this conservative assumption was be assessed by performing a sensitivity study wherein the weld residual stresses are retained in the crack initiation calculation but are removed from the through-wall cracking calculation. In this sensitivity study, we performed analyses of both the Beaver Valley and the Palisades RPVs at two embrittlement levels each (32 EFPY and the Ext-B embrittlement conditions). The effect of relieving the residual stresses in the through-wall cracking calculations was to entirely negligible, reducing the TWCF values by less than 1% (on average). This limited sensitivity of the TWCF values on residual stresses occurs because the crack driving force cause by the residual stress is very small relative to that caused by the combination of thermal and pressure loading.

9.2.1.2.3 Embrittlement Shift Model

The embrittlement shift model relates compositional and neutron exposure variables to the amount by which irradiation shifts the Charpy V-notch (CVN) transition temperature curve to higher temperatures. FAVOR adopts a model developed under an NRC Research contract by Eason in 2000 [Eason]. Since that time a similar, albeit not identical, embrittlement trend curve had been adopted by the American Society for Testing and Materials in the E900-02 standard [ASTM E900]. A sensitivity study was, therefore, performed to assess the effect of adopting the ASTM embrittlement trend curve, rather than that proposed by Eason (again analyzing Beaver Valley and Palisades at two different embrittlement levels). The ASTM E900-02 embrittlement shift model produces TWCF estimates that are systematically lower (approximately one-third) of those estimated using the Eason shift model. This reduction in TWCF is almost entirely attributable to the existence of a "long-term bias" in the Eason model that does not exist in the ASTM E900-02 model. Activity is currently underway within ASTM Committee E10.02 to revise the E900 model. Representatives of both the industry and the NRC are involved in this code committee

work, and the committee is expected to publish a revised model that incorporates features of both the current Eason and E900-02 relationships. Thus, for the purposes this report, we have continued to use the Eason correlation and accepted this approach as slightly conservative. At such time as a consensus emerges from the E10.02 Code committee process, it will be a simple matter to assess the effect of the new embrittlement shift model on the TWCF values reported herein. However, based on this sensitivity study, we expect this effect to be small (less than a factor of 3 reduction in TWCF).

9.2.1.2.4 Embrittlement Shift Uncertainty Treatment

In FAVOR, the uncertainty of the embrittlement shift model is not sampled. As argued in [*EricksonKirk-SS*], this approach is appropriate because the uncertainty in the embrittlement shift model arises as a result of uncertainties in the input variables to the embrittlement shift model (i.e., copper content, nickel content, phosphorus content, and fluence), which are sampled in FAVOR. This is demonstrated by the results in Figure 9.6, which were generated as follows:

(1) Median values were assigned to all of the input variables to the Eason embrittlement shift equation (except for fluence).

(2) The FAVOR uncertainty distributions for Cu, Ni, P, and fluence were sampled about these medians for fluence medians ranging from 0.25×10^{19} to 5×10^{19} n/cm^2.

(3) At each different fluence value, 1,000 sets (Cu, Ni, P, and fluence) were simulated. Each set was used to estimate a value of embrittlement shift using the Eason embrittlement model. The standard deviation of these 1,000 embrittlement shift estimates was calculated and plotted in Figure 9.6.

The uncertainties simulated by FAVOR agree well with those in the embrittlement shift data used by Eason to develop the model. The lower uncertainties associated with lower fluence values results from FAVOR setting to zero simulations of embrittlement shift that are negative, which is physically unrealistic.

This information confirms the appropriateness of the FAVOR approach to uncertainty simulation for this model. Simulation of both the embrittlement shift model uncertainties and the uncertainties in the input variables would produce a model that simulated a greater magnitude of uncertainty in embrittlement shift than is observed in test data.

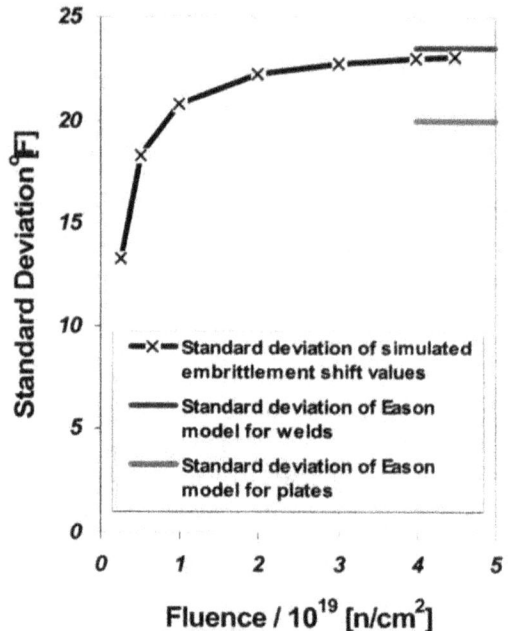

Figure 9.6. Comparison of embrittlement shift uncertainties simulated by FAVOR (blue line with X symbols) with the uncertainties in the experimental embrittlement shift database used by Eason to construct the model

9.2.1.2.5 Chemical Composition Re-Sampling for Welds

In welds, a gradient of properties is expected to exist through the thickness of the RPV because of through-wall changes in copper content. These copper content changes arise from the fact that, given the large volume of weld metal needed to fill an RPV weld, manufacturers often needed to use weld wire from multiple weld wire spools to completely fill the groove. Lack of control of the process used to copper plate the weld wires (a step taken for corrosion control)

resulted in wide variability in copper coating thickness from spool to spool (variability that is manifested in measurable variations in Cu content through the RPV wall thickness). These copper variations produce variations in sensitivity to irradiation embrittlement, and consequent variations in resistance to fracture though the vessel wall.

FAVOR adopts a weld composition gradient model wherein the Cu content is re-sampled in a through-wall cracking calculation every time the crack passes the ¼ thickness, the ½ thickness, and the ¾ thickness locations in the vessel wall. A four-weld layer model was developed based on considerations of the volume of weld metal needed to fill an RPV weld. To assess the effect of this model on TWCF, a sensitivity study was performed wherein the Cu resampling in FAVOR was turned off. Again, the sensitivity study included analysis of Beaver Valley and Palisades at two different embrittlement levels. The results of this study show that turning off the FAVOR 4-weld layer model increase the estimated TWCF by a small amount (factor of 2.5 on average).

9.2.1.2.6 Crack Face Pressure

As part of the peer review, Dr. Schultz noted that FAVOR had inappropriately not accounted for the effects of crack face pressure loading (see Appendix B, Reviewer Comment #23). FAVOR Ver. 04.1 (which was used to generate all of the results reported in Chapter 8) now accounts for the effects of crack face pressure. The effect of including crack-face pressure on non-SO-1 transients is a negligible (a 0% to 6% increase in CPTWC) because pressure does not contribute significantly to the failure probability of these transients. For SO-1 transients, larger increases (25% to 75%) in the CPTWC are seen. The effect of including crack face pressure in an integrated analysis of PTS risk (all transients) is, however, small. An analysis of Beaver Valley at 60 EFPY showed that including crack face pressure increased the estimated TWCF by only 6%.

9.2.1.2.7 Upper Shelf Toughness Model

In FAVOR Version 03.1, upper shelf fracture toughness values (J_{Ic}, J-R) were estimated through correlations with Charpy V-notch energy. These empirical relationships had very low correlation coefficients and high scatter, reflecting the different underlying physical processes that control Charpy energy and fracture toughness on the upper shelf. Comments from the peer review group (see Comment #40, Appendix B) questioned the appropriateness of this approach. After reviewing the existing FAVOR model and other available alternatives, the staff adopted a new upper shelf model and implemented it in FAVOR Version 04.1 to address this concern. This new model does not rely on Charpy correlations in any way, and features an explicit treatment of the uncertainty in upper shelf toughness (both the ductile initiation toughness as measured by J_{Ic} and the resistance to further crack extension as measured by J-R). Additionally, the new model links transition toughness and upper shelf toughness properties, a relationship motivated by trends in fracture toughness data and physical considerations, and a feature the FAVOR Version 03.1 models did not have. This upper shelf model is based on work recently completed by EPRI [EricksonKirk 04]. Details of the FAVOR implementation of this new model can be found in [*EricksonKirk-PFM*] and [*Williams*].

The new upper shelf model does not change the TWCF values in any substantive way. On average, the TWCF values estimated using the new model are ~5% lower than the values estimated using the correlative approaches used in FAVOR 03.1. However, the linkage between transition toughness and upper shelf toughness properties in the new model has eliminated FAVOR predictions of physically implausible results (e.g., predicting that flaws in a particular axial weld (say Axial Weld A) of the RPV beltline contribute more to the TWCF than do flaws in another axial weld (say Axial Weld B) even though the toughness of Axial Weld A exceeds that of Axial Weld B).

9.2.2 Sensitivity Studies Performed to Assess the Applicability of the Results in Chapter 8 to PWRs in General

As detailed in [*EricksonKirk-SS*], the following sensitivity studies were performed to assess the applicability of the TWCF results presented in Chapter 8 to PWRs *in general*:

- method for simulating increased levels of embrittlement

- assessment of the applicability of these results to forged vessels

- effect of vessel thickness

The results of these sensitivities are summarized in the following sections.

9.2.2.1 Simulating Increased Levels of Embrittlement

Use of more realistic models and input values than were used in the calculations that provide the technical basis for the current PTS Rule produces a considerable reduction in the estimated values of TWCF. As detailed in Table 8.4, at 60 EFPY (an operational lifetime beyond that anticipated after a single license extension), the TWCF values estimates for the three study plants lie between 10^{-11} and 10^{-8} events/year. However, the through-wall cracking frequency limit recommended in Chapter 10 as being consistent with Regulatory Guide 1.174 is 10^{-6} events/year. Consequently, to develop a reference temperature based screening limit (see Chapter 11), it was necessary to somehow artificially increase the level of embrittlement of the vessels and, thereby, the estimated TWCF values so that they would approach the 10^{-6} events/year limit. In the baseline calculations reported in Chapter 8, embrittlement was artificially increased by increasing EFPY (increasing time) and extrapolating fluence in linear proportion to time. An alternative procedure for artificially increasing embrittlement would be to allow the temporal and irradiation exposure parameters to remain within realistic ranges and, instead, increase the unirradiated transition temperature (the $RT_{NDT(u)}$)

of the beltline materials. To determine what effect these two procedures have on estimated TWCF values, we performed a sensitivity study using the Beaver Valley and Palisades plants. In this sensitivity study, the 32 EFPY analyses reported in Table 8.4 were treated as a baseline above which embrittlement was increased. Increases in embrittlement achieved by increasing EFPY/time are also reported in Table 8.4. Each EFPY/time increase in this table can be quantified as an increase in the reference temperature by subtracting from the reference temperature associated with a particular EFPY/time increment the reference temperature associated with 32 EFPY. In this sensitivity study, we compared the TWCF increases produced by these EFPY/time-driven reference temperature increases with TWCF increases driven by simply increasing the $RT_{NDT(u)}$ of the beltline materials by some fixed increment. Figure 9.7 shows the result of this analysis, which demonstrates that the EFPY/time method of artificially increasing embrittlement results in TWCF estimates that exceed those produced by the alternative method of increasing $RT_{NDT(u)}$.

It must be emphasized that both of these procedures (as well as any other alternative procedures) extrapolate outside of the empirical bounds of the database used to establish the embrittlement shift model. We selected the EFPY/time extrapolation method over the $RT_{NDT(u)}$ extrapolation method because the embrittlement shift model includes explicitly both time and irradiation exposure variables. During the development of this model, the known physical bases for time/exposure trends were explicitly considered, and this knowledge was incorporated into the functional form of the model [Eason]. Thus, there is some reason to expect that time and irradiation exposure variables will extrapolate better than the fracture toughness before irradiation begins (as quantified by $RT_{NDT(u)}$), which was not considered in the development of the embrittlement shift model.

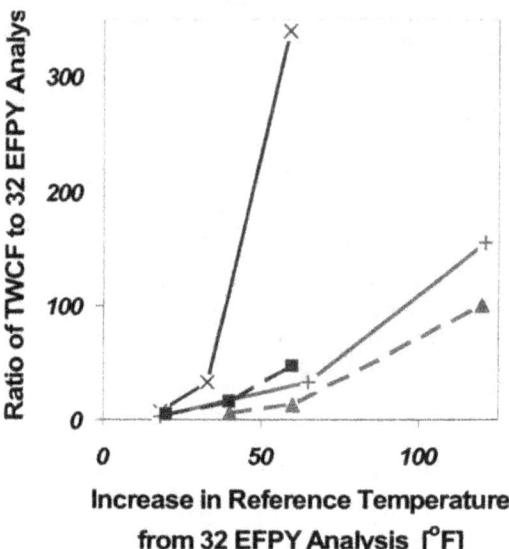

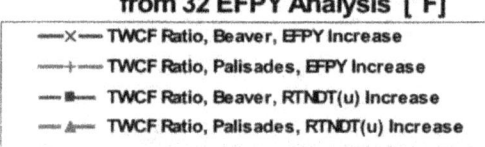

Figure 9.7. Effect of different methods to artificially increase embrittlement on the predicted TWCF values

9.2.2.2 Applicability to Forged Vessels

All three of our study plants are plate vessels. However, 21 of the operating PWRs have beltline regions made of ring-forgings. As such, these vessels have no axial welds. The lack of the large axially oriented axial flaws from such vessels indicates that they should, in general, have much lower values of TWCF than a comparable plate vessel of equivalent embrittlement. However, forgings have a population of embedded flaws that is particular in density and size to their method of manufacture. Additionally, under certain conditions forgings are subject to subclad cracking associated with the deposition of the austenitic stainless steel cladding layer. Thus, to investigate the applicability of the results reported in Chapter 8 to forged vessels, we performed a number of analyses on vessels using properties ($RT_{NDT(u)}$, Cu, Ni, P) and flaw populations appropriate to forgings.

Appendix G details the technical basis for the distributions of flaws used in these sensitivity studies. The distribution of embedded forging flaws is based on destructive examination of an RPV forging [Schuster 02]. These flaws are similar in both size and in density to plate flaws. The distribution of subclad cracks is based on a review of the literature on subclad flaws, in particular that appearing in a summary article [Dhooge 78]. Subclad cracks occur as dense arrays of shallow cracks extending into the vessel wall from the clad to basemetal interface to depths limited by the heat affected zone (~0.08-in. (~2mm)). These cracks are oriented normal to the direction of welding for clad deposition, producing axially oriented cracks in the vessel beltline. They are clustered where the passes of strip clad contact each other. Subclad flaws are much more likely to occur in particular grades of pressure vessel steels that have chemical compositions that enhance the likelihood of cracking. Forging grades such as A508 are more susceptible than plate materials such as A533. High levels of heat input during the cladding process also enhance the likelihood of subclad cracking.

9.2.2.2.1 Embedded Forging Flaw Sensitivity Study

This sensitivity study was constructed as follows:

(1) Two sets of forging properties were selected: those of the Sequoyah 1 and Watts Bar 1 RPVs [RVID2]. These properties were selected because they are among the most irradiation-sensitive of all the forging materials in RVID.

(2) Two hypothetical models of forged vessels were constructed based on our existing models of the Beaver Valley and Palisades vessels. In each case, the hypothetical forged vessels were constructed by removing the axial welds and combining these regions with the surrounding plates to make "forgings." These "forgings" were assigned the properties from Step 1.

(3) A FAVOR analysis of each vessel/forging combination from Steps 1 and 2 was

analyzed at two embrittlement levels: 32 EFPY and Ext-B. Thus, a total of 2^3 (or 8) FAVOR analyses were performed (2 material property definitions x 2 vessel definitions x 2 embrittlement levels).

On average, the TWCF of the "forging" vessels was only 3% of the plate welded vessels; at most, it was 15%. These reductions are consistent with those expected when the large axial weld flaws are removed from the analysis.

9.2.2.2.2 Subclad Crack Sensitivity Study

This sensitivity study was constructed as follows:

(1) One set of forging properties was selected: that of the Sequoyah 1 RPV [RVID2].

(2) One hypothetical model of a forged vessel was constructed based on our existing model of the Beaver Valley vessel. The hypothetical forged vessel was constructed by removing the axial welds and combining these regions with the surrounding plates to make a "forging." This "forging" was assigned the properties from Step 1.

(3) A FAVOR analysis of each vessel/forging combination from Steps 1 and 2 was analyzed at three embrittlement levels: 32 EFPY, 60 EFPY, and Ext-B. Thus, a total of 3 FAVOR analyses were performed (1 material property definition x 1 vessel definition x 3 embrittlement levels).

At 32 and 60 EFPY the TWCF of the "forging" vessels was ~0.2% and 18% of the plate welded vessels. However, at the much higher embrittlement level represented by the Ext-B condition the "forging" vessels had TWCF values 10 times higher than that characteristic of plate welded vessels at an equivalent level of embrittlement. While these very high embrittlement levels are unlikely to be approached in the foreseeable future, these results indicate that a more detailed assessment of vessel failure probabilities associated with subclad cracks would be warranted should a subclad cracking prone forging ever in future be subjected to very high embrittlement levels.

9.2.2.3 Effect of RPV Wall Thickness on TWCF

In Section 8.5.2.4.1, we noted in the FAVOR results for primary side pipe breaks a potential effect of vessel wall thickness on the conditional probability of through-wall cracking. This affect can be expected for the following reasons:

- The magnitude of thermal stress scales in proportion to the thickness, with thicker vessels generating higher levels of thermal stress. Figure 9.8 shows the effect of this increased thermal stress on the applied driving force to fracture associated with a large-diameter pipe break. This effect will tend to increase the probability of through-wall cracking for thicker vessels.

- Because thicker vessels will have a larger volume of plate material and a larger weld fusion line area, they will also have a larger number of flaws. This effect will also tend to increase the probability of through-wall cracking for thicker vessels.

- There is more distance in a thicker vessel over which an initiated crack can arrest, thereby not failing the vessel. Also, thicker vessels would tend to have more weld layers with different Cu contents. This effect will tend to reduce the probability of through-wall cracking for thicker vessels.

To investigate the effect of these first two factors (the third could not be investigated without modifying the structure of the FAVOR code), we increased the thickness of the Beaver Valley vessel from 7.875-in. (20-cm) (its actual thickness) in 5 increments up to 11-in. (27.9-cm) (characteristic of the thickest PWRs in service, see Figure 9.9). For each of these 5 thicker versions of Beaver Valley, we used FAVOR to estimate the CPTWC of the following four transients (all of which are dominant contributors to the TWCF of Beaver Valley):

- BV9: 16-in. diameter hot leg break

- BV56: 4-in. diameter surge line break

- BV126: stuck-open safety relief valve that recloses after 100 minutes resulting in repressurization of the primary system

- BV102: main steam line break

Figure 9.10 shows that increasing the vessel wall thickness increases the CPTWC for all four transients. Recalling that these CPTWC values would be weighted by their bin frequencies (and those of other transients) to obtain a TWCF estimate, these results suggest that through a wall thickness of 9.5-in. (24.13-cm) (thicker than all but three of the in-service PWRs), the integrated effect of wall thickness on TWCF should be modest (factor of ~3 increase at most) relative to our analyses (see Chapter 8) of one 7.875-in. (20-cm) thick vessel and two 8.5-in. (21.6-cm) thick vessels. For vessels of greater wall thicknesses, a plant-specific analysis is warranted to properly capture all aspects of increased vessel wall thickness on TWCF. However, given that the three plants of 11-in. (27.9-cm) and greater thickness are Palo Verde Units 1, 2, and 3, and these vessels have very low embrittlement projected at either EOL or EOLE, the practical need for such plant-specific analysis is mitigated. It can also be noted that using the TWCF results from Chapter 8 will overestimate the TWCF of the seven thinner operating PWRs (7-in. (17.78-cm) thick or less).

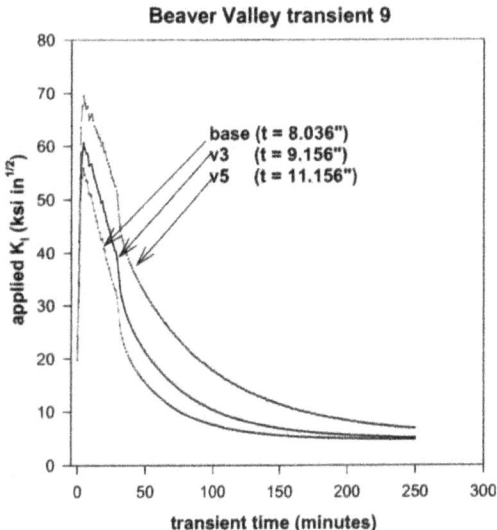

Figure 9.8. Effect of vessel wall thickness on the variation of applied-K_I vs. time for a 16-in. (40.64-cm) diameter hot leg break in Beaver Valley. The flaw has the following dimensions: $\mathcal{L}$=0.35-in., $2a$=0.50-in., $2c$=1.5-in. ($\mathcal{L}$=8.89-mm, $2a$=12.7-mm, $2c$=38.1-mm)

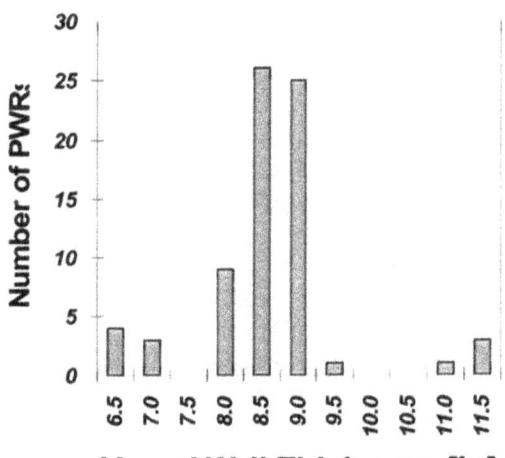

Figure 9.9. Distribution of RPV wall thicknesses for PWRs currently in service [RVID2]

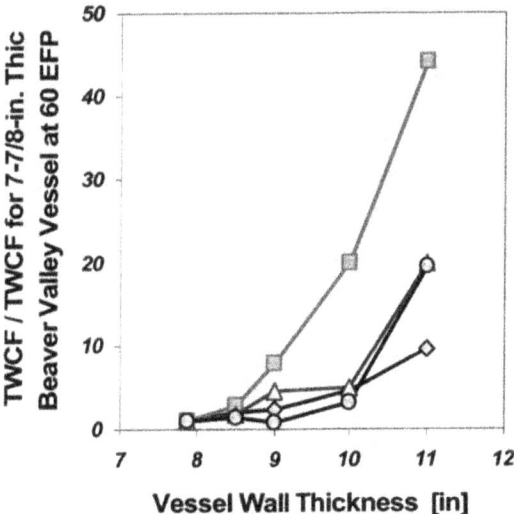

—◇— BV9 - 16" Hot Leg Break
—□— BV56 - 4" Surge Line Break
—△— BV102 - MSLB
—○— BV126 - Stuck open SRV, re-closes after 100 minutes

Figure 9.10. Effect of vessel wall thickness on the TWCF of various transients in Beaver Valley (all analyses at 60 EFPY)

9.2.3 Summary and Conclusions

This section summarized sensitivity studies on our PFM model (and on PFM-related variables) performed with two aims in mind:

- To provide confidence in the ***robustness*** of our PFM model we assessed the effect of credible model and input perturbations on TWCF estimates:

    o flaw distribution (size and density of simulated flaws)

    o residual stresses assumed to exist in the RPV wall

    o embrittlement shift model: model used and treatment of uncertainties

    o re-sampling of chemical composition variables at the ¼T, ½T, and ¾T locations for welds

    o crack face pressure

    o upper shelf toughness model

- To provide confidence that the results of our calculations for three specific plants can be **_generalized_** to apply to all PWRs, we performed sensitivity studies to assess the influence of factors not fully considered in our baseline TWCF estimates (see Chapter 8):

  o method for simulating increased levels of embrittlement

  o assessment of the applicability of these results to forged vessels

  o effect of vessel thickness

In the former category, all effects were negligible or small. The small effects included our adoption of an embrittlement shift model different from that in ASTM E900-02 (which increases TWCF by ~3x) and our model that accounts for distinctly different Cu contents in different weld layers (which reduces TWCF by ~ 2.5x relative to the assumption that the mean value of Cu does not vary through the vessel thickness). Neither of these effects is significant enough to warrant a change to our baseline model, or to recommend a caution regarding its robustness.

Sensitivity studies in the latter category suggest the following minor cautions regarding the applicability of the results in Chapter 8 to PWRs *in general*:

- In general, the TWCF of forged PWRs can be assessed using the Chapter 8 results by ignoring the TWCF contribution of axial welds. However, should changes in future operating conditions result in a forged vessel being subjected to very high levels of embrittlement, a plant-specific analysis to assess the effect of subclad flaws on TWCF would be warranted.

- For PWRs with thicknesses of 7.5 to 9.5-in. (19.05 to 24.13-cm), the TWCF results in Chapter 8 are realistic. The Chapter 8 results overestimate the TWCF of the seven thinner vessels (wall thicknesses below 7-in. (17.78-cm)) and underestimate the TWCF of Palo Verde Units 1, 2, and 3, all of which have wall thicknesses above 11-in. (27.94-cm). However, these vessels have very low

embrittlement projected at either EOL or EOLE, suggesting little practical effect of this underestimation.

9.3 Plant-to-Plant Differences in Design/Operational Characteristics that Impact PTS Transient Severity

This section describes an effort in which we examined the plant design and operational characteristics of five additional high-embrittlement plants. Our aim was to identify whether the design and operational features that are the key contributors to PTS risk (see Section 8.6) vary significantly enough in the larger population of PWRs to question the generality of our results. Full details of this work are reported elsewhere [**_Whitehead-Gen_**].

In this activity, we focused on several plants beyond the three for which we have conducted detailed plant-specific analyses to assess PTS risk. To identify which additional plants to study, Table 9.5 was constructed early in 2002. At the time, we understood from our plant-specific analyses of Oconee that circumferential welds did not contribute significantly to through-wall cracking. Therefore, we calculated a reference temperature metric for each plant equal to the sum of the un-irradiated RT_{NDT} plus the embrittlement shift after 40 years of operation [Eason] calculated for the most irradiation-sensitive region in the beltline (i.e., most irradiation-sensitive axial weld, plate, or forging; circumferential welds were excluded). This metric, shown as a column in Table 9.5, provided an approximate ranking of the PTS sensitivity of the plants based on information we had available at the time. Since the goal of this activity was to determine whether the design and operational features that we have identified as being the key contributors to PTS risk (see Section 8.6) vary significantly enough in the larger population of PWRs to question the generality of our findings from Chapter 8, we felt it important to select the most embrittled plants from the list. In the end, we selected the following five plants:

- Salem 1 (W-4[1]) [comparable to Beaver Valley (W-3[2])]

- TMI 1 (B&W[3]) [comparable to Oconee]

- Ft. Calhoun (CE[4]) [comparable to Palisades]

- Diablo Canyon 1 (W-4) [comparable to Beaver Valley]

- Sequoyah 1 (W-4) [comparable to Beaver Valley]

Following identification of the study plants, we conducted the following three activities:

- A questionnaire was developed to elicit PTS-relevant information about the additional PWRs.

- Responses to the questionnaire were examined to determine whether results from the detailed analyses were generically applicable to the additional PWRs.

- Conclusions were generated as to the generic applicability of the detailed results.

We compared potentially important design and operational features (as related to PTS) of these five PWRs to the same features from the three plants on which we have performed detailed analyses to determine whether these features are similar or different. Based on these comparisons, we made judgments regarding the appropriateness of treating the results presented in Chapter 8 as being representative of PWRs *in general*.

Section 9.3.1 details the questionnaire we developed and sent to the five plants, while Section 9.3.2 details our analysis of the results we obtained. Combined observations and overall conclusions are provided in Section 9.3.3.

9.3.1 Generalization Questionnaire

Based on the insights obtained during an examination of the results from the three plant-specific studies, the analysts identified five general event scenarios for which plant design and operational features should be obtained. Plant design and operational features were examined to identify those that play a role in determining the importance of these five overcooling scenarios.

Table 9.6 identifies the scenarios and their corresponding plant design and operational features. Once the scenarios and the design and operational features were identified, a questionnaire was constructed. Collection of the information via this questionnaire was facilitated by an industry representative working under the auspices of the Electric Power Research Institute (EPRI).

9.3.2 Analysis of Collected Information

Our analysis of the plant design and operational information collected via the questionnaire entails both PRA/HRA and TH information. Judgmental analysis of the comparable design and operational information between Oconee, Beaver Valley, and Palisades and the generalization plants (i.e., Ft. Calhoun, TMI, Diablo Canyon, Sequoyah, and Salem) was performed to determine if there are any differences that would be expected to have a significant impact on any conclusions that would be reached by the activity if it were to be performed in detail (i.e., to the same level of rigor as was done in the plant-specific analyses). The following subsections summarize the results of the PRA/HRA (9.3.2.1) and TH judgmental analyses (9.3.2.2)

---

[1]   W-4 denotes a Westinghouse 4-loop design.
[2]   W-3 denotes a Westinghouse 3-loop design.
[3]   B&W denotes Babcock and Wilcox.
[4]   CE denotes Combustion Engineering.

9.3.2.1   PRA/HRA Judgmental Analyses

For **secondary breaches,** the following observations were made:

- For generalization issue (GI) 1[‡‡‡‡‡], each of the generalization plants is similar to or better than their corresponding detailed plant. Thus, for GI 1, we conclude that there would be no significant adverse differences between the generalization plants and their corresponding detailed plant.

- For GI 2, each of the generalization plants is similar to their corresponding detailed plant. Thus, for GI 2, we conclude that there would be no significant adverse differences between the generalization plants and their corresponding detailed plant.

- For GI 3, each of the generalization plants is similar to their corresponding detailed plant with one possible exception. For Salem, it appears that early isolation opportunities exist; however, exactly when these occur is not clear. Nonetheless, since Salem's procedures are based on Westinghouse Owners Group (WOG) Emergency Response Guidelines, it is expected that Salem is similar to its corresponding detailed analyzed plant, Beaver Valley. Thus, for GI 3, we conclude that there would be no significant adverse differences between the generalization plants and their corresponding detailed plant.

[‡‡‡‡‡]   GI # refers to the number assigned to each generic issue. For example, GI 1 refers to *number of MSIVs* and GI 26 refers to *emergency operating procedure (EOP) criteria for initiation of feed–and–bleed.*

Table 9.5. Plant list for generalization study

Tolerance to a PTS Challenge		Plant Name	NSSS Vendor	Most Embrittled Material	$RT_{NDT(u)}$ + Irradiation Shift at 40 years [°F]	Vessel Manufacturer
	1	Salem 1	Westinghouse	Plate	204	Combustion Engineering
	2	Beaver Valley 1	Westinghouse	Plate	194	Combustion Engineering
	3	TMI-1	Babcock & Wilcox	Axial Weld	186	Babcock & Wilcox
	4	Fort Calhoun	Combustion Engineering	Axial Weld	181	Combustion Engineering
	5	Palisades	Combustion Engineering	Axial Weld	179	Combustion Engineering
	6	Calvert Cliffs 1	Combustion Engineering	Axial Weld	178	Combustion Engineering
	7	Diablo Canyon 1	Westinghouse	Axial Weld	171	Combustion Engineering
	8	Diablo Canyon 2	Westinghouse	Plate	170	Combustion Engineering
	9	Sequoyah 1	Westinghouse	Forging	167	Rotterdam Dockyard
	10	Watts Bar 1	Westinghouse	Forging	164	Rotterdam Dockyard
	11	St. Lucie 1	Combustion Engineering	Axial Weld	164	Combustion Engineering
	12	Surry 1	Westinghouse	Axial Weld	163	Babcock & Wilcox
	13	Indian Point 2	Westinghouse	Plate	162	Combustion Engineering
	14	Ginna	Westinghouse	Forging	161	Babcock & Wilcox
	15	Point Beach 1	Westinghouse	Axial Weld	159	Babcock & Wilcox
	16	Farley 2	Westinghouse	Plate	158	Combustion Engineering
	17	Mcguire 1	Westinghouse	Axial Weld	158	Combustion Engineering
	18	Oconee 1	Babcock & Wilcox	Axial Weld	157	Babcock & Wilcox
	19	North Anna 2	Westinghouse	Forging	155	Rotterdam Dockyard
	20	Shearon Harris	Westinghouse	Plate	153	Chicago Bridge & Iron
	21	North Anna 1	Westinghouse	Forging	153	Rotterdam Dockyard
	22	Cook 2	Westinghouse	Plate	152	Chicago Bridge & Iron
	23	Salem 2	Westinghouse	Axial Weld	148	Combustion Engineering
	24	Crystal River 3	Babcock & Wilcox	Axial Weld	141	Babcock & Wilcox
	25	Calvert Cliffs 2	Combustion Engineering	Plate	139	Combustion Engineering
	26	Robinson 2	Westinghouse	Plate	138	Combustion Engineering
	27	Cook 1	Westinghouse	Axial Weld	138	Combustion Engineering
	28	Farley 2	Westinghouse	Plate	133	Combustion Engineering
	29	Farley 1	Westinghouse	Plate	133	Combustion Engineering
	30	Arkansas Nuclear 1	Babcock & Wilcox	Axial Weld	129	Babcock & Wilcox

The estimated tolerance to a PTS challenge increases as the number in the next column increases (i.e., plants with the lowest ranking have the most embrittled materials).

Notes:

Plants analyzed in the PTS reevaluation effort.

Plants compared in the Generalization activity.

Table 9.6 Important PTS scenarios and corresponding plant design and operational features

	Scenario Types				
	Secondary Breach	**Secondary Overfeed**	**LOCA Related**	**PORV and SRV Related**	**Feed and Bleed Related**
Generalization Issues (Number)	Number of MSIVs (1)	Information on the feed (MFW and AFW or emergency feedwater (EFW)) capabilities to the steam generators including inventory of water available to continue MFW or AFW/EFW (8)	Allowable range of safety injection water temperatures (11)	Number and sizes of PORVs and SRVs, whether each plant operates with PORV block valves normally shut, and if there are any auto-operation features of the PORVs (20)	Number of AFW/EFW pumps/flow paths versus minimum success criteria for adequate feed to the steam generators (hints to reliability of AFW/EFW and, hence, probability for going to feed-and-bleed) (25)
	Isolation capability with regards to other paths (2)	Information on normal steam generator inventory (9)	Information to estimate recirculation water temperature (12)	Instrumentation available (e.g., acoustic monitors, differential pressure, etc.) to identify open PORVs or SRVs and to notice if they have reclosed (21)	Emergency operating procedure (EOP) criteria for initiation of feed-and-bleed (26)
	Identification of procedures, steps, and location of steps within procedures that ensure likelihood of early identification and isolation of faulted steam generators (3)	Information on possible feed temperatures for all feed sources (especially how cold they could be) (10)	Safety injection/accumulators water source size (i.e., inventory) (13)	Procedures for addressing LOCAs resulting from stuck-open PORVs or SRVs (22)	Number of PORVs opened out of total available (or even SRVs if pumps can open SRVs) when in feed-and-bleed mode (27)
	Operator training or procedural allowances that support early isolation of steam generators (4)		Safety injection flow rate versus LOCA break size (14)	Procedures for addressing the sudden reclosure of such valves, including safety injection (SI) throttling/termination guidance (23)	Number of HPI pumps used in feed-and-bleed and is actual flow rate equivalent to number of pumps (28)
	Location and size of steamline flow restrictors (5)		Charging, high-pressure injection (HPI), and low-pressure injection (LPI) shutoff heads (15)	Operating characteristics of the charging system when pressurizer level goes back high (e.g., stop, keep running) (24)	
Key Assumptions Relative to MSLB Analysis	Auxiliary feedwater (AFW) and main feedwater (MFW) control during steamline break (or similar) (6)		Actuation requirements for containment spray and flow rate once running (16)		
	Determination of whether turbine-driven AFW pump (auto) isolates in MSLB (7)		Impact on HPI, LPI, and charging when sump switchover occurs (which pumps on vs. off) (17)		
			Any significant changes in flow rates going from injection to recirculation (18)		
			Accumulator (e.g., safety injection tank (SIT), core flood tank (CFT)) discharge pressure (19)		

9-22

- For GI 4, each of the generalization plants is similar to their corresponding detailed plant with one possible exception. For Salem, it appears that training supports early action, even though it is unclear exactly when the actions would occur. Since Salem's procedures are based on Westinghouse Owners Group (WOG) Emergency Response Guidelines, it is expected that Salem is similar to its corresponding detailed analyzed plant, Beaver Valley. Thus, for GI 4, we conclude that there would be no significant adverse differences between the generalization plants and their corresponding detailed plant.

- GI 5 is not a PRA/HRA issue. This issue is examined in section 9.3.2.2.

- For GI 6, each of the generalization plants is similar to or as good as their corresponding detailed plant. Thus, for GI 6, we conclude that there would be no significant adverse differences between the generalization plants and their corresponding detailed plant.

- For GI 7, each of the generalization plants is similar to their corresponding detailed plant with one exception. For TMI the turbine-driven AFW pump is not automatically isolated while it is automatically isolated for the corresponding detailed analyzed plant, Oconee. Thus, for GI 7, this could increase the importance of a faulted steam generator for the Babcock & Wilcox (B&W) generalization plant.

From the observations provided above, only GI 7 has the potential for a significant adverse difference between the generalization plants and their corresponding detailed plant — and that only for the B&W generalization plant (i.e., TMI). However, when observations for GI 3 and GI 4 are considered in combination, we expect the importance of the GI 7 difference to be minimal, since operators would be expected to isolate the feed flow. Thus, we conclude that for secondary breaches, no significant adverse differences exist.

For **secondary overfeed**, the GIs are not PRA/HRA issues. These issues are examined in section 9.3.2.2.

For **LOCA-related**, the GIs are not PRA/HRA issues. These issues are examined in the in section 9.3.2.2.

For **PORV- and SRV-related**, the following observations are made:

- For GI 20, generic data were used to estimate the probabilities associated with the sticking open and subsequent closure of either PORVs or SRVs [Poloski 99]. No significant differences are expected for Westinghouse and B&W plants. For the Combusting Engineering (CE) generalization plant, Fort Calhoun, we might expect a higher estimated probability of having a stuck-open valve. This expectation comes from the fact that Fort Calhoun experienced one of the two stuck-open valve events that were used to estimate the generic probability of a stuck-open valve (1.6E-3). If we approximate the probability by using one event in the 12 years covered by [Poloski 99] (the most conservative interpretation of the data), we get approximately 0.08. Using this approximate value for Fort Calhoun, the probability associated with stuck-open valves would increase by about a factor of 50. This ignores the fact that there may be appropriate reasons to combine both generic PWR experience and the Fort Calhoun plant-specific experience (such as through a Bayesian analysis) or to obtain other information to arrive at a more realistic estimate of a stuck-open valve event at Fort Calhoun.

In an effort to determine a more realistic estimate, additional information was obtained with the help from staff at Fort Calhoun Station about the SRV opening event that actually happened in 1992, subsequent analyses of the root cause, and the corrective actions. This additional information [LER 92-023, LER 92-028, and NRC-IR] including phone conversations with plant staff, revealed that the causes of the actual event are well-understood, and actions have been taken that should make Fort Calhoun no more susceptible to SRV demand events than other PWRs. In particular, the event was caused by both a SRV setpoint drift as a result of movement of an adjusting nut during valve vibrations that resulted in a lower setpoint for valve opening, and determination that setpoint calibration of the SRVs at an outside laboratory was not being done under laboratory conditions (particularly temperature conditions) that sufficiently approximated actual plant installation conditions closely enough. This latter situation was unknowingly contributing to the SRV setpoint being lower than what was specified.

The SRVs at Fort Calhoun are manufactured by Crosby (one of the manufacturers used in other plants), so Fort Calhoun is not unique from this perspective. The specific corrective actions included adding a torque setting for the adjusting nut that did not exist in the procedures, adding a locking nut that prevents inadvertent movement of the adjusting nut, and changes in the laboratory setup and procedures during valve calibration that now allow for sufficient approximation of actual installation conditions. Additionally, Fort Calhoun, like other plants, has lowered the plant's high-pressurizer pressure trip setpoint, making it less likely to cause an SRV demand.

Considering the use of a valve manufacturer not uncommon among PWRs, changes in the plant's high-pressure setpoint to be like other PWRs, the specific "fixes" for the identified Fort Calhoun SRV problems, and a history of no subsequent SRV events or significant problems at Fort Calhoun since 1992, we conclude that no evidence exists to suggest that Fort Calhoun is any more susceptible to SRV events than other PWRs. Hence, our best estimate of Fort Calhoun's frequency of stuck-open SRV events looking to the future, is that Fort Calhoun can be treated as among the "generic" population of PWRs, and the generic value used for such events in our PTS models can

be used for Fort Calhoun. Hence, there is no identifiable frequency difference to be considered in this generalization study.

Thus, for GI 20, we conclude that there would be no significant adverse differences between the generalization plants and their corresponding detailed plant.

- For GI 21, except for possibly Salem, all plants have multiple indications to know when pressurizer PORV/SRVs are open and/or reclose. Thus, it would be appropriate to postulate that for Salem, there might be some increase in the human error probability (HEP) associated with the failure to throttle because operators have less direct indication of stuck-open valves (e.g., no acoustic monitors) and, thus, less indication of valve reclosure than for Beaver Valley (the corresponding detailed plant). Without a detailed analysis of the specifics associated with stuck-open valves that reclose at Salem, it is difficult to estimate the amount of increase in the throttling HEP. Nonetheless, given the fact that there are indications available at Salem (although they are neither as redundant nor as direct as for other plants), we expect the HEP for failure to throttle should not increase by more than a factor of 5 (at most). Thus, for GI 21, we conclude that Salem is the only generalization plant that might have a significant adverse difference compared to the corresponding detailed plant.

- For GI 22, it appears that procedural guidance is sufficiently similar among all plants. From this similarity, we do not expect significant differences in operator response or large delays in attempting to isolate paths (e.g., >15–20 minutes). Thus, for GI 22, we conclude that there would be no significant adverse differences between the generalization plants and their corresponding detailed plant.

- For GI 23, all plants have throttling guidance and specific steps; particularly once a transition to the appropriate procedure occurs. For the very rapid rise in RCS pressure and subcooling that would occur with an unexpected/sudden reclosure of PORVs or SRVs, it would seem that there is likely to be some delay in responding to the very quick transition from a saturated RCS to a filled RCS (as we have seen for the analyzed plants). Thus, for GI 23, we conclude that there would be no significant adverse differences between the generalization plants and their corresponding detailed plant.

- For GI 24, all plants require (or appear to require) manual action to control charging flow. Thus, for GI 24, we conclude that there would be no significant adverse differences between the generalization plants and their corresponding detailed plant.

From the observations provided above, one potential difference has been found between the detailed analysis plants and the generalization plants. For Salem, the frequency could increase by at most a factor of 5 (GI 21).

For **feed-and-bleed-related**, the following observations are made:

- For GI 25, all plants appear to have a similar "over-capacity" of feed than what is needed for sufficient heat removal. Hence, losing all feedwater and having to go to feed-and-bleed would seem similarly "unlikely." To test this, information in Table D-5 of NUREG/CR-5500, Vol. 1 [Poloski 98] was examined. From this examination, we found that for B&W plants, the generalization plant (TMI) has an AFW/EFW unavailability that is a factor of 1.2 higher than the detailed plant (Oconee). For the Westinghouse plants, the unavailability is either lower for the generalization plants (Diablo Canyon and Salem) or higher by a factor of 1.1 (for Sequoyah) compared to the detailed plant (Beaver Valley). For the CE plants, the unavailability for the generalization plant (Ft. Calhoun) is a factor of 26 higher than the detailed analysis plant (Palisades). However, this does not include credit for the diesel-driven AFW pump at the generalization plant. If we conservatively assign a 0.1 probability of failure to the

diesel-driven pump, this difference becomes a factor of 3. Thus, for GI 25, we conclude that only the CE generalization plant would have a frequency that is somewhat higher than its detailed analysis plant.

- For GI 26, all plants have specific criteria that direct the operators to go to feed-and-bleed. While there are some differences in the specifics, it is unlikely that such specifics would substantially affect the operators' response. Thus, for GI 26, we conclude that there would be no significant adverse differences between the generalization plants and their corresponding detailed plant.

- GI 27 is not a PRA/HRA issue. This issue is examined in in section 9.3.2.2.

- GI 28 is not a PRA/HRA issue. This issue is examined in section 9.3.2.2.

From the observations provided above, one potential difference has been found between the detailed analysis plants and the generalization plants. For Fort Calhoun, the frequency could increase by about a factor of 3 (GI 25).

9.3.2.2   TH Judgmental Analyses

9.3.2.2.1   Introduction

To facilitate the performance of the individual judgmental TH analyses, the five general scenarios identified in Table 9.6 of Section 9.3.1 were recategorized into four basic groups based on (1) more global examination of the dominant types of scenarios in more detail and the less-dominant scenarios, (2) the TH characteristics of the scenarios in the group, and (3) the systems that determine the downcomer fluid temperature behavior. These groups are described in the following subsections.

9.3.2.2.1.1 Group 1: Large-Diameter Pipe Breaks

Group 1 consists of LOCAs with a break diameter of 8-in. (20.32-cm) or greater. This group of LOCAs results in rapid system cooldown and complete system depressurization. The operator trips the reactor coolant pumps in these transients because of loss of primary system subcooling. The high- and low-pressure injection systems are running at or near pump runout conditions within several minutes of initiation. The safety injection tanks also discharge within several minutes. With the combined flow of the injection systems and safety injection tank discharge, the downcomer is filled with subcooled water after the initial blowdown for the duration of the transient[§§§§§]. The downcomer fluid temperature is principally determined by the flow from the high- and low-pressure injection systems, the safety injection tank discharge, and the initial temperature of the water used in the injection systems.

9.3.2.2.1.2 Group 2: Small- to Medium-Diameter Pipe Breaks

Group 2 consists of LOCAs with a break diameter of 2.0 to 5.7-in. (5.08 to 14.37-cm). This group of LOCAs results in slower cooldown and depressurization than the Group 1 transients. For this break diameter range, the balance between break flow and ECCS injection flow governs the primary system cooldown and depressurization rate. The operator trips the reactor coolant pumps in these transients because of loss of primary system subcooling, although there is some trip time variation for different break sizes. Safety injection tank discharge and initiation of low-pressure injection occur later in the sequence, relative to Group 1 transients. In cases where the break diameters are small, low-pressure injection flow may not be initiated at all. Also, the safety injection tanks may not totally discharge, again depending on the break size. In this range of break sizes, the system pressure limits the rate of high- and

---

§§§§§   The term "transient" is used in its generic sense to represent the occurrence of a set of events that lead to a specific outcome

low-pressure injection system injection to the reactor system. The downcomer fluid conditions are principally determined by the break diameter, the flow from the high- and low-pressure injection systems, the safety injection tank discharge, and the initial temperature of the water used in these systems. The break location plays a role in the downcomer fluid conditions. In the case of a cold leg break, some of the ECCS goes directly out the break instead of into the downcomer, resulting in warmer downcomer fluid temperatures over an equivalent-sized hot leg break. Note that the use of feed-and-bleed can be considered to "fit" within this group, since this involves one or more open pressurizer valves (hence, like a LOCA) with successful safety injection. Since feed-and-bleed can be controlled by the operator, it cannot be worse than an equivalent-sized break.

9.3.2.2.1.3 Group 3: Stuck-Open Valves in the Primary System that Reclose

Group 3 consists of transients involving stuck-open primary side SRVs that reclose. This group of transients results in cooldown and depressurization characteristics of a LOCA with a diameter at the low end of the Group 2 range. Once the valve recloses, the system heats up as a result of the loss of primary system coolant flow out the valve, and repressurizes as a result of charging or high-pressure injection flow. The operator trips the reactor coolant pumps in these transients because of loss of primary system subcooling, although there may be some time separation when individual pumps are tripped depending on the trip criteria used. In Group 3 transients, low-pressure injection flow is not initiated. Safety injection tanks do not generally totally discharge because the system remains at relatively high pressure, compared to Groups 1 and 2. The high-pressure injection system is not operating near pump runout conditions, especially once the valve recloses. In this range of break sizes, the break flow limits the rate of high-pressure injection system injection to the reactor system.

9.3.2.2.1.4 Group 4: Main Steam Line Breaks and Other Secondary Side Failures

Group 4 consists of main steam line breaks and other secondary side failures (e.g., valve openings, overfeed). This group of transients results in overcooling of the primary system through the steam generator loop affected by the failure of the steam line or other secondary fault. The response of these events is determined by numerous factors, including break location and operator actions. If the operator isolates the affected steam generator within a reasonable time, the primary system cooldown stops. The secondary side pressure equalizes with the containment pressure (slightly above atmospheric), and the secondary side fluid is near saturation temperature (somewhat subcooled as a result of adverse containment conditions). On the primary side, the operator does not trip the reactor coolant pumps, as subcooling is not lost; however, if the break is inside containment, the reactor coolant pumps are manually tripped as a result of adverse containment conditions. High-pressure injection starts but does not operate at runout conditions, as the primary system pressure remains high. Low-pressure injection initiation and safety injection tank discharge do not occur. The downcomer fluid conditions generally remain subcooled throughout the transient.

Included in Group 4 are transients involving stuck-open secondary side SRVs and overfeeds. Like the main steam line break, this group of transients results in overcooling of the primary system through the steam generator loop affected by the stuck-open valve or overfeed. The cooldown rate is much slower because the flow through the valve is much lower than the flow through the failed steam line, and the consequences of any overfeed are not significant, particularly if isolated by the time the SG(s) are full. The operator does not trip the reactor coolant pumps, as subcooling is not lost. High-pressure injection starts but does not operate at runout conditions, as the primary system pressure remains high. Low-pressure injection initiation and safety injection tank

discharge are not likely to occur. The downcomer fluid conditions generally remain subcooled throughout the transient.

9.3.2.2.2 Analysis

The approach used for the plant TH generalization is to compare key design features in conjunction with the RELAP5 TH results for the Oconee, Beaver Valley, and Palisades plants against the comparable designs in the generalization plants to determine whether there are any differences that would have a significant impact on the downcomer fluid temperature prediction. System pressure is considered in those transients where repressurization occurs. Further information and data on the four groups of TH sequences is presented in [*Whitehead-Gen*].

9.3.2.2.2.1 Group 1: Large Diameter Pipe Breaks

Group 1 sequences result in the most rapid cooldown and depressurization of any of the dominant sequences analyzed for the Oconee, Beaver Valley, and Palisades plants. System cooldown and depressurization is essentially complete by about 150 seconds for 16-in. (40.64-cm) diameter LOCAs. For 8-in. (20.32-cm) LOCAs, the time for system depressurization to occur is longer because the break area is a factor of 4 lower than in the case of a 16-in. (40.64-cm) break. For the 8-in. (20.32-cm) break, the system depressurizes to 1.38 MPa [200 psia] in about 300 seconds for the Beaver Valley and Palisades plants. For Oconee, the system depressurizes to under 1.38 MPa [200 psia] in about 600 seconds.

Similar downcomer temperature characteristics are expected in the generalization plants, factoring in the plants' power level, primary system volume and ECCS design differences. For the CE designs, the comparable plants are Fort Calhoun and Palisades. Some differences are found in the injection system capacities and safety injection tank water volume as a result of the difference in power level between these plants, although differences in the reactor vessel volume may also be a factor as a key function of the safety injection tanks is to refill the reactor vessel after blowdown. In any event, the safety injection tanks are designed to refill the system in large-break LOCAs.

In the case of B&W plants, the Oconee and TMI plants are comparable. These plants have about the same power level (2,568 MWt for Oconee compared to 2,530 MWt for TMI). The ECCS flow and safety injection tank volumes are comparable, which is not surprising, given that these plants operate at about the same power level.

The comparable Westinghouse plants are Beaver Valley, Diablo Canyon, Sequoyah, and Salem. These plants have significant basic design differences, including the core power level and number of loops in the plant. The core power level in Beaver Valley is 2,652 MWt compared to 3,338 MWt for Diablo Canyon (Unit 1) and 3,411 MWt for the Salem and Sequoyah plants. Beaver Valley is a 3-loop design, while Diablo Canyon, Salem, and Sequoyah are 4-loop designs. As a result, the system volume for Beaver Valley is less than the 4-loop plants[7]. The Beaver Valley plant has three safety injection tanks (one for each loop), compared to four injection tanks for the other plants. As noted earlier, reactor vessel volume is a factor since a key function of the tanks is to refill the vessel after blowdown. Because of the higher power levels, ECC injection flow is higher in the comparison plants compared to Beaver Valley.

The initial water temperature in the high- and low-pressure injection system and safety injection tanks is a factor in the cooldown rate and in the final downcomer fluid temperature. A review of the data obtained from the generalization plants show that the temperatures used in the plant analyses for Oconee, Beaver Valley, and Palisades is in the range of injection temperatures used in all plants. All the plants operate with injection temperatures within a range set in the plant technical specifications,

which is represented by the temperatures used in the analysis.

In summary, no differences in the plant system designs have been found that will cause significant differences in the downcomer fluid temperature from a thermal-hydraulic perspective. It is possible that there will be temperature variations attributable to the power level (i.e., MWt), although breaks in the range of 8 to 16-in. (20.32 to 40.64-cm) are sufficiently large that the water injected into the system as a result of combined high- and low-pressure injection and safety injection tank discharge largely governs the downcomer fluid temperature. Also, the conditional probability of vessel failure is at a maximum in this break size diameter range, as discussed in Sections 8.5.2.4.1 and 9.1.2.1 of this report.

9.3.2.2.2.2 Group 2: Small- to Medium-Diameter Pipe Breaks

The Group 2 sequences result in a slower cooldown and depressurization rate compared to the Group 1 dominant sequences for the Oconee, Beaver Valley, and Palisades plants. No general behavior pattern emerges in downcomer temperature for this mix of transients compared to the Group 1 transients. This lack of a general pattern is attributable to variations in such factors as break location, assumed injection temperature, and initial reactor power level. In addition, different operator actions, pump shutoff heads, and trip setpoints are also factors.

Although the downcomer temperature results are highly variable among the plant types, generalization among plants by a given vendor can still be made. In the range of break sizes from 2.0 to 5.7-in. (5.08 to 14.37-cm) from hot full-power conditions, the rate of injection is limited by the size of the break, particularly as the break sizes becomes smaller. As a result, variations in reactor power level have more of an impact on downcomer temperature predictions compared to Group 1. Safety injection tank discharge and low-pressure injection flow initiation occur later, if at all.

---

[7] The plant design factors in the power level when selecting ECCS injection and safety injection tank capacities.

The tendency of the injection flow to be limited by the break flow in Group 2 transients also limits the amount of energy that can be discharged through the break. Higher-power systems have a larger system volume with more steel mass and more water in the steam generators on the secondary side. Consequently, for a given break size, the higher-power systems should result in a slower cooldown and depressurization rate and, hence, somewhat warmer downcomer temperatures, particularly during depressurization, given comparable ECC injection rates. In general, the cooldown rate should be slower for the Salem, Sequoyah, and Diablo Canyon plants (compared to Beaver Valley), as these plants operate at higher reactor power relative to Beaver Valley. Conversely, a reactor system that operates at lower power could have a faster cooldown rate, which is the situation between the Palisades and Fort Calhoun plants. However, the capacity of the high- and low-pressure injection systems is smaller and generally scaled to the core power. Comparing Palisades and Fort Calhoun, for example, the high-pressure injection system pump at Palisades has about twice the flow capacity as at Fort Calhoun, so these plants should have comparable depressurization and cooldown rates. Once the system has depressurized and reached an equilibrium pressure, the downcomer temperature becomes comparable among the plants and is principally governed by the injection water temperature.

For hot zero power conditions, downcomer temperature behavior should be less sensitive to the power level, simply because the power level is low. For the analyzed plants, the assumed power level is 0.2% of rated core power (about 5 MWth) for hot zero power operation. If analyses were performed for the generalization plants, the models could be initialized to the same power level. In this case, the difference among plants of similar design would be small.

An issue that needs to be considered for the thermal-hydraulic generalization is the switchover of the ECCS injection suction from the refueling water storage tank (or equivalent) to the containment sump. The increase in downcomer fluid temperature later in the transient is attributable to this switchover at a point in time after system cooldown and depressurization has occurred, so the downcomer temperature is governed by the injection temperature. Many times, however, vessel failure is predicted to occur *before* switchover of ECCS suction. As a result, ECCS suction switchover to the containment sump is generally unimportant to the vessel failure prediction.

In summary, break flow and energy released through the break govern the rate of cooldown and depressurization in the reactor system. For hot full-power cases, the cooldown and depressurization rates are expected to be slower for reactor systems that operate at higher powers and faster for systems that operate at lower powers. However, since the flow capacity of the high-pressure injection pumps at Fort Calhoun is about one-half that of Palisades, all generalization plants should have depressurization and cooldown rates that are comparable to their corresponding detailed analysis plant. The difference in cooldown and depressurization rates should have less of an impact on downcomer temperature if the transient begins from hot zero power operation.

It should be noted that the feed-and-bleed LOCA scenarios have a thermal-hydraulic behavior that is similar to the small LOCA described above.

9.3.2.2.2.3 Group 3: Stuck-Open Valves in the Primary System

Transients involving stuck-open primary side SRVs that reclose have cooldown and depressurization characteristics of a LOCA with a diameter at the low end of the Group 2 range. A key difference, however, is the reclosure of the stuck-open valve after significant cooldown and depressurization has occurred. Once the valve recloses, rapid system repressurization occurs as a result of continued operation of the high-pressure injection system or charging system. The rate of repressurization depends on the flow characteristics of the high-pressure injection or charging pumps. The operator action to control system pressure by controlling the high-pressure injection system pumps is important to determining system response in this group of transients.

The system cooldown and depressurization rates are governed by the capacity of the PORVs or SRVs, power level, system volume, and ECCS injection temperatures/rates. For the B&W design, the Oconee PORV and SRV capacities are slightly larger than the TMI capacities, so the cooldown and depressurization rates would be slightly faster for Oconee. For the Westinghouse designs, the capacity of the Beaver Valley PORV is higher than Sequoyah and Salem, even though the reactor power for both Salem and Sequoyah is more than 750 MWth higher. The cooldown and depressurization rates for Salem and Sequoyah would be slower, and the downcomer fluid temperature would remain higher throughout the transient if the PORV fails. The results are similar, comparing the relief valve capacity for these plants, as Beaver Valley has a higher relief capacity than Sequoyah or Salem.

Compared to Beaver Valley, the Diablo Canyon PORV has a 25% higher flow capacity. However, the reactor power is also about 25% higher, so the cooldown and depressurization rates would be about the same for both plants if the PORV fails. In the case of the SRVs, Beaver Valley has a higher capacity valve than Diablo Canyon, so the cooldown and depressurization rates for Diablo Canyon should be slower than for Beaver Valley.

For the CE designs, Fort Calhoun has a higher SRV capacity per valve than Palisades, even though its core power is lower. As a result, the cooldown and depressurization rates for Fort Calhoun are higher than for Palisades, given failure of a single valve. Palisades has large PORVs, but operates with closed block valves that prevent the function of pressure relief through these valves, so no comparison is made using PORV capacity for these plants.

As in the case of the Group 2 LOCAs, downcomer temperature behavior should be less

sensitive to the power level for hot zero power conditions, simply because the power level is low for the reasons cited at the end of the Group 2 discussion.

In contrast to the Group 2 transients, late stage repressurization and operator actions to control the subcooling and system pressure must be factored into the evaluation. In LOCAs, the system pressure is low and does not play a significant role in the prediction of vessel failure. However, in the case of a stuck-open primary relief valve that subsequently recloses, the primary repressurizes (without operator intervention), and the resulting pressure rise can drive cracks through the vessel wall. The pump head of the high-pressure injection system is also a factor in determining the primary pressure. The Oconee, Beaver Valley, Diablo Canyon, and TMI plants have high-head pumps that can repressurize the system to the setpoint of the PORV or pressurizer SRV. The Palisades, Fort Calhoun, Sequoyah, and Salem plants have low-head pumps that can repressurize the system to the range of 8.9 to 10.3 MPa (1,290 to 1,500 psia). However, the charging systems of these plants can also repressurize the system, albeit at a slower rate. Primary system reheating after the valve recloses as a result of decay heat also contributes to system repressurization. For hot zero power cases, the system can also repressurize after the valve recloses, although throttling of the high-pressure injection system allows the system to eventually depressurize.

Operators are trained to control system pressure and subcooling by controlling high-pressure injection flow and to reestablish normal charging and letdown flow (see Table 9.7, GI 23). The criteria used to establish when the operator starts high-pressure injection system throttling and continues to throttle varies significantly from plant-to-plant. It is not possible to generalize system response to the variety of possible throttling strategies without further analysis.

In summary, the system cooldown and depressurization rates are higher for Oconee (B&W) and Beaver Valley (W-3) than for the generalization plants from the same NSSS vendor (i.e., the generalization plants are warmer). However, Fort Calhoun (CE) has higher system cooldown and depressurization rates than its corresponding detailed analysis plant, Palisades. The impact of high-pressure injection system throttling strategies among the plants is discussed in Section 9.3.2.1.

9.3.2.2.2.4 Group 4: Main Steam Line Breaks and Other Secondary Side Failures

Group 4 transients includes large steam line breaks and stuck-open secondary side valves, as well as consideration of overfeeds such as the unexpected opening of the feed regulating valves. The secondary breaches can vary from double-ended guillotine breaks of the main steam line to a single stuck-open turbine bypass valve. There are many factors that influence the thermal-hydraulic response of the reactor system during such events.. Key factors are operator actions, the location of the break, and steam line flow restrictors. If the operator can isolate the affected steam generator in a reasonable amount of time, primary system cooldown is stopped and there may not be a primary system overcooling problem. In all plants, the operator is instructed to isolate the affected steam generator, and training and procedures support early operator actions (see more on this above under the PRA/HRA discussion). In order for main steam line breaks and other secondary faults to become a PTS problem, feedwater must be continued to the affected steam generator.

Break location is another factor in system response during a main steam line break transient. Plant response is different depending on whether the break is inside or outside containment because of effects on reactor trip, containment spray actuation, safety injection and reactor coolant pump trips, and other adverse condition issues. If the break/stuck valve is downstream of the MSIV, the valves should close and the primary system cooldown is stopped. While the MSIV closure setpoints vary from plant-to-plant, they all close relatively early in the transient. Note that some B&W plants (such as Oconee) do not have MSIVs, so the break location is less important. If the break

occurs inside containment, the operators should trip the RCPs in response to adverse containment conditions. In general, RCP trip makes conditions worse as the downcomer fluid is not as well-mixed as when the pumps are running so lower downcomer fluid temperatures may result. The flow restrictors (if available) are in place to limit the break flow during steam line breaks and determine the cooldown rate. Note that the B&W plants (Oconee and TMI) do not have flow restrictors, and the break flow is determined by the flow area of the steam line.

Starting with the B&W plants designs (Oconee and TMI) some comparisons and observations are made. Both plants use the once-through steam generator design and have comparable power levels (2,568 MWt for Oconee and 2,533 MWt for TMI). The steam generator water mass in the Oconee plant is estimated between 35,000 to 40,000 lbm (15,875 to 18,143 kg), while TMI is estimated between 42,000 and 45,000 lbm (19,050 and 20,411 kg). Neither plant has flow restrictors, so the steam line break flow is limited by steam line size (34-in. (86.4-cm) for Oconee, and 24-in. (61.0-cm) for TMI). Since the steam line flow area is smaller in TMI, the break flow is expected to be less than at Oconee, thus leading to a slower primary side cooldown. In addition, neither the Oconee nor TMI plants have MSIVs, so the break location is relatively unimportant. Both plants have main feedwater automatically isolated after an MSLB, so main feedwater temperature and flow rate are unimportant.

On the primary system side, the high-pressure injection system has a major effect on downcomer fluid temperature during a main steam line break transient. The two B&W plants have similar high-pressure injection systems. Based on an overall general comparison, the Oconee and TMI plants are expected to have similar thermal-hydraulic responses to an MSLB transient. Given that TMI has smaller-diameter steam lines, the average downcomer fluid temperature is expected to be slightly warmer than at Oconee.

Next, comparisons are made between the two CE plants: Palisades and Ft. Calhoun. Both plants utilize vertical U-tube steam generators. These two plants have significantly different power levels (2,530 MWt for Palisades and 1,500 MWt for Ft. Calhoun). Consequently, Ft. Calhoun has smaller steam generators. The normal full power water mass in the steam generator for Palisades is 142,138 lbm (64,472 kg), compared to 82,000 lbm (37,194 kg) for Ft. Calhoun. Both plants have flow restrictors at the steam generator outlets with a flow area of approximately 2.0 ft^2 (0.18 m^2). In Palisades, the MFW is typically isolated by the operator; however, MFW is runback automatically if the operator does not take control in time. In Ft. Calhoun, MFW is isolated automatically during an MSLB. Auxiliary feedwater temperature can vary from 294 to 311 K (70 to 100°F). The Palisades analysis uses a nominal temperature of 305 K (90°F). In the Palisades plant, a control system limits the total AFW flow to the affected steam generator. In other plants, this type of control system is not used, so total AFW flow to a single steam generator is possible.

The high-pressure injection pumps at Palisades have a shutoff head of 8.9 MPa (1,291.7 psia), while Ft. Calhoun pumps are slightly higher at 9.6 MPa (1,390 psia). However, both plants have charging pumps capable of pressurizing the primary system to above the PORV setpoint. Note that Palisades normally operates with the PORV block valves closed. The flow capacity of the Palisades HPI pumps is about twice that of the Ft. Calhoun pumps. The Ft. Calhoun plant probably has a smaller primary side fluid volume than Palisades, consistent with the difference in power level.

Based on an overall general comparison, the Palisades and Ft. Calhoun plants are expected to have similar thermal-hydraulic responses to an MSLB transient.

Finally, comparisons are made between the Westinghouse-designed plants, Beaver Valley (3-loop), Diablo Canyon (4-loop), Sequoyah (4-loop), and Salem (4-loop). All plants utilize vertical U-tube steam generators. The power

levels vary from 2,652 MWt for Beaver Valley to 3,411 MWt for Sequoyah and Salem. Note that the power levels are larger on the 4-loop plants than on the 3-loop Beaver Valley plant. The steam generator mass varies from 100,000 lbm (45,360 kg) for Salem to 115,000 lbm (52,160 kg) for Diablo Canyon. All plants use a flow restrictor at the steam generator outlet. For the 4-loop plants, the flow area is 1.4 ft^2 (0.13 m^2), but is much larger (4.7 ft^2 (0.44 m^2)) on the 3-loop Beaver Valley plant. Based on its larger flow restrictor, Beaver Valley is expected to have a much faster cooldown rate than the other Westinghouse plants.

The main feedwater temperature for the Westinghouse plants is typically around 497 K (435°F), and decreases to 311 K (100°F) after a reactor trip. In all four plants, main feedwater should automatically trip on a main steam line break. Auxiliary feedwater temperature varies from 275 to 322 K (35 to 120°F) among the four plants. The Beaver Valley analysis uses a temperature of 295 K (72°F). In all four plants, the AFW is capable of maintaining steam generator level even during an MSLB.

The four plants have somewhat different high-pressure injection systems. At Beaver Valley, the charging and high-pressure injection systems use the same pumps. These pumps have a shutoff head greater than 18 MPa (2,600 psia) and are capable of pressurizing the primary system to above the PORV setpoint. The other Westinghouse plants use high-head charging pumps but intermediate-pressure HPI pumps. These intermediate-pressure pumps have a shutoff head of approximately 10.3 MPa (1,500 psia). The minimum HPI temperature varies from 275 to 289 K (35 to 60°F) among the four plants. In the Beaver Valley analysis, 283 K (50°F) was used for HPI temperature.

Based on an overall general comparison, the four Westinghouse plants are expected to have similar thermal-hydraulic responses to an MSLB transient.

Stuck-open valves on the secondary side are equated to smaller steam line breaks. Transients with stuck-open secondary side (turbine bypass, atmospheric dump, and safety relief) valves are less severe thermal-hydraulically than the larger steam line breaks discussed above. For all plants evaluated, all secondary side valves can be isolated with the exception of the SRVs.

In summary, the generalization plants should be warmer (or about the same) when compared to the plants analyzed in detail.

The simple overfeeds are worth a brief mention. In these events, an unexpected overfeed of one or more SGs occurs. If such an overfeed condition is allowed to continue for many tens of minutes, the secondary temperature will ultimately drive toward the main condenser water temperature (~311 K (100°F)) following a plant trip and likely isolation of warming (i.e., steam addition) of the feedwater. This causes depressurization and cooldown of the primary system. However, as discussed in the above comparable PRA/HRA section, the likelihood of a continuing overfeed, which would involve failure of automatic high SG level trips backed by operator action to either close feed valves or shutdown pumps as necessary, makes such an event very unlikely. Further, the plant-specific plant analyses show that the PTS challenge, if the feed is not controlled even until the SGs are completely full, is not significant. For these reasons, simple overfeed scenarios are not important and, hence, not discussed any further.

9.3.3 Combined Observations and Overall Conclusion

Group 1 (Large-Diameter Primary Side Pipe Breaks): No differences were found that would cause significant changes in either the progression or frequencies of the PTS scenarios. From the TH perspective, no differences in the plant system designs were found that would cause significant changes in the downcomer fluid temperature. While some temperature variations could be expected because of the initial power level, breaks in this range are sufficiently large that the water injected into the system due to combined high-

and low-pressure injection and safety injection tank discharge should largely govern the downcomer fluid temperature. Thus, we expect that the generalization plants can be bounded (or represented) by the detailed analysis plants.

Group 2 (Small- to Medium-Diameter Primary Side Pipe Breaks): No differences were found that would cause significant changes in either the progression or frequency of the pipe break LOCAs. For the feed-and-bleed LOCAs, the only identified difference affected the frequency for the CE generalization plant (i.e., Fort Calhoun). The frequency for these types of scenarios could be higher by a factor of ~3; however, this increase would not prevent the generalization plants from being bounded (or represented) by the detailed analysis plants. All generalization plants should have depressurization and cooldown rates associated with pipe break and feed-and-bleed transients that are comparable to their corresponding detailed analysis plant. Thus, we expect that the generalization plants can be bounded (or represented) by the detailed analysis plants.

Group 3 (Stuck-Open Valves on the Primary Side that May Later Reclose): The progression of accident scenarios should be the same across all plants. However, the frequencies associated with these scenarios could increase by at most a factor of 5 for one of the Westinghouse plants (i.e., Salem). The importance of this factor of 5 increase at Salem was approximated by increasing the failure probability assigned to the operator fails to throttle basic event in the Beaver Valley model and requantifying the Beaver Valley results. The total point estimate for Beaver Valley increased by a factor of 1.02; thus, we conclude that this difference is unimportant.

Only Fort Calhoun is expected to have a downcomer temperature that is cooler than its corresponding detailed analysis plant (Palisades). The downcomer temperature for the other generalization plants is actually expected to be somewhat warmer. Given the expected Fort Calhoun results, a surrogate analysis was performed. This analysis used the Palisades TH model, adjusting the model to account for the differences in thermal power to primary system volume and size of the relief valve opening(s). Results from the analysis indicated that Fort Calhoun would have a lower downcomer temperature, as expected. The results from the surrogate TH calculation were then analyzed using FAVOR and the Palisades embrittlement map. Results from the FAVOR calculation indicated an increase in conditional probability of through-wall cracking. While this resulted in much higher TWCFs for Fort Calhoun than for Palisades for the same type of sequence, the TWCFs were still small in an absolute sense (low E-08/yr or lower range). These values are comparable to but not higher than the highest TWCFs estimated for all types of sequences (LOCAs, SRV openings, MSLBs, etc.), which are also in the E-08/yr range. Thus, the TWCF of Fort Calhoun can be bounded by Palisades.

Group 4 (Main Steam Line Breaks and Secondary Side Breaks, in General):
No differences were found that would cause significant differences in either the progression or frequency of the PTS scenarios. The downcomer temperature for the generalization plants should be about the same (Westinghouse and CE) or warmer (B&W). Thus, we expect that the generalizations plants can be bounded (or represented) by the detailed analysis plants.

These combined observations support the overall conclusion that the TWCF estimates produced for the detailed analysis plants are sufficient to characterize (or bound) the TWCF estimates for the five generalization plants and, thus, by inference, PWRs *in general*.

9.4 Consideration of External Events

9.4.1 Introduction

In examining the potential for a revised PTS screening limit, it is important to also consider the potential risk from external events. External events are those in which spatial interactions may be important to the propagation of the accident sequence, and these can contribute to the PTS risk. External events include such scenarios as those involving fires, floods, high winds and tornados, and seismic events, among others. As an example, a fire could start in an electrical cabinet causing the spurious opening of one or more secondary relief valves such as turbine bypass (steam dump) valves, which could induce a serious overcooling and a potential PTS concern depending on subsequent plant equipment and operator responses. Since external events can affect multiple plant equipment and operator actions as well, they could be important to PTS.

Because (1) the specific effects of external events are very plant-specific (e.g., into which rooms the water from an internal flood propagates and, thus, what equipment is affected), and (2) since these analyses can be resource-intensive, requiring the gathering of significant spatial information about each plant, it was not practical to perform plant-specific external event PTS analyses. Instead, conservative analyses were performed with the goal of *bounding* the potential PTS TWCFs from external events. This is in contrast to the internal event PTS analyses results, which are generally "best-estimate" analyses meant to determine a realistic assessment of PTS TWCFs attributable to scenarios initiated by such events as turbine trips, loss of feedwater, etc. (i.e., internal events). In contrast, the contribution from external events was assessed by using conservative assumptions to bound the PTS TWCFs from external events and, hopefully, demonstrates that the bounding TWCFs from external events are at least no higher than the highest best-estimate internal events TWCFs. Such a result would provide reasonable assurance that the total external event-caused

PTS TWCF is no worse than the total internal event-caused PTS TWCF (which is as high as the low E-8/yr range at 60 EFPY based on the three detailed plant analyses).

As a result, the numerical results from the external events analyses (described in detail in [*Kolaczkowski-Ext*] and which contains the references to the other documents cited here) should not be taken as best-estimate or realistic values; they are intended to provide bounding TWCF estimates for the pertinent external event scenarios. Also note that in following this approach, no particular plant was taken as a representative model for the analysis (with the exception of earthquake hazard, where H.B. Robinson and Diablo Canyon were used as surrogates). Therefore, because these results are intended to bound the worst situation that might arise at virtually any plant, they may be extremely conservative for many plants. The degree of conservatism cannot be determined without performing plant-specific analyses.

9.4.2   Approach

A multi-faceted approach was used to gain insight as to the potential contribution of external events to the PTS TWCFs. This approach included the following:

(1) A review was performed of the late 2001 – early 2002 version of the Calvert Cliffs PRA model, with cooperation from the utility, which includes not only core damage scenarios, but also PTS scenarios. The model includes contributions from both internal and external events for both core damage frequencies and PTS TWCFs and can offer insight into the potential importance of external events.

(2) As further evidence of the potential importance of external events, a review of licensee event reports (LERs) was performed of actual overcooling events in U.S. plant operating experience covering a recent approximately twenty year period.

(3) Further, a review was conducted of a sampling of (just two) individual plant examinations for external events (IPEEE)

submittals, one for Salem and one for Ginna, to determine what insights could be gained from those studies that might be applicable to PTS.

(4) With all of the above as background, it was nonetheless decided that additional analytical analyses were necessary to be able to bound the potential TWCFs from external event overcooling scenarios.

9.4.3   Findings Based on the Reviews

The late 2001 – early 2002 version of the Calvert Cliffs PRA suggests that the TWCFs as a result of PTS caused by external events are low compared to that caused by internal events (i.e., less than 10%). The PRA shows fire as the external event of greatest concern. While this is an indicator of the potential relative contributions, it is only one plant's result and the finding is subject to some modifications that would need to be made to the model in order to be more comparable to the three analyses conducted as part of this work. For instance, the Calvert Cliffs model needs modifications in the areas of the sequences being modeled, and some human failure probabilities may need to be reconsidered during certain external events. Additionally, the latest CPTWC information from this study needs to be reflected in any update of the Calvert Cliffs PRA. Hence, while encouraging, the relative importance of external events to the PTS TWCFs cannot be generically determined based on this one input alone.

The LER review of events occurring in a recent 20-year period identified a total of 128 PTS-relevant (i.e., cooldown) events. Of these, only three events could be potentially categorized as involving an external event, although only one (a switchgear fire) was clearly an external event (LER No. 26989002). This evidence suggests that external events will be involved in no more than approximately 2% of all PTS occurrences. While this is a valuable insight in that it suggests that experience shows that cooldowns are more likely to be caused by internal events rather than external events, it still does not address the potential TWCFs from external events even if they do occur less frequently. This is because external events could still lead to more serious scenarios with higher CPTWC values, thereby resulting in potentially higher TWCFs.

The two IPEEEs were originally conducted to determine core damage frequencies as a result of undercooling (rather than overcooling events); hence, there were very limited insights from these reports applicable to PTS. Nonetheless, during the review of the IPEEEs, one general type of interaction between external events and effects of interest to PTS was noted to be included in both studies. This was a fire-induced opening of one or more pressurizer PORVs — a possible serious overcooling event. This indicates that any estimation of the external event contribution to PTS needs to include consideration of spurious actions such as that described as a result of fire scenarios. However, no other meaningful insights were gained from reviewing the two IPEEEs that would be applicable to this PTS work.

9.4.4   Additional Analyses

9.4.4.1   Overview

The above reviews provided some insights with regard to how important external events may be to PTS. However, the set of insights was incomplete. As a result, additional analytical analyses were performed. These additional analyses involved comparisons of the following factors:

(1) TWCF results from the internal events analyses for the three plants

(2) conservatively estimated corresponding external event TWCF results

This comparative analysis was structured based on the following *broad* types of overcooling scenarios analyzed in this PTS work:

- *Category 1: Loss-of-Coolant Accidents (LOCAs)*. These are scenarios that involve primary system breaches (such as pipe breaks and open pressurizer valves) but without any secondary anomalies or faults.

- *Category 2: Secondary Anomalies or Faults*. These are scenarios that involve such events as stuck-open secondary valves, main steam line breaks, and steam generator overfeeds but without any primary system anomalies or faults.

- *Category 3: Coexisting LOCA - Secondary Faults*. These are scenarios that involve both primary system breaches and secondary faults at the same time.

As required, the analyses further divided these broad categories of scenarios into more specific types of scenarios. Table 9.7 summarizes all types of scenarios for which TWCF comparisons were made. These were examined for both full-power and hot zero power conditions. For each type of scenario, conservative judgments were made with regard to the type of external event that could directly contribute to the cause of such a scenario. In addition, conservative estimates were made with regard to the applicable external event frequencies, plant equipment responses, and operator effects. With regard to operator actions, little or no credit was given in these analyses in response to the external event-induced PTS challenges; this further contributed to the conservative estimations of external event TWCFs, thereby making them artificially more important. Finally, the resulting TWCFs from both internal event contributions and the conservatively assessed external event contributions were compared. The following is provided as just one example of such a comparison.

9.4.4.2   A Representative Comparison

Category 1 - LOCAs; Scenario Type #3: In this scenario, a small LOCA (with an equivalent diameter of ~1.5 to 3-in. (~3.8 to 7.6-cm)) occurs as a result of a pipe break, and everything else functions as designed. (Other small LOCAs, such as those caused by an open PORV, are a different scenario type that is analyzed elsewhere.) By this, we mean that HPI operates (so cold water enters the vessel downcomer region) and the system likely continues to provide full flow, since throttling criteria are not likely to be met for most breaks in this size range during the time period of interest to PTS when large temperature gradients occur across the vessel wall. It is assumed the operator does shut down the RCPs as procedurally required (this is worse for PTS since there is less mixing of the primary coolant), and there are no secondary anomalies or other operator errors that induce secondary complications.

Table 9.8 summarizes the major inputs and resulting TWCFs from such a scenario caused by a random small-break LOCA (i.e., an internal event initiator) based on results from the three plant analyses.

Table 9.7. Scenarios covered under the external event analyses

Overall Scenario Category	Scenario Types
Category 1: LOCAs	Large LOCA pipe break
	Medium LOCA pipe break
	Small LOCA pipe break
	Scenario with single stuck-open pressurizer PORV
	Scenario with single stuck-open pressurizer SRV
	Scenario with two stuck-open pressurizer PORVs
	Scenario with two stuck-open pressurizer SRVs
	Scenario with two stuck-open pressurizer PORVs that reclose
	Scenario with one or two stuck-open pressurizer SRVs that reclose
	Total loss of secondary heat sink with subsequent use of feed-and-bleed
	Small LOCA, or PORV or SRV opening, with initial loss of primary system injection
Category 2: Secondary Anomalies or Faults	Steam generator(s) overfeeds
	Uncontrolled secondary depressurization to feed steam generator(s) with condensate
	Two or fewer valves open upstream of MSIVs
	Turbine bypass (steam dump) valves open downstream of MSIVs
	Large steamline break upstream of MSIVs
	Large steamline break downstream of MSIVs
Category 3: Coexisting LOCA - Secondary Faults	Consideration of combinations of above

Table 9.8. Small-break LOCA internal event results

Scenario	Internal Event Frequency (yr^{-1})	CPTWC at 60 EFPY	Internal Event TWCF (yr^{-1})
Small LOCA at Full Power	Up to 1E-3	Up to 1E-5	Up to 2E-9*
Small LOCA at Hot Zero Power	Up to 2E-5	<1E-4 (conservative estimate)	<2E-9

* Highest CPTWC does not necessarily correspond to the highest frequency shown, so one cannot simply multiply the highest frequency in the table with the highest CPTWC shown in the table.

Consideration was given to how external events might directly induce a small pipe break LOCA. Seismic, flooding, fire, high wind/tornado, and other (e.g., aircraft crash) external events were considered. In large part because of the nature of the primary coolant system and containment designs, and their relative location to the rest of the plant (e.g., a fire in the auxiliary building should not be able to induce a pipe break in the primary coolant housed inside the containment), we concluded that only a seismic event might be able to induce a small pipe break LOCA. Hence an analysis of a seismic-induced small pipe break LOCA was conducted.

Possible Seismic-Small Loca Scenario:

For the small LOCA case, a 0.3g high confidence of low probability of failure (HCLPF) is assumed to be representative of the seismic strength of the primary piping and other components for which failure as a result of a seismic event could result in a small LOCA. This corresponds to the review-level earthquake (RLE) peak ground acceleration for most plants in the IPEEE program. Most (if not all) IPEEEs concluded that primary piping and components have higher seismic strengths than that corresponding to a 0.3g HCLPF; thus, use of the 0.3g HCLPF in this analysis is conservative. It is further assumed that both β_R and β_u (which define the uncertainty in the HCLPF) are 0.3 (typical), giving a median fragility of about 0.5g. Using the H.B. Robinson site as a surrogate for Eastern plants, because it has the largest hazard of any Eastern PWR, this corresponds to a mean accidence frequency of 1.6E-4/yr. An analysis was performed using the SAPHIRE computer code to convolve the above fragility information with the revised Lawrence Livermore National Laboratory (LLNL) hazard curve for H.B. Robinson, resulting in a mean seismic-induced small pipe break LOCA frequency estimated to be 1.1E-4/yr.

As an additional sensitivity, the hazard curve for Diablo Canyon was also used as representative of a high-seismicity site. A corresponding HCLPF for a small pipe break LOCA at such a site was assumed to be 0.5g, because of the more rugged plant design (higher RLE). Maintaining β_R and β_u of 0.3, and convolving this fragility information for a small pipe break LOCA with the mean hazard curve from the Diablo Canyon IPEEE submittal results in a mean seismic-

induced small pipe break LOCA frequency of 5.0E-4/yr[******].

Using a value of 0.02 (i.e., 2%) as the fraction of the year the plant is at HZP conditions, as done in the internal events analysis, yields 1E-5/yr as the highest estimated frequency (5.0E-4/yr from above x 0.02 = 1E-5/yr) of a seismic event causing a small pipe break LOCA while the plant is at HZP conditions.

By using the frequencies conservatively estimated above, and the same maximum CPTWC from the internal events analyses of the three plants (the CPTWC will be the same whether the event is caused by an internal event initiator or a seismic event), the corresponding seismically induced small pipe break LOCA TWCFs are as shown in Table 9.9.

Note that the conservative external event contributions to the TWCFs for this type of accident are either less than or not significantly greater than the internal event TWCFs.

9.4.5 Overall Findings

In spite of the conservative nature of the external event analyses, no external event scenarios were found where the TWCFs significantly exceed that of the worst internal event scenarios (contributions from LOCA-type and SRV open-reclose-type accidents) as discussed in detail in the companion report [*Kolaczkowski-Ext*]. From that report, and as reiterated in this summary section, the highest total best-estimate TWCF across all internal event scenarios for the three plants analyzed at 60 EFPY is approximately 2E-8/yr and is used as part of the basis for proposing revised PTS Rule criteria. The comparable *bounding* total TWCF across all external event scenarios is also approximately 2E-8/yr. Therefore, given the bounding nature of the external event analyses, there is

---

[******] The hazard curve in the Diablo Canyon IPEEE is given in terms of peak spectral acceleration in the range of 3.5–8Hz. This was converted to a zero-period peak ground acceleration by dividing the accelerations by a factor of 2.

considerable assurance that the external event contribution to overall TWCF as a result of PTS is at least no greater than the highest best-estimate contribution from internal events. In fact, given the conservative probabilities and dependencies assumed in the external event analyses, with the addition of little or no credit for any operator actions for the external event scenarios, it is more likely that the "realistic" external event contribution to overall TWCF is much less than the highest internal event contribution. It is, therefore, our view that the contribution of external initiating events to the overall TWCF attributable to PTS is enveloped by the internal event results. Hence, for general purposes, it is recommended that the overall PTS TWCF can be estimated by neglecting the potential contribution from external events. To the extent it may be necessary or desirable, individual plants could provide a detailed external events PTS analysis to ensure that the plant staff understands the specific contributions to PTS TWCF from external events.

Table 9.9. Small-break LOCA TWCF comparison

Scenario	Internal Event Frequency (yr⁻¹)	CPTWC at 60 EFPY	Internal Event TWCF (yr⁻¹)	Bounding External Event Frequency (yr⁻¹)	Bounding External Event TWCF (yr⁻¹)
Small LOCA at Full Power	Up to 1E-3	Up to 1E-5	Up to 2E-9	5E-4	5E-9
Small LOCA at Hot Zero Power	Up to 2E-5	<1E-4 (conservative estimate)	<2E-9	1E-5	<1E-9

9.5 Summary of Generalization Studies

In this chapter, we examined the applicability of the TWCF estimates presented in Chapter 8 for Oconee Unit 1, Beaver Valley Unit 1, and Palisades to PWRs *in general*. The information presented focused on the following topics:

- Sensitivity studies performed on the TH and PFM models to engender confidence in both the robustness of the results presented in Chapter 8 and their applicability to PWRs *in general*.

- An examination of the plant design and operational characteristics of five additional plants to determine whether the design and operational features that are the key contributors to PTS risk vary significantly enough in the general plant population to question the generality of our results.

- An examination of the effects of external events (e.g., fires, floods, earthquakes) to PTS risk.

Except for a few situations that are not expected to occur, none of these analyses revealed any reason to question the applicability of the results presented in Chapter 8 to the general population of operating PWRs in the United States. The information developed in these analyses is summarized as follows:

TH Sensitivity Studies

- Changes to the RELAP heat transfer coefficient model to account for low-flow situations where mixed convection heat transfer may be occurring in the downcomer were made based on the Petukhov-Gnielinski heat transfer correlation. This change in the heat transfer coefficient increases the CPTWC by a factor ~3 (averaged across all transients analyzed) compared to using the default heat transfer correlations in RELAP5/MOD3.3 Version ei. There is some variability from the average CPF factor, depending upon the transient being considered.

PFM Sensitivity Studies

- An examination of the effects of all postulated credible perturbations to our PFM model revealed no effects significant enough to warrant a change to our baseline model, or to recommend a caution regarding its robustness.

- In general, the TWCF of forged PWRs can be assessed using the Chapter 8 results (for plate welded PWRs) by ignoring the TWCF contribution of axial welds. However, should changes in future operating conditions result in a forged vessel being subjected to very high levels of embrittlement (far beyond any currently anticipated at EOL or EOLE) a plant-specific analysis to assess the effect of subclad flaws on TWCF would be warranted.

- For PWRs with vessel thicknesses of 7.5 to 9 .5-in. (19.05 to 24.13-cm), the TWCF results in Chapter 8 are realistic. The Chapter 8 results overestimate the TWCF of the seven thinner vessels (with wall thicknesses below 7-in. (17.78-cm)) and underestimate the TWCF of Palo Verde Units 1, 2, and 3, all of which have wall thicknesses above 11-in (27.94-cm). However, these vessels have very low embrittlement projected at either EOL or EOLE, suggesting little practical effect of this underestimation.

Plant Design and Operational Characteristics

- *Large-Diameter Primary Side Pipe Breaks*: No differences were found that would cause significant changes in either the progression or frequencies of the PTS scenarios. Additionally, no differences in the plant system designs were found that would cause significant changes in the downcomer fluid temperature.

- *Small- to Medium-Diameter Primary Side Pipe Breaks*: No differences were found that would cause significant changes in either the progression or frequency of the pipe break LOCAs. For the feed-and-bleed LOCAs, the only difference that was found affected the frequency for the CE

generalization plant (i.e., Fort Calhoun). The frequency for these types of scenarios could be higher by a factor of ~3; however, this increase would not prevent the generalization plants from being bounded (or represented) by the detailed analysis plants.

- *Stuck-Open Valves on the Primary Side that May Later Reclose*: The progression of the accident scenarios should be the same across all plants. While, the frequency associated with this type of scenarios could increase at some Westinghouse plants, the integrated effect of this increase was determined to be small. Fort Calhoun is expected to have a downcomer temperature that is cooler than its corresponding detailed analysis plant (Palisades) because of the smaller size of the plant. The downcomer temperature for the other generalization plants is actually expected to be somewhat warmer. PFM calculations performed to quantify the effect of the colder temperatures in Ft. Calhoun determined that while the conditional through-wall cracking probabilities would increase (as expected), the increase was not so substantial as to prevent the Palisades plant analysis from upper-bounding the Ft. Calhoun plant analysis. Thus, the colder downcomer temperature for smaller plants was not viewed as impeding the applicability of the TWCF values in Chapter 8 to PWRs in general.

- *Main Steam Line and other Secondary Side Breaks*: No differences were found that would cause significant differences in either the progression or frequency of the PTS scenarios.

- *Summary*: These observations support the conclusion that the Chapter 8 TWCF estimates produced can be used to characterize (or bound) the TWCF of PWRs in general.

External Events

- No external event scenarios were found where the TWCFs significantly exceed that of the worst internal event scenarios (contributions from LOCA-type and SRV open-reclose-type accidents). Given the bounding nature of the external event analyses, there is considerable assurance that the external event contribution to overall TWCF as a result of PTS does not exceed than the highest best-estimate contribution from internal events. Given the conservative probabilities and dependencies assumed in the external event analyses, with the addition of little or no credit for any operator actions for the external event scenarios, it is more likely that the "realistic" external event contribution to overall TWCF is much less than the highest internal event contribution. Therefore, the contribution of external initiating events to the overall TWCF attributable to PTS can be considered negligible.

10 Risk-Informed Reactor Vessel Failure Frequency Acceptance Criteria

10.1 Introduction

As discussed in Chapter 2, the current PTS Rule establishes a series of steps that PWR licensees must perform. The initial step involves a deterministic evaluation of the RPV's RT_{PTS} for welds and plate materials (RT_{NDT} evaluated at EOL). If the computed RT_{PTS} values exceed the screening limit established in 10 CFR 50.61, licensees are directed to accomplish reasonably practicable neutron flux reduction to avoid exceeding the screening limit during the RPV's licensed life. Plants for which the computed RT_{PTS} values still exceed the screening limit, even with neutron flux reduction, are required, at least 3 years before exceeding the criteria, to submit a plant-specific safety analysis demonstrating that the risk associated with PTS events is acceptably low. Regulatory Guide 1.154 [RG 1.154], describes one acceptable method for performing such safety analyses.

Two key aspects of the PTS safety analysis approach described in RG 1.154 are the estimation of RPV TWCF and comparison of the estimated TWCF with an acceptance criterion of 5×10^{-6} per reactor year (ry). Neither RG 1.154 nor Enclosure A to SECY-82-465 [SECY-82-465] provides a detailed discussion regarding this specific value, although Enclosure A to SECY-82-465 does argue that an even higher TWCF value (i.e., 1×10^{-5}/ry) is consistent with the then-proposed Safety Goal Policy guidelines on "core melt frequency" and the desire that the core melt frequency ascribable to "one sequence" (such as PTS) should be a small fraction of the overall core melt frequency. Based on the assessed likelihood of potential PTS challenges, predicted TH response of the plant, and predicted behavior of the RPV, the RT_{NDT} screening limits recommended by the staff in 1982 and subsequently incorporated in

10 CFR 50.61 were determined to be consistent with a TWCF of around 5×10^{-6}/ry.

The NRC has established a considerable amount of guidance on the use of risk information in regulation since it issued SECY-82-465 and published the original PTS Rule. In light of this more recent guidance, and as part of the PTS technical basis reevaluation project, the staff has identified and assessed options for a risk-informed criterion for the reactor vessel failure frequency (RVFF) associated with PTS (currently specified in RG 1.154 in terms of TWCF). The assessment includes a scoping study of the issue of containment performance during PTS accidents, which has implications for the specification of the acceptance criterion. The resulting conclusions and their bases are provided in this chapter.

10.2 Current Guidance on Risk-Informed Regulation

Key documents published since the issuance of the original PTS Rule include the Commission's Safety Goal Policy Statement (issued in 1986); a June 1990 Staff Requirements Memorandum (SRM) [NRC 90]; and RG 1.174 [RG 1.174], as well as the associated revision of Chapter 19 of NUREG-0800, "Standard Review Plan for the Review of Safety Analysis Reports for Nuclear Power Plants (LWR Edition)" (SRP) [NRC 98b].

The Safety Goal Policy Statement [NRC FR 86] defines qualitative goals and quantitative health objectives (QHOs) for the acceptable risk of nuclear power plant operations. The QHOs address the prompt fatality risk to individuals, and the cancer fatality risk to society. For both the individual and societal risks, the QHOs are defined to ensure that the public health and safety risk arising from nuclear power plant operations is a very small fraction (0.1% or less) of the total risk to the public.

The June 1990 SRM [NRC 90] discusses subsequent Commission decisions with respect to the policy statement. Of particular interest, the SRM establishes a subsidiary core damage frequency (CDF) goal of 1×10^{-4}/ry. At the time it was developed, this subsidiary goal, as well as the qualitative safety goals and QHOs, was intended for use in generic agency decisions such as rulemakings. It was not aimed at plant-specific applications.

RG 1.174 [RG 1.174] and SRP Chapter 19 [NRC 98b] describe a risk-informed process by which licensee-proposed license amendments that act to change regulatory requirements can be submitted, reviewed, and, if appropriate, approved. Toward that end, RG 1.174 fulfills the following purposes:

- Describe a set of general principles for this process.

- Extend the policies established in the Safety Goal Policy Statement, by providing a large early release frequency (LERF) subsidiary objective and making use of the QHOs in plant-specific decision-making.

- Provide a set of probabilistic guidelines defining acceptable changes in CDF and LERF associated with proposed reductions in regulatory requirements.

RG 1.174 applies to voluntary changes to a plant's licensing basis. However, it provides a general template for improving consistency in regulatory decisions in areas in which the results of risk analyses are used to help justify regulatory action. The principles of integrated, risk-informed decision-making (involving consideration of risk information, defense-in-depth, safety margins, and uncertainties) discussed in that RG apply broadly to risk-informed regulatory activities. RG 1.174 provides acceptance guidelines for changes in CDF and LERF. These guidelines were developed to provide assurance that proposed increases in CDF and LERF are small and consistent with the intent of the Safety Goal

Policy Statement. If the baseline risk can be shown to be acceptable (as indicated by a total mean CDF of less than 1×10^{-4}/ry and a total mean LERF less than 1×10^{-5}/ry), applications for plant changes leading to small increases in mean CDF (up to 1×10^{-5}/ry) and mean LERF (up to 1×10^{-6}/ry) will be considered for regulatory approval.

The relationship between the RG 1.174 LERF criterion and the QHOs is discussed in Appendix A to NUREG/CR-6595 [Pratt 99]. In particular, that appendix argues that, for certain large early releases (involving the release of 2.5% to 3% of the reactor's iodine and/or tellurium inventory within 4 hours of accident initiation), a LERF of 1×10^{-5}/ry roughly corresponds to the prompt fatality QHO (currently around 5×10^{-7}/yr). The calculations supporting NUREG/CR-6094 [Hanson 94] and SECY-93-138 [SECY-93-138] are cited as the basis for these conclusions.

The staff's current activities on Option 3 for risk-informing 10 CFR Part 50, as described in SECY-00-0198 [SECY-00-0198], takes advantage of the groundwork laid by RG 1.174. The Option 3 framework being developed employs the total mean CDF and mean LERF guidelines mentioned above (1×10^{-4}/ry and 1×10^{-5}/ry, respectively). The framework also provides guidelines to limit the CDF and LERF associated with any single accident type from being a large fraction of the plant's total CDF and LERF.

10.3 Containment Performance During PTS Accidents

As discussed in Section 10.1, the current TWCF criterion of 5×10^{-6}/ry provided in RG 1.154 was established to ensure that the risk associated with PTS is a small fraction of the acceptable level of risk established by the Safety Goals and is consistent with the philosophy of distributing risk among accident types. However, the relationship between this criterion and the CDF and LERF guidelines established in RG 1.174 and those proposed in the draft Option 3 framework is not clear because there is currently an incomplete understanding regarding the progression of an accident following a postulated PTS-induced RPV failure.

10.3.1 Previous Research Results

Several previous research efforts have addressed potential PTS-induced RPV failure modes and their effects on core cooling and containment integrity. In the late 1970s and 1980s, large-scale experiments, in which prototypic RPVs were subjected to pressure and temperature transients characteristic of PTS loadings, were conducted as part of the NRC-sponsored Heavy Steel Section Technology (HSST) research program. These experiments demonstrated three potential outcomes of a PTS event (depending on the particulars of the transient, material embrittlement, etc.):

- No cracks initiate, and the vessel remains intact.

- A crack initiates, propagates to some depth into the entire vessel wall, and stops. The vessel remains intact with little additional deformation.

- A crack initiates and propagates entirely through the vessel wall. In addition to large openings in the reactor vessel, this outcome involves significant additional deformation of the vessel.

In the context of RPVs, the third outcome presents a potentially significant challenge to core cooling and containment integrity.

In the mid-1980s, following the promulgation of the initial versions of 10 CFR 50.61 and RG 1.154, the NRC sponsored a number of studies on the risk associated with PTS. One such study, documented in NUREG/CR-4483 [Simonen 86], evaluated the current state of knowledge regarding post-vessel failure accident progression. The study considered such issues as the axial and azimuthal extent of crack propagation, depressurization of the reactor coolant system, RPV vertical movement resulting from postulated full circumferential breaks of the vessel wall, and the possibility of missiles generated during the RPV failure. From the perspective of an RVFF acceptance

criterion, NUREG/CR-4483 offers two key findings:

(1) The possibility of axial cracks propagating into embrittled circumferential welds and then propagating along these welds cannot be neglected.

(2) The effects of PTS-induced missiles (including the RPV in extreme cases) are likely to be contained within the concrete barriers surrounding the RPV.

In 2001, the NRC sponsored a study of the potential structural consequences of PTS events. This study [Theofanous 2001] assumed the instantaneous opening of a very large axially oriented hole (4-m x 0.4-m, ~2,480-in.^{2}) in the RPV as a postulated result of PTS. Under these conditions, and given the relatively low energy of the fluid, the impulse on the RPV and piping resulting from the blowdown was predicted to be within the bounds of a design-basis safe-shutdown earthquake (SSE). However, the study did not model either the effects of internal structures (fuel supports, fuel assemblies, etc.) on the blowdown loads, or the possible effects of blowdown on the internal structures themselves.

The study also explored a simplified crack opening model that predicts a small hole (~110-in^2 (0.07-m^2)) resulting from a postulated 157.48-in. (4-m) long axial crack, rather than the very large hole ($\sim2,480$-in^2 (1.6-m^2)) assumed in the analysis of blowdown loads. The study found that ECCS injection would not be challenged by a crack (and predicted hole area) of this size. However, the study did not address either the possibility of more extensive axial crack propagation, or the possibility of circumferential cracks that could challenge the ECCS. The staff's evaluation, summarized in Section 10.3.2, addresses these issues.

On July 18, 2002, the Advisory Committee on Reactor Safeguards (ACRS) wrote a letter on the issue of PTS acceptance criteria [Apostolakis 02]. The letter noted that the LERF criterion provided in RG 1.174 is not a proper starting point for PTS considerations, since the "...source terms used to develop the current goal do not reflect the air-oxidation phenomena that would be a likely outcome of a PTS event."

The concern with air-oxidation events is associated with potential scenarios where fuel cooling has been lost and the fuel rods are exposed to air (as opposed to steam). Should such a situation arise, some portion of the reactor fuel will eventually be oxidized in an air environment. Based upon currently available information, this oxidation is expected to result in release fractions for key fission products (ruthenium being of primary concern) that may be significantly (e.g., a factor of 20) larger than those associated with fuel oxidation in steam environments, and these larger release fractions could lead to a larger number of prompt fatalities than predicted for non-PTS risk-significant scenarios.

10.3.2 Post-RPV Failure Scenarios Scoping Study

In order to support the assessment of options for an RVFF acceptance criterion (see Section 10.4 for a description of the options considered), the staff conducted a limited scoping study of PTS-induced post-RPV failure scenarios. The specific aim of the study was to develop an initial qualitative assessment of the potential impact (both positive and negative) of the unique characteristics of such scenarios on the likelihood of severe source terms, especially source terms beyond those typically assessed for non-PTS-associated risk-significant scenarios.

The study involved the structured identification of technical issues underlying the assessment of the margins to core damage and large early release following potentially significant PTS-induced RPV failure scenarios (dominant scenarios for the pilot plants addressed by the PTS reevaluation project are discussed in Chapter 8 of this report), and the collection and evaluation of currently available information relevant to these issues. Of particular interest was the identification of PTS-unique physical mechanisms that could lead to dependent failures of accident mitigation features. To better inform the evaluation, a small number

of limited-scope TH and structural calculations were performed.

The scoping study focused on differences between post-PTS-induced RPV failure accident progression and accident progression associated with non-PTS core damage events. Thus, in addition to the previously mentioned air-oxidation issue, the scoping study addressed issues associated with the development and characteristics of the postulated opening in the RPV, the resulting blowdown forces, the effect on key structural components (e.g., the RPV, containment penetrations), and the potential for damaging missiles. Table 10.1 lists and briefly describes the issues addressed.

To support the identification and semi-quantitative analysis of the issues, an accident progression event tree (APET) was developed. This tree, shown in Figure 10.1, identifies potentially important phenomena and possible scenarios following PTS-induced RPV failure.††††††

In general, the APET explicitly addresses the issues listed in Table 10.1. Two notable exceptions are the issues of missiles and early overpressure. Regarding missiles, activities performed as part of the scoping study indicate that the possibility of a PTS-induced RPV failure leading to energetic missiles that could affect important top events in the APET (i.e., those associated with containment isolation, sprays, and ECCS) is sufficiently remote to allow exclusion of this issue from the APET. Missile generation attributable to a PTS event would result in an object being directed laterally into the reactor vessel cavity wall by the blowdown forces associated with the breach in the RPV. For a missile to affect the containment spray systems, ECCS systems or containment penetrations, it would have to traverse a tortuous

---

†††††† Note that the APET includes branches for issues whose uncertainties are more epistemic in character (e.g., the blowdown forces associated with a given break size), as well as branches associated with issues for which the uncertainties are more aleatory in character (e.g., the availability of ECCS).

path through tight clearances of the RPV cavity (between the reactor vessel and the concrete of the cavity wall). It would then have to hit an extremely small target (either ECCS piping, containment penetration or containment spray piping). The missile's energy would be dissipated through its multiple contacts with the RPV cavity wall, as well as the distance it traveled.

Table 10.1. Post-RPV-failure technical issues

Dominant PTS scenarios	This issue concerns the relative likelihood and characteristics of the scenarios predicted to contribute most to PTS-induced RPV failure. The characteristics of the PTS scenario (e.g., pressure, temperature, timing) directly affect the issues of crack propagation, blowdown forces, and ECCS status (see below).
Relative contribution of axial and circumferential welds	This issue concerns the relative frequencies of PTS-induced RPV failures attributable to flaws in axial welds vs. flaws in circumferential welds. The orientation of the crack affects crack propagation and the characteristics of the resulting hole.
Crack propagation, hole size, hole location	This issue concerns the characteristics of the crack and the resulting hole in the RPV (including the rate of opening and the shape of the hole). This issue directly affects the issues of blowdown forces, fuel coolability, and fuel environment (see below).
Blowdown forces	This issue concerns the pressure differential driving fluid out of the RPV and the associated forces on the RPV, its internals, and connected piping. This issue directly affects the issues of containment isolation, missiles, ECCS status, core status, and fuel dispersal (see below).
Containment isolation	Early failure of containment isolation (e.g., by the failure of containment penetrations) is a contributing factor to the occurrence of a large early release.
Missiles	This issue concerns the possibility of a PTS-induced RPV failure leading to energetic missiles that could affect accident progression. This issue directly affects the issues of ECCS status and containment spray status (see below).
ECCS status (injection, recirculation)	This issue concerns the reliability of ECCS (given that ECCS was working prior to RPV failure). Potential contributors to ECCS failure include random hardware failure, failure to switch over properly to recirculation, failure of ECCS piping, and containment sump clogging.
Containment spray status	Early failure of containment spray is a contributing factor to the occurrence of a large early release. This issue concerns the reliability of containment spray (given that ECCS was working prior to RPV failure). Potential contributors to failure include random hardware failure, failure of piping (attributable to missiles), and containment sump clogging.
Core status (intact, distorted, disrupted)	This issue concerns whether the fuel geometry is distorted or severely disrupted as a result of the blowdown forces associated with a PTS-induced RPV failure.
Fuel dispersal	This issue concerns the location of fuel, should it be dispersed from the core as a consequence of a PTS-induced RPV failure.
Fuel coolability	This issue concerns fuel coolability, given its location and the core status.
RPV water level	This issue concerns the availability of water to cool the fuel (even if the ECCS is not working). It is affected by a number of factors, including the characteristics of the RPV cavity and the inventory of water available.
Fuel environment (steam, air)	This issue concerns the possibility of large-scale air oxidation of fuel. It is strongly dependent on the development of the accident scenario.
Early overpressure	This issue concerns the possibility of early containment failure attributable to (1) overpressures resulting from PTS-induced RPV failure events, and (2) overpressure caused by other mechanisms (e.g., hydrogen combustion).

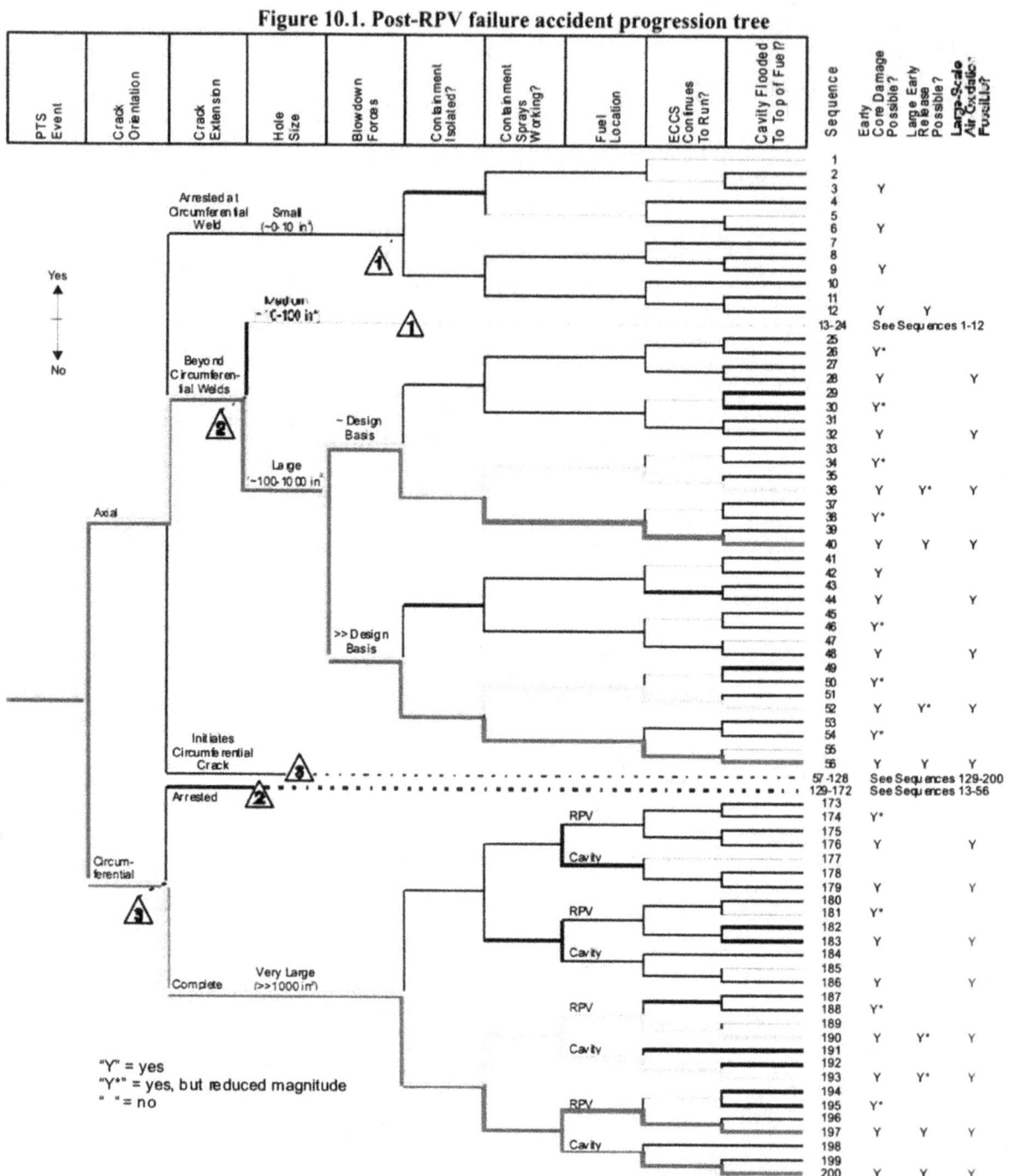

Figure 10.1. Post-RPV failure accident progression tree

"Y" = yes
"Y*" = yes, but reduced magnitude
" " = no

Therefore, there is little chance that the missile would possess the energy to damage the ECCS, containment spray system, or any containment penetrations. Additional activities regarding missiles included a review of NUREG/CR-4483 [Simonen 86] in light of currently available information on missile generation and penetration potential, a review of the reactor cavity designs of the plants considered in this study, and limited calculations to estimate plastic strains associated with a postulated, instantaneous large ($\sim$4 m x 0.3 m, 1,728 in.^{2}) hole in the side of a representative RPV.

To address scenarios involving early overpressure, limited-scope RELAP5 calculations (performed for a representative plant) were performed. These calculations indicate that the initial containment pressure rise associated with a range of PTS-induced RPV failures should be small, relative to the containment design pressure. PTS-initiated scenarios involving large amounts of hydrogen generation are possible (e.g., see Scenario 56 in the APET), but are not likely to lead to failure of either large, dry containments or ice condenser containments. The former are capable of withstanding the overpressure associated with a severe accident hydrogen burn, and the principal failure mode of the hydrogen igniters for the latter is a loss of station power, which is not a concern for PTS scenarios. (Loss of power is, of course, an issue for core overheating scenarios typically addressed by PRAs, in which possible RPV failures occur after core damage.)

Figure 10.1 identifies scenarios that have the potential to lead to source terms significantly worse than those associated with risk-significant, non-PTS related accident scenarios. Scenarios that are judged to have a possibility of leading to an early (e.g., less than 4 hours after RPV failure) release with a severe source term (i.e., a source term associated with large-scale air-oxidation of fuel) are highlighted in red. Scenarios that are judged to have a possibility of leading to an early release with a containment-spray-scrubbed, air-oxidation source term are highlighted in yellow.

Table 10.2 summarizes the key characteristics associated with each of the highlighted scenarios. The common characteristics of these scenarios are also shared with risk-significant non-PTS scenarios: they require the loss of fuel cooling (either from ECCS or from water in the reactor cavity), the loss of containment isolation, and, in the case of the most severe scenarios, the loss of containment spray. Table 10.2 also provides a summary assessment of the conditional likelihood of each scenario, given the occurrence of a PTS event.

The discussion in Table 10.2 identifies two classes of plants, including (1) those for which it is expected that, following a PTS-initiated RPV failure, the reactor cavity will be flooded above the top of the active fuel, and (2) all other plants. For the first class, it is believed that, for all scenarios identified by the APET, the conditional probability of PTS-induced fuel damage and subsequent large early release is extremely small (i.e., less than 0.001).

For the second class of plants, the most important APET postulated scenarios appear to be Scenarios 96, 100, 118, and 125. These scenarios all involve the following factors:

- an initial crack in an axial weld that propagates to the circumferential weld, and then initiates a circumferential crack

- blowdown forces above those anticipated for design-basis events

- the possibility of containment penetration failures as a result of RPV movement

- the possibility of ECCS failure attributable to RPV movement

Table 10.3 identifies the key differences between the four scenarios and their assessed likelihoods. A likelihood rating of "extremely small" corresponds to a conditional probability less than 0.001, while a rating of "very small" corresponds to a conditional probability less than 0.01, and a rating of "small" corresponds to a conditional probability less than 0.1.

Table 10.2. Potentially risk-significant post-RPV failure accident progression scenarios

Scena rio.	Characteristics	Potential Consequential Failures[b]	Independent Failures[c]	Conditional Probability Rating[d,e]
36	- Axial crack that extends beyond circumferential weld - Medium-to-large (~100-1,000 in^2) hole in RPV - Blowdown forces within design basis - Failed containment isolation - Operating containment spray - Loss of fuel cooling		- Containment Isolation - ECCS	Extremely small
40	- Axial crack that extends beyond circumferential weld - Medium-to-large (~100-1000 in^2) hole in RPV - Blowdown forces within design basis - Failed containment isolation - Failed containment spray - Loss of fuel cooling		- Containment Isolation - Containment Spray - ECCS	Extremely small
52	- Axial crack that extends beyond circumferential weld - Medium-to-large (~100-1000 in^2) hole in RPV - Blowdown forces greater than design basis - Failed containment isolation - Operating containment spray - Loss of fuel cooling	- Containment Penetration - ECCS piping		- Extremely small for plants where cavity flooding above the top of the fuel is expected - May be very small for other plants, depending on effect of blowdown forces
56	- Axial crack that extends beyond circumferential weld - Medium-to-large (~100-1000 in^2) hole in RPV - Blowdown forces greater than design basis - Failed containment isolation - Failed containment spray - Loss of fuel cooling	- Containment Penetration - ECCS piping	- Containment Spray	Extremely small
80	- Axial crack that initiates a circumferential crack that arrests after limited propagation - Medium-to-large (~100-1000 in^2) hole in RPV - Blowdown forces within design basis - Failed containment isolation - Operating containment spray - Loss of fuel cooling		- Containment Isolation - ECCS	Extremely small
84	- Axial crack that initiates a circumferential crack that arrests after limited propagation - Medium-to-large (~100-1000 in^2) hole in RPV - Blowdown forces within design basis - Failed containment isolation - Failed containment spray - Loss of fuel cooling		- Containment Isolation - Containment Spray - ECCS	Extremely small
96	- Axial crack that initiates a circumferential crack that arrests after limited propagation - Medium-to-large (~100-1000 in^2) hole in RPV - Blowdown forces greater than design basis - Failed containment isolation - Operating containment spray - Loss of fuel cooling	- Containment Penetration - ECCS piping		- Extremely small for plants where cavity flooding above the top of the fuel is expected - May be small to very small for other plants, depending on effect of blowdown forces
100	- Axial crack that initiates a circumferential crack that arrests after limited propagation - Medium-to-large (~100-1000 in^2) hole in RPV - Blowdown forces greater than design basis - Failed containment isolation - Failed containment spray - Loss of fuel cooling	- Containment Penetration - ECCS piping	- Containment Spray	- Extremely small for plants where cavity flooding above the top of the fuel is expected - May be very small to extremely small for other plants, depending on effect of blowdown

Scenario	Characteristics	Potential Consequential Failures[b]	Independent Failures[c]	Conditional Probability Rating[d,e]
				forces
118	- Axial crack that initiates a circumferential crack that subsequently progresses around the entire RPV - Very large (>>1000 in^2) hole - Blowdown forces greater than design basis - Failed containment isolation - Operating containment spray - Majority of fuel retained in RPV - Loss of fuel cooling	- Containment Penetration - ECCS piping		- Extremely small for plants where cavity flooding above the top of the fuel is expected - May be small to very small for other plants, depending on effect of blowdown forces
121	- Axial crack that initiates a circumferential crack that subsequently progresses around the entire RPV - Very large (>>1000 in^2) hole - Blowdown forces greater than design basis - Failed containment isolation - Operating containment spray - Majority of fuel dispersed into reactor cavity - Loss of fuel cooling	- Containment Penetration - ECCS piping		- Extremely small for plants where cavity flooding above the top of the fuel is expected - May be very small to extremely small for other plants, depending on effect of blowdown forces
125	- Axial crack that initiates a circumferential crack that subsequently progresses around the entire RPV - Very large (>>1000 in^2) hole - Blowdown forces greater than design basis - Failed containment isolation - Failed containment spray - Majority of fuel retained in RPV - Loss of fuel cooling	- Containment Penetration - ECCS piping	- Containment Spray	- Extremely small for plants where cavity flooding above the top of the fuel is expected - May be very small to extremely small for other plants, depending on effect of blowdown forces
128	- Axial crack that initiates a circumferential crack that subsequently progresses around the entire RPV - Very large (>>1000 in^2) hole - Blowdown forces greater than design basis - Failed containment isolation - Failed containment spray - Majority of fuel dispersed into reactor cavity - Loss of fuel cooling	- Containment Penetration - ECCS piping	- Containment Spray	Extremely small
152	- Circumferential crack that arrests - Medium-to-large (~100-1000 in^2) hole in RPV - Blowdown forces within design basis - Failed containment isolation - Operating containment spray - Loss of fuel cooling		- Containment Isolation - ECCS	Extremely small
156	- Circumferential crack that arrests - Medium-to-large (~100-1000 in^2) hole in RPV - Blowdown forces within design basis - Failed containment isolation - Failed containment spray - Loss of fuel cooling		- Containment Isolation - Containment Spray - ECCS	Extremely small
168	- Circumferential crack that arrests - Medium-to-large (~100-1000 in^2) hole in RPV - Blowdown forces greater than design basis - Failed containment isolation - Operating containment spray - Loss of fuel cooling	- Containment Penetration - ECCS piping		- Extremely small for plants where cavity flooding above the top of the fuel is expected - May be very small to extremely small for other plants, depending on effect of blowdown forces
172	- Circumferential crack that arrests - Medium-to-large (~100-1000 in^2) hole in RPV - Blowdown forces greater than design basis	- Containment Penetration - ECCS piping	- Containment Spray	Extremely small

Scenario	Characteristics	Potential Consequential Failures[b]	Independent Failures[c]	Conditional Probability Rating[d,e]
	- Failed containment isolation - Failed containment spray - Loss of fuel cooling			
190	- Circumferential crack that progresses around the entire RPV - Very large (>>1000 in^2) hole - Blowdown forces greater than design basis - Failed containment isolation - Operating containment spray - Majority of fuel retained in RPV - Loss of fuel cooling	- Containment Penetration - ECCS piping		- Extremely small for plants where cavity flooding above the top of the fuel is expected - May be very small to extremely small for other plants, depending on effect of blowdown forces
193	- Axial crack that initiates a circumferential crack that subsequently progresses around the entire RPV - Very large (>>1000 in^2) hole - Blowdown forces greater than design basis - Failed containment isolation - Operating containment spray - Majority of fuel dispersed into reactor cavity - Loss of fuel cooling	- Containment Penetration - ECCS piping		Extremely small
197	- Axial crack that initiates a circumferential crack that subsequently progresses around the entire RPV - Very large (>>1000 in^2) hole - Blowdown forces greater than design basis - Failed containment isolation - Failed containment spray - Majority of fuel retained in RPV - Loss of fuel cooling	- Containment Penetration - ECCS piping	- Containment Spray	Extremely small
200	- Axial crack that initiates a circumferential crack that subsequently progresses around the entire RPV - Very large (>>1000 in^2) hole - Blowdown forces greater than design basis - Failed containment isolation - Failed containment spray - Majority of fuel dispersed into reactor cavity - Loss of fuel cooling	- Containment Penetration - ECCS piping	- Containment Spray	Extremely small

Table 10.3. Key APET scenarios

Scenario	Circumferential Crack Arrested?	Containment Spray Status	Likelihood Rating
96	Yes	Operating	Very small to small
100	Yes	Failed	Extremely small to very small
118	No	Operating	Very small to small
125	No	Failed	Extremely small to very small

The ratings are based largely on the following considerations:

- Containment spray operation is not expected to be adversely affected by the occurrence of a PTS event. In fact, its reliability may be higher than for non-PTS risk-significant scenarios, since support system availability is not generally a concern for PTS scenarios.[††††††]

- As shown in Chapter 8, PTS scenarios generally involve situations where the RCS is at relatively low temperature. Consequently, the stored energy in the RCS is relatively low, and there is little driving force to directly cause the damage postulated in the scenarios.

- An initial assessment of the RPV deformation associated with a (conservatively assumed) instantaneous hole opening in the RPV indicates that substantial deformations will not occur and, therefore, the movement of the pipes connected to the RPV will be limited by the gap between the RPV and the cavity wall.

- Since reactor vessel movement attributable to blowdown forces is limited, damage of ECCS piping, containment spray or containment penetrations is not expected. The limited vessel movement would be

---

[††††††] This assessment is based on an assumption that any potential recirculation sump clogging issues, as identified under GSI-191, are addressed.

compensated for by the pipe ductility, long runs of piping with many bends, and the hanger and support systems.

Table 10.3 is based upon currently available information. Resolution of the following key uncertainties could affect the assessment:

- the likelihood that an axial crack will indeed initiate a propagating circumferential crack

- the potential effect of "external events" (e.g., earthquakes) and other environmental hazards (e.g., internal fires) on PTS-induced LERF that were not addressed in the scoping study

10.4   Acceptance Criteria Options

The staff has developed two sets of options for PTS-associated RVFF acceptance guidelines. The first set of options concerns the specific definition of RPV failure to be used. The second concerns possible quantitative acceptance limits for that metric. Note that any potential changes to the RT_{NDT} screening limits discussed in Chapter 11 may affect RVFF, but are not likely to affect the conditional probability of core damage (given a PTS-induced RPV failure) or the conditional probability of large, early release (given a PTS-induced core damage event). Thus, they will likely have little effect on the level of defense-in-depth against PTS challenges already provided by the current rule.

The following two options were considered for defining RPV failure:

(1) RPV failure occurs when a PTS-induced crack penetrates the RPV wall (i.e., RVFF = TWCF).

(2) RPV failure occurs when a PTS event initiates a crack in the RPV wall (i.e., RVFF = Vessel Crack Initiation Frequency, or VCIF).

The first option uses the current definition of RPV failure. The second reflects the position adopted by non-U.S. regulatory bodies.

In developing the possible quantitative acceptance limits for RVFF (denoted by RVFF*), the staff considered the following four options:

A. RVFF* = 5 x 10^{-6}/ry
B. RVFF* = 1 x 10^{-5}/ry
C. RVFF* = 1 x 10^{-6}/ry
D. RVFF* << 1 x 10^{-6}/ry

Option A is suggested by the current value in RG 1.154. Option B is suggested by current guidelines on CDF provided by RG 1.174 and the Option 3 framework for risk-informing 10 CFR Part 50. Option C is suggested by current guidelines on LERF provided by RG 1.174 and the Option 3 framework for risk-informing 10 CFR Part 50. Option D is suggested by the possibility of significantly worse consequences for PTS events (as opposed to other risk-significant scenarios), as discussed by the July 2002 letter from ACRS [Bonaca 02].

10.5 Conclusions

The staff's analysis has led to the following conclusions regarding the establishment of a criterion for RVFF:

(1) The analysis supports a definition of RVFF as being equivalent to TWCF (i.e., for PTS considerations, RPV "failure" can be defined as an occurrence of a through-wall crack). This conclusion is based on the following two factors:

(a) TWCF is a more direct measure than VCIF of the likelihood of events with potentially significant public health consequences. This is desirable from a risk-informed decision-making perspective.

(b) The uncertainties associated with the prediction of a through-wall crack (under PTS conditions) are only slightly larger than those associated with the prediction of crack initiation (also under PTS conditions). For example, at the 10 CFR 50.61 RT_{PTS} screening limit, the separation between the 50th and 95th percentiles in the distribution of VCIF

ranges from 0.8 to 1.8 orders of magnitude, while the separation between the 50th and 95th percentiles in the distribution of TWCF ranges from 0.9 to 2.6 orders of magnitude. This slight increase in uncertainty is a natural and expected consequence of a cleavage failure mechanism and does not reflect a state of knowledge limitation regarding crack arrest. (See [EricksonKirk-PFM] for details of the crack arrest model.)

(2) The analysis supports an acceptance criterion for RVFF, RVFF*, of 1x10^{-6}/ry. This is based on the following observations:

(a) The conditional probability of an unscrubbed, large early release with a large air-oxidation source term (given a PTS-induced RPV failure) appears to be very small (i.e., less than 0.01). It is particularly small for plants where water in the reactor cavity (following a PTS-induced RPV failure) will cover the fuel. For plants with larger cavities, the low probability of the scenario is largely attributable to the independence and reliability of containment sprays.

(b) The assessment underlying the above observation does not account for potential dependencies associated with PTS-events initiated by "external events" (e.g., earthquakes) or internal fires.

(c) For plants with cavities such that fuel cooling is not assured following a PTS-induced RPV failure, the APET (Figure 10.1) identifies the most probable scenarios where limited fuel damage might occur, even if ECCS operates as designed.

Observation (a), taken in isolation, supports the use of an RVFF* based on considerations of core damage consistent with those proposed in current activities for risk-informing 10 CFR Part 50 [SECY-00-0198]. However, Observation (b) identifies a potentially significant uncertainty regarding the margin between PTS-induced RPV failure and large early release, and Observation (c) raises a potential concern regarding defense-in-depth. Therefore, RG 1.174 guidelines on CDF supporting a value for $RVFF^*$ of 1×10^{-5} events/year may not have sufficient justification, whereas the scoping study developed for RG 1.174 guidelines on LERF is more defensible given currently available information. This rationale supports our recommended value of 1×10^{-6} events/year for $RVFF^*$, which is consistent with the RG 1.174 guidelines on LERF.

When assessing the acceptability of the PTS-associated risk at a given plant, the mean value of the plant's PTS-induced $RVFF$ (i.e., the mean $TWCF$) should be compared with $RVFF^*$. This conclusion is based on how other NRC risk-informed decisions use risk information (e.g., see RG 1.174).

(3) Should additional work be performed to address the key post-RPV failure accident progression uncertainties identified in this study, the following issues are of principal importance:

(a) the likelihood that a PTS-induced axial crack will, upon reaching a circumferential weld, turn and progress along the circumferential weld

(b) the likelihood of PTS-induced containment isolation failure (especially failures associated with failure of containment penetrations) and ECCS failure (especially ECCS piping failures)

(c) the magnitude of potential source terms and consequences associated with PTS events

(d) substantiation of conditional probability values in Table 10.2 and Table 10.3

(e) the impact of external events on PTS-induced LERF.

It is anticipated that state-of-knowledge improvements in any of these areas will strengthen this study's conclusions regarding the margin between a PTS-induced RPV failure and consequent large early releases. Although not quantified,

several aspects of our analysis performed to support an $RVFF^*$ value 1×10^{-6} events/year have a known conservative bias. The following is a summary of a few of these areas identified earlier in this chapter:

- Given the relatively low energy of the fluid following a postulated PTS event, the impulse on the RPV and piping resulting from a blowdown was predicted to be within the bounds of a design-basis SSE. The limited vessel movement from a blowdown forces would be compensated for by the pipe ductility, long runs of piping with many bends, and the hanger and support systems. For these reasons, damage of ECCS piping or containment penetrations is not expected.

- Missile generation attributable to a postulated PTS event would result in an object being directed laterally into the reactor vessel cavity wall by the blowdown forces associated with the breach in the reactor vessel. For a missile to affect the containment spray system or containment penetrations, it would have to traverse a tortuous path through tight clearances of the reactor vessel cavity. The missile's energy would be dissipated by multiple contacts with the reactor cavity wall, as well as the distance it travels, and it would have to hit an extremely small target to render the containment spray system inoperable.

- Through-wall crack frequency is assumed to equal core damage, which is assumed to equal a release. The through-wall cracks may cover a wide spectrum of sizes, from very large to very small. Very small cracks would result in only minor leakage that would not significantly challenge the reactor safety systems.

11 Reference Temperature (*RT*)-Based PTS Screening Criteria

11.1 Introduction

In Chapter 8, we presented our baseline estimates of the variation of TWCF in the three study plants over a range of embrittlement levels. These estimates demonstrated that the challenge to the structural integrity of the RPV posed by the dominant transient classes (i.e., large-diameter primary side pipe breaks, stuck-open primary side valves that later reclose, and breaks of the main steam line) is approximately equal (at equivalent levels of embrittlement) across the three plants. We also identified why the structural integrity challenges posed by these dominant transients are *not expected* to vary from plant-to-plant, and are *not expected* to be influenced by factors that may differ between the three study plants and the general population of PWRs (see Sections 8.5.2.4.5, 8.5.3.4.3, and 8.5.4.4.2, respectively). This finding was further reinforced in Section 9.3, which included a survey of five additional plants having high levels of embrittlement. This survey assessed the factors in these plants that could influence either the severity of the transients or the frequency of their occurrence, with the aim of identifying the potential for situations in the general PWR population having greater severity and/or frequency than in the three study plants. The survey's outcome supported the view presented in Chapter 8. In the great majority of cases, the severity and frequency of transients in the general PWR population is no greater, and is often less, than in the three study plants. A few situations were identified where greater severities or frequencies did occur, but never both. Thus, the effect of these situations not being considered in the baseline TWCF results presented in Chapter 8 can be regarded as negligible.

Overall, the evidence presented in both Chapter 8 and Chapter 9 supports the use of the TWCF values presented in Table 8.5, together with the reactor vessel failure frequency acceptance criterion of 1×10^{-6} events per year proposed in Chapter 10 to develop a materials-based screening limit applicable to PWRs *in general*. In this chapter, we propose such a limit, making use of the reference temperature (*RT*) metrics also found in Table 8.5. As illustrated in Figure 8-4, an *RT* establishes a material's resistance to fracture, the variability in this resistance, and how this resistance varies with temperature. Since *RT* values can be estimated from information on vessel materials available in the RVID database [RVID2], as well as surveillance programs conducted in accordance with Appendix H to 10 CFR Part 50, they provide a means to estimate the fracture resistance of vessel materials and how this resistance diminishes with increased neutron irradiation.

The remainder of the chapter is organized as follows:

- Section 11.2 addresses *RT* metrics. We review the discussion of Section 8.4.1, which concerns the characteristics an *RT* metric needs so that it can be expected to correlate/predict the probability of vessel failure. This section also includes a critique of how well the *RT* metric currently used in 10 CFR 50.61, RT_{PTS}, meets these characteristics.

- In Section 11.3, we develop relationships between the RT_{AW}, RT_{PL}, and RT_{CW} metrics (see Table 8.5) and TWCF.

- Section 11.4 includes our proposed PTS screening criteria derived from the relationship developed in Section 11.3. We discuss the applicability of these screening criteria to PWRs in general, and we assess the proximity of currently operating PWRs to this proposal at both end of license (40 years of operation) and end of license extension (60 years of operation).

11.2   Reference Temperature (*RT*) Metrics

As discussed in Section 8.4.1, in order to correlate and/or predict a RPV's resistance to fracture, we need some measure of the fracture resistance of the materials in the vessel at the location of the flaws in the vessel. *RT* values characterize fracture resistance, as illustrated in Figure 8-4. In Section 8.4.1, we proposed three *RT* metrics (RT_{AW}, RT_{PL}, and RT_{CW}), each of which is associated with a different flaw population (flaws on the axial weld fusion lines, flaws in plates, and flaws on the circumferential weld fusion lines, respectively). These three *RT* metrics were defined as follows (see Eq. 8-1, Eq. 8-2, and Eq. 8-3 for mathematical definitions):

- The **axial weld reference temperature** RT_{AW} characterizes the RPV's resistance to fracture initiating from flaws found along the axial weld fusion lines. It corresponds to the maximum RT_{NDT} of the plate/weld that lies to either side of each weld fusion lines, and is weighted to account for differences in weld fusion line length (and, therefore, the number of simulated flaws).

- The **plate reference temperature** RT_{PL} characterizes the RPV's resistance to fracture initiating from flaws found in plates that are not associated with welds. It corresponds to the maximum RT_{NDT} occurring in each plate, and is weighted to account for differences in plate volumes (and, therefore, the number of simulated flaws).

- The **circumferential weld reference temperature** RT_{CW} characterizes the RPV's resistance to fracture initiating from flaws found along the circumferential weld fusion lines. It corresponds to the maximum RT_{NDT} of the plate/weld that lies to either side of each weld fusion lines, and is weighted to account for differences in weld fusion

line length (and, therefore, the number of simulated flaws).

We proposed these **three** different *RT*s in recognition of the fact that the probability of vessel fracture initiating from these three different flaw populations varies considerably as a result of the following known factors.

- Different regions of the vessel have flaw populations that differ in size (weld flaws are considerably larger than plate flaws), density (weld flaws are more numerous than plate flaws), and orientation (axial and circumferential welds have flaws of corresponding orientations, whereas plate flaws may be either axial or circumferential). The driving force to fracture depends on both flaw size and flaw orientation, so different vessel regions experience different fracture driving forces.

- The degree of irradiation damage suffered by the material at the flaw tips varies with location in the vessel because of differences in chemistry and fluence.

These differences indicate that it is impossible for a single *RT* to accurately represent the RPV's resistance to fracture in the general case. Indeed, this is precisely the liability associated with the 10 CFR 50.61 *RT* value RT_{PTS}. 10 CFR 50.61 defines RT_{PTS} as the maximum RT_{NDT} of any region in the vessel (a region is an axial weld, a circumferential weld, a plate, or a forging) evaluated at the peak fluence occurring in that region. Consequently, the RT_{PTS} value currently assigned to a vessel may only coincidentally correspond to the toughness properties of the material region responsible for the bulk of the TWCF, as illustrated by the following examples:

- Out of 71 operating PWRs, 14 have their RT_{PTS} values established based on circumferential weld properties [RVID2]. However, our results show that the probability of a vessel failing as a consequence of a crack in a circumferential weld is extremely remote because of the lack of through-wall fracture driving force associated with circumferentially oriented cracks. For these 14 vessels, the RT_{PTS} value is unrelated to any material that has any significant chance of causing vessel failure.

- Out of 71 operating PWRs, 32 have their RT_{PTS} values established based on plate properties [RVID2]. Certainly, plate properties influence vessel failure probability; however, the 10 CFR 50.61 practice of evaluating RT_{PTS} at the peak fluence occurring in the plate is likely to estimate a toughness value that cannot be associated with any large flaws because the location of the peak fluence may not correspond to an axial weld fusion line. While the RT_{PTS} value for these 32 vessels is related to a material that contributes significantly to the vessel failure probability, it is likely that RT_{PTS} has been overestimated (perhaps significantly so) because the fluence assumed in the RT_{PTS} calculation does not correspond to the fluence at a likely flaw location.

- Out of 71 operating PWRs, 10 have their RT_{PTS} values established based on forgings [RVID2]. Forged vessels do not have axial welds, and consequently do not have the large flaws associated with axial weld fusion lines that account for a large portion of the TWCF. As discussed in Section 9.2 of this report and in [*EricksonKirk-SS*], flaws in forgings arise either as a consequence of the forging process itself or as "subclad" defects associated with the stainless steel cladding. Forging flaws are approximately equivalent to plate flaws in terms of both size and density, while subclad flaws occur as dense arrays of axially oriented flaws with a depth of ≈0.08-in. (≈2mm). Our sensitivity studies show that at an equivalent level of embrittlement, a forged vessel will have a through-wall cracking frequency that is *at most* ~15% that of an equivalent plate vessel (with axial welds). Thus, while forgings do contribute to the risk of vessel failure, the RT_{PTS} value for a forging-limited plant could considerably exceed the 10 CFR 50.61 screening criteria and still have a TWCF value below that of a plate vessel.

- Out of 71 operating PWRs, 15 have their RT_{PTS} values established based on axial weld properties [RVID2]. It is only for these vessels where the RT_{PTS} value is clearly associated with a material region that contributes significantly to the vessel failure probability, and is evaluated at a fluence that is clearly associated with a potential location of large flaws.

11.3 Relationship between *RT* Metrics and TWCF

11.3.1 Weighted *RT* Values

The information in Table 8.5 provides the percent contribution to the total TWCF attributable to axial weld flaws, circumferential weld flaws, and plate flaws. We use this information in Table 11.1 to determine the TWCF attributable to each flaw population. Figure 11-1 shows the relationships between the weighted *RT* metrics RT_{AW}, RT_{PL}, and RT_{CW} (described in Section 8.4.1 and quantified by Eq. 8-1, Eq. 8-2, and Eq. 8-3) and the TWCF values presented in Table 11.1. At a fixed reference temperature, the TWCF increases ≈50-fold between circumferential weld flaws and plate flaws, and ≈100-fold between plate flaws and axial weld flaws, reflecting the differences in fracture driving force caused by the different flaw sizes and orientations associated with the three flaw populations. The close agreement between TWCF values for different plants shown in Figure 11-1 is attributable to two factors:

- the similarity in both the frequency of, and the structural integrity challenge posed by, the most aggressive transients (i.e., large-diameter primary side pipe breaks, stuck-open primary side valves that later reclose, and breaks of the main steam line), as discussed in Section 8.5

- the fact that the weighted *RT* metrics appropriately reflect the toughness of the vessel at the location of postulated flaws

The fits shown in Figure 11-1 can be combined to estimate the TWCF of other PWRs, as follows:

Eq. 11-1 $\qquad TWCF_{TOTAL} = TWCF_{AXIAL-WELD} + \alpha_{PL} \cdot TWCF_{PLATE} + TWCF_{CIRC-WELD}$

where

$TWCF_{AXIAL-WELD} = 4\text{x}10^{-26} \cdot \exp\{0.0585 \cdot (RT_{AW} + 459.69)\}$ (see Eq. 8-1 for RT_{AW})

$\alpha_{PL} = 1.7$, $\qquad TWCF_{PLATE} = 4\text{x}10^{-29} \cdot \exp\{0.064 \cdot (RT_{PL} + 459.69)\}$ (see Eq. 8-2 for RT_{PL})

$TWCF_{CIRC-WELD} = 3\text{x}10^{-27} \cdot \exp\{0.051 \cdot (RT_{CW} + 459.69)\}$ (see Eq. 8-3 for RT_{CW})

Table 11.1. Contributions of different flaw populations to the TWCF values estimated by FAVOR Version 04.1

EFPY	Weighted Reference Temperatures [°F]			Maximum Reference Temperatures [°F]			% TWCF Due to Flaws in			Mean TWCF, events/yr.			
	RT_{AW}	RT_{CW}	RT_{PL}	$RT_{MAX\text{-}AW}$	$RT_{MAX\text{-}CW}$	$RT_{MAX\text{-}PL}$	Axial Welds	Circ Welds	Plates	Total	Axial Welds	Circ Welds	Plates
Oconee Unit 1													
32	134	136	72	152	175	79	100.00%	0.00%	0.00%	2.30E-11	2.30E-11	0.00E+00	0.00E+00
60	149	156	83	171	193	89	99.90%	0.10%	0.00%	6.47E-11	6.46E-11	6.47E-14	0.00E+00
Ext-Oa	200	207	134	232	251	136	99.83%	0.16%	0.00%	1.30E-09	1.30E-09	2.08E-12	0.00E+00
Ext-Ob	227	229	164	263	281	170	99.81%	0.11%	0.08%	1.16E-08	1.16E-08	1.28E-11	9.28E-12
Beaver Valley Unit 1													
32	171	243	217	192	243	243	68.44%	0.33%	31.23%	8.89E-10	6.08E-10	2.93E-12	2.78E-10
60	188	272	244	210	272	272	39.19%	0.72%	60.09%	4.84E-09	1.90E-09	3.48E-11	2.91E-09
Ext-Ba	203	301	273	225	301	301	15.69%	1.74%	82.55%	2.02E-08	3.17E-09	3.51E-10	1.67E-08
Ext-Bb	226	354	324	250	354	354	9.21%	6.18%	84.62%	3.00E-07	2.76E-08	1.85E-08	2.54E-07
Palisades													
32	210	201	165	212	201	189	99.95%	0.05%	0.00%	4.90E-09	4.90E-09	2.45E-12	0.00E+00
60	227	215	181	230	215	205	99.97%	0.04%	0.00%	1.55E-08	1.55E-08	6.20E-12	0.00E+00
Ext-Pa	271	259	231	277	259	259	99.91%	0.02%	0.08%	1.88E-07	1.88E-07	3.76E-11	1.50E-10
Ext-Pb	324	335	293	333	335	335	98.62%	0.01%	1.37%	1.26E-06	1.24E-06	1.26E-10	1.73E-08

Note: See Eq. 8-1, Eq. 8-2, and Eq. 8-3 for reference temperature definitions.

In Eq. 11-1, the RT values are expressed in °F; the formula converts Fahrenheit to Rankine to prevent the introduction of negative numbers to the exponential terms. The TWCF attributable to plate flaws is multiplied by a factor of 1.7 to prevent a systematic underestimation of the TWCF results for Beaver Valley. Averaged across all embrittlement levels analyzed, Eq. 11-1 overpredicts the Oconee, Beaver Valley, and Palisades results by 65%, 1%, and 25%, respectively. Figure 11-3 compares the FAVOR 04.1 TWCF estimates with the predictions of Eq. 11-1, showing good agreement overall.

11.3.2 Maximum RT Values

The TWCF estimation formula (Eq. 11-1) developed in the preceding Section is based on weighted RT values; it provides a means to estimate with reasonable accuracy how TWCF changes with embrittlement level. However, information from construction drawings regarding the dimensions and placement of the welds, plates, and forgings in the beltline region is needed to estimate the weighted reference temperatures (RT_{AW}, RT_{CW}, and RT_{PL}) used in Eq. 11-1, *in addition to* information available in the RVID database concerning chemical composition, fluence, and the RT_{NDT} before irradiation [RVID2]. While this additional information is readily available to licensees, and indeed has been docketed with the NRC, not having this information available in one place for all PWRs makes it difficult to estimate TWCF using Eq. 11-1 for the operating fleet. Conversely, the *maximum* reference temperatures RT_{MAX-AW}, RT_{MAX-CW}, and RT_{MAX-PL} that are used to estimate the weighted reference temperatures (RT_{AW}, RT_{CW}, and RT_{PL}, respectively) can be evaluated based only on information in RVID. Consequently, in Figure 11-2, we examine the relationships between these maximum reference temperatures and the TWCF values presented in Table 11.1 for each of the three flaw populations. The uncertainty in the correlations of TWCF with maximum RT values exceeds slightly the uncertainty in the correlations of TWCF with weighted RT values (compare Figure 11-2 to Figure 11-1). Nonetheless, the relationships in Figure 11-2 do provide a basis for estimating TWCF when only the information in RVID is available. The fits shown in Figure 11-2 can be combined to estimate the TWCF of other PWRs, as follows:

$$\text{Eq. 11-2} \qquad TWCF_{TOTAL} = \alpha_{AW} \cdot TWCF_{AXIAL-WELD} + \alpha_{PL} \cdot TWCF_{PLATE} + TWCF_{CIRC-WELD}$$

where

$$\alpha_{AW} = 1.6, \quad TWCF_{AXIAL-WELD} = 3\text{x}10^{-27} \cdot \exp\{0.0605 \cdot (RT_{MAX-AW} + 459.69)\}$$

$$\alpha_{PL} = 1.7, \quad TWCF_{PLATE} = 9\text{x}10^{-27} \cdot \exp\{0.0543 \cdot (RT_{MAX-PL} + 459.69)\}$$

$$TWCF_{CIRC-WELD} = 4\text{x}10^{-29} \cdot \exp\{0.0561 \cdot (RT_{MAX-CW} + 459.69)\}$$

(see Eq. 8-1, Eq. 8-2, and Eq. 8-3 for the definitions of RT_{MAX-AW}, RT_{MAX-PL}, and RT_{MAX-CW}, respectively)

In Eq. 11-2, the RT values are again expressed in °F; the formula converts Fahrenheit to Rankine to prevent the introduction of negative numbers to the exponential terms. The TWCF attributable to axial weld flaws and to plate flaws are multiplied by factors of 1.6 and 1.7, respectively, to prevent a systematic underestimation of the TWCF results of Palisades and of Beaver Valley, respectively. Averaged across all embrittlement levels analyzed, Eq. 11-2 overpredicts the Oconee, Beaver Valley, and Palisades results by 278%, 1%, and 2%, respectively. Figure 11-4 compares the FAVOR 04.1 TWCF estimates with the predictions of Eq. 11-2. As expected, based on the lower correlation coefficients of the TWCF *vs.* maximum RT relationships shown in Figure 11-2, the estimation accuracy of Eq. 11-2 is not quite as good as that of Eq. 11-1.

11.4 Proposed *RT*-Based Screening Limits

A *RT*-based screening limit can be established by setting the total TWCF in either Eq. 11-1 or Eq. 11-2 equal to the reactor vessel failure frequency acceptance criterion of 1×10^{-6} events per year proposed in Chapter 10. In the following two subsections we propose two *RT*-based screening limits: first in Section 11.4.1 for plate vessels (which have axial welds), and second in Section 11.4.2 for forged vessels (which do not have axial welds). In both sections, we compare our proposed screening limits to the *RT* values for currently operating PWRs at both EOL and EOLE. This section concludes with a discussion of the need for margins when using these screening limits to assess operating PWRs (see Section 11.4.3).

11.4.1 Plate Vessels

Plate vessels are made up of axial welds, plates, and circumferential welds, so in principal flaws in all of these regions will contribute to the through-wall cracking frequency. However, as revealed by our results (see Table 8.5) and as reflected in Eq. 11-1 and Eq. 11-2, the contribution of flaws in circumferential welds to TWCF is negligible relative to that of flaws in axial welds and in plates. A *RT*-based screening limit for PTS can therefore be derived from Eq. 11-1 by the following procedure:

(1) Set RT_{CW} to a fixed value.

(2) Set $TWCF_{TOTAL}$ to the 1×10^{-6} value proposed in Chapter 10.

(3) Solve the equation to establish (RT_{AW}, RT_{PL}) pairs that satisfy equality.

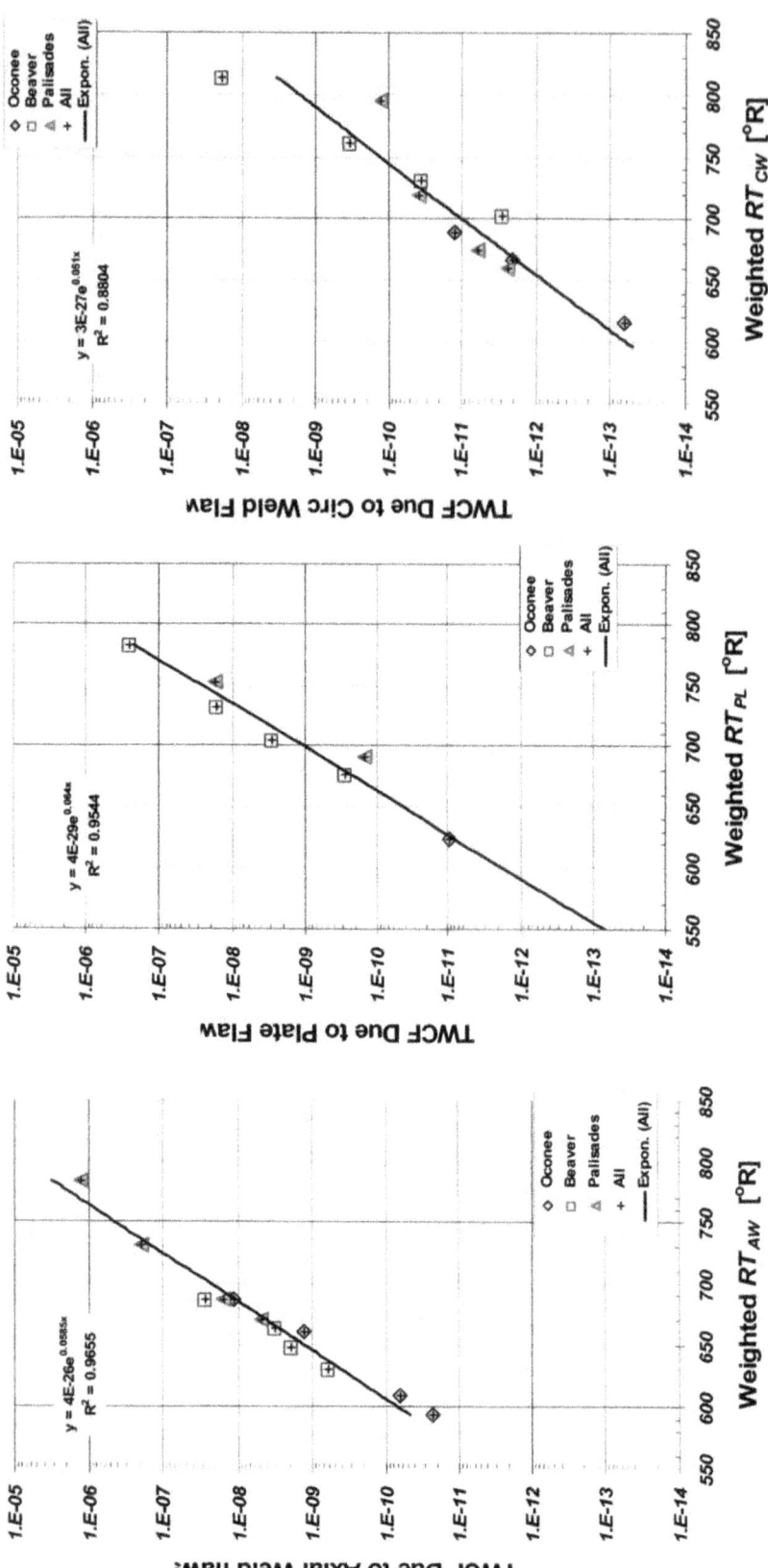

Figure 11-1. Correlation of through-wall cracking frequencies with weighted reference temperature metrics for the three study plants ($°R = °F + 459.69$)

11-8

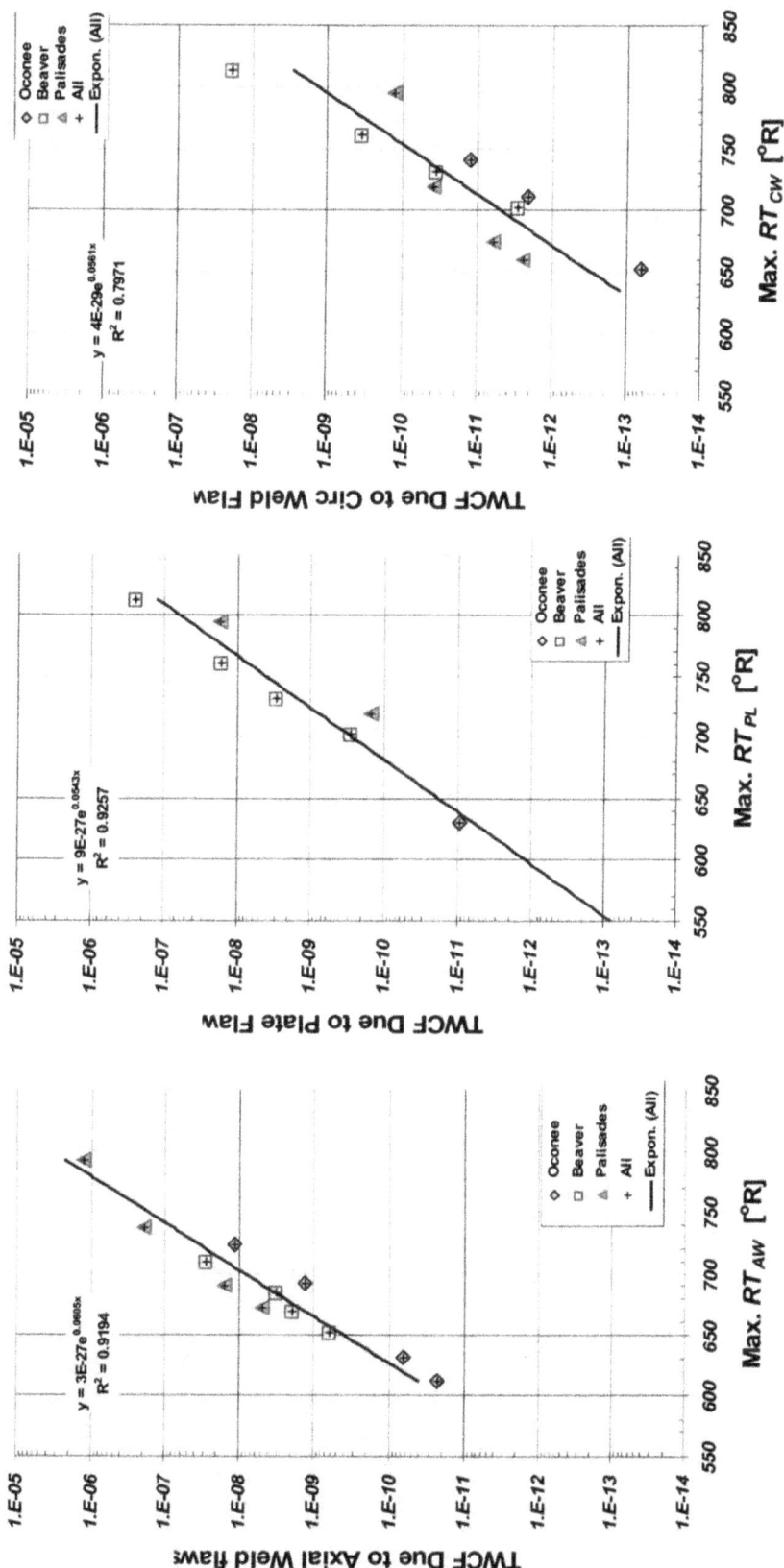

Figure 11-2. Correlation of through-wall cracking frequencies with maximum reference temperature metrics for the three study plants (°R = °F + 459.69)

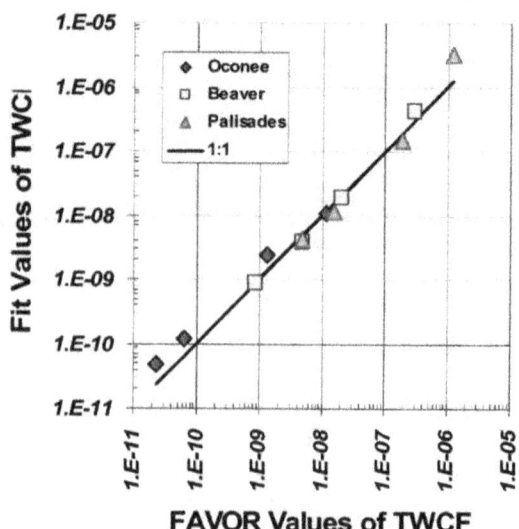

Figure 11-3. Comparison of FAVOR 04.1 TWCF estimates with TWCF values estimated using weighted *RT* values (Eq. 11-1)

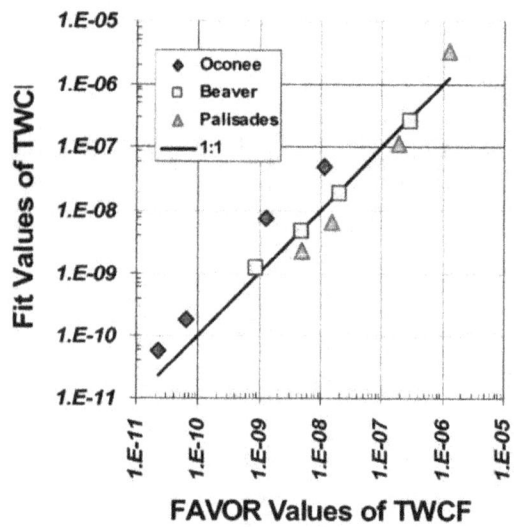

Figure 11-4. Comparison of FAVOR 04.1 TWCF estimates with TWCF values estimated using maximum *RT* values (Eq. 11-2)

As graphically illustrated in Figure 11-5, this procedure establishes a locus of (RT_{AW}, RT_{PL}) pairs. In the region of the graph between the locus and the origin, the TWCF is below the 1×10^{-6} acceptance criterion, so these combinations of RT_{AW} and RT_{PL} would be considered acceptable and require no further analysis. In the region of the graph outside of the locus, the TWCF is above the 1×10^{-6} acceptance criterion, indicating the need for additional analysis or other measures to justify continued plant operation. Figure 11-5 also indicates the effects of the RT_{CW} value (left-hand graph) and the $TWCF_{TOTAL}$ value (right-hand graph) on the position of the RT_{AW} vs. RT_{PL} locus. As previously mentioned, the RT_{CW} value has little effect on the location of the 1×10^{-6} locus for any RT_{CW} value that is likely to occur within the foreseeable future.

Figure 11-6 provides loci of (RT_{MAX-AW}, RT_{MAX-PL}) similar to those shown in Figure 11-5, but based instead on Eq. 11-2 (that is, on maximum RT values rather than on weighted RT values). These loci are used to assess the condition of currently operating PWRs relative to RT-based screening limits derived from the results of this investigation because maximum RT values can be estimated using only the information available in the RVID database [RVID2]. We assess the condition of operating PWRs at EOL (40 years, or 32 EFPY) and EOLE (60 years of operation, or 48 EFPY). The ID fluence at EOLE was assumed to be 1.5 times the value reported in RVID at EOL. This assumption implies that no changes in core loading will be made during the period of license extension. Were any licensee to change their core loading (e.g., remove their halfnium suppression to increase power), these changes would be reflected in both calculated fluence values and in the results of the surveillance programs conducted under Appendix H to 10 CFR Part 50, and so could easily be accounted for by recalculating the various RT metrics based on these different input values.

The results of these calculations are reported in Appendix D and are compared to the proposed screening limit for plate vessels in Figure 11-7. At EOL, at least 70°F (21°C) and up to 290°F (143°C) separate operating PWRs from the proposed screening limit; these values reduce by between 10 and 20°F (5.5 to 11°C) at EOLE. The wide separation of operating plants at EOL from these proposed screening limits contrasts sharply with the current regulatory situation (see Figure 1.1), where some operating plants lie within less than a single degree Fahrenheit of the

10 CFR 50.61 RT_{PTS} screening limits. This increase in estimated "distance" from a RT screening limit occurs as a direct consequence of the more accurate models used throughout this investigation. Figure 11-8 points out that these improvements can, equivalently, be quantified in terms of a reduction in the estimated annual frequency of through-wall cracking associated with operating PWRs. As shown in the figure, even at EOLE no currently operating plant is projected to exceed a annual TWCF of 1×10^{-7} (again, most plants have projected TWCFs far below this value, see Figure 11-8).

11.4.2 Forged Vessels

Forged vessels are comprised of forgings and circumferential welds; they contain no axial welds and so there can be no contribution to TWCF from the RT_{MAX-AW} term in Eq. 11-2. While we have not performed a detailed analysis of a forged vessel, the sensitivity studies on forging flaw distributions reported in Section 9.2 of this report and in [**EricksonKirk-SS**] support the use of the RT_{MAX-PL} term (evaluated using forging properties) in Eq. 11-2 to estimate the contribution of TWCF of forgings.

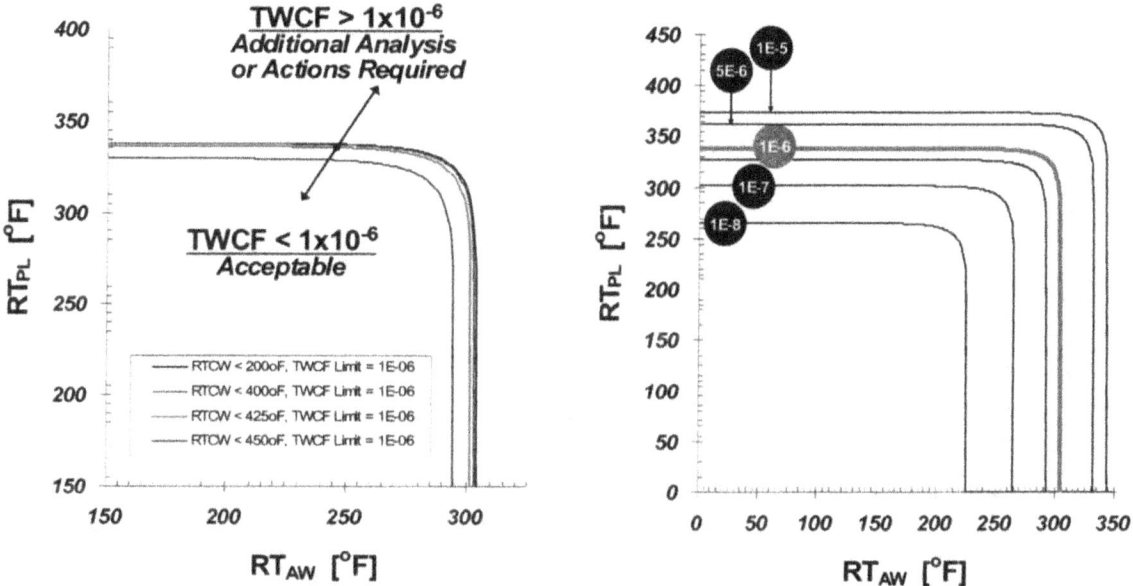

Figure 11-5. Weighted RT-based screening criterion for plate vessels based on Eq. 11-1
(Left: Effect of RT_{CW} value for a fixed $TWCF_{TOTAL}$ value of 1×10^{-6};
Right: Effect of $TWCF_{TOTAL}$ for a fixed RT_{CW} value of 300°F (149°C))

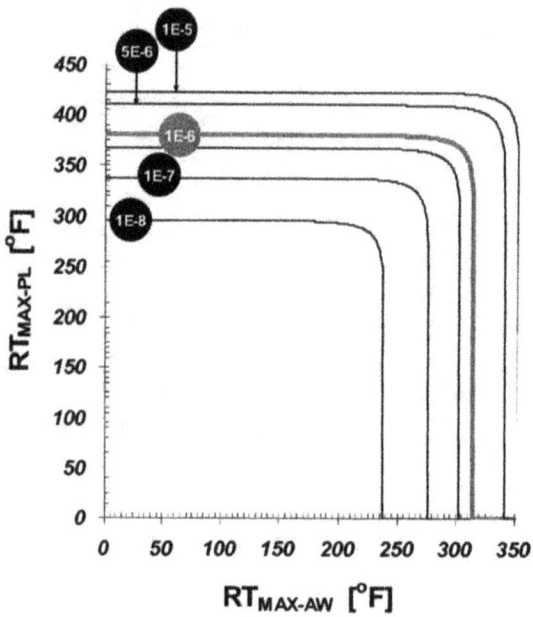

Figure 11-6. Maximum *RT*-based screening criterion for plate vessels based on Eq. 11-2

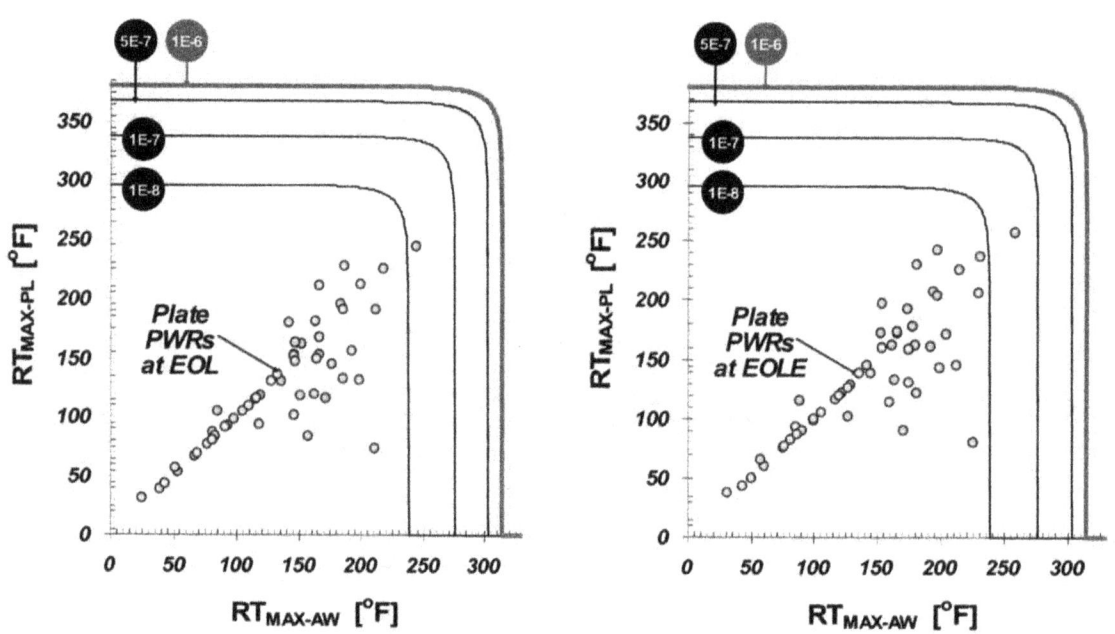

Figure 11-7. Comparison of the maximum *RT*-based screening limit for plate vessels based on Eq. 11-2 with assessment points for all operating PWRs at EOL (32 EFPY, 40 operating years) (left) and EOLE (48 EFPY, 60 operating years) (right) (Plant RT values estimated from information in [RVID2]. RT_{MAX-CW} is 300°F (149°C) for both graphs, exceeding the calculated RT_{MAX-CW} value for any plant at EOL or EOLE.)

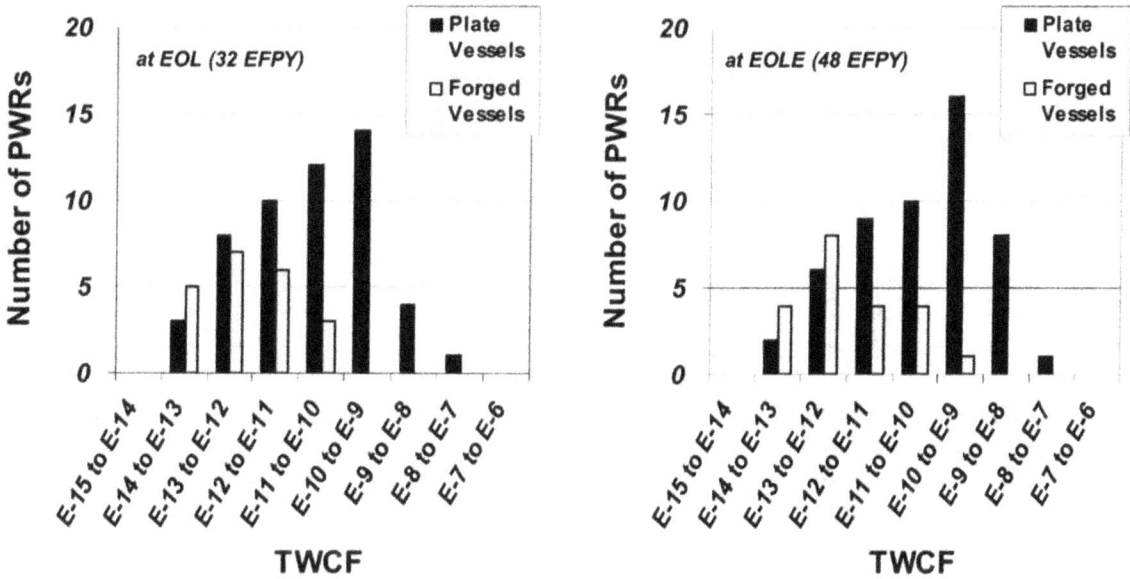

Figure 11-8. TWCF values for operating PWRs estimated using Eq. 11-1 at EOL (left) and EOLE (right) (Values for individual plants are reported in Appendix D.)

Figure 11-9 provides the locus of (RT_{MAX-CW}, RT_{MAX-PL}) pairs that can be used to assess the compliance of forged vessels with the reactor vessel failure frequency limit of 1×10^{-6} events/year proposed in Chapter 10. Figure 11-9 is interpreted in the same way as the proposed screening limit for plate vessels (Figure 11-6).

Figure 11-10 compares this proposed screening limit with the RT_{MAX-CW} and RT_{MAX-PL} values for currently operating forged vessels at EOL and at EOLE (see Appendix D for plant-specific values of RT_{MAX-CW} and RT_{MAX-PL}). These results demonstrate that no forged plant is anywhere close to screening limits based on a reactor vessel failure frequency limit of 1×10^{-6} events/year (see also Figure 11-8, which expresses these results in terms of frequency, rather than in terms or reference temperature).

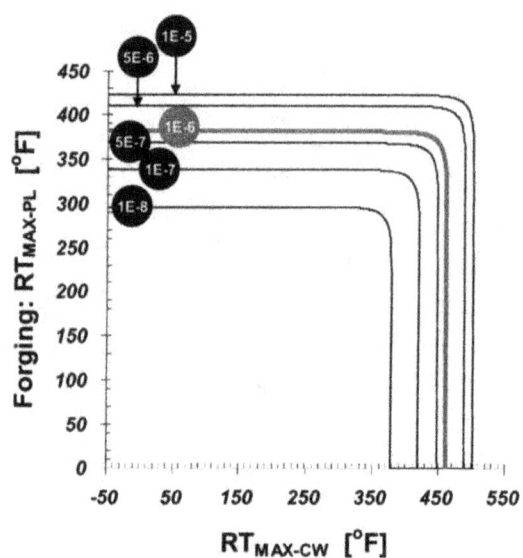

Figure 11-9. Maximum *RT*-based screening criterion for forged vessels based on Eq. 11-1, illustrating the effect of $TWCF_{TOTAL}$

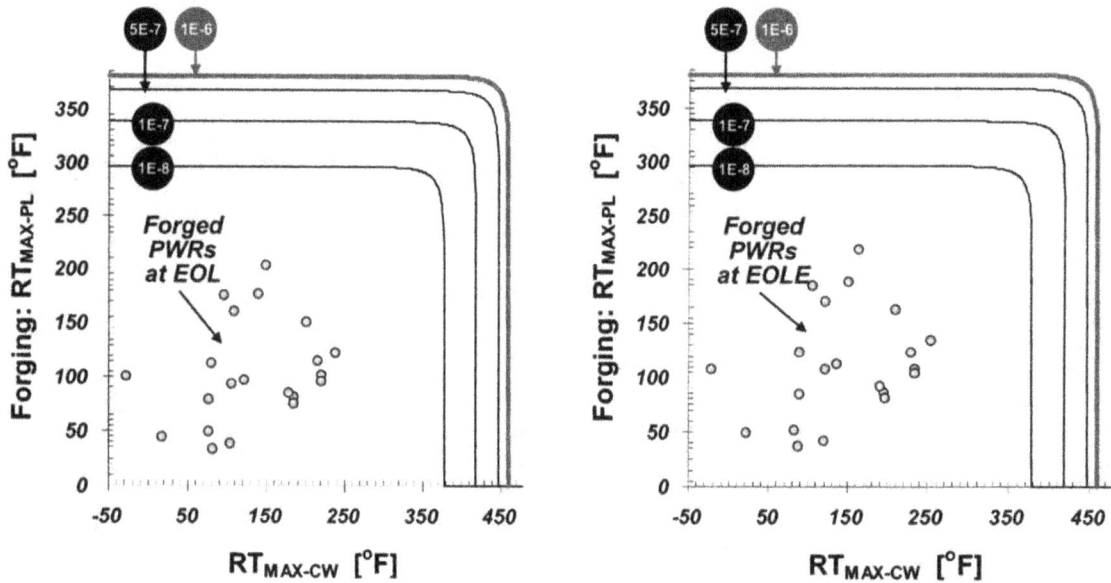

Figure 11-10.   Comparison of maximum *RT*-based screening limit for forged vessels based on Eq. 11-2 with operating PWRs at EOL (32 EFPY, 40 operating years) (left) and EOLE (48 EFPY, 60 operating years) (right) (Plant *RT* values estimated from information in [RVID2]. RT_{MAX-PL} is estimated based on forging properties.)

11.4.3 Need for Margin

Aside from relying on different *RT* metrics, the PTS screening limits proposed in Figure 11-6 and Figure 11-9 differs from the 10 CFR 50.61 RT_{PTS} screening limit by the absence of a "margin term." Use of a margin term is appropriate to account (at least approximately) for factors that occur in application that were not considered in the analyses upon which these proposed screening limits are based. For example, the 10 CFR 50.61 margin term (see **Eq. 2-4**) accounts for uncertainty in copper, in nickel, and in initial RT_{NDT}. However, as summarized in Chapter 7 and discussed in detail by [**EricksonKirk-PFM**], our model explicitly considers uncertainty in all of these variables, and represents these uncertainties as being larger (a conservative representation) than would be appropriate in any plant-specific application of the proposed screening limit. Consequently, use of the 10 CFR 50.61 margin term with the screening limits proposed in Figure 11-6 and Figure 11-9 would be inappropriate.

In general, the following additional reasons suggest that use of any margin term with the proposed screening limits is inappropriate:

(1) The *TWCF* values used to establish the screening limit represent 90th percentile values or greater (see Figure 8-3).

(2) Chapter 8 and Chapter 9 demonstrate that the results from our three plant-specific analyses apply to PWRs in general.

(3) Certain aspects of our modeling cannot be reasonably represented as "best estimates." On balance, there is a conservative bias to these non-best estimate aspects of our analysis, as discussed in the following section.

11.4.4 Non-Best Estimate Aspects of the Model

Throughout this project, every effort has been made to perform a "best estimate" analysis. Nonetheless, comparison of the analytical models upon which the screening limits proposed in Sections 11.4.1 and 11.4.2, with the actual situation being assessed, reveals that certain features of that situation have not been represented as realistically as possible. These parts of the model may be judged as providing either a conservative representation (i.e., tending to increase the estimated TWCF) or a nonconservative representation (i.e., tending to decrease the estimated TWCF) relative to the actual situation in service. Table 11.2 summarizes these conservatisms and nonconservatisms, which are discussed in greater detail in Section 11.4.4.1 and Section 11.4.4.2, respectively. This discussion does not include factors that our models do not accurately represent when these inaccuracies have been demonstrated not to significantly influence the TWCF results. This information demonstrates that, on balance, more

conservatisms than nonconservatisms remain in the model, suggesting the appropriateness of applying the proposed screening limits (see Figure 11-6 and Figure 11-9) without an additional margin term.

11.4.4.1 Residual Conservatisms

In the reactor vessel failure frequency limit

- The reactor vessel failure frequency limit of 1×10^{-6} events/year was established based on the assumption that through-wall cracking of the RPV will produce a large early release in all circumstances. As discussed in Chapter 10, through-wall cracking of the RPV is likely to lead to core damage, but large early release is unlikely because of reactor safety systems and the multiple barriers that block radioactive release to the environment (e.g., containment). Current guidelines on core damage frequency provided by RG 1.174 and the Option 3 framework for risk-informing 10 CFR Part 50 suggest a reactor vessel failure frequency limit of 1×10^{-5} events/year [RG1.174]. As illustrated in Figure 11-6 and Figure 11-9 changing from a 1×10^{-6} to a 1×10^{-5} limit would increase all of the proposed *RT* limits by $\approx 40°F$ (22°C)

Table 11.2. Non-best estimate aspects of the models used to develop the RT-based screening limits for PTS shown in Figure 11-5 and Figure 11-9

Situation in Service	Potential Conservatism in the Analytical Model
If the vessel fails, what happens next?	The model assumes that all failures produce a large early release; however, in the APET (Ch. 10), most sequences lead only to core damage.
	An initiated axial crack is assumed to instantly propagate to infinite length. In reality, the crack length will be finite and limited to the length of a single shell course because the cracks will most likely arrest when they encounter higher toughness materials in either the adjacent circumferential welds or plates.
	An initiated circumferential crack is assumed to instantly propagate 360° around the vessel ID. In reality, the crack length is limited because the azimuthal fluence variation places strips of tougher material in the path of the extending crack.
How the many possible PTS initiators are binned, and how TH transient are selected to represent each bin to the PFM analysis.	When uncertainty of how to bin existed, consistently conservative decisions were made
Characterization of secondary side failures	The minimum temperature of main steam line break inside containment is modeled as ~50°F (28°C) colder than it can be because containment pressurizes as a result of the steam escaping from the break.
	Stuck-open valves on the secondary side are conservatively modeled in Palisades.
Through-wall attenuation of neutron damage	Attenuation is assumed to be less-significant than measured in experiments.
Model of material unirradiated toughness and chemical composition variability.	The statistical distributions sampled produce more uncertainty than could ever occur in a specific weld, plate, or forging.
Correction for systematic conservative bias in RT_{NDT}	Model corrects for mean bias, but over represents uncertainty in RT_{NDT}.
Embrittlement shift model	Model used produces systematically higher TWCF than that estimated by the embrittlement shift model adopted by ASTM.
Flaw model	All defects found were assumed to be planar.
	Systematically conservative judgments were made when developing the flaw distribution model.
Interdependency of between initiation toughness and arrest toughness.	Model employed allows all initiated flaws a chance to propagate into the vessel.
Extrapolation of irradiation damage	Most conservative approach taken (increasing time, vs. increasing unirradiated RT_{NDT}).

Situation in Service	Potential Non-Conservatism in the Analytical Model
If the vessel fails, what happens next?	The potential for air oxidation has been ignored.
External PTS initiators	The potential for external events (e.g., fires, earthquakes) initiating PTS transients has been ignored. A conservative bounding analysis (see Section 9.4) estimates the effect of external events to be at most a factor of 2 increase in TWCF, but the likely increase is expected to be much less than 2x.
Through-wall chemistry layering	Model assumes that the mean level of copper can change four times through the vessel wall thickness. If copper layering is not present, the TWCF would increase.

In the PRA model

- In the PRA binning process, when there was uncertainty regarding what bin to place a particular scenario in, the scenario was intentionally binned in a conservative manner. Thus, the loading severity has a tendency toward being overestimated.

In the thermal-hydraulics model

- The temperature of water held in the safety injection accumulators was assumed to be 60°F (15.6°C). These accumulators are inside containment and (so) exist at temperatures of 80–90°F (26.7–32.2°C) in the winter and above 110°F (43.3°C) in the summer. Again, this conservative estimate of injection water temperature increases the magnitude of the thermal stresses that occur during of pipe breaks and reduces the fracture resistance of the vessel steel.

- When a main steam line breaks inside of containment the release of steam from the break pressurizes the containment structure to ~50psi (335 kPa). Consequently, the minimum temperature for MSLBs is bounded by the boiling point of water at ~50psi (335 kPa), or ~260°F (126.7°C). However, our models of secondary side breaks do not account for pressurization of containment, so the minimum temperature calculated by RELAP for these transients is 212°F (100°C), or approximately 50°F (28°C) too cold. This conservative estimate of the minimum temperature associated with an MSLB increases the magnitude of the thermal stresses that occur during pipe breaks and reduces the fracture resistance of the vessel steel.

In the fracture model

- Once a circumferential crack initiates, it is assumed to instantly propagate 360° around the vessel wall. However, full circumferential propagation is highly unlikely because of the azimuthal variation in fluence, which causes alternating regions of more embrittled and less embrittled material to exist circumferentially around the vessel wall. Thus, our model tends to overestimate the extent of cracking initiated from circumferentially oriented defects because it ignores this natural crack arrest mechanism.

- Once an axial flaw initiates, it is assumed to instantly become infinitely long. In reality, it only propagates to the length of an axial shell course (~8 to 12–ft (~2.4 to 3.7-m)), at which point, it encounters tougher material and arrests. Even though a shell course is very long, flaws of finite length tend to arrest more readily than do flaws of infinite length because of systematic differences in the through-wall variation of crack driving force. Because of this approximation, our model tends to overestimate the likelihood of through-wall cracking.

- As detailed in Section 4.2.3.1.3 of [*EricksonKirk-PFM*] and in [English 02], the adopted FAVOR model of how fluence attenuates through the RPV wall is conservative relative to experimental data.

- As detailed in Section 4.2.2.2 of [*EricksonKirk-SS*] and in Appendix D to [*EricksonKirk-PFM*], the statistical distributions of Cu, Ni, P, and RT_{NDT} sampled by FAVOR overestimate the degree of uncertainty in these variables relative to what can actually exist in any particular weld, plate, or forging.

- While the FAVOR model corrects (on average) for the systematic conservative bias in RT_{NDT}, the model overestimates the uncertainty associated with the fracture toughness transition temperature metric.

- As detailed in Section 9.2.1.2.3, the embrittlement shift model adopted by FAVOR systematically overestimates the TWCF relative to the embrittlement shift model currently recommended by the ASTM (an international consensus body).

In the flaw model

- In the experimental data upon which the flaw distribution is based, all detected defects were modeled as being crack-like and, therefore, potentially deleterious to the fracture integrity of the vessel. However, many of these defects are actually volumetric rather than planar, making them either benign or, at a minimum, much less of a challenge to the fracture integrity of the vessel. Thus, the model we have adopted overestimates the seriousness of the defect population in RPV materials, which leads to overly pessissimistic assessments of the fracture resistance of the vessel.

- FAVOR incorporates an interdependence between initiation and arrest fracture toughness values premised on physical arguments (see Sections 5.3.1.1 and 5.3.1.2 of [*EricksonKirk-PFM*]). While the staff believes these models are appropriate, this view is not universally held (see reviewer comment 40D in Appendix B). The alternative model, with no interdependence between initiation and arrest fracture toughness values, would reduce the estimated values of TWCF.

- As detailed in Section 9.2.2.1, we have simulated levels of irradiation damage beyond those occurring over currently anticipated lifetimes using the most conservative available techniques.

11.4.4.2   Residual Non-Conservatisms

In the reactor vessel failure frequency limit

- Air oxidation. The LERF criterion provided in RG 1.174, which was used to establish the 1×10^{-6}/ry TWCF limit, assumes source terms that do not reflect scenarios where fuel cooling has been lost, exposing the fuel rods to air (rather than steam). Should such a situation arise, some portion of the reactor fuel would eventually be oxidized in an air environment, which would result in release fractions for key fission products (ruthenium being of primary concern) that may be significantly (e.g., a factor of 20) larger than those associated with fuel oxidation in steam environments. These larger release fractions could lead to larger numbers of prompt fatalities than predicted for non-PTS risk-significant scenarios. Nonetheless, the APET developed in Chapter 10

demonstrates that the number of scenarios where air oxidation is possible is extremely small, certainly far smaller than the number of scenarios where only core damage (not LERF) is the only plausible outcome. Thus, the nonconservatism introduced by not explicitly considering the potential for air oxidation is more than compensated for by the conservatism of establishing a TWCF limit based on LERF when many accident sequences can only plausibly result in core damage.

In the PRA model

- External initiating events. As detailed in Section 9.4, our analysis hast not considered the potential for a PTS transient to be started by an initiating event external to the plant (e.g., fire, earthquake). The bounding analyses reported in Section 9.4 demonstrate that this would increase the TWCF values reported herein by at most a factor of 2. However, the bounding nature of our external events analysis suggests strongly that the actual effect of ignoring the contribution of external initiating events would be much smaller than 2x.

In the fracture model

- Through-wall chemistry layering. As detailed in Section 9.2.1.2.5, FAVOR models the existence of a gradient of properties through the thickness of the RPV because of through-wall changes in copper content. These copper content changes arise from the fact that, given the large volume of weld metal needed to fill an RPV weld, manufacturers often need to use weld wire from multiple weld wire spools (having different amounts of copper coating) to completely fill the groove. The model adopted in FAVOR resamples the mean copper content of the weld at the ¼T, ½T, and ¾T locations through the thickness. This resampling increases the probability of crack arrest because it allows the simulation of less irradiation-sensitive materials, which could arrest the running crack before it fails the vessel. If these weld layers did not occur in a real vessel, the TWCF would increase

relative to those reported herein by a small
factor (~2.5 based on the limited sensitivity
studies performed).

12 Summary of Findings and Considerations for Rulemaking

The investigation documented by this report reevaluates the technical basis of the PTS Rule and its associated screening criteria. Our approach considers the factors that influence the risk of vessel failure during a PTS event, while accounting for uncertainties as an integrated part of a quantitative PRA. Two central features of our approach are a focus on the use of realistic input values and models (wherever possible), and an *explicit* treatment of uncertainties (to the greatest extent practicable). Thus, our approach differs markedly from that employed in developing 10 CFR 50.61, in which many aspects of the analysis included intentional and unquantified conservatisms, and uncertainties were *implicitly* treated by incorporating them into the models.

In this chapter, we summarize the results of our findings in the following four areas:

- baseline analysis of the likelihood of PTS-induced RPV failure at three plants (Oconee 1, Beaver Valley, and Palisades), as presented in Chapter 8

- examination of the applicability of the results from Chapter 8 to PWRs *in general*, as presented in Chapter 9

- assessment of a annual per plant limit on through-wall cracking frequency that is consistent with current NRC guidelines on risk-informed regulation, as presented in Chapter 10

- use of information from Chapters 8, 9, and 10 to develop a reference temperature (RT)-based PTS screening criteria, as presented in Chapter 11

This chapter concludes with a short discussion of considerations for rulemaking and possible regulatory implications of this work beyond those associated with 10 CFR 50.61.

12.1 Plant-Specific Baseline Analysis of the PTS Risk at Oconee Unit 1, Beaver Valley Unit 1, and Palisades

Chapter 8 provided the results of plant-specific analyses of Oconee Unit 1, Beaver Valley Unit 1, and Palisades. In the following list, which summarizes the information presented in Chapter 8, the *conclusions* are shown in *bold italics*, while supporting information is shown in regular type:

- ***The degree of PTS challenge for currently anticipated lifetimes and operating conditions is low.***

  o Even at the end of license extension (60 operational years, or 48 EFPY at an 80% capacity factor), the mean estimated through-wall cracking frequency (*TWCF*) does not exceed 2×10^{-8}/year for the plants analyzed. Considering that the Beaver Valley and Palisades RPVs are constructed from some of the most irradiation-sensitive materials in commercial reactor service today, these results suggest that, provided that operating practices do not change dramatically in the future, the operating reactor fleet is in little danger of exceeding either the limit on *TWCF* of 5×10^{-6}/yr expressed by Regulatory Guide 1.154 [RG 1.154] or the 1×10^{-6}/yr value recommended in Chapter 10, even after license extension.

- ***Mean TWCF values are in fact upper bounds.***

  o Because of the skewness characteristic of the *TWCF* distributions that arise as a result of the physical processes responsible for steel fracture, mean *TWCF* values correspond to the 90th percentile (or higher) of the *TWCF* distribution. Thus, the mean *TWCF* values we report in this chapter are appropriately regarded as upper bounds to the uncertainty distribution on TWCF.

- *Axial flaws, and the toughness properties that can be associated with such flaws, control nearly all of the TWCF.*

  o Axial flaws are much more likely to propagate through-wall than circumferential flaws because the applied driving force to fracture increases continuously with increasing crack depth for an axial flaw. Conversely, circumferentially oriented flaws experience a driving force peak mid-wall, providing a natural crack arrest mechanism. It should be noted that crack initiation from circumferentially oriented flaws is likely; it is only their through-wall propagation that is much less likely (relative to axially oriented flaws).

  o It is, therefore, the toughness properties that can be associated with axial flaws that control nearly all of the TWCF. These include the toughness properties of plates and axial welds at the flaw locations. Conversely, the toughness properties of both circumferential welds and forgings have little effect on TWCF because these can be associated only with circumferentially oriented flaws.

- *Transients involving primary side faults are the dominant contributors to TWCF. Transients involving secondary side faults play a much smaller role.*

  o The severity of a transient is controlled by a combination of three factors:

    - the initial cooling rate, which controls the thermal stress in the RPV wall

    - the minimum temperature of the transient, which controls the resistance of the vessel to fracture

    - the pressure retained in the primary system, which controls the pressure stress in the RPV wall

  o The significance of a transient (i.e., how much it contributes to PTS risk) depends on these three factors and on the likelihood of the transient occurring.

  o Our analysis considered transients in the following classes:

    - primary side pipe breaks
    - stuck-open valves on the primary side
    - main steam line breaks
    - stuck-open valves on the secondary side
    - feed-and-bleed
    - steam generator tube rupture
    - mixed primary and secondary initiators

  o Table 12.1 summarizes our results for these transient classes in terms of both transient severity indicators and the likelihood of the transient occurring. The color-coding of table entries indicates the contribution (or not) of these factors to the TWCF of the different classes of transients. This summary indicates that the risk-dominant transients (medium- and large-diameter primary side pipe breaks, and stuck-open primary side valves that later reclose) all have multiple factors that, in combination, result in their significant contribution to TWCF.

    - For medium- to large-diameter primary side pipe breaks, the fast to moderate cooling rates and the low downcomer temperatures (generated by the rapid depressurization and emergency injection of low-temperature makeup water directly to the primary) combine to produce a high-severity transient. Despite the moderate to low likelihood of transient occurrence, the severity of these transients (if they occur) makes them significant contributors to the total TWCF.

    - For stuck-open primary side valves that later reclose, the repressurization associated with valve reclosure

12-2

coupled with low temperatures in the primary combine to produce a high-severity transient. This coupled with a high likelihood of transient occurrence makes stuck-open primary side valves that later reclose significant contributors to the total TWCF.

Table 12.1. Factors contributing the severity and risk dominance of various transient classes.

Transient Class		Transient Severity			Transient Likelihood	TWCF Contribution
		Cooling Rate	Minimum Temperature	Pressure		
Primary Side Pipe Breaks	Large Diameter	Fast	Low	Low	Low	Large
	Medium Diameter	Moderate	Low	Low	Moderate	Large
	Small Diameter	Slow	High	Moderate	High	~0
Primary Stuck-Open Valves	Valve Recloses	Slow	Moderate	High	High	Large
	Valve Remains Open	Slow	Moderate	Low	High	~0
Main Steam Line Break		Fast	Moderate	High	High	Small
Stuck-Open Valve(s), Secondary Side		Moderate	High	High	High	~0
Feed-and-Bleed		Slow	Low	Low	Low	~0
Steam Generator Tube Rupture		Slow	High	Moderate	Low	~0
Mixed Primary & Secondary Initiators		Slow	Mixed		Very Low	~0
Color Key	Enhances TWCF Contribution		Intermediate		Diminishes TWCF Contribution	

- The small or negligible contribution of all secondary side transients (MSLBs, stuck-open secondary valves) results directly from the lack of low temperatures in the primary system. For these transients, the minimum temperature of the primary for times of relevance is controlled by the boiling point of water in the secondary (212°F (100°C) or above). At these temperatures, the fracture toughness of the RPV steel is sufficiently high to resist vessel failure in most cases.

- *Credits for operator action, while included in our analysis, do not influence these findings in any significant way.* Operator action credits can dramatically influence the risk-significance of *individual* transients. Appropriate credits for operator action, therefore, need to be included as part of a "best estimate" analysis because there is no way to establish *a priori* if a particular transient will make a large contribution to the total risk. Nonetheless, the results of our analyses demonstrate that the *overall effect* of these operator action credits on the *total TWCF* for a plant is small, for the following reasons:

  o Medium- and Large-Diameter Primary Side Pipe Breaks: No operator actions are modeled for any break diameter because, for these events, the safety injection systems do not fully refill the upper regions of the RCS. Consequently, operators would never take action to shut off the pumps.

  o Stuck-Open Primary Side Valves that May Later Reclose: Reasonable and appropriate credit for operator actions (throttling of HPI) has been included in the PRA model. However, the influence of these credits on the estimated values of vessel failure probability attributable to SO-1 transients is small because the operator actions credited only prevent repressurization when SO-1 transients initiate from HZP conditions and when

the operators act promptly (within 1 minute) to throttle HPI. Complete removal of operator action credits from the model increases the total risk associated with SO-1 transients only slightly.

  o Main Steam Line Breaks: For the overwhelming majority of MSLB transients, vessel failure is predicted to occur between 10 and 15 minutes after transient initiation because it is within this timeframe that the thermal stresses associated with the rapid cooldown reach their maximum. Thus, all of the long-time effects (isolation of feedwater flow, timing of HSSI control) that can be influenced by operator actions have no effect on vessel failure probability because these factors influence the progression of the transient after failure has occurred (if it occurs). Only factors affecting the initial cooling rate (i.e., plant power level at transient initiation, break location inside or outside of containment) can influence the CPTWC values. These factors are not influenced in any way by operator actions.

- *Because the severity of the most significant transients in the dominant transient classes are controlled by factors that are common to PWRs in general, the TWCF results presented in this chapter can be used with confidence to develop revised PTS screening criteria that apply to the entire fleet of operating PWRs.*

  o Medium- and Large-Diameter Primary Side Pipe Breaks: For these break diameters, the fluid in the primary cools faster than can the wall of the RPV. In this situation, *only* the thermal conductivity of the steel and the thickness of the RPV wall control the thermal stresses and, thus, the severity of the fracture challenge. Perturbations to the fluid cooldown rate controlled by break diameter, break location, and season of the year do not play a role. Thermal conductivity is a physical property, so it is very consistent for all

RPV steels, and the thicknesses of the three RPVs analyzed are typical of PWRs. Consequently, the TWCF contribution of medium- to large-diameter primary side pipe breaks is expected to be consistent from plant-to-plant and can be well-represented for all PWRs by the analyses reported herein.

o Stuck-Open Primary Side Valves that May Later Reclose: A major contributor to the risk-significance of SO-1 transients is the return to full system pressure once the valve recloses. The operating and safety relief valve pressures of all PWRs are similar. Additionally, as previously noted, operator action credits affect the total risk associated with this transient class only slightly.

o Main Steam Line Breaks: Since MSLBs fail early (within 10–15 minutes after transient initiation), only factors affecting the initial cooling rate can have any influence on CPTWC values. These factors include the plant power level at event initiation and the location of the break (inside or outside of containment). These factors are not influenced in any way by operator actions.

12.2 Applicability of these Plant Specific Results to Estimating the PTS Risk at PWRs in General

In Chapter 9, we examined the applicability of the TWCF estimates presented in Chapter 8 for Oconee Unit 1, Beaver Valley Unit 1, and Palisades to PWRs *in general*. The information presented focused on the following topics:

• Sensitivity studies performed on the TH and PFM models to engender confidence in both the robustness of the results presented in Chapter 8 and their applicability to PWRs *in general*.

• An examination of the plant design and operational characteristics of five additional plants to determine whether the design and

operational features that are the key contributors to PTS risk vary significantly enough in the general plant population to question the generality of our results.

• An examination of the effects of external events (e.g., fires, floods, earthquakes) to PTS risk.

Except for a few situations that are not expected to occur, none of these analyses revealed any reason to question the applicability of the results presented in Chapter 8 to the general population of operating PWRs in the United States. The information developed in these analyses is summarized as follows:

TH Sensitivity Studies

• Changes to the RELAP heat transfer coefficient model to account for low-flow situations where mixed convection heat transfer may be occurring in the downcomer were made based on the Petukhov-Gnielinski heat transfer correlation. This change in the heat transfer coefficient increases the CPTWC by a factor ~3 (averaged across all transients analyzed) compared to using the default heat transfer correlations in RELAP5/MOD3.3 Version ei. There is some variability from the average CPF factor, depending upon the transient being considered.

PFM Sensitivity Studies

- An examination of the effects of all postulated credible perturbations to our PFM model revealed no effects significant enough to warrant a change to our baseline model, or to recommend a caution regarding its robustness.

- In general, the TWCF of forged PWRs can be assessed using the Chapter 8 results (for plate welded PWRs) by ignoring the TWCF contribution of axial welds. However, should changes in future operating conditions result in a forged vessel being subjected to very high levels of embrittlement (far beyond any currently anticipated at EOL or EOLE) a plant-specific analysis to assess the effect of subclad flaws on TWCF would be warranted.

- For PWRs with vessel thicknesses of 7.5 to 9 .5-in. (19.05 to 24.13-cm), the TWCF results in Chapter 8 are realistic. The Chapter 8 results overestimate the TWCF of the seven thinner vessels (with wall thicknesses below 7-in. (17.78-cm)) and underestimate the TWCF of Palo Verde Units 1, 2, and 3, all of which have wall thicknesses above 11-in (27.94-cm). However, these vessels have very low embrittlement projected at either EOL or EOLE, suggesting little practical effect of this underestimation.

Plant Design and Operational Characteristics

- *Large-Diameter Primary Side Pipe Breaks*: No differences were found that would cause significant changes in either the progression or frequencies of the PTS scenarios. Additionally, no differences in the plant system designs were found that would cause significant changes in the downcomer fluid temperature.

- *Small- to Medium-Diameter Primary Side Pipe Breaks*: No differences were found that would cause significant changes in either the progression or frequency of the pipe break LOCAs. For the feed-and-bleed LOCAs, the only difference that was found affected the frequency for the CE

generalization plant (i.e., Fort Calhoun). The frequency for these types of scenarios could be higher by a factor of ~3; however, this increase would not prevent the generalization plants from being bounded (or represented) by the detailed analysis plants.

- *Stuck-Open Valves on the Primary Side that May Later Reclose*: The progression of the accident scenarios should be the same across all plants. While, the frequency associated with this type of scenarios could increase at some Westinghouse plants, the integrated effect of this increase was determined to be small. Fort Calhoun is expected to have a downcomer temperature that is cooler than its corresponding detailed analysis plant (Palisades) because of the smaller size of the plant. The downcomer temperature for the other generalization plants is actually expected to be somewhat warmer. PFM calculations performed to quantify the effect of the colder temperatures in Ft. Calhoun determined that while the conditional through-wall cracking probabilities would increase (as expected), the increase was not so substantial as to prevent the Palisades plant analysis from upper-bounding the Ft. Calhoun plant analysis. Thus, the colder downcomer temperature for smaller plants was not viewed as impeding the applicability of the TWCF values in Chapter 8 to PWRs in general.

- *Main Steam Line and other Secondary Side Breaks*: No differences were found that would cause significant differences in either the progression or frequency of the PTS scenarios.

- *Summary*: These observations support the conclusion that the Chapter 8 TWCF estimates produced can be used to characterize (or bound) the TWCF of PWRs in general.

- No external event scenarios were found where the TWCFs significantly exceed that of the worst internal event scenarios (contributions from LOCA-type and SRV open-reclose-type accidents). Given the bounding nature of the external event analyses, there is considerable assurance that the external event contribution to overall TWCF as a result of PTS does not exceed than the highest best-estimate contribution from internal events. Given the conservative probabilities and dependencies assumed in the external event analyses, with the addition of little or no credit for any operator actions for the external event scenarios, it is more likely that the "realistic" external event contribution to overall TWCF is much less than the highest internal event contribution. Therefore, the contribution of external initiating events to the overall TWCF attributable to PTS can be considered negligible.

12.3 An Anual Per-Plant Limit on Through-Wall Cracking Frequency Consistent with Current Regulatory Guidance on Risk-Informed Regulation

The analysis presented in Chapter 10 produced the following conclusions regarding the establishment of an annual per-plant limit on through-wall cracking frequency (i.e., a criterion for RVFF):

(1) The analysis supports a definition of RVFF as being equivalent to TWCF (i.e., for PTS considerations, RPV "failure" can be defined as an occurrence of a through-wall crack). This conclusion is based on the following two factors:

(a) TWCF is a more direct measure than VCIF of the likelihood of events with potentially significant public health consequences. This is desirable from a risk-informed decision-making perspective.

(b) The uncertainties associated with the prediction of a through-wall crack (under PTS conditions) are only slightly larger than those associated with the prediction of crack initiation (also under PTS conditions). For example, at the 10 CFR 50.61 RT_{PTS} screening limit, the separation between the 50th and 95th percentiles in the distribution of VCIF ranges from 0.8 to 1.8 orders of magnitude, while the separation between the 50th and 95th percentiles in the distribution of TWCF ranges from 0.9 to 2.6 orders of magnitude. This slight increase in uncertainty is a natural and expected consequence of a cleavage failure mechanism and does not reflect a state of knowledge limitation regarding crack arrest. (See [EricksonKirk-PFM] for details of the crack arrest model.)

(2) The analysis supports an acceptance criterion for RVFF, RVFF*, of 1×10^{-6}/ry. This is based on the following observations:

(a) The conditional probability of an unscrubbed, large early release with a large air-oxidation source term (given a PTS-induced RPV failure) appears to be very small (i.e., less than 0.01). It is particularly small for plants where water in the reactor cavity (following a PTS-induced RPV failure) will cover the fuel. For plants with larger cavities, the low probability of the scenario is largely attributable to the independence and reliability of containment sprays.

(b) The assessment underlying the above observation does not account for potential dependencies associated with PTS-events initiated by "external events" (e.g., earthquakes) or internal fires.

(c) For plants with cavities such that fuel cooling is not assured following a PTS-induced RPV failure, the APET (Figure 10.1) identifies the most probable scenarios where limited fuel damage might occur, even if ECCS operates as designed.

Observation (a), taken in isolation, supports the use of an *RVFF** based on considerations of core damage consistent with those proposed in current activities for risk-informing 10 CFR Part 50 [SECY-00-0198]. However, Observation (b) identifies a potentially significant uncertainty regarding the margin between PTS-induced RPV failure and large early release, and Observation (c) raises a potential concern regarding defense-in-depth. Therefore, RG 1.174 guidelines on CDF supporting a value for *RVFF** of 1×10^{-5} events/year may not have sufficient justification, whereas the scoping study developed for RG 1.174 guidelines on LERF is more defensible given currently available information. This rationale supports our recommended value of 1×10^{-6} events/year for *RVFF**, which is consistent with the RG 1.174 guidelines on LERF.

When assessing the acceptability of the PTS-associated risk at a given plant, the mean value of the plant's PTS-induced *RVFF* (i.e., the mean *TWCF*) should be compared with *RVFF**. This conclusion is based on how other NRC risk-informed decisions use risk information (e.g., see RG 1.174).

(3) Should additional work be performed to address the key post-RPV failure accident progression uncertainties identified in this study, the following issues are of principal importance:

(a) the likelihood that a PTS-induced axial crack will, upon reaching a circumferential weld, turn and progress along the circumferential weld

(b) the likelihood of PTS-induced containment isolation failure (especially failures associated with failure of containment penetrations) and ECCS failure (especially ECCS piping failures)

(c) the magnitude of potential source terms and consequences associated with PTS events

(d) substantiation of conditional probability values in Table 10.2 and Table 10.3

(e) the impact of external events on PTS-induced LERF

It is anticipated that state-of-knowledge improvements in any of these areas will strengthen this study's conclusions regarding the margin between a PTS-induced RPV failure and consequent large early releases. Although not quantified, several aspects of our analysis performed to support an RVFF* value 1×10^{-6} events/year have a known conservative bias. The following is a summary of a few of these areas identified earlier in this chapter:

- Given the relatively low energy of the fluid following a postulated PTS event, the impulse on the RPV and piping resulting from a blowdown was predicted to be within the bounds of a design-basis SSE. The limited vessel movement from a blowdown forces would be compensated for by the pipe ductility, long runs of piping with many bends, and the hanger and support systems. For these reasons, damage of ECCS piping or containment penetrations is not expected.

- Missile generation attributable to a postulated PTS event would result in an object being directed laterally into the reactor vessel cavity wall by the blowdown forces associated with the breach in the reactor vessel. For a missile to affect the containment spray system or containment penetrations, it would have to traverse a tortuous path through tight clearances of the reactor vessel cavity. The missile's energy would be dissipated by multiple contacts with the reactor cavity wall, as well as the distance it travels, and it would have to hit an extremely small target to render the containment spray system inoperable.

- Through-wall crack frequency is assumed to equal core damage, which is assumed to equal a release. The through-wall cracks may cover a wide spectrum of sizes, from very large to very small. Very small cracks would result in only minor leakage that would not significantly challenge the reactor safety systems.

12.4 A Reference Temperature Based PTS Screening Criteria

In Chapter 11, we proposed the use of different reference temperatures (*RT*) metrics to characterize the resistance of an RPV to fracture initiating from different flaws at different locations in the vessel:

- To characterize the contribution of flaws in **axial welds** to vessel fracture probability, we have proposed two reference temperature metrics: RT_{AW} and RT_{AW-MAX}. RT_{AW-MAX} can be estimated for any plant based solely on the information contained in the NRC's RVID database [RVID], while estimation of RT_{AW} requires information from plant drawings concerning the dimensions and placement of axial welds in the beltline region of the RPV.

- To characterize the contribution of flaws in **plates** to vessel fracture probability, we have proposed two reference temperature metrics: RT_{PL} and RT_{PL-MAX}. RT_{PL-MAX} can be estimated for any plant based solely on the information contained in the NRC's RVID database [RVID], while estimation of RT_{PL} requires information from plant drawings concerning the dimensions and placement of plates in the beltline region of the RPV.

- To characterize the contribution of flaws in **circumferential welds** to vessel fracture probability we have proposed two reference temperature metrics: RT_{CW} and RT_{CW-MAX}. RT_{CW-MAX} can be estimated for any plant based solely on the information contained in the NRC's RVID database [RVID], while estimation of RT_{CW} requires information from plant drawings concerning the dimensions and placement of circumferential welds in the beltline region of the RPV.

These different *RT* values were proposed in recognition of the fact that the probability of vessel fracture starting from different flaw populations varies considerably as a result of factors that are both understood and predictable:

- Different regions of the vessel have flaw populations that differ in size (weld flaws are considerably larger than plate flaws) and orientation (axial and circumferential welds have flaws of corresponding orientations, whereas plate flaws may be either axial or circumferential). The driving force to fracture depends on both flaw size and flaw orientation, so different vessel regions experience different fracture driving forces.

- The degree of irradiation damage suffered by the material at the flaw tips varies with location in the vessel as a result of differences in chemistry and fluence.

Correlations between these *RT*-metrics and the TWCF attributable to axial weld flaws, plate flaws, and circumferential weld flaws showed little plant-to-plant variability as a result of the general similarity of PTS challenge between plants detailed in Chapters 8 and 9 and summarized in Sections 12.2 and 12.3. The following two relationships were developed based on these correlations:

TWCF estimated from weighted RT metrics

$$TWCF_{TOTAL} = TWCF_{AXIAL-WELD} + \alpha_{PL} \cdot TWCF_{PLATE} + TWCF_{CIRC-WELD}$$

where

$$TWCF_{AXIAL-WELD} = 4\text{x}10^{-26} \cdot \exp\{0.0585 \cdot (RT_{AW} + 459.69)\} \text{ (see Eq. 8-1 for } RT_{AW})$$

$$\alpha_{PL} = 1.7, \quad TWCF_{PLATE} = 4\text{x}10^{-29} \cdot \exp\{0.064 \cdot (RT_{PL} + 459.69)\} \text{ (see Eq. 8-2 for } RT_{PL})$$

$$TWCF_{CIRC-WELD} = 3\text{x}10^{-27} \cdot \exp\{0.051 \cdot (RT_{CW} + 459.69)\} \text{ (see Eq. 8-3 for } RT_{CW})$$

TWCF estimated from maximum RT metrics

$$TWCF_{TOTAL} = \alpha_{AW} \cdot TWCF_{AXIAL-WELD} + \alpha_{PL} \cdot TWCF_{PLATE} + TWCF_{CIRC-WELD}$$

where

$$\alpha_{PL} = 1.6, \quad TWCF_{AXIAL-WELD} = 3\text{x}10^{-27} \cdot \exp\{0.0605 \cdot (RT_{MAX-AW} + 459.69)\}$$

$$\alpha_{PL} = 1.7, \quad TWCF_{PLATE} = 9\text{x}10^{-27} \cdot \exp\{0.0543 \cdot (RT_{MAX-PL} + 459.69)\}$$

$$TWCF_{CIRC-WELD} = 4\text{x}10^{-29} \cdot \exp\{0.0561 \cdot (RT_{MAX-CW} + 459.69)\}$$

(see Eq. 8-1, Eq. 8-2, and Eq. 8-3 for the definitions of RT_{MAX-AW}, RT_{MAX-PL}, and RT_{MAX-CW}, respectively)

In these relationships, all temperatures are in °F. *RT*-based screening limits were established by setting the total TWCF in these equations equal to the reactor vessel failure frequency acceptance criterion of $1\text{x}10^{-6}$ events per year proposed in Chapter 10. Two different *RT*-based screening limits were developed from each of the above relationships: one for plate welded vessels based on axial weld and plate properties (the contribution of circumferential welds at realistic embrittlement levels is so small that it can be neglected), and one for forged vessels based on circumferential weld and plate properties (there are no axial welds in these vessels so their contribution to TWCF is, by definition, zero). Figure 12-1 provides graphical representations of these screening criteria along with an assessment of all operating PWRs relative to limits based on the maximum *RT* embrittlement metrics[§§§§§§]. In these figures,

the region of the graph between the red locus and the origin has TWCF values below the $1\text{x}10^{-6}$ acceptance criterion, so these combinations of reference temperatures would be considered acceptable and require no further analysis. In the region of the graph outside of the red locus, the TWCF is above the $1\text{x}10^{-6}$ acceptance criterion, indicating the need for additional analysis or other measures to justify continued plant operation.

To compare the condition of currently operating PWRs with this proposed screening limit, we used the information in the RVID database [RVID2] to estimate values of RT_{MAX-AW}, RT_{MAX-PL}, and RT_{MAX-CW} for each operating PWR. At EOL, at least 70°F (21°C) and up to 290°F (143°C) separate operating PWRs from the proposed screening limit; these values reduce by between 10 and 20°F (5.5 to 11°C) at EOLE. Even at EOLE, no plate-welded PWR is projected to exceed an annual TWCF of $1\text{x}10^{-7}$ (again, most plants have projected TWCFs far below this value, see Figure 11-8). Additionally, no forged plant is anywhere close to the limit of $1\text{x}10^{-6}$ events per year at either EOL or EOLE. This separation of operating plants from the proposed

---

[§§§§§§] Maximum *RT* embrittlement metrics are used in these comparisons because these metrics can be estimated based only on the information in RVID. In principal PTS limits based on weighted *RT* embrittlement metrics should provide a somewhat more accurate estimate of plant risk.

screening limits can be compared with the current situation where the most embrittled plants are within 1°F of the 10 CFR 50.61 screening limit. As noted in Sections 9.2.2.2 and 9.2.2.3, these *RT*-based screening limits apply to PWRs in general subject to the following three provisos:

- When assessing a forged vessel where the forging has a very high reference temperature (RT_{PL} above 225°F (107°C)) *and* the forging is believed to be susceptible to subclad cracking, a plant-specific analysis of the TWCF produced by the subclad cracks should be performed. However, no forging is projected to reach this level of embrittlement, even at EOLE.

- When assessing an RPV having a wall thickness of 7-in. (18-cm) or less (7 vessels), the proposed *RT* limits are conservative.

- When assessing an RPV having a wall thickness of 11-in. (28-cm) or greater, the proposed *RT* limits may be nonconservative. For the three plants meeting this criterion, either the *RT* limits would need to be reduced or known conservatisms in the current analysis would have to be removed to demonstrate compliance with the TWCF limit of 1×10^{-6} event/year.

Aside from relying on different *RT* metrics than 10 CFR 50.61, the proposed revision to the PTS screening limit differs from that used currently in the absence of a "margin term." Use of a margin term is appropriate to account (at least approximately) for factors that occur in application that were not considered in the analysis upon which the screening limit is based. For example, the 10 CFR 50.61 margin term accounts for uncertainty in copper, in nickel, and in initial RT_{NDT}. However, our model considers explicitly uncertainty in all of these variables, and represents these uncertainties as being larger (a conservative representation) than would be appropriate in any plant-specific application of the proposed screening limit. Consequently, use of the 10 CFR 50.61 margin term with the new screening limits is inappropriate. In general, the following additional reasons suggest that use of

any margin term with the proposed screening limits is inappropriate:

(1) The *TWCF* values used to establish the screening limit represent 90th percentile values or greater (see Figure 8-3).

(2) Chapter 8 and Chapter 9 demonstrate that the results from our three plant-specific analyses apply to PWRs in general.

(3) Certain aspects of our modeling cannot be reasonably represented as "best estimates." On balance, there is a conservative bias to these non-best estimate aspects of our analysis. Residual conservatisms and nonconservatisms in our model are as follows:

Conservatisms

(a) The assumption that all vessel failures lead to LERF, when in fact many would lead only to core damage.

(b) The assumption that once initiated all circumferential cracks instantly propagate 360° around the vessel ID. In reality, crack length is limited because the azimuthal fluence variation places strips of tougher material in the path of the extending crack.

(c) The assumption that once initiated, an axial crack will instantly propagate to infinite length. In reality, crack length is finite and limited to the length of a single shell course because axial cracks most likely arrest when they encounter higher toughness materials in either the adjacent circumferential welds or plates.

(d) The systematically conservative judgments made when placing potential PTS initiators into bins.

(e) The systematic underestimation of the minimum temperature associated with secondary side breaks (MSLBs) because the pressurization of containment (attributable to steam escaping from the break) is not modeled.

(f) The attenuation of neutron damage by steel in the vessel wall is assumed to be less than that measured in experiments.

(g) The distributions used to represent the statistical uncertainty in unirradiated transition temperature and chemical composition variables contain more uncertainty than could ever occur in a given weld, plate, or forging.

(h) The systematic modeling overestimation in the uncertainty in used to correct for the mean bias in the RT_{NDT} index temperature.

(i) The production of systematically higher TWCF values by the model used to estimate the increase in RT_{NDT} index temperature caused by irradiation damage (compared to those estimated by the model adopted by ASTM).

(j) The flaw model assumption that all defects are planar (when many are actually volumetric), as well as the use of systematically conservative judgments when developing the flaw

model (in the absence of definitive evidence).

(k) Use of the most conservative available extrapolation schemes when the effects of irradiation damage were extrapolated forward in time.

Nonconservatisms

(a) The fact that the small potential for air oxidation has been ignored.

(b) The fact that the small possibility of external events (e.g., fire) initiating PTS has been ignored.

(c) The assumption that the mean level of copper can change four times through the vessel wall thickness, consistent with measurements made on thick-section RPV welds. (If copper layering is not present, the TWCF would actually increase slightly.)

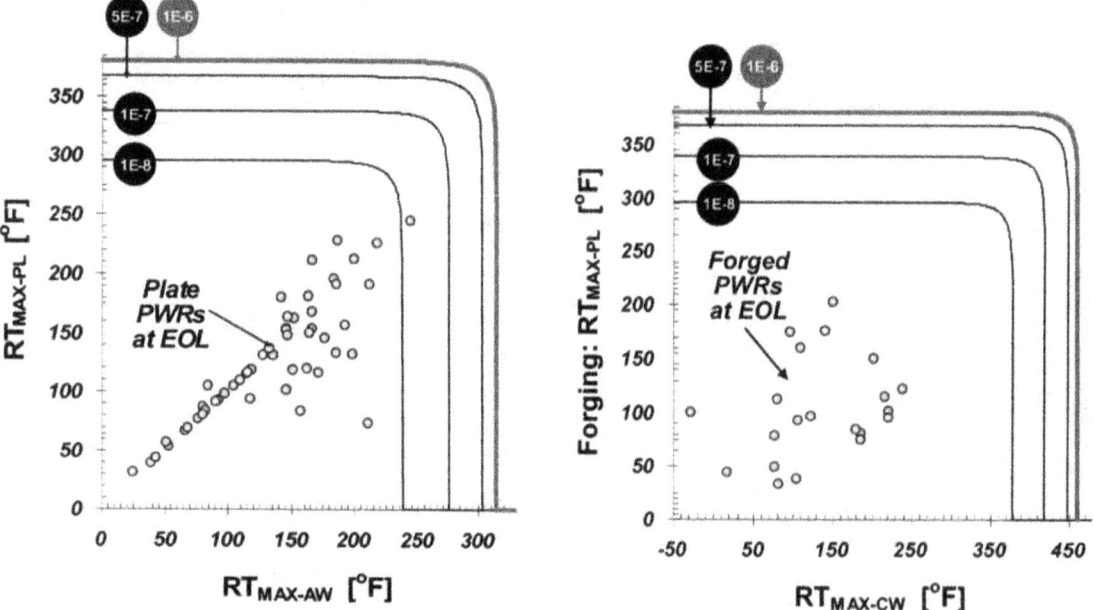

Figure 12-1. Comparison of *RT*-based screening limit (curves) with assessment points for operating PWRs at EOL in plate vessels (left) and forged vessels (right)

12.5   Considerations for Rulemaking

The calculations reported herein demonstrate
that PTS events are associated with an extremely
small risk of vessel failure, suggesting the
existence of considerable safety margin in the
current PTS Rule. The magnitude of this margin
appears to justify consideration of rulemaking.
Should rulemaking proceed, it appears feasible
to use improved (i.e., more risk-informed)
metrics to represent RPV embrittlement. The
metrics proposed herein reflect the principal
contributors to PTS-induced RPV failure.
A numeric value can be established for an
RT-based screening limit based on the
information provided herein, as well as
considerations of risk in current NRC guidance
and other non-PTS-related risk-informed
regulatory activities.

While numerous factors should be addressed in
any revision of 10 CFR 50.61, our research
shows that a significant increase in the PTS
screening limit can be justified. Such a change
could be implemented without imposing
on licensees either new material testing
requirements or new inspection programs.

13 References

13.1 Citations Summarized by this Report

The following three sections provide the citations that are summarized by this report (see also Figure 4-1). Taken together, these documents provide complete documentation of the NRC's PTS reevaluation project. When these reports are cited in the text, the citations appear in *italicized boldface* to distinguish them from the related literature citations.

13.1.1 Probabilistic Risk Assessment

Kolaczkowski-Oco   Kolaczkowski, A.M., et al., "Oconee Pressurized Thermal Shock (PTS) Probabilistic Risk Assessment (PRA)," 9-28-2004, available in the NRC's Agencywide Documents Access and Management System (ADAMS) under Accession #ML042880452.

Kolaczkowski-Ext   Kolaczkowski, A. et al., "Estimate of External Events Contribution to Pressurized Thermal Shock (PTS) Risk," Letter Report, 10-1-2004, available in ADAMS under Accession #ML042880476.

Siu 99   Sui, N., "Uncertainty Analysis and Pressurized Thermal Shock: An Opinion," U.S. Nuclear Regulatory Commission, 1999, available in ADAMS under Accession #ML992710066.

Whitehead-PRA   Whitehead, D.L. and A.M. Kolaczkowski, "PRA Procedures and Uncertainty for PTS Analysis," NUREG/CR-6859, U.S. Nuclear Regulatory Commission, 12-31-2004.

Whitehead-BV   Whitehead, D.L., et al., "Beaver Valley Pressurized Thermal Shock (PTS) Probabilistic Risk Assessment (PRA)," 9-28-2004, available in ADAMS under Accession #ML042880454.

Whitehead-Gen   Whitehead, D.W., et al., "Generalization of Plant-Specific Pressurized Thermal Shock (PTS) Risk Results to Additional Plants," 10-14-2004, available in ADAMS under Accession #ML042880482.

Whitehead-Pal   Whitehead, D.L., et al., "Palisades Pressurized Thermal Shock (PTS) Probabilistic Risk Assessment (PRA)," 10-6-2004, available in ADAMS under Accession #ML042880473.

13.1.2 Thermal-Hydraulics

Arcieri-Base   Arcieri, W.C., R.M. Beaton, C.D. Fletcher, and D.E. Bessette, "RELAP5 Thermal-Hydraulic Analysis to Support PTS Evaluations for the Oconee-1, Beaver Valley-1, and Pallisades Nuclear Power Plants," NUREG/CR-6858, U.S. Nuclear Regulatory Commission, 9-30-2004.

Arcieri-SS	Arcieri, W.C., et al., "RELAP5/MOD3.2.2Gamma Results for Palisades 1D Downcomer Sensitivity Study," August 31, 2004, available in ADAMS under Accession #ML061170401.
Bessette	Bessette, D.E., "Thermal-Hydraulic Evaluations of Pressurized Thermal Shock," NUREG-1809, U.S. Nuclear Regulatory Commission, 5-30-2005.
Chang	Chang, Y.H., K. Almenas, A. Mosleh, and M. Pour-Gol, "Thermal-Hydraulic Uncertainty Analysis in Pressurized Thermal Shock Risk Assessment: Methodology and Implementation on Oconee-1, Beaver Valley, and Palisades Nuclear Power Plants," NUREG/CR-6899, U.S. Nuclear Regulatory Commission.
Fletcher	Fletcher, C.D., D.A. Prelewicz, and W.C., Arcieri, "RELAP5/MOD3.2.2γ Assessment for Pressurized Thermal Shock Applications," NUREG/CR-6857, U.S. Nuclear Regulatory Commission, 9-30-2004.
Junge	"PTS Consistency Effort," Staff Letter Report to file, 10-1-2004, available in ADAMS under Accession #ML042880480.
Reyes-APEX	Reyes, J.N., et al., "Final Report for the OSU APEX-CE Integral Test Facility," NUREG/CR-6856, U.S. Nuclear Regulatory Commission, 12-16-2004.
Reyes-Scale	Reyes, J.N., et al., "Scaling Analysis for the OSU APEX-CE Integral Test Facility," NUREG/CR-6731, U.S. Nuclear Regulatory Commission, 11-30-2004.

13.1.3 Probabilistic Fracture Mechanics

Dickson-Base	Dickson, T.L., and S. Yin, "Electronic Archival of the Results of Pressurized Thermal Shock Analyses for Beaver Valley, Oconee, and Palisades Reactor Pressure Vessels Generated with the 04.1 Version of FAVOR," ORNL/NRC/LTR-04/18, 10-15-2004, available in ADAMS under Accession #ML042960391
Dickson-UG	Dickson, T.L., and P.T.Williams, "Fracture Analysis of Vessels Oak Ridge, FAVOR v04.1, Computer Code: User's Guide," NUREG/CR-6855, U.S. Nuclear Regulatory Commission, 10-21-2004.
EricksonKirk-PFM	EricksonKirk, M.T., "Probabilistic Fracture Mechanics: Models, Parameters, and Uncertainty Treatment Used in FAVOR Version 04.1," NUREG-1807, U.S. Nuclear Regulatory Commission, 1-26-2005.
EricksonKirk-SS	EricksonKirk, M.T., et al., "Sensitivity Studies of the Probabilistic Fracture Mechanics Model Used in FAVOR Version 03.1," NUREG-1808, U.S. Nuclear Regulatory Commission, 11-30-2004.
Kirk 12-02	EricksonKirk, M.T., "Technical Basis for Revision of the Pressurized Thermal Shock (PTS) Screening Limit in the PTS Rule (10 CFR 50.61)," December 2002, available in ADAMS under Accession #ML030090626.

Malik	Malik, S.N.M., "FAVOR Code Versions 2.4 and 3.1: Verification and Validation Summary Report," NUREG-1795, U.S. Nuclear Regulatory Commission, 10-31-2004.
Simonen	F.A. Simonen, S.R. Doctor, G.J. Schuster, and P.G. Heasler, "A Generalized Procedure for Generating Flaw Related Inputs for the FAVOR Code," NUREG/CR-6817, Rev. 1, U.S. Nuclear Regulatory Commission, October 2003, available in ADAMS under Accession #ML051790410.
Williams	Williams, P.T., and T.L. Dickson, "Fracture Analysis of Vessels Oak Ridge, FAVOR v04.1: Computer Code: Theory and Implementation of Algorithms, Methods, and Correlations," NUREG/CR-6854, U.S. Nuclear Regulatory Commission, 10-21-2004.

13.2   Literature Citations

10 CFR 50.61	Title 10, Section 50.61, of the *Code of Federal Regulations*, "Fracture Toughness Requirements for Protection Against Pressurized Thermal Shock Events," promulgated June 26, 1984.
10 CFR Part 50 App. H.	Appendix H to Title 10, Part 50, of the *Code of Federal Regulations*, "Reactor Vessel Material Surveillance Program Requirements."
ASME NB2331	ASME NB-2331, 1998 ASME Boiler and Pressure Vessel Code, Rules for Construction of Nuclear Power Plants, Division 1, Subsection NB, Class 1 Components, American Society of Mechanical Engineers.
ASTM E23	ASTM E23, "Standard Test Methods for Notched Bar Impact Testing of Metallic Materials," American Society for Testing and Materials, 1998.
ASTM E185	ASTM E185-94, "Standard Practice for Conducting Surveillance Tests for Light-Water Cooled Nuclear Power Reactor Vessels," American Society for Testing and Materials, 1998.
ASTM E208	ASTM E208, "Standard Test Method for Conducting Drop-Weight Test to Determine Nil-Ductility Transition Temperature of Ferritic Steels," American Society for Testing and Materials, 1998.
ASTM E399	ASTM E399, "Test Method for Plane-Strain Fracture Toughness Testing of Metallic Materials," American Society for Testing and Materials, 1998.
ASTM E900	ASTM E900-02, "Standard Guide for Predicting Radiation-Induced Transition Temperature Shift in Reactor Vessel Materials, E706 (IIF)," American Society for Testing and Materials, 2002.
ASTM E1221	ASTM E1221-96, "Standard Test Method for Plane-Strain Crack-Arrest Fracture Toughness, K_{Ia}, of Ferritic Steels," American Society for Testing and Materials, 1996.
ASTM E1921	ASTM E1921-02, "Test Method for Determination of Reference Temperature, T_o, for Ferritic Steels in the Transition Range," American Society for Testing and Materials, 2002.
Apostolakis 02	Apostakolis, G.E.., Chairman, Advisory Committee on Reactor Safeguards (ACRS), U.S. Nuclear Regulatory Commission, "Risk Metrics and Criteria

for Reevaluating the Technical Basis of the Pressurized Thermal Shock Rule," ADAMS ML0220406120, July 18, 2002.

Bass 04   Bass, B.R., et al., "Experimental Program for Investigating the Influence of Cladding Defects on Burst Pressure," ORNL/NRC/LTR-04/13, NRC Adams Number ML042660206, 2004.

Bonaca 03   Bonaca, M.V., Chairman, Advisory Committee on Reactor Safeguards (ACRS), U.S. Nuclear Regulatory Commission, "Pressurized Thermal Shock (PTS) Reevaluation Project: Technical Bases for Potential Revision to PTS Screening Criteria," February 21, 2003.

Brothers 63   Brothers, A.J., and S. Yukawa, "The Effect of Warm Prestressing on Notch Fracture Strength," *Journal of Basic Engineering,* March 1963, p. 97.

Charpy   Charpy, M.G., "Note sur l'Essai des Metaux à la Flexion par Choc de Barreaux Entailles," *Soc. Ing. Francais,* June 1901, p. 848.

Cheverton 85a   Cheverton, R.D., et al., "Pressure Vessel Fracture Studies Pertaining to the PWR Thermal-Shock Issue: Experiments TSE-5, TSE-5A, and TSE-6," NUREG/CR-4249 (ORNL-6163), Oak Ridge National Laboratory, June 1985.

Cheverton 85b   Cheverton, R.D., et al., Pressure Vessel Fracture Studies Pertaining to the PWR Thermal-Shock Issue: Experiment TSE-7," NUREG/CR-4303 (ORNL-6177), Oak Ridge National Laboratory, August 1985.

Chopra 06   Chopra, O.K., et al., "Crack Growth Rates of Irradiated Austenitic Stainless Steel Weld Heat Affected Zone in BWR Environments," NUREG/CR-6891, U.S. Nuclear Regulatory Commission, January 2006.

Congleton 85   Congleton, J., T. Shoji, and R.N. Parkins, "The Stress Corrosion Cracking of Reactor Pressure Vessel Steel in High-Temperature Water" *Corrosion Science,* Vol. 25, No. 8/9: 1985.

CSAU   Boyack, B., et al., "Quantifying Reactor Safety Margins – Application of Code Scaling, Applicability, and Uncertainty Evaluation Methodology to a Large-Break Loss of Coolant Accident," NUREG/CR-5249, U.S. Nuclear Regulatory Commission, December 1989.

Dhooge 78   A. Dhooge, R.E. Dolby, J. Sebille, R. Steinmetz, and A.G. Vinckier, "A Review of Work Related to Reheat Cracking in Nuclear Reactor Pressure Vessel Steels," *International Journal of Pressure Vessels and Piping,* Vol. 6, 1978, pp.329–409.

Dickson 87   Dickson, T.L., "Sensitivity of Probabilistic Fracture Mechanics Analysis Results to Thermal-Hydraulic Variations," March 24, 1987.

Dickson 99   Dickson, T.L., et al., "Evaluation of Margins in the ASME Rules for Defining the P-T Curve for an RPV," *Proceedings of the ASME Pressure Vessel and Piping Conference,* 1999.

Dickson 02   Dickson, T.L. and Simonen, F.A., "The Impact of an Improved Flaw Model on Pressurized Thermal Shick Evaluation," *Proceedings of the ASME Pressure Vessel and Piping Conference,* Vancouver, British Columbia, 2002.

Dickson 03   Dickson, T.L. and Simonen, F.A., "The Sensitivity of Pressurized Thermal Shock Results to Alternative Models for Weld Flaw Distributions,"

	Proceedings of the ASME Pressure Vessel and Piping Conference, Cleveland, Ohio, 2002.
Dickson 03b	Bass, B.R., T.L. Dickson, P.T. Williams, A.-V. Phan, and K.L. Kruse, "Verification and Validation of the FAVOR Code: Deterministic Load Variables," Oak Ridge National Laboratory Report, ORNL/NRC/LTR-04/11, March 2004.
Eason	Eason, E., et al., "Updated Embrittlement Trend Curve for Reactor Pressure Vessel Steels," *Transactions of the 17th International Conference on Structural Mechanics in Reactor Technology (SMiRT 17)*, Prague, Czech Republic, August 17–22, 2003.
English 02	English, C., and W. Server, "Attenuation in US RPV Steels – MRP-56," Electric Power Research Institute, June 2002.
EPRI 94	EPRI Report TR-103837, "PWR Reactor Pressure Vessel License Renewal Industry Report, Revision 1," Electric Power Research Institute, July 1994
EricksonKirk 04	EricksonKirk, MarjorieAnn, "*Materials Reliability Program: Implementation Strategy for Master Curve Reference Temperature, T_o (MRP-101),*" EPRI, Palo Alto, CA, and U.S. Department of Energy, Washington, DC: 2004. 1009543.
Fang 03	Fang T., and M. Modarres, "Probabilistic and Deterministic Treatments for Multiple Flaws in Reactor Pressure Vessel Safety Analysis," *Transactions of the 17th International Conference on Structural Mechanics in Reactor Technology (SMiRT 17)*, August 17–22, 2003, Prague, Czech Republic.
Fletcher 84	Fletcher, C. D., et. al., RELAP5 Thermal-Hydraulic Analyses of Pressurized Thermal Shock Sequences for the Oconee-1 Pressurized-Water Reactor, NUREG/CR-3761, June 1984.
GL9201R1	Generic Letter 92-01 Revision 1, "Reactor Vessel Structural Integrity, 10 CFR 50.54(f)," U.S. Nuclear Regulatory Commission, 1992.
GL9201R1S1	Generic Letter 92-01 Revision 1, "Reactor Vessel Structural Integrity," U.S. Nuclear Regulatory Commission, May 19, 1995.
Hanson 94	A.L. Hanson et al., "Calculations in Support of a Potential Definition of Large Release," NUREG/CR-6094, U.S. Nuclear Regulatory Commission, May 1994.
Hurst 85	Hurst, P., D.A. Appleton, P. Banks, and A.S. Raffel. "Slow Strain Rate Stress Corrosion Tests on A508-III and A533B Steel in De-Ionized and PWR Water at 563K" *Corrosion Science*, Vol. 25, No. 8/9: 1985.
IAEA 90	"Stress Corrosion Cracking of Pressure Vessel Steel in PWR Primary Water Environments." *Proceedings of the Third International Atomic Energy Agency Specialists' Meeting on Subcritical Crack Growth*, U.S. Nuclear Regulatory Commission (NRC), Moscow, 14–17 May 1990.
INEEL 00a	INEEL staff review of LERs for the Oconee PTS analysis conducted during March–April, 2000, based on keywords "overcooling," "thermal shock," and "excessive cooling." This includes a draft letter report, "Human Performance Insights for Overcooling Events in Support of PTS," D. Gertman and M. Parrish, INEEL, March 7, 2000.

Kasza 96	Kasza, K.E., et al., "Nuclear Plant Generic Aging Lessons Learned (GALL)," NUREG/CR-6490, U.S. Nuclear Regulatory Commission, October 1996.
Khaleel 00	Khaleel, M.A., et al., "Fatigue Analysis of Components for 60-Year Plant Life," NUREG/CR-6674, U.S. Nuclear Regulatory Commission, June 2000.
Kirk 01a	Kirk, M.T., M.E. Natishan, and M. Wagenhofer, "Microstructural Limits of Applicability of the Master Curve," 32nd Volume, ASTM STP-1406, R. Chona, Ed., American Society for Testing and Materials, 2001.
Kirk 01b	Kirk, M., and M.E. Natishan, "Shift in Toughness Transition Temperature Due to Irradiation: ΔT_o vs. ΔT_{41J}, A Comparison and Rationalization of Differences," Proceedings of the IAEA Specialists Meeting on Master Curve Technology, Prague, Chech Republic, September 2001
Kirk 02a	Kirk, M. T., M.E. Natishan, and M. Wagenhofer, M., "A Physics-Based Model for the Crack Arrest Toughness of Ferritic Steels," Fatigue and Fracture Mechanics, 33rd Volume, ASTM STP-1417, W.G. Reuter and R.S. Piascik, Eds., American Society for Testing and Materials, 2002.
LER 92-023	Fort Calhoun Station, Docket No. 50-285, Licensee Event Report 92-023, submitted via letter from Omaha Public Power District to the USNRC on August 3, 1992.
LER 92-028	Fort Calhoun Station, Docket No. 50-285, Licensee Event Report 92-028, submitted via letter from Omaha Public Power District to the USNRC on September 21, 1992.
Marshall 82	"An Assessment of the Integrity of PWR Vessels," 2nd report by a study group under the chairmanship of D.W. Marshall, United Kingdom Atomic Eenergy Authority, 1982.
Meyer 03	Meyer, T., B. Bishop, P. Kotwicki, and N. Palm, "Materials Reliability Program: Pressurized Thermal Shock Sensitivity Studies Using the FAVOR Code (MRP-96)," Electric Power Research Institute, November 2003.
Natishan 01	Natishan, M.E.N., Materials Reliability Program (MRP) Establishing a Physically Based, Predictive Model for Fracture Toughness Transition Behavior of Ferritic Steels (MRP-53), Electric Power Research Institute, 2001. 1003077.
NEI Comments	NEI Letter, dated June 23, 2003, from A. Marion to N. Chokshi. "Review of NRC Draft Report entitled Technical Basis for Revision of the Pressurized Thermal Shock (PTS) Screening Limit in the PTS Rule (10 CFR 50.61)."
NRC FR 86	51 FR 28044, August 4, 1986, and 51 FR 30028, August 21, 1986 (republication of 51 FR 28044 in its entirety at the Commission's request), "Safety Goals for the Operations of Nuclear Power Plants: Policy Statement."
NRC MEMO 82	Memorandum dated August 30 1982 from M. Vagans to S. Hanauer (DST/NRR).
NRC MTEB 5.2	METB 5-2, Branch Technical Position, "Fracture Toughness Requirements," Rev. 1, U.S. Nuclear Regulatory Commission, July 1981.

NRC 90   SRM - SECY-00-0077, STAFF REQUIREMENTS - SECY-00-0077 - "Modifications to the Reactor Safety Goal Policy Statement," U.S. Nuclear Regulatory Commission, June 27, 2000.

NRC 98b   NUREG-0800 (SRP Ch. 19), "Standard Review Plan for the Review of Safety Analysis Reports for Nuclear Power Plants," Chapter 19, Severe Accidents, U.S. Nuclear Regulatory Commission.

NRC 00   U.S. Nuclear Regulatory Commission, Technical Basis and Implementation Guidelines for A Technique for Human Event Analysis (ATHEANA), NUREG-1624, Rev. 1, U.S. Nuclear Regulatory Commission, May 2000.

NRC-IR   Inspection Report 50-285/92-18, U.S. Nuclear Regulatory Commission, August 6, 1992.

NRR Comments   Comments on [Kirk 12-02] provided from NRR to RES, March 2003.

NUREG/BR-0167   "Software Quality Assurance Program and Guidelines," Office of Information Resources Management, U.S. Nuclear Regulatory Commission, February 1993.

ORNL 85a   Oak Ridge National Laboratory, Pressurized Thermal Shock Evaluation of the Calvert Cliffs Unit 1 Nuclear Power Plant, NUREG/CR-4022, ORNL/TM-9408, for the U.S. Nuclear Regulatory Commission, September 1985.

ORNL 85b   Oak Ridge National Laboratory, Pressurized Thermal Shock Evaluation of the H.B. Robinson Unit 2 Nuclear Power Plant, NUREG/CR-4183, ORNL/TM-9567, for the U.S. Nuclear Regulatory Commission, September 1985.

ORNL 86   Oak Ridge National Laboratory, "Preliminary Development of an Integrated Approach to the Evaluation of Pressurized Thermal Shock as Applied to the Oconee Unit 1 Nuclear Power Plant, NUREG/CR-3770, ORNL/TM-9176, for the U.S. Nuclear Regulatory Commission, May 1986.

Poloski 98   J.P. Poloski et al., "Reliability Study: Auxiliary/Emergency Feedwater Systems, 1987–1995," NUREG/CR-5500, U.S. Nuclear Regulatory Commission, August 1998.

Poloski 99   Poloski, J.P., Marksberry, D.G., Atwood, C.L., and Galyean, W.J., "Rates of Initiating Events at U.S. Nuclear Power Plants: 1987-1995," NUREG/CR-5750, February 1999.

Pratt 99   Pratt W.T., et al., "An Approach for Estimating the Frequencies of Various Containment Failure Modes and Bypass Events," NUREG/CR-6595, U.S. Nuclear Regulatory Commission, October 2004.

PREP   "PREP4: Power Reactor Embrittlement Program, Version 1.0," Electric Power Research Institute, 1996. SW-106276.

PRODIGAL   Chapman, O.V.J., and F.A. Simonen, "RR-PRODIGAL – A Model for Estimating Probabilities of Defects in Welds," NUREG/CR-5505, U.S. Nuclear Regulatory Commission, October 1998.

Randall 87   Randall, P.N., "Basis for Revision 2 of the USNRC Reg. Guide 1.99, Radiation Embrittlement in Nuclear Pressure Vessel Steels: An International Review (2nd Volume)," ASTM STP-909, L.E. Steele, Ed., 1987.

RELAP 99	RELAP5/MOD3 Code Manual, Volume IV: Models and Correlations, June 1999.
RELAP 01	RELAP5/MOD3.3 Code Manual – Vol III: Developmental Assessment Problems, December 2001
RG 1.162	Regulatory Guide 1.162, "Thermal Annealing of Reactor Pressure Vessel Steels," U.S. Nuclear Regulatory Commission, February 1996.
RG 1.154	Regulatory Guide 1.154, "An Approach for Using Probabilistic Risk Assessment in Risk-Informed Decisions on Plant-Specific Changes to the Licensing Basis," U.S. Nuclear Regulatory Commission, January 1987.
RG 1.174 Rev 1	Regulatory Guide 1.174, Revision 1 "Format and Content of Plant-Specific Pressurized Thermal Shock Safety Analysis Reports for Pressurized-Water Reactors," U.S. Nuclear Regulatory Commission, November 2002.
RG 1.190	Regulatory Guide 1.190, "Calculational and Dosimetry Methods for Determining Pressure Vessel Neutron Fluence," U.S. Nuclear Regulatory Commission, March 2001.
RG 1.99	Regulatory Guide 1.99, Rev. 2, "Radiation Embrittlement of Reactor Vessel Materials," U.S. Nuclear Regulatory Commission, May 1988.
Rolfe	Rolfe, S.T., and J.T. Barson, *Fracture and Fatigue Control in Structures: Applicatins of Fracture Mechanics, Second Edition*, Prentice-Hall, 1987.
Rippstein 89	Rippstein, K., and H. Kaesche. "The Stress Corrosion Cracking of a Reactor Pressure Vessel Steel in High-Temperature Water at High Flow Rates," *Corrosion Science*, Vol. 29, No. 5: 1989
Ruther 84	Ruther, W.E., W.K. Soppet, and T.F. Kassner, "Evaluation of Environmental Corrective Actions," *Materials Science and Technology Division Light-Water-Reactor Safety Research Program: Quarterly Progress Report, October–December 1983*, NUREG/CR-3689, Vol. IV, ANL-83-85, Argonne National Laboratory, for the U.S. Nuclear Regulatory Commission, August 1984.
RVID2	Reactor Vessel Integrity Database, Version 2.1.1, U.S. Nuclear Regulatory Commission, July 6, 2000.
SAPHIRE	Systems Analysis Programs for Hands-on Integrated Reliability Evaluations (SAPHIRE) Version 7.0, Idaho National Engineering and Environmental Laboratory.
SECY-82-465	SECY-82-465, "Pressurized Thermal Shock," U.S. Nuclear Regulatory Commission, November 23, 1982.
SECY-93-138	SECY-93-138, "Recommendation on Large Release Definition," U.S. Nuclear Regulatory Commission, June 10, 1993.
SECY-00-0198	SECY-00-0198, "Status Report on Study of Risk-Informed Changes to the Technical Requirements of 10 CFR Part 50 (Option 3) and Recommendations on Risk-Informed Changes to 10 CFR 50.44 (Combustible Gas Control)," U.S. Nuclear Regulatory Commission, September 14, 2000.
SECY-02-0092	SECY-02-0092, "Status Report: Risk Metrics and Criteria for Pressurized Thermal Shock," U.S. Nuclear Regulatory Commission, May 30, 2002.

Schuster 02   Schuster, G.J., "Technical Letter Report – JCN-Y6604 – Validated Flaw Density and Distribution Within Reactor Pressure Vessel Base Metal Forged Rings," Pacific Northwest National Laboratory, for U.S. Nuclear Regulatory Commission, December 20, 2002.

Shaw 88   Shaw, R.A., et al., "Development of a Phenonmena Identificatioin and Ranking Table (PIRT) for Thermal-Hydraulic Phenomena During a PWR LBLOCA," NUREG/CR-5074, August 1988.

Simonen 86   Simonen, F.A., et al., "Reactor Pressure Vessel Failure Probability Following Through-Wall Cracks Due to Pressurized Thermal Shock Events," NUREG/CR-4483, U.S. Nuclear Regulatory Commission, March 1986.

Spiggs 85   Spriggs, G.D., Koenig, J. E., Smith, R.C., "TRAC-PF1 Analyses of Potential Pressurized Thermal Shock Transients at Calvert Cliffs Unit 1,". NUREG/CR-4109, February 1985

Strosnider 94   Strosnider, J., et al., "Reactor Pressure Vessel Status Report," NUREG-1511, U.S. Nuclear Regulatory Commission, 1994.

Swanson 87   Swanson, L.W., and I. Catton, "PWR Annulus Thermal-Hydraulics Important to Analysis of Pressurized Thermal Shock," *Nuclear Engineering and Design*, 102, 105–114, 1987

Theofanous 01   Theofanous, T.G., Dinh, A.T., Yuen, W.W., Nourgaliev, R.R., Dinh, T.N., "Consequences of Postulated PTS-Induced Brittle Failure of a Pressurized Water Reactor Vessel," University of California, Santa Barbara, CRSS-SA-01/4, April 5, 2001.

Travers 03   Travers, W.D., "Pressurized Thermal Shock (PTS) Reevaluation Project: Technical Bases for Potential Revision to PTS Screening Criteria," U.S. Nuclear Regulatory Commission, March 28, 2003.

Tregoning 05   Tregoning, R., Abramson, L., and Scott, P., "Estimating Loss-of-Coolant Accident (LOCA) Frequencies through the Elicitation Process," United States Nuclear Regulatory Commission, NUREG-1829, 2005.

Wagenhofer 01   Wagenhofer, M., and M.E. Natishan, "A Micromechanical Model for Predicting Fracture Toughness of Steels in the Transition Region," *33rd Volume, ASTM STP-1417*, Reuter and Piascik, Eds., American Society for Testing and Materials, 2002.

Wallin 93a   Wallin, K., "Irradiation Damage Effects on the Fracture Toughness Transition Curve Shape for Reactor Vessel Steels," *Int. J. Pres. Ves. & Piping*, 55, pp. 61–79, 1993.

Wallin 98b   Wallin, K., and R. Rintamaa, "Master Curve Based Correlation Between Static Initiation Toughness K_{Ic} and Crack Arrest Toughness K_{Ia}," *Proceedings of the 24th MPA-Seminar,* Stuttgart, October 8–9, 1998.

Westinghouse 99   "WOG Pilot-Plant Application of the EPRI Alternative Method for Reactor Vessel PTS," WCAP-15156, Westinghouse Electric Company, LLC, Nuclear Services Division, June 1999.

WRC 175   "PVRC Recommendations on Toughness Requirements for Ferritic Materials." Welding Research Council Bulletin No. 175, PVRC Ad Hoc Group on Toughness Requirements, August 1972.

Woods 01   Woods, R., N. Siu, A. Kolaczkowski, and W. Galyean, "Selection of Pressurized Thermal Shock Transients To Include in PTS Risk Analysis," *IJPVP*, 78 (2001) 179–183.

Zuber 89   Zuber, N. et al., "Quantifying Reactor Safety Margins, NUREG/CR-5249," December 1989.

NRC FORM 335
(9-2004)
NRCMD 3.7

U.S. NUCLEAR REGULATORY COMMISSION

1. REPORT NUMBER
(Assigned by NRC, Add Vol., Supp., Rev., and Addendum Numbers, if any.)

BIBLIOGRAPHIC DATA SHEET
(See instructions on the reverse)

NUREG-1806, Vol.1

2. TITLE AND SUBTITLE

Technical Basis for Revision of the Pressurized Thermal Shock (PTS) Screening Limit in the PTS Rule (10 CFR 50.61): Summary Report

3. DATE REPORT PUBLISHED

MONTH	YEAR
August	2007

4. FIN OR GRANT NUMBER

5. AUTHOR(S)

Mark EricksonKirk, Mike Junge, William Arcieri, B. Richard Bass, Robert Beaton, David Bessette, T.H.(James) Chang, Terry Dickson, C. Don Fletcher, Alan Kolaczkowski, Shah Malik, Todd Mintz, Claud Pugh, Fredric Simonen, Nathan Siu, Donnie Whitehead, Paul Williams, Roy Woods, Sean Yin

6. TYPE OF REPORT

Technical

7. PERIOD COVERED *(Inclusive Dates)*

6-99 to 6-06

8. PERFORMING ORGANIZATION - NAME AND ADDRESS *(If NRC, provide Division, Office or Region, U.S. Nuclear Regulatory Commission, and mailing address; if contractor, provide name and mailing address.)*

Division of Fuel, Engineering, and Radiological Research
Office of Nuclear Regulatory Research
U.S. Nuclear Regulatory Commission
Washington, DC 20555-0001

9. SPONSORING ORGANIZATION - NAME AND ADDRESS *(If NRC, type "Same as above"; if contractor, provide NRC Division, Office or Region, U.S. Nuclear Regulatory Commission, and mailing address.)*

Division of Fuel, Engineering, and Radiological Research
Office of Nuclear Regulatory Research
U.S. Nuclear Regulatory Commission
Washington, DC 20555-0001

10. SUPPLEMENTARY NOTES

M. EricksonKirk, NRC Project Manager

11. ABSTRACT *(200 words or less)*

During plant operation, the walls of reactor pressure vessels (RPVs) are exposed to neutron radiation, resulting in localized embrittlement of the vessel steel and weld materials in the core area. If an embrittled RPV had a flaw of critical size and certain severe system transients were to occur, the flaw could very rapidly propagate through the vessel, resulting in a through-wall crack and challenging the integrity of the RPV. The severe transients of concern, known as pressurized thermal shock (PTS), are characterized by a rapid cooling of the internal RPV surface in combination with repressurization of the RPV. Advancements in our understanding and knowledge of materials behavior, our ability to realistically model plant systems and operational characteristics, and our ability to better evaluate PTS transients to estimate loads on vessel walls led the NRC to realize that the earlier analysis, conducted in the course of developing the PTS Rule in the 1980s, contained significant conservatisms.

This report summarizes 21 supporting documents that describe the procedures used and results obtained in the probabilistic risk assessment, thermal hydraulic, and probabilistic fracture mechanics studies conducted in support of this investigation. Recommendations on toughness-based screening criteria for PTS are provided.

12. KEY WORDS/DESCRIPTORS *(List words or phrases that will assist researchers in locating the report.)*

pressurized thermal shock, probabilistic fracture mechanics, nuclear reactor pressure vessel pressurized water reactor

13. AVAILABILITY STATEMENT

unlimited

14. SECURITY CLASSIFICATION

(This Page)

unclassified

(This Report)

unclassified

15. NUMBER OF PAGES

16. PRICE

NRC FORM 335 (9-2004)

Federal Recycling Program